Handbook on the Assessment of Learning Disabilities
Theory, Research, and Practice

H. Lee Swanson

Handbook on the Assessment of Learning Disabilities:
Theory, Research, and Practice

Advisory Editor

Steven R. Forness, Ed.D.
Director of Mental Retardation and Developmental Disabilities Program, Principal, Neuropsychiatric Hospital School, Professor of Psychiatry and Biobehavioral Sciences, UCLA School of Medicine, Los Angeles

Handbook on the Assessment of Learning Disabilities:
Theory, Research, and Practice

Edited by
H. Lee Swanson, Ph.D.
Professor,
Department of Educational Psychology, Faculty of Education,
University of British Columbia, Vancouver, British Columbia

8700 Shoal Creek Boulevard
Austin, Texas 78758

© 1991 by H. Lee Swanson

All rights, including that of translation, reserved. No part of this publication may be reproduced, stored in a retrieval system, or transmitted in any form or by any means, electronic, mechanical, recording, or otherwise, without the prior written permission of the publisher.

Printed in the United States of America

Library of Congress Cataloging in Publication Data
Main entry under title:

Handbook on the assessment of learning disabilities: theory, research, and practice / H. Lee Swanson.
    p.   cm.
Includes bibliographical references.
ISBN 0-89079-406-5
1. Learning disabilities—Diagnosis.   I. Swanson, H. Lee, 1947–

[DNLM: 1. Learning Disorders—diagnosis.   WS 110 H23694]
RJ496.L4.H36 1990
616.85'88075—dc20
DNLM/DLC
for Library of Congress   89-13458
                                                                                          CIP

8700 Shoal Creek Boulevard
Austin, Texas 78758

Contents

Preface		vii
Contributors		xi

Part I Current Perspectives

1✓	Introduction: Issues and Concerns in the Assessment of Learning Disabilities *H. Lee Swanson*	1
2✓	Issues and Problems Related to the Assessment of Learning Disabilities *Howard S. Adelman and Linda Taylor*	21
3✓	Assessment for Instruction *John Wills Lloyd and Barbara J. Blandford*	45
4	Assessing Subtypes of Learning Abilities *G. Reid Lyon and Jane M. Flynn*	59

Part II Assessment Models and Domains

5	Dynamic Assessment *Annemarie Sullivan Palincsar, Ann L. Brown, and Joseph C. Campione*	75
6	Behavioral Assessment of Learning Disabilities *Thomas C. Lovitt*	95
7✓	Neuropsychological Assessment of Childhood Learning Disabilities *John E. Obrzut and Carol A. Boliek*	121
8	Reading Disability: Assessment Issues *Keith E. Stanovich*	147
9	A Cognitive Approach to Assessing the Mathematical Difficulties of Children Labeled "Learning Disabled" *Arthur J. Baroody and Herbert P. Ginsburg*	177
10	Language Assessment *Doris J. Johnson and Patricia A. Croasmun*	229
11✓	Assessment Strategies Inspired by Genetic Epistemology *D. Kim Reid*	249
12	Assessment of Metacognitive Research in Learning Disabilities: Theory, Research and Practice *Bernice Y. L. Wong*	265
13	Assessment of Social Cognition: Review of Research in Learning Disabilities *Tanis Bryan*	285

| 14 | Assessing Temperament
Barbara K. Keogh and Cynthia Ratekin Bess | 313 |

Part III Assessment and Intervention

15	Cognitive-Behavioral Assessment and Intervention *Clayton E. Keller*	331
16	Psychopharmacological Assessment and Intervention *Kenneth D. Gadow*	351
17	The Role of Standardized Tests in Planning Academic Instruction *Donald D. Hammill and Brian R. Bryant*	373
18	A Critique of Assessment Methodology *Kenneth A. Kavale and Nancy A. Mundschenk*	407

Index 433

Preface

There are two reasons for assessment in the field of learning disabilities: to enhance communication and to improve instruction. Assessing children with learning disabilities should facilitate communication between practitioners and researchers regarding the needs of those suspected of having learning disabilities. In addition, all assessment procedures should provide further treatment recommendations and outcome predictions. If assessment does not improve communication about the needs of the learner or provide valid directions for prevention and treatment, one must question its usefulness.

A review of the literature on assessment of children with learning disabilities strongly suggests that current assessment procedures do not meet these criteria. The term "learning disabilities" rarely describes more than academic difficulties and, of even more concern, does not appear to tie into any theoretical framework related to the learning process. That is, students who are suspected of having learning disabilities are usually not assessed within the framework of the learning process. Many professionals have unquestioningly accepted current systems of assessment as entities with proven validity and usefulness. Although our measurement tools and tests typically undergo arduous evaluations of their reliability and validity, such tools are only a small (or in some cases a nonsignificant) part of the assessment process. The major purpose behind the assessment process, at least in this context, is to solve and remediate problems unique to students with learning disabilities. This is done by considering various theoretical frameworks or models in which to judge information that has been gathered.

Given the importance of assessment, a handbook on this area is of importance. There is also a personal motivation behind the publication of *Handbook on the Assessment of Learning Disabilities: Theory, Research, and Practice*, which requires some explanation. Several years ago, I participated in placing a child into a learning disabilities resource room. I discovered among the participating professionals making recommendations for the child's educational future that the information relied on in the assessment was based almost exclusively on test results. Although the school psychologist tempered her discussion by noting the validity and reliability of the various tests as well as the outcomes of these test scores"plugged" into various discrepancy formulas, and the regular classroom teacher confirmed some of the discussion about the child with observational and informal measures, there did not appear to be a clear sense of a learning model (or alternative models) that put into perspective the child's learning abilities. It also appeared to me that the tests (WISC-R, Woodcock-Johnson) used to assess performance were being chosen because they were in vogue in this particular school district. This puzzled me because I thought that a well-founded theory dictates the choice of measurement instruments for assessment. When I asked the staffing team what the models of learning were behind these various instruments and what insights these current instruments provided that could not be provided by other measures, I was given an uncomfortable stare. After a period of silence I told them that "I was sorry for losing my head" and agreed reluctantly with them that these instruments were good predictors of how the child would perform in the classroom.

Three things happened to me after this meeting. First, I was not invited to participate in a school staffing by that school district again. Second, my thoughts about how to understand learning disabilities started to become more closely linked to models of learning. Finally, I began to realize that if contributions are to be made to help those children suspected of a learning disability one must have a bigger picture of assessment that goes beyond the selection of tasks that are used by school districts.

Although I cannot do much about the first outcome, I feel a responsibility, as many professionals do, in tackling the latter problems. I feel one means of approaching these latter problems is to identify individuals who wrestle with issues related to understanding the cognitive abilities of learning disabled students. Thus, instead of writing a book exclusively about my own research and theories on assessing learning disabilities (a small book, by necessity), I proposed to tackle the editing of a handbook. The contributing authors of the various chapters for this text were chosen because of their clear research expertise in various domains, as well as for their familiarity with learning disabilities and the education process.

The purpose of this handbook is to bring the process of assessment into various theoretical perspectives. This is done by considering issues related to assessment from various perspectives. The volume is organized around some broad notions about the assessment of learning disabilities. Assessment is defined as the collection of data for the purpose of solving a problem. Of course, the problems are diverse and include such issues as determining why some children have learning disabilities and others do not, which instructional program best matches a particular child's needs, which variables are the most important in understanding learning disabilities, and so on.

As suggested by the above vignette, some frustration exists in the assessment of learning disabilities because current techniques appear to operate in somewhat of a theoretical and research vacuum. Although previous handbooks on assessment provide some notions about various testing measures, there is little discussion given to conceptual models. Unfortunately, the separation of conceptual framework and measurement is apparent in diagnostic and case study work-ups of children with learning disabilities in the schools. This handbook attempts to provide various frameworks in which tasks related to assessment can be used. The handbook is written from the perspective that the assessment of individuals with suspected learning disabilities should be grounded in psychological science and committed to the goal of advancing the knowledge about such individuals. The work argues that the application of scientific knowledge should be the basis of all assessment practice and documents this argument by presenting the scientific underpinnings of practice within the field.

The handbook is divided into three parts. Part I provides an overview of issues related to assessment, research, and instructional planning. Part II encompasses the major portion of the text by focusing on specific "researchable" models of assessment. Part III focuses on the "intervention perspective" of the assessment process. A critique and overview of each chapter in the three sections will be provided in Chapter 1. The handbook is designed for graduate students seeking exposure to the field of learning disabilities. I hope that this handbook will become an important reference work that researchers and practitioners in the field of learning disabilities will consult for current scientific knowledge.

A number of people have influenced my thinking in organizing this book. Most importantly, I wish to thank the contributors and reviewers of the various chapters. I particularly thank Drs. Bill Watson, Annette Tessier, and Jack Little who shaped many of my clinical notions about what assessment is and what it is supposed to be. I also greatly appreciate Marie Linvill and Steve Forness for their excellent editorial insights.

H. L. S.

Contributors

Howard S. Adelman, Ph.D.
University of California, Los Angeles

Arthur Baroody, Ph.D.
University of Illinois, Champaign

Cynthia R. Bess, Ph.D.
University of California, Los Angeles

Barbara J. Blandford, Ph.D.
University of Virginia

Carol A. Boliek, Ph.D.
Department of Speech and Hearing Sciences, University of Arizona, Tucson

Ann L. Brown, Ph.D.
University of California, Berkeley

James H. Bryan, Ph.D.
Northwestern University, Evanston, Illinois

Tanis Bryan, Ph.D.
University of Illinois at Chicago, Chicago

Brian R. Bryant, Ph.D.
Director of Research, PRO-ED, Inc., Austin, Texas

Joseph C. Campione, Ph.D.
University of California, Berkeley

Patricia A. Croasmun, Ph.D.
Northwestern University, Evanston

Jane M. Flynn, Ph.D.
Gunderson Medical Foundation, LaCrosse, WI

Kenneth D. Gadow, Ph.D.
State University of New York, Stony Brook

Herbert P. Ginsburg, Ph.D.
Teachers College, Columbia University, New York

Donald D. Hammill, Ed.D.
President, PRO-ED, Inc., Austin, Texas

Kenneth A. Kavale, Ph.D.
University of Iowa, Iowa City

Clayton E. Keller, Ph.D.
University of Minnesota, Duluth

Doris S. Johnson, Ph.D.
Northwestern University, Evanston

Barbara K. Keogh, Ph.D.
University of California, Los Angeles

John Wills Lloyd, Ph.D.
University of Virginia

Thomas C. Lovitt, Ed.D.
University of Washington, Seattle

G. Reid Lyon, Ph.D.
University of Vermont, Burlington

Nancy A. Mundschenk, Ph.D.
University of Iowa, Iowa City

John E. Obrzut, Ph.D.
University of Arizona, Tucson

Annemarie Sullivan Palincsar, Ph.D.
University of Michigan, Ann Arbor

D. Kim Reid, Ph.D.
Independent researcher/writer

Keith E. Stanovich, Ph.D.
Oakland University, Rochester, Michigan

H. Lee Swanson, Ph.D.
University of British Columbia, Vancouver, British Columbia

Linda Taylor, Ph.D.
University of California, Los Angeles

Bernice Y. L. Wong, Ed.D.
Simon Fraser University, Burnaby, British Columbia

PART I

Current Perspectives

CHAPTER 1

Introduction: Issues in the Assessment of Learning Disabilities

H. LEE SWANSON

The concept of learning disabilities rests on two assumptions: (a) learning difficulties are not due to inadequate opportunity to learn or to significant physical or emotional disorders, but to basic disorders in psychological processes and (b) these processing deficits are a reflection of neurological, constitutional, and/or biological factors. Although these assumptions may seem straightforward, there is a problem in putting them into operation (see Brown & Campione, 1986; Farnham-Diggory, 1986; Keogh, 1988; Wong, 1987, for further discussion). For example, concerns arise regarding the meaningfulness of the term "learning disabilities," at least as a diagnostic label (Keogh, 1987; Shepard, 1983), as well as the criteria for identifying children with these disabilities (Shepard, Smith, & Vojir, 1983; Wong, 1986). In addition, some authors suggest that there is little reason to believe that the characteristics or needs of children so identified are different from those of nonachievers (e.g., Ysseldyke, Algozzine, Richey, & Graden, 1983). It is my assumption that many of these criticisms are related to problems with assessment, rather than to how one might conceptualize a learning disability. Thus, if one is to address adequately the operational issues that confront the field of learning disabilities, then one must grapple with issues related to assessment. It is in this spirit that this handbook was developed. In this chapter, I seek to distill ideas that unify what otherwise might appear to be a collection of unintegrated chapters on the assessment of learning disabilities. I shall conclude with a discussion of themes that seem to run consistently throughout the book.

THE GOAL OF ASSESSMENT

The term "assessment" is used in many different ways by the authors of this book. As an integrator, I face the difficult task of trying to decide whether to impose a definition of assessment on all these contributions, and thereby risk misinterpreting the intent of a particular author's chapter, or to provide no definition at all and thereby provide a review of the chapters with no integrating theme. Because I believe there is a way to summarize the contributions of this text, I shall discuss the goal of assessment, as well as provide a definition.

The remediation of learning disabilities is the goal of assessment. In the field of medicine, it is traditional to speak of assessment as being directly related to intervention. The illness model generally presupposes some cause of learning difficulties, a particular battery of diagnostic tests, some information about prognosis, and knowledge of possible treatment. Unfortunately, as psychologists and educators test LD (learning disabled) students' classroom competence, they confront several issues that obscure the goal of assessment, and therefore, remediation. Some of these issues are related to legal and social concerns (see Chapter 2, by Adelman & Taylor), but other important issues arise: (1) The lack of an adequate taxonomy of classroom learning makes it difficult to compare results gathered on students with learning disabilities in different situations and to gauge those results in a specific classroom. (2) There is a lack of theoretical perspectives from which to approach the complex transaction of students with learning disabilities and their educational needs. (3) There is a limited number of valid and reliable instruments available for observing the behavior of students with learning disabilities in natural settings. I shall return to these issues later.

Traditionally, identification of learning disabilities has relied primarily on uncovering a discrepancy between expected achievement and intellectual ability. One means of determining discrepancies between potential and actual performance is to compare the scores of children with learning disabilities on different standardized tests. These discrepancies are quantified using (a) informal judgements, (b) grade-level expectancies and the degree to which a child deviates from grade-level expectancy, (c) mathematical formulas that emphasize current achievement, IQ, or mental age,

(d) standard score discrepancies, and/or (e) regression formulas that account for the effects of scores regressing toward the mean. The reliance on standardized tests to determine performance discrepancies is based on the assumption that latent sources of individual differences are related to mathematically derived constructs (i.e., factors). Although interpretations of mathematically derived constructs are unequivocal (Carroll, 1983), the goal of such procedures is to isolate global constellations of the strengths and weaknesses in functioning of students with learning disabilities. In a practical sense, it is assumed that standardized tests assess individual differences along some continuum and that test items reflect an educationally relevant construct; otherwise, the tests would be of little interest or value as a means of determining discrepancies in performance of students with learning disabilities.

Although the psychometric approach does predict fairly well the stability of performance discrepancies (McKinney & Speece, 1986; Speece, McKinney, & Appelbaum, 1985), it may be difficult to define the mental processes necessary for effective learning, to identify subprocesses underlying academic tasks, as well as global processes required for school learning, and to provide a link between theories of learning and educational practice. Furthermore, it has been suggested that standardized tests have questionable ecological validity. For example, rarely have data from traditional psychometric procedures accounted for an adequate amount of variation in criterion-task performance (Hunt, 1983). In addition, correlations between composite scores and measures of academic and occupational success have ranged from only 0.30 to 0.50 (Jencks, 1977). It can also be argued that the supposed performance discrepancies between children with and those without learning disabilities on traditionally used tests, such as the Wechsler Intelligence Scale for Children-Revised (WISC-R; see Kavale & Forness, 1984), are suspect.

Perhaps the most serious limitation to the use of standardized tests as a means of assessing the performance discrepancies in students with learning disabilities is that these measures obscure the specific discrepancies we are trying to find. We know, for example, that students with learning disabilities perform less well than students who are not learning disabled on many standardized measures. Recognizing this, of course, most practitioners in the field of learning disabilities have focused on the differential deficit; that is, a greater deficit revealed on one (or more) test or subtest than on another. Unfortunately, these differential deficits in performance do not necessarily represent a "specific" discrepancy in actual performance. They may instead reflect generalized performance deficits of students with learning disabilities, coupled with the fact that one or some of the subtest items measure these generalized deficits better than others do (Stanovich, 1986). Thus, for example, low scores on an achievement subtest and average or above-average performance on an IQ test cannot be interpreted as indicating a meaningful or true discrepancy.

In search of a better conceptualization for assessing performance (discrepancies) of students with learning disabilities, the chapters in this book may have much to offer. It is not my intent in outlining some of these contributions, however, to suggest that standardized tests or discrepancy notions be abandoned, but rather to put them into perspective. The fact is that the field of learning disabilities will continue to use and rely on standardized tests to determine performance patterns (unless, of course, there is some breakthrough in the assessment of individual differences). Thus, the suggestions in these chapters are meant to be integrated with current psychometric practice.

ASSESSMENT DEFINED

I shall make the assumption that assessment is a *goal-directed problem-solving process* that uses various measures within a theoretical framework. It is a goal-directed activity that operates on some very loose definitional notions about what is a learning disability and what is the best way to operationalize this subgroup of the school population. As presented in this book, assessment is also a variable process that depends on the questions asked, the type of student with learning disabilities involved, and a myriad of social, developmental, and contextual factors. Although the goal of this assessment process is the remediation of learning disabilities, assessment cannot be reduced to a finite set of specific steps or rules.

However, I believe there is a structure to the assessment process. This structure underlying assessment can be delineated in the form of assumptions that can be made regarding the nature of the data to be obtained (for example, which test to choose) and the uses to which the resulting data are put (for example, information used for educational remediation). But, of course, many of the assumptions related to data and its use are open to disagreement. Thus, some discussion of important issues is necessary.

ISSUES IN ASSESSMENT PRACTICE

ISSUES OF THEORY

One issue is the theoretical relationship between measurement and assessment. In Chapter 18, Kavale and Mundschenk argue that meager theoretical development has shrouded and made ineffectual the data collected on students with learning disabilities. They suggest that what we have in the field of learning disabilities is a system of broad assumptions that lack a theoretical structure in which to organize and interpret the empirical information that has been gathered. Learning disability constructs lack an exact analysis and, therefore, the majority of instruments that assess students with learning disabilities lack adequate construct validity. These authors further state that most measures commonly used in assessment batteries reflect a form of psychometric engineering that obscures the poor conceptual basis of the test. Thus, the authors suggest that inadequate measurement has been a major impediment in the field. Unfortunately, the field of learning disabilities focuses primarily on enhancing measurement procedures, via testing, rather than anchoring these observations at a theoretical level.

No doubt, the lack of theory creates a number of practical problems in the assessment of learning disabilities. For example, suppose one accepts the notion that a child may have a learning disability. What test should be used to assess the presence of a disability without overrating or underrating the child's learning potential? Overrating or extending our data would lead to a false-positive diagnostic error: the child is not learning disabled. A false-positive error results from falsely concluding, based on testing performance, that the child possesses, for example, the language skills necessary for regular classroom understanding. The child could answer correctly on a vocabulary subtest, "What does nuisance mean?" without understanding what he or she has answered. Furthermore, it is possible to administer a test in such a way that the probability of an accurate assessment is enhanced. Unfortunately, these very same conditions can increase the risk of underrating the child's performance, leading to a false-negative conclusion that the child does have some learning disability. A false-negative error consists of a false conclusion that a child has not yet acquired adequate vocabulary for regular classroom functioning. Although the child possesses this capability, he or she fails to perform because of selective attention, metacognition, or other problems. Possibly, the test demands more from the child than required in the educational context. Thus, the testing procedure may lead to conclusions based on inadequate or inaccurate information. As can be inferred from Kavale and Mundschenk's chapter, a theoretical framework is needed that will decrease the likelihood of these kinds of errors.

ISSUES OF CLASSIFICATION

Disagreement over the definition of the term "learning disabilities" and the wide variation in the criteria used to identify students with learning disabilities makes it difficult to integrate the findings related to assessment (Keogh, 1983; 1987; Shephard et al, 1983; also see Chapter 8, by Stanovich). Indeed, it has been argued that the heterogeneity of failure conditions found among "LD" students is about the only factor universally agreed upon in the field. In addition, researchers usually use samples of LD students from remedial programs or from the bases of diagnosis made by school districts. Such variations present difficulties in reviewing research on assessment in the area of learning disabilities. Lyon and Flynn (Chapter 4) address this issue.

Lyon and Flynn see classification as critical in producing meaningful constructs to account for learning behavior. Characteristics of useful classification systems for learning disabilities should be theory driven, developed from adequately defined samples and tasks that have adequate psychometric properties, and obtained from clusters of relatively high external and internal validity. Such is not the case with a number of subtype studies in the field (see Lyon, 1985, for further discussion).

Lyon and Flynn argue that the identification of subgroups of individuals with learning disabilities can be useful, both scientifically and clinically, primarily because validated classification systems provide a less heterogeneous data set for analysis and description. Classification provides a foundation for theory development, communication, and prediction. Thus, the field of learning disabilities could benefit from the appropriate application of classification efforts, most directly related to issues of treatment, to such a heterogeneous population. Lyon and Flynn appropriately observe that subtype research will not have an impact on the field unless longitudinal research is implemented. Longitudinal research is necessary to determine if the symptomatology of the subtype remains stable over time, regardless of the developmental and educational constraints that are imposed on the group. These samples of children must be selected from the general population without prior designations of learning disabilities. These children should be studied over time with a wide range of theoretically relevant assessments in a variety of teaching and learning contexts.

POLITICAL AND SOCIAL ISSUES

Another issue relates to the social and political arena. Adelman and Taylor's analysis suggests that assessment procedures are linked to policy issues. That is, decisions related to who is labeled as learning disabled go beyond the existing data (e.g., Ysseldyke, Algozzine, Richey, & Graden, 1983). Indeed, as noted by the authors, some relevant data may be ignored in order to arrive at decisions that match political and economic values. The root of the problem, as these authors see it, is that very little time has been devoted to a classification scheme that delineates the field (also see Lyon & Flynn). There are also issues related to how best to match instruction to the learner and whose view should prevail (e.g., parents, teacher, and/or funding source). A typical assessment situation that has political implications is related to selecting testing instruments. One may argue that unless certain procedures or instruments are perfected, these tools should not be used in assessment practices, but in many cases the alternative procedures cause more harm than good. For example, in place of the use of IQ data, some attempts to classify students with learning disabilities have used screening and rating scales that have produced many false-positive classifications.

ISSUES RELATED TO TESTS AND INSTRUCTION

If tests are simply tools and if the effectiveness of such tools can be assessed by means of sophisticated statistics, why is there so much controversy or criticism over a lack of assessment models? If psychologists and educators know the referral question they are attempting to answer and the kind of data to collect, and have some notion of the problem's solution, then it would seem that an adequate assessment model can be used. This logic seems straightforward, but does not deal with the real problems. The real problem, as suggested by Hammill and Bryant (Chapter 17), revolves around the use of tests and the conclusions drawn from them.

Hammill and Bryant provide an excellent overview of what a test is, the frame of reference for tests, types of norms, and issues related to reliability and validity. Due to the passage of PL 94-142, there are a number of tests available from commercial publishers that attempt to measure attainment skills. Their review focuses on the nature of standardized tests and how they can be used to improve instruction. Although the authors see standardized tests as helpful in terms of providing a reference of student performance, such measures are cleary inadequate as aids in planning intervention. Furthermore, in their analysis of tests that are used to facilitate academic instruction, they have found that the majority of frequently used measures are inadequately standardized (e.g., reliability and/or validity information are insufficient). The authors further state that standardized measures are inappropriate for instructional purposes because they deliberately induce variance (discrimination between individuals of poor and good abilities) and provide a limited sample of items.

Lloyd and Blandford (Chapter 3) make a similar point that formal tests do not direct teachers to relevant instruction. They further suggest that the instruction of students with learning disabilities cannot be based on psychometric characteristics. They argue that there is little correspondence between the goals and objectives of formal assessment data and daily lesson plans. Although research in special education is replete with examples of matching individual student characteristics with specific instructional treatments, the research has not supported a teaching method based on student traits (however, see Lyon, 1985). Certainly, in the area of modality preference, research has not supported the assumption that teaching to modality strength increases reading performance.

The authors go on to argue that if prior assessment of student characteristics does not lead to effective instructional planning, then assessment should be directed to the types of tasks to be mastered. They outline three components of instructional assessment that must be considered: (1) direction, (2) skills to be taught, and (3) how instruction should be delivered. Important procedures to be considered in task performance of the assessment are task analysis (target objective divided into skills), trial teaching (experimental procedure where the teacher determines if the instruction is producing the desired responses), and interviews with students.

MODELS OF ASSESSMENT

Debates on the usefulness of psychological constructs to learning disabilities have taken place for some time (see Chapter 3, by Lloyd & Blanford). A traditional assessment model of learning disabilities is based on the assumptions that (1) individuals can be characterized by attributes that can be placed at some point on a continuum, (2) individuals have different amounts or quantities of the same attribute, and (3) there is a true placement (score) on the continuum of attributes that can be approximated by test data. Implicit in this model, at least as carried out in practice, is that behavior is determined by internal factors—constructs or traits. Typically some applications of these notions have been illustrated through what is popularly called "diagnostic-prescriptive teaching." The objective of this assessment approach includes determining: (1) the cause of the learning disability for purposes of classification, (2) diagnostic information about a student's style of learning and psychological processes, and (3) academic content needs for instructional purposes.

Cogent examples of such an assessment process would use standardized instruments to identify a child's strengths and weaknesses on subtest items, followed by extrapolation of the information to provide a plan for instruction. This approach stresses the diagnosis of specific constructs, such as memory, and the training and instruction in specific abilities, which are assumed to improve academic functioning. For example, the model of the Illinois Test of Psycholinguistic Abilities, which had considerable influence in the historical development of the field of learning disabilities, was based on the assumption that the cause of the learning problem is a failure within the child, and that strengthening the weak area will improve learning. A seminal review by Hammill and Larsen (1974) on the efficacy of psycholinguistic training concluded that this assumption has not proven effective.

It could be argued that earlier assessment models that were connected to various psychometric measures were flawed because several mental components are involved in the learning process. At the least, one may safely conclude that for some children, testing instruments might not be totally appropriate for providing information about learning problems or for prescribing instructional activities. Thus, assessment procedures could be rendered more effective for programming if many aspects (constructs) of behavior within several instructional contexts are considered. An assessment model of this nature is beyond the scope of traditional models of testing. Let us briefly consider other approaches to assessment.

DYNAMIC ASSESSMENT

Dynamic assessment can be distinguished from traditional assessment models in three ways: (1) the social context in which learning occurs, (2) the flexibility with which learning occurs, and (3) the prescription of appropriate instruction. Palincsar, Brown, and Campione (Chapter 5) broadly define dynamic assessment as involving a testing procedure that attempts to modify an examinee's performance level by providing structured cues or instruction with items. Unlike traditional testing, in dynamic testing score changes are not viewed as threatening test validity. In fact, proponents of dynamic testing postulate that validity will increase. For example, Vygotsky (1978) proposed that the modifiability of an individual's performance is a valid prediction of future learning. Vygotsky recommended testing the level of potential development by administering test-related training and cues along with the items. He further hypothesized that the assessment of ability is more validity measured by two scores, the actual development level (i.e., initial performance level) and the zone of potential (performance gain).

Palincsar et al. review several recent applications of dynamic testing that have been guided by somewhat different theoretical orientations, but all models focus on the "modifiability" of constructs. These models emphasize the modifiability of cognitive structures (Feuerstein), learning-potential status (Budoff), upper limits of performance (Carlson), and flexibility that students learn to use what they have been taught (Campione & Brown). They review some relevant studies that have assessed the predictive validity of procedures using a dynamic assessment model and found that initial unaided performance underestimates what children could achieve with minimal assistance. The authors emphasize that the point of dynamic assessment is to qualify learning potential, *not* to identify children in terms of learning.

As an extension of dynamic assessment research, the authors provide an excellent overview of reciprocal teaching in which through a social dialogue the child comes to assume an active role in the learning process. Reciprocal teaching serves as an assessment approach because it allows the child to self test his or her understanding of the material, to clarify and understand material, and to monitor the flow of information so that it is tailored to instructional needs.

NEUROPSYCHOLOGICAL ASSESSMENT

Obrzut and Boliek (Chapter 7) present an alternative view of assessment that focuses on underlining neuropsychological dysfunction. A neuropsychological focus for learning disabilities derives from the demonstrated relationship between learning and brain structure and functions. Neuropsychological assessment delineates the nature and significance of cognitive deficits that are unique and specific to the child. The authors contend that children who have difficulty in their ability to organize, coordinate, and integrate and/or synthesize stimuli will experience academic failure due to an underlying cerebral dysfunction. They view learning disabilities as persisting with age and such children as failing to respond to normal classroom instruction.

The authors present a brief historical framework for assessment. Within this framework, they provide a rationale for a test battery. The aim of this battery is to investigate the functional structure of the brain by analyzing behavioral responses. The authors note that many psychologists do not have training in the use of neuropsychological evaluation and are unfamiliar with the behavioral correlates thought to be associated with a dysfunction in various anatomical structures. In addition, the most popular standardized neuropsychological assessment batteries (e.g., Luria-Nebraska Neuropsychological Battery, Halstead-Reitan Neuropsychological Test Battery) considered useful in diagnosing learning disabilities, provide little educationally relevant information. Although neuropsychological test batteries have been found to discriminate among normal, LD, and brain-damaged children; they have certain limitations. For example, the reliability and validity data is scarce, and the factor structure of many of the batteries is in question. There are also a number of confounding variables related to age, language, and memory.

One intervention procedure that has some "roots" in neuropsychological models of learning is drug medication. It is assumed that drug intervention indirectly enhances academic performance either by enhancing a compensatory mechanism, improving general cognitive functions, or reversing a specific brain mechanism that has an adverse effect on performance. Some individuals thus believe that medication makes a child more responsive to educational instruction. Gadow's review (Chapter 16) suggests that stimulant drugs do increase academic productivity in hyperactive children, and, in all probability, in learning disabled children. Although the results of short-term intervention studies suggest that stimulant medications do not appear to improve reading, arithmetic, and spelling achievement significantly, some moderate results have been found in handwriting. The results of long-term interventions are even less robust, suggesting that drug therapy does not enhance academic achievement. The combination of drug intervention with behavioral programs have led some researchers to a number of interesting conclusions: (1) combined intervention programs are more effective if they focus on academic task performance, (2) there is a limited interaction possible between drug and behavior therapy because they affect behavior in a similar way, and (3) behavior-oriented programs that focus on specific academic behaviors are more effective than contingency management in general, and the former programs are minimally influenced by drugs. Overall, the efficacy studies suggest that combined academically oriented and behavioral interventions are superior to stimulant medication alone. Although stimulant drugs enhance a number of learning-related behaviors (attention span) and academic productivity, they do not appear to add much to academically oriented behavior-intervention programs.

A BEHAVIORAL MODEL

Another important model of assessment focuses primarily on observational (attention, amount of eye contact to task) and situational (environment) events. Although no single summary describes behavioral assessment, it usually focuses on five categories:

1. Deficiencies in information or required behavior
2. Behavioral excesses
3. Inappropriate environmental stimulus control
4. Inappropriate self-generated stimulus control
5. Problematic reinforcement contingencies

Lovitt (Chapter 6) provides an excellent overview of the behavioral assessment model for students with learning disabilities. Perhaps the term "behavioral approach" is somewhat of a misnomer because all assessment approaches focus on behavior. The behavioral approaches to date may be characterized by their directness and the frequency of data collection. Important questions for assessment using this approach are What specific educational tasks are important for the child to learn? What are the sequential steps in the learning of this task? and What specific behaviors does the child need to perform this task? Lovitt has pointed out the wide range of uses of behavioral assessments, such as screening students, placing them in the proper instructional level, evaluating short-term and long-term objectives, follow-up, program evaluation, and differentiation of learning needs. Behavior assessment extends beyond the classroom to pinpointing the needs of students in vocational, recreational, and community settings.

There are few variations of behavioral models that attempt to identify cognitions that are involved in functional relations. Keller (Chapter 15) provides a comprehensive review of assessment and intervention from a cognitive–behavioral perspective. Assessment from this perspective provides information on covert thinking that may relate to overt behaviors, provides information on how coping mechanisms develop, and confirms the effects of intervention. This approach emphasizes that an individual's thoughts and behaviors are critically related to intervention. The focus of intervention is on altering events around these behaviors in order to better understand causal relations. These interventions are directed at manipulating psychological, environmental, and supportive prompts that influence the behavior. Methodological concerns related to this form of assessment revolve around the accuracy of information presented, the direct effects of intervention procedures on cognitive processes, and the concurrent validity of what is being measured across assessment instruments.

DOMAINS OF ASSESSMENT

CONCEPTUAL DEVELOPMENT

An adequate understanding of learning disabilities requires an explanation of the interactions between macrodevelopment (changes that take place over a substantial period of time) and microdevelopment (changes that occur in a relatively short period of time). The former describes the nature of change, and the latter focuses primarily on the mechanisms through which change occurs. Unlike a behavioral account of learning disabilities, which may be characterized as reflecting response chains, a developmental epistemologist believes all learning is structural (i.e., learning results from qualitative changes in mental representations). These structures reflect representations and concepts, but also strategies and skills. As noted in Chapter 11, by Reid, the process oriented research stimulated from an epistemological viewpoint has not been abundant in the field of learning disabilities. The research that is available, however, suggests that persons with learning disabilities follow the same stage-like behaviors as normals, but with developmental delays. The little research that does exist suggests that students with learning disabilities have difficulty learning to do complex tasks. These difficulties reflect processing inefficiencies rather than deficits. That is, students with learning disabilities experience a period of stagnation in which they fail to reflect on or gain a conscious understanding of their task performance. The importance of Reid's analysis is the notion that children with learning disabilities are active problem solvers who do engage in strategic behaviors, but they do not operate at a level where they use abstract general principles.

LANGUAGE

In Chapter 10, Johnson and Croasmum provide a model of language assessment that draws from Bloom and Lahey's (1978) paradigm of "form, content, and use." The features and characteristics of words are referred to as the **form** of language and these basic elements include phonology, morphology, and syntax. The **content** incorporates meaning and various components of semantics. The **use** of language involves pragmatic functions and the ways in which different social situations affect the linguistic forms one uses in attempts at communication. The authors suggest that primary areas of assessment include semantics, syntax, morphology, and pragmatics.

The authors see the assessment process as addressing the question Is the child developing language normally? No doubt, this question is not answered easily because the role of language acquisition varies. The authors suggest that diagnosis should occur over time and that no single test or series of tests adequately capture this variation. The authors outline the various levels of assessment (e.g., screening, eligibility for services, planning for intervention, diagnostic teaching), but more importantly, suggest that language is only one form of representation and the relations between language and other processes, such as conceptualization, must be investigated. Thus, impaired language in students with learning disabilities is viewed as occurring with other processing deficits. Language should be assessed in combination with both standardized and informal language sampling.

METACOGNITION

Wong (Chapter 12) provides an overview of the importance of metacognition to theory, research, and instructional practice. A focus on metacognition is in contrast with traditional assessment models, which have viewed learning disabilities as isolated cognitive deficits, such as perceptual or attentional disorders. The metacognitive orientation suggests that learning disabilities are more general than previously thought. Wong indicates that one problem with the metacognitive approach is that it makes learning disabilities more general in nature and thus undermines the specificity of the problems of children with learning disabilities (also see Chapter 8, by Stanovich). Thus, metacognitive problems should be considered a byproduct or a second-order problem of lower-order processing problems. Furthermore, reading studies reviewed by Wong suggest that high-order metacognitive knowledge develops adequately after students have mastered low-order decoding mechanics. Regardless of these issues, the results of metacognitive intervention have been positive and suggest the need to generalize beyond traditional academic domains (e.g., reading). Although interventions have been somewhat sophisticated, the assessment devices are still underdeveloped. Some promising metacognitive assessment tools are emerging, which may serve as models for professionals in the field of learning disabilities.

SOCIAL INTERACTION

Another assessment focus that has developed tremendously within the past decade is social cognition. This approach specializes in teaching the child to behave in a socially competent or adaptable manner. The importance of social cognition in defining learning disabilities has been noted by the Interagency Committee on Learning Disabilities (1987), which indicated that such children manifest difficulties in social skills. Chapter 13, by Bryan, provides a timely analysis of the extant literature on social cognition: specifically in the areas of perspective taking, moral development, and social problem solving.

In interpreting these results, Bryan gives specific concern to the psychometric properties of the instruments used. Issues related to reliability and validity were raised as well as the narrowness in social situations represented. Of particular interest in Bryan's analysis is the relationship between social cognition, IQ, and achievement. On the whole, the majority of studies that find that children with learning disabilities do poorly on measures of social cognition are *not* related to intelligence (IQ) or to the experience of academic failure. The author concludes her analysis by suggesting that the construct validity of social cognition measures will be enhanced if other constructs (e.g., memory, attention) are left out of the analysis.

TEMPERAMENT

There is increasing evidence that the achievements in school of children with learning disabilities are not limited to experiences related only to cognition. Rather, children experience a series of continuing interactions with peers, teachers, and task demands. These interactions involve a range of personal characteristics, including behavioral style and temperament. Although there are few studies on the temperament of students with learning disabilities, such variables in individual differences are appealing for a number of reasons. First, children's temperament characteristics have a number of associations with school performance, such as how teachers assign grades, and instructional interactions. Second, temperament is differentiated from personality, cognition, and motivation and is a fairly stable individual characteristic.

The implication of Keogh and Bess's chapter (Chapter 14) is that one must look at the "goodness of fit" between the contextual demand of the schools and the child's temperament. The authors note, however, that despite considerable support for the goodness of fit notion there has been limited demonstration of its power. A specific problem in this kind of research is that there is a limited amount of variance among school environments. There are some additional problems related to implementing a temperament analysis of children with learning disabilities. First, there are a number of different theoretical formulations that influence how temperament should be assessed. Second, temperament may be expressed differently in various settings (home and school) and various individuals may have different perceptions of the same behavior.

READING

Stanovich (Chapter 8) suggests that at the heart of most definitions of learning disabilities, especially as applies to dyslexia, is the assessment of a severe discrepancy between aptitude and achievement. Considerable research has been done validating the appropriateness of this discrepancy criterion, but it suffers from not being able to separate readers with learning disabilities from poor readers. Furthermore, the field is characterized as plunging itself into the areas of educational practice and diagnosis without setting itself on a firm empirical foundation.

Stanovich reviews research designs that compare ability groups and suggests that the research has produced equivocal results. Part of the problem is that the majority of studies have dealt with general processing, which is intertwined with general constructs as intelligence (see also chapter by Wong for further discussion). These findings create difficulties because the notion of specificity is lost in our conceptualization of learning disabilities. Deficits that might best support the notion of specificity are processes that are not under the direction of higher level cognitive structures and those that are domain specific. IQ is seen as irrelevant to the notion of a reading problem. Thus, it is necessary to formulate a concept of reading disabilities that is independent of any notion of IQ. One candidate is phonological processing.

There is voluminous information that phonological deficits are the basis for dyslexia. Research on phonological deficits shows that normal readers are comparable to reading-level-matched controls in phonological processing, whereas dyslexic readers are inferior to reading-level-matched controls. Furthermore, the dyslexic group may be characterized as representing compensatory processing (superior vocabulary, general knowledge sensitivity) when compared with reading-level-matched controls.

Stanovich discusses a phonological core variable difference model in which reading problems represent a multidimensional continuum rather than a clustering of subskills in which reading problems move from a processing deficit localized to phonological core to global deficits of the developmentally lagging poor reader. This model accounts for variation in reading in which it is assumed that all poor readers have a phonological deficit, but processing deficits emerge as one drifts in multidimensional space from pure dyslexics toward nondyslexic poor readers. Thus, a straightforward prediction in these studies is that the IQ–reading discrepancy should be greater in subjects who have more specific deficits and that more processing deficits are found as one moves closer to the ordinary space. The notion of a *continuum* is emphasized, rather than a discrete classification about reading disabilities.

The author also suggests that if liberal classification criteria are used, then the dyslexic sample will be hard to locate. That is, the wider the net is cast, the greater will be difficulties in distinguishing dyslexic readers from other readers. Although Stanovich creates the argument that construct validity exists for the concept of dyslexia, there are some problems. For example, there are no data suggesting that the discrepancy-defined dyslexic reader responds differently to various educational treatments than do ordinary poor readers.

MATHEMATICS

Treatment as it relates to cognition is the focus of Baroody and Ginsburg's chapter (Chapter 9). According to Baroody and Ginsburg, assessment is viewed as a means to understand what students know and make informed instructional decisions. Instruction is seen as going beyond categorizing children and providing information that is useful in planning instruction. Their chapter focuses on instructionally induced learning disabilities.

The results of inappropriate instruction are reviewed extensively in terms of a gap between (a) formal instruction and the child's existing informal knowledge, (b) concrete informal mathematics and the relatively formal abstract instruction, and (c) instructional conditions that force the child into a passive role of assimilating knowledge. The authors detail an assessment of learning disabilities that includes an analysis of formal knowledge, individual patterns in the accuracy and efficiency of skills, as well as problem-solving processes (solution strategies, error patterns), learning potential, metacognitive knowledge, belief systems, and the nature of the child's instruction. Thus, their chapter makes the point that the assessment of mathematics is related directly to the evaluator's view of learning as it relates to instruction, learning, and cognition.

ASSESSMENT PERSPECTIVE

The theme that underlies most of the chapters in this book is that the assessment of the performance of students with learning disabilities must be directed by a theoretically based strategy that assesses educational potential. Assessing the potential for learning of children with learning disabilities, as suggested by some authors in this book, is done by assessing their adaptation to the goals and expectations of their environment. They are evaluated in relation to their potential within a social or learning context. Children are affected directly by obvious and by covert contingencies (e.g., classroom supports, cognitive constraints). Thus, an adequate assessment approach emphasizes the child's environmental interactions, along with the analysis of behavioral interactions and a focus on developmental structures, biological constraints, and cognitive factors.

As suggested by these chapters, there is a long list of needs for students with learning disabilities. Some of these students do not monitor their learning well, cannot generate phonological codes effectively when processing visual information, have poor metacognitive skills, cannot negotiate social situations well, and so on. Depending on one's assessment bias, one might say that the student with learning disabilities is unable to think logically or symbolically, fails to access a language system adequately, has a context–temperament mismatch, lacks adaptive behaviors, and so on. Unfortunately, there is, to date, an overriding tendency to treat information on students with learning disabilities in light of students who are functioning adequately in the regular classroom. For example, children of various cognitive abilities are given the same task, which is assumed to be well suited for testing a given competence. The student who performs well is said to possess that skill or capacity; the student who fails is viewed as deficient in the task. There is an implicit assumption that the various instruments provide an accurate assessment of the skill or capacity in question. A review of the chapters in this text does much to challenge this assumption. When diverse tests are used, standard tests are modified, or experimental training, testing, and teaching are introduced, educators begin to glimpse what a child with learning disabilities can do. No doubt, certain tests underscore the fact that some children, when compared with their "normal" peers, seem to differ in their ability to negotiate a particular domain (for example, reading, mathematics). This cannot be denied. But to the extent that an educator makes it possible to determine what a "typical" student with learning disabilities can do, one can then determine what might underlie the child's learning difficulty. From there, we can begin to formulate an educational program.

In conclusion, I would suggest that current assessment practices of the performance of children with learning disabilities are insensitive to how such children learn. Although current research has suggested that learning disabilities can be inferred from task performance on ability and achievement measures, especially if these performance discrepancies are consistently demonstrated across related tasks, as a general rule it is dangerous to make inferences about learning from test performance. To do that requires discounting a variety of plausible sources of poor performance (e.g., generalized performance deficit, production deficiencies, recognition of test). Unfortunately, these variables are confounded hopelessly in current assessment practices used to determine performance of students with learning disabilities and thus an accurate diagnostic interpretation of score differences is unlikely. A contrasting approach, as suggested in this book, is to focus on complex models of learning that are sensitive to the current literature on cognition, temperament, language, neuropsychology, and so on. The concept of assessment favored in this handbook is a broad and inclusive one covering much more than the traditional or more narrowly defined view of learning disabilities. Each chapter is written from existing theoretical bases within each psychological domain. Each chapter provides a basis on which the strengths and weaknesses of other models can be judged.

REFERENCES

Bloom, L., & Lahey, M. (1978). Language development and language disorders. NY: John Wiley & Sons.
Brown, A. L., & Campione, J. C. (1986). Psychological theory and the study of learning disabilities. *American Psychologist, 14*, 1059–1068.
Carroll, J. B. (1983). Studying individual differences in cognitive abilities: Through and beyond factor analysis. In R. Dillon & R. Schneck (Eds.), *Individual differences in cognition* (pp. 1-28). New York: Academic Press.
Farnham-Diggory, S. (1986). Time, now, for a little serious complexity. In S. J. Ceci (Ed.), *Handbook of cognitive, social, and neurological aspects of learning* (pp. 207–238). Hillsdale, NJ: Erlbaum.

Hammill, D., & Larsen, S. (1974). The effectiveness of psycholinguistic training. *Exceptional Children, 41*, 5–14.
Hunt, E. (1983). On the nature of intelligence. *Science, 35*, 141–146.
Interagency Committee on Learning Disabilities (1987). Learning Disabilities: A report to Congress.
Jencks, C. (1977). *Who gets ahead?* New York: Basic Books.
Kavale, K. A., & Forness, S. R. (1984). A meta-analysis of the validization of Wechsler Scale Profile and Recategorizations. *Learning Disability Quarterly, 7*, 136–156.
Keogh, B. K. (1983). Classification, compliance and confusion. *Journal of Learning Disabilities, 16*(1), 25.
Keogh, B. K. (1987). Learning disabilities: In defense of a construct. *Learning Disabilities, 3*(1), 4–9.
Keogh, B. K. (1988). Diversity in search of order. In M. Wang, M. Reynolds, & H. Walberg (Eds.), *Handbook of special education research and practice, Vol. 2*. Oxford: Pergamon Press.
Lyon, G. R. (1985). Identification and remediation of learning disability subtypes: Preliminary findings. *Learning Disabilities Focus, 1*, 21–35.
McKinney, J. D., & Speece, D. L. (1986). Academic consequences and longitudinal stability of behavioural subtypes of learning disabled children. *Journal of Educational Psychology, 78*, 365–372.
Shepard, L. A. (1983). The role of measurement in educational policy: Lessons from the identification of learning disabilities. *Educational Measurement: Issues and Practice, 2*(3), 4–8.
Shepard, L. A., Smith, M. L., & Vojir, C. P. (1983). Characteristics of pupils identified as learning disabled. *American Educational Research Journal, 20*, 309–331.
Speece, D. L., McKinney, J. D., & Appelbaum, M. I. (1985). Classification and validation of behavioural subtypes of learning-disabled children. *Journal of Educational Psychology, 77*, 67–77.
Stanovich, K. (1986). Matthew effects in reading: Some consequences of individual differences in the acquisition of literacy. *Reading Research Quarterly, 21*, 360–387.
Vygotsky, L. S. (1978). *Mind in society: The development of higher psychological processes.* (M. Cole, V. John-Steiner, S. Scribner, & E. Souberman, Eds. and Trans.). Cambridge: Harvard University Press.
Wong, B. Y. L. (1986). Problems and issues in the definition of learning disabilities. In J. K. Torgeson & B. Y. L. Wong (Eds.), *Psychological and educational perspectives on learning disabilities* (pp. 3–26). Orlando, FL: Academic Press.
Wong, B. Y. L. (1987). Conceptual and methodological issues in interventions with learning disabled children and adults. In S. Vaughn & C. S. Bos (Eds.), *Research in learning disabilities: Issues and future directions* (pp. 185–202). Austin, TX: PRO-ED.
Ysseldyke, J. E., Algozzine, B., Richey, L., & Graden, J. (1983). Declaring students eligible for disability services: Why bother with the data? *Learning Disability Quarterly, 5*(1), 37–43.

CHAPTER 2

Issues and Problems Related to the Assessment of Learning Disabilities

HOWARD S. ADELMAN
LINDA TAYLOR

Widespread controversy surrounds assessment for learning disabilities. Some concerns stem from methodological, conceptual, and ethical issues and problems; others arise from sociopoliticoeconomic considerations. A broad range of fundamental concerns that must be understood and addressed in using assessment in research and practice are highlighted. Specifically stressed are controversies over what should be assessed and when and how assessment should be carried out. Also underscored is that interpreting the meaning of findings remains problematic. Concerns over privacy rights and negative consequences are reviewed. Finally, most assessment activity is seen as having the potential to be controversial because decisions to assess and decisions stemming from the data gathered often involve conflicting vested interests.

WHAT DO WE WANT TO ASSESS?

In terms of practice and most research in the field, assessment serves four major functions: classification (especially diagnostic classification), *selection* (especially placement and group assignment), *specific treatment planning,* and *evaluation* of intervention (Figure 2-1). Conflicts arise over what should be assessed with respect to these functions because of ongoing debates over who should be identified as learning disabled, what "models" for understanding human behavior should guide research and practice in the field, how problems should be remedied, what is involved in matching instruction to the learner, and what constitutes appropriate accountability and evaluation of efficacy.

WHO IS TO BE IDENTIFIED

The most fundamental issue in the field remains: Who should be classified as learning disabled? Different answers to this question lead to different assessment practices. At one extreme, there are those who argue this is a nonissue. They see no value in the term either because they believe there is no such thing as a specific learning disability or because they prefer to focus on improved teaching for all who have learning problems rather than separately classifying some as having a disability. At the other extreme are those who have adopted the term as a synonym for any learning problem. In between are those who want to reserve the term for a specific subgroup manifesting learning problems. Among this last group, some want the label to designate only chronic conditions of a "presumed neurological origin" (e.g., a central nervous system dysfunction) that interferes with learning and development. Others use the label to encompass various learning problem syndromes or attributes in which they are interested. The longstanding debate over definition reflects this classification issue; so does the lack of consensus over how to operationalize the construct (Adelman & Taylor, 1986a; Keogh, 1987; Lyon, 1987; Silver, 1988).

In 1984, members of a U.S. Task Force concluded "a learning disability cannot be identified by any one criterion such as (a) a list of behavioral characteristics; (b) a test score(s); (c) evidence about possible dysfunction in a psychological process; (d) the inability to identify other reasons for a student's failure in school; (e) identification of an etiological factor; or (f) a discrepancy between aptitude and achievement" (Chalfant, 1985, p. 12). While there seems to be widespread agreement with this conclusion, there is considerably less agreement with their view that, "By using all of these factors . . . the probability of accurately identifying LD students will be increased" (p. 12).

The problem is not just that the focus has been limited to assessing one or another of the above criteria; it is also that the conceptual and empirical work required to evolve a valid differential diagnostic process has not been done in the field of learning disabilities (Adelman, 1979a; Senf, 1986). At the root of this problem is the fact that too little attention has been devoted to

2. Issues and Problems Related to the Assessment of Learning Disabilities

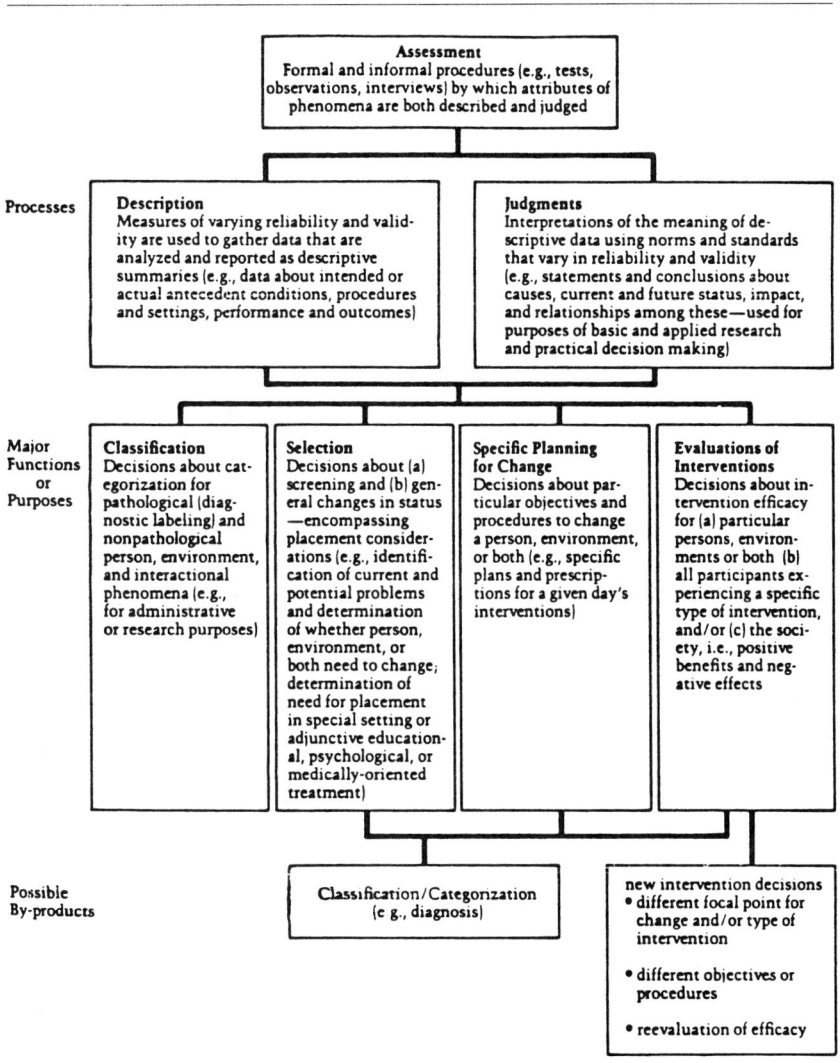

Figure 2-1. Assessment processes and purposes. From H. S. Adelman & L. Taylor, *An introduction to learning disabilities* (1986), with the kind permission of the publisher, Scott, Foresman & Co.

the theoretical problem of developing a classification scheme that delineates the phenomena defining the field.

Arguments over what to assess in order to identify whom to study and treat will continue unabated in the absence of agreement about a theory-based classification scheme. Such a scheme would conceptually differentiate learning disabilities from other major types of learning problems manifested by individuals with at least average intelligence. It would also pave the way to a concise and coherent approach to classification of subtypes not only within the group with learning disabilities (Lyon, 1985), but in other major learning problem groupings as well. For instance, we have suggested that a system of classification be developed that contrasts learning problems that are not the result of internal pathology with those that are (e.g., Adelman, 1971; Adelman & Taylor, 1986a; 1986b). Besides helping the field counter its person-oriented pathological bias, such a scheme could have a significant role in reversing the debilitating trend toward learning disabilities becoming synonymous with all learning problems. And reversing this trend is essential to reducing the heterogeneity in research samples and improving the quality of intervention studies.

CONTRASTING MODELS GUIDING ASSESSMENT IN RESEARCH AND PRACTICE

In general, concern has been raised that the focus of prevailing assessment procedures encompasses too narrow a range of factors. This criticism has been voiced more strongly as new models have emerged to challenge the prevailing view that sees the causes and correction of learning problems in terms of *person* variables (i.e., in terms of pathology [disorders and "illness"] or lack of readiness). Competing models focus on the *environment* (also emphasizing either pathology or deficiencies) or the *interaction* or transactions between person and environment.

Of the three models, only the *person* model has been used extensively to guide research and practice in the field of learning disabilities. It has focused assessment on physiological and psychological correlates of pathology, developmental deficits, or both. But, as can be seen in books on special education and neuropsychological assessment, this focus has been restricted to a delimited set of variables associated with behavior and learning (see Gaddes, 1985; Salvia & Ysseldyke, 1985; Swanson & Watson, 1982). As a result, some researchers have suggested broadening the range of correlates assessed to include factors associated with social skills, temperament and cognitive style, and a variety of cognitive and metacognitive variables.

Because of dissatisfaction with the prevailing person-oriented model, the work of researchers who focus on the *environment* has taken on prominence. This work is concerned with assessing home and school variables to clarify the role they play in the cause and correction of learning problems in general and learning disabilities in particular (see Barclay, 1983; Freund, Bradley, & Caldwell, 1979; Moos, 1979).

Going a step further, *interaction* oriented investigators hope to determine the degree to which the interplay of person and environment must be accounted for in understanding cause and correction (Adelman & Feshbach, 1971; Bandura, 1978; Coles, 1987; Sameroff, 1985). Those who have adopted an interactional (transactional, reciprocal determinist) orientation argue that they have subsumed, not rejected the other two models.

WHAT IS TO BE REMEDIED?

When it comes time to plan the specifics of an intervention, formal and informal assessment procedures are used. These include tests, observations, interviews, and trial teaching. Prevailing assessment procedures reflect contrasting views toward treatment that have dominated the field of learning disabilities. Ultimately, the purpose of all remediation is to improve functioning related to such basics as reading, language, mathematics, and interpersonal functioning. Advocates of a particular orientation argue for their procedures and sometimes argue against assessment procedures reflecting other orientations. To understand why requires an understanding of opposing views about what is to be remedied.

Essentially, three treatment viewpoints dominate current assessment practices: (1) the underlying abilities orientation, (2) the observable skills orientation, and (3) the metacognitive or general learning strategies orientation. And as facets of this last orientation have evolved, they have offered another perspective on the underlying abilities view. Each orientation defines treatment needs in different terms and thus specifies a different central focus for assessment.

Advocates of the underlying abilities orientation (sometimes called the process or diagnostic–prescriptive model) postulate that learning problems result from disabilities related to specific areas of development such as perceptual, motor, linguistic, and memory functions. Thus, they focus on assessing these areas in planning treatment. That is, they assume the underlying disabilities must be corrected or compensatory strategies must be acquired so that basics can be learned. Available tests and research based on this orientation have been criticized severely. In particular, research and logical analyses suggest that treatments based on such tests as the Developmental Test of Visual Perception and the Illinois Test of Psycholinguistic Abilities are highly suspect (see reviews by Arter & Jenkins, 1979; Coles, 1978). In response, it has been argued that such criticism is not evidence that the basic premises of the underlying abilities orientation are invalid (Colarusso, 1987; Snart, 1985). The poor validity of a given test says little about the theory upon which it is based. Recognizing this, some critics have directed their arguments against the theoretical assumptions of the approach. For instance, Carnine and Woodward (1988) assert, "After 40 years of research (related to such assumptions), with little to show for it, many have finally come to view this elusive deficit as a myth" (p. 234). Despite such assertions, the ultimate value of theories about how underlying deficits affect learning is yet to be determined. As discussed below, recent emphasis on cognitive and temperament components related to learning problems has generated a renewed, although redirected, interest in underlying abilities.

Those who follow an observable skills orientation focus on specific knowledge and skills that have not yet been learned by the individual. That is, they focus directly on the basics (including traditional readiness–prerequisite skills). Thus, skill-oriented assessments use procedures such as standardized achievement tests, unstructured, informal skill diagnostic tests, observation of daily performance, and criterion-referenced evaluations. Controversy over this orientation has included arguments about what skills should be assessed and over assumptions about whether all assessed skills need to be taught formally. In addition, motivation theorists argue there are instances when factors such as avoidance motivation and anxiety interfere with skill performance, and these must be dealt with before a valid assessment of skill deficiencies can be made. Those with an underlying abilities orientation suggest that underlying ability deficits can interfere with learning skills and that by not looking for underlying problems, interveners fail to address important prerequisites for correcting some individuals' learning problems.

Those who pursue metacognitive or general learning strategy approaches focus on the awareness and control learners can produce over the learning process. Some interveners emphasize metacognitive skills (Brown & Campione, 1986); others distinguish metacognitive knowledge from metacognitive experiences (Flavell, 1985; Garner, 1987). The most used procedures in assessing metacognitive knowledge and cognitive monitoring are verbal interviews and error detection. Procedures are chosen with reference to strategies an intervener sees as most relevant to school learning and is prepared to train the student to use (e.g., see Wiener, 1986). Such assessment procedures have been criticized both methodologically and conceptually (e.g., problems of reliability and validity related to interviews, debates over what strategies can and should be taught).

The interest in cognitive components underlying learning problems goes beyond metacognitive knowledge and cognitive monitoring (e.g., Swanson, 1988). As can be seen in the "dynamic" assessment movement, there are a variety of cognitive skills and processes that have been identified as the appropriate focus for remedial intervention (e.g., Campione & Brown, 1987; Feuerstein, 1979). Because this movement has had limited exposure but appears to be gaining considerable momentum, it warrants a bit more discussion here.

Dynamic assessment is described as a reaction to static (i.e., conventional psychometric) approaches to measuring intelligence. Static approaches are criticized for treating IQ as a trait rather than a score, thereby equating it with learning ability and ignoring the nature of underlying mechanisms of cognitive development and functioning and the influence of handicapping conditions and cultural bias. Moreover, static approaches and techniques are criticized as too limited for planning interventions.

In terms of what should be assessed, the dynamic assessment movement wants to go beyond conventional psychometric techniques in order to determine "the operation of basic psychological processes presumed responsible for acquisition of the information requested on standard tests" (Campione & Brown, 1987; p. 82). Feuerstein and his colleagues (Feuerstein, Rand, Jensen, Kaniel, & Tzuriel, 1987) stress that their approach to dynamic assessment provides not only data on cognitive functioning but on "structural cognitive modifiability ... the very structural nature of the cognitive processes that directly determine cognitive functioning in more than one area of mental activity" (pp. 42–43). Their intent is to assess the efficiency of operation of specific cognitive processes, not just to measure enhanced performance and/or the magnitude of response to instruction (see Lidz, 1987). Because dynamic assessment involves prompting/teaching, it also is used to identify intervention approaches that seem to work well with the individual being assessed. Thus, the products of the assessment are seen as providing information on both *what* and *how to teach*. In order to gather such data, the process is designed and implemented as an intervention to improve performance. Improved performance is interpreted as an indication of the learner's real capabilities and ability to change (e.g., learning potential). Because the content focus of dynamic assessment is on underlying processes, critics of the underlying abilities orientation simply reiterate arguments about the validity of measures and of underlying theoretical assumptions.

In general, it is to be expected that issues surrounding prevailing orientations to remediation will not be resolved in the near future. Thus, although specific instruments may be discredited, advocates of each orientation will continue to use assessment procedures that reflect their approach to treatment and will continue to criticize each other. At the same time, advocates of environmental and transactional models can be expected to escalate their criticism and propose alternative assessment procedures.

DIFFERENT VIEWS OF HOW BEST TO MATCH INSTRUCTION TO THE LEARNER

In addition to assessment differences resulting from treatment orientations, different views about how to design instruction for specific learners lead to divergent perspectives about what needs to be assessed. For instance, concern has been raised that assessment for *individualized* as contrasted with *personalized* instruction results in an inadequate instructional design (e.g., Adelman & Taylor, 1983; 1986b).

To clarify the point, **individualization** typically emphasizes detecting a student's deficiencies by monitoring daily performance on learning tasks and then modifying instruction to address the deficiencies. In addition, some approaches, such as dynamic assessment, attempt to assess the best teaching approach for a given child. In most cases, however, a major shortcoming of assessment guided by the concept of individualized instruction is that it overemphasizes developmental deficiencies and underemphasizes the importance of assessing motivation, especially intrinsic motivation. This is not surprising, given how little systematic attention researchers and practitioners have paid to the concept of intrinsic motivation as it relates to the causes and correction of learning and behavior problems. (This oversight may account for the lack of maintenance and generalization of effects found in the majority of studies of training strategies designed to improve learning, problem solving, and social skills.)

In contrast, the concept of personalization could broaden the focus of assessment. As we define it, **personalization** encompasses individualization. The concept stresses the importance of designing intervention to match not only current capabilities of the learner but also levels of motivation, especially intrinsic motivation. This latter emphasis is seen as critical, given the degree to which intrinsic motivation can profoundly affect current, as well as long-term performance and learning (Adelman, 1978; Deci & Chandler, 1986). Thus, the major implication of the concept of personalization for assessment and correction of learning problems is that formal and systematic procedures are needed to address motivation.

ACCOUNTABILITY AND EVALUATING EFFICACY

It is not uncommon to hear professionals in the field of learning disabilities say, "If it works, use it!" Unfortunately, there rarely is adequate evidence about what really works when the standards used are long-term outcomes rather than short-term effects.

Assessment plays a major role in efforts to answer the basic question: Are interventions for learning disabilities effective? Although some may prefer to ignore this question, two facts make this impossible. First, evaluative research is essential to improve interventions. Second, this is an age of accountability, and therefore, evaluation increasingly is mandated by legislation and government regulations.

Problems arise, however, because of limitations in measurement capability. Comprehensive evaluation requires a range of valid procedures, and development of such procedures requires considerable financial commitment. Because of the costs, evaluation usually remains a token item in most budgets.

Issues arise because of different views about the appropriate focus of evaluation (e.g., Is it sufficient to gather data on person variables? Should long-term outcomes be measured as well as immediate effects?) and about the best way to proceed in gathering and interpreting data (e.g., What specific measures and design should be used? Should there be an emphasis on minimizing the negative effects of evaluation?). Because there are different views, issues arise over whose perspective should determine the evaluation focus, methods, and interpretive standards. That is, should the views of teachers, parents, students, researchers, or funding agencies prevail? Stated more boldly, whose biases or vested interests should prevail? Conflicts between vested interests are addressed further later in the chapter.

WHEN TO ASSESS

There has been considerable controversy over the premature use of assessment practices. Some critics have argued that the proper implementation of corrective interventions can eliminate the need for specialized assessment in many cases. Other criticism has been directed at the use of procedures before they have been developed adequately. Another line of concern has stressed that multistage, as contrasted with single stage, decision making provides a better framework to guide assessment practices.

WHAT SHOULD PRECEDE ASSESSMENT?

Critics concerned about premature person-focused assessment have argued that major efforts to improve programs should come first. In this context, we recall Hobbs' (1975) views on screening. "Ideally, special screening programs to identify health problems and developmental difficulties of children should not be necessary. All children regardless of economic status should be able to participate in a comprehensive health maintenance program" (pp. 90–91). And, we would add, they should be enrolled in comprehensive psychoeducationally oriented school programs. That is, once children arrive in kindergarten and the elementary grades, the need for screening is secondary to the need to develop classroom programs to match learners' levels of motivation and development. Advocates suggest that preventive and early-age intervention programs should reduce the number of learning and behavior problems and provide improved in situ screening to identify those who continue to require special help, thereby reducing the need for special assessment.

There are a substantial number of advocates for improving programs as the first step in a screening sequence for learning problems (see review by Adelman, 1989). In essence, it is argued that, before assessment, programs to ameliorate learning problems should enhance regular learning and instruction for all children and remedy problems that arise as soon as possible and with the least intervention needed. It is recognized that accomplishment of these goals requires broadening the psychoeducational nature of regular school interventions (e.g., personalizing instruction) and increasing the availability of support mechanisms for academic learning (e.g., volunteer aides, peer tutoring, computers). Proponents also stress the need for programs to train and provide consultation for teachers regarding what interventions to pursue before referring a student for special education (e.g., prereferral interventions).

Despite advocacy for improving programs as a first step in screening, the idea remains relatively uninvestigated. An example of the type of study needed is one in which a representative sample of preschool, kindergarten, and primary school programs (across socioeconomic groups) is upgraded to improve their capability to provide personalized and remedial instruction. The proportion of children subsequently found to manifest problems in these settings would then be compared with those identified in a matched control sample of standard programs. Data from this comparison would indicate the efficacy of the experimental settings in preventing some types of problems. Identification of learning problems in each classroom would involve no more than establishing criteria for daily performance and noting those who do not meet the criteria over a period of several weeks. Students in the experimental and control samples would be followed into the upper elementary grades to determine the degree to which false-positive and false-negative identifications were made. After this first study, a second could determine whether identification sensitivity and specificity are improved by adding formal assessment screening procedures to the experimental programs.

SHOULD WE WAIT FOR VALID TOOLS?

As reviewers have consistently noted, most learning disability assessment practices raise major concerns with respect to their validity as diagnostic and prescriptive tools (e.g., Coles, 1978; Salvia & Ysseldyke, 1985). There are few who would argue that a procedure should not be used until it is perfected (if it ever could be). The consensus is that, despite inadequacies, many assessment tools can provide useful information to guide decision making—if they are properly chosen and used. But what constitutes proper choice and use?

At the very least, most will agree that an assessment procedure should meet the minimal standards set forth by the American Psychological Association and the American Educational Research Association (see "Standards for Educational and Psychological Tests," 1974). From an ethical and legal perspective, a practice should do more good than harm. In this context, it has been argued that some psychometric and rating-scale procedures for massive screening are used in ways that produce so many false-positive errors that they probably cause more harm than good and should not be used (Adelman, 1982; 1989). In California, based on the *Larry P. v. Riles* court decision, the Los Angeles Unified School District has taken the extreme position of placing a moratorium on use of IQ test data in special education placement decisions.

When an assessment procedure is seen as meeting minimal standards and providing useful information, there are still the problems that the data gathered will be limited and perhaps erroneous. There are no satisfactory solutions for these problems. A common suggestion is that additional data be gathered that might at least disconfirm false-positive findings. Ethically, it has been stressed that all concerned parties should be alerted to the limitations of the findings and the tentative nature of recommendations and conclusions based on the data. With respect to gathering disconfirming data, there is growing advocacy for viewing decision making as a multi-stage rather than single stage process.

SINGLE VS. MULTI-STAGE DECISION MAKING

Although some assessors find it necessary and/or convenient to assess and make decisions in one or two sessions, such a single stage approach has been a matter of concern. For example, with respect to screening, it is generally acknowledged that after a potential problem has been identified subsequent steps must be taken to confirm or disconfirm the problem. Critics warn, however, that diagnoses and placement decisions often may be made solely on the basis of first-level screening data. Furthermore, even when the best available assessment procedures are used, initial decisions about placement and special programming may be in error and should be confirmed or disconfirmed expeditiously through daily in situ assessment.

Similar arguments have been raised about ways to improve the diagnosis of learning disabilities and of learning disability subgroups. For instance, researchers have suggested that separating out those whose learning problems are due to central nervous system disorders requires some type of sequential filtering system (Adelman, 1971; Lindsay & Wedell, 1982; Wissink, Kass, & Ferrell, 1975). Increasingly, sequential or multistage assessments are advocated as one way to work on improving decision accuracy, including reducing the number of persons wrongly diagnosed as having learning disabilities.

HOW TO ASSESS

Conventional psychometric approaches and techniques have raised a variety of concerns about validity. A common example already noted is that, under formal assessment conditions, poor performance among problem populations may be due to low or negative (avoidance) motivation resulting from high anxiety or negative attitudes. And these factors and cultural differences are seen as negatively affecting the performance of persons from certain cultural backgrounds. That is, the assessment results for such persons are seen as contaminated and cannot be taken at face value. Thus, critics argue that it is impossible to know whether failure to demonstrate specific knowledge, abilities, or skills represents a real deficiency. The implications of this point for research and intervention are profound.

Within the psychometric tradition, efforts to deal with this criticism have stressed accounting for contaminants when interpreting findings, improving task content and administration to reduce biasing conditions (including frequent reassessments), and going beyond standardized administration to assess how much more the individual can do (e.g., allowing additional time, adding a brief prompting/teaching facet to the process). Going a step further, those in the dynamic assessment movement have argued for alternative procedures designed to assess how much more the individual can do when comprehensively prompted and taught. That is, they have pursued a highly interventionistic approach to assessment. The assessor is seen as "an active intervener who monitors and modifies the interaction with the learner in order to induce successful learning. The learner is prodded, directed, and reinforced into a role of active seeker and organizer of information" (Lidz, 1987; pp. 3–4).

CONVENTIONAL VS. INTERVENTIONIST ASSESSMENT

To underscore the fundamental issue involved here, it is useful to contrast nondynamic (conventional) with what can be described broadly as interventionist assessment. The term **interventionist** goes beyond dynamic assessment to encompass a wide variety of assessor activity designed to determine whether the person assessed can perform at a higher level. In terms of how to assess, interventionist assessment is designed to move beyond the nondynamic/static approach found in typical psychometric testing. The assessor assumes a highly active "testing the limits" stance with a view to encouraging an increased level of performance. The process often takes the form of an assess–teach–reassess approach, involving a reasonable interval of time for learning to take place.

Advocates of interventionist assessment state that the intent is not to replace but to supplement prevailing assessment procedures. They stress that they are seeking data not available through prevailing approaches (e.g., data on performance capability in a teaching situation, information on teaching approaches that appear to be effective with the learner).

Critics raise questions about the underlying assumptions and the validity of interpretations made in relation to interventionist assessment. For example, with respect to assumptions underlying dynamic assessment, they question whether deficient functions found in the cognitive processes of input, elaboration, and output can be modified to a significant extent during an assessment procedure. With respect to the validity of interpretations, they question whether performance changes primarily reflect motivational rather than cognitive modifiability.

CONDITIONS FOR ASSESSMENT

There are a variety of options in deciding how to assess. Stimulus and response conditions may vary in terms of the number and complexity of variables assessed, whether they are simulated or natural, and whether they are formal or informal. Variations also appear with respect to degree of ambiguity and subjectivity, standardization of administration, obtrusiveness, and reactive impact, and with regard to similarities and differences between the assessor and the assessed (e.g., in terms of race, cultural background, socioeconomic status, gender).

Although it is recognized that variations in practice influence both the form of assessment activity and the findings, there is little agreement about the nature and scope of such influences. Thus, there continue to be major debates over how to produce the best data in a given circumstance. The problem, of course, is akin to that of how best to match instruction to the learner.

WHAT DO THE FINDINGS MEAN?

As we have suggested, decisions about what data to gather are determined by views about what one wants to assess. Regardless of what one wants to assess, however, the actual data provide only a description of observed behavior. One does not observe intelligence or perception or attention deficits or minimal central nervous system dysfunction. One sees responses to stimuli or noncompliance with rules and directions (e.g., test answers or refusal to do a task), or one receives reports of poor performance and misbehavior. Concerns therefore arise that assessment and decision making procedures may lead to

- inadequate descriptions of a phenomenon (e.g., Does the procedure provide information relevant to the types of interpretations and judgments we want to make? Does the procedure measure what it says it does? Only what it says it does? All of what it says it does? Does it provide new information?)

- invalid interpretations and judgments of phenomena (e.g., Are inferences justified? Are appropriate norms and standards available?)
- invalid decisions (e.g., How relevant are data for decisions to be made?)

If one sets out to assess cognitive deficiencies, for example, one wants to be able to discuss findings in terms of such deficiencies and to judge the nature and scope of deficiencies based on appropriate norms and standards.

VALIDITY AND UTILITY

Deficiencies with regard to validity and utility generate controversy not only about what findings mean but about the value of assessment per se. The crux of the problem can be appreciated by awareness that, although the reliability of an assessment procedure can be established in a relatively technical and objective way, validation requires a great deal of rational and subjective activity. As Cronbach (1970) stressed with respect to assessing constructs, "Construct validity is established through a long-continued interplay between observation, reasoning, and imagination.... The process of construct validation is the same as that by which scientific theories are developed" (p. 142). Because determining a procedure's validity and utility is difficult and costly, assessors find themselves having to use the "best" that is available—even though the best may not be very good. The inevitable result has been criticism of procedures and decisions based on them.

NORMS AND STANDARDS

The problem of determining meaning is compounded by the inadequacy of available norms and the lack of consensus regarding standards used in interpreting assessment data. To understand the problem, it is important to appreciate the nature of the interpretive/judgmental process in assessment, and this requires an appreciation of the way standards and norms are used.

For our purposes **standards** refers to values or a theoretical idea used in making judgments about what has been assessed. Such judgments involve conclusions about what was assessed with respect to consistency with some theory, whether a problem exists, and whether something is good or bad. **Norms** are not standards (i.e., they are not value or theoretical statements). Formal norms are based on research and systematic observation. In practice, any set of previous findings (including nonsystematic observations over years of professional practice) might constitute a set of norms with which to compare assessment data. After formal or informal norms are used, it is commonplace to apply some set of standards to make judgments about good and bad. This can happen so quickly that it may not be apparent that judgments have been made. For example, a score from a test or rating scale that falls above or below some predetermined average may be quickly translated into a judgment that the performance was unacceptably low and indicative of significant underachievement, developmental lag, or pathology. This is understandable, especially with tests of achievement and developmental indices. However, it is important not to lose sight of the fact that a value judgment—a standard—has been used. The use of norms by themselves does not lead to the judgment of good or bad.

All in all, controversy seems inevitable given that assessors must rely on inadequate procedures and norms and given the lack of consensus about standards used in making judgments about learning and behavior problems (Buros, 1974; Coles, 1987; Schrag & Divoky, 1975). And the criticism is justified when professionals proceed in uncritical ways. As Buros (1974) noted, practitioners

"seem to have an unshakable will to believe the exaggerated claims of test authors and publishers. If these users were better informed regarding the merits and limitations of their testing instruments, they would probably be less happy and successful in their work. The test user who has faith—however unjustified—can speak with confidence in interpreting test results and making recommendations. The well-informed test user cannot do this; [this person] knows that the best of our tests are still highly fallible instruments which are extremely difficult to interpret with assurance in individual cases. Consequently, [the user] must interpret test results cautiously with so many reservations that others wonder whether [s]he really knows what [s]he is talking about" (p. xxxvii).

ETHICAL CONCERNS

Impetus for ethical concerns about negative aspects of assessment of learning disabilities has come from reported misuses and abuses of test data. Criticism has come from political conservatives, liberals, and civil libertarians. At the center of the controversy is the traditional tension between society's rights, responsibilities, and needs and individuals' rights and freedoms. Critics have argued that individual rights and liberties are not sufficiently safeguarded and have pushed for greater legal protection of rights and due process. This is leading to improvements in consent procedures.

Another line of ethical criticism stresses the errors, costs, and "negative side effects" of assessment. Some critics stress psychological, social, economic, and possible physical harm to individuals; others point out that subgroups are discriminated against; and a few have raised the specter of the quality of life in society being significantly lowered by institutionalizing assessment practices. In contrast, some professionals underscore that it is a core ethical responsibility of professionals to use assessment practices to maximize benefits for individuals and society (Adelman, 1979b). These matters can be highlighted by briefly discussing concerns about privacy rights and negative consequences of assessment.

PRIVACY

With respect to privacy rights, there is a dual concern: invasion of privacy and misuse of information. These concerns arise when the information is considered highly sensitive and could lead to diagnoses and evaluations that are perceived negatively. The situation is especially volatile when assessment is carried out primarily to serve society or institutional objectives.

Power to assess—to obtain and use information about others—is power to shape lives. Legally and ethically, there is a need to keep such power in check. At issue is the nature of the control a person ought to have over the gathering and disclosure of information about himself or herself. In other words, when should society be able to mandate assessment and, in the process, infringe on individual rights? Stated this way, the question is seen as one aspect of the broader concern over when society should be allowed to coerce individuals and thereby deny a variety of rights and freedoms (Adelman & Taylor, 1988; Robinson, 1974). From this issue springs a variety of questions. What kind of information is it reasonable to gather on an individual? What safeguards exist with respect to highly personal and sensitive information? What types of records should be kept and who should have access to them? What restrictions should be placed on how information can be used? Is parental consent sufficient when children don't want to be assessed?

The complexity of ethical concerns is well illustrated when individuals come for help. A request for help may be seen as consent to gather data on anything the assessor sees as relevant. Given adequate theory and evidence about what is relevant, it would be a relatively clear-cut matter to explain what is needed and why as a basis for eliciting informed consent. Unfortunately, the state of knowledge regarding psychoeducational problems is not sophisticated enough to specify what information is absolutely needed. Thus, assessors develop their own criteria for what should be assessed. Some feel free to pursue anything that intuitively seems significant at the moment. Although well-meaning, they may pry into embarrassing and painful areas of a person's life to gather data that, ironically, may be irrelevant. Some data gathered amounts to little more than gossip, with no significant meaning for dealing with the problem. Such data can be even more harmful when it is used inappropriately (e.g., to prescribe treatment).

For a variety of political and legal reasons, many school systems have moved away from presumptions of consent. In the United States, this movement has been accelerated by federal law (i.e., the Family Educational Rights and Privacy Act of 1974). The apparent result has been that (1) less assessment data are gathered and circulated in schools, (2) consent is sought more frequently when a need for assessment exists, and (3) due process is being emphasized with respect to student and parent access to records and for complaints and corrections of data that may be inappropriate or in error.

Critics caution, however, that the burden of protecting rights still falls mostly on those assessed. Consumer advocates advise students or parents to object if they dislike either what is asked or the procedures. In doing so, however, there is a risk of being refused services or having the objection interpreted as defensiveness, hostility, or lack of cooperation.

The situation is further complicated where procedures have become routine and institutionalized. Under such circumstances, those involved may see neither a "rights" issue nor a need for consent. For example, physicians, psychologists, educators, and a variety of other personnel in schools, clinics, and agencies routinely administer tests and questionnaires with little or no explanation about why the information is needed or about any limitations with respect to the procedures' validity. When procedures have become a natural part of an institution's operations, those administering them may be genuinely unaware of invading privacy or coercing. Those who are assessed may assume the experience must be essential, and any discomfort is a necessary "negative side effect."

NEGATIVE CONSEQUENCES

Every major intervention has some negative consequence. Assessment is no exception. It is customary to speak of "negative side effects," but this wording tends to ignore errors and economic costs and is more appropriately applied to minor and perhaps low-probability phenomena. Negative consequences encompass the range of potentially significant harm that may occur.

Negative consequences related to assessment, such as extreme anxiety, may occur during the process or may be an immediate or long-term outcome. It is widely recognized that persons who are assessed and labeled may be stigmatized, isolated, and excluded from important experiences, and this may negatively affect motivation and hinder full and healthy development. Evidence suggests that certain subgroups are more likely than others to experience such negative effects (e.g., see Mercer & Brown, 1973; Swanson & Watson, 1982). Civil rights hearings and court cases have highlighted the intentional and unintentional cultural and sex-role bias of formal assessment. Unfortunately, little data exist on the frequency of negative consequences, including inevitable errors, or about financial costs to individuals and to taxpayers.

Illich (1976) and others have warned that the cost to society may be more than financial. He has argued that overreliance on professionals leads to alarming incapacity among individuals and natural support systems to cope with problems. The rapid rise in number of children diagnosed as having learning disabilities, and the highly specialized (and sometimes inappropriate) treatments prescribed may be a poignant example of such effects.

From a practical perspective, concern over negative consequences generally centers on how to minimize negative effects and be certain that benefits outweigh harm. Often at issue is whether the positive is outweighing the negative. There does seem to be widespread agreement, however, about the following guidelines. (1) Assessors are obligated at least to be aware of potential negative consequences, such as immediate and long-term harm to individuals, groups, and society. (2) Where consent is sought, assessors are required ethically and often legally to inform prospective consenters of potential positive and negative consequences. (3) As they attempt to maximize benefits, assessors are obligated to minimize potential negative effects. (4) Although they cannot follow a student around to prevent self-fulfilling prophecies, they are expected to take steps to correct and guard records and equip students and parents to protect and advocate for themselves. (5) Assessors are expected to acknowledge whenever findings are inconclusive and not rationalize or dismiss uncertainties and incongruities in findings.

WHO DECIDES? THE POLITICS OF ASSESSMENT

Not only is decision making the final outcome of assessment, but decisions are made at each stage of the assessment process. For example, in planning assessment, there are decisions about the need for and the focal point of assessment and about what procedures to use. In many instances, these matters are resolved so routinely that those involved hardly are aware that decisions were made. In other cases, heated arguments arise. An already noted instance is the debate over the appropriateness of preschool screening programs to detect learning disabilities. (Can it be done appropriately?)

Pivotal to all such debates are considerations about criteria and procedures for decision making. Where there is disagreement, a particularly critical concern is Who decides what the criteria and procedures should be?

When the objectives of the individual are compatible with other involved parties (e.g., parent, teacher, society), the question of who decides about criteria and procedures may be of little concern. However, when ideas and interests conflict, who decides becomes profoundly important. The problem of conflicting interests is reflected in the extensive concern raised about society's ability to exercise control through psychological and educational interventions (e.g., Adelman & Taylor, 1986b; 1988; Coles, 1978; Mnookin, 1985; Robinson, 1974; Schrag & Divoky, 1975). At one extreme, it is argued there are times when society must put its needs before individual rights by pursuing certain activities designed to maintain itself (e.g., compulsory testing); at the other extreme, it is argued that activities that jeopardize individuals' rights (e.g., coercion, invasion of privacy) are never justified. For many persons, however, neither extreme is acceptable, especially with respect to minors.

Without agreeing or disagreeing with a particular position, one can appreciate the importance of the debate for our field. Specifically, it serves to heighten awareness that (1) no society is devoid of some degree of coercion in dealing with its members (e.g., no right or liberty is absolute), and that such coercion has been seen as especially justified in intervening with minors; (2) interventions such as assessment can be used to serve the vested interests of subgroups in a society at the expense of other subgroups (e.g., to deprive minorities, the poor, females, and legal minors of certain freedoms and rights); and (3) informed consent and due process of law are central to the protection of individuals when there are conflicting interests at stake (e.g., about who or what should be blamed for a problem and be expected to carry the brunt of corrective measures). This awareness and greater sensitivity to conflicts among those with vested interests in interventions are essential if children are to be adequately protected from abuse by those with power to exercise control over them.

Usually, control of decision making is maintained by those with greatest authority in a situation. This is a questionable practice when those in authority have no legitimate basis for assuming power or have interests that conflict with those of other participants. The former circumstance includes instances when professionals assess and prescribe outside their area of competence or in areas where the state of knowledge precludes sufficient expertise and when professionals inappropriately assume consent of participants. The latter circumstance includes instances where professionals' values or financial interests are at variance with those seeking services and when society pursues its rights and responsibilities at the expense of the rights and liberties of individuals.

It is when ideas and interests conflict that the "political" facets of assessment are underscored. Power conflicts and imbalances are apparent when those with authority are in a position to have their vested psychological, social, political, or economic interests prevail in decision making even though those without such authority dislike the decisions and indicate their dissatisfaction.

Authority stems from various psychological and sociopoliticoeconomic factors, which may or may not be institutionalized and legitimized. Therefore, political facets of assessment are not limited to power imbalances stemming from legislated authority. The overt political facets of assessment are seen in the many instances when assessments are required by organizational (government, school, industry) policies and when assessment data are used for planning, evaluating, and policy-making purposes. Covert political facets are potentially present in all other assessment activity. What is being described is any power imbalance inappropriately detrimental to the interests of one or more participants.

Concerns have been raised about the decision-making role of those assessed, especially persons presumed to be less than competent, which seems often to be the case for children and those having learning or emotional problems. Currently, the role students, clients, and their advocates should play in decision making is being debated in legal and professional circles (e.g., Melton, Koocher, & Saks, 1983; Mnookin, 1985; Taylor & Adelman, 1986). Efforts to ensure protection for those denied a decision-making role have been reflected in court cases and various advocacy programs. Improved guidelines should soon emerge clarifying both the legitimate bases for denying individuals decision-making power and the protection safeguarding their interests when others have decision-making power. Because overt and covert power imbalances appear inevitable, stringent protection of individual rights is essential. There must be understanding of and commitment to ethical principles by professionals and society as a whole if abuses are to be constrained.

CONCLUDING COMMENTS

A great deal of controversy surrounds assessment in the field of learning disabilities. Although some of the controversy is about the deficiencies and limitations of specific procedures, broader concerns and criticism have been directed at the way assessment is used to shape research and practice and related policy decisions. Even when relatively objective assessment data are used, decisions referencing the data often are extremely subjective. This is not surprising given that most decisions in the field involve considerations that go well beyond availability of valid data. More often than not, complex sociopoliticoeconomic value questions are involved. Indeed, in some cases, seemingly relevant data are ignored in order to arrive at a decision the decision makers see as viable and beneficial (cf. Woodhead, 1988). Thus, controversy is inevitable, and as Thorndike and Hagen (1977) have aptly stated, "The wisdom of the decider is crucial" (p. 20).

REFERENCES

Adelman, H. S. (1971). The not so specific learning disability population. *Exceptional Children, 37*, 528–533.
Adelman, H. S. (1978). The concept of intrinsic motivation: Implications for practice and research related to learning disabilities. *Learning Disability Quarterly, 1,* 43–54.
Adelman, H. S. (1979a). Diagnostic classification of LD: A practical necessity and a procedural problem. *Learning Disability Quarterly, 2,* 56–62.
Adelman, H. S. (1979b). Diagnostic classification of LD: Research and ethical perspectives. *Learning Disability Quarterly, 2,* 5–16.
Adelman, H. S. (1982). Identifying learning problems at an early age: A critical appraisal. *Journal of Clinical Child Psychology, 11,* 255–261.
Adelman, H. S. (1989). Prediction and prevention of learning disabilities: Current state of the art and future directions. In L. Bond & B. Compas (Eds.), *Primary prevention and promotion in the schools*. Newbury Park, CA: Sage.
Adelman, H. S., & Feshbach, S. (1971). Predicting reading failure: Beyond the readiness model. *Exceptional Children, 37,* 349–354.
Adelman, H. S., & Taylor, L. (1983). *Learning disabilities in perspective*. Glenview, IL: Scott, Foresman.
Adelman, H. S., & Taylor, L. (1986a). The problems of definition and differentiation and the need for a classification schema. *Journal of Learning Disabilities, 19,* 514–520.
Adelman, H. S., & Taylor, L. (1986b). *An introduction to learning disabilities*. Glenview, IL: Scott, Foresman.
Adelman, H. S., & Taylor, L. (1988). Clinical child psychology: Fundamental intervention questions and problems. *Clinical Psychology Review, 8,* 637–665.
Arter, J.A., & Jenkins, J. R. (1979). Differential diagnosis—Prescriptive teaching: A critical appraisal. *Review of Educational Research, 49,* 517–555.
Bandura, A. (1978). The self system in reciprocal determinism. *American Psychologist, 33,* 344–358.
Barclay, J. R. (1983) *Barclay Classroom Assessment System*. Los Angeles: Western Psychological Services.
Brown, A. L., & Campione, J. C. (1986). Psychological theory and the study of learning disabilities. *American Psychologist, 14,* 1059–1068.
Buros, O. K. (Ed.) (1974). *Tests in print II*. Highland Park, NJ: Gryphon.
Campione, J. C., & Brown, A. L. (1987). Linking dynamic assessment with school achievement. In C. S. Lidz (Ed.), *Dynamic assessment: An interactional approach to evaluating learning potential*. New York: Guilford Press.
Carnine, D., & Woodward, J. (1988). Paradigms lost: Learning disabilities and the new ghost in the old machine. *Journal of Learning Disabilities, 21,* 233–236.

Chalfant, J. C. (1985). Identifying learning disabled students: A summary of the National Task Force Report. *Learning Disabilities Focus, 1,* 9–20.
Colarusso, R. P. (1987). Diagnostic-prescriptive teaching. In M. Wang, M. Reynolds, & H. Walberg (Eds.), *The handbook of special education: Research and practice.* Oxford, England: Pergamon Press.
Coles, G. S. (1978). The learning disabilities test battery: Empirical and social issues. *Harvard Educational Review, 48,* 313–340.
Coles, G. S. (1987). *The learning mystique: A critical look at "learning disabilities."* New York: Pantheon.
Cronbach, L. J. (1970). *Essentials of psychological testing,* 3rd ed. New York: Harper & Row.
Deci, E. L., & Chandler, C. L. (1986). The importance of motivation for the future of the LD field. *Journal of Learning Disabilities, 19,* 587–594.
Feuerstein, R. (1979). *The dynamic assessment of retarded performers.* Baltimore: University Park Press.
Feuerstein, R., Rand, Y., Jensen, M. R., Kaniel, S., & Tzuriel, D. (1987). Prerequisites for assessment of learning potential: The LAPD model. In C. S. Lidz (Ed.), *Dynamic assessment: An interactional approach to evaluating learning potential.* New York: Guilford Press.
Flavell, J. J. (1985). *Cognitive development.* Englewood Cliffs, NJ: Prentice-Hall.
Freund, J. H., Bradley, R. H., & Caldwell, B. M. (1979). The home environment in the assessment of learning disabilities. *Learning Disability Quarterly, 2,* 39–51.
Gaddes, W. H. (1985). *Learning disabilities and brain function: A neuropsychological approach.* 2nd ed. New York: Springer-Verlag.
Garner, R. (1987). *Metacognition and reading comprehension.* Norwood, NJ: Ablex.
Hobbs, N. (1975). *The futures of children: Categories, labels, and their consequences.* San Francisco: Jossey-Bass.
Illich, I. (1976). *Medical nemesis.* New York: Pantheon.
Keogh, B. K. (1987). Learning disabilities: In defense of a construct. *Learning Disabilities Research, 3,* 4–9.
Larry P. v. Riles, 343 FSupp. 1306 (N.D. Calif., 1972).
Lidz, C. S. (Ed.) (1987). *Dynamic assessment: An interactional approach to evaluating learning potential.* New York: Guilford Press.
Lindsay, G. A., & Wedell, K. (1982). The early identification of educationally "at risk" children revisited. *Journal of Learning Disabilities, 15,* 212–217.
Lyon, G. R. (1985). Identification and remediation of learning disability subgroups: Preliminary findings. *Learning Disabilities Focus, 1,* 21–35.
Lyon, G. R. (1987). Severe discrepancy: Theoretical psychometric, developmental, and educational issues. *Learning Disabilities Research, 3,* 10–11.
Melton, G. B., Koocher, G. P., & Saks, M. (Eds.) (1983). *Children's competence to consent.* New York: Plenum.
Mercer, J. R., & Brown, W. C. (1973). Racial differences in IQ: Fact or artifact? In C. Seena (Ed.), *The fallacy of IQ.* New York: Third Press.
Mnookin, R. H. (1985). *In the interest of children: Advocacy, law reform and public policy.* New York: W. H. Freeman.
Moos, R. (1979). *Evaluating educational environments.* San Francisco: Jossey-Bass.
Robinson, D. N. (1974). Harm, offense, and nuisance: Some first steps in the establishment of an ethics of treatment. *American Psychologist, 29,* 233–238.
Salvia, J., & Ysseldyke, J. E. (1985). *Assessment in special and remedial education.* 3rd ed. Boston: Houghton Mifflin.
Sameroff, A. J. (1985). Environmental factors in the early screening of children at

risk. In W. K. Frankenburg, R. N. Emde, & J. W. Sullivan (Eds.), *Early identification of children at risk: An international perspective*. New York: Plenum.
Schrag, P., & Divoky, D. (1975). *The myth of the hyperactive child & other means of child control*. New York: Pantheon.
Senf, G. M. (1986). LD research in sociological and scientific perspective. In J. K. Torgesen & B. Y. L. Wong (Eds.), *Psychological and educational perspectives on learning disabilities*. Orlando, FL: Academic Press.
Silver, L. B. (1988). A review of the federal government's Interagency Committee on Learning Disabilities report to the Congress. *Learning Disabilities Focus, 3*, 73–80.
Snart, F. (1985). Cognitive-processing approaches to the assessment and remediation of learning problems: An interview with J. P. Das and Reuven Feuerstein. *Journal of Psychoeducational Assessment, 3*, 1–14.
Standards for educational and psychological tests (1974). Washington, D. C.: American Psychological Association.
Swanson, H. L. (1988). Toward a metatheory of learning disabilities. *Journal of Learning Disabilities, 21*, 196–209.
Swanson, H. L., & Watson, B. L. (1982). *Educational and psychological assessment of exceptional children*. St. Louis: Mosby.
Taylor, L., & Adelman, H. S. (1986). Facilitating children's participation in decisions that affect them: From concept to practice. *Journal of Clinical Child Psychology, 15*, 346–351.
Thorndike, R. L., & Hagen, E. P. (1977). *Measurement and evaluation in psychology and education*, 4th ed. New York: Wiley.
Wiener, J. (1986). Alternatives in the assessment of the learning disabled adolescent: A learning strategies approach. *Learning Disabilities Focus, 1*, 97–107.
Wissink, J. F., Kass, C. E., & Ferrell, W. R. (1975). A Bayesian approach to the identification of children with learning disabilities. *Journal of Learning Disabilities, 8*, 158–166.
Woodhead, M. (1988). When psychology informs public policy: The case of early childhood intervention. *American Psychologist, 43*, 443–454.

CHAPTER 3

Assessment for Instruction
JOHN WILLS LLOYD
BARBARA J. BLANDFORD

Academic difficulties are a hallmark of students identified as learning disabled. Deficits in oral language, reading, spelling, composition, computation, handwriting, and other areas may be confirmed in the formal assessment required by eligibility and triennial review procedures. In addition to showing how well pupils perform in comparison with their peers on general measures of academic endeavor, formal assessment may also reveal how well they perform in specific areas of endeavor (i.e., on subtests of a diagnostic instrument). However, one of the principal purposes of assessment—assessment for instructional planning—is poorly served by the use of formal assessment data, even by diagnostic instruments.

Although the relationship between assessment and instruction has regularly been of concern to special educators (cf., Bateman, 1964), information provided by formal assessment does not usually enable teachers to plan detailed and relevant instruction. For example, Schenck (1980) found that long- and short-term goals and objectives on individualized education programs are, at best, only partially based on formal assessment data. Furthermore, there is little correspondence among formal assessment reports and daily lesson plans (D'Amato & Dean, 1987). Thus, assessment and instruction have been uncoupled (Meyers, 1988; Meyers, Pfeffer, & Erlbaum, 1985).

We suspect that much of this problem is the result of the forms of assessment that have traditionally been practiced in the field of learning disabilities. We contend that there has been an overemphasis on assessment of traits (e.g., intelligence), abilities (e.g., auditory processing), and developmental stages (e.g., conservation). This emphasis has propagated what Engelmann (1967) characterized as inclusive and irrelevant explanations. Inclusive explanations describe problems in such broad terms that only nebulous teaching recommendations can be drawn from them; for example, when assessment reveals that the reason a student is not learning reading skills is a problem in auditory discrimination, the direct solution is to teach auditory discrimination. Irrelevant explanations cast problems in such a way that instruction is not implied; for example, when assessment reveals that the cause of a student's failure to learn certain arithmetic skills is that he or she has not progressed to the formal operations stage, no specific instruction is implied (the solution is to await his or her development of concepts characteristic of that stage).

In this chapter we provide an alternative view of assessment, one that specifies an integrated relationship between assessment and instruction (Heron & Heward, 1982; Howell & Morehead, 1987). After discussing our view of the purposes of assessment for instruction, we propose methods of student and environmental assessment that provide information that can be applied directly to the teaching–learning situation.

PURPOSES OF INSTRUCTIONAL ASSESSMENT

There are three main purposes of instructional assessment. One purpose is to identify the areas of instructional need; this is the **direction** of instruction. The second is to determine the skills and sequence of skills to be taught; this is the **starting point** of instruction. The third is to ascertain **how to deliver** instruction. The fourth is to determine whether instruction is succeeding; this permits **correction** of instruction.

IDENTIFYING AREAS OF INSTRUCTIONAL NEED

By determining the direction of instruction, we mean that the teacher or other assessor must ascertain what broad areas of instruction are the appropriate foci for teaching for an individual pupil. These broad areas of instruction may include speaking clearly, following directions, decoding in reading, comprehending written material, writing legible text, spelling written words, composing written material, computing numbers, comprehending numerical statements, writing numerical statements, solving algorithms, and appropriately asserting one's position.

In large part, the direction of instruction is predetermined because schools are charged with teaching these skills to virtually all pupils. However, pupils with learning disabilities may have difficulties with performance in certain areas. Thus, assessment identifies the direction in which instruction should proceed. These are essentially the goals of instruction (e.g., to improve computing).

In providing such direction, formal assessment results* attain perhaps their greatest utility. Judgments about areas on which to focus can be appropriately influenced by comparing a pupil's performance to local or national norms. This is essentially accomplished during eligibility meetings. However, knowing the direction in which instruction should proceed is insufficient when planning an educational program.

IDENTIFYING SPECIFIC SKILL DEFICITS

In addition to knowing the direction of instruction, the teacher must know where along the ray described by that direction to initiate instruction. We assume that there are many component skills for any given area of endeavor and that these can be ordered sequentially on the basis of which are learned earlier than others or which are required by others. Given this assumption, teachers must identify the component skills on which instruction must be focused. These are essentially the objectives of instruction.

Although some formal instruments purport to assess performance at this level of specificity, they do so only in a cursory fashion. For example, an instrument may have subscores for addition, subtraction, multiplication, division, fractions, measurement, money, and several other areas within arithmetic. Despite the fact that this is a more fine grained analysis than is provided in ascertaining the direction of instruction, it is not specific enough to allow the teacher to know that instruction must focus on specific deficits (e.g., subtraction with regrouping that involves zeros) or teaching certain strategies.

To ascertain this starting point the teacher must have trial tasks that sample the skills and subskills along a hierarchy and rules about placement decisions based on pupil performance on the trial tasks (Howell, 1986). Although some instructional programs could provide such tasks and guidelines, placement tests are used more often. Thus, in most cases, teachers must develop them.

SELECTING INSTRUCTIONAL DELIVERY PROCEDURES

In addition to knowing in what area and on what specific tasks instruction should focus, teachers must know some things about how instruction is

---

*Some less formal assessment methods, particularly *curriculum-based assessment*, have been proposed as means for providing such direction. Hopwever, these methods become far more formal in such applications because they depend on use of *norms* (Shinn, Tindal, & Stein, 1988).

most appropriately delivered. We assume that the initial approach to this question is to deliver instruction in ways that are consistent with evidence about the most effective teaching practices (e.g., Brophy & Good, 1986; Rosenshine & Stevens, 1986). However, specific features of such instruction may have to be adjusted to maximize the performance of pupils with learning disabilities. For example, some pupils may require more detailed manipulation of practice or reinforcement schedules or may respond more appropriately when the pace of instruction is held constant rather than varied.

We see decisions about the delivery of instruction as empirical matters. That is, they can be answered best by manipulating variables and ascertaining the effects of these manipulations. Obviously, to accomplish this, one must collect data about performance and make teaching decisions based on those data.

MONITORING THE EFFECTS OF INSTRUCTION

Once instruction has begun, assessment should not end. To do so would be analogous to choosing an appropriate direction and starting point but then traveling with one's eyes closed. Progress toward goals and objectives must be monitored. Assessment of this sort should have both a formative and a summative nature. It should shape instruction on the basis of pupil performance, causing modifications in it. Modifications may come in many forms; for example, progress-monitoring data may reveal that (a) target levels of performance have been reached and that a maintenance strategy (e.g., distributed practice) should be adopted, (b) progress has faltered and different teaching procedures should be investigated (e.g., changes in reinforcement density), or (c) progress is continuing at a satisfactory rate and current practices should be continued.

Some instructional programs provide periodic progress-monitoring checks. In most cases, however, teachers must assess progress by devising and administering instruments. The latter case has been helped mightily by the emphasis on systems for monitoring progress (Deno, 1985; Howell & Morehead, 1987).

ASSESSMENT OF THE STUDENT

Much of the assessment practiced in learning disabilities focuses on the learner. One hope of such assessment is that some characteristic of the learner will indicate what kind of instruction she or he should receive. A more appropriate application of the assessment of learners is to ascertain their level of performance in relation to a given task. This is consistent with the recommendation that diagnosis focus on instruction (Engelmann,

Granzin, & Severson, 1979). Engelmann and his colleagues proposed examining learner performance with the assumption that pupils will form responses using the minimum amount of information possible. Thus, if a task allows more than one response, the pupil will use the response that requires the least knowledge. To examine this, teachers must vary the task systematically so that the learner must respond using maximum knowledge. This is done by creating tasks that admit to one and only one interpretation—"faultless" instruction (Engelmann & Carnine, 1982). Learners who fail under a maximum knowledge test can be safely assumed to have atypical learning characteristics or knowledge deficits.

In the first of the following sections we discuss the matching of instruction to student characteristics. In the second we discuss the use of pupil assessment data that is drawn almost directly from the instructional situation. In the third we discuss the use of student performance data as a means of monitoring instructional progress.

CHARACTERISTICS OF THE LEARNER

The history of special education is replete with examples of special educators' efforts to match individual student's characteristics with specific instructional treatments (Mann, 1979). The aptitude–treatment interaction model appeals to educators because of the necessarily individualized nature of the teaching methods; individualization of instruction has long been a key concept in the field of special education. Research on aptitude–treatment interactions is extensive, but has not supported the conventional wisdom that selecting a teaching method on the basis of student traits (abilities, personality characteristics) will result in greater achievement (Lloyd, 1984).

Tarver and Dawson (1978), for example, reviewed the literature on modality preference and the teaching of reading. They concluded that modality preference does not interact significantly with method of teaching reading. In other words, teaching to pupils' strengths will not necessarily increase their reading achievement. Despite the disclaimers of some (e.g., Dunn, 1988), other examinations of the same literature (e.g., Arter & Jenkins, 1979; Cronbach & Snow, 1977; Kavale & Forness, 1987; Larrivee, 1981; Ysseldyke, 1973) reveal essentially the same results. Perhaps more circumspect analyses will provide such guidance (see Lyon and Flynn, Chapter 4).

If a priori assessment of student characteristics does not lead to effective instructional planning and practices, what assessment methods should teachers and educational diagnosticians use? Discussions of assessment for instruction generally call for assessment of the pupil's interaction with instructional tasks. We turn to those proposals now.

TASK PERFORMANCE

Instead of examining learners' traits, other features, such as their interaction with tasks, should be the focus of assessment because these provide teachers with information relevant to instruction (Dickenson, 1980). The remainder of this section will focus on recommendations about the use of tasks in assessing students for the purposes of instructional planning. Task analysis, trial teaching, and interviews are considered.

Task analysis

Dickenson (1980), Hughes (1982), Howell, Kaplan, and O'Connell (1979), and Lloyd (1979) suggested using a task-analysis method for assessing student performance. Hughes (1982) defined task analysis as "the classification of target objectives into their component skills for purposes of identifying the prerequisites of what is to be learned" (p. 273). Tasks may be analyzed in any of several ways (Hughes, 1982; Resnick & Ford, 1978). Given a task analysis, a teacher or diagnostician can assess student performance by ascertaining whether the pupil can perform adequately on each of the various component skills. For example, Howell (1986) provided the task-analysis specification of sentence combining skills in composition that is shown in Table 3-1. Such an analysis would permit assessment, as illustrated in the bottom right corner of the table. Assessment tasks would be devised for each of the component skills (as suggested by the objectives for each) and administered. The component skills on which the pupil cannot perform well would constitute targets for further instruction.

Trial Teaching

Feuerstein, Rand, and Hoffman (1979), Hamilton (1983), Schworm and Abelseth (1981), and Zigmond and colleagues (Zigmond & Miller, 1986; Zigmond, Vallecorsa, & Silverman, 1983) discussed trial teaching, another direct method of assessing students for instruction. In trial teaching, teachers gather information that will enable them to determine if instruction is producing the desired responses from students or at what level pupils function appropriately.

The teacher might make decisions about placement by using trial-teaching procedures. Lovitt and Hansen (1976) provided an example of using such procedures. They placed pupils in reading texts by assessing correct oral reading rate, incorrect oral reading rate, and correct comprehension answers on sample passages selected from a reading series. Based on decision rules (e.g., "Place a pupil in the highest level reader in which his average correct rate was between 45–65 wpm, his average incorrect rate

Table 3-1. Specifications for the Task, "Combines Sentences in Writing"

	Conditions			
	WITH PROMPTS (I)		SPONTANEOUSLY (II)	
	PROFICIENCY		PROFICIENCY	
Content	ACCURACY (1)	FLUENCY (2)	ACCURACY (1)	FLUENCY (2)
Coordinate Structures (A)	I.A.1	I.A.2	II.A.1	II.A.2
Adverbial Structures (B)	I.B.1	I.B.2	II.B.1	II.B.2
Restrictive Noun Noun Modifiers (C)	I.C.1	I.C.2	II.C.1	II.C.2
Noun Substitutes (D)	I.D.1	I.D.2	II.D.1	II.D.2

EXAMPLE	TASK		STUDENT A	STUDENT B
I.B.1	Combine sentences with prompts by adverbial structures with 100% accuracy		pass	pass
I.B.2	Combine sentences with prompts by using adverbial structures correctly in 5 seconds (fluency)		pass	pass
II.B.1	Combine sentences spontaneously by using adverbial structures with 100% accuracy		fail	pass
II.B.2	Combine sentences spontaneously by using adverbial structures correctly in 10 seconds (fluency)		fail	fail

From "Direct Assessment of Academic Performance" by K. W. Howell, 1986, *School Psychology Review*, 15, 329. Copyright 1986 by the National Association of School Psychologists. Reprinted by permission.

was between 4–8 wpm, and his average comprehension score between 50–75%" p. 350), pupils were assigned to particular readers.

Similarly, Zigmond et al. (1983) proposed that the teacher present a lesson under typical conditions and gather data on each child's performance. Then the teacher should systematically manipulate parts of the presentation. For example, size and composition of student groups, instructional techniques, types of materials used, distribution of practice, and amount of teacher involvement could be altered. With each manipulation, the teacher collects data to evaluate the success of the teaching. By completion of the trial teaching assessments, the teacher will have a record of how each student responds under various conditions. Of course, the possibility of order and practice confounds will render these data primarily of heuristic value.

Interviews

Another means of assessment for instruction involves interviewing individual students about how they perform learning tasks. Lloyd and Loper (1986) described how interviews and observations could be used to assess metacognitive skills such as project planning, strategy application, task monitoring, error correction, and overall task evaluation. Interview questions are asked to ascertain whether pupils are aware of the use of such strategies. A think-aloud assessment could be used to ascertain whether pupils apply the strategies.

Wiener (1986) provided a comprehensive set of informal instruments to assess strategies students use in the following areas: producing written work, test taking, note taking, and gaining information from a text. The instruments are combinations of questionnaires and checklists. The instrument for assessing written work, for instance, asks the student to respond to aspects of his or her previous knowledge of writing and of the specific topic, planning of the paper, and reviewing and rewriting of the paper. By assessing learning strategies, the teacher can determine if a student requires instruction in certain strategy areas, and what particular strategies need to be taught.

Instructional assessment of the types described in the previous paragraphs provides teachers with a means of identifying where instruction should begin and initial hypotheses about how instruction should be delivered. However, collecting data after instruction has been initiated is equally important for effective teaching.

MONITORING PROGRESS

Although it has its roots in work produced during the genesis of the field of learning disabilities (e.g., Lindsley, 1964; Lovitt, 1967; Starlin, 1971), progress monitoring has received great emphasis recently as a part of the *curriculum-based assessment* movement (Deno, 1985). Appropriate monitoring of progress has two facets: frequent assessment of individual pupil performance on the actual tasks that are being taught and adjustment of instruction based on the teacher's judgments about the data collected (Howell & McCollum-Gahley, 1986). (Although the collection of progress-monitoring data makes it possible for the teacher to manipulate teaching procedures as an experimenter would in single-subject research [Murphy & Bryan, 1980; Repp & Lloyd, 1980], it is not usually necessary to do so. In fact, the teacher will most often use such assessment data to ascertain the effects of one or two interventions and then will often administer them in ways that produce order confounders. This does not mitigate the conclusions that the teacher can draw about whether a given student is or is not progressing; it only reduces the confidence with which similar interventions can be expected to succeed with other pupils under other conditions.)

Although some instructional programs include periodic progress assessments, these are not common. For this reason, teachers often have to adopt extant progress-monitoring systems such as those available from the Precision Teaching Project (1977). More often, however, teachers must construct assessment instruments themselves. This can readily be accomplished by using materials from the ongoing curriculum. Detailed treatments of progress-monitoring procedures, rationale, and effects are available elsewhere (Deno, 1986; Deno & Mirkin, 1977; Fuchs & Fuchs, 1986; Howell & Morehead, 1987).

SUMMARY

Instruction of students clearly cannot follow simply from a priori assessment of student characteristics. Assessment for instruction should include the use of task analysis, trial teaching, interviews, and ongoing data collection. However, when teachers assess students for instructional planning, they must consider more than just the immediate, student-centered situation. The total environment of the classroom can affect a child's learning. In the next section we consider aspects of environmental assessment.

ASSESSMENT OF THE ENVIRONMENT

Academic instruction of and learning by students with learning disabilities do not occur in a vacuum; rather, they take place in a school environment replete with teachers, other adults, and peers. It is reasonable to assume that the physical environment, social ecology, and components of instruction found in this environment affect a student's learning. It is apparent, then, that environmental conditions must be assessed so the teacher can plan effective instruction (Graham, 1985; Hardin, 1978).

PHYSICAL ENVIRONMENT

Assessment of physical variables such as classroom size and seating arrangement; numbers of teachers and pupils; number, kind, and location of instructional materials and educational equipment; daily class schedules; and noise and activity levels is important (Gable & Trout, 1985; Heron & Heward, 1982). The setting in which teaching and learning occur can be measured using checklists or interviews (Gable & Trout, 1985). Effects of the physical environment can be assessed by using trial teaching procedures.

SOCIAL ENVIRONMENT

Individuals and groups who interact with a particular student have important roles in establishing the social atmosphere and student–student and student–teacher interactions within the classroom. Peer relationships and classroom dynamics can be assessed through sociograms and reaction inventories. Questions on a reaction inventory could include "How do you feel about your school day?" and "If you could spend your time in any way you would like, what would you do?" (Hardin, 1978, p. 18). In addition, frequent, direct observations (Heron & Heward, 1982) can increase a teacher's knowledge of social classroom factors, further enabling her or him to identify specific needs for each student and to establish intervention priorities.

Teachers are regularly considered to be among the people most responsible for socializing children, therefore maintaining an important and prominent role in children's lives (Graham, 1985). Teachers' background characteristics can greatly influence their decisions about appropriate instruction of students with learning disabilities. General educational beliefs and prior life experiences of a teacher can affect how he or she chooses to teach students (e.g., how he or she puts content in sequence; Graham, 1985). Teachers must be aware of their personal characteristics and how they could influence their instructional decisions. Self-assessment is an important component of increasing teachers' awareness (Hardin, 1978).

To assess their direct influence on students, Hardin (1978) suggests that teachers videotape parts of their school day and then view the tape to evaluate their interactions with pupils. Teachers working in a team-teaching situation may observe one another to obtain similar information.

Heron and Heward (1982) emphasize that the gathered data will enable the teacher to ascertain the student's current level of functioning, choose a starting point at which to begin instruction, and evaluate the student's future performance against a base line. The authors emphasize that a key to successful ecological assessment lies with the teacher's knowing when environmental information is necessary to conduct successful instructional planning for a particular student.

INSTRUCTIONAL ENVIRONMENT

Assessment of the instructional environment completes the range of ecological measures necessary to make an effective assessment–intervention link (Lentz & Shapiro, 1986). Gelzheiser and Leonard (1987) suggest assessment of four salient environmental areas: exposure to instruction, quality and appropriateness of the instruction implemented, quality and appropriateness of the curriculum, and student response to instruction.

For example, in the area of exposure to instruction, the teacher should gather information on student absences and tardiness and presence of health or other impairments that limit the child's instructional time. Also important is assessment of student time spent engaged in academics—How much time does the teacher allocate for academic work and how much opportunity does the student have to respond academically (Gelzheiser & Leonard, 1987; Lentz & Shapiro, 1986)? Assessment of these factors may be done through examination of school records and direct observation (Gelzheiser & Leonard, 1987; Lentz & Shapiro, 1986).

In the area of quality and appropriateness of the instruction implemented, information on clarity of directions, use of modeling and examples, amount of practice provided, and other instructional variables gleaned from the effective instruction literature is important to collect (Gelzheiser & Leonard, 1987; Lentz & Shapiro, 1986; Ysseldyke & Christenson, 1987). Lentz and Shapiro (1986) recommend evaluating these aspects of instruction through direct observations, teacher interviews, and inspection of students' academic products. The Instructional Environment Scale (TIES) (Ysseldyke & Christenson, 1987) is designed to enable teachers or other professionals to describe the instructional environment for an individual student. The information gathered about the instructional environment coupled with information on a student's academic skills allows the teacher to plan effective interventions.

Gelzheiser and Leonard (1987) described two ways in which environmental assessment is directly linked to instruction. First, the assessment procedure itself focuses on the student's actual performance rather than inferring from typical assessment results how the student might perform. Second, teachers can modify the learning environment almost immediately after assessment has taken place, thereby enhancing the potential for achievement by students with learning disabilities.

SUMMARY

Formal testing procedures do not provide teachers with sufficient information to plan instruction for students with learning disabilities. Formal assessment procedures should be supplemented if not supplanted by other means of assessing students that allow teachers to use pertinent information to plan instruction for each student; appropriate methods for instructional planning include task-analysis, trial-teaching, and interview procedures. During the course of instruction, procedures for monitoring pupil progress should be implemented; these procedures should be used by teachers to modify instruction on the basis of its effects on pupils' performance. Throughout the assessment–instructional process, the physical, social, and instructional environment of student learning should also be assessed; environmental assessment provides teachers with additional information to consider in instructional planning for students with learning disabilities.

REFERENCES

Arter, J. A., & Jenkins, J. R. (1979). Differential diagnosis—prescriptive teaching: A critical appraisal. Review of *Educational Research, 49*, 517–555.
Bateman, B. D. (1964, November). Techniques in diagnosis and remediation of school learning problems. Paper presented at the Wisconsin School Psychologists' Institute, Madison.
Brophy, J., & Good, T. L. (1986). Teacher behavior and student achievement. In M. C. Wittrock (Ed.), *Handbook of research on teaching* (3rd ed., pp. 328–375). New York: Macmillan.
Cronbach, L. J., & Snow, R. E. (1977). *Aptitudes and instructional methods.* New York: Irvington.
D'Amato, R. C., & Dean, R. S. (1987). Psychological reports, individual education programs, and daily lesson plans: Are they related? *Professional School Psychology, 2*, 93–101.
Deno, S. (1985). Curriculum–based measurement: The emerging alternative. *Exceptional Children, 52*, 219–232.
Deno, S. L. (1986). Formative evaluation of individual student programs: A new role for school psychologists. *School Psychology Review, 15*, 358–374.
Deno, S. L., & Mirkin, P. K. (1977). *Data–based program modification: A manual.* Reston, VA: Council for Exceptional Children.
Dickenson, D. J. (1980). The direct assessment: An alternative to psychometric testing. *Journal of Learning Disabilities, 13*, 472–476.
Dunn, R. (1988). Teaching students through their perceptual strengths or preferences. *Journal of Reading, 31*, 304–309.
Engelmann, S. (1967). Relationship between psychological theories and the act of teaching. *Journal of School Psychology, 5*, 93–100.
Engelmann, S., & Carnine, D. (1982). *Theory of instruction: Principles and applications.* New York: Irvington.
Engelmann, S., Granzin, A., & Severson, H. (1979). Diagnosing instruction. *Journal of Special Education, 13*, 355–363.
Feuerstein, R., Rand, Y., & Hoffman, M. B. (1979). *The dynamic assessment of retarded performers: The learning potential assessment device, theory, instruments, and techniques.* Baltimore: University Park Press.
Fuchs, L. S., & Fuchs, D. (1986). Effects of systematic formative evaluation: A meta–analysis. *Exceptional Children, 53*, 199–208.
Gable, R., & Trout, B. (1985). Measurement of the teaching process in education and treatment programs for exceptional youth. *Education and Treatment of Children, 8*, 297–320.
Gelzheiser, L. M., & Leonard, K. (1987). Assessing the learning environment for mathematics. *Journal of Reading, Writing, and Learning Disabilities International, 3*, 41–52.
Graham, S. (1985). Teaching basic academic skills to learning disabled students: A model of the teaching–learning process. *Journal of Learning Disabilities, 18*, 528–534.
Hamilton, J. L. (1983). Measuring response to instruction as an assessment para-

digm. In K. D. Gadow & I. Bailer (Eds.), *Advances in Learning and Behavioral Disabilities* (Vol. 2, 111–133). Greenwich, CT: JAI Press.
Hardin, V. B. (1978). Ecological assessment and intervention for learning disabled students. *Learning Disability Quarterly, 12,* 15–20.
Heron, T. E., & Heward, W. L. (1982). Ecological assessment: Implications for teachers of learning disabled students. *Learning Disability Quarterly, 5,* 117–125.
Howell, K. W. (1986). Direct assessment of academic performance. *School Psychology Review, 15,* 324–335.
Howell, K. W., Kaplan, J. S., & O'Connell, C. Y. (1979). *Evaluating exceptional children: A task analysis approach.* Columbus, OH: Merrill.
Howell, K. W., & McCollum–Gahley, J. (1986). Monitoring instruction. *Teaching Exceptional Children, 19,* 47–49.
Howell, K. W., & Morehead, M. K. (1987). *Curriculum–based evaluation for special and remedial education: A handbook for deciding what to teach.* Columbus, OH: Merrill.
Hughes, S. (1982). Another look at task analysis. *Journal of Learning Disabilities, 15,* 273–275.
Kavale, K. A., & Forness, S. R. (1987). Substance over style: Assessing the efficacy of modality testing and teaching. *Exceptional Children, 54,* 228–239.
Larrivee, B. (1981). Modality preference as a model for differentiating beginning reading instruction: A review of the issues. *Learning Disability Quarterly, 4,* 180–188.
Lentz, F. E., Jr., & Shapiro, E. S. (1986). Functional assessment of the academic environment. *School Psychology Review, 15,* 346–357.
Lindsley, O. R. (1964). Direct measurement and prosthesis of retarded behavior. *Journal of Education, 147,* 62–81.
Lloyd, J. (1979). Ascertaining the reading skills of atypical learners. In D. A. Sabatino & T. L. Miller (Eds.), *Describing learner characteristics of handicapped children and youth* (pp. 293–332). New York: Grune & Stratton.
Lloyd, J. W. (1984). How shall we individualize instruction—or should we? *Remedial and Special Education, 5*(1), 7–15.
Lloyd, J. W., & Loper, A. B. (1986). Measurement and evaluation of task–related learning behaviors: Attention to task and metacognition. *School Psychology Review, 15,* 336–345.
Lovitt, T. C. (1967). Assessment of children with learning disabilities. *Exceptional Children, 34,* 223–239.
Lovitt, T. C., & Hansen, C. L. (1976). Round one—Placing the child in the right reader. *Journal of Learning Disabilities, 9,* 347–353.
Mann, L. S. (1979). *On the trail of process: A historical perspective on cognitive processes and their training.* New York: Grune & Stratton.
Meyers, J. (1988). Diagnosis diagnosed: Twenty years after. *Professional School Psychology, 3,* 123–134.
Meyers, J., Pfeffer, J., & Erlbaum, V. (1985). Process assessment: A model for broadening assessment. *Journal of Special Education, 19,* 73–89.
Murphy, R. J., & Bryan, A. J. (1980). Multiple–baseline and multiple probe designs: Practical alternatives for special education assessment and evaluation. *Journal of Special Education, 14,* 325–335.
Precision Teaching Project. (1977). *Materials directory.* Great Falls, MT: Precision Teaching Project.
Repp, A. C., & Lloyd, J. (1980). Evaluating educational changes with single–subject designs. In J. Gottlieb (Ed.), *Educating mentally retarded persons in the mainstream* (pp. 73–105). Baltimore: University Park Press.
Resnick, L. B., & Ford, W. W. (1978). The analysis of tasks for instruction: An

information-processing approach. In A. C. Catania & T. A. Brigham (Eds.), *Handbook of applied behavior analysis: Social and instructional processes* (pp. 378–409). New York: Irvington.

Rosenshine, B., & Stevens, R. (1986). Teaching functions. In M. C. Wittrock (Ed.), *Handbook of research on teaching* (3rd ed., pp. 376–391). New York: Macmillan.

Schenck, S. J. (1980). The diagnostic/instructional link in individualized education programs. *Journal of Special Education, 14,* 337–345.

Schworm, R. W., & Abelseth, J. L. (1981). Evaluating instructional interactions: How do we begin teaching? *Learning Disability Quarterly, 4,* 101–111.

Shinn, M. R., Tindal, G. A., & Stein, S. (1988). Curriculum-based measurement and the identification of mildly handicapped students: A research review. *Professional School Psychology, 3,* 69–85.

Starlin, C. (1971). Evaluating progress toward reading proficiency. In B. D. Bateman (Ed.), *Learning disorders* (Vol. 4, pp. 389–465). Seattle: Special Child.

Tarver, S. G., & Dawson, M. M. (1978). Modality preference and the teaching of reading: A review. *Journal of Learning Disabilities, 11,* 5–17.

Wiener, J. (1986). Alternatives in the assessment of the learning disabled adolescent: A learning strategies approach. *Learning Disabilities Focus, 1,* 97–107.

Ysseldyke, J. E. (1973). Diagnostic-prescriptive teaching: The search for aptitude-treatment interactions. In L. Mann & D. A. Sabatino (Eds.), *First review of special education* (Vol. 1, p. 5–32). Philadelphia: JSE Press.

Ysseldyke, J. E., & Christenson, S. L. (1987). Evaluating students' instructional environments. *Remedial and Special Education, 8*(3), 17–24.

Zigmond, N., & Miller, S. E. (1986). Assessment for instructional planning. *Exceptional Children, 52,* 501–509.

Zigmond, N., Vallecorsa, A., & Silverman, R. (1983). *Assessment for instructional planning in special education.* Englewood Cliffs, NJ: Prentice-Hall.

CHAPTER 4

Assessing Subtypes of Learning Abilities*

G. REID LYON
JANE M. FLYNN

This chapter addresses issues and trends related to the classification of individuals with learning disabilities into subgroups and subtypes. The terms "subgroups" and "subtypes" are frequently used interchangeably in the literature on learning disabilities. However, from a classification perspective, it is more accurate to speak of subgroups when referring to major classes within a population, and to subtypes when partitioning each class into smaller distinct groups of individuals who share common characteristics. For example, by definition the population with learning disabilities is composed of several major subgroups identified on the basis of handicapping condition (e.g., oral language disorders, basic reading disorders, arithmetic calculation disorders, written language disorders, etc.). A number of these subgroups have themselves been found to contain smaller subtypes (e.g., oral language disorders are subdivided further into receptive [listening] and expressive [speaking] language disorders). While most of the discussion in this chapter is devoted to subtype identification, the

---

*The preparation of this article was made possible by a Research Scientist grant to Reid Lyon from the Gunderson Medical Foundation, La Crosse, WI, and by a grant from the Initial Teaching Alphabet Foundation, Roslyn Heights, NY, to Jane Flynn. The authors wish to thank Tanya Prindle and Mary Vaassen for critical comments on drafts of this article.

reader should note that the same theoretical and methodological requirements apply to the partitioning of a population into subgroups. Since classification research in the behavioral sciences typically relies on assessment activities for the measurement of subtype characteristics, the general theme of the book will be preserved in this chapter. However, our understanding of how best to assess and identify homogeneous groupings of individuals with learning disabilities is limited, albeit emerging (see Speece, in press, for a well reasoned discussion of this issue). Thus, it is premature to write of assessing subtypes of learning disabilities, particularly if this implies a mature diagnostic and identification process that has demonstrated clinical utility and scientific validity.

It is not too early, however, to discuss the characteristics of useful and valid procedures for distinguishing, ordering, sorting, and naming entities within a population. In doing so, we can provide guidelines for evaluating current research on classification of learning disabilities with an eye toward making improvements in future subtyping efforts.

With this as background, this chapter is organized to address first the overarching concept of classification and to delineate the critical features of valid and reliable subtype research studies. Following this discussion, two studies of children with learning disabilities are reviewed to illustrate how different methods can be applied to a variety of classification questions. The studies have also been selected to reflect improvements in the application of multivariate classification procedures and clinical partitioning models, respectively. This review is selective rather than exhaustive, for three reasons. The first relates to the usual space constraints encountered in textbooks. The second and more fundamental reason is to avoid redundancy. The literature on subtyping of learning disabilities is voluminous, comprising over 100 classification studies since 1963 (Hooper & Willis, 1989). Various aspects of this literature have been reviewed since 1981 (Doehring, Trites, Patel, & Fiedorowicz, 1981; Fisk & Rourke, 1983; Harris, 1982; Lyon, 1983, 1985a, 1985b; Lyon & Risucci, 1988; McKinney, 1984, 1988; Satz & Morris, 1981), with the most comprehensive review recently completed by Hooper and Willis (1989). Third, given the availability of these recent reviews, it seems appropriate to focus our commentary on selected "second-generation" subtyping studies that are either in progress or have been published since 1988. As stated earlier, the investigations chosen for review reflect improvements over studies carried out during the past decade and can serve as useful models for future subtyping research.

Finally, the chapter concludes with suggestions for conducting classification (subtyping) research within a developmental, longitudinal perspective. We will stress the position that this perspective will be necessary if subtyping research is to contribute meaningfully to the ultimate understanding and assessment of learning disabilities.

RATIONALE FOR CLASSIFICATION RESEARCH

Classification plays a pivotal role in producing operationally meaningful accounts of human learning and behavior. In a general sense, classification is inextricably linked to human cognition and basic conceptual ability; mankind has evolved through the ability to distinguish, order, and describe similarities and differences among people, objects, and events.

Classification serves a significant scientific function by structuring domains of study for more precise description and inquiry. For example, the classification of plant characteristics forms one of the cornerstones of botany, while the classification of diseases serves as the structural foundation for medicine. Within the social and behavioral sciences, classifications of intellectual, behavioral, and social characteristics serve as the basis for descriptions of different dimensions and categories of mental retardation and the psychopathologies. In essence, by creating classifications, the scientist establishes the foundation for theory development, communication, and prediction. Kendall (1975) underscored these fundamental properties of classification when he wrote: "Theories and therapeutic claims have no more chance of surviving than buildings if they are not built on secure foundations. Developing reliable diagnostic criteria and a classification may be tedious ... but provides the foundations on which all else will depend" (p. vii).

For a number of reasons, the field of learning disabilities could benefit from the appropriate application of classification efforts. For example, it is apparent that the category of learning disabilities represents an extraordinarily diverse population of disabled learners who will form a continuous distribution across the majority of tasks designed to assess their characteristics. Unless well-designed attempts are made to classify this diverse group of individuals into relatively homogeneous subtypes, research findings will continue to be obscured by contaminating factors associated with heterogeneity (Keogh, 1986; Lyon, 1987). In addition, identification of subtypes of learning disabilities could provide insight into the assessment of useful clinical dimensions and their treatment (Lyon & Moats, 1988; Lyon, Moats, & Flynn, 1988; Rourke, 1985). Moreover, identification of specific subtype patterns of performance across cognitive, linguistic, academic, and social/behavioral measures within the context of longitudinal designs can enhance knowledge of meaningful developmental continuities and their relationship to school learning (Lyon, 1987; Lyon & Risucci, 1988).

CHARACTERISTICS OF USEFUL CLASSIFICATION SYSTEMS

A review of the development of classification systems in the behavioral and social sciences suggests that if a classification is to have predictive and communicative power, it should (1) be theory driven (Fletcher & Morris, 1986; Kavale & Forness, 1987; Lyon, 1987; Skinner, 1981); (2) be based on variables that have theoretical relevance and adequate psychometric properties (Aldenderfer & Blashfield, 1986; Lyon & Risucci, 1988); (3) be developed on samples that are operationally defined (Fletcher & Morris, 1986; Speece, in press); (4) be replicable and internally valid (Blashfield & Draguns, 1976; Skinner, 1981); and (5) be externally valid and thus useful for description, prediction, and clinical practice (Lyon et al., 1988; Lyon & Risucci, 1988). In addition, if multivariate cluster-analysis procedures are used to create a classification, several critical decisions must be made with respect to inclusion rules for subtype membership and how individuals within subtypes are judged to be "similar." Specific issues related to multivariate classification procedures are beyond the scope of this chapter. Interested readers are referred to Aldenderfer and Blashfield (1986) and Speece (in press) for excellent reviews of cluster-analysis principles and practices. For now, the general characteristics of useful and valid classification systems are briefly highlighted.

CLASSIFICATIONS AS THEORY-DRIVEN HYPOTHESES

While classification research can be useful in the recognition of types within heterogeneous populations (e.g., the population with learning disabilities), the opportunity for misuse of methods to identify subgroups and subtypes with learning disabilities is substantial. Contrary to common perceptions, obtaining a classification solution is not functionally dependent on logic or theory. Subtypes can literally be identified within any data set regardless of the theoretical significance of the classification solution or the measurement qualities of the variables selected to represent the content domain. It is for this reason that rigorous efforts should be applied to delineating, in an a priori fashion, the scope, purpose, and theoretical basis for the classification study. In this context, the investigator can formulate theory-driven hypotheses. These hypotheses, in turn, should lead to tentative descriptions of anticipated subtypes, identification of the type of data needed to search logically for the predicted subtypes, and specification of relationships between predicted subtypes and variables not used in the classification (e.g., treatment outcomes).

VARIABLE SELECTION

Once theory-driven hypotheses have been developed to specify the possible range and nature of the subtype solution, both classification and validation (external) variables are selected. Variables designated as classification variables are chosen to assess the critical attributes of the predicted subtypes. The selection of the specific type of classification variables depends on the purposes of the subtyping effort. For example, the set of classification variables that would allow one to identify a general type of learning disability would differ from the measures needed to distinguish specific forms of memory deficits. In essence, classification variables are selected to provide the best assessment of the phenotypic expression of the hypothesized subtypes.

Validation variables are selected to test hypotheses relevant to relationships among subtypes and relationships between subtypes and external criteria (e.g., assessment of subtype-by-treatment interactions). In the main, these variables are used to establish descriptive and predictive validities (Fletcher, 1985; Lyon, 1985; Lyon & Risucci, 1988).

Variable selection is a complex process and should be guided by informed theoretical, psychometric, and developmental perspectives. As a general guideline for subtyping studies, variables should be selected on the basis of

1. Their theoretical coherence and ability to permit unconfounded and fine-grained analysis of hypothesized subtypal attributes and constructs;
2. Their relationship to known paths of development within the content domain being studied. This ensures that the measurement of a subtypal attribute or construct is appropriate to the developmental level of the individuals in the sample. If this condition is not met, floor or ceiling effects would be observed;
3. Evidence that the variables constitute valid measurements of the attributes or constructs critical to the hypothesized classification solution;
4. Evidence that the variables possess adequate reliability; and
5. Evidence that classification and validation variables accomplish nonredundant assessments of the subtypal attributes or constructs under study. This type of evidence can be obtained through application of appropriate factor-analysis and other data-reduction procedures.

SAMPLE SELECTION IN SUBTYPE RESEARCH

Although the identification and description of distinct subtypes of learning disabilities has potential for theory refinement and the testing of hypotheses related to cause, diagnosis, and treatment, the scientific advantages of subtype methods have been largely unrealized because of sampling problems. It is well documented that present exclusionary definitions of learning disabilities contain ambiguous identification criteria that limit the ability to make standardized diagnostic decisions (Fletcher & Morris, 1986; Kavale & Forness, 1988; Lyon & Risucci, 1988). In the main, individuals with learning disabilities identified according to current definitional practices vary widely with respect to IQ, age, socioeconomic status, severity of academic and information-processing deficits, as well as factors related to educational history, motivation, and social adjustment. This is particularly true when "school-identified" children with learning disabilities are selected for study because interpretations of criteria for learning disabilities differ significantly within and between states and school systems (Lyon, 1987).

Such diversity does not bode well for making systematic observations that can be replicated precisely by others. For example, reviews of the major studies of learning disability subtypes carried out to date reveal that fewer than 20% of the investigations are comparable or even can be compared with respect to critical subject marker variables (e.g., IQ, age, socioeconomic status) (Hooper & Willis, 1989; Lyon & Risucci, 1988; McKinney, 1988). No doubt, this extreme variability in sample characteristics precludes replication of subtype solutions and limits the generalizability of findings to the population with learning disabilities as a whole.

The pronounced lack of coherent and consistent sampling strategies indicates a need to examine the manner in which subjects are selected for subtype research. Fortunately, some progress is currently being made in this regard. For example, Keogh (1986) has introduced the concept of "marker" variables to ensure adequate measurement and description of persons with learning disabilities who are under study. However, it is doubtful that even strict use of marker variables will significantly improve our ability to understand findings from subtyping studies unless the sampling net is cast wide enough to enable comparisons between children who meet standard criteria for learning disabilities and children who have learning problems but who do not meet traditional exclusionary criteria (e.g., children with mental retardation, attentional deficits, emotional disturbance). This is because we do not yet know whether children selected according to traditional definitions actually differ from one another beyond their performance on the selection criteria. Until this is known, conducting subtyping studies with selected samples of students with learning disabilities may produce artificial distinctions within groups of underachievers. Finally, because age, developmental history, and educational experiences have a critical role in how learning abilities and disabilities are expressed at any given time, samples should be selected to permit longitudinal study. This issue will be addressed in a later section of this chapter.

RELIABILITY AND INTERNAL VALIDITY OF SUBTYPES

Not only must samples be appropriately selected and described to permit independent replication, the types identified in studies of learning disability subtyping must also be replicable and internally valid. Basically stated, for a classification solution to have explanatory power, it must be reliable, replicable, homogeneous, and provide adequate coverage of the population being studied. **Reliability** refers to the degree to which experts or methods of grouping individuals agree on the assignment of individuals to subtypes. **Replicability** refers to the degree to which the subtype solution can be identified in new samples drawn from the same population. Replicability is also assessed by determining whether similar subtypes can be identified by using different variables to measure the same content domain and/or by employing different classification techniques. **Homogeneity** refers to the cohesiveness of the obtained subtypes. Do the subjects that are assigned to a subtype closely resemble one another with respect to performance on the classification variables or are the subtypes "loosely" organized? **Coverage** concerns the extent to which a subtype solution accounts for members of the population being studied. More specifically, how many subjects are assigned to the obtained subtypes and how many subjects appear to be "outliers" from the boundaries of the classification? The reader is referred to Morris, Satz, and Blashfield (1981) for a comprehensive overview of internal validation principles and studies.

EXTERNAL VALIDATION OF SUBTYPES OF LEARNING DISABILITIES

External validation is the continuous evaluation of the generalizability of a classification solution, its prognostic accuracy, its descriptive capability, and its clinical utility (Fletcher & Morris, 1986; Lyon, 1985a). From a methodological standpoint, external validity studies address the degree to which obtained subtypes can be differentiated on external criteria or variables that were not employed in the original classification. For example, prognostic and clinical utility could be demonstrated by hypothesizing and confirming subtype-by-task and/or subtype-by-treatment interactions (Lyon, 1985a, 1985b). Descriptive power can be demonstrated by showing convergent and discriminant validities for the obtained subtypes across measures hypothesized to reflect critical theoretical and clinical dimensions (Satz & Morris, 1981). Clinical validity can be established by demonstrating that clinicians can employ the subtype solution in practical settings and situations (Wilson & Risucci, 1986). External validation is essential to the use of classification methods of individuals with learning disabilities. This is because any subtypes that are identified within the population with learning disabilities reflect somewhat arbitrary distinctions within heterogeneous continuous distributions. The relevance of any particular set of distinctions is confirmed or disconfirmed by application of the external validation procedures addressed here. This point is addressed in greater detail below.

INTERPRETIVE NECESSITIES IN CLASSIFICATION RESEARCH ON LEARNING DISABILITIES

To reiterate, the application of classification methods to the heterogeneous population with learning disabilities may yield a number of benefits, most notably a more refined description of the sample that will enhance both theory building and clinical applications. However, researchers and clinicians need to understand that subtypes of learning disabilities typically reflect abstract and artificial distinctions among subjects. This is because subjects with learning disabilities vary in their measured abilities along dimensions rather than falling into discrete categories (Ellis, 1985; Olson, Kliegel, Davidson, & Foltz, 1985; Stanovich, 1988). As such, for any processing and/or academic skill measured, children will differ from one another along a continuous distribution, not "clump" together in syndromes marked by distinctive boundaries. No doubt, this distribution will be characterized by substantial heterogeneity. Because of such variability among subjects, classification methods can be applied to identify relative homogeneity within the distribution and to identify dimensions of similarities and differences on tasks composing the content domain. It is important to note that subtypes can change in appearance depending upon where the investigator or clinician arbitrarily sets the "cut points" for inclusion in a particular subtype. It is for this reason that internal and external validity studies play such a crucial role in research on learning disabilities classification.

SUMMARY

Classification research is complex and requires a long-term commitment for both theoretical and methodological reasons. Theory formulation and the identification of a reliable and valid subtype solution are intimately related. Theory drives the development of hypotheses and the selection of variables within relevant content domains, and external validation studies provide objective feedback with respect to the ability of the theory to predict, describe, and support clinical activity.

As noted earlier, the majority of "first-generation" studies of learning disability subtypes failed to meet many of the requirements for classification research discussed here. However, recent and ongoing investigations appear more capable of generating replicable and valid observations related to subtype structure within the population with learning disabilities. Two examples from these contemporary research efforts are reviewed to demonstrate advances in classification work with individuals with learning disabilities and to show how different methods can be employed to uncover subtype structure within heterogeneous samples. The first research program that is discussed provides an example of theory-driven subtype research carried out within the context of a multivariate classification framework. The second study demonstrates the value of clinically generated subtype efforts that rely on external validation treatment studies to test relevant theoretical hypotheses.

IDENTIFYING SUBTYPES WITH MULTIVARIATE CLASSIFICATION METHODS

A large number of studies during the past decade have employed multivariate classification methods to identify subtypes of learning disabilities within heterogeneous samples (see Hooper & Willis, 1989). Several reviews of this work indicate that the studies are generally limited by inadequate theory formulation, sampling problems, inadequate measurement of the content domain, and insufficient external validation (Kavale & Forness, 1987; Lyon & Risucci, 1988; McKinney, 1988). More recent classification studies have been designed to account for these design flaws and a review of one ongoing investigation may offer guidance for future subtyping efforts.

THE YALE/HASKINS LABORATORY PROGRAM PROJECT

The primary goal of the current studies within this federally funded program project is to develop and validate classifications of reading disabilities both in relation to a broader spectrum of learning problems and to more specific cognitive and linguistic abilities. These investigations are being carried out under the direction of B. Shaywitz and associates (Shaywitz et al., 1987). The specific studies within this classification project are designed to (1) identify subtypes of reading performance within a large sample of children with learning difficulties whose deficient academic performance is below expectations in reading and/or mathematics, or who meet accepted criteria for attention deficit hyperactive disorder (ADHD); (2) address the neuroanatomical correlates of reading disabilities via external validation studies utilizing magnetic resonance imaging of the brain; (3) provide a quantitative index of shared electrophysiological activity through the use of electroencephalographic coherence analysis, and to use these data in external validation studies of identified subtypes; (4) examine the emergence of subtypes of reading disability in an epidemiological sample and within a longitudinal context; and (5) investigate individuals within reading disability subtypes who have affected family members in order to clarify possible genetic influences on reading development.

The theoretical viewpoint guiding this classification research holds that reading is dependent upon language, that language processes and abilities form a biologically coherent system or module that is distinct from other cognitive processes, and hence, that most reading problems involve language-related deficiencies (Fodor, 1983; Liberman & Shankweiler, 1985; Mann, 1986). Modularity within the linguistic system is also hypothesized, with specific deficiencies potentially occurring with a single component (e.g., the phonological component, the semantic component, the syntactic component). Accordingly, subtypes should result from deficiencies in different components.

Specific a priori hypotheses generated from this theoretical background have been stated to predict the number of specific subtypes as well as expected reading and neurophysiological characteristics. Moreover, additional a priori hypotheses predict that children with reading disabilities will not perform differently from normal controls on measures designed to test competing nonlanguage theories of reading disorder.

In order to test these hypotheses, the Yale/Haskins group has selected or developed theoretically relevant classification and validation measurement variables to determine whether reading disability involves deficits only within the language system, or occurs simultaneously with deficiencies in cognitive, perceptual, and attentional domains that are orthogonal to the linguistic system. The classification design also calls for the measurement variables to be assessed for psychometric adequacy and redundancy.

The sample selected for study in the Yale/Haskins project is large and diverse. More specifically, the sampling net has been cast widely enough to answer questions related to (1) the specificity of reading disorder and its relation to intelligence, (2) the concomitant influences of attentional and arithmetic disorders on reading achievement, and (3) the differentiation of disabled from nondisabled individuals.

The classification method used in the Yale/Haskins project is intimately related to the theoretical model, which provides the rationale for the subtyping effort and the hypotheses that have been posed. More specifically, because a desired outcome of the program project is to classify children according to one set of problems (e.g., patterns of reading disorders, patterns of reading and math disorders) followed by a more specific partitioning within subgroups to identify subtypes, heirarchical agglomerative and iterative classification methods are being employed. Furthermore, the investigators have selected similarity measures to define how subjects will be judged as "alike" on the basis of their specific theoretical hypotheses. For example, correlation coefficients are employed to identify subgroups and subtypes with specific profiles on the classification variables without regard to the severity of the deficits displayed. A second similarity coefficient based upon Squared Euclidean Distance is used to identify both subtype patterns (profile shape) of performance on classification variables, as well as the severity of deficits manifested by different subtypes (elevation). Finally, the Yale/Haskins scientists have designed this classification study in such a way as to ensure a fair test of the question "do subtypes actually exist?" Furthermore, if subtypes are identified, the classification method has established procedures to test for the reliability of the solution and to determine if the subtypes have content, concurrent, and predictive validity.

As noted, the Yale/Haskins project is currently being conducted and complete data will not be available for several years. The point to be stressed, however, is that whatever results are obtained, a well-grounded theory has led to specifically stated a priori hypotheses that are open to disconfirmation, and to the selection of theoretically relevant assessment domains and test instruments. If predictions are not supported by the data, the investigators can systematically determine if null findings are related to a faulty theory, an inadequate test of the hypotheses, and/or an inadequate assessment of theoretically relevant subtype characteristics (Skinner, 1981).

IDENTIFICATION AND EXTERNAL VALIDATION OF CLINICALLY GENERATED SUBTYPES

Clinical-inferential subtyping studies have frequently been criticized on the basis of their limited diagnostic reliability and minimal external validity (see Lyon, 1983; McKinney, 1984; Satz & Morris, 1981). However, a recent series of clinically based studies that identify subtypes according to children's performance on direct measures of reading and spelling have generated some confidence in nonempirical classification procedures through strong external validation studies. Since these types of studies suggest ecological validity to many practitioners, a review of one such effort is provided to show examples of clinical subtype assessment and treatment procedures.

THE LOVETT RESEARCH PROGRAM

A study by Lovett, Barron, and Ransby (1988) exemplifies clinical classification research that is theory driven and uses direct measures of reading behaviors to subtype children and predict response to differential treatments. Based on Chall's (1983) reading-stage theory, Lovett hypothesized that children fail in reading either because of difficulties in word recognition accuracy (Stage 1) or reading fluency (Stage 2). Within this context, Lovett and her associates have identified two subtypes of disabled readers, accuracy disabled and rate disabled, on the basis of the subjects' performance on multiple measures of single-word recognition and contextual reading.

Given that it is generally desirable to classify children based on nonredundant measures, a word about Lovett's use of multiple measures to assess similar constructs is in order. As Lovett et al. (1988) point out, standardized tests of word recognition vary significantly in the regularity, number, and complexity of words used as stimuli. Thus, to avoid classification artifact due to the idiosyncratic content of different instruments, children were classified as accuracy disabled only if they performed in a substandard fashion on four of five measures of untimed word recognition. Children with rate disability were classified on similar criteria for reading speed. In light of these procedures, Lovett's classification research appears to have substantial ecological validity, particularly with respect to the clinical assignment of children to subtypes according to patterns of academic performance based on reading-stage theory and the measures used to determine reading patterns.

After being assigned to subtypes, 110 children received systematic instruction as part of an external validation program. Before initiating instruction, a priori hypotheses were generated that predicted how children in each subtype would respond to different teaching procedures. After hypothesis generation, children were assigned to 40 hours of remediation in either: (1) a decoding skills program (DS), which emphasized single-word recognition for both regular and exception words; (2) an oral and written language program (OWLS), which stressed contextual reading, listening and reading comprehension, vocabulary development, syntactical elaboration, and written composition; or (3) a classroom survival skills program (CSS), which consisted of instruction in skills unrelated to reading development (e.g., social skills, organizational strategies).

Before and after the intervention program, children were administered a set of external validation measures that assessed critical reading and linguistic skills relevant to constructs of the stage theory that guided subtype construction and the statement of hypotheses. Lovett's results suggest that children who fail at reading at different developmental stages do respond to differentiated reading programs based on pretreatment subtype profiles. For example, pretest and posttest results for exception-word reading revealed that children with accuracy disability differed from their control (CSS) peers only in the decoding skills (DS) program, while children with rate disability differed from their peers in the CSS program under both DSS and OWLS conditions.

The Lovett studies are important for a number of reasons. First, the classification system was based on direct observation of reading behaviors and was also guided by a developmental perspective. Second, multiple measures of reading behavior were used to classify children into subtypes, thus avoiding classification artifacts associated with sizable differences in the standardized test stimuli used to assess reading accuracy and fluency. Third, a large number of disabled readers, matched for IQ and age, were assigned randomly to clearly defined reading treatments and a nonreading control treatment that provided equal time and attention. Fourth, project teachers implemented all three treatments, thus controlling for teacher differences. Finally, remediation sessions were randomly monitored and coded to ensure that the treatment sessions were carried out systematically and according to the experimental protocol.

DEVELOPMENTAL CLASSIFICATION OF LD SUBGROUPS AND SUBTYPES

We have attempted to point out in this chapter that the identification of subgroups and subtypes with learning disabilities can be both scientifically and clinically useful primarily because validated types can provide a less heterogeneous data set for study and description. However, in our view, cross-sectional classification studies with school- or clinic-identified subjects with learning disabilities will not have a significant impact because of the sampling problems alluded to earlier and because of developmental factors. Because the definitional problems that characterize the field of learning disabilities are not likely to be reduced in the near future, the identification of subgroups and subtypes of learning disabilities can best be accomplished when guided by a developmental longitudinal perspective. Within this context, representative samples of children selected randomly from the general population without a priori designation as learning disabled could be studied over time with a wide range of theoretically relevant assessments and in a variety of teaching and clinical contexts. Thus, developmentally appropriate descriptions of the attributes of individuals who are or who are not achieving academically and/or socially could be obtained, thus delineating critical characteristics that may be manifested differently over time. The methods discussed in this chapter could then be applied to identify subgroups within the general population studied, followed by an attempt to delineate subtypes and assess their stability over time.

Because of the developmental nature of the learning process, it could be hypothesized that learning disabilities would be expressed in different ways at different age levels. Furthermore, it should be expected that some subtypes of individuals with learning disabilities would not differ initially from normal learners or from other subtypes in some measured abilities but may show differences in these or other abilities at older ages. Moreover, the type of remediation or instructional experience a child has had over time could certainly be expected to modify subtype characteristics. The point is that unless a developmental and longitudinal perspective is used to guide classification research, gains in our understanding of children's learning differences will be minimal, at best.

CONCLUSIONS

While some advances have been made in identifying the factors that are critical for methodologically sound classification research, substantial ground remains to be covered before a particular subtype model or specific subtyping procedures can be recommended for assessment purposes. At present, the identification of subtypes of learning disabilities appears to have greater utility for research practices than for clinical applications. For example, subtyping efforts can aid in the identification of multimodal score distributions within heterogeneous groups with learning disabilities, thus providing a more accurate description of samples than typically accomplished by contrasting group methods. In addition, when classification procedures are applied within the context of longitudinal and developmental studies of learning disabilities, the tendency to rely on exclusionary definitions for subject selection purposes can be reduced significantly. The primary research advantage obtained through longitudinal classification is the elimination of a priori assumptions about learning disabilities. As Kavale (1987) has pointed out, with no presumptions about learning disabilities, the data obtained would be neutral and open to objective interpretation.

Finally, for assessment findings to relate meaningfully to clinical treatment options and predicted outcomes, the phenotypic or behavioral expression of learning disabilities must ultimately be clearly defined and categorized in an ecologically valid manner (Lyon et al., 1988). To this end, subtype research must capitalize on what we know about theoretically driven dynamic assessment procedures, the developmental nature of the content to be learned, and the methodological requirements for longitudinal classification research (Lyon & Moats, 1988; Lyon & Risucci, 1988).

REFERENCES

Aldenderfer, M. S. & Blashfield, R. K. (1986). *Cluster Analysis*. Beverly Hills, CA: Sage Publications.
Blashfield, R. K. & Draguns, J. (1976). Evaluative criteria for psychiatric classification. *Journal of Abnormal Psychology, 85*, 140–150.
Chall, J. (1983). *Learning to Read: The Great Debate*. New York: McGraw-Hill.
Doehring, D. G., Trites, R. L., Patel, P. G. & Fiedorowicz, C. A. M. (1981). *Reading Disabilities: The Interaction of Reading, Language and Neuropsychological Deficits*. New York: Academic Press.
Ellis, A. W. (1985). The cognitive neuropsychology of developmental (and acquired) dyslexia: A critical survey. *Cognitive Neuropsychology, 2*, 169–205.
Fisk, J. L. & Rourke, B. P. (1983). Neuropsychological subtyping of learning disabled children: History, methods, implications. *Journal of Learning Disabilities, 9*, 529–531.
Fletcher, J. M. (1985). Memory for verbal and non-verbal stimuli in learning disability subgroups: Analysis by selective reminding. *Journal of Experimental Child Psychology, 40*, 244–259.
Fletcher, J. M. & Morris, R. (1986). Classification of disabled learners: Beyond exclusionary definitions. In S. J. Ceci (Ed.), *Handbook of Cognitive, Social, and Neuropsychological Aspects of Learning Disabilities* (pp. 55–80). Hillsdale, NJ: Erlbaum.
Fodor, J. N. (1983). *Modularity of Mind*. Cambridge, MA: MIT Press.
Harris, A. J. (1982). How many kinds of reading disabilities are there? *Journal of Learning Disabilities, 15*, 456–460.
Hooper, S. R. & Willis, W. G. (1989). *Learning Disability Subtyping: Neuropsychological Foundations, Conceptual Models, and Issues in Clinical Differentiation*. New York: Springer-Verlag.
Kavale, K. A. & Forness, S. R. (1987). Substance over style: Assessing the efficacy of modality testing and teaching. *Exceptional Children, 54*, 228–239.
Kavale, K. A. & Forness, S. R. (1988). The far side of heterogeneity: A critical analysis of empirical subtyping research in learning disabilities. *Journal of Learning Disabilities, 20*, 374–382.
Kendall, R. E. (1975). *The Role of Diagnosis in Psychiatry*. London: Blackwell Scientific Publications.
Keogh, B. K. (1986). A marker system for describing learning disability samples. In S. J. Ceci (Ed.), *Handbook of Cognitive, Social and Neuropsychological Aspects of Learning Disabilities* (pp. 81–94). Hillsdale, NJ: Erlbaum.
Liberman, I. & Shankweiler, D. (1985). Phonology and the problems of learning to read and write. *Remedial and Special Education, 6*, 8–17.
Lovett, M. W., Barron, R. W. & Ransby, M. J. (1988). Treatment, subtype, and word type effects in dyslexic children's response to remediation. *Brain and Language, 34*, 328–349.
Lyon, G. R. (1983). Subgroups of learning disabled readers: Clinical and empirical identification. In H. R. Myklebust (Ed.), *Progress in Learning Disabilities* (Vol. 5, pp. 103–134). New York: Grune & Stratton.

Lyon, G. R. (1985a). Educational validation of learning disability subtypes. In B. P. Rourke (Ed.), *Neuropsychology of Learning Disabilities*: Essentials of subtype analysis (pp. 228–256). New York: Guilford Press.

Lyon, G. R. (1985b). Identification and remediation of learning disability subtypes: Preliminary findings. *Learning Disabilities Focus, 1*, 21–35.

Lyon, G. R. (1987). Learning disabilities research: False starts and broken promises. In S. Vaughn and C. Bos (Eds.), *Research in Learning Disabilities: Issues and Future Directions* (pp. 69–85). San Diego: College-Hill Press.

Lyon, G. R. & Moats, L. C. (1988). Critical issues in the instruction of the learning disabled. *Journal of Consulting and Clinical Psychology, 6*, 830–835.

Lyon, G. R., Moats, L. C. & Flynn, J. (1988). From assessment to treatment: Linkages to interventions with children. In M. Tramontana and S. Hooper (Eds.), *Issues in Child Neuropsychology: From Assessment to Treatment* (pp. 113–142). New York: Plenum Press.

Lyon, G. R. & Risucci, D. (1988). Classification issues in learning disabilities. In K. A. Kavale (Ed.), *Learning Disabilities: State of the Art and Practice* (pp. 44–70). San Diego: College-Hill Press.

Mann, V. (1986). Why some children encounter reading problems. In J. Torgesen & B. Wong (Eds.), *Psychological and Educational Perspectives on Learning Disabilities, 17*, 43–50.

McKinney, J. D. (1984). The search for subtypes of specific learning disabilities. *Journal of Learning Disabilities, 17*, 43–50.

McKinney, J. D. (1988). Research on conceptually and empirically derived subtypes of specific learning disabilities. In M. C. Wang, M. C. Reynolds, & H. J. Walberg (Eds.), *The Handbook of Special Education: Research and Practice* (pp. 268–282). Oxford: Pergamon Press.

Morris, R., Satz, P. & Blashfield, R. K. (1981). Neuropsychology and cluster analysis: Potentials and problems. *Journal of Clinical Neuropsychology, 3*, 77–79.

Olson, R. K., Kliegel, R., Davidson, B. J. & Foltz, G. (1985). Individual and developmental differences in reading disability. In T. G. Waller (Ed.), *Reading Research: Advances in Theory and Practice* (Vol. 4, pp. 1–64). London: Academic Press.

Rourke, B. P. (1985). *Neuropsychology of Learning Disabilities: Essentials of Subtype Analysis*. New York: Guilford Press.

Satz, P. & Morris, R. (1981). Learning disability subtypes: A review. In F. J. Piroxxolo & M. C. Wittrock (Eds.), *Neuropsychological and Cognitive Processes in Reading* (pp. 109–141). New York: Academic Press.

Shaywitz, B., Liberman, I. Y., Fletcher, J. M., Shaywitz, S., Liberman, A., Duncan, J., Salsberg, B., & Pauls, D. (1987). *Psycholinguistic and Biological Mechanisms in Dyslexia*. Grant No: HD 21888-02. The National Institutes of Health, Department of Health and Human Services, Bethesda, MD.

Skinner, H. (1981). Toward the integration of classification theory and methods. *Journal of Abnormal Psychology, 90*, 68–87.

Speece, D. L. (in press). Methodological issues in cluster analysis: How clusters become real. In H. L. Swanson & B. K. Keogh (Eds.), *Learning Disabilities: Theoretical and Research Issues*. Hillsdale, NJ: Erlbaum.

Stanovich, K. E. (1988). Explaining the differences between the dyslexia and the garden-variety poor reader: The phonological-core variable-difference model. *Journal of Learning Disabilities, 21*, 590–604.

Wilson, B. C. & Risucci, D. A. (1986). A model for clinical-quantitative classification. Generation I: Application to language-disordered preschool children. *Brain and Language, 7*, 281–309.

PART II

Assessment Models and Domain

CHAPTER 5

Dynamic Assessment

ANNEMARIE SULLIVAN PALINCSAR
ANN L. BROWN
JOSEPH C. CAMPIONE

Consider the following vignettes, first from the perspective of the child, then from the perspective of the examiner, and finally from the perspective of an adult (parent or teacher) observing but not interacting with the child.

Vignette 1: The child is seated with an examiner and presented a page that has five rows of letters, with eight letters in each row. At the end of each row of letters are four blank lines. The examiner tells the child that she is to look at the letters in each row and then figure out what letters belong in the blank spaces. The task is structured in such a way that, with each problem, the relationship among the letters is increasingly more complicated. The child, with furrowed brow, examines the first row of letters (GWHWIWJW _ _ _ _) pointing to each letter. After a few moments, she smiles, and proceeds to fill in the blank spaces (KWLW). She moves on to the second problem (PZUFQZFV _ _ _ _). She puzzles over it, looks to the examiner who shrugs her shoulders and gently urges "just try your best." After several minutes the child proceeds to write four letters, that appear to be random, on the lines provided. She follows the same course for each of the remaining three problems, spending less time with each problem. After the child has left the room, the examiner scores the page, consults a table of norms and notes that the student is below age level on letter-series completion. The examiner adds that the child has "a low threshold for frustration."

Vignette 2: The same child, having successfully completed Problem #1 is presented with Problem #2. After a few unsuccessful minutes, the examiner asks the child, "Is this problem like any other that you have seen before?" The child responds, "I thought it was like this one but it doesn't work." The examiner urges the child to "read the letters in the problem out loud.... Did you hear a pattern in the letters?" This prompt failing, the examiner continues with "Are there any letters written more than once in the problem? Which ones? Does this give you any ideas about how to continue?" With this prompt, there is a smile of recognition and the child successfully completes the problem. When she is presented with the third problem, a problem identical in nature to the second, she is heard to say, "Oh, I know how to do this one... which letters are here more than one time?" The session continues with the examiner presenting problems either similar to the one presented previously, or differing in degree of difficulty. With each problem, the examiner provides, as needed, a series of prompts facilitating the child's successful completion of the problem. After the child leaves the room, the examiner notes, "quickly internalized use of prompts, indicated good maintenance and was quick to transfer to novel problems, showed persistence, eager to try another 'harder one.'"*

These two vignettes illustrate the difference between a common assessment task administered in a static manner (Vignette 1) and one administered in a dynamic manner (Vignette 2). This chapter focuses on dynamic assessment, including its definition, models of dynamic assessment, the application of the principles of dynamic assessment to instruction, and the implications of dynamic assessment for research and practice.

THE DEFINITION OF DYNAMIC ASSESSMENT

Dynamic assessment is actually a term used to characterize a number of distinct approaches that feature guided learning for the purpose of determining a learner's potential for change. In contrast to more traditional and static procedures that focus on the products of assessment, dynamic assessment is concerned with the different ways in which individuals who earned the same score achieved that score. In contrast to static measures, which reveal only those abilities that are completely developed, dynamic measures are concerned with how well a child performs once given assistance. Hence, dynamic assessment provides a *prospective* measure of performance, indicating abilities that are in the process of developing. The nature and extent of the assistance the child requires is *predictive* of how the child will perform independently in the future. The response the child makes to the assistance that is provided aids in *prescribing* effective instruction (Brown, Campione, & Weber, & McGilly, in press; Day, 1986; Lidz, 1987).

With these shared goals in mind, we will explore several approaches to dynamic assessment, focusing on distinguishing features of each. (The

---

*The problem and hint sequence presented in this vignette were adapted from Ferrara, Brown, & Campione (1986).

reader is referred to Lidz [1987] for a comprehensive review of contemporary dynamic assessment programs.) We begin with the work of Feuerstein as he is generally acknowledged to have coined the term, "dynamic assessment," and is one of its chief proponents.

MODELS OF DYNAMIC ASSESSMENT

FEUERSTEIN

Feuerstein suggests that cognitive growth is the result of *incidental* and *mediated* learning. While incidental learning is a consequence of the child's exposure to the changing environment, it is mediated learning to which Feuerstein attributes greater importance. "Mediated learning is the training given to the human organism by an experienced adult who frames, selects, focuses, and feeds back an environmental experience in such a way as to create appropriate learning sets" (Feuerstein, 1969, p. 6). Through interactions in which supportive others (parents, teachers, siblings, peers) guide problem-solving activity and structure the learning environment, the child gradually internalizes structuring and regulatory activities of his or her own.

Feuerstein proposes that the principal reason for the poor performance of many disadvantaged adolescents is the absence of consistent mediated learning experiences in their earlier developmental histories. This "deprivation" results in poor performance on a broad array of academic tasks; however, Feuerstein submits that, provided intensive mediated learning experiences, these same learners will show improvement. In contrast, students whose poor academic profile is the result of organic brain damage or retardation would be expected to profit less from these "re-mediation" experiences.

Driven by the belief that traditional psychometric devices could not tap the child's ability to acquire knowledge, Feuerstein developed the *Learning Potential Assessment Device* (LPAD; Feuerstein, 1980) to measure low-achieving students' ability to profit from instruction. The goal of the LPAD is to "produce changes in the very structural nature of the cognitive processes that directly determine cognitive functioning" (Feuerstein et al., 1979, p. 42). Hence, the LPAD was designed as an intervention to serve two functions: (1) to produce changes in the child's performance in order to be able to assess the child's degree of modifiability and (2) to remediate deficiencies in problem solving and thus serve as the basis for remediation after assessment.

To achieve this dual purpose, Feuerstein selected tasks that he felt require higher mental processes that are accessible to change and that permit the detection of minimal change. The LPAD is constructed around such tasks as matrix problems, span tests, and embedded-figure tasks. In this respect, the LPAD bears a strong resemblance to numerous traditional and static measures of IQ. However, Feuerstein substantially modifies the testing situation.

When administering the LPAD, the examiner assumes the roles of teacher/observer while the examinee becomes learner/performer. In this role, the examiner is interacting in a flexible and individualized manner with the examinee; "The examiner constantly intervenes, makes remarks, requires and gives explanations, whenever and wherever they are necessary, asks for repetition, sums up experiences, anticipates difficulties and warns the child about them, and creates insightful reflective thinking in the child . . ." (Feuerstein et al., 1979, p. 102).

Because the purpose of the assessment is not to predict future performance based on a score, but rather to depict the modifiability of cognitive structures and the source of deficits in learning, the results are to be considered in terms of a *cognitive map*. Features of the cognitive map that are to guide analysis of the interactions and results include the following:

- *Content*—examinee's familiarity with content

- *Modality*—verbal, pictorial, numerical, etc.

- *Phase*—a mental act can be divided into three phases: input, elaboration, and output. Failure may occur during any one or during all phases.

- *Operations*—strategies or sets of rules that facilitate problem solving

- *Level of complexity*—quantity and quality of information

- *Level of abstraction*—"the distance between the mental act and the object or events upon which it operates" (Feuerstein et al., 1979, p. 124)

- *Level of efficiency*—e.g., a high level of complexity attributable to a lack of familiarity may lead to relatively inefficient handling of the task. Factors such as fatigue and anxiety can also lead to inefficiency.

Guided by this cognitive map, the examiner seeks to specify the nature of the child's problem, asking questions about (for example), the role that familiarity of content plays in the child's success or failure, the phase or phases with which the child experiences difficulty, the strategies the child employs, and the efficiency of learning. In this assessment process, the primary indication that structural change has occurred is the decreased dependence on the examiner's help. This help can be described both in terms of amount and type. Improvement in the examinee is the goal in this model of dynamic assessment, because it is this improvement that permits one to make a statement regarding modifiability of the learner.

There are several criticisms of LPAD as an assessment procedure. One is related to the need for clarification regarding such constructs as "cognitive structure." It is unclear what it means to modify "the structural nature of cognitive functioning" (Brown et al., in press; Lidz, 1987).

A second concern is related to the clinical and, in many respects, intuitive nature of assessment using the LPAD. The open-ended flexibility of this procedure suggests that its success is largely a reflection of the skill of the examiner. A final concern is that the emphasis on very general skills leads to a significant problem with regard to transfer (Bransford, Delclos, Vye, Burns, & Hasselbring, 1987; Brown et al., in press). The tasks and materials used in the LPAD intentionally bear little resemblance to school-like activities. It is quite possible for children to show improvement in their ability to deal with these activities without showing concurrent gains on academic tasks. In contrast to the recent trends toward curriculum-based assessment (cf. *Exceptional Children*, 1985, Vol. 52(3)), Feuerstein's procedure is divorced from the content and context of classrooms. Despite these criticisms, Feuerstein is to be acknowledged for the impetus he has provided in the reexamination of special education assessment and placement practices in this country.

VYGOTSKY

Central to Vygotsky's theory of development is the *zone of proximal development*, or "the distance between the actual developmental level as determined by independent problem solving and the level of potential development as determined through problem solving under adult guidance, or in collaboration with more capable peers" (Vygotsky, 1978, p. 86). Hence, Vygotsky argued that one cannot understand the child's developmental level without considering both the actual level of development as well as the potential level of development.

The static tests of development that are typically in use today, at best, inform us regarding the child's actual level of development. Such an approach, in the words of Vygotsky, means that

we focus on what the child has and knows today. Using this approach, we can establish only what has already matured, we can determine only the level of the child's actual development. To determine the state of the child's development on this basis alone, however, is insufficient. The state of development is never defined only by what has matured. If the gardener decides only to evaluate the matured or harvested fruits of the apple tree, he cannot determine the state of his orchard. The maturing trees must also be taken into consideration. Correspondingly, the psychologist must not limit his analysis to functions that have matured; he must consider those that are in the process of maturation. . . . the zone of proximal development. How can this be accomplished?

When we determine the level of actual development, we use tasks that require independent resolution. These tasks function as indices of fully formed or fully matured functions. How then do we apply this new method? Assume that we have determined the mental age of two children to be eight years. However, we do not stop with this. Rather, we attempt to determine how each of these children solve tasks that were meant for older children. We assist each child through demonstration, through leading questions, and by introducing the initial elements of the task's solution. With this help or collaboration from the adult, one of these children solves problems characteristic of a twelve year old while the other solves problems only at a level typical of a nine year old. This difference between the child's mental ages, this difference between the child's actual level of development and the level of performance that he achieves in collaboration with the adult, defines the zone of proximal development. In this example, the zone can be expressed by the number 4 for one child and by the number 1 for the other. Can we assume that these children stand at identical levels of mental development, that the state of their development coincides? Obviously not. (Vygotsky, 1934/1986, pp. 203–204)

There are several research programs in this country that are based on Vygotsky's theory. The three that we will consider in this chapter have been conducted by Budoff and colleagues, Carlson and colleagues, and Campione and Brown and colleagues. While each of these programs employ an approach that can be characterized as "test–train–test," to the extent that some form of guided learning occurs between the administration of a test before and after instruction, they differ in terms of what that guidance entails and what the goal of the assessment procedure is. (For a more comprehensive analysis of these programs, see Brown et al., in press.)

BUDOFF

Budoff's approach is based on a conceptualization of intelligence that stresses trainability. We illustrate his approach using a block building task. The child first completes a test on several block designs (pretest). The child then enters the training phase. Training consists of presenting a problem and, if the child is unable to solve it, providing a series of increasingly explicit prompts until the solution is reached. In the case of the block design task the prompts draw the child's attention to the correspondence between his or her construction and the construction on the design card. After the training phase, the child is tested again (posttest).

Budoff has used the responses of children to this guided learning experience to characterize three types of learners: (a) *high scorers*, those who performed adequately on the pretest; (b) *nongainers*, those who experienced difficulty with the pretest and demonstrate little or no gain after instruction; and (c) *gainers*, those who indicate marked gains following instruction. As in any discussion of "gain scores," it is difficult to know how to compare the child who solves no problems on the pretest and six problems on the posttest with the child who solves five problems on the pretest and six problems on the posttest. In fact, Budoff has recently turned to a linear continuum model to describe the results of guided learning assessments (Budoff, 1987). However, Budoff has reported interesting findings with regard to gainer–nongainer status. For example, middle class children in special education classes tend to be nongainers, whereas special education classes serving primarily lower class children have a higher incidence of gainers. In addition, Budoff has found learning-potential status to be a successful predictor of performance on concept learning tasks, performance with a specially constructed math curriculum, and adaptation to mainstreaming.

CARLSON AND COLLEAGUES

What distinguishes the model of Carlson and his colleagues (Bethge, Carlson & Wiedl, 1982; Carlson & Widaman, 1986; Carlson & Wiedl, 1978, 1979, 1980, 1988) is the integration of specific interventions within the testing procedure. By modifying the testing procedures, they attempt to determine which procedures are better estimates of the upper limits of competence. Theirs is an interactive approach to assessment in which they analyze the effects of *personal factors* (e.g., motivation, cognitive factors), *task requirements*, and *diagnostic approaches* (e.g., strategy use) on the problem-solving process. In a manner similar to that used by Budoff, there is a sequence of procedures that guides the assessment process and is designed to test the limits of the child's ability: (1) The child is provided simple feedback regarding whether or not he or she has correctly solved the problem. (2) The child is prompted to verbalize how he or she attempted to achieve solution. (3) The child is encouraged to verbalize while attempting to solve the problem. (4) The child is provided with an explanation regarding why a particular solution is correct or incorrect, including the principles involved in task completion. And (5) Completion of the task is modeled for the child, with a verbal explanation.

Carlson and his colleagues report that the testing-the-limits procedures yield higher estimates of ability than do standardized test results and that the more intrusive procedures inducing children to reflect, explain, and elaborate on their responses (3, 4, and 5) increase test performance (Carlson & Wiedl, 1988). An additional outcome of this procedure worth noting is the reduction of test anxiety on the part of children (Bethge et al., 1982).

Bethge at al. suggest that changes in such affective variables may well contribute to differences in cognitive performance.

CAMPIONE AND BROWN

A third research program, influenced in part by interpretations of Vygotsky's writings, and driven in large measure by questions regarding learning and transfer processes has been conducted by Campione and Brown and their colleagues. The principal purpose of their assessment model (Brown & Ferrara, 1985; Brown & French, 1979; Bryant, Brown, & Campione, 1983; Campione, in press; Campione & Brown, 1984; Campione, Brown, & Ferrara, 1982; Campione, Brown, Ferrara, & Bryant, 1984; Campione, Brown, Ferrara, Jones, & Steinburg, 1985; Ferrara, 1987; Ferrara, Brown, & Campione, 1986) is to determine the facility with which students learn from others and the flexibility with which they use what they have learned. Hence, their procedure assumes the following form. Students are first pretested to determine their prior knowledge of a particular domain. There is then a match between the students and the task they are presented so that they are successful with easier tasks but do not perform well on the harder tasks. As the students attempt each problem the examiner/teacher provides a series of hints (similar to those illustrated in the vignette at the beginning of this chapter) until they solve the problem. The early hints are general, metacognitive prompts encouraging the student to, for example, "think of similar problems," and "plan ahead," while later hints are more specific to the demands of the task. For example, one of the final hints of the series-completion problem (described in the opening vignette of this chapter) is to provide the student a template that illustrates the relationship among the various letters in the sequence while the examiner verbalizes this relationship. This phase of the assessment process continues until the child can solve an array of target problems with no help. The amount of help each student needs is interpreted to be an estimate of learning efficiency within that domain at that particular time.

After achieving independent learning, students are then given a series of transfer problems that vary in terms of their similarity to the items originally learned. The purpose at this point in the assessment is to determine the extent of lateral transfer (Gagne, 1965) students can achieve. These transfer problems are classified as "near," "far," or "very far," depending upon the number of transformations performed on the initial learning problem. For example, in the series-completion problems, the transformations include repetitions and alphabetical ordering of the letters.

Once again, the student is provided help, but only the help necessary to achieve solution of the transfer problem. The amount of help needed is used to estimate students' "transfer propensity" in the specific domain, which in turn is regarded as a measure of the extent to which students understand the procedures they have been taught during the prompted assessment phase. To what extent can they access and modify the problem-solving procedures in flexible ways?

To summarize the principal results of investigations of this dynamic assessment model: There is evidence of concurrent validity to the extent that grade-school children of higher academic ability required less help to learn rules and principles and transferred use of these rules to novel problems more readily than did students of lower academic ability. In addition, differences between ability groups were greater on transfer measures than on the initial learning problems; that is, higher ability students showed greater degrees of lateral transfer while students who were academically weak had difficulty applying what they learned to the novel but related situations (Campione et al., 1985; Ferrara et al., 1986).

Studies examining the predictive validity of these procedures were conducted with preschool children using either series completion or matrix problems (Bryant, 1982; Bryant et al., 1983). The children were first given a series of pretests measuring both general ability (using the Wechsler Preschool and Primary Scale of Intelligence [WPPSI] and Raven Progressive Matrices [Raven's]) as well as task-specific competence (unaided performance on the problem types to be included in the dynamic assessment phase). The children then participated in the dynamic assessment sessions, including the prompted learning, maintenance, near transfer, and far transfer problems described above. The principal question in this investigation was related to the change from pretest to posttest performance. What were the best predictors of this gain score: the static scores derived from the general ability measures and measures of entering competence or the dynamic scores (i.e., the learning and transfer measures)?

The results indicated that the initial unaided performance of the children was a significant underestimate of what the children could achieve with minimal assistance. There were sizable differences in the gain scores. Regression analyses conducted to determine the best predictors of this gain score indicated that the estimated IQ score and Raven score were related to the gain score, accounting together for about 36% of their variance. However, the learning and transfer scores still accounted for an additional 39% of the variance in the matrix task. In summary, the learning and transfer measures provided further significant diagnostic information. Furthermore, if one considers the simple correlations, the assisted learning and transfer scores were better predictors of gain than were either of the static measures. Finally, the results of these investigations supported earlier studies, which indicated that, despite the fact that children had learned the same problem with the same criterion, they differed dramatically in terms of how flexibly they could apply this new knowledge. Children achieving lower scores on the ability measures demonstrated less flexible knowledge use than children scoring higher on these measures.

It is important to emphasize at this point that in this research program the goal of quantifying learning potential has been for theoretical and empirical purposes, not for the purpose of identifying children in terms of their initial learning and transfer ability. To suggest that the measures arising from this research suggest stable learning characteristics would be to repeat the error of reifying test scores as cognitive entities. In addition, it would imply a belief in very general learning factors, wherein the problem of transfer once again arises. It is because of these issues that Brown and Campione and their research team have begun to explore the principles of dynamic assessment within academic contexts. We return to this research, following a discussion of comparative research conducted by Bransford and his research team.

BRANSFORD AND COLLEAGUES

While the dynamic assessment research of Bransford and his colleagues is extensive (Bransford et al., 1987; Burns, Vye, Bransford, Delclos, & Ogan, 1987; Vye, Burns, Delclos, & Bransford, 1987) and notable on a number of dimensions, we discuss but one facet of their work in this chapter. This is their recent work comparing the Feuerstein model of mediated assessment with the graduated prompting developed by Campione and Brown and their colleagues (Bransford et al., 1987).

In this work, young children are first assessed with static IQ measures and those whose score is more than one standard deviation below the mean proceed to the next phase. In this phase, the children are engaged in verbal, quantitative, or performance tasks and receive graduated prompting, similar to that described in the accounts of the research of Brown, Campione, and colleagues. The graduated prompts method involves providing children with a series of prompts or hints, arranged from general to explicit, to teach the child completion of the task. One prompt is given with each attempt. Children who attain criterion performance after this phase, are considered able to learn with relevant experience or motivation. Children who fail to reach a criterion proceed to the third phase of assessment—mediated dynamic assessment. In this phase, the child is first familiarized with the materials used in the task, then given task-specific rules and procedures tailored to his or her individual needs, and finally is given feedback on the adequacy of performance.

Their principal findings indicate that static measures do not predict performance well, both the graduated prompts and mediated assessment methods produce learning, and mediated dynamic assessment produces more transfer than graduated prompts. This last finding makes more salient the different outcomes one would expect from these two forms of dynamic assessment. Since variation on transfer efficiency is the major diagnostic element in graduated prompting, good transfer in everyone would negate the predictive validity of this procedure. Furthermore, since mediated dynamic assessment is, in essence, intensive instruction, and one expected outcome of good instruction is transfer, one would expect to find more transfer after the use of mediated assessment.

There is an additional outcome of the work conducted by the Vanderbilt team that is worthy of note. In a study conducted by Vye et al. (1987), the researchers showed segments of assessment sessions to two groups of teachers. One saw two segments for a child during static assessment; the second saw one segment of a static assessment and one of a dynamic assessment. The teachers then completed a questionnaire in which they rated the child's task involvement, specific task performance, and general competence. Teachers reported the children as moderately involved in both conditions. With regard to task performance and general competence, they rated the children low on both dimensions following the static assessment condition. Those who continued to view the static assessment session, continued to rate the child low on these features; whereas those who saw the dynamic assessment segment after the static assessment session, rated the child much higher. Finally, when the static–static sessions were followed by the viewing of a third (dynamic assessment) session, these teachers' ratings increased to the level of the original static–dynamic group. When we consider that information about children's abilities to learn has an important role in teachers' and parents' expectations, these findings have significant educational implications.*

In summary thus far, dynamic assessment procedures reveal a different picture of individual competence than do static procedures. Static measures tend to underestimate many children's ability to learn in a domain in which they initially performed poorly. Learning and transfer scores are better predictors of gain than are static measures. Furthermore, these dynamic scores continue to account for variance even when static scores are used as covariates. Furthermore, dynamic assessment approaches have attempted to combine assessment with instruction, for while students are being evaluated, they are also being taught something about the target

---

*There is an additional piece of research that serves as an interesting postscript to the study of Burns et al. (1987) in which teachers had the opportunity to observe children in dynamic and static assessment situations and reported more favorable impressions from the dynamic session(s). Hoy and Retish (1986) conducted a study in which teachers were asked to rate the usefulness of written psychoeducational reports of static and dynamic assessment procedures. The teachers rated neither type particularly useful and made no distinction, in terms of usefulness, between the two types of reports. The most useful way in which to communicate the results of assessment constitutes a significant research issue.

domain. Finally, the dynamic assessment research underscores the importance of teaching flexible knowledge use, particularly, with special education populations. In the final portion of this chapter we pursue this assessment–intervention link (Meyers, Pfeffer, & Erlbaum, 1985) by examining research in which many of the features of dynamic assessment have been embedded in particular academic domains. Our first example is from early mathematics.

LINKING ASSESSMENT AND INSTRUCTIONAL PROCEDURES

GUIDED LEARNING AND TRANSFER IN EARLY MATHEMATICS

Ferrara (1987) conducted a study in which she applied the principles of dynamic assessment to examining the mathematical performance of young children. Ferrara first developed a test to assess kindergartener's knowledge about numbers, including the basic principles of counting, the ability to "count on" and count backward from a given number, and to generate a set when given a number. The children were also administered the mathematics subtest of the Stanford Early School Achievement Test (SESAT). The correlation between Ferrara's knowledge measure and the SESAT was 0.71.

In the next phase of her research, each child and the tester/teacher worked together to solve word problems that the child could not solve independently. A prototypical problem follows:

Miss Piggy is starting out with 4 pennies in her purse (briefly displayed and taken away), and I'm putting 3 more pennies into the purse (displayed and added to the hidden display). *Now* how many pennies are there *altogether* in the purse?

When the child experienced difficulty, the tester/teacher provided a sequence of hints that ranged from simply informing the child that his or hers was a good try but not quite right, to representing the problem numerically, to demonstrating and explaining the complete solution to the problem. There were eight hints in a complete hint sequence. At what point the tester/teacher began the hinting process depended upon the child's level of performance with the given problem. Once the solution was reached, problems of the same type were presented, measuring with each problem the amount of aid needed to complete the problem successfully. This continued until the child could solve this problem type, at which time the child was presented transfer problems. Near transfer problems involved new combinations of familiar quantities but with different characters and contexts, whereas very far transfer problems included missing addend problems. Once again, what was scored during the interactive transfer sessions was the amount of help the child needed when attempting to solve these transfer problems independently.

Following the learning and transfer sessions, a posttest was administered, determining how much the child had learned during the course of the guided learning sessions. Once again, the scores were examined to determine which variables or combinations of variables best predicted gain scores. The main findings were that the dynamic scores were better predictors of gain (mean correlation = 0.57) than were static knowledge and ability scores (mean correlation = 0.38). Furthermore, regression analysis indicated that while static scores accounted for 22.2% of the variance in gain scores, the addition of the dynamic scores accounted for an additional 33.7% of the variance, with transfer performance accounting for 32% of the variance.

In addition to predicting how well these young students would do within the math domain, and in addition to the instruction that the children received during this assessment process, there was yet another outcome of considerable value. The assessment process yielded specific information about the kinds of help these various children needed to be successful with these mathematical problems. By organizing these hints in a qualitative way, their effects could be used to inform remedial instruction. For example, Ferrara was able to determine the effectiveness of simply giving students an opportunity to correct their initial responses in comparison with providing verbal memory aids (i.e., reminding students of the quantities involved in the problem) to actually helping children to structure the problems. It is easy to envision the value of such recommendations to teachers and parents.

GUIDED LEARNING AND READING

The domain of reading is a particularly appropriate one in which to examine the themes of dynamic assessment and the links between assessment and instruction. Recent reading theory and research emphasize the highly interactive nature of reading performance; "Reading is the process of constructing meaning through the interaction among the reader, the text, and the context of the reading situation" (Wixson & Lipson, 1986, p. 132). This interaction has been found to vary as a function of numerous factors: the reader's prior knowledge (Anderson, Reynolds, Schallert, & Goetz, 1977), the structure of the text (Stein & Glenn, 1979), motivation (Butkowsky & Willows, 1980), and the difficulty of the text (Lipson, Irwin, & Poth, 1986). Such an understanding of reading suggests an agenda quite different from the traditional assessment agenda applied to the case of reading disability. Rather than administering an array of aptitude, achievement, and diagnostic measures to determine the deficits displayed by the child, assessment is focused on determining the conditions under which the child can and does experience reading success (Wixson & Lipson, 1986).

Since this is a fairly new perspective on reading and reading disability, there are few assessment models that have been investigated from this perspective. However, the work of Paratore and Indrisano (1987) is illustrative. Rather than assessing a series of subskills in reading, they assess students' ability and inclination to use such strategies as activating background knowledge, building relationships among ideas presented in text and using text structure to organize and recall text. The materials used in the assessment are representative of the kinds of materials that are used in classrooms. The assessment itself follows a test–teach–test paradigm. For example, to assess the student's use of text structure to organize and recall information, the student is presented a passage to read. The student is then asked to retell the story. The number of idea units recalled as well as the organization of the recall is evaluated. The student is then shown a "map" that depicts the structure of the text (e.g., comparison–contrast, problem–solution, cause–effect). The student is then asked to reread the story, focusing on the events outlined on the map. After this reading, the student is once again asked to retell the story. If the student continues to display limited recall, she or he is guided to use the map for the purpose of note taking. This step is followed by another recall measure. The results of this assessment procedure can be used to identify the strategies the reader currently deploys, to identify strategies that would assist the reader, and to determine responsiveness to strategy instruction. Paratore and Indrisano's model is principally one of assessment.

In a second illustration we discuss a model that is principally instructional but with implications for assessment: reciprocal teaching. Similar to much of the dynamic assessment research discussed in this chapter, the design of reciprocal teaching was informed by Vygotsky's theory that a zone of proximal development is created, sustained, and extended in a social situation (Brown & Palincsar, in press; Palincsar & Brown, 1984; in press). Vygotsky argued that thinking is a social activity, initially shared between people but gradually internalized to reappear again as individualized achievement (Vygotsky, 1978; Wertsch, 1980). Indeed, Vygotsky proposed that through social dialogue, it is possible for the child to participate in strategic activity without understanding it completely. Through repeated and shared dialogues, the child comes to discover the import of the more knowledgable participant's utterances and his or her own responses.

Reciprocal teaching then, assumes the form of a dialogue in which teachers and students take turns leading discussions about shared text. The discussions are structured by the use of four activities that are practiced as strategies in the dialogues: predicting, questioning, summarizing, and clarifying. Generally, these four activities are used to structure the discussion in the following manner: The person who is serving as the discussion leader for a portion of text begins by asking *questions* pertinent to the material read. Other members of the group respond to the questions and suggest additional questions, which are also answered. The discussion leader then *summarizes* the same portion of text and other members of the group are invited to comment or elaborate upon the summary. If there were points in the text that were unclear (e.g., concepts, vocabulary, references), these are discussed for the purpose of achieving *clarity*. Finally, the group determines if there are clues as to upcoming content and these *predictions* are discussed. While these particular strategies are useful for supporting the dialogues, it is the teacher who supports the students' participation in the dialogues. This support varies according to the ability of the students and the difficulty of the text.

The effectiveness of reciprocal teaching has been investigated in a number of studies conducted over the past seven years. In each study the intervention period occurred over a relatively extensive period (20 to 60 days), the older students (middle school) were at least two years behind on standardized measures of reading comprehension and the younger students (primary) were identified as "at risk" for academic difficulty, progress was measured not only be evaluating students' participation in the dialogues, but also by assessments of comprehension of novel text and strategy use, and measures of long-term maintenance and generalization were included.

Focusing on the independent tests of comprehension, students typically scored approximately 30% on these measures before the intervention. If we regard criterion performance as achieving a score of 75 to 80% correct on four of five consecutive days, approximately 80% of the students across ages attained criterion performance. Furthermore, with the older population, maintenance was demonstrated for up to a year after instruction (Brown & Palincsar, 1982; Brown, Palincsar, Ryan, & Slattery, work in progress); progress was generalized to other classroom activities, specifically science and social studies; and the students improved approximately two years on standardized measures of comprehension (Palincsar & Brown, 1984). The young students have demonstrated comparable gains on the criterion-referenced measures but not on the standardized measures. We believe that this is an artifact of the nature of standardized measures in the early grades. Tests of reading are primarily tests of decoding skills, practiced out of context. Tests of listening are primarily following directions, auditory sequencing, and rote recall of facts. Because of this mismatch between instruction (in comprehension) and assessment (of decoding, rote recall, etc.), the improvement indicated on the other measures employed in these studies has not been demonstrated on the standardized tests.

How is reciprocal teaching an assessment procedure? First, the strategies themselves provide the students the opportunity to self-test their understanding of the text. If the student is unable to summarize the text, this may well be an indication that there is difficulty understanding the text and remedial action is called for. This self-monitoring is, of course, not only useful in the context of the group discussions but, more importantly, is useful to independent reading of text. The strategies induce the reader to engage in the kinds of activities (i.e., reviewing and integrating content, anticipating information, resolving confusion) in which skilled readers engage (Bereiter & Bird, 1987).

Second, the dialogues provide a window on the manner in which the children approach text for the purpose of making sense of it. As the discussion leader frames the summary and other participants comment on it, the teacher is privy to the decisions the children have made with regard to what was important in the text. As the group generates predictions, the teacher acquires some sense of the extent, accuracy, and organization of the knowledge the children have regarding the content at hand. The clarifications the children request inform the teacher about the features of text to which they attend. For example, when the dialogues first begin the children generally request clarification of "hard words" (even if they are unimportant to understanding the text). As instruction proceeds, the children begin to discriminate among words that are important to understanding the text and clarifications are more frequently focused on ideas in the text.

Third, the dialogues provide the opportunity to assess the children's responsiveness to instruction and to adjust instruction as needed. In these dialogues, the teacher is monitoring the engagement of each student in the discussions, providing feedback that is tailored to the individual's participation and providing the assistance that is needed for the child to join the discussion successfully. Because reciprocal teaching usually occurs in small but heterogeneous groups, the teacher's involvement in the instruction varies with each child and changes over the course of instruction. The teacher's goal is to transfer responsibility for the comprehension activity to the students as soon as they are able to assume this responsibility. Because the teacher is focused on this transfer, the teacher is engaged in ongoing diagnosis and adjustment of instruction in response to student's needs. Since reciprocal teaching was designed as an intervention to be used in small group instruction (groups have generally ranged in size from six to eight but have reached eighteen), we continue to explore ways in which the principles of reciprocal teaching can be incorporated in whole-class instruction (Palincsar & Brown, work in progress).

CONCLUSION

There have been numerous and sustained calls for changes in assessment practices, particularly assessment practices that lead to the identification and placement of children in programs for the handicapped or at-risk (Meisels, 1987; Shepard & Smith, 1988; Swanson, 1984; Meyers, et al., 1985). While the concerns that are voiced are often couched in terms of the technical adequacy of the instruments and procedures that have historically been used for these purposes, nevertheless, underlying these concerns are questions of an ethical nature. In what procedures can we have the confidence to make the "educational career decisions" (Mehan, Hertweck, & Meihls, 1986) to which assessment typically leads?

There is a common set of assumptions about learners and learning underlying dynamic assessment models that distinguish dynamic assessment from more traditional procedures: (1) The social contexts in which learning occurs significantly influence the learning process. (2) Learners can learn to be more efficient learners and assessment should measure this flexibility. And (3) The real value in assessment lies in the ability to prescribe rather than to predict.

Dynamic assessment research, for the purpose of translating this model of assessment into assessment procedures, is still in its infancy in many respects. For example, the dynamic assessment procedures described in this chapter require fairly extensive commitments of time to the assessment process. Shepard & Glass (1981) have called our attention to the alarmingly high costs associated with evaluation. Research identifying the most critical components of dynamic assessment, as well as research defining the specificity of the domain in which dynamic assessment must be conducted to be instructionally useful, are extremely important at this juncture. Perhaps most complementary to these efforts will be research focused on the integration of instruction and assessment.

REFERENCES

Anderson, R. C., Reynolds, R. E., Schallert, D. L., & Goetz, E. T. (1977). Frameworks for comprehending discourse. *American Educational Research Journal, 14*, 367–381.
Bereiter, C., & Bird, M. (1987). Use of thinking aloud in identification and teaching of reading comprehension strategies. *Cognition & Instruction, 2*,(2) 131–156.
Bethge, H., Carlson, J. S., & Wiedl, K. H. (1982). The effects of dynamic assessment procedures on Raven matrices performance, visual search behavior, text anxiety and test orientation. *Intelligence, 6*, 89–97.
Bransford, J. D., Delclos, V. R., Vye, N. J., Burns, M. S., & Hasselbring, T. S. (1987). Approaches to dynamic assessment: Issues, data and future directions. In C. S. Lidz (Ed.), *Dynamic assessment: Foundations and fundamentals*. New York: Guilford Press.

Brown, A. L., Campione, J. C., Weber, L. S., & McGilly, K. (in press). Interactive learning environments: A new look at assessment and instruction. Paper commissioned by the Commission on Testing and Public Policy. University of California at Berkeley.

Brown, A. L., & Ferrara, R. A. (1985). Diagnosing zones of proximal development: An alternative to standardized testing? In J. Wertsch (Ed.), *Culture, communication and cognition: Vygotskian perspectives* (pp. 273–305). New York: Cambridge University Press.

Brown, A. L., & French, L. A. (1979). The cognitive consequences of education: School experts or general problem solvers. Commentary on "Education and cognitive development: The evidence from experimental research" by Sharp, Cole & Lave. *Monographs of the Society of Research in Child Development, 44*, (1–2, Serial No. 178).

Brown, A. L., & Palincsar, A. S. (in press). Guided cooperative learning and individual knowledge acquisition. In L. B. Resnick (Ed.), *Knowing and learning: Issues for a cognitive psychology of instruction*. Hillsdale, NJ: Erlbaum.

Brown, A. L., & Palincsar, A. S. (1982). Inducing strategic learning from texts by means of informed, self-control training. *Topics in Learning and Learning Disabilities, 2*(1), 1–17.

Bryant, N. R. (1982). *Preschool children's learning and transfer of matrices problems: A study of proximal development*. Unpublished master's thesis, University of Illinois.

Bryant, N. R., Brown, A. L., & Campione, J. C. (April, 1983). *Preschool children's learning and transfer of matrices problems: Potential for improvement*. Paper presented at the Society for Research in Child Development meetings, Detroit.

Budoff, M. (1987). Measures for assessing learning potential. In C. S. Lidz (Ed.), *Dynamic assessment: Foundations and fundamentals* (pp. 173–195). New York: Guilford Press.

Burns, M. S., Vye, N. J., Bransford, J. D., Delclos, V. R., & Ogan, T. (1987). *Static and dynamic measures of learning in young handicapped children*. (Tech. Report No. 8). Vanderbilt University, John F. Kennedy Center for Research on Education and Human Development.

Butkowsky, S., & Willows, D. (1980). Cognitive-motivational characteristics of children varying in reading ability: Evidence for learned helplessness in poor readers. *Journal of Educational Psychology, 72*, 408–422.

Campione, J. C. (in press). Assisted assessment: A taxonomy of approaches and an outline of strengths and weaknesses. *Journal of Learning Disabilities*.

Campione, J. C., & Brown, A. L. (1984). Learning ability and transfer propensity as sources of individual differences in intelligence. In P. H. Brooks, R. Sperber, & C. McCauley (Eds.), *Learning and cognition in the mentally retarded*. (pp. 137–150). Baltimore: University Park Press.

Campione, J. C., Brown, A. L., & Ferrara, R. A. (1982). Mental retardation and intelligence. In R. J. Sternberg (Ed.), *Handbook of human intelligence*. New York: Cambridge University Press.

Campione, J. C., Brown, A. L., Ferrara, R. A., & Bryant, N. R. (1984). The zone of proximal development: Implications for individual differences and learning. In B. Rogoff & J. Wertsch (Eds.), *New directions for cognitive development: The zone of proximal development* (pp. 77–91). San Francisco: Jossey-Bass.

Campione, J. C., Brown, A. L., Ferrara, R. A., Jones, R. S., & Steinburg, E. (1985). Breakdown in flexible use of information: Intelligence-related differences in transfer following equivalent learning performance. *Intelligence, 9*, 297–315.

Carlson, J. S., & Widaman, K. F. (1986). Eysenck on intelligence: A critical perspective. In S. Modgil & C. Modgil (Eds.), *Hans Eysenck: Consensus and controversy* (pp. 103–132). Philadelphia: The Falmer Press.

Carlson, J. S., & Wiedl, K. H. (1978). The use of testing-the-limits procedures in the assessment of intellectual capabilities in children with learning difficulties. *American Journal of Mental Deficiency, 82*, 559–564.

Carlson, J. S., & Wiedl, K. H. (1979). Toward a differential testing approach: Testing-the-limits employing the Raven matrices. *Intelligence, 3*, 323–344.

Carlson, J. S., & Wiedl, K. H. (1980). Applications of a dynamic testing approach in intelligence assessment: Empirical results and theoretical formulations. *Zeitschrift fur Differentielle und Diagnostiche Psychologie, 1*(4), 303–318.

Carlson, J. S., & Wiedl, K. H. (1988). The dynamic assessment of intelligence. In H. C. Haywood & D. Tzuriel (Eds.), *Interactive assessment*. Hillsdale, NJ: Erlbaum.

Day, J. D. (1986). Teaching summarization skills: Influences of student ability level and strategy difficulty. *Cognition & Instruction, 3*(3), 193–210.

Ferrara, R. A. (1987). *Learning mathematics in the zone of proximal development: The importance of flexible use of knowledge*. Ph.D. dissertation, Department of Psychology, University of Illinois at Urbana-Champaign.

Ferrara, R. A., Brown, A. L., & Campione, J. C. (1986). Children's learning and transfer of inductive reasoning rules: Studies in proximal development. *Child Development, 57*(5), 1087–1099.

Feuerstein, R. (1969). [The instrumental enrichment method: An outline of theory and technique.] Unpublished paper. Jerusalem: Hadassah-Wizo-Canada Research Institute.

Feuerstein, R. (1979). *The dynamic assessment of retarded performers: The learning potential assessment device, theory, instruments, and techniques*. Baltimore: University Park Press.

Feuerstein, R. (1980). *Instrumental enrichment: An intervention program for cognitive modifiability*. Baltimore: University Park Press.

Gagne, R. M. (1965). *The conditions of learning*. New York: Holt, Rinehart & Winston.

Hoy, M. P., & Retish, P. M. (1986). A comparison of two types of assessment reports. *Exceptional Children, 51*(3), 225–229.

Lidz, C. S. (Ed.) (1987). *Dynamic assessment: Foundations and fundamentals*. New York: Guilford Press.

Lipson, M. Y., Irwin, M., & Poth, E. (1986). The relationship between metacognitive self-reports and strategic reading behavior. In J. Niles & R. Lalik (Eds.), *Solving problems in literacy: Learners, teachers, and researchers* (pp. 214–221). Thirty-fifth Yearbook of the National Reading Conference. Rochester, NY: National Reading Conference.

Mehan, M., Hertweck, A., & Meihls, J. L. (1986). *Handicapping the handicapped: Decision making in students' educational careers*. Stanford, CA: Stanford University Press.

Meisels, S. J. (1987). Uses and abuses of developmental screening and school readiness testing. *Young Children, 42*(2), 4–73.

Meyers, J., Pfeffer, J., & Erlbaum, V. (1985). Process assessment: A model for broadening assessment. *The Journal of Special Education, 19*(1), 73–89.

Palincsar, A. S., & Brown, A. L. (in press). Classroom dialogues to promote self-regulated comprehension. In J. Brophy (Ed.), *Teaching for Meaningful Understanding and Self-regulated Learning* (Vol. 1). Greenwich, CT: JAI Press.

Palincsar, A. S., & Brown, A. L. (1984). Reciprocal teaching of comprehension-fostering and comprehension-monitoring activities. *Cognition & Instruction, 1*(2), 117–175.

Paratore, J. R., & Indrisano, R. (1987). Intervention assessment of reading comprehension (pp. 778–782). *The Reading Teacher, 40*(8), 778–782.
Shepard, L. A., & Glass, M. L. (1981). The identification, assessment, placement, and remediation of perceptual and communication disordered children. Boulder, CO: Laboratory of Educational Research, University of Colorado.
Shepard, L. A., & Smith, M. L. (1988). Escalating academic demand in kindergarten: Counter-productive policies. *The Elementary School Journal, 89*(2), 135–145.
Swanson, H. L. (1984). Process assessment of intelligence in learning disabled and mentally retarded children: A multidirectional model. *Educational Psychologist, 19*(3), 149–162.
Stein, N. L., & Glenn, C. G. (1979). An analysis of story comprehension in elementary school children. In R. O. Freedle (Ed.), *Advances in discourse processes,* Vol. 2: New directions in discourse processing. Norwood, NJ: Ablex.
Tucker, J. A. (Ed.) (1985). Curriculum-based assessment. *Exceptional Children, 52*(3).
Vye, N. J., Burns, M. S., Delclos, V. R., & Bransford, J. D. (1987). A comprehensive approach to assessing intellectually handicapped children (pp. 327–359). In C. S. Lidz (Ed.), *Dynamic assessment: An interactional approach to evaluating learning potential.* New York: Guilford Press.
Vygotsky, L. S. (1978). *Mind in society: The development of higher psychological processes.* Edited by M. Cole, V. John-Steiner, S. Scribner, and E. Souberman. Cambridge: Harvard University Press.
Vygotsky, L. S. (1934/1986). *Thought and Language.* Edited by A. Kozulin. Cambridge: MIT Press.
Wertsch, J. V. (1980). The significance of dialogue in Vygotsky's account of social, egocentric, and inner speech. *Contemporary Educational Psychology, 5,* 150–162.
Wixson, K. K., & Lipson, M. Y. (1986). Reading (dis)abilities: An interactionist perspective. In T. E. Raphael (Ed.), *Contexts of school-based literacy* (pp. 131–148). New York: Random House.

CHAPTER 6

Behavioral Assessment of Learning Disabilities

THOMAS C. LOVITT

This chapter discusses the arrangement of behavioral approaches to assess aspects of instructional programs for students with learning disabilities. Before describing those approaches, however, a few words are in order about the term, "behavioral assessment." This is a rather presumptuous and smug label, for most people in the business of assessment would think that *their* approaches had something to do with behaviors. To date, I have never heard of a nonbehavioral method.

Behavioral assessments such as the ones explained in this chapter have existed under many names. Perhaps the originators of that school were the *operant conditioners* of the 1950s and 1960s who obtained frequent measures of pecking, clawing, and scratching. Later, the *behavior modifiers* in the 1960s and 1970s relied on behavioral assessments as they directly recorded talk outs, out of seats, and tantrums. At about the same time, advocates of *precision teaching* extended behavioral assessments to record directly and frequently the rates of reading, writing, calculating, spelling, and other academic behaviors. Supporters of *formative evaluation* in the 1970s and 1980s latched onto aspects of behavioral measurement, particularly the component of frequent measurement. Most recently, proponents of *curriculum-based assessment* have adopted the direct component of behavioral assessment.

Certainly there are differences between these types of behavioral assessment, and the professionals who promote one form or the other are often quick to inform us that the differences are not subtle. But in the interests of parsimony and clarification, there appear to be two distinguishing features that are shared by all the aforementioned procedures, and set them apart from other types of assessment that may be behavioral but do not use the word.

The most important of these uniform features is the matter of directness. Behavioral assessors would advise teachers to measure the behaviors about which they are concerned. If, for example, a teacher was most interested in a boy's ability to read Book F of the Lippincott reading series, she would obtain data as he read from that book, not from a different level of that series, the same level in another series, and certainly not from an achievement test. The second feature of many behavioral approaches that distinguish them from other types of monitoring, is the attribute of frequency. In most of their assessments, data are obtained on a number of occasions.

In this chapter, the arrangement of behavioral assessments in eight educational situations is explained. Most of the examples are with learning disabled youngsters of elementary age. The following topics are discussed in this chapter: screening, placement, evaluation of a short-term objective, evaluation of a long-term objective, follow-up of students, evaluation of programs, differentiation of types of students, and comparison of a behavioral assessment with a normative assessment.

SCREENING YOUNGSTERS FOR SPECIAL SERVICES

Initially in this section a screening approach with first grade youngsters is explained; then, a behavioral approach for nondiscriminatory assessment is discussed. As for the former, the teacher of 29 first graders wished to assess their performances on four prereading skills that she believed should be developed early in the year. Her screening took place the first week in October.

These are the four attributes the teacher identified: "see letter, say letter"; "see letter, say sound"; "see picture, say sound"; and "listen to word, write letter for initial sound." In order to obtain data on these skills, the teacher developed formats for administering the tests. For the "see letter, say letter" assessment, she randomly printed all the letters of the alphabet on an 8 1/2 by 11 sheet of paper. There were 10 rows and 6 columns of letters, thus all the letters appeared about three times. That same sheet was used for the "see letter, say sound" assessment. For the "see picture, say sound" evaluation, the teacher assembled a set of cards that showed pictures of objects such as an apple, ball, cup, and dog. The teacher used the same pictures for the "listen to word, write initial letter assessment."

To acquire data on the four activities, the teacher conducted 1-minute timings. For the "see letter, say letter" component, students were given the sheet of letters and told to say the names of the letter on the top row and progress from left to right, then move to the second row, and so forth. Pupils were asked to say as many as they could in 1 minute. They were given the same sheet for the second feature and instructed to say as many of the letter sounds as possible in 1 minute. For the "see picture, say sound" assessment, the youngsters were shown one picture at a time and told to name the initial sound of the picture. For the last component, pupils listened to the teacher pronounce words and they wrote the letter that corresponded to the first letter in the words.

The teacher then graphed those data, the four correct rates for each of the 29 children. The average correct rates per minute were as follows: 24 letters said from letters; 5.3 sounds said from letters; 9 sounds said from pictures; and 2 letters written from words.

When the teacher studied those data from individual children, it was apparent that two youngsters were off the mark and would require extra assistance if they were to become proficient by the end of the semester. One was a boy and one a girl. Interestingly, the teacher had suspected, before the screening, that the boy was in trouble, but she had no idea that the girl's performances were so low.

Reacting to those data, the teacher arranged daily exercises for the pair of students on the four components in an attempt to raise their performance levels to the mean of the class. The boy reached the targets for the four skills in 4, 16, 7, and 2 days; the girl in 8, 6, 9, and 8 days.

The second part of this set is an explanation of a screening instrument designed by Kunzelmann (1976) that was intended to be nondiscriminatory. Purportedly, it did not discriminate youngsters on the basis of race, but did so on their ability to learn.

For his assessment, Kunzelmann developed formats to obtain data from youngsters in three areas: reading, mathematics, and spelling. For each subject, exercises were designed at grade levels from 1 through 6. Stories for these grade levels were printed on 8 1/2 by 11 sheets. For math, problems taught at the various grade levels were printed on similar sheets, and for spelling, words at the various grade levels were written on these sheets.

To acquire data, Kunzelmann required youngsters to respond to materials at their grade level for 1 minute for 5 consecutive days. For each youngster then, five correct rates were acquired in reading, math, and spelling.

These correct rates were then charted, and revealed three measures: two "performance" scores and one "learning" score. Performance scores were the youngster's first and fifth rates; those might have been 20 and 25 correct responses per minute. The "learning" score took into account all five of the student's rates. To calculate that figure, a trend line was drawn through the correct rates and a percentage was obtained that reflected the amount of growth throughout a week. If a student's scores were changing at a 10% pace per week, that was described as a x1.1 acceleration.

To summarize, performance scores, derived from single measures, gave static indications of achievement (like achievement tests); whereas the learning score, determined by all five scores, provided a dynamic index of achievement (unlike achievement tests).

Table 6-1 offers data about reading for white and minority students from grades 1 through 6. Shown in the table are averages for the groups' first and last performance scores and their average learning scores. Also indicated are the numbers in each group, their standard deviations, and calculated t and probability values. These data revealed that the average first and last performance scores for the white students were all higher than those of minority youngsters. When learning scores were taken into account, however, the means for the minority children were higher for students in grades 1, 4, 5, and 6.

With respect to statistical significance, all but two of the performance measures reached significance beyond the .05 level, all favoring the Caucasian students. As for the learning scores, none of the means reached significance beyond the .05 level. Thus Kunzelmann could make a convincing case that when a measure of growth, or "learning," as he referred to it, was taken into account, as much progress was shown by minority students as was indicated by white pupils.

PLACEMENT OF YOUNGSTERS AT INSTRUCTIONAL LEVELS

The study reviewed here is the first in a series of four. It was carried out several years ago with boys with learning disabilities between the ages of 8 and 11 at the Experimental Education Unit (EEU), University of Washington. The purpose of the project was to place them at proper instructional reading levels (Lovitt & Hansen, 1976a).

From previous data it appeared that when children were placed with books in which their correct rates were between 45 and 65 words per minute, their incorrect rates from 4 to 8 words per minute, and their comprehension scores no less than 50%, they were able to progress when rather basic, straightforward instruction was provided. It was the aim of this project, therefore, to place youngsters with the highest reader in a series in which those conditions were met, and follow their progress throughout a year. (See the following three projects.)

To carry out the placement, the students were required to read orally from eight different books representing grade levels of 1.5 to 6.0 from the

Table 6-1. Performance and Learning Comparisons of Caucasions vs. Minorities In Reading

Grade	Ethnic	No.	Performance(First)				Performance(Last)				Learning			
			MEAN	SD	T-TEST	P VALUE	MEAN	SD	T-TEST	P VALUE	MEAN	SD	T-TEST	P VALUE
1	White	1302	7	14.1			52	22.5			1.27	.65		
	Minority	130	5	12.2	1.27	.21	50	40.4	.79	.43	1.49	1.55	-1.60	.11
2	White	1319	31	26.3			63	34.0			1.42	.53		
	Minority	126	24	26.0	2.71	.007	57	32.2	2.06	.04	1.39	.32	.84	.40
3	White	1194	55	28.0			89	42.7			1.35	.37		
	Minority	131	46	25.7	3.61	<.0005	79	41.8	2.41	.02	1.33	.28	.71	.48
4	White	1188	64	29.6			100	36.9			1.35	.25		
	Minority	118	49	30.6	5.18	<.0005	85	43.8	3.60	<.0005	1.40	.25	-1.92	.06
5	White	1149	54	28.5			105	38.1			1.45	.34		
	Minority	127	42	28.7	4.50	<.0005	83	29.6	5.82	<.0005	1.47	.55	-.45	.65
6	White	931	63	30.9			107	39.3			1.40	.40		
	Minority	121	50	27.7	4.83	<.0005	94	38.8	3.44	.001	1.45	.38	-1.20	.23

SD = standard deviation.

Lippincott reading series. They read 100-word selections from each book for five consecutive days.

The pupils also responded to six comprehension questions after reading each selection: two recall, two sequential, and two inferential. Recall questions pertained to facts from the story, whereas sequential questions were about the order of events. Inferential questions dealt with interpretation and synthesis.

Correct and incorrect oral reading rates and correct percentage scores for answering comprehension questions were graphed, and the teacher studied these data to determine the appropriate reading level for each pupil.

Data from MF's reading performances are presented in Figure 6-1. The top graph indicates his correct and incorrect rates for reading in each of the texts, and the lower graph shows his correct percentage for answering questions. The range of MF's averages were as follows: correct rates, from 23.4 (Book J) to 53.4 (Book D); incorrect rates, 10.5 (Book J) to 6.8 (Books D and E); comprehension percentages, 95.8 (Book D) to 50.0 (Book I). Although there were fluctuations in performance noted within each book, his scores were generally better in the lower level texts. When these data were analyzed, MF was placed with Book D for instruction.

This behavioral placement technique was used with 14 boys at the EEU over a 2-year period. During the first year, five reading samples were obtained from each text. When these data were analyzed, researchers learned that three samples per text were sufficient to determine an appropriate instructional reading level; therefore, students were required to read only three passages during the second year.

EVALUATION OF A SHORT-TERM OBJECTIVE

This study, the second in the series, was conducted with seven intermediate-age boys at the EEU who were involved in the preceding research. This is an explanation of how a behavioral assessment can be arranged to evaluate an instructional method over a short period of time.

As explained in the previous report, each student was assigned to the highest book in the Lippincott series in which his correct rate was between 45 and 65 words per minute, his incorrect rate between 4 and 8 words per minute, and his comprehension score above 50%.

After placement, each day the youngsters read orally a selection of 500 words and answered several comprehension questions (Lovitt & Hansen, 1976b). The students who read from lower level texts were given 30 questions: 10 recall, 10 sequential, and 10 inferential. Students assigned to higher level books were given 20 questions: 5 recall, 5 sequential, 5

6. Behavioral Assessment of Learning Disabilities 101

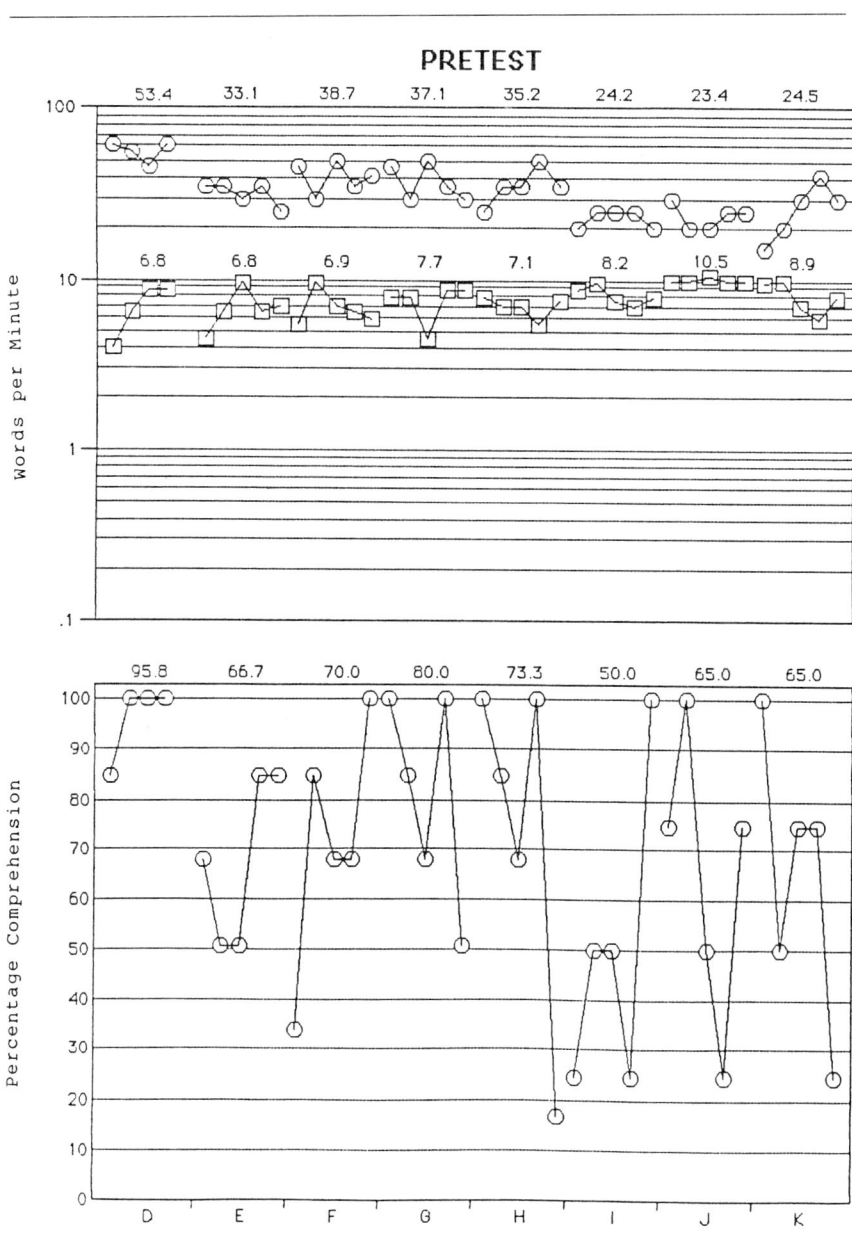

Figure 6-1. MF's reading score. In the top graph, circles indicate correct rates and boxes, incorrect rates. Percent correct data for answering comprehension questions are shown in the bottom chart.

inferential, and 5 vocabulary. Pupils at all levels read the questions silently and wrote their answers. Short answers were required for the recall, sequential, and inferential questions, and a multiple-choice format was adopted for the vocabulary questions.

An "ABA" design was arranged to evaluate the intervention in this investigation. During the A or base-line condition, students received minimal feedback with respect to their efforts. In the second or B phase, the skip-and-drill technique was introduced; each student was informed that he could skip one fourth of his text if on any day his oral reading and comprehension performances showed a 25% improvement over his average base-line scores.

If a pupil did not skip for four days, drill procedures of three types, depending upon his performance, were instituted. If his correct rate did not surpass the average base-line rate by 25%, he was required to read several 100-word passages orally from his daily assignment until his performance met this criterion. If a student's incorrect rate was not 25% lower than the average base-line rate, he practiced phrases in which his error words were embedded. If a boy did not answer 25% more comprehension questions than he had during the base-line phase he was required to redo his incorrect answers. These drill procedures continued each day until the student skipped.

After this skip-and-drill intervention, base–line procedures—return to A phase—were reestablished. Students read orally and answered questions as they had initially; the skip-and-drill provisions were not in effect.

Throughout the base-line phase the average oral correct and incorrect rates for the group were 50.7 and 3.1 words per minute. During the skip-and-drill phase, the average correct and incorrect rates were 60.0 and 2.9 words per minute. The correct rates for all students were higher and the incorrect rates for four of seven students were lower from the base-line to intervention phase.

As for comprehension scores, the group's average was 65.9% for the base-line period and 77.8% during the second condition. Comprehension scores of all pupils improved when the skip–and–drill procedure was scheduled.

When the skip-and-drill intervention was removed in the third phase, the performances of the students generally were maintained. In fact, the average oral reading rates and comprehension percentages of some students actually improved during this condition.

Figure 6-2 shows MF's daily oral reading and comprehension scores throughout the three phases of the project. As illustrated, all three aspects of his reading were influenced by the skip-and-drill intervention, and they generally were maintained in Phase 3 when the intervention was removed.

6. Behavioral Assessment of Learning Disabilities

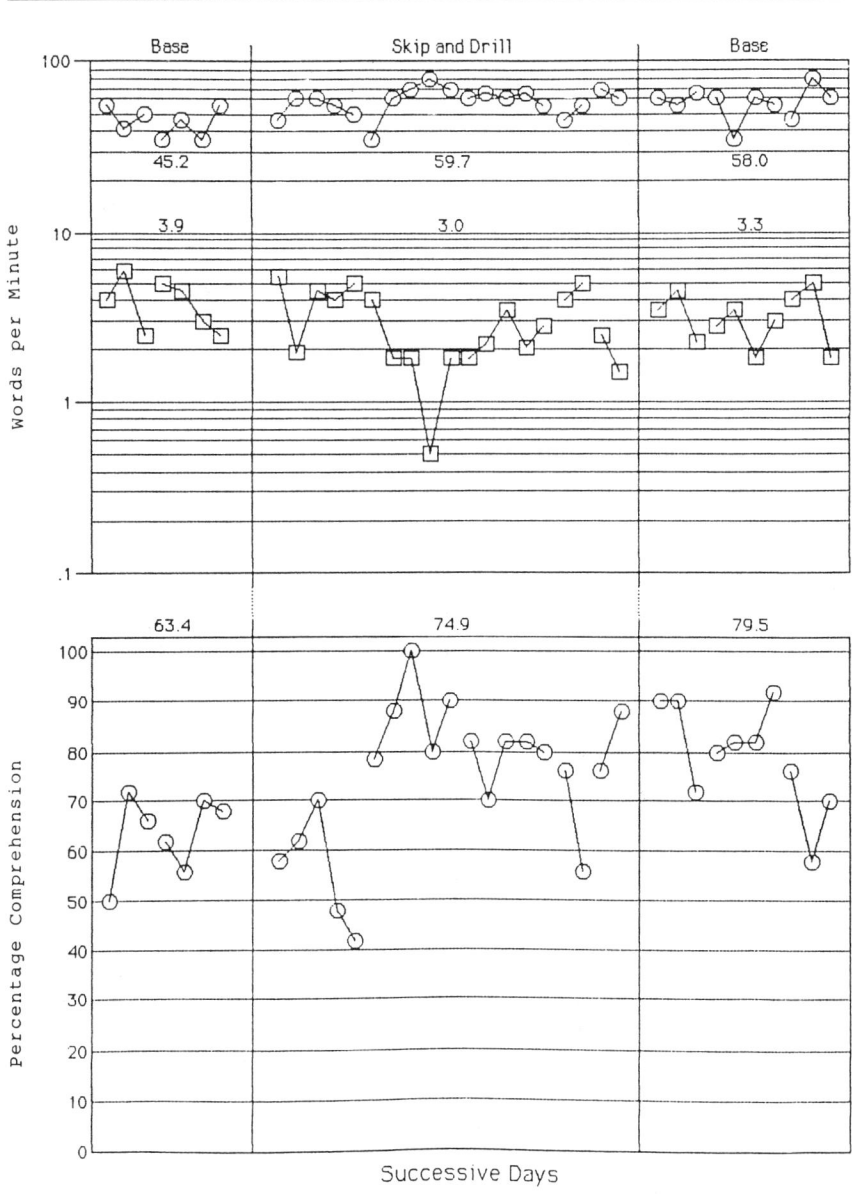

Figure 6-2. MF's reading scores for three phases of the project.

EVALUATION OF A LONG-TERM OBJECTIVE

Described here is a behavioral approach for evaluating a reading program with a pretest–posttest design. This is the third project in a series of four that relied on behavioral measures to track the reading progress of the same boys with learning disabilities.

The pretest data for this program were used to place youngsters at their appropriate reading levels. These data were obtained in October of a school year. (Refer to Figure 6-1 for MF's placement data.) Recall that for the placements, the boys read five times from eight levels of the Lippincott reading series, and after each passage, answered a set of comprehension questions.

Data were plotted for each session; that is, five sessions for each of the eight levels. After placement, the youngsters were involved in the skip-and-drill technique, the project that preceded this one.

In June of that year the youngsters once again read the passages orally and responded to the comprehension questions. Figure 6-3 shows data from MF's reading performances during that posttest. A few observations from these data are pointed out. For one, MF's correct and incorrect oral reading rates and comprehension percentages for all levels improved from October to June. With respect to changes in correct rates, the largest were for Book F and the smallest for Book J. The average word-per-minute change was 28.5. His largest and smallest incorrect rate changes were observed in Books G and in D and H; his average change was 4.6 words per minute. MF's comprehension scores were generally all 100% during the posttest, whereas they were more variable in the first administration of the readings.

It should be noted that the configurations of the correct rate data were quite similar in the two administrations of the readings. This is particularly obvious for Book K, when, on the pretest, MF's lowest score was on the first day followed by a steady acceleration until the fifth day. A similar pattern was noted during the posttest. That same arrangement of correct rates during the pretest and posttest was noted for the other six boys.

Another observation from these data was that regardless of the boys' placement levels (i.e., D through K), the greatest correct rate improvements from first to second administration were in the lower books. For four boys their biggest improvement was in Book D, for two in F, and for one in Book I. The reverse was also true; for four boys their least change was noted in Book J, and for three, this occurred in Book K.

6. Behavioral Assessment of Learning Disabilities

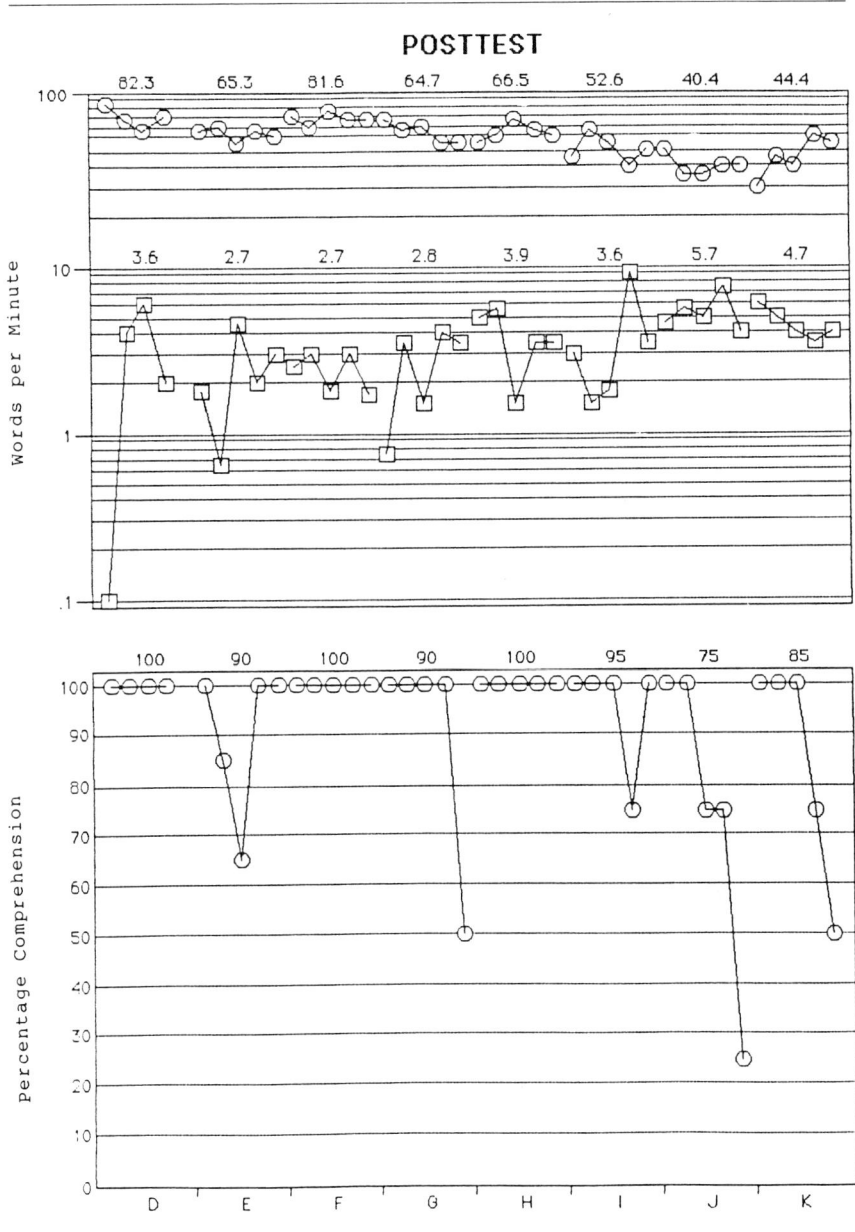

Figure 6-3. MF's posttest reading scores.

FOLLOW-UP OF STUDENTS
FROM SPECIAL PROGRAMS

This is the fourth and last project with the same youngsters with learning disabilities who were involved in classes at the EEU (Leone, Lovitt, & Hansen, 1981). The first explained the placement procedure, and the second the evaluation of the skip-and-drill technique. The third part in this series was the evaluation of the year-long reading program. This last part shows how a behavioral assessment can be arranged to follow-up students.

This study, conducted in the summer of 1979, followed up youngsters with learning disabilities five or six years after they attended a special class at the EEU. At the time of the Leone et al. survey, the pupils were in either the 10th, 11th, or 12th grade in their regular school district.

In this project, data were obtained on some of the seven boys from the EEU class of 1973–1974 and a few pupils from the class of 1972–1973, a total of 10. In addition to gathering information from the students with learning disabilities, data were acquired from six schoolmates with no learning disabilities whom the former boys had asked to participate.

Considerable data were gathered for this research. Boys with learning disabilities and their cohorts were interviewed, and data were obtained from their school records. In the context of this chapter, however, only the behavioral measures that were taken are explained.

For the follow-up, boys with learning disabilities read orally from books they had read during their stay at the EEU: Lippincott Books I and J. These data are shown in Figure 6-4. Note that pretest and posttest data, as explained in previous write-ups, are presented, in addition to data from those texts five or six years after the boys left the EEU. The data from Book I are on the left and those from Book J are on the right in each section of the figure. The top data illustrate correct rates, and the bottom lines depict incorrect rates. The vertical line and the top and bottom horizontal lines indicate the range of scores, and the circle, the mean score. The number above each line is the mean score. Note further that follow-up data were reported for both classes at the EEU: 1972–1973 and 1973–1974. Those years are written beneath their respective ranges.

The six boys with no learning disabilities also read from the two Lippincott texts, and when their reading rates were compared with those of the pupils with learning disabilities, the scores of the former boys, as shown in Figure 6-5, were always higher. (In Figure 6-5, data of boys with learning disabilities from both classes were combined.) The mean scores for the boys with and those without learning disabilities in Lippincott Books I and J were 130 and 160, and 114 and 150.

The boys with and without learning disabilities also read a news article and a passage from the sports page of the Seattle Times. The average rates

6. Behavioral Assessment of Learning Disabilities

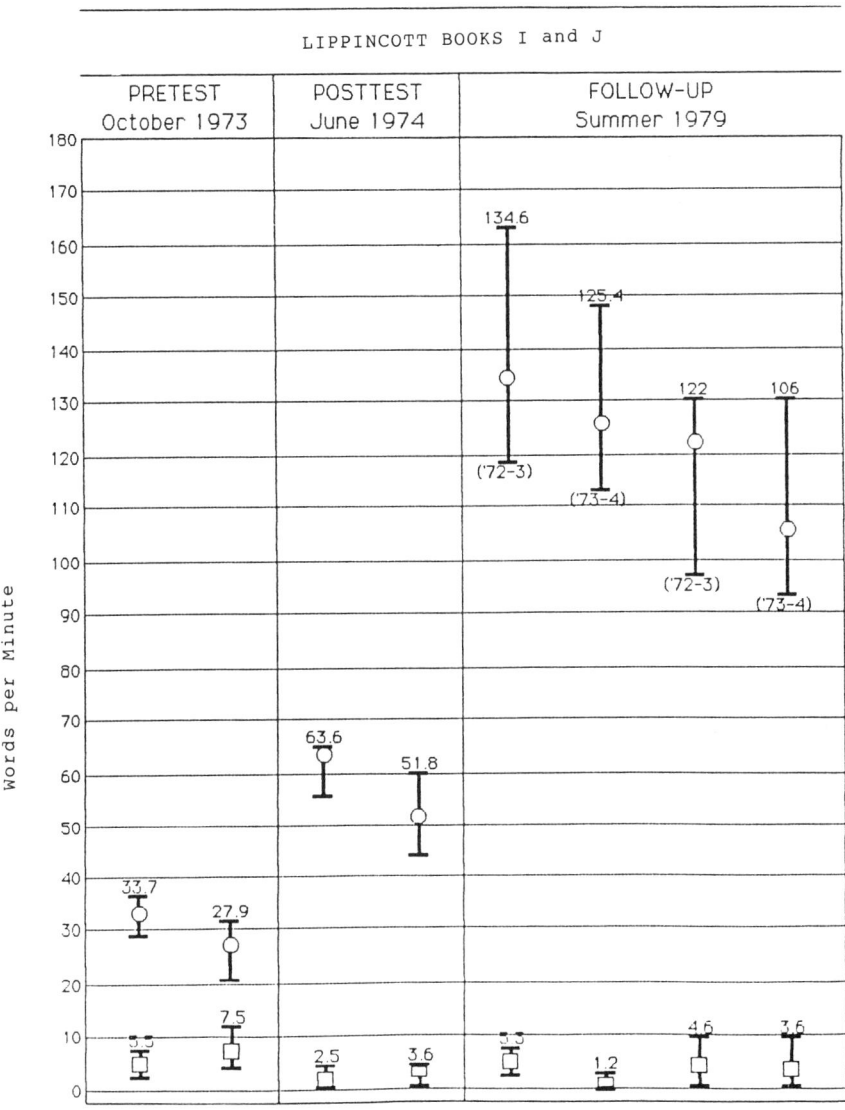

Figure 6-4. Reading scores with Books I and J.

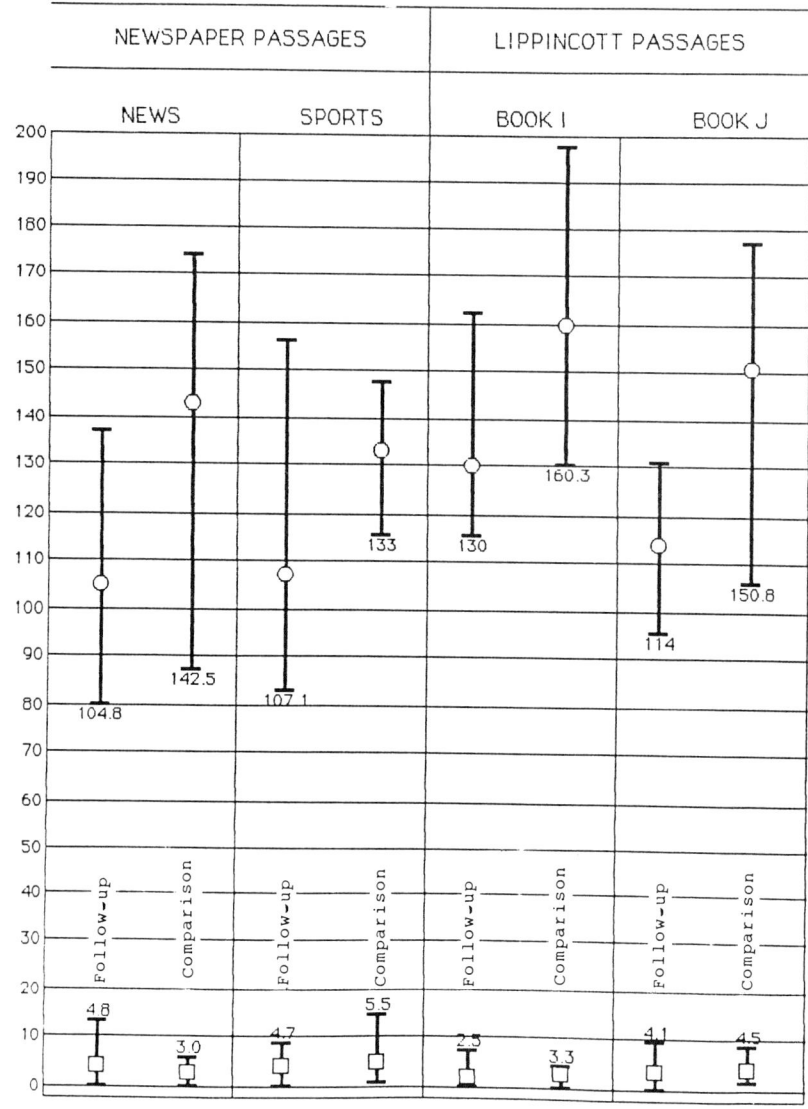

Figure 6-5. Comparison of reading scores for boys with and those without learning disabilities.

of the students for reading those sections were 104 and 142, and 107 and 133.

Educators could extend this type of assessment when following up youngsters by similarly measuring their performances in other areas. Just as rate-per-minute data were gathered in this research to assess reading, evaluators could easily acquire data in aspects of mathematics, writing, spelling and other subjects.

EVALUATION OF PROGRAMS

Explained here is a description of the Student Progress Inventory (SPI), a curriculum-based assessment of reading, spelling, and mathematics. Materials for the SPI were developed in each of the three subjects from first- through sixth-grade levels.

In reading, the selections were from the Holt reading series. Passages from levels 1 through 6 were selected that corresponded to the readability level for that grade according to the Fry readability scale (1972). In another effort to validate the reading levels of the stories, several children read the six passages and their correct and incorrect rates per minute for the readings were charted. These data indicated that generally, the correct rates of the students decreased from the lowest to the highest level, and the opposite was noted for incorrect rates. Based on these data and the readability scores, the investigators were confident that the reading material was progressively more difficult from the first- to sixth-grade text.

For the spelling assessment, 30 words were chosen for grade levels 1 through 6. They were the most frequently used words from six commercial spelling programs. In an effort to indicate that the words from list one to list six were progressively more difficult, several children were required to spell a few words from each list. These data revealed that the correct rates of the children generally decreased from the first through the highest level, and the opposite was true for the incorrect rates.

For the mathematics assessment, problem types most frequently taught by teachers at the various grades were selected. For the first grade, the problems involved simple addition and subtraction; for second grade, more difficult addition and subtraction problems were chosen. For third grade, still more advanced addition and subtraction problems were selected, and for fourth grade, addition, subtraction, and multiplication problems were chosen. At fifth grade, problems from all four processes were included, and for the sixth grade assessment, more difficult problems from the four processes were given.

A booklet containing these stories, word lists, and problems was given to teachers, and they were asked to familiarize themselves with the materials at the various levels. In October, teachers projected the levels at which they expected each student to perform by the end of the year. A teacher might anticipate, for example, a third-grade reading level, a second-grade level in spelling, and a fourth-grade level in mathematics, for a child. Once those levels were determined, children were assessed in October, December, March, and June with materials of the corresponding difficulty.

There were exceptions to this approach when youngsters performed higher or lower than a preset band of rates during the first assessment. Those students were shifted to materials from a grade above or below in the subject in which their rates were out of the range. During subsequent testing periods, they were assessed at the adjusted levels.

For the reading evaluation pupils read the same passage twice for 1 minute during each session, and were told their correct and incorrect words-per-minute rates after both readings. Data from only the second reading, however, were recorded. These identical procedures were followed for the mathematics assessment.

In spelling, pupils wrote the first five words on the list as they were pronounced by an examiner, and then told how well they did. Then, they were asked to write all 30 words, 1 at a time. The latter performance was timed and these data recorded as correct and incorrect letter sequences per minute.

Three studies were carried out with the SPI materials, and were reported by Lovitt and Fantasia (1983). In the first, data from 182 children with learning disabilities in five school districts who were in Precision Teaching (PT)-type classes were gathered. These data appear in Table 6-2. The mean percent difference score was a combination of the mean scores for correct and incorrect rates from the first to the last assessment. The mean slope accuracy score was a combination of the correct and incorrect rate accelerations (as per the Kunzelmann, 1976, project) across the four assessments. Note that the greatest difference in both measures was in reading.

For Study 2, performances of 13 youngsters with learning disabilities in a PT class were compared to those of 13 youngsters with learning disabilities who were not involved with PT. All the children were instructed in self-

Table 6-2. Summary Data for Study 1: Youngsters with Learning Disabilities in All Five Locations

	Mean Percent Difference	Mean Slope Accuracy
Reading	42.4	x1.66
Math	9.0	x1.20
Spelling	18.3	x1.37

contained classes in the same school district. Summary data from these students are shown in Table 6-3. As indicated, the mean difference scores and the slope accuracy scores of pupils in the PT classes were greater than those of students with learning disabilities in non-PT situations in all three subjects.

For the third study, data from 14 students with learning disabilities in a PT class were compared with those of youngsters with no learning disabilities who did not receive PT-type instruction. Their data, summarized in Table 6-4, show that the mean percent difference scores in reading and

Table 6-3. Summary Data for Study 2: Children with Learning Disabilities (LD) in PT Classes vs. Children with Learning Disabilities in Non-PT Classes

	Mean Percent Difference	Mean Slope Accuracy
PTLD		
Reading	8.57*	x1.48
Math	.92	x1.07
Spelling	11.20	x1.26
Non-PTLD		
Reading	1.71	x1.25
Math	-1.58	x1.05
Spelling	6.38	x1.17

*$p<.01$ (dependent measures t-test)

Table 6-4. Summary Data for Study 3: Children with Learning Disabilities (LD) in PT Classes vs. Children with No Learning Disabilities in Non-PT Classes

	Mean Percent Difference	Mean Slope Accuracy
PTLD		
Reading	7.58*	x1.75
Math	1.58	x1.31
Spelling	11.83	x1.46
Non-PTNonhandicapped		
Reading	1.81	x1.41
Math	1.76	x1.20
Spelling	8.19	x1.65

*$p<.05$ (dependent measures t-test)

spelling, and the mean slope accuracy scores in reading and math of the youngsters with learning disabilities were higher than those for the students with no learning disabilities.

DIFFERENTIATION OF TYPES OF STUDENTS

Shinn and Marston (1985) demonstrated how behavioral assessments could discriminate among three types of youngsters: mildly handicapped, Chapter 1, and regular. The students in their research were from grades 4, 5, and 6.

To obtain data in reading, youngsters read orally from reading texts selected by their districts. For spelling, they wrote words that corresponded to their grade levels. In mathematics, they calculated problems that were appropriate for their grade levels, and for writing, they wrote stories from story starters that were suitable for the various grades. Data from these assessments were transformed to correctly read words (reading), correctly written letter sequences (spelling), correctly written digits (math), and correctly written words (writing).

The reading data, which were for 1 minute, are summarized for the three groups in Table 6-5. Spelling, writing, and math data are summarized in Tables 6-6, 6-7, and 6-8. The spelling and math data were for 2 minutes, and written expression data for 3 minutes. Also provided in those tables, along with the average scores, are standard deviations, and F and p values.

Note that in every subject except math, the rates were higher from grade 4 to 5 and 5 to 6 for all three types of students. The highest rates in all four subjects were from regular students, and the lowest from the mildly handicapped. The rates of the mildly handicapped were most discrepant from those of Chapter 1 students in reading and spelling and the least in mathematics. With respect to statistical significance, the differences were beyond the .001 level for the three types of students in all four subjects at each grade level. As for variability, as indicated by standard deviations, there did not appear to be significant differences across types of students when all grade levels and subjects were taken into account.

COMPARISON OF BEHAVIORAL AND NORMATIVE ASSESSMENTS

Currently, achievement tests are the most widely scheduled technique for evaluating pupil progress. In many schools an achievement test is administered at the beginning and the end of the year. Scores from those tests are

Table 6-.5 A Comparison of Mildy Handicapped Students Receiving Special Education, Chapter 1, and Regular Education Services in Reading, Grades 4 to 6

Grade	Group	Mean No. of Words Read Correctly	SD	F Value	p value
	Mildly handicapped	33.7	17.1	35.29	.001
4	Chapter 1	65.9	28.0		
	Regular education	117.9	35.2		
	Mildly handicapped	56.4	39.7	20.90	.001
5	Chapter 1	101.0	33.2		
	Regular education	128.2	30.7		
	Mildly handicapped	75.2	36.2	22.87	.001
6	Chapter 1	125.2	27.9		
	Regular education	162.3	37.9		

SD = standard deviation.

Table 6-6. A Comparison of Mildy Handicapped Students Receiving Special Education, Chapter 1, and Regular Education Services in Spelling, Grades 4 to 6

Grade	Group	Mean No. of Words Read Correctly	SD	F Value	p value
	Mildly handicapped	35.3	18.9	24.49	.001
4	Chapter 1	60.7	24.3		
	Regular education	93.3	14.9		
	Mildly handicapped	51.7	33.0	22.23	.001
5	Chapter 1	90.3	32.8		
	Regular education	115.4	20.3		
	Mildly handicapped	72.6	29.1	15.29	.001
6	Chapter 1	109.3	26.2		
	Regular education	124.3	16.6		

SD = standard deviation.

Table 6-7. A Comparison of Mildy Handicapped Students Receiving Special Education, Chapter 1, and Regular Education Services in Written Expression, Grades 4 to 6

Grade	Group	Mean No. of Words Read Correctly	SD	F Value	p value
4	Mildly handicapped	13.5	8.1	9.41	.001
	Chapter 1	22.9	11.9		
	Regular education	30.5	12.2		
5	Mildly handicapped	20.6	10.2	12.51	.001
	Chapter 1	37.0	12.2		
	Regular education	44.5	20.1		
6	Mildly handicapped	27.1	15.2	5.44	.001
	Chapter 1	41.7	13.6		
	Regular education	43.6	12.7		

SD = standard deviation.

Table 6-8. A Comparison of Mildy Handicapped Students Receiving Special Education, Chapter 1, and Regular Education Services in Grade Level Math Computation, Grades 4 to 6

Grade	Group	Mean No. of Words Read Correctly	SD	F Value	p value
4	Mildly handicapped	25.7	12.3	8.29	.001
	Chapter 1	30.3	12.0		
	Regular education	44.0	15.1		
5	Mildly handicapped	21.2	12.0	23.54	.001
	Chapter 1	35.4	13.3		
	Regular education	55.7	20.6		
6	Mildly handicapped	32.8	13.8	9.73	.001
	Chapter 1	44.2	15.3		
	Regular education	58.4	16.1		

SD = standard deviation.

intended to reflect abilities in reading, spelling, arithmetic, and other subjects.

These scores are used for various purposes, one of which is to evaluate teacher competencies. They are also considered when making placement decisions: whether to assign students to special or regular classes, to one grade or another, or to high or low reading groups. At other times, scores from achievement tests are used to communicate progress of pupils to their parents, teachers, administrators, or themselves.

Several years ago Eaton and Lovitt (1972) arranged a situation to compare data from achievement tests and a behavioral assessment. In the fall and spring of the year the Metropolitan Achievement Test (MAT) and Wide Range Achievement Test (WRAT) were administered to a group of youngsters with learning disabilities. These data are shown in Table 6-9. Moreover, direct and daily data were obtained from the children in reading throughout the year; that is, correct and incorrect rates from the books to which they were assigned.

When the behavioral method was used to place children at one level or another, they were required to read a number of books from different grade levels for several days, as was explained in the second project in this chapter. Their correct and incorrect performance rates from those texts were graphed each day. After several days, these data were analyzed and books were selected for initial reading instruction based on the youngsters' performance. Those fall placement levels are noted in Table 6-9 as are the levels at which the pupils were reading in the spring.

A number of interesting observations can be made from these data. First of all, it was apparent that the scores from the two achievement tests did not agree. The tests given in the fall disagreed by more than half a grade level for three of the six children. The most discrepant scores were obtained by a pupil who received a 2.4 rating on one test and a 4.4 on the other. The scores of the two tests in the spring disagreed four out of six times, when the same standard was used. The widest difference for a pupil on the two tests at that time was 4.7 years.

It was also obvious that the achievement tests and the behavioral approach did not agree with respect to placement. The behavioral assessment agreed with an achievement test, within half a grade level, on only three of six occasions. Those agreements were all with the MAT.

A comparison of the book level at which students were reading at the end of the year with their spring achievement test scores revealed concurrence for four of six pupils. There were two agreements for each achievement test.

As for pupil growth throughout the year, all of them gained when their MAT scores were considered: spring scores were higher than fall scores. According to the WRAT, however, there was no growth for two pupils and a worsening of performance for another. When the behavioral assessment

Table 6-9. Reading Scores for Youngsters with Learning Disabilities

Child	Metropolitan Achievement Test		Wide Range Achievement Test		Actual Placement		
	FALL	SPRING	FALL	SPRING	BOOK	FALL	SPRING
Paul L.	1.0	2.7	2.7	2.5	Lippincott	—	2-2
	P²	E			Palo Alto	Book 3	—
					Bank Street	Primer	2-2
Paul R.	2.6	4.0	2.5	2.5	Bank Street	2-1	3-1
	E	I			Scott Foresman	2-1	4-1
John	1.1	4.0	KG 7	8.7	Lippincott	Pre-primer	2-1
	P	E			Palo Alto	—	Book 11
Fred	1.6	2.5	1.9	1.9	Merrill	—	Book 5
	E	E			Bank Street	Primer	2-2
Jenni	2.4	6.8	4.4	4.8	Lippincott	3-1	Book 5
	E	I			Laidlaw	3-1	Book 5
					McMillan	1-3	Book 5
Phil	Non low enough	1.7	KG 5	1.9	Lippincott	Pre-primer	1-1
		P			Bank Street	—	1-1

P = Primary battery
P² = Primary² battery
E = Elementary Battery
I = Intermediate Battery

was considered, all children improved. Furthermore, since graphs were kept for each student, this improvement was indicated in three ways: their correct rates increased from fall to spring, their incorrect rates went down, and they read from more difficult material as the year progressed. Achievement tests provided only a grade-level difference score as a measure of improvement.

DISCUSSION

There are several reasons for considering behavioral approaches such as those explained here to evaluate and monitor aspects of instruction.

1. The measures are direct, they pertain to behaviors that teachers intend to teach. Therefore, the content validity of these measures is extremely high.

2. These behavioral data can be gathered by teachers or others who work with children. Although it is important to administer the assessments consistently and carefully, it is not necessary to be a certified psychometrician.

3. The data from these measures can serve as local norms at various grade levels. Teachers at each level would know at the beginning of the year the extent to which their students should achieve in certain subjects by the end of the year. If these behavioral data were obtained over an extended period of time, the local norms could be adjusted.

4. The information from these behavioral assessments is relatively easy to communicate to children, their parents, and others. It is simple to understand what is meant by a "correct oral reading rate of 140 words per minute." Moreover, communication of this type is more honest than telling parents that their child reads "at a fourth grade level." Although it appears to be straightforward to speak in terms of "grade level equivalents," they are greatly influenced by which standardized test was given. As pointed out earlier, the scores from various tests are not always in agreement.

5. The data from behavioral assessments, particularly if they are obtained frequently, can prompt instructional decisions. With data of this type teachers are apprised of the extent to which objectives are being mastered, and can accordingly, advance pupils to different levels, schedule interventions, or make other instructional decisions.

6. These behavioral data are quite suitable for developing individualized education program objectives. It is far more precise to state that a pupil will be able to "say facts at a rate of 15 per minute from passages in a Lippincott Book D" than to say that his "ability to comprehend material will increase by one grade level."

As for the disadvantages of using behavioral assessments, they are difficult to identify, but there are some considerations that should be taken into account.

1. It takes time and effort to prepare behavioral assessments. Since they pertain to local curriculum it is not possible to look up a few measures in a catalogue and then order and administer them.
2. For behavioral assessments, teachers must pinpoint what they intend to teach, because that is what they should measure. Some teachers may not want to be pinned down.
3. It may be difficult to compare pupil progress from one locale to another if behavioral assessments have been arranged, for the data would probably pertain to different attributes.
4. It might take more time to administer some behavioral assessments than it does some franchised tests, for not all of the former can be administered to groups, as is often the case with many of the current, paper-and-pencil–type assessments.
5. It may be difficult for districts that rely on behavioral measures to communicate with their state departments about pupil performance, for these officials are accustomed to dealing with achievement test data.

The basic purpose of this chapter was to point out the wide range of uses of behavioral assessments. That approach was used to screen youngsters, to place them at proper instructional levels, to evaluate short- and long-term objectives, to follow–up on youngsters, to evaluate programs, and to differentiate types of youngsters.

Behavioral assessments can be used for instructional purposes beyond those described in this chapter. For example, a behavioral assessment is now being developed that will provide information on the extent to which mildly handicapped adolescents are able to function in their communities. For this assessment my colleagues and I selected two reading pinpoints in each of three areas—vocational, community, and recreational—and developed formats for obtaining oral reading and comprehension data in those attributes. We are now administering the assessment to groups of mildly handicapped adolescents. Later, we will obtain data from nonhandicapped adolescents and from workers in jobs of the type the mildly handicapped might eventually hold. Initially, these data will show the degree to which the mildly handicapped compare with nonhandicapped peers and workers in those types of reading. Based on these comparative data, we hope to design materials and procedures that will assist mildly handicapped citizens to acquire skills necessary to survive in the world outside of school.

REFERENCES

Eaton, M., & Lovitt, T. C. (1972). Achievement tests vs. direct and daily measurement. In G. Semb (Ed.), *Behavior analysis and education-1972*. Lawrence, KS: University of Kansas Press.

Fry, E. (1972). Reading instruction for classroom and clinic. New York: McGraw-Hill.

Kunzelmann, H. (1976). Unpublished data from a nondiscriminatory testing approach.

Leone, P., Lovitt, T., & Hansen, C. (1981). A descriptive follow-up study of learning disabled boys. *Learning Disability Quarterly, 4*, 152-162.

Lovitt, T. C., & Hansen, C. L. (1976a). Round one—Placing the child in the right reader. *Journal of Learning Disabilities, 6*, 347-353.

Lovitt, T. C., & Hansen, C. L. (1976b). The use of contingent skipping and drilling to improve oral reading and comprehension. *Journal of Learning Disabilities, 9*, 481-487.

Lovitt, T. C., & Fantasia, F. (1983) A precision teaching project with learning disabled children. *Journal of Precision Teaching, 3*(4), 85-91.

Shinn, M., & Marston, D. (1985). Differentiating mildly handicapped, low-achieving, and regular education students: A curriculum-based approach. *Remedial and Special Education 6*(2), 31-38.

CHAPTER 7

Neuropsychological Assessment of Childhood Learning Disabilities

JOHN E. OBRZUT
CAROL A. BOLIEK

It has been fairly well established that learning disability is the most prevalent form of handicapping condition being diagnosed in our public schools today. Prevalence estimates in the range of 10 to 15% have been reported in the literature, with no indication of a trend reversal. While there is much agreement that learning disabilities account for a high percentage of special education placements, there is relatively little agreement on factors such as cause, definition, screening, assessment, and remediation of this condition (Heaton, 1988). This state of affairs has arisen because in the past, researchers and professionals have considered children with learning disabilities as a homogeneous population and thus have accounted inadequately for the vast heterogeneity of learning disorders.

It is apparent from the literature that although there is basic agreement on a fairly broad definition of learning disabilities, the confusion results from failure of researchers to operationalize systematically the concepts of the definition across studies. While most authors have adhered to an exclusionary definition of learning disabilities, which includes children of average and sometimes above-average intelligence with no sensory incapacity, emotional disturbance, educational or cultural deprivation, but who display a significant discrepancy between measured ability and academic performance, few of the studies have provided precise data on many of these variables. For example, in their review of the literature, Barclay and Hagen (1982) found that many studies involving populations with learning disabilities tended to ignore significant differences in factors such as the quantity and quality of academic performance, differences in social–emotional functioning, motivation and learning styles, and perhaps more importantly, differences in the presence or absence of "soft" or "hard" neurological signs found among children with learning disabilities. Moreover, the issue of heterogeneity of samples of learning disabilities is further complicated when one considers the developmental perspective in academic performance. This perspective suggests that performance is based on the interaction between learning tasks and the motivational level of the child (Doehring, 1976). In essence, patterns of strengths and weaknesses may change with age, and thus may make it more difficult to distinguish primary from secondary deficits, particularly with regard to assessments conducted during middle to late childhood (Heaton, 1988).

NEUROPSYCHOLOGICAL PERSPECTIVE

Acknowledging the factors mentioned above, we are of the opinion that learning disorders reflect central processing deficits that selectively interfere with the organization, integration, analysis, and synthesis of verbal and/or nonverbal information. We argue in particular, that learning disabilities are specific in nature and basically result from underlying neuropsychological dysfunction. The evidence concerning children with learning disabilities tends to support such a position, as summarized recently by Coplin and Morgan (1988). These authors concluded that from the study of the subtype literature learning disorders "persist with age, fail to respond to normal classroom instruction, and occur cross-culturally in similar patterns" (p. 616).

A neuropsychological model for learning disabilities derives from demonstrated relationships between learning modalities and associated brain structures and functions (see Obrzut, 1981, for a review). Thus we agree with those who contend that children who have difficulty in their ability to organize, coordinate, integrate, and/or synthesize stimuli will experience academic failure due to an underlying cerebral dysfunction. For example, as Rourke (1975) has concluded, one crucial factor limiting the satisfactory adaptation of children with learning disabilities is cerebral dysfunction.

Although the causes of the cerebral dysfunction are currently unknown, they may range from acquired cerebral damage to neurodevelopmental anomalies to chemical imbalances. In any case, the assumption is that specific learning disabilities result from disturbed information processing abilities rather than from a generalized cognitive deficit. Neuropsychological assessment procedures, therefore, can be used to evaluate specific information-processing strengths and weaknesses in children with suspected central nervous system (CNS) dysfunction. In essence, neuropsychological assessment is designed to delineate the nature and significance of cognitive deficits that are unique and specific to each child's learning problem (Taylor, 1988). Although neuropsychological test batteries have been found to discriminate among normal children, those with learning disabilities, and those with brain damage with a high degree of predictive accuracy, they have certain limitations, which will be pointed out later in this chapter.

Within this context this chapter will attempt to address a number of relevant issues with regard to the neuropsychological assessment of children who experience learning disabilities due to CNS dysfunction. First, a brief historical perspective of neuropsychological assessment of learning disabilities will be provided, with a focus on defining what constitutes a learning disability and the importance of understanding the neuroanatomical structure and function of the brain as it relates to the learning process. Second, a conceptual framework for the neuropsychological assessment of learning disabilities will be presented. Within this framework will be a discussion of the rationale for a test battery, including the general aims of neuropsychological assessment, followed by comment on the generalization of test findings and limitations of using fixed-battery approaches. Finally, a proposed set of neuropsychological procedures will be presented that are available for use with children who experience learning disabilities. With the use of these procedures it is hoped that a more thorough understanding of the cognitive profile of each child with learning disabilities will emerge, so that the practitioner will have a better understanding of how best to remediate the specific learning problem.

HISTORICAL PERSPECTIVE OF NEUROPSYCHOLOGICAL ASSESSMENT OF LEARNING DISABILITIES

Obrzut (1981) originally indicated that a multitude of factors have contributed to the growing interest in clinical neuropsychology in the schools. A number of other authors recently have underscored these factors as being significantly responsible for this increased activity in child neuropsychology of populations with learning disabilities (see, for example, Hynd,

Snow, & Becker, 1986b; Tramontana & Hooper, 1988). To summarize, the primary impetus has been the federal legislation, Public Law 94-142 (Federal Register, 1976), the Education for All Handicapped Children Act, mandating public schools to provide programs for all handicapped children from birth to 21 years of age. As a result, federal funding is directly related to the number of differentially diagnosed children, including those with learning disabilities and receiving special instructional services. This means that the need to identify children with conditions such as developmental dyslexia or aphasia has increased the clinician's reliance on comprehensive clinical assessment procedures such as those advocated in this chapter. These procedures are presumed to both identify specific neurodevelopmental disorders and to help devise appropriate educational plans (Tramontana & Hooper, 1988). In addition, the survival rates for children suffering neurological trauma has increased substantially over the past decade because of advances in medical care; this has created a greater need for assessment of neuropsychological sequences in these children. Finally, the call for neuropsychological assessment of children has increased because evidence exists that developmental learning and behavioral disorders have a neuropsychological basis in cases due to anomalies in normal neurological development and in cases due to some early traumatic event (Hynd & Obrzut, 1986).

Since clinical differentiation of learning disorders must encompass some assessment of neuropsychological functioning, the clinician will be called upon to provide a differential assessment based on brain–behavior relationships. However, as Tramontana and Hooper (1988) have pointed out, there are important differences in brain–behavior relationships between children and adults and, thus, an appropriate assessment of these relationships in children "cannot be based simply on scaled-down versions of assessment methods used with adults" (p. 4). The choice of tests in each case should depend on the questions being asked about a particular child and should be selected to elucidate brain–behavior relationships as they exist at various points in a child's developmental sequence.

According to Tramontana and Hooper (1988), the history of assessment in child neuropsychology indicates that the goals of such assessment have shifted from a static emphasis on diagnosing brain lesions to more of a focus on the analysis of functional deficits with a concomitant emphasis on the relationship between assessment results and the child's capacity to deal with important tasks in daily functioning. One example of this trend is in the neuropsychological assessment of learning disabilities, which has dealt with understanding each child's unique learning style in the school environment. Thus it seems necessary that practitioners view learning problems in terms of the functional status of the brain by using neuropsychological assessment and remedial procedures with these children. But while the concept of learning disabilities is frequently acknowledged, the precise definition and population characteristics of these children is often at variance from one author to another.

DEFINITION AND CHARACTERISTICS OF LEARNING DISABILITIES

The National Joint Committee for Learning Disabilities (NJCLD), acknowledging the widespread acceptance of neurodevelopmental evidence in the cause of learning disabilities published a definition that, it presumed, would reflect the underlying nature of the disorder. The NJCLD defined learning disabilities as a "generic term that refers to a heterogeneous group of disorders manifested by significant difficulties in the acquisition and use of listening, speaking, reading, writing, reasoning or mathematical abilities. These disorders are intrinsic to the individual and *presumed to be due to central nervous system dysfunction*" (Hammill, Leigh, McNutt, & Larsen, 1981). The Committee agreed that even though a learning disability may occur concomitantly with other handicapping conditions (e.g., sensory impairment, mental retardation, social and emotional disturbance) or environmental influences (e.g., cultural differences, insufficient/inappropriate instruction, psychogenic factors), it is not the direct result of those conditions or influences. The NJCLD also agreed that while "hard signs" of brain damage were not necessary in order to diagnose a child as having learning disabilities, no child should be labeled "learning disabled" unless there was CNS involvement. By stating that "learning disabilities" is a generic term the Committee made it clear that a variety of disorders comprise the clinical category of learning disabilities. Given the heterogeneous nature of this syndrome, it is perhaps easy to understand the lack of unanimity among studies of learning disabilities in the literature.

One of the major reasons for the lack of conclusive evidence with regard to populations with learning disabilities is that, although there is an enormous volume of literature available on the topic, relatively few of the studies have used well-defined samples of children with learning disabilities. The heterogeneous nature of these samples selected in most research does not allow for valid generalization to occur across studies. As Obrzut and Boliek (1988) have pointed out in another context, sample selection has included individuals from both public school as well as clinic and hospital settings. Children chosen from the latter institutions are often very different (i.e., more severe) with regard to their presenting symptoms. Therefore, the results derived from these populations are inconsistent with the results of studies that use school populations. Groups with learning disabilities drawn from school populations have generally been selected on the basis of criteria for placement in special education classes according to federal and state guidelines. A multidisciplinary team including a certified school psychologist participates in the child's diagnosis and resulting special class placement. Although there is basic agreement on a fairly broad definition of learning disabilities (see above), there is much less agreement on the specific criteria used among professionals interested in the diagnosis of children with learning disabilities.

STRUCTURE AND RELATED FUNCTIONS OF THE BRAIN

It is obvious that an adequate understanding of the structure and function of the brain is necessary when using neuropsychological screening and assessment techniques in the diagnosis of children with learning disorders. However, according to recent surveys (e.g., Hynd, Quackenbush, & Obrzut, 1980; Leavell & Lewandowski, 1988), many psychologists do not have specific training in the use of neuropsychological evaluation procedures and are unfamiliar with the behavioral correlates thought to be associated with dysfunction in the various anatomical structures. Although space does not permit a detailed description of the complex neurostructures of the brain in this chapter, several in-depth sources are available and are recommended for use by the practitioner (Gaddes, 1985; Kolb & Whishaw, 1980; Lezak, 1983; Tarnopol & Tarnopol, 1977; Woodruff & Baisden, 1986). However, in order for the reader with virtually no background in brain structure and function to derive some insight into cerebral functioning, a cursory description of some basic features of the cortex are presented.

The cerebrum consists of two hemispheres that are almost, but not quite, mirror images of each other. The right and left hemispheres are connected by the corpus callosum and the anterior commissure, two pathways of neural fibers, that allow for interhemispheric communication.

The patterns of functional localization in the cortex are organized along two spatial planes: (1) the lateral plane, which cuts through homologous (corresponding position) areas of both hemispheres and (2) the longitudinal plane, which runs from the front to the back of the cortex. Thus, the primary sensory and motor centers are homologously positioned within the cortex of each hemisphere in a mirror image relationship. The centers in each cerebral hemisphere mediate the activities of the contralateral half of the body with the exception of the visual and auditory systems, which are more complex and are explained in more detail elsewhere (Obrzut, 1981).

Another kind of organization across the lateral plane differentiates the localization of primary cognitive functions. In nearly all right-handed individuals, the left hemisphere is thought to process in a sequential analytic linguistic mode, while the right hemisphere processes in a parallel holistic spatial nonlinguistic mode (Witelson, 1977). In general, left hemisphere dysfunction gives rise to speech and related language disorders and disorders of symbol formulation. On the other hand, right hemisphere dysfunction leads to difficulties in spatial orientation, perceptual integration of visual and spatial components, and analysis and synthesis of nonverbal conceptual material. As Teeter (1986) suggests, "if a child shows significantly depressed motor speed and consistent sensory imperceptions on the right side of the body, the functional status of the left hemisphere is thought to be impaired. If other higher level cognitive disabilities, such as significantly low verbal IQ (compared to performance IQ) and reading deficits are also found, then they are most likely a result of left hemisphere dysfunction" (p. 195).

The longitudinal organization of the brain refers to the division of each hemisphere into the four lobes: frontal, parietal, temporal, and occipital. The lobes represent anatomical regions, but provide a useful reference for functional localization; although some functionally definable areas overlap two or even three lobes (Kolb & Whishaw, 1980). The division of the hemispheres are also thought of as anterior and posterior regions. Theoretically, the left and the right sides may be characterized as the verbal and nonverbal sides, and the anterior and posterior portions as the motor and sensory areas, respectively. However, in reality there is much integration of different functional components within and across the lobes.

CONCEPTUAL FRAMEWORK FOR NEUROPSYCHOLOGICAL ASSESSMENT OF LEARNING DISABILITIES

As we noted earlier, the primary purpose of conducting a neuropsychological evaluation of a child suspected of experiencing a learning disability is to determine if the profile of abilities and disabilities is consistent with a learning disability caused by CNS dysfunction. Thus, one should conduct a neuropsychological assessment to try to determine whether the child's difficulties are due to neurological dysfunction. Such an assessment can provide information both in the identification of specific underlying dimensions of dysfunction in subtypes of learning disabilities and in the formulation of specific remedial plans. In addition, neuropsychological assessment of learning disabilities can be instrumental in the area of developmental precursors of learning disabilities, neuroanatomical and neurodevelopmental factors, as well as relevant aptitude and treatment interactions (Tramontana & Hooper, 1988).

The aim of clinical neuropsychological assessment, according to Rourke, Bakker, Fisk, and Strang (1983), is to investigate the functional status of the brain by analyzing behavioral responses on a variety of tests. It is in this context that a broad range of behaviors are sampled to provide information concerning the functional integrity of specific neural structures and cortical systems of the brain that mediate mental processes (Teeter, 1986). Ultimately, the main objective in neuropsychological evaluation is to provide descriptive information to aid in the understanding of brain–behavior relationships. This information can then be used to design individualized remedial programs for the child with brain dysfunction, such as those with learning disabilities.

RATIONALE FOR NEUROPSYCHOLOGICAL TEST PROCEDURES FOR LEARNING DISABILITIES

Neuropsychological test batteries have been designed to assess global brain functioning, as well as to evaluate the presence of deficits in specific, focalized areas of the cortex. Although different approaches are used in neuropsychological assessment, a comprehensive approach would include measures of cognitive, language, sensory-perceptual, motor, and reasoning abilities. The rationale for comprehensive testing is to investigate the nature and extent of cognitive impairments that accompany learning disabilities. According to Taylor (1988), a battery that is comprehensive will make it possible to identify the kinds of skill deficits that frequently occur in children with learning disabilities (e.g., deficiencies in language and memory and inconsistencies in performance across various cognitive dimensions). However, while the three most popular standardized neuropsychological assessment batteries for use with school-aged children (Luria-Nebraska Neuropsychological Battery–Children's Revision, Reitan-Indiana, and Halstead-Reitan Neuropsychological Test Battery) are useful in diagnosing learning disabilities, they provide little educationally relevant information (Hynd, Obrzut, Hayes, & Becker, 1986a). Also, these batteries, especially the Halstead-Reitan Neuropsychological Test Battery for older children (9 to 14 years), have many measures that appear contaminated because of high correlations with intellectual ability (Seidenberg, Giordani, Berent, & Boll, 1983).

RELIABILITY AND VALIDITY OF NEUROPSYCHOLOGICAL TEST BATTERIES

Although fixed batteries have represented the most commonly used approaches in adult neuropsychological assessment (See Hynd et al., 1986b), some researchers have found these test batteries to be inadequate for a number of reasons, primarily related to their psychometric properties. For example, the Halstead-Reitan Batteries have been criticized for the scarce amount of reliability and validity data (Sattler, 1988), confounding between language and nonlanguage deficits as well as memory functions being underrepresented (Crosson & Warren, 1982), and subtests that are insufficiently specific in regard to functions they assess and the underlying cerebral correlates of those functions (Goldstein, 1984). The Luria-Nebraska Neuropsychological Test Battery has been also criticized for its weak reliability across clinical settings (Adams, 1980), and lack of construct and predictive validity (Goldstein, 1984). In addition, the scales have been found to be heterogeneous, so the clinician cannot interpret specific functions, and some scales omit important functions they should measure. The result may be that many scales do not measure the function they were designed to measure (Crosson & Warren, 1982). Finally, because the battery is language oriented, it is inappropriate for use with aphasia patients (Goldstein, 1984).

The Halstead-Reitan and Luria-Nebraska Neuropsychological test batteries for children are downward extensions of the adult versions, as noted earlier. Basically, there is little evidence to support the validity of either test battery in localizing early brain injury or in specifying other lesion characteristics in children with brain damage (Hynd et al., 1986b). In addition, there seems to be substantial overlap between general intelligence and overall performance on these fixed test batteries. For example, Snow, Hynd, and Hartlage (1984) found that the capacity of the Luria-Nebraska–Children's Revision to discriminate the severity of learning disabilities is greatly reduced once IQ and overall academic achievement is controlled. However, both test batteries have been found to discriminate effectively between children with documented brain damage, children with learning disabilities, and normal controls, and, at least in a general diagnostic sense, the two batteries yield highly comparable results (i.e., Teeter, Boliek, Obrzut, & Malsch, 1986; Townes, Turpin, Martin, & Goldstein, 1980). In reviewing the literature Tramontana and Hooper (1988) have suggested that the independent contributions to assessment by these batteries presumably involve tasks that measure basic motor and sensory-perceptual abilities. Nevertheless, in the case of children with learning disabilities, the discriminate validity of these test batteries does not appear to be better than what one would achieve with administration of standard psychoeducational test instruments.

There has been also a general dearth of research into the precise nature of the underlying functions (construct validity) that may be detected by neuropsychological test batteries with populations with learning disabilities. One recent study by Gamble, Mishra, and Obrzut (1988), who conducted a factor analysis on the scores of the Halstead-Reitan Test Battery obtained from children with learning disabilities, found that the factor structure did not meet the overall construct paradigm as conceptualized by the author of the battery. Specifically, analysis of the data yielded the following four factors: verbal intelligence, psychomotor speed, achievement, and memory. In addition, because fixed batteries are designed to assess broad measures of neuropsychological functioning, supplementary information is further required in order to address individual referral questions and provide in-depth information about specific deficits (Tramontana & Hooper, 1988; Stoddart & Knights, 1986). Thus, given that the current neuropsychological test batteries might not be representative of the manifestation of learning disabilities, and given the recent awareness of subtypes of learning disabilities, incorporating the Halstead-Reitan and Luria-Nebraska subtests with supplementary neuropsychological tests may be the best practice when viewing the large diversity of learning disabilities in a school-aged population.

In summary, current neuropsychological test batteries can provide a standard data base on which different clinical groups can be compared. Specifically, these batteries can discriminate effectively between normal children and those with documented brain damage. However, children with learning disabilities have presumed, as opposed to direct, evidence of brain dysfunction. Therefore, the fixed-battery approach may be limited in its usefulness for assessing this clinical population. Furthermore, as Taylor (1988) has recently indicated, neuropsychological test batteries have certain limitations. The most obvious shortcomings are the lack of adequate reliability data and the lack of construct validity of the individual subtests or on the factorial composition of the batteries as a whole. That is, there is an absence of evidence that the tests are useful in explaining independent sources of variance in IQ or in academic abilities. Finally, since neuropsychological test batteries for children lack a firm grounding in developmental neuropsychology, it is difficult to assess developmental changes in test performance by this approach. Teeter (1986) argues that "the importance of this fact cannot be underestimated, as the confounding effects of developmental factors can result in the misdiagnosis and misunderstanding of the range of variability in normal development for many neuropsychological abilities' (p. 93). Thus, there is an especially great need for continued research with child clinical populations using neuropsychological assessment approaches.

NEUROPSYCHOLOGICAL ASSESSMENT PROCEDURES FOR USE IN CHILDREN WITH LEARNING DISABILITIES

While the fixed-battery approach to neuropsychological assessment is based on a standard set of test procedures, there are other general approaches (i.e., eclectic test batteries, qualitative approaches, process-oriented approaches and special purpose measures) to neuropsychological assessment which allow for more flexibility in the selection and administration of individual subtests. A detailed review of these approaches is beyond the scope of this chapter, but the reader can refer to Tramontana and Hooper (1988), for a general discussion of this topic. Suffice it to say that there are major differences among these approaches primarily in the rationale and guiding principles of assessment, and in the relative emphasis given to quantitative versus qualitative methods of analysis.

We argue, as do others, that the use of neuropsychological procedures with special child populations such as those with learning disabilities should be conceptualized differently from procedures commonly used with adult patients. The needs of educators are for a neuropsychological evaluation that reflects developmentally relevant and instructionally meaningful information for purposes of intervention.

A variety of eclectic batteries have emerged since the mid-1970s and involve selecting a number of standardized tests to measure a range of neuropsychological functions. The selection of tests to be routinely given in a thorough neuropsychological examination, depends on the theoretical framework and the conceptualization of important neuropsychological components. For example, Bigler (1988) recently suggested that an eclectic assessment should include components from pediatric neurological examinations as well as neuropsychological measures. In addition, Bigler (1988) points out that tasks should vary according to age and development. Herskowitz and Rosman (1982) have developed some developmental parameters for several neurological/neuropsychological tasks, such as tactile perception and motor fluency (i.e., finger tapping). Based on the Pediatric Neurological Exam, the examiner could measure the integrity of basic neurological functioning such as tactile discrimination, auditory and visual acuity, and a variety of cerebellar functions and primary and peripheral motor functions (i.e., gait, posture, muscle tone, strength, resistance, reflex, fine motor control, and dexterity).

Bigler (1988) further suggests that a full assessment should include the following components: motor, sensory-perception, spatial-perception, memory (verbal/nonverbal, long- and short-term), graphomotor, language (receptive and expressive), and cognitive functions.

The Michigan Neuropsychological Test Battery (Smith, 1975) represents another example of an eclectic assessment approach and includes a variety of scales that measure motor skills, visual perception, memory, receptive language, and cognition. The prescribed tasks include the Purdue Pegboard, Symbol Digit Modalities Test, Visual Organization Test, Benton Visual Retention Test, Color Naming, Memory for Unrelated Sentences, Peabody Picture Vocabulary Test, Raven's Coloured Matrices, and the Wechsler Intelligence Scale for Children-Revised (WISC-R).

The Victoria Battery presents a slightly different approach to assessing child neuropsychological functions (Gaddes, 1980, 1985). The various subtests were included in the battery based on the work of Arthur Benton and Otfried Spreen (Gaddes, 1980). The battery provides a variety of tests that can be selected and can vary from clinic to clinic and the training perspective of the examiner. Intelligence, visual–spatial–constructional, auditory perception, tactile, sensorimotor integration, body image, and motor function are the primary areas measured using this approach.

There are numerous eclectic assessment approaches like the examples previously described. Obrzut (1981) originally described a procedure for child neuropsychological assessment based on a hierarchy of information processing as developed by Johnson and Myklebust (1967). This model considers the developmental stages of learning acquisition via a hierarchy of information processing involving sensation, perception, memory, symbolization, and conceptualization. Obrzut suggested that a breakdown at any level of this hierarchy could result in learning difficulties. Hynd and Cohen (1983) expanded the proposed assessment approach in an effort further to establish an organized and systematic method for the evaluation of neuropsychological functioning of children with learning disorders.

This framework suggests that by carefully selecting various measures, one may assess strengths and weaknesses across the domains of information processing, mentioned above, systematically and efficiently, and in a manner more directly related to a specific subtype of learning disabilities (Hynd, Connor, Neeves, 1988). Thus, as Hynd et al. (1986a) point out, the assessment becomes less time consuming than traditional neuropsychological batteries, less redundant, and more germane to the referral question. However, one must be acquainted with a variety of assessment procedures across these domains and be knowledgeable in learning and development theory.

The neuropsychological assessment will then consist of subtests or items from clinically established batteries, as well as special tests or subtests developed on an experimental basis for investigating levels of information processing. In assessing children with learning disabilities, especially good candidates for inclusion in the assessment, are cognitive measures that vary somewhat independently from IQ or other aspects of cognitive functioning, yet are predictive of specific types of academic failure (Taylor, 1988).

Upon reviewing this assessment procedure and proposed task selection, one can see the hierarchical progression of neuropsychological demands beginning with sensation and concluding with cognition-conceptualization and subsequent academic performance (Hynd & Cohen, 1983). Each of the information processing levels will be further described in the following section, including associated tests as described previously (Obrzut, 1981;

Hynd & Cohen, 1983), with the addition of several other components (i.e., attention, memory) and associated tasks recommended for use with populations with learning disabilities.

SENSORY ACUITY

Sensation represents the lowest level of the information processing hierarchy as the involvement is the initial activation of sensory neurostructures (Obrzut, 1981). At the sensation level basic acuity is examined for primary sensory modalities. Table 7-1 represents a selection of associated tasks that can be used in measuring sensory integrity. The goal at this level is to rule out visual, hearing, and tactile sensory deficits. If acuity screening results are questionable, further examination should be conducted by audiologists and/or ophthalmologists to determine the extent and nature of acuity loss.

SENSORY RECOGNITION AND PERCEPTUAL FUNCTIONS

The organization and integration of sensory input represents the second level of the information-processing model. Perceptual recognition and perception at this level involves visual, auditory, tactile, and kinestetic processing (Obrzut, 1981). Again, referring to Table 7-1, some suggested tasks are presented. All of these tasks require oral and/or motor responses by the child. Therefore, the examiner must be sensitive to any output dysfunction that may interfere with performance of these tasks.

MOTOR FUNCTIONING

Gross and fine motor functioning are important components of the assessment process. If dysfunction is noted at the various levels of the motor domain it is likely that performance on tasks requiring perception, symbolization, and conceptualization could be confounded with motor and motor integration deficits. Table 7-2 presents a selection of tasks that tap a variety of levels of motor functioning. Performance on several of these tasks can be derived from observation of the child, pediatric exams, and/or occupational–physical therapy evaluations. The goal of assessing motor functioning is to assess cerebellar integrity, sensorimotor integration, and the identification of apraxia (sensorimotor loss). Motor assessment should also include the oral-motor domain, which is commonly assessed during a speech–language evaluation conducted by a speech pathologist.

Table 7-1. Sensation Acuity and Perception: Selected Procedures.

Sensation

AUDITORY

Acuity screening—pure tone audiometric exam
Double simultaneous auditory stimulation

VISUAL

Visual acuity
Ocular motility—eye movements
Visual field testing—visual inattention or neglect

TACTILE

Touch sensation—ability to detect light touch
Two-point tactile discrimination

DEVELOPMENTAL AND MEDICAL HISTORY

Sensory, Recognition, and Perception

AUDITORY

Sensory-perceptual exam–Auditory—Reitan
Speech Sounds Perception Test
Seashore Rhythm Test
Acoustical-Motor Organization–Rhythm Test—Luria Nebraska Neuropsychological Battery–Children's Revision (LNNB-CR)
Tests of central auditory abilities

VISUAL

Bender Visual-Motor Gestalt Test
Bender Visual Retention Test
Beery Visual-Motor Integration Test
Visual Scale—Luria Nebraska Neuropsychological Battery–Children's Revision (LNNB-CR)
Sensory Perception Exam–Visual Tasks—Reitan
Embedded Figures Test

TACTILE-KINESTHETIC

Finger agnosia
Fingertip number writing
Tactile form recognition test
Sensory Perceptual Exam–Tactile Component—Reitan
Tactile finger localization
Fingertip symbol writing
Tactile Scale—Luria Nebraska Neuropsychological Battery–Children's Revision (LNNB-CR)
Tactile performance test

Table 7-2. Motor Functioning: Selected Procedures.

General Physical

Muscle tone and posture
Grip strength—hand dynamometer
Resistance
Reflex assessment (upper and lower extremities)

Gross Motor

Gait appraisal
Heel-to-shin movements
Tanden walking
Balance tests

Fine motor

Finger-tapping test
Dexterity
Finger to nose orientation
Motor scale items—Luria Nebraska Neuropsychological Battery–Children's Revision (LNNB-CR)

Sensory-Motor Integration

Trail-making test
Purdue Pegboard
Visual-manual reaction time
Auditory-manual reaction time
Motor scale items—Luria Nebraska Neuropsychological Battery–Children's Revision (LNNB-CR)
Progressive figures test
Beery Visual-Motor Integration Test

ATTENTION

Attention skills are similar to motor functioning in the overall evaluation of neuropsychological abilities. As Barkley (1988) states "Attention plays a key role not only in the evaluation of other neuropsychological functions but also in the proficiency of these functions" (p. 147). However, as Crary, Voeller, and Haak (1988) point out, there are few tests that tap the various attentional dimensions and the potential influence on cognitive tasks such as language. Table 7-3 provides a list of selected procedures for measuring attentional characteristics in children. The tasks have been derived from reviewing the literature of experts in the area of memory research (i.e., Barkley, 1988; Piontrowski & Calfee, 1979; Douglas & Peters, 1979; Milich

Table 7-3. Attention Functioning: Selected Procedures.

Behavior Rating Scales

Conners Rating Scale
Edelbrock Child Assessment Profile–Overactive Profile
Preschool Behavior Questionnaire–Hyperactivity–Distractibility Scale
Attention Deficit Disorder–Hyperactivity (ADD-H) Comprehensive Teacher Rating Scale
Revised Behavior Problem Checklist—Motor Excess Scale

Reaction Time Tests

Continuous Performance Tasks

Children's Checking Task, sustained and span of attention
Underling Test
Trail-making test—sustained and span of attention
Mazes—impulsivity and sustained attention

Other Tests of Attention

Matching familiar figures—concentration and impulsivity
Goldman–Fristoe–Woodcock Selective Attention Test—auditory, attention, distractibility
Flowers–Costello Tests of Central Auditory Abilities—selective, auditory attention
WISC-R—freedom from distractibility factor

& Kramer, 1984). It is important to consider the complexity and multidimensional nature of memory, and for the purposes of this discussion these issues have been greatly simplified. The relevant components of attention relative to an evaluation should include the following: overall alertness, focused attention or selective attention, sustained attention, and span of attention (simultaneous stimulation) (Barkley, 1988). As can be seen by examining Table 7-3, many of the tests currently in use tap a variety of attentional domains. Therefore, it is important that the examiner be familiar with theoretical models of attention and employ task analysis procedures when using any of these tests.

MEMORY

According to the previously discussed information processing hierarchy (Johnson & Myklebust, 1967), memory constitutes the third level and involves a complex system for the retrieval of perceptual information from previous experiences. Theoretical memory models are varied and extremely complex, much like attentional models discussed previously. Again for the purposes herein, the procedures have been selected on a simplified level of current memory theory and research. Boyd (1988) suggests that tasks should include multiple trial learning and selective reminding procedures using both verbal and nonverbal material. He also suggests examining the child's incidental memory and memory capacity abilities. Boyd presents an excellent table of assessment instruments and type of memory evaluated such as long- and short-term memory, input modality and output modality. Table 7-4 represents a somewhat condensed version of Boyd's presentation and includes only tests and subtests most commonly in use with children with learning disabilities. The reader is encouraged to review Boyd's presentation and associated discussion regarding memory assessment with children. The evaluator should record how the child responds to items tapping short- and long-term memory and should compare performance between tasks that involve language stimuli versus nonlanguage stimuli. In addition, method of response (i.e., verbal and visual–motor) should also be considered.

PSYCHOLINGUISTIC FUNCTIONING

Language functioning is dependent upon the development of all information-processing levels from sensation to conceptualization. As language develops and becomes more complex, so does the extent and nature of the assessment process. Bates, Benigni, Bretherton, Camainoi, and Volterra (1979) have emphasized the period of language readiness that constitutes the period of time between birth and formal language processes. Crary et al. (1988) have described language in the context of three general stages including the prelinguistic stage, lexical expansion stage, and the grammatical expansion stage. The prelinguistic stage is marked by the infant's ability to communicate basic biological needs and respond to voice, people, and objects (Alegria & Noirot, 1978; Lieberman, 1967). Grammatical expansion is described as increased semantic and phonological knowledge and production of language (Crary et al., 1988). Finally, grammatical expansion involves the growth and refinement of all grammatical structures of language (Crary et al., 1988). These authors suggest that a neurolinguistic approach to assessment should be based on the three general language stages and should include both language content measures such as syntax, and morphology as well as language functions (i.e., naming and comprehension). Table 7-5 presents assessment procedures designed to evaluate various language components. Again, it becomes very important for the examiner to become familiar with developmental aspects of language acquisition and task-analysis procedures in order to

Table 7-4. Memory Function: Selected Procedures.

Short-Term Auditory Memory

Digit Span—WISC-R
Numerical Memory I & II—McCarthy
Memory for Digits—Stanford-Binet Intelligence Scale–Revised (SB-R)
Number Recall—Kaufman Assessment Battery for Children (K-ABC)
Numbers Reversed—Woodcock–Johnson Psychoeducational Battery (WJPB)
Memory for Sentences—SB-R
Verbal Memory I & II—McCarthy
Word Order—K-ABC
Sentence Imitation—Detroit Test of Learning Aptitude-2 (DTLA-2)
Oral Directions—DTLA-2
Memory for Sentences—WJPB
Word Sequences—DTLA-2
Memory Items—Memory Scale—Luria Nebraska Neuropsychological Battery–Children's Revision (LNNB-CR)

Short-Term Visual-Spatial Memory

Coding—WISC-R
Memory for Objects—SB-R
Bead Memory—SB-R
Pictoral Memory—McCarthy
Face Recognition—K-ABC
Hand Movements—K-ABC
Spatial memory—K-1ABC
Design Reproduction—DTLA-2
Object Sentences—DTLA-2
Letter Sequences—DTLA-2
Target Test—Reitan
Category Test—Reitan
Memory Items–Memory Scale—LNNB-CR
Benton Revised Visual Retention Test

Long-Term Auditory Memory

Information Scale—WISC-R
Arithmetic Scale—WISC-R
Intelligence Scale—LNNB-CR

Table 7-4. (Continued)

Long-Term Visual Memory

Object Assembly Scale—WISC-R
Faces and Places—K-ABC*
Knowledge Cluster—WJPB*

Tactile Memory

Tactile Performance Test—Reitan
Hand Movements—K-ABC

*These subtests require a verbal response but are elicited with visual pictures, which may tap a visual memory representation.

---

ensure an accurate interpretation of language performance. Crary et al. (1988) also suggest identifying and employing various subtests and scales that measure language content and functions in a systematic fashion to produce a multidimensional and diagnostically sound psycholinguistic evaluation.

COGNITIVE AND ACADEMIC FUNCTIONING

Measures of cognitive functioning represent symbolism and conceptualization components of the information processing hierarchy. The tasks involved in a cognitive evaluation involve complex and highly integrative neuropsychological functions. Traditionally, this is the level where most evaluations begin in the case of a referral for learning disabilities. Whereas cognitive functioning is sensitive to development and neuropsychological integrity, there are certain diagnostic limitations when used as the sole measure of neuropsychological functioning. Bigler (1988) suggests that some inferences about neuropsychological processes can be derived from cognitive measures. Specifically, in the efficacy of cognitive instruments to identify impaired ability patterns in children with neuropsychological disorders (Kaufman, Long, & O'Neal, 1986). However, cognitive measures cannot provide a complete perspective of functioning because there are only limited or no measures of motor, sensory, language, or memory abilities (Bigler, 1988). Table 7-6 presents the most widely used cognitive instruments from which performance patterns and normative group comparisons can be derived.

Table 7-5. Psycholinguistic Functioning: Selected Procedures.

Screening Measures

Aphasia Screening Test—Reitan
Peabody Picture Vocabulary—Revised
Northwestern Syntax Screening Test
Token Test for Children
Fluency and Articulation Tests
Receptive Language Scale—Luria Nebraska Neuropsychological Battery–Children's Revision (LNNB-CR)
Expressive Language Scale—LNNB-CR
Boston Naming Test
Speech Perception Test
Blending Test—Woodcock–Johnson Psychoeducational Battery (WJPB)

Language—Functional Asymmetries

Dichotic Listening Tasks
Visual Half-Field Tasks
Concurrent Verbal Manual Tasks

Formal Assessment Batteries

Boston Aphasia Examination
Illinois Test of Psycholinguistic Abilities
Clinical Evaluation of Language Functions
Test of Language Development

ACHIEVEMENT

Like cognition, achievement requires the child to process and integrate symbolic and conceptual information. Achievement testing should involve a comprehensive assessment of all academic areas to address patterns of performance regarding strengths and weaknesses on academic materials. Table 7-6 briefly lists some of the most commonly used instruments at this time. When testing academic performance it is important to look at patterns of performance that may be related to neuropsychological patterns found previously. In addition, achievement testing should involve direct observations of a child attempting academic tasks within the classroom setting including the child's approach to the task, concentration, strategies employed, and frustration levels. In addition, achievement measures should also include testing of limits, teaching of new tasks and practice information. The goal of achievement testing is to identify levels

Table 7-6. Cognitive Functioning and Achievement: Selected Procedures.

Screening Instruments and Scales

Category Test—Reitan
Intellectual Scale—Luria Nebraska Neuropsychological Battery–Children's Revision (LNNB-CR)
Raven Coloured Matrices
Slossen Intelligence Test

Formal Batteries

Wechsler Intelligence Scale for Children-Revised (WISC-R)
Stanford–Binet Intelligence Scale-Revised (SB-R)
Kaufman Assessment Battery for Children (K-ABC)
McCarthy Scales of Children's Abilities

Achievement—Comprehensive Batteries

Peabody Individual Achievement Test
Woodcock–Johnson Psychoeducational Battery
Kaufman Assessment Battery for Children–Achievement Section

Achievement—Reading

Durrell Analysis of Reading Difficulties
Gates–McKillop Reading Mastery Tests
Woodcock Reading Mastery Test

Achievement—Math

Key Math Diagnostic Tests

Achievement—Written Language

Test of Written Language (TOWL)
Test of Early Written Language (TEWL)

of academic functioning, but more importantly, to relate neuropsychological strengths and weaknesses to actual academic performance. It is at this juncture that a thorough evaluation can potentially yield information upon which to build effective remediation and/or compensation strategies for the future academic growth of the referred child.

CONCLUSIONS

There are some distinct advantages to an eclectic approach to neuropsychological assessment. First, tasks can be selected on an individual basis to evaluate specific deficit areas in question. In addition, if tests are selected carefully the result may be less testing time overall as compared to a full neuropsychological battery and potentially a more in-depth understanding of specific neuropsychological deficits (Stoddart & Knights, 1986). As Tramontana and Hooper (1988) suggest, there is a distinct need for a "core" set of neuropsychological procedures that could serve as a consistent basis for screening. The eclectic approach as recommended in this chapter, although highly dependent on the training and level of expertise of the examiner, provides this basis for screening of populations with learning disabilities and should serve as a model for evaluation and clinical practice.

REFERENCES

Adams, K. M. (1980). In search of Luria's battery: A false start. *Journal of Consulting and Clinical Psychology, 48*, 511-516.

Alegria, J., & Noirot, E. (1978). Neonate orientation behavior towards the human race. *International Journal of Behavioral Development, 1*, 291-312.

Barclay, C. R., & Hagen, J. W. (1982). The development of mediated behavior in children: An alternative view of learning disabilities. In J. P. Das, R. F. Mulcahy, & A. E., Wall (Eds.), *Theory and research in learning disabilities* (pp. 61-83). New York: Plenum Press.

Barkley, R. A. (1988). Attention. In M. G. Tramontana & S. R. Hooper (Eds.), *Assessment issues in child neuropsychology* (pp. 145-176). New York: Plenum Press.

Bates, E., Benigni, L., Bretherton, I., Camaioni, L., & Volterra, V. (1979). *The emergence of symbols: Cognition and communication in infancy.* New York: Academic Press.

Bigler, E. D. (1988). The role of neuropsychological assessment in relation to other types of assessment with children. In M. G. Tramontana & S. R. Hooper (Eds.), *Assessment issues in child neuropsychology* (pp. 67-91). New York: Plenum Press.

Boyd, T. A. (1988). Clinical assessment of memory in children: A developmental framework for practice. In M. G. Tramontana & S. R. Hooper (Eds.), *Assessment issues in child neuropsychology* (pp. 177-204). New York: Plenum Press.

Coplin, J. W., & Morgan, S. B. (1988). Learning disabilities: A multidimensional perspective. *Journal of Learning Disabilities, 21*, 614-622.

Crary, M. A., Voeller, K. K. S., & Haak, N. J. (1988). Questions of developmental neurolinguistic assessment. In M. G. Tramontana & S. R. Hooper (Eds.), *Assessment issues in child neuropsychology* (pp. 249-279). New York: Plenum Press.

Crosson, B., & Warren, R. L. (1982). Use of the Luria-Nebraska Neuropsychological Battery in aphasia: A conceptual critique. *Journal of Consulting and Clinical Psychology, 50*, 22-31.

Doehring, D. G. (1976). Evaluation of two models of reading disability. In R. M. Knights & D. J. Bakker (Eds.), *The neuropsychology of learning disorders* (pp. 405-412). Baltimore: University Park Press.

Douglas, V. I., & Peters, K. G. (1979). Toward a clearer definition of the attentional deficit of hyperactive children. In G. A. Hale & M. Lewis (Eds.), *Attention and cognitive development* (pp. 173-248). New York: Plenum Press.
Federal Register (1976). Education of handicapped children and incentive grants programs. (Vol. 41, p. 46977). Bethesda, M.D.: U.S. Department of Health, Education and Welfare.
Gaddes, W. H. (1980). *Learning disabilities and brain function: A neuropsychological approach.* New York: Springer-Verlag.
Gaddes, W. H. (1985). *Learning disabilities and brain function: A neuropsychological approach* (2nd ed.). New York: Springer-Verlag.
Gamble, C. M., Mishra, S. P., & Obrzut, J. E. (1988). Construct validity of neuropsychological instrumentation with a learning disabled population. *Archives of Clinical Neuropsychology, 3,* 359-368.
Goldstein, G. (1984). Comprehensive neuropsychological assessment batteries. In G. Goldstein & M. Hersen (Eds.), *Handbook of psychological assessment* (pp. 181-210). New York: Pergamon Press.
Hammill, D. D., Leigh, J. E., McNutt, G., & Larsen, S. C. (1981). A new definition of learning disabilities. *Learning Disability Quarterly, 4,* 336-342.
Heaton, R. K. (1988). Introduction to the special series. *Journal of Consulting and Clinical Psychology, 56,* 787-788.
Herskowitz, J., & Rosman, N. P. (1982). *Pediatrics, neurology, and psychiatry: Commonground.* New York: Macmillan.
Hynd, G. W., & Cohen, M. (1983). *Dyslexia: Neuropsychological theory, research, and clinical differentiation.* New York: Grune & Stratton.
Hynd, G. W., Connor, R. T., & Nieves, N. (1988). Learning disabilities subtypes: Perspectives and methodological issues in clinical assessment. In M. G. Tramontana & S. R. Hooper (Eds.), *Assessment issues in child neuropsychology* (pp. 281-312). New York: Plenum Press.
Hynd, G. W., & Obrzut, J. E. (1986). Clinical child neuropsychology: Issues and perspectives. In J. E. Obrzut & G. W. Hynd (Eds.), *Child neuropsychology: Clinical practice.* (Vol. 2). (pp. 3-14). Orlando, FL: Academic Press.
Hynd, G. W., Obrzut, J. E., Hayes, F., & Becker, M. G. (1986a). Neuropsychology of childhood learning disabilities. In D. Wedding, A. M. Horton, Jr., & J. Webster (Eds.), *The neuropsychology handbook: Behavioral and clinical perspectives* (pp. 456-485). New York: Springer Publishing Company.
Hynd, G. W., Snow, J. H., & Becker, M. G. (1986b). Neuropsychological assessment in clinical child psychology. In B. B. Lahey & A. Kazdin (Eds.), *Advances in clinical child neuropsychology* (Vol. 9). New York: Plenum Press.
Hynd, G. W., Quackenbush, R., & Obrzut, J. E. (1980). Training school psychologists in neuropsychology: Current practices and trends. *Journal of School Psychology, 18,* 148-153.
Johnson, D., & Myklebust, H. (1967). *Learning disabilities; Educational principles and practices.* New York: Grune & Stratton.
Kaufman, A. S., Long, S. W., & O'Neal, M. R. (1986). Topical review of the WISC-R for pediatric neuroclinicans. *Journal of Child Neurology, 1,* 89-98.
Kolb, B., & Whishaw, I. Q. (1980). *Fundamentals of human neuropsychology.* San Francisco: W. H. Freeman.
Leavell, C., & Lewandowski, L. (1988). Neuropsychology in the schools: A survey report. *School Psychology Review, 17,* 147-155.
Lezak, M. D. (1983). *Neuropsychological assessment* (2nd ed.). New York: Oxford Press.

Lieberman, P. (1967). *Intonation, perception and language.* Cambridge, MA: MIT Press.
Milich, R., & Kramer, J. (1984). Reflections on impulsivity: An empirical investigation of impulsivity as a construct. In K. Gadlow & I. Bialer (Eds.), *Advances in learning and behavioral disabilities* (Vol. 3, pp. 57-94). Greenwich, CT: JAI Press.
Obrzut, J. E. (1981). Neuropsychological procedures with school-age children. In G. W. Hynd & J. E. Obrzut (Eds.), *Neuropsychological assessment and the school-age child: Issues and procedures.* (pp. 237-275). New York: Grune & Stratton.
Obrzut, J. E., & Boliek, C. A. (1988). Dichotic listening and learning disabilities. In K. H. Hugdahl (Ed.), *Handbook of dichotic listening: Theory, methods, and research* (pp. 475-511). Chichester, England: John Wiley and Sons.
Piontrowski, D., & Calfee, R. (1979). Attention in the classroom. In G. Hale & M. Lewis (Eds.), *Attention and cognitive development* (pp. 297-330). New York: Plenum Press.
Rourke, B. P. (1975). Brain-behavior relationships in children with learning disabilities: A research program. *American Psychologist, 30,* 911-920.
Rourke, B. P., Bakker, D. J., Fisk, J. L., & Strang, J. D. (1983). *Child neuropsychology: An introduction to theory, research, and clinical practice.* New York: Guilford Press.
Sattler, J. M. (1988). *Assessment of children* (3rd ed.). San Diego: Jerome M. Sattler.
Seidenberg, M., Giordani, B., Berent, S., & Boll, T. J. (1983). IQ Level and Performance on the Halstead-Reitan Neurological Test Battery for Older Children. *Journal of Consulting and Clinical Psychology, 51,* 406-413.
Smith, A. (1975). Neuropsychological testing in neurological disorders. In W. J. Friedlander (Ed.), *Advances in neurology* (Vol. 7, pp. 49-110). New York: Raven Press.
Snow, J. H., Hynd, G. W., & Hartlage, L. C. (1984). Difference between mildly and more severely learning-disabled children on the Luria-Nebraska Neuropsychological Battery-Children's Revision. *Journal of Psychoeducational Assessment, 2,* 23-28.
Stoddart, C., & Knights, R. M. (1986). Neuropsychological assessment of children: Alternative approaches. In J. E. Obrzut & G. W. Hynd (Eds.), *Child neuropsychology: Clinical practice* (Vol. 2, pp. 229-243). Orlando, FL: Academic Press.
Tarnopol, L., & Tarnopol, M. (1977). *Brain function and reading disabilities.* Baltimore: University Park Press.
Taylor, H. G. (1988). Neuropsychological testing: Relevance for assessing children's learning disabilities. *Journal of Consulting and Clinical Psychology. 56,* 795-800.
Teeter, P. A. (1986). Standard neuropsychological batteries for children. In J. E. Obrzut & G. W. Hynd (Eds.), *Child neuropsychology: Clinical practice* (Vol. 2) (pp. 187-227). Orlando, FL.: Academic Press.
Teeter, P. A., Boliek, C. A., Obrzut, J. E., & Malsch, K. (1986). Diagnostic utility of the critical level formula and clinical summary scales of the Luria-Nebraska Neuropsychological Battery-Children's Revision with learning-disabled children. *Developmental Neuropsychology, 2,* 125-135.
Townes, B. D., Turpin, E. W., Martin, D. C., & Goldstein, D. (1980). Neuropsychological correlates of academic success among elementary school children. *Journal of Consulting and Clinical Psychology, 6,* 675-684.
Tramontana, M. G., & Hooper, S. R. (1988). Child neuropsychological assessment: Overview of current status. In M. G. Tramontana & S. R. Hooper (Eds.), *Assessment issues in child neuropsychology.* (pp. 3-38). New York: Plenum Press.
Witelson, S. F. (1977). Early hemisphere specialization and interhemisphere plasticity: An empirical and theoretical review. In S. J. Segalowitz & F. A. Gruber (Eds.),

Language development and neurological theory. (pp. 213-287). New York: Academic Press.

Woodruff, M. L., & Baisden, R. H. (1986). Theories of brain functioning: A brief introduction to the study of the brain and behavior. In D. Wedding, A. M. Horton, Jr., & J. Webster (Eds.), *The neuropsychology handbook: Behavioral and clinical perspectives* (pp. 23-58). New York: Springer Publishing.

CHAPTER 8

Reading Disability: Assessment Issues

KEITH E. STANOVICH

The learning disability now identified variously as dyslexia (and/or reading disability, specific reading retardation, developmental reading disorder; the terms are used interchangeably here) was brought to general attention by the turn-of-the-century clinical reports of Pringle Morgan (1896) and James Hinshelwood (1895) (among others) in Great Britain, and termed "congenital word blindness." Subsequent to these early reports, the most influential single investigator was Samuel Orton (1925, 1928, 1937), who contributed numerous clinical cases, theoretical speculation about proximal causation, and suggestions for treatment techniques. However, a focus on assessment issues did not occur until the introduction of the generic term "learning disabilities" in the early 1960s (Kirk, 1963; Lerner, 1985), and was spawned by concerns with providing services for children with Learning Disabilities—the bulk of whom suffered from reading difficulties of varying degrees of severity (Bateman, 1979; Gaskins, 1982; Kirk & Elkins, 1975; Lerner, 1975).

During the 1960s and 1970s, several proposed definitions of reading disability had considerable influence on both research and debates on delivery of service. The definition of the World Federation of Neurology had many features that became canonical for many researchers and practitioners. Specific developmental dyslexia was characterized as "A disorder manifested by difficulty in learning to read despite conventional instruction, adequate intelligence, and socio-cultural opportunity. It is dependent upon fundamental cognitive abilities which are frequently of constitutional origin" (Critchley, 1970).

This particular definition highlighted the well-known "exclusionary criteria" that subsequently caused much dispute in discussions of dyslexia (e.g., Applebee, 1971; Ceci, 1986; Doehring, 1978; Eisenberg, 1978; Rutter, 1978). These exclusionary criteria were carried over into the definition of learning disability employed in the landmark Education for All Handicapped Children Act (Public Law [PL] 94-142) passed in 1975: "Specific learning disability means a disorder in one or more of the basic psychological processes involved in understanding or in using language spoken or written, which may manifest itself in an imperfect ability to listen, think, speak, read, write, spell, or to do mathematical calculations. The term includes such conditions as perceptual handicaps, brain injury, minimal brain dysfunction, dyslexia, and developmental aphasia. The term does not include children who have learning problems which are primarily the result of visual, hearing, or motor handicaps, of mental retardation, of emotional disturbance, or of environmental, cultural, or economic disadvantage."

The National Joint Committee for Learning Disabilities (NJCLD) responded to criticisms of the exclusionary criteria by proposing that "These disorders are intrinsic to the individual and presumed to be due to central nervous dysfunction. Even though a learning disability may occur concomitantly with other handicapping conditions (e.g., sensory impairment, mental retardation, social and emotional disturbance) or environmental influences (e.g., cultural differences, or inappropriate instruction, psycholinguistic factors), it is not the direct result of those conditions or influences" (Hammill, Leigh, McNutt, & Larsen, 1981), thus emphasizing that the mere presence of other impairments or of environmental deprivation should not exclude children from being categorized as learning disabled. The Interagency Committee on Learning Disabilities established by the U.S. Health Research Extension Act of 1985 (Kavanagh & Truss, 1988) accepted the essentials of the NJCLD definition, but added disorders of social skills to the listing of learning disabilities and indicated that learning disabilities may also occur with attention deficit disorder.

THE FOCUS ON SEVERE DISCREPANCY

All of these professional and legal definitions highlight the same salient feature: the fact that a dyslexic child has an "unexpected" disability in the domain of reading, one not predicted by their general intellectual competence and socioeducational opportunities. Practically, this has meant a statistical assessment of the difference between their objectively measured reading ability and general intelligence (Frankenberger & Harper, 1987; Kavale, 1987; Kavale & Nye, 1981; Reynolds, 1985; Shepard, 1980). Typically, very little effort is expended in ascertaining whether adequate instruction has been provided or whether the child suffers from sociocultural disadvantage—in short, in ascertaining whether the disability is "intrinsic to the individual." So much conceptual confusion has surrounded the more operational discrepancy criterion that researchers and theoreticians have been reluctant to take on the potential additional complications of the other criteria.

In short, despite repeated admonitions that the diagnosis of reading disability should be multidimensional (Johnson, 1988; McKinney, 1987; Senf, 1986; Tindal & Marston, 1986), in actual educational and clinical practice it is the assessment of a discrepancy between aptitude and reading achievement that is the key defining feature (Frankenberger & Harper, 1987). Reynolds (1985) notes that across the numerous legal, professional, and research definitions of learning disabilities, five major components recur with great frequency: failure to achieve, psychological process disorders, exclusionary criteria, etiology, severe discrepancy. However, "The severe discrepancy criterion is the most widely applied across the states," probably because "Severe discrepancy is easily measured relative to other components of the definition of learning disability" (pp. 38–39). As Shepard (1980) argues, "All learning disability definitions, either by connotation or denotation, rest on this discrepancy between achievement and ability" (p. 80). Referring to the expert testimony and public discussion during the development of PL 94-142, Reynolds (1984–85) concludes that "the only consensus regarding the characteristics of this 'thing' called learning disability, was that it resulted in a major discrepancy between what you would expect academically of learning disabled children and the level at which they are actually achieving" (p. 452).

Although numerous side issues and points of contention surround the classification of children as reading disabled, the core disputes concern the operationalization and theoretical justification of the discrepancy criterion. These disputes surrounding the discrepancy criterion can be classified into two types. First, there are statistical and measurement complications involved in the operationalization of severe discrepancy. Many early attempts at defining severe discrepancy for purposes of educational classification were psychometrically naive. Several of these early classification practices served to undermine the definitional clarification that various agencies and professional bodies were striving to achieve. For example, discrepancy formulas that ignore regression artifacts subvert the attempt not to exclude the possible simultaneous occurrence of reading disability and low IQ. With the use of appropriate statistical knowledge, many of the difficulties encountered in applying a severe discrepancy criterion are, at least in theory, easily remediable.

Much more problematic have been challenges to the conceptual assumptions that underlie the motivation to create a category of reading disability in the manner of the definitions outlined above. The vast majority of poor readers in the schools are, of course, not characterized by severe discrepancies between their reading ability and assessed intelligence (Eisenberg, 1979). Their below-average reading performance is predictable from their general cognitive abilities. They are what Gough and Tunmer (1986) term "garden-variety" poor readers—by mathematical necessity much more numerous than discrepancy-defined poor readers.

One of the fundamental premises that has provided the impetus for the development of classifications such as dyslexia or developmental reading disorder has been the assumption that such children are qualitatively different from garden-variety poor readers. Since classifications such as dyslexia or developmental reading disorder have been employed for purposes of educational treatment and for purposes of educational funding, it would be desirable for qualitative differentiation to occur in a variety of domains. That is, strong justification for a discrepancy-based classification would derive from studies showing that these different types of poor readers employ somewhat different information-processing operations while reading, that they have different educational prognoses, and that they show different responses to treatment than do garden-variety poor readers. Lack of such an empirical differentiation would certainly question the wisdom of expending such great effort to differentiate poorly achieving children along the lines outlined above.

Part of the reason for the malaise and soul-searching that periodically overtake researchers and practitioners in the area of reading disabilities (Coles, 1978, 1987; Lyon, 1987; Senf, 1986; Stanovich, 1989; Swanson, 1988; Vaughn & Bos, 1987; Vellutino, 1979) is that the field plunged ahead into the domains of educational practice and diagnosis without setting itself on a firm foundation by first unequivocally demonstrating the empirical differentiability that would establish construct validity for the concept of reading disability. We will review below the evidence that does exist.

Our review of the literature will focus on two classes of controversy surrounding the construct of dyslexia: What is the best way to operationalize severe discrepancy? and What is the empirical evidence that would justify the need to assess achievement/aptitude discrepancies for the purposes of educational classification?

OPERATIONALIZING SEVERE DISCREPANCY

The field of reading disabilities has come to accept the fact that it is wedded to the discrepancy notion if, as has been the case, it insists on differentiating between types of poor readers. Attempts to discourage the use of discrepancy formulas (Board of Trustees of the Council for Learning Disabilities, 1987) will only result in dependence on much less reliable clinical judgments (Reynolds, 1985) and will almost inevitably result in samples of "dyslexic" children who are not differentiable from other poor readers who are not so labeled. (As will be discussed, such a lack of differentiation will fuel criticism of the use of the reading disability category in research and in practice.) Although advances in neuropsychology (e.g., Hynd & Semrud-Clikeman, 1989), and in theories of human abilities (Ceci, in press; Gardner, 1983; Sternberg, 1985; Swanson, 1987, 1988) may one day change this situation, at present we are tied to a definition that involves the use of quantitative data obtained from standardized psychometric instruments.

In the history of research and diagnosis of reading disabilities, the assessment of achievement below that expected has been operationalized in four different ways (Cone & Wilson, 1981; Reynolds, 1984–85, 1985; Shepard, 1980; Wilson & Cone, 1984). The first, which classifies anyone more than two grade levels below current grade placement as reading disabled, involves no discrepancy from aptitude and so is inconsistent with almost all current conceptions of reading disability. A more popular method is to define reading disability as an achievement discrepancy from an expected grade-equivalent, the latter based on some formula containing a measure of mental age or IQ. There are two fundamental problems with such formulas. First, they often ignore the fact that the standard deviation of grade equivalent distributions increases with age, leading to greater numbers of older children being classified as disabled if a constant criterion is used (Cone & Wilson, 1981; Shepard, 1980). Secondly, they do not take into account regression effects because they assume a perfect correlation between IQ and achievement (Cone & Wilson, 1981; Reynolds, 1985; Shepard, 1980; Wilson & Cone, 1984).

A third technique, the z-score discrepancy method (Cone & Wilson, 1981; Shepard, 1980), obviates the problems involved in assessing discrepancies in grade-equivalent units (which have a number of undesirable properties; see Reynolds, 1981) but still fails to correct for the imperfect correlation between ability and achievement. In contrast, the fourth class of technique, the regression discrepancy method (Reynolds, 1984–1985, 1985; Rutter & Yule, 1975; Shepard, 1980) is psychometrically the most justifiable. Here, the discrepancy is calculated from an expected achievement level based on the regression of reading achievement on the aptitude measure, thus taking into account the imperfect correlation between achievement and aptitude. McKinney (1987; see also, Yule, 1984) has demonstrated how, in an actual data set, the regression discrepancy method identifies a more uniform distribution of children across the IQ range than does the z-score method, a desirable characteristic given the logic of what a learning disability is supposed to be, and also given that most recent definitions allow for the simultaneous occurrence of a reading disability with low intelligence. The z-score discrepancy method, in contrast to the regression method, overidentifies high IQ children and underidentifies low IQ children, a pattern of identification that has fueled social criticism of the learning disabilities concept (Coles, 1987; Senf, 1986). As Yule (1984) notes: "Where scarce remedial resources are provided according to the degree of a child's underachievement, the less able child will be doubly disadvantaged unless regression techniques are used" (p. 234).

Despite its many advantages, the regression method does have some drawbacks. It can require some sophistication to apply and several precautions regarding test standardization are critical (Reynolds, 1984–1985, 1985; Shepard, 1980). However, the existence of some helpful computer programs (e.g., Reynolds & Stowe, 1985) serves to ease the conceptual load on practitioners. The current state of knowledge in brain science and in the psychology of individual differences—in combination with the logical constraints imposed by our previous conceptualizations of what a reading disability is (see below and Stanovich, 1986a, 1988b)—guarantees that we will have to live with discrepancy formulas for some time to come. It is thus worthwhile for clinicians to become conversant with this technique for measuring discrepancy and for researchers to continue to clarify the complications involved in its application (Cone & Wilson, 1981; Reynolds, 1984–1985; Shepard, 1980). The issue of how to measure the discrepancy is actually a relatively straightforward concern when compared with the conceptual complications involved in trying to establish construct validity for the concept of reading disability itself. We now turn to this complicated and contentious issue.

THE CONSTRUCT VALIDITY OF THE CONCEPT OF DYSLEXIA

From the beginning, what has fueled both theoretical interest in reading disability and has justified differential educational treatment has been the assumption that the reading difficulties of the dyslexic individual stem from problems different from those characterizing the garden-variety poor reader (to use Gough & Tunmer's [1986] term); or, alternatively, if they stem from the same factors, that the degree of severity is so extreme for the dyslexic individual that it constitutes, in effect, a qualitative difference.

The experimental contrasts that have operationalized the idea of qualitative difference and/or differential causation in the literature have been dominated by two different designs. One is the reading-level match design (see Bradley & Bryant, 1978, 1985; Bryant & Goswami, 1986), in which an older group of dyslexic children is matched for reading level with a younger group of nondyslexic children. The cognitive characteristics and reading subskills of the two groups are then compared. The logic here is fairly straightforward. If the reading subskills and cognitive characteristics of the two groups do not match, then it would seem that they are arriving at their similar reading levels via different routes, and this would support the idea of a qualitatively different developmental model for dyslexic readers (although there are numerous conceptual and methodological complications surrounding this inference; see Bryant & Goswami, 1986; Goswami & Bryant, in press; Jackson & Butterfield, 1989). In contrast, if the reading subskill profiles of the two groups are identical, this would seem to undermine the rationale for the different educational treatment of dyslexic children and for their theoretical differentiation. If dyslexic children are reading just like any other child who happens to be at their reading level, and are using the same cognitive skills to do so, why should we consider their reading behavior to be so special?

The second major design—one pertinent not only to theoretical issues but also to the educational politics of reading disability—is to compare dyslexic children with children of the same age who are reading at the same level, but who are not labeled dyslexic. (Adapting the terminology of Gough & Tunmer [1986], this design will be termed the "garden-variety control" design.) Again, the inferences drawn are relatively straightforward. If the reading subskills and cognitive characteristics of the two groups do not match, then it would seem that the two groups are arriving at their similar reading levels via different routes. In contrast, if the reading subskill profiles of the two groups are identical, this would certainly undermine the rationale for the different educational treatment of dyslexic children and would make dyslexic children considerably less interesting theoretically. As Fredman and Stevenson (1988) state, if "there is no clear distinction between the groups in terms of how they read, then the practice of identifying a special group of poor readers for special attention may no longer be necessary" (p. 105).

Only recently has the learning disabilities field accumulated an appreciable amount of data from these two critical designs. It was not until the mid-1970s that we had the data from the groundbreaking epidemiological comparison of dyslexic and garden-variety poor readers conducted by

Rutter and Yule (1975), and only in the past 10 years or so has their data been supplemented by other garden-variety control investigations. Additionally, only recently have enough studies employing reading-level matches been accumulated so that patterns were discernible.

Unfortunately, when the necessary empirical data did begin to accumulate in the past few years, the data were not always convergent. Empirically, there are reading-level match studies that have revealed similar processing profiles (Baddeley, Logie, & Ellis, 1988; Beech & Harding, 1984; Treiman & Hirsh-Pasek, 1985) and those that have identified differences (Baddeley, DiBenedetto, 1983; Olson, Kliegl, Davidson, & Foltz, 1985; Olson, Wise, Conners, Rack, & Fulker, 1989; Snowling, 1980; Snowling, Stackhouse, & Rack, 1986). Similarly, garden-variety comparisons have supported qualitative similarity (Fredman & Stevenson, 1988; Siegel, 1988; Taylor, Satz, & Friel, 1979) and difference (Jorm, Share, Maclean, & Matthews, 1986; Rutter & Yule, 1975; Silva, McGee, & Williams, 1985).

THE PHONOLOGICAL-CORE VARIABLE-DIFFERENCE MODEL

These mixed results have troubled many in the field because they relate to some of the foundational assumptions of the concept of dyslexia as it is used in both research investigations and educational practice. Nevertheless, if we step back from the minutia of the experimental details and look for patterns, there are trends discernible in the admittedly somewhat confusing data base. I have described these trends within the context of what I have termed the phonological-core variable-difference framework (Stanovich, 1988a). The model rests on a clear understanding of the assumption of specificity in definitions of dyslexia (see Hall & Humphreys, 1982; Stanovich, 1986a, 1986b). This assumption underlies all discussions of the concept of dyslexia, even if it is not explicitly stated. It is the idea that a child with this type of learning disability has a brain/cognitive deficit that is reasonably specific to the reading task. That is, the concept of dyslexia requires that the deficits displayed by such children not extend too far into other domains of cognitive functioning. If they did, this would depress the constellation of abilities we call intelligence and thus reduce the reading/intelligence discrepancy that is central to all the definitions reviewed above.

A major problem in the area of reading disabilities is that much research and theory about individual differences in the cognitive processes related to reading has undermined the assumption of specificity (see Stanovich, 1986a, 1988b). Hypotheses have been advanced that characterize the child with reading disabilities as deficient in global processes such as general linguistic awareness, comprehension, strategic functioning, rule learning, active/inactive learning, and generalized metacognitive functioning. The problem with all of these is that they are central processes (Fodor, 1983), too critically intertwined with other aspects of intellectual functioning (Sternberg, 1985). Any hypothesis that attempts to explain dyslexia while at the same time undermining the assumption of specificity (that the disability is localized in only a thin slice of the cognitive domain, rather than in more global aspects of intellectual functioning) will lead to a crisis in the application of the concept of dyslexia. Metacognition and strategic functioning as explanations of reading disability cause just such a crisis. Metacognition is the sine qua non of almost all recent theories of intelligence. Deficient metacognitive functioning means lower intelligence, which reduces the achievement/aptitude discrepancy, which takes the child out of the reading disability category.

This, by the way, is not to say that a large number of poor readers do not have metacognitive problems or that the recent focus on metacognitive training is inappropriate. Indeed, many school-labeled children with learning disabilities may be characterized by metacognitive and strategic problems, but they are probably not typical of those who meet strict psychometric criteria for the dyslexic classification (see also, Shephard, Gelzheiser, & Solar, 1985). The former group of children are numerous and are well-known to the teacher consultants who staff learning disability and learning resource centers across the country. They have problems with study skills; and by all indications they can benefit to a considerable extent from interventions based on experimental work in the area of strategic and metacognitive processing. But for the reasons outlined above, they should not be considered dyslexic.

The best candidates for key processing mechanisms underlying reading disability will be those that are somewhat modular, roughly in Fodor's (1983) sense. He conceptualizes modular systems as those that are fast, automatic, and informationally encapsulated. The latter is the most important aspect of modularity and means that a module operates autonomously: that it is not under the direction of higher-level cognitive structures and is not supplemented by real-world knowledge. For our purposes, the important point is that modular processes are not strongly interactive with central processes; they may provide data for central-processing procedures but they do not direct those central procedures, nor are they directed by them. This means that a modular system may fail without disrupting the operations of central processes that do not depend on its output; and also that efficiently functioning central processes cannot remedy a module that is functioning inefficiently.

In short, the key deficit in dyslexia must be a vertical faculty rather than a horizontal faculty (see Fodor, 1983); that is, a domain-specific process

(Cossu & Marshall, 1986) rather than a process that operates across a variety of domains. Critically, modular processes can fail without necessarily degrading certain central processes of the type needed for adequate performance on intelligence tests. For this, and other reasons, many investigators have located the proximal locus of dyslexia at the word-recognition level (e.g., Aaron, 1989; Gough & Tunmer, 1986; Morrison, 1984, 1987; Perfetti, 1985; Siegel, 1985, 1988; Siegel & Faux, 1989; Stanovich, 1986b, 1988b; Vellutino, 1979). Recent research has indicated that at least in adults, word recognition is modular to a large extent (Gough, 1983; Seidenberg, 1985a, 1985b; Stanovich & West, 1983). That is, when reading clear, nondegraded text that is well within their reading ability, the word-recognition processes of adults appear to be relatively automatic and autonomous—executing without the need for supplementary contextual information. In addition, there is a developmental trend away from supplementing processes of direct visual access with additional knowledge such as contextual expectancies (Gough, 1983; Seidenberg, 1985a, 1985b; Stanovich & West, 1983; Stanovich, Nathan, West, & Vala-Rossi, 1985). One key to fluent reading then, appears to be the development of an autonomously functioning module at the word-recognition level.

Thus, much recent research has been directed at isolating the locus of the flaw in the word-recognition module of the dyslexic reader. Research in the past 10 years has focused intensively on phonological processing abilities. It is now well established that dyslexic children display deficits in various aspects of phonological processing. They have difficulty making explicit reports about sound segments at the phoneme level, they display naming difficulties, their utilization of phonological codes in short-term memory is inefficient, and their categorical perception of certain phonemes may not be normal (Cossu, Shankweiler, Liberman, Katz, & Tola, 1988; Kamhi & Catts, 1989; Liberman & Shankweiler, 1985; Lieberman, Meskill, Chatillon, & Schupack, 1985; Mann, 1986; Pennington, 1986; Pratt & Brady, 1988; Wagner & Torgesen, 1987; Werker & Tees, 1987; Williams, 1984, 1986; Wolf & Goodglass, 1986). Importantly, there is increasing evidence that the linkage from phonological processing ability to reading skill is a causal one (Bradley & Bryant, 1985; Liberman & Shankweiler, 1985; Lundberg, Frost, & Peterson, 1988; Maclean, Bradley, & Bryant, 1987; Stanovich, 1986b, 1988b; Wagner, 1988; Wagner & Torgesen, 1987). Both longitudinal correlation investigations (Bradley & Bryant, 1985; Maclean, Bryant, & Bradley, 1987; Perfetti, Beck, Bell, & Hughes, 1987; Stanovich, Cunningham, & Cramer, 1984; Torneus, 1984) and experimental investigations (Bradley & Bryant, 1985; Fox & Routh, 1984; Lundberg, Frost, & Peterson, 1988; Treiman & Baron, 1983) have indicated a causal connection. Presumably, lack of phonological sensitivity makes the learning of grapheme-to-phoneme correspondences very difficult.

The tendency to view the primary causal locus of dyslexia as deficient phonological processing (Bradley & Bryant, 1985; Kamhi & Catts, 1989; Liberman & Shankweiler, 1985; Wagner & Torgesen, 1987) has positive implications for future developments in early diagnosis. Some of the most diagnostic of the phonological processing tasks that are strongly predictive of reading failure can be administered to children at very young ages, before they attend school (Berninger, Thalberg, DeBruyn, & Smith, 1987; Blachman, 1989; Bradley & Bryant, 1985; Fox & Routh, 1975; Maclean et al., 1987; Stanovich, Cunningham & Cramer, 1984; Williams, 1984). As further work refines these tasks and they are developed as psychometric instruments, clinicians will have greater ability to diagnose reading disability at younger ages than is now possible. Importantly, early prevention efforts based on remediating phonological processes have generally met with success (Blachman, 1989; Bradley, 1987; Bradley & Bryant, 1985; Lundberg et al., 1988).

In short, there is now voluminous evidence indicating that phonological deficits are the basis of the dyslexic performance pattern. This is an oversimplification, since it ignores—at least temporarily—the possibility of core deficits in the realm of orthographic processing. I believe that there is growing evidence for the utility of distinguishing a group of dyslexics who have severe problems in accessing the lexicon on a visual/orthographic basis (see Stanovich, in press; Stanovich & West, 1989). Suggestive evidence comes from the work on acquired reading disability that has revealed the existence of surface dyslexia (Patterson, Marshall, & Coltheart, 1985) and from multivariate investigations indicating that efficient phonological processing is a necessary but not sufficient condition for attaining advanced levels of word recognition skill (Juel, Griffith, & Gough, 1986; Tunmer & Nesdale, 1985).

But as regards orthographic processing deficits, two crucial caveats are in order. First, there is a very large body of evidence indicating that this group of children must be numerically quite smaller than the group with phonological difficulties (Aaron, 1989; Freebody & Byrne, 1988; Gough & Hillinger, 1980; Liberman, 1982; Liberman & Shankweiler, 1985; Pennington, 1986; Perfetti, 1985; Rayner & Pollatsek, 1989; Vellutino, 1979). Logically, they must be very small in number since they have not obscured the identification of phonological problems in samples that were not preselected for subtypes. Secondly, I believe that the problem encountered by these children is not similar to the "visual perception" problems popular in the early history of the study of dyslexia, but now widely recognized to have been overstated (Aman & Singh, 1983; Morrison, Giordani, & Nagy, 1977; Stanovich, 1986a; Vellutino, 1979). The actual problems in orthographic processing must be much more subtle and localized than these older views suggested.

EVIDENCE FOR THE DIFFERENTIABILITY OF DYSLEXIC AND GARDEN-VARIETY POOR READERS

The critical processing differences that distinguish dyslexic readers from garden-variety poor readers can now be considered within the context of the two critical designs that were introduced earlier. First, the base-line performance of garden-variety poor readers has become considerably clarified in recent years. It appears that on a wide variety of reading-related cognitive tasks, the performance of garden-variety poor readers mirrors that of younger, skilled children who are reading at the same level (Stanovich, Nathan, & Vala-Rossi, 1986; Stanovich, Nathan, & Zolman, 1988). Compared to chronological-age peers, they do display deficits in phonological processing, but these are in addition to other processing and cognitive deficits (See Aaron, 1989).

In contrast, discrepancy-defined dyslexic readers are actually inferior in phonological processing compared to reading-level controls, but they do not have as many other cognitive deficits when compared with controls matched for chronological age (Baddeley et al., 1982; Bradley & Bryant, 1978; Holligan & Johnston, 1988; Kochnower et al., 1983; Olson et al., 1985; Olson et al., 1989; Siegel & Faux, 1989; Siegel & Ryan, 1988; Snowling, 1980, 1981; Snowling, Stackhouse, & Rack, 1986). Although there are some exceptions to this pattern (Beech & Harding, 1984; Treiman & Hirsch-Pasek, 1985), Olson, Wise, Conners, and Rack (in press) have recently reported a meta-analysis of this literature that explains most of the extant discrepancies.

In the reading–level–match design, the fact that the dyslexic subjects are matched with the younger controls on reading ability means that we might characterize the processing pattern of the dyslexic children as displaying compensatory processing. In a match based on reading comprehension, because of their inferior phonological skills, the older dyslexic children should display inferior word-recognition skill, but should also demonstrate superior vocabulary, memory, and real-world knowledge—the latter skills and knowledge presumably balancing the inferior word-recognition skills to yield the equivalent reading comprehension performance (see Aaron, 1989; Bruck, 1988). A match based on a word-recognition test should yield complementary results. The older dyslexic children matched at the word-recognition level, should display superior reading comprehension.

For the majority of dyslexic children with a phonological core deficit, a word-recognition match with a younger group of nondyslexic controls should reveal another pattern of ability tradeoffs: deficits in phonological sensitivity and in the phonological mechanisms that mediate lexical access, but superior visual/orthographic mechanisms and orthographic knowledge. Several investigations have shown this predicted pattern (Baddeley et al., 1982; Baron & Treiman, 1980; Bradley & Bryant, 1978; Kochnower et al., 1983; Olson et al., 1985; Snowling, 1980, 1981).

Compared with the data deriving from the reading-level design, it has been more difficult to differentiate dyslexic subjects in garden-variety designs. While some garden-variety comparisons have supported the idea of qualitative difference (Horn & O'Donnell, 1984; Jorm et al., 1986; Rutter & Yule, 1975; Silva et al., 1985), other investigations have demonstrated that it can often be surprisingly difficult to differentiate discrepancy-defined dyslexic readers from garden-variety poor readers (Fredman & Stevenson, 1988; Siegel, 1988; Taylor, Satz, & Friel, 1979).Nevertheless, some research has provided indications of the compensatory processing pattern when dyslexic subjects and garden-variety poor readers are matched on reading comprehension: poorer word recognition but superior "horizontal faculties" on the part of the dyslexic individuals (Aaron, 1989; Bloom et al., 1980; Fredman & Stevenson, 1988; Seidenberg et al., 1985). Similarly, dyslexic children matched with garden-variety controls on word-recognition skill have displayed superior reading comprehension and horizontal faculties (see Bloom, Wagner, Reskin, & Bergman, 1980; Ellis & Large, 1987; Jorm et al., 1986; Silva et al., 1985).

In the phonological-core variable difference model, the term variable differences refers to the key performance contrasts between the garden-variety and the dyslexic poor reader. As outlined above, the cognitive status of the garden-variety poor reader is well described by a developmental lag model (Stanovich et al., 1988). Cognitively, they are remarkably similar to younger children reading at the same level. A logical corollary of this pattern is that the garden-variety reader will have a wide variety of cognitive deficits when compared to controls matched for chronological age who are reading at normal levels. However, it is important to understand that the garden-variety poor reader does share the phonological problems of the dyslexic reader, and these deficits appear also to be a causal factor in their poor reading (Perfetti, 1985; Stanovich, 1986b). But for the garden-variety reader the deficits—relative to chronological age controls —extend into a variety of domains (see Ellis & Large, 1987), and some of these (e.g., vocabulary, language comprehension), may also be causally linked to reading comprehension. Such a pattern does not characterize the dyslexic subject, who has a deficit localized in the phonological core.

The phonological-core variable-difference model assumes multidimensional continuity for reading ability in general and for all its related cognitive subskills. That is, it conceives of all of the relevant distributions of reading-related cognitive skills as being continuously arrayed in a multidimensional space and not distributed in clusters. There is considerable evidence from a variety of different sources supporting such a continuity assumption (Ellis, 1985; Jorm, 1983; Olson et al., 1985; Scarborough, 1984; Seidenberg et al., 1985; Share, McGee, McKenzie, Williams, & Silva, 1987; Silva et al., 1985). However, the fact that the distribution is a graded continuum does not render the concept of dyslexia scientifically useless, as many critics would like to argue. Ellis (1985) has drawn the analogy with obesity. No one doubts that it is a very real health problem, despite the fact that it is operationally defined in a somewhat arbitrary way by choosing a criterion in a continuous distribution.

The framework of the phonological-core variable-difference model meshes nicely with the multidimensional continuum notion. Consider the following characterization: As we move in the multidimensional space—from the dyslexic to the garden-variety poor reader—we will move from a processing deficit localized in the phonological core to the global deficits of the developmentally lagging garden-variety poor reader. Thus, the actual cognitive differences that are displayed will be variable depending upon the type of poor reader who is the focus of the investigation. The differences on one end of the continuum will consist of deficits located only in the phonological core (the dyslexic subject) and will increase in number as we run through the intermediate cases that are less and less likely to pass strict psychometric criteria for dyslexia. Eventually we will reach the part of the multidimensional space containing relatively "pure" garden-variety poor readers who clearly will not qualify for the label dyslexic (by either regression or exclusionary criteria), will have a host of cognitive deficits, and will have the cognitively immature profile of a developmentally lagging individual.

This framework provides an explanation for why almost all processing investigations of reading disability have uncovered phonological deficits, but also why some investigations have found deficits in other areas as well (see Stanovich, 1988b). This outcome is predictable from the fact that the phonological-core variable-difference model posits that virtually all poor readers have a phonological deficit, but that other processing deficits emerge as one drifts in the multidimensional space from "pure" dyslexic individuals toward garden-variety poor readers. Thus, the model's straightforward prediction is that the studies that reveal a more isolated deficit will be those with more psychometrically select dyslexic readers. In short, the reading/IQ discrepancy of the subject populations should be significantly greater in studies displaying more specific deficits. Presumably, studies finding deficits extending beyond the phonological domain are in the "fuzzy" area of the multidimensional space and are picking up the increasing number of processing differences that extend beyond the phonological domain as one moves toward the garden-variety area of the space.

In summary, the research literature on the comparative cognitive characteristics of dyslexic children does provide some support for the construct validity of the concept of dyslexia. However, several critical caveats are in order. First, we must always be cognizant that continuity characterizes the distribution of reading ability and that of various reading-related subskills. We should not let connotations of discreteness creep into our thinking about reading disability merely because we have imposed a discrete classification system upon an underlying continuum of ability.

A second related point is that the continuity inherent in the distribution of reading skill will make it difficult to differentiate dyslexic children if liberal classification criteria are used. Indeed, the failure to separate dyslexic subjects from garden-variety controls in many investigations (e.g., Siegel, 1988; Taylor et al., 1979) still provides justification for the argument that IQ discrepancies have no useful role in discussions of reading difficulty (Seidenberg, Bruck, Fornarolo, & Backman, 1986; Siegel, 1988, 1989). While it has proven easier to demonstrate that dyslexic children are differentiable from younger controls in reading-level designs (see Olson et al., in press), it still appears that such a differentiation is only achieved when the dyslexic subjects are psychometrically very select—that is, when they display extremely severe discrepancies (see Stanovich et al., 1988). As has previously been argued: "Only by exercising some restraint and specificity in our application of the label will we arrive at a concept that has some scientific and educational utility" (p. 109, Stanovich, 1986a), "It is only by isolating the true outliers that researchers can hope to obtain the evidence for specificity that the dyslexia concept requires if it is to be of scientific and practical utility.... Groups who have pushed for ever-more-inclusive definitions of dyslexia ... are indirectly undermining the concept. The wider the net that is cast, the greater will be the difficulties in distinguishing dyslexia from other educational designations (e.g., borderline retardation). Lack of restraint in applying the label is in part responsible for the failure of researchers to demonstrate consistently that the performance profiles of disabled subjects differ reliably from those of other poor readers" (p. 387, Stanovich, 1986b). It is noteworthy that the seminal Rutter and Yule (1975) epidemiological investigation—one of the more successful demonstrations of differences in a garden-variety control design—adopted a criterion that resulted in approximately 3.7% of their sample being classified as specifically reading retarded.

LINGERING PROBLEMS OF CONSTRUCT VALIDITY

While the review of research on the cognitive differentiability of dyslexic children just concluded does seem to support the construct validity of the concept of dyslexia, there is still inadequate data on other foundational assumptions. For example, outside of the pioneering work of Lyon (1985), there is very little data on differential response to treatment. There are, for instance, no good data indicating that discrepancy-defined dyslexics respond differently to various educational treatments than do garden-variety poor readers of the same age or than younger nondyslexic children reading at the same level (Pressley & Levin, 1987; van der Wissel, 1987). Although more data exist on the issue of differential developmental growth curves for reading, the data is contradictory. Rutter and Yule (1975) found a differential prognosis for specifically disabled and garden-variety poor readers. The garden-variety poor readers displayed greater growth in reading but less growth in arithmetic ability than the specifically disabled children. However, this finding of differential reading growth rates has not been replicated in some other studies (Labuda & DeFries, 1989; McKinney, 1987; Share et al., 1987; van der Wissel & Zegers, 1985).

Until convincing data on these two issues are provided, the utility of the concept of developmental reading disorder will continue to be challenged because the field of reading disabilities will have no rebuttal to assertions that it is more educationally and clinically relevant to define reading disability without reference to IQ discrepancy (Seidenberg et al., 1986; Siegel, 1988, 1989). For example, Share, McGee, and Silva (1989) still see fit to argue that "It may be timely to formulate a concept of reading disability which is independent of any consideration of IQ. Unless it can be shown to have some predictive value for the nature of treatment or treatment outcome, considerations of IQ should be discarded in discussions of reading difficulties" (p. 100). No amount of clinical evidence, case studies, or anecdotal reports will substitute for the large-scale experimental demonstrations that, as compared with groups of garden-variety poor readers, discrepancy-defined poor readers show differential response to treatment and prognosis, and for further evidence that the reading-related cognitive profiles of these two groups are reliably different.

DEEPER CONCEPTUAL PROBLEMS: THE ISSUE OF INTELLIGENCE

Unfortunately, the conceptual problems surrounding the concept of reading disability do not end with considerations of discrepancy measurement and validation. Increasingly, researchers are raising questions not merely about the statistical procedures necessary to define severe discrepancy reliably, but with the foundational benchmark from which discrepancy is measured: intelligence (Hessler, 1987; Siegel, 1988, 1989). Indeed, it is surprising that for so long the concept of intelligence received so little discussion in the literature on learning disabilities. Researchers and practitioners in this field seem not to have realized that it is a foundational concept for the study of reading disability. As currently defined, IQ is a superordinate construct for the classification of a child as reading disabled. Without a clear conception of the construct of intelligence, the notion of a reading disability, as currently defined, dissolves into incoherence.

The problem is that one would be hard-pressed to find a concept more controversial than intelligence in all of psychology. It has been the subject of dispute for decades, and this shows no signs of abating. Current work on individual differences in intelligent functioning continues to produce exciting findings and interesting theories (Baron, 1985; Ceci, in press; Ceci & Liker, 1986; Sternberg, 1985, 1988), but no consensual view of the intelligence concept (Sternberg & Detterman, 1986). Even though much progress has been made in both empirical and theoretical domains, quite fundamental disputes remain. For example, some investigators have recently emphasized more contextualized approaches to the study of intelligence (Ceci, in press; Ceci & Liker, 1986; Sternberg, 1985, 1988; Sternberg & Wagner, 1986), whereas others have been advocating more decontextualized biological approaches (Vernon, 1987).

Yet despite the controversy surrounding intelligence in the cognitive, developmental, and psychometric literature, it was adopted as a foundational construct for the definition of dyslexia. The choice of IQ test performance as the base line from which to measure achievement discrepancies was accepted by teachers, clinicians, professional organizations, and government agencies in the absence of much critical discussion or research evidence. Until quite recently the field seems never to have grappled very seriously with the question of why the benchmark should have been IQ (although see Reed [1970] for an early discussion of the complications involved in the discrepancy definition).

One reason why professional assent to the use of IQ test scores in the discrepancy definition was given so readily derived from the belief that IQ scores were valid measures of intellectual potential. One major problem, however, was that most psychometricians, developmental psychologists, and educational psychologists long ago gave up the belief that IQ test scores measured potential in any valid sense. Indeed, standard texts in educational measurement and assessment routinely warn against interpreting IQ scores as measures of intellectual potential (Anastasi, 1988; Cronbach, 1984; Thorndike, 1963). As Eisenberg (1978) argues, "There is no better reason for assuming that the measured IQ represents intellectual potential than that reading level reflects reading potential" (p. 37).

At their best, IQ test scores are gross measures of current cognitive functioning (Detterman, 1982). Indeed, many theorists would dispute even this characterization. Siegel (1988, 1989), for example, attacks the representativeness of several of the typical tasks that are on IQ tests and gives the outlines of the objections of many theorists. As Lyon (1987) notes "Tacitly ingrained within this assumption is the notion that learning-disabled children can attain levels of achievement commensurate with their IQ if they were assessed and taught properly. However, both the assumption of discrepancy and the implicit message that it connotes stand on shaky conceptual and logical grounds.... we do not know whether psychometric discrepancies tell us anything of value about how children respond to instruction" (pp. 78–79).

But even if we were to concede that the idea of measuring aptitude/achievement discrepancies is a valid educational procedure, there are other more educationally relevant choices for a benchmark than IQ. As the work of several investigators has suggested (Aaron, 1989; Carver, 1981; Gillet & Temple, 1986; Hood & Dubert, 1983; Royer, Kulhavy, Lee, & Peterson, 1986; Spring & French, 1990; Sticht & James, 1984), measuring the discrepancy between reading comprehension and listening comprehension would seem to have been a more logical choice in the first place. Certainly a discrepancy calculated in this way seems to have more face validity and educational relevance than the traditional procedure (Aaron, 1989; Durrell & Hayes, 1969; Spache, 1981). Children who understand written material less well than they would understand the same material if it were read to them appear to be in need of educational intervention. Presumably, their listening comprehension exceeds their reading comprehension because word-recognition processes are inefficient and are a "bottleneck" that impedes comprehension (Perfetti, 1985; Perfetti & Lesgold, 1977).

There are, of course, several obstacles to implementing procedures of measuring reading disability by referring to discrepancies from listening comprehension. For example, while several individual measures of listening comprehension ability have been published (CTB/McGraw-Hill, 1985; Durrell & Hayes, 1969; Spache, 1981), it may be the case that none have been standardized across the range of ages, or attained the psychometric properties, to serve as an adequate measure from which to assess discrepancy (Johnson, 1988; but see Aaron, 1989). Nevertheless, it may be worth the research effort to develop such instruments further, because assessing discrepancies from listening comprehension could help to mitigate many of the paradoxes that plague discrepancy measures based on the more nebulous concept of intelligence. For example, it has often been pointed out that changes in the characteristics of the IQ test being used will result in somewhat different subgroups of children being identified as discrepant and also alter the types of processing deficits that they will display in comparison studies (e.g., Bowers, Steffy, & Tate, 1988; Lindgren, DeRenzi, & Richman, 1985; Reed, 1970; Shankweiler, Crain, Bradley, & Macaruso, in press; Siegel & Heaven, 1986; Stanley, Smith, & Powys, 1982; Torgesen, 1985; Vellutino, 1978).

Also, despite many recommendations that performance IQ measures provide "fairer" measures of the reading potential of disabled children (e.g., Siegel & Heaven, 1986; Stanovich, 1986a), it is not at all clear that the spatial abilities, fluid intelligence, and problem-solving abilities tapped by most performance tests provide the best measures of the potential to comprehend verbal material. To the contrary, it would appear that verbally loaded measures and/or listening comprehension would provide the best estimates of how much a dyslexic child could get from written text if their deficient decoding skills were to be remediated. As Hessler (1987) notes: "There are different types of intelligence, and they predict academic achievement differently.... In fact, the performance score accounts for so little academic achievement that there is reason to question its relevance for use as an ability measure to predict academic achievement. It is therefore a mistake to use any test of intelligence as an ability measure for predicting academic achievement in a severe discrepancy analysis simply because it is called a test of intelligence, cognitive ability, scholastic aptitude, or whatever, without demonstrating some ability to predict academic achievement" (p. 45). Consistent with this interpretation, van der Wissel (1987) has demonstrated via data simulation that the extent to which an IQ subtest separates dyslexic from garden-variety children is *inversely* related to how highly the subtest correlates with reading achievement. It is a paradoxical situation indeed when the indicators that best make this subgroup discrimination are those that do not relate to the criterion performance that drew professional attention in the first place: reading failure.

Of course, the common recommendation against the use of verbally loaded tests stems from the either tacit or explicit assumption that the reading difficulties themselves may lead to depressed performance on such measures. Some recognition of these "Matthew effects" involved in reading (that is rich-get-richer and poor-get-poorer effects, see Stanovich, 1986b) is thus implicit in this recommendation. But such a suggestion tacitly undermines the whole notion of discrepancy measurement by weakening the distinction between aptitude and achievement; for it serves to remind us that while the logic of the learning disabilities field has implicitly given all the causal power to IQ—that is, it is reading that is considered discrepant from IQ rather than IQ that is discrepant from reading—this is a vast oversimplification, because there are potent effects running in both directions. As Senf (1986) notes, "Logically, we are imputing more validity to the predictor (IQ) than we are to the resulting behavior (achievement)" (p. 39). Doehring, Trites, Patel, Fiedorowicz (1981) argue similarly: "The usual definitions of developmental dyslexia do not recognize the interactive development of reading, language, and cognition.... Cognitive and language abilities essential to reading could be excluded from the measures used to define normal intelligence, but we will not be entirely sure what these abilities are until there is a comprehensive theory of human ability that provides a firmer basis for defining intelligence. Even then we will have to recognize the probability that the difficulty in learning to read has, itself, impaired the development of important aspects of intelligence such as vocabulary and comprehension" (p. 6).

Much evidence has now accumulated to indicate that reading itself is a moderately powerful determinant of vocabulary growth, verbal intelligence, and general comprehension ability (Juel, 1988; Share & Silva, 1987; Share et al., 1989; Stanovich, 1986b; Stanovich & West, 1989). These Matthew effects highlight a further problematic aspect of discrepancy-based classification. Do we really want to withhold certain types of educational treatments from children whose poor reading is accompanied by equally subpar IQs (or listening comprehension) when we know that the poor reading may at least in part be a direct cause of the low IQs and listening-comprehension ability? The possibility of a Matthew effect precludes us from assuming that the poor listening comprehension or verbal intelligence could not be enhanced by better reading.

As Hessler argues: "Using a nonverbal test of intelligence because an individual has better nonverbal cognitive abilities than verbal cognitive abilities does not, of course, remove the importance of verbal processing and knowledge structures in academic achievement; it only obscures their importance and perhaps provides unrealistic expectations for an individual's academic achievement" (p. 46). Lyon (1987) presses a similar point: "Many samples of learning-disabled children are selected for study on a basis of a discrepancy between the Performance IQ derived from the WISC-R and measures of academic achievement. Unfortunately, the Performance IQ, and even the Full Scale IQ, bear little psychometric relationship to measures of academic achievement, particularly in the oral language, reading, and written language domains, thus negating the predictive power attributed to discrepancies between measures of nonverbal intelligence and school learning" (pp. 78–79). If we do not like some of the logical implications of such arguments, then it becomes even more useful to move toward measuring discrepancies from listening comprehension and to move away from implicating conceptions of intelligence in our definitions of dyslexia.

SUMMARY AND CONCLUSIONS

Since the heart of most definitions of developmental dyslexia is the assessment of a severe discrepancy between aptitude and achievement, it is not surprising that considerable research attention has focused on validating the appropriateness of the severe discrepancy criterion. While much progress has been made in eliminating the statistical artifacts in how we classify children as having aptitude/achievement discrepancies, it has been much more difficult to demonstrate the construct validity of discrepancy as a basis for classification. However, discrepancy-based classification has recently been bolstered by long overdue research indicating that it is possible to differentiate dyslexia from garden-variety poor reading. However, this trend is stronger in studies employing reading-level matches with younger children than it is in studies employing garden-variety controls of the same chronological age as the dyslexic children. Also, successful differentiation is only achieved when fairly strict psychometric criteria are employed. Thus, further work on the cognitive differentiability of discrepancy-defined poor readers is still urgently needed.

It is also unfortunate that we still have no good evidence that dyslexic children differ either in their prognosis or their response to treatment from poor readers without severe discrepancies. A further problem is that there are a variety of conceptual and psychometric paradoxes surrounding the concept of intelligence that by logical necessity transfer to reading disability definitions that are based on such a construct. It was suggested that researchers further explore the possibility of using listening comprehension as perhaps a more ecologically valid and less controversial base line from which to measure reading discrepancies. Some recent research on the processing of oral versus written language will aid in our exploration of the potential of such an alternative base line (Aaron, 1989; Carver, 1981; Daneman & Blennerhassett, 1984; Danks & End, 1987; Hood & Dubert, 1983; Royer et al., 1986; Spring & French, 1990; Sticht & James, 1984).

The increasing tendency to locate the proximal cause of reading disability in the language domain (see Kamhi & Catts, 1989) has potential implications for assessment. Processing problems at the phonological level have been increasingly singled out as the most salient cause of reading disabilities. Such a localization for the disability raises the possibility of assessing, before school entry, the critical phonological skills that are necessary prerequisites to the development of adequate reading skill. Successful remediation based on such early assessment is already an empirically demonstrated fact (Blachman, 1989; Bradley, 1987; Bradley & Bryant, 1985; Lundberg et al., 1988).

REFERENCES

Aaron, P. G. (1989). *Dyslexia and hyperlexia*. Dordrecht, The Netherlands: Kluwer Academic.
Aman, M., & Singh, N. (1983). Specific reading disorders: Concepts of etiology

reconsidered. In K. Gadow & I. Bialer (Eds.), *Advances in learning and behavioral disabilities* (Vol. 2, pp. 1–47). Greenwich, CT: JAI Press.
Anastasi, A. (1988). *Psychological testing* (6th ed.). New York: Macmillan.
Applebee, A. N. (1971). Research in reading retardation: Two critical problems. *Journal of Child Psychology and Psychiatry, 12,* 91–113.
Baddeley, A. D., Ellis, N. C., Miles, T. R., & Lewis, V. J. (1982). Developmental and acquired dyslexia: A comparison. *Cognition, 11,* 185–199.
Baddeley, A. D., Logie, R., & Ellis, N. C. (1988). Characteristics of developmental dyslexia. *Cognition, 30,* Austin, TX: PRO-ED. 197–227.
Baron, J. (1985). *Rationality and intelligence.* Cambridge: Cambridge University Press.
Baron, J., & Treiman, R. (1980). Use of orthography in reading and learning to read. In J. F. Kavanagh & R. L. Venezky (Eds.), *Orthography, reading, and dyslexia.*
Bateman, B. (1979). Teaching reading to learning disabled and other hard-to-teach children. In L. Resnick & P. Weaver (Eds.), *Theory and practice of early reading* (Vol. 1, pp. 227–259). Hillsdale, NJ: Erlbaum.
Beech, J., & Harding, L. (1984). Phonemic processing and the poor reader from a developmental lag viewpoint. *Reading Research Quarterly, 19,* 357–366.
Berninger, V. W., Thalberg, S. P., DeBruyn, I., & Smith, R. (1987). Preventing reading disabilities by assessing and remediating phonemic skills. *School Psychology Review, 16,* 554–565.
Blachman, B. A. (1989). Phonological awareness and word recognition: Assessment and intervention. In A. G. Kamhi & H. W. Catts (Eds.), *Reading disabilities* (pp. 133–158). Austin, TX: PRO-ED.
Bloom, A., Wagner, M., Reskin, L., & Bergman, A. (1980). A comparison of intellectually delayed and primary reading disabled children on measures of intelligence and achievement. *Journal of Clinical Psychology, 36,* 788–790.
Board of Trustees of the Council for Learning Disabilities. (1987). The CLD position statements. *Journal of Learning Disabilities, 20,* 349–350.
Bowers, P., Steffy, R., & Tate, E. (1988). Comparison of the effects of IQ control methods on memory and naming speed predictors of reading disability. *Reading Research Quarterly, 23,* 304–319.
Bradley, L. (1987, December). *Categorising sounds, early intervention and learning to read: A follow-up study.* Paper presented at the meeting of the British Psychological Society, London.
Bradley, L., & Bryant, P. E. (1978). Difficulties in auditory organization as a possible cause of reading backwardness. *Nature, 271,* 746–747.
Bradley, L., & Bryant, P. E. (1985). *Rhyme and reason in reading and spelling.* Ann Arbor: University of Michigan Press.
Bruck, M. (1988). The word recognition and spelling of dyslexic children. *Reading Research Quarterly, 23,* 51–69.
Bryant, P. E., & Goswami, U. (1986). Strengths and weaknesses of the reading level design: A comment on Backman, Mamen, and Ferguson. *Psychological Bulletin, 100,* 101–103.
Carver, R. P. (1981). *Reading comprehension and reading theory.* Springfield, IL: Charles C Thomas.
Ceci, S. J. (1986). *Handbook of cognitive, social, and neuropsychological aspects of learning disabilities* (Vol. 1). Hillsdale, NJ: Erlbaum.
Ceci, S. J. (in press). *A bio-ecological approach to intelligence.* Englewood Cliffs, NJ: Prentice-Hall.
Ceci, S. J., & Liker, J. K. (1986). A day at the races: A study of IQ, expertise, and cognitive complexity. *Journal of Experimental Psychology: General, 115,* 255–266.

Coles, G. S. (1978). The learning-disabilities test battery: Empirical and social issues. *Harvard Educational Review, 48,* 313–340.
Coles, G. S. (1987). *The learning mystique.* New York: Pantheon.
Cone, T. E., & Wilson, L. R. (1981). Quantifying a severe discrepancy: A critical analysis. *Learning Disability Quarterly, 4,* 359–371.
Cossu, G., & Marshall, J. C. (1986). Theoretical implications of the hyperlexia syndrome: Two new Italian cases. *Cortex, 22,* 579–589.
Cossu, G., Shankweiler, D., Liberman, I. Y., Katz, L., & Tola, G. (1988). Awareness of phonological segments and reading ability in Italian children. *Applied Psycholinguistics, 9,* 1–16.
Critchley, M. (1970). *The dyslexic child.* London: William Heinemann Medical Books.
Cronbach, L. J. (1984). *Essentials of psychological testing* (4th ed.). New York: Harper & Row.
CTB/McGraw-Hill. (1985). *Listening test.* Monterey, CA: CTB/McGraw-Hill.
Daneman, M., & Blennerhassett, A. (1984). How to assess the listening comprehension skills of prereaders. *Journal of Educational Psychology, 76,* 1372–1381.
Danks, J. H., & End., L. J. (1987). Processing strategies for reading and listening. In R. Horowitz & S. J. Samuels (Eds.), *Comprehending oral and written language* (pp. 271–294). San Diego: Academic Press.
Detterman, D. (1982). Does "g" exist? *Intelligence, 6,* 99–108.
Doehring, D. G. (1978). The tangled web of behavioral research on developmental dyslexia. In A. L. Benton & D. Pearl (Eds.), *Dyslexia* (pp. 123–135). New York: Oxford University Press.
Doehring, D. G., Trites, R. L., Patel, P. G., & Fiedorowicz, C. A. M. (1981). *Reading disabilities: The interaction of reading, language, and neuropsychological deficits.* New York: Academic Press.
Durrell, D., & Hayes, M. (1969). *Durrell listening-reading series.* New York: Psychological Corporation.
Eisenberg, L. (1978). Definitions of dyslexia: Their consequences for research and policy. In A. L. Benton & D. Pearl (Eds.), *Dyslexia* (pp. 29–42). New York: Oxford University Press.
Eisenberg, L. (1979). Reading disorders: Strategies for recognition and management. *Bulletin of the Orton Society, 29,* 39–55.
Ellis, A. W. (1985). The cognitive neuropsychology of developmental (and acquired) dyslexia: A critical survey. *Cognitive Neuropsychology, 2,* 169–205.
Ellis, N., & Large, B. (1987). The development of reading: As you seek so shall you find. *British Journal of Psychology, 78,* 1–28.
Fodor, J. (1983). *Modularity of Mind.* Cambridge: MIT Press.
Fox, B., & Routh, D. K. (1975). Analyzing spoken language into words, syllables, and phonemes: A developmental study. *Journal of Psycholinguistic Research, 4,* 331–342.
Fox, B., & Routh, D. K. (1984). Phonemic analysis and synthesis as word attack skills: Revisited. *Journal of Educational Psychology, 76,* 1059–1064.
Frankenberger, W., & Harper, J. (1987). States' criteria and procedures for identifying learning disabled children: A comparison of 1981/82 and 1985/86 guidelines. *Journal of Learning Disabilities, 20,* 118–121.
Fredman, G., & Stevenson, J. (1988). Reading processes in specific reading retarded and reading backward 13-year-olds. *British Journal of Developmental Psychology, 6,* 97–108.
Freebody, P., & Byrne, B. (1988). Word-reading strategies in elementary school children: Relations to comprehension, reading time, and phonemic awareness. *Reading Research Quarterly, 23,* 441–453.

Gardner, H. (1983). *Frames of mind*. New York: Basic Books.
Gaskins, I. (1982). Let's end the reading disabilities/learning disabilities debate. *Journal of Learning Disabilities, 15*, 81–83.
Gillet, J. W., & Temple, C. (1986). *Understanding reading problems: Assessment and instruction* (2nd ed.). Boston: Little, Brown.
Goswami, U., & Bryant, P. E. (1989). The interpretation of studies using the reading level design. *Journal of Reading Behavior, 21*, 413–424.
Gough, P. B. (1983). Context, form, and interaction. In K. Rayner (Ed.), *Eye movements in reading* (pp. 203–211). New York: Academic Press.
Gough, P. B., & Hillinger, M. L. (1980). Learning to read: An unnatural act. *Bulletin of the Orton Society, 30*, 171–176.
Gough, P. B., & Tunmer, W. E. (1986). Decoding, reading, and reading disability. *Remedial and Special Education, 7*, 6–10.
Hall, J., & Humphreys, M. (1982). Research on specific learning disabilities: Deficits and remediation. *Topics in Learning and Learning Disabilities, 2*, 68–78.
Hammill, D., Leigh, J. McNutt, G., & Larsen, S. (1981). A new definition of learning disabilities. *Learning Disability Quarterly, 4*, 336–342.
Hessler, G. L. (1987). Educational issues surrounding severe discrepancy. *Learning Disabilities Research, 3*, 43–49.
Hinshelwood, J. (1895). Word-blindness and visual memory. *Lancet, 2*, 1564–1570.
Holligan, C., & Johnston, R. S. (1988). The use of phonological information by good and poor readers in memory and reading tasks. *Memory & Cognition, 16*, 522–532.
Hood, J., & Dubert, L. A. (1983). Decoding as a component of reading comprehension among secondary students. *Journal of Reading Behavior, 15*, 51–61.
Horn, W. F., & O'Donnell, J. (1984). Early identification of learning disabilities: A comparison of two methods. *Journal of Educational Psychology, 76*, 1106–1118.
Hynd, G., & Semrud-Clikeman, M. (1989). Dyslexia and neurodevelopmental pathology: Relationships to cognition, intelligence, and reading skill acquisition. *Journal of Learning Disabilities, 22*, 204–220.
Jackson, N. E., & Butterfield, E. C. (1989). Reading Level Match Designs; Myths and Realities. *Journal of Reading Behavior, 21*, 387–412.
Johnson, D. J. (1988). Review of research on specific reading, writing, and mathematics disorders. In J. F. Kavanagh & T. J. Truss (Eds.), *Learning disabilities: Proceedings of the national conference* (pp. 79–163). Parkston, MD: York Press.
Jorm, A. (1983). Specific reading retardation and working memory: A review. *British Journal of Psychology, 74*, 311–342.
Jorm, A., Share, D., Maclean, R., & Matthews, R. (1986). Cognitive factors at school entry predictive of specific reading retardation and general reading backwardness: A research note. *Journal of Child Psychology and Psychiatry, 27*, 45–54.
Juel, C. (1988). Learning to read and write: A longitudinal study of 54 children from first through fourth grades. *Journal of Educational Psychology, 80*, 437–447.
Juel, C., Griffith, P. L., & Gough, P. B. (1986). Acquisition of literacy: A longitudinal study of children in first and second grade. *Journal of Educational Psychology, 78*, 243–255.
Kamhi, A., & Catts, H. (1989). *Reading disabilities: A developmental language perspective*. Austin, TX: PRO-ED.
Kavale. K. A. (1987). Theoretical issues surrounding severe discrepancy. *Learning Disabilities Research, 3*, 12–20.
Kavale, K., A. & Nye, C. (1981). Identification criteria for learning disabilities: A survey of the research literature. *Learning Disability Quarterly, 4*, 363–388.
Kavanagh, J. F., & Truss, T. J. (Eds.). (1988). *Learning disabilities: Proceedings of the national conference*. Parkston, MD: York Press.
Kirk, S. (1963). *Behavioral diagnosis and remediation of learning disabilities*. Paper

presented at the Conference on the Exploration into the Problems of the Perceptually Handicapped Child. Evanston, IL: Fund for the Perceptually Handicapped Child.

Kirk, S., & Elkins, J. (1975). Characteristics of children enrolled in the child service demonstration centers. *Journal of Learning Disabilities, 8*, 630–637.

Kochnower, J., Richardson, E., & DiBenedetto, B. (1983). A comparison of the phonic decoding ability of normal and learning disabled children. *Journal of Learning Disabilities, 16*, 348–351.

Labuda, M., & DeFries, J. C. (1989). Differential prognosis of reading-disabled children as a function of gender, socioeconomic status, IQ, and severity: A longitudinal study. *Reading and Writing: An Interdisciplinary Journal, 1*, 25–36.

Lerner, J. (1975). Remedial reading and learning disabilities: Are they the same or different? *Journal of Special Education, 9*, 119–131.

Lerner, J. (1985). *Learning disabilities* (4th ed.). Boston: Houghton Mifflin.

Liberman, I. (1982). A language-oriented view of reading and its disabilities. In H. Mykelbust (Ed.), *Progress in learning disabilities* (Vol. 5, pp. 81–101). New York: Grune & Stratton.

Liberman, I. Y., & Shankweiler, D. (1985). Phonology and the problems of learning to read and write. *Remedial and Special Education, 6*, 8–17.

Lieberman, P., Meskill, R. H., Chatillon, M., & Schupack, H. (1985). Phonetic speech perception deficits in dyslexia. *Journal of Speech and Hearing Research, 28*, 480–486.

Lindgren, S. D., De Renzi, E., & Richman, L. C. (1985). Cross-national comparisons of developmental dyslexia in Italy and the United States. *Child Development, 56*, 1404–1417.

Lundberg, I., Frost, J., & Peterson, O. (1988). Effects of an extensive program for stimulating phonological awareness in preschool children. *Reading Research Quarterly, 23*, 263–284.

Lyon, G. R. (1985). Educational validation studies of learning disability subtypes. In B. P. Rourke (Ed.), *Neuropsychology of learning disabilities* (pp. 228–253). New York: Guilford Press.

Lyon, G. R. (1987). Learning disabilities research: False starts and broken promises. In S. Vaughn & C. S. Bos (Eds.), *Research in learning disabilities* (pp. 69–85). Austin, TX: PRO-ED.

Maclean, M., Bryant, P., & Bradley, L. (1987). Rhymes, nursery rhymes, and reading in early childhood. *Merrill-Parker Quarterly, 33*, 255–281.

Mann, V. (1986). Why some children encounter reading problems. In J. Torgesen & B. Wong (Eds.), *Psychological and educational perspectives on learning disabilities* (pp. 133–159). New York: Academic Press.

McKinney, J. D. (1987). Research on the identification of learning-disabled children: Perspectives on changes in educational policy. In S. Vaughn & C. Bos (Eds.), *Research in learning disabilities* (pp. 215–233). Austin, TX: PRO-ED.

Morgan, W. P. (1896). A case of congenital word-blindness. *British Medical Journal, 2*, 1378.

Morrison, F. (1984). Word decoding and rule-learning in normal and disabled readers. *Remedial and Special Education, 5*, 20–27.

Morrison, F. J. (1987). The nature of reading disability: Toward an integrative framework. In S. Ceci (Ed.), *Handbook of cognitive, social, and neuropsychological aspects of learning disabilities* (pp. 33–62). Hillsdale, NJ: Erlbaum.

Morrison, F., Giordani, B., & Nagy, J. (1977). Reading disability: An information processing analysis. *Science, 196*, 77–79.

Olson, R., Kliegl, R., Davidson, B., & Foltz, G. (1985). Individual and developmental differences in reading disability. In T. Waller (Ed.), *Reading research: Advances in theory and practice* (Vol. 4, pp. 1–64). London: Academic Press.

Olson, R., Wise, B., Conners, F., & Rack, J. (in press). Organization, heritability, and remediation of component word recognition and language skills in disabled readers. In T. Carr & B. A. Levy (Eds.), *Reading and its development: Component skills approaches*. New York: Academic Press.

Olson, R., Wise, B., Conners, F., Rack, J., & Fulker, D. (1989). Specific deficits in component reading and language skills: Genetic and environmental influences. *Journal of Learning Disabilities, 22*, 339–348.

Orton, S. T. (1925). "Word-blindness" in school children. *Archives of Neurology and Psychiatry, 14*, 581–615.

Orton, S. T. (1928). Specific reading disability—strephosymbolia. *Journal of the American Medical Association, 90*, 1095–1099.

Orton, S. T. (1937). *Reading, writing, and speech problems in children*. New York: Norton.

Patterson, K., Marshall, J., & Coltheart, M. (1985). *Surface dyslexia*. London: Erlbaum.

Pennington, B. F. (1986). Issues in the diagnosis and phenotype analysis of dyslexia: Implications for family studies. In S. D. Smith (Ed.), *Genetics and learning disabilities* (pp. 69–96). Austin, TX: PRO-ED.

Perfetti, C. A. (1985). *Reading ability*. New York: Oxford University Press.

Perfetti, C. A., Beck, I., Bell, L., & Hughes, C. (1987). Phonemic knowledge and learning to read are reciprocal: A longitudinal study of first grade children. *Merrill-Palmer Quarterly, 33*, 283–319.

Perfetti, C. A., & Lesgold, A. M. (1977). Discourse comprehension and sources of individual differences. In M. Just & P. Carpenter (Eds.), *Cognitive processes in comprehension* (pp. 141–183). Hillsdale, NJ: Erlbaum.

Pratt, A. C., & Brady, S. (1988). Relation of phonological awareness to reading disability in children and adults. *Journal of Educational Psychology, 80*, 319–323.

Pressley, M., & Levin, J. R. (1987). Elaborative learning strategies for the inefficient learner. In S. J. Ceci (Ed.), *Handbook of cognitive, social, and neuropsychological aspects of learning disabilities* (Vol. 2, pp. 175–212). Hillsdale, NJ: Erlbaum.

Rayner, K., & Pollatsek, A. (1989). *The psychology of reading*. Englewood Cliffs, NJ: Prentice-Hall.

Read, J. C. (1970). The deficits of retarded readers—Fact or artifact? *The Reading Teacher, 23*, 347–357.

Reynolds, C. R. (1981). The fallacy of "two years below grade level for age" as a diagnostic criterion for reading disorders. *Journal of School Psychology, 19*, 350–358.

Reynolds, C. R. (1984–1985). Critical measurement issues in learning disabilities. *Journal of Special Education, 18*, 451–475.

Reynolds, C. R. (1985). Measuring the aptitude-achievement discrepancy in learning disability diagnosis. *Remedial and Special Education, 6*, 37–55.

Reynolds, C. R., & Stowe, M. (1985). *Severe discrepancy analysis*. Philadelphia: TRAIN, Inc.

Royer, J., Kulhavy, R., Lee, S., & Peterson, S. (1986). The relationship between reading and listening comprehension. *Educational and Psychological Research, 6*, 299–314.

Rutter, M. (1978). Prevalence and types of dyslexia. In A. Benton & D. Pearl (Eds.), *Dyslexia: An appraisal of current knowledge* (pp. 5–28). New York: Oxford University Press.

Rutter, M., & Yule, W. (1975). The concept of specific reading retardation. *Journal of Child Psychology and Psychiatry, 16*, 181–197.

Scarborough, H. S. (1984). Continuity between childhood dyslexia and adult reading. *British Journal of Psychology, 75*, 329–348.

Seidenberg, M. (1985a). Lexicon as module. *Behavioral and Brain Sciences, 8*, 31–32.
Seidenberg, M. (1985b). The time course of information activation and utilization in visual word recognition. In D. Besner, T. Waller, & G. MacKinnon (Eds.), *Reading research: Advances in theory and practice* (Vol. 5, pp. 199–252). New York: Academic Press.
Seidenberg, M. S., Bruck, M., Fornarolo, G., & Backman, J. (1985). Word recognition processes of poor and disabled readers. Do they necessarily differ? *Applied Psycholinguists, 6*, 161–180.
Seidenberg, M. S., Bruck, M., Fornarolo, G., & Backman, J. (1986). Who is dyslexic? Reply to Wolf. *Applied Psycholinguistics, 7*, 77–84.
Senf, G. F. (1986). LD Research in sociological and scientific perspective. In J. K. Torgeson & B. Y. L. Wong (Eds.), *Psychological and educational perspectives on learning disabilities* (pp. 27–53). Orlando, FL: Academic Press.
Shankweiler, D., Crain, S., Brady, S., & Macaruso, P. (in press). Identifying the causes of reading disability. In P. B. Gough (Ed.), *Reading acquisition*. Hillsdale, NJ: Erlbaum.
Share, D. L., McGee, R., McKenzie, D., Williams, S., & Silva, P. A. (1987). Further evidence relating to the distinction between specific reading retardation and general reading backwardness. *British Journal of Developmental Psychology, 5*, 35–44.
Share, D. L., McGee, R., & Silva, P. (1989). IQ and reading progress: A test of the capacity notion of IQ. *Journal of the American Academy of Child and Adolescent Psychiatry, 28*, 97–100.
Share, D. L., & Silva, P. A. (1987). Language deficits and specific reading retardation: Cause or effect? *British Journal of Disorders of Communication, 22*, 219–226.
Shepard, L. (1980). An evaluation of the regression discrepancy method for identifying children with learning disabilities. *Journal of Special Education, 14*, 79–91.
Shepherd, M. J., Gelzheiser, L. M., & Solar, R. A. (1985). How good is the evidence for a production deficiency among learning disabled students? *Journal of Educational Psychology, 77*, 553–561.
Siegel, L. S. (1985). Psycholinguistic aspects of reading disabilities. In L. Siegel & F. Morrison (Eds.), *Cognitive development in atypical children* (pp. 45–65). New York: Springer-Verlag.
Siegel, L. S. (1988). Evidence that IQ scores are irrelevant to the definition and analysis of reading disability. *Canadian Journal of Psychology, 42*, 201–215.
Siegel, L. S. (1989). IQ is irrelevant to the definition of learning disabilities. *Journal of Learning Disabilities, 22*, 469–478.
Siegel, L. S., & Faux, D. (1989). Acquisition of certain grapheme-phoneme correspondences in normally achieving and disabled readers. *Reading and Writing: An Interdisciplinary Journal, 1*, 37–52.
Siegel, L. S., & Ryan, E. B. (1988). Development of grammatical-sensitivity, phonological, and short-term memory skills in normally achieving and learning disabled children. *Developmental Psychology, 24*, 28–37.
Siegel, L. S., & Heaven, R. K. (1986). Categorization of learning disabilities. In S. J. Ceci (Ed.), *Handbook of cognitive, social, and neuropsychological aspects of learning disabilities* (Vol. 1, pp. 95–121). Hillsdale, NJ: Erlbaum.
Silva, P. A., McGee, R., & Williams, S. (1985). Some characteristics of 9-year-old boys with general reading backwardness or specific reading retardation. *Journal of Child Psychology and Psychiatry, 26*, 407–421.
Snowling, M. (1980). The development of grapheme-phoneme correspondence in normal and dyslexic readers. *Journal of Experimental Child Psychology, 29*, 294–305.
Snowling, M. (1981). Phonemic deficits in developmental dyslexia. *Psychological Research, 43*, 219–234.

Snowling, M., Stackhouse, J., & Rack, J. (1986). Phonological dyslexia and dysgraphia—A developmental analysis. *Cognitive Neuropsychology, 3,* 309–339.
Spache, G. D. (1981). *Diagnostic reading scales.* Monterey, CA: CTB/McGraw-Hill.
Spring, C., & French, L. (1990). Identifying reading-disabled children from listening and reading discrepancy scores. *Journal of Learning Disabilities, 23,* 53–58.
Stanley, G., Smith, G., & Powys, A. (1982). Selecting intelligence tests for studies of dyslexic children. *Psychological Reports, 50,* 787–792.
Stanovich, K. E. (1986a). Cognitive processes and the reading problems of learning disabled children: Evaluating the assumption of specificity. In J. Torgesen & B. Wong (Eds.), *Psychological and educational perspectives on learning disabilities* (pp. 87–131). New York: Academic Press.
Stanovich, K. E. (1986b). Matthew effects in reading: Some consequences of individual differences in the acquisition of literacy. *Reading Research Quarterly, 21,* 360–407.
Stanovich, K. E. (1988a). Explaining the differences between the dyslexic and the garden-variety poor reader: The phonological-core variable-difference model. *Journal of Learning Disabilities, 21,* 590–612.
Stanovich, K. E. (1988b). The right and wrong places to look for the cognitive locus of reading disability. *Annals of Dyslexia, 38,* 154–177.
Stanovich, K. E. (1989). Learning disabilities in broader context. *Journal of Learning Disabilities, 22,* 287–297.
Stanovich, K. E. (in press). Speculations on the causes and consequences of individual differences in early reading acquisition. In P. Gough (Ed.), *Reading acquisition.* Hillsdale, NJ: Erlbaum.
Stanovich, K. E., Cunningham, A. E., & Cramer, B. (1984). Assessing phonological awareness in kindergarten children: Issues of task comparability. *Journal of Experimental Child Psychology, 38,* 175–190.
Stanovich, K. E., Nathan, R., & Vala-Rossi, M. (1986). Developmental changes in the cognitive correlates of reading ability and the developmental lag hypothesis. *Reading Research Quarterly, 21,* 267–283.
Stanovich, K. E., Nathan, R. G., West, R. F., & Vala-Rossi, M. (1985). Children's word recognition in context: Spreading activation, expectancy, and modularity. *Child Development, 56,* 1418–1429.
Stanovich, K. E., Nathan, R. G., & Zolman, J. E. (1988). The developmental lag hypothesis in reading: Longitudinal and matched reading-level comparisons. *Child Development, 59,* 71–86.
Stanovich, K. E., & West, R. F. (1983). On priming by a sentence context. *Journal of Experimental Psychology: General, 112,* 1–36.
Stanovich, K. E., & West, R. F. (1989). Exposure to print and orthographic processing. *Reading Research Quarterly, 24,* 402–433.
Sternberg, R. (1985). *Beyond IQ: A triarchic theory of human intelligence.* Cambridge: Cambridge University Press.
Sternberg, R. J. (1988). *The triarchic mind.* New York: Viking.
Sternberg, R. J., & Detterman, D. K. (1986). *What is intelligence?* Norwood, NJ: Ablex.
Sternberg, R. J., & Wagner, R. K. (1986). *Practical intelligence.* Cambridge: Cambridge University Press.
Sticht, T. G., & James, J. H. (1984). Listening and reading. In P. D. Pearson (Ed.), *Handbook of reading research* (pp. 293–317). New York: Longmen.
Swanson, H. L. (1987). Severe discrepancy: Some thoughts from cognitive psychology. *Learning Disabilities Research, 3,* 57–63.
Swanson, H. L. (1988). Toward a metatheory of learning disabilities. *Journal of Learning Disabilities, 21,* 196–209.

Taylor, H. J., Satz, P., & Friel, J. (1979). Developmental dyslexia in relation to other childhood reading disorders: Significance and clinical utility. *Reading Research Quarterly, 15*, 84–101.

Thorndike, R. L. (1963). *The concepts of over- and under-achievement.* New York: Teachers College, Columbia University.

Tindal, G., & Marston, D. (1986). Approaches to assessment. In J. K. Torgeson & B. Y. L. Wong (Eds.), *Psychological and educational perspectives on learning disabilities* (pp. 55–84). Orlando, FL: Academic Press.

Torgesen, J. (1985). Memory processes in reading disabled children. *Journal of Learning Disabilities, 18*, 350–357.

Torneus, M. (1984). Phonological awareness and reading: A chicken and egg problem? *Journal of Educational Psychology, 70*, 1346–1358.

Treiman, R., & Baron, J. (1983). Phonemic-analysis training helps children benefit from spelling-sound rules. *Memory & Cognition, 11*, 382–389.

Treiman, R., & Hirsh-Pasek, K. (1985). Are there qualitative differences in reading behavior between dyslexics and normal readers? *Memory and Cognition, 13*, 357–364.

Tunmer, W. E., & Nesdale, A. R. (1985). Phonemic segmentation skill and beginning reading. *Journal of Educational Psychology, 77*, 417–427.

van der Wissel, A. (1987). IQ profiles of learning disabled and mildly mentally retarded children: A psychometric selection effect. *British Journal of Developmental Psychology, 5*, 45–51.

van der Wissel, A., & Zegers, F. E. (1985). Reading retardation revisited. *British Journal of Developmental Psychology, 3*, 3–9.

Vaughm, S., & Bos, C. S. (1987). *Research in learning disabilities: Issues and future directions.* Austin, TX: PRO-ED.

Vellutino, F. (1978). Toward an understanding of dyslexia: Psychological factors in specific reading disability. In A. L. Benton & D. Pearl (Eds.), *Dyslexia* (pp. 59–111). New York: Oxford University Press.

Vellutino, F. (1979). *Dyslexia: Theory and research.* Cambridge, MA: MIT Press.

Vernon, P. A. (Ed.). (1987). *Speed of information-processing and intelligence.* Norwood, NJ: Ablex.

Wagner, R. K. (1988). Causal relations between the development of phonological processing abilities and the acquisition of reading skills: A meta-analysis. *Merrill-Palmer Quarterly, 34*, 261–279.

Wagner, R. K., & Torgesen, J. K. (1987). The nature of phonological processing and its causal role in the acquisition of reading skills. *Psychological Bulletin, 101*, 192–212.

Werker, J. F., & Tees, R. C. (1987). Speech perception in severely disabled and average reading children. *Canadian Journal of Psychology, 41*, 48–61.

William, J. (1984). Phonemic analysis and how it relates to reading. *Journal of Learning Disabilities, 17*, 240–245.

Williams, J. P. (1986). The role of phonemic analysis in reading. In J. T. Torgesen & B. Wong (Eds.), *Psychological and educational perspectives on learning disabilities* (pp. 399–416). New York: Academic Press.

Wilson, L. R., & Cone, T. (1984). The regression equation method of determining academic discrepancy. *Journal of School Psychology, 22*, 95–110.

Wolf, M., & Goodglass, H. (1986). Dyslexia, dysnomia, and lexical retrieval: A longitudinal investigation. *Brain and Language, 28*, 154–168.

Yule, W. (1984). The operationalizing of "underachievement"—doubts dispelled. *British Journal of Clinical Psychology, 23*, 233–234.

CHAPTER 9

A Cognitive Approach to Assessing the Mathematical Difficulties of Children Labeled "Learning Disabled"

ARTHUR J. BAROODY
HERBERT P. GINSBURG

The nature of assessment is determined explicitly or implicitly by an evaluator's view of learning and cognition. A theory of learning and cognition defines the goals of instruction and so dictates what is important to examine. This, in turn, shapes the conduct of assessment. This chapter uses the perspective of cognitive theory to examine the mathematical assessment of children classified as learning disabled (e.g., see Davis, 1984; Nesher, 1986; Shuell, 1986).

The chapter begins by discussing different views of learning disabilities and what view is most practical for educational assessment. It then provides an overview of how children learn mathematics, why they often encounter learning difficulties, and what difficulties elementary students commonly encounter. It ends with general implications for assessing

Preparation of this chapter was supported, in part, by a grant (No. MDR-8470191) from the National Science Foundation awarded to H. P. Ginsburg and A. J. Baroody and a grant from the University of Illinois Research Board awarded to A. J. Baroody.

mathematical difficulties and a case study that illustrates the difficulties all too commonly faced by children classified as learning disabled.

Unfortunately, the term mathematical learning disability is not used with precision (e.g., Allardice & Ginsburg, 1983; Blankenship, 1988; Cawley, 1985b; Coles, 1978; Farnham-Diggory, 1978). In theory (e.g., DeRuiter & Wansart, 1982; Kaliski, 1962; Kosc, 1974; Rourke & Finlayson, 1978; Rourke & Strang, 1983; Share, Moffitt, & Silva, 1988; Strauss & Kephart, 1955), such disabilities are due to an organic brain dysfunction, perhaps so minimal as to be difficult or impossible to detect by current diagnostic methods. Certainly, there are children who experience difficulty learning mathematics as a result of a neurological impairment (see, e.g., Deloche & Seron, 1987; Luria, 1969; Strauss & Lehtinen, 1947). Assessing the learning needs of children with real handicaps requires the cooperation of medical, psychological, and educational professionals (Sharma, 1985; Tucker, 1985). However, such students comprise a very small proportion of the children classified as learning disabled (e.g., Tucker, 1985), and including in this classification children without clear signs of an organic dysfunction is a questionable practice at best (e.g., Algozzine & Ysseldyke, 1986; Blankenship, 1988; Cawley, 1985a; Ysseldyke & Algozzine, 1983).

In his classification scheme, Kosc (1974) distinguished between organically based impairments and learning deficits (Kidron, 1985). Dyscalculia refers to specific disturbances in learning mathematical concepts or computations associated with an organic dysfunction. Developmental dyscalculia implies a genetic or congenital impairment (e.g., Kosc, 1970), and acquired dyscalculia is the result of brain damage or dysfunction occurring after birth (e.g., Sears, 1986). Acalculia refers to a general and severe deficiency in mathematical learning, and oligocalculia refers to a general depression of mathematical ability. Kosc (1974) labels learning deficits—failure to achieve potential because of inadequate instruction, illness, emotional problems, and so forth—pseudo-dyscalculia, pseudo-acalculia, or pseudo-oligocalculia.

Like others who propose minimal brain damage as an explanation for learning difficulties, Kosc (1974) classified as impaired children with "soft signs" of neurological dysfunction. In contrast to "hard signs" (e.g., an abnormal electroencephalogram or brain-wave pattern), soft signs (developmental abnormalities such as fine and gross motor-coordination deficiencies, mixed or confused laterality, strabismus, defective or slow speech development, short attention span, and general awkwardness) are not clear indications of brain damage (Coles, 1978). Reviews of the literature (e.g., Coles, 1978) fail to find a convincing link between soft signs ("evidence" of minimal brain damage) and learning problems. In brief, many children are labeled as impaired on the basis of questionable evidence.

Many children labeled learning disabled, perhaps most, are in David

Elkind's words "curriculum disabled," not organically impaired (e.g., Hendrickson, 1983). In other words, such children have learning difficulties because mathematics is not taught in a psychologically appropriate manner. Moreover, it is likely that ineffective instruction compounds the learning difficulties of children with genuine neurological involvement (e.g., Hayes, 1985a; Kosc, 1974). Given that the neurological concept of learning disability is often misapplied, this chapter focuses on the assessment of learning difficulties in a general sense, especially those resulting from inappropriate instruction.

COGNITIVE VIEW OF LEARNING AND COGNITION

MENTAL STRUCTURES

In a cognitive view, genuine learning is not simply a matter of absorbing information, and knowledge is not merely a copy of reality (e.g., Baroody, 1987a). Instead, a child actively constructs a representation of reality (a mental structure). Initially, the representation will be incomplete or inaccurate from an expert's perspective, but with the appropriate experiences, it can become progressively more complete and accurate. Sophisticated representations permit more flexible reasoning and more effective problem solving than do unsophisticated representations (e.g., Davis, 1983). Indeed, with development, thinking can change qualitatively (e.g., an insight can provide a fresh and more powerful perspective). Furthermore, the effective use of knowledge depends on the development of structures that serve an executive function (e.g., the monitoring of performance) and personality structures (e.g., interests that energize performance).

Conceptual Knowledge

Like other "consequential knowledge" (Sternberg, 1984a, 1984b), mathematical knowledge is not simply a collection of facts and procedures to be memorized through repeated practice. It includes a highly structured body of information replete with relationships. According to cognitive theory, children construct mental structures (schemata) to represent important regularities in their experiences. Anderson (1984) defines a schema as a representation of relationships, which can summarize information about many particular cases. It provides a system "for recognizing recurring sets of features" (Anderson, 1980, p. 254) and a framework for assimilating new facts or relationships (Shuell, 1986).

Strategies

Mathematical knowledge also includes strategies for applying existing knowledge and making sense of new situations (problem-solving skills). According to cognitive theory, children construct mental structures to deal effectively with their environment and learn more about it. Indeed, Piaget defined a schema as an organized pattern of actions (Ginsburg & Opper, 1988). Strategies can be task specific (e.g., a counting-on routine used to compute sums) or broadly applied (e.g., memorization devices like labeling and rehearsing information or heuristics like drawing a picture in order to help understand a problem) (e.g., Pressley, Goodchild, Fleet, Zajchowski, & Evans, 1989).

Metacognition

Conceptual knowledge and strategies are not sufficient to ensure their effective use in completing assignments, learning new material, solving problems, and so forth (cf. Palinscar, 1986). There must be an awareness of what resources a task requires and oversight or regulation of resource use (e.g., Baker & Brown, 1984; Reeve & Brown, 1985). Knowledge about one's own knowledge (concepts, learning strategies, or thinking processes) and the active monitoring and regulation of learning and cognitive processes is called metacognition (e.g., Brown, 1978; Flavell, 1976; Flavell & Wellman, 1977). In brief, metacognitive knowledge permits self-regulated learning and problem solving.

Affect

According to Piaget and Inhelder (1969), cognition and affect are complementary aspects of behavior. The affective elements (needs, feelings, and interests) energize or motivate action and thus exert a tremendous influence on learning (Reyes, 1984). Beliefs link cognition and affect in that they are assumptions about the self or world that prompt certain actions (Baroody, 1987a). In brief, affective factors and belief structures shape an individual's disposition to learn and to use knowledge.

PROCESSES OF CHANGE

Understanding and strategies are actively constructed by relating new experiences to what is already known or by combining existing pieces of knowledge. Both processes involve making a connection (insight), and both are mechanisms for making schemata more complete and accurate.

Assimilation and Accommodation

Learners filter new information in terms of what they already know. The process of interpreting and incorporating new information in terms of existing knowledge is called "assimilation" (e.g., Piaget, 1964). During the process of assimilation, a child may encounter aspects of the new experiences that do not fit existing structures exactly. This creates a disequilibrium, which requires an adjustment. Adjusting existing concepts or strategies to meet the demands of a new experience is called **accommodation**. Through the complementary processes of assimilation and accommodation, then, knowledge structures become enriched and more responsive to the environment. That is, they provide a more complete and accurate understanding of reality or way of responding to it. In this view, learning is not merely a process of adding information, it is a process that transforms mental structures (DeRuiter & Wansart, 1982).

Integration

By reflecting on experiences, a child may relate or integrate existing but previously isolated aspects of knowledge. This can occur when an experience causes two schemata to come into conflict (e.g., see Figure 9-1). The resulting disequilibrium induces the schemata to reorganize into a single new schema that is more complete and accurate.

Figure 9-1. Integration of conflicting geometry schemata.

Rule 1 (learned as a result of earlier shape-recognition training): "A square and a rectangle are <u>different</u> shapes."	←————→ CONFLICT caused by a request to analyze the characteristics of a square ("A square has four sides, the opposite sides are parallel, the sides meet at a right angle, all sides—including opposite sides—are equal"). The resulting disequilibrium induces a reorganization.	Rule 2 (learned in a recent geometry lesson): "A rectangle is a parallelogram (four-sided shape with equal and parallel opposite sides), with adjoining sides that meet at a right angle."

↓

New (more complete and accurate) rule:
"A square <u>is</u> a special kind of <u>rectangle</u>; it is different from the broader category of rectangles in that all—not simply opposite—sides are equal."

INFORMAL MATHEMATICAL KNOWLEDGE

Preschool Development

Research (e.g., Baroody, 1987a; Court, 1920; Fuson & Hall, 1983; Gelman & Gallistel, 1978; Ginsburg, 1989; Starkey & Gelman, 1982) shows that the development of mathematical knowledge begins well before children enter school. This *informal* knowledge is based, in large part, on counting experiences and provides an important basis for learning formal (school-taught, largely written or symbolic) mathematics. Rule-governed errors such as counting "eighteen, nineteen, *tenteen*," suggests that preschoolers do not merely absorb information or imitate solutions passively but actively construct their mathematical knowledge (Ginsburg, 1989).

Personal Mathematics of Schoolchildren

Even after children begin school, they often continue to rely on their informal mathematics instead of doing mathematics the way it is taught (e.g., Resnick & Ford, 1981). That is, children do not simply imitate and quickly adopt adult strategies or patterns of thought (Brownell, 1935). For example, despite the emphasis in many schools on memorizing the number facts, children persist in computing (e.g., Baroody, 1985; Carpenter & Moser, 1984). In fact, regardless of the teacher, mathematics curriculum, community, or country, children—at least initially—rely on counting to compute sums, differences, and products (see, e.g., Ginsburg, Posner, & Russell, 1981; Ginsburg & Russell, 1981; Kouba, 1986). Schoolchildren invent and rely on informal arithmetic procedures because these methods allow them to cope with their environment in a meaningful manner.

Strengths and Limitations

Informal mathematics enables children to exhibit surprising strengths. For example, cognitive research (e.g., Carpenter, 1986; Carpenter & Moser, 1983; Riley, Greeno, & Heller, 1983) indicates that young children have previously unsuspected problem-solving skills. Even kindergartners and first-graders can solve simple addition and subtraction word problems by using counting strategies that model the meaning of a problem. On the other hand, informal mathematical knowledge may not be complete, coherent, or logical (see, e.g., Baroody & Ginsburg, 1986; Piaget, 1965). A significant inconsistency, for example, is that even when young children can deal effectively with quantitative questions involving small numbers, they cannot always do so with large numbers (e.g., Gelman, 1972).

FORMAL MATHEMATICS

School-Taught Mathematics

Formal mathematics, which is taught in school and which uses written symbols, can greatly extend children's ability to deal with quantitative issues. Indeed, the mathematical skills and concepts taught in the primary grades are not only the foundation for learning more advanced mathematics later in school but are basic "survival skills" in our technologically oriented society. This formal mathematics is powerful in various ways. It is a highly precise and logical body of knowledge. Written algorithms (step-by-step procedures) greatly increase calculation efficiency, especially with larger quantities, and provide a long-lasting record. However, the extent to which children benefit from formal instruction depends on how well it meshes with their thinking.

Informal Mathematics: A Foundation for Formal Mathematics

Though formal mathematics can greatly extend their capabilities, children cannot immediately comprehend abstract instruction. In a cognitive view, the meaningful learning of school mathematics involves the assimilation of information, not merely its absorption. A basis for assimilating school-taught mathematical knowledge is children's informal mathematical knowledge. Mathematical symbols, computational algorithms, and formulas can make sense to children if this formal mathematics can be connected to their existing, personal, counting-based knowledge of mathematics.

SCHEMA DEVELOPMENT

Weak Versus Strong Schemata

Anderson (1984) differentiates between weak and strong schemata. A weak schema contains a collection of facts that are largely unconnected or unrelated. This greatly limits a child's ability to use existing knowledge to learn new material or to solve problems. For example, with isolated pieces of knowledge, the child cannot reason out an answer but must rely on looking up a precedent: a similar, previous experience. If a looked-up response is incorrect, the child has no other avenues (connections) to explore and may simply give up or resort to guessing. If a problem is changed even superficially from what was learned, the child—if simply not stumped—may relate the "novel" problem to a different (and inappropriate) precedent. In other words, because weak schemata include knowledge narrow in scope, they provide an uncertain basis for reasoning and may yield inconsistent responses.

On the other hand, a strong schema involves well-connected knowledge. This enables a child to coordinate a wide range of information to comprehend new material and to solve problems. A strong schema implies that comprehension is principle driven (general in scope) and that predictions can be derived (reasoned out) in a logical and consistent fashion.

Developmental Trends

Applied to the development of mathematical thinking, the weak versus strong schema distinction should be thought of as a continuum rather than as a dichotomy (Baroody & Ginsburg, 1986). Indeed, cognitive research indicates that with any mathematical content, learners generally progress from concrete to abstract conceptions, from incomplete to complete knowledge, and from unsystematic to systematic thinking (e.g., Baroody, 1987a; Crowley, 1987; Lunkenbein, 1985; van Erp & Heshusius, 1986). That is, for a first grader learning to add or a college student learning calculus, understanding begins imprecisely with the apparent. Initial cognitive structures, which emerge from concrete activities and are based on global perceptions, can be characterized as intuitive or infralogical (e.g., Lunkenbein, 1985). But this intuitive, unanalyzed, impressionistic knowledge is context bound, spotty, and unsystematic (e.g., Ginsburg, 1989; Lunkenbein, 1985); reasoning is idiosyncratic and prototypical. In brief, initial knowledge may be characterized as a weak schema.

Only gradually does knowledge in a particular domain become relatively abstract, complete, and systematic. In time, a student begins to abstract and formulate the properties and relationships of a domain. Initially, such knowledge may not form a coherent system and may be limited in scope and logically inconsistent. Reasoning still remains more descriptive or precedent-driven than truly deductive. Further advances in development entail recognizing and defining precise properties and logical relationships and organizing this information into an axiomatic system. Now a student is capable of seeing logical implications and reasoning deductively. For a few, mathematical knowledge is taken a step further. Properties and relationships are formally defined in terms of abstract symbols, which can be used to build a self-contained system of deductions of increasing complexity (Davis & Hersh, 1981). Thus, schemata can range from weak (intuitive or infralogical) to relatively weak (principled but unsystematic) to relatively strong (principled and systematic) to strong (principles formally defined).

The Case of Number-Combination Knowledge

Like other consequential mathematical knowledge, the essence of number-combination knowledge is structure (Baroody, 1988c). It would make sense, then, that the evolution of this knowledge and its proficient use would depend upon the elaboration of schemata. Initially, children may assimilate arithmetic problems (e.g., "five plus three" or 5 + 3) to existing but inadequate structures and respond ineffectively. As they notice regularities or find connections between bits of information, children construct more adequate (complete and integrated) schemata. The discovery of a relationship or the integration of knowledge can produce sudden qualitative changes in performance (e.g., the mastery of a whole set of related combinations). Thus, children need not practice each combination to make a "copy" of individual facts. As schemata become stronger, they can generate solutions to new as well as familiar problems automatically and confidently.

Before children master the number facts, a mental-addition task (a timed test) may amount to an estimation exercise (Baroody, 1989c). That is, children may use their existing knowledge of number and arithmetic to devise strategies for making educated guesses (Baroody, 1983). Initially, a child's strategy may be based on extremely limited information, perhaps unrelated to his or her existing informal incrementing concept of addition: Adding something to a collection makes it larger. Moreover, the strategy may be used in a highly mechanical or indiscriminate manner. For example, some children with little or no understanding of addition may rely on a strategy of stating one of the addends for all arithmetic problems (e.g., Baroody, 1988a, 1989c; Ilg & Ames, 1951). (Line A in Table 9-1 summarizes the kind of responses that can be expected from one such strategy.) Some of these children appear to assimilate or interpret an unfamiliar arithmetic question such as "5 + 2 = ?" as a number-comparison query, which results in the systematic error of responding with the larger addend (see Line B in Table 9-1) (e.g., Baroody, 1989c). Initially, then, mental arithmetic may be governed by incomplete, disconnected, and inflexible knowledge, characteristics of a weak schema.

At some point, children "see" the connection between mental addition and their informal arithmetic knowledge (i.e., assimilate the formal addition terminology to their informal incrementing concept) and realize that an addend must be increased. Children commonly exploit their existing counting knowledge for this purpose. More specifically, they realize that they can use their well-learned number-after knowledge to respond (e.g., "Five plus one is just the number after five: six") (e.g., Baroody, 1985). Initally, the strategy based upon an incrementing concept may not be very sophisticated (see Line C in Table 9-1). Because they view addition as

Table 9-1. Patterns of Responses to Six Problems for Different Mental Addition Strategies

	Response Patterns					
Strategy	5 + 0	0 + 5	5 + 1	1 + 5	5 + 3	3 + 5
	MECHANICAL ESTIMATION STRATEGIES					
A. State last addend	0	5	1	5	3	5
B. State larger addend	5	5	5	5	5	5
	INTERMEDIATE ESTIMATION STRATEGIES					
C. Add one to last	1	6	2	6	4	6
D. Add one to first	6	1	6	2	6	4
E. Add one to larger	6	6	6	6	6	6
	ADVANCED ESTIMATION AND EXACT ANSWER STRATEGIES					
F. Zero rule + add one to larger*	5	5	6	6	6	6
G. "True" estimation for non-one problems[†]	5	5	6	6	7, 8 or 9	7, 8 or 9

*Though the zero rule ($N + 0$ or $0 + N = N$) may have as its origin the mechanical state-the-larger-addend estimation strategy, it is now no longer an estimation strategy. It is used selectively to generate the exact sums of combinations involving zero.
[†]The schema for generating answers to combinations involving one (the number-after rule) is now no longer an estimation strategy, because it is used selectively to generate the exact sum of these combinations.

making an initial amount larger (e.g., Weaver, 1982), some children may simply add 1 to the *first* addend (see Line D in Table 9-1). For example, because they interpret 1 + 5 as "one *and five more*," a child may respond: "Two." A more sophisticated child will realize that a sum must be larger than either addend and use the prescription: increase the *larger* addend by one (e.g., in Line E of Table 9-1, 1 + 5: "Six").

With experience and feedback, children discriminate among different types of problems, recognize that a single strategy is not always appropriate, and invent strategies more appropriate for each type of problem. For example, by assimilating formal expressions involving zero to their informal knowledge that adding nothing to a collection leaves it unchanged, children can make sense of symbolic problems such as 5 + 0. Now, a child can distinguish between combinations involving zero and other combinations and respond differently to each (see Line F in Table 9-1).

Moreover, children also begin to differentiate between combinations involving one (e.g., 5 + 1) and those involving larger numbers (e.g., 5 + 3). This can occur when children recognize a discrepancy between the results of their estimation strategy (state the number after the larger addend) and their informal understanding that adding one and more than one to a number cannot have the same sum. At this point, they may conclude that an add-one-to-the-larger strategy is appropriate only for problems involving one (Baroody, 1989c). For problems involving the addition of more than one, a child devises a more genuine estimation strategy such as choosing a number (2 to 6) more than the larger addend (see Line G in Table 9-1). For the problem 7 + 4 = ?, for example, the child now rejects eight as inappropriate and chooses from a range of numbers just beyond it (Baroody, 1983).

With further insights and practice, schemata become more elaborate, interconnected, and automatic and hence provide a basis for more effective problem solving (cf. Anderson, 1984; Greeno, 1978; Kaye, 1986; Norman & Rumelhart, 1975; Resnick & Ford, 1981). For example, because of their informal incrementing concept of addition, children do not realize that addition is commutative: Addend order is irrelevant to the outcome (e.g., Baroody & Gannon, 1984). As a result, they view 6 + 2 and 2 + 6 as different problems (six and two more and two and six more) with *different* sums (see, e.g., Siegel, 1957). Once they discover that addition is commutative, children may learn an unknown combination such as 2 + 6 = 8 with little or no practice because they know it is equivalent to a known fact (6 + 2 = 8).

On timed tests, schemata may serve as a basis for evaluating, sorting, and processing different types of problems (cf. Svenson & Hedenborg, 1979). Those for addition are depicted in Figure 9-2* (Baroody, 1988c). As schemata become automatic, they can serve as a component for processing unknown addition combinations and the combinations of other operations. For example, children typically learn the doubles such as 5 + 5 quickly, and many discover that they can use this knowledge to reason out the sum for near doubles, like 5 + 6, that they do not know. More specifically, they use existing knowledge to construct a "doubles-plus-one" thinking strategy: Retrieve the sum of the double (Schema 5) and then use the number-after rule (Schema 3) to increment the retrieved sum by one. In effect, existing

---

*In fact, by screening out nonretrieved responses, Svenson (1985) found that her data formed three plateaus. Combinations involving 1 and 2 had relatively quick response times that suggested an incrementing process. These data are consistent with the *number*-after rule and the skip-the-next-number rule described in Figure 9-2. Moreover, large-addend-first combinations (e.g., 5 + 3 and 9 + 6) had faster latencies than commuted counterparts (e.g., 3 + 5 and 6 + 9) by a *constant* amount. These data suggest that retrieving the sums of small-addend-first combinations involved a process of transforming addend order. This supports the view that a schema embodying the commutativity principle is an integral aspect in mentally processing basic addition combinations. That is, because of a commutativity schema, two related facts may be represented by a single entry in long-term memory. For example, 2 + 6 = 8 and 6 + 2 = 8 might not be stored as two separate associations but as a single 2, 6, 8 association. Even if some combinations are learned initially as separate facts, acquisition of the commutative relationship may induce a reorganization in the mental representation of basic addition (and multiplication) combinations.

Figure 9-2. Addition schemata.[1]

---

(1) If the operation sign is plus, then addend order is irrelevant: Focus on the key term regardless of its position (Commutativity Principle.)[2]

↓

(2) If zero and a number are added, then the sum is the number ($N + 0$ or $0 + N = N$ Rule).

↓

(3) If one and a number are added, then the sum is the term after the larger number in the count sequence (*Number* -After Rule).

↓

(4) If two and a number are added, then the sum is the term after the next term of the larger number in the count sequence (Skip-N Rule).

↓

(5) If a number is added to itself, then access the associative network (Identity Comparison).[3]

↓

(6) If a larger number and a smaller number are added, then access the associative network (Magnitude Comparison).[4]

↓

(7) If a smaller number and a larger number are added, then transform the addends and access the associative network (Transformation Process).

---

[1]The schemata form a hierarchical checklist by which an expert evaluates addition problems. Schema 1 has priority over the rest.
[2]Unlike subtraction, where order is constrained, the commutativity schema permits attention to focus on key terms in the following order of importance: zero, one, two, and (large) number.
[3]The associative network would consist of an association-enriched representation of the number sequence.
[4]Making an identity judgment should be easier than determining which term is larger (making a magnitude comparison). Ties often have faster reaction times than nonties. If further work does not confirm a tie effect, Schemata 5 and 6 could be combined: If a larger number and itself or a smaller number are added; then access the associative network.

---

schemata are compiled to construct a new schema for a particular class of combinations. Extant knowledge of addition combinations can also serve as data for subtraction (e.g., $5 + 3 = 8$, therefore, $8 - 5$ is 3) and multiplication (e.g., knowledge of the addition doubles such as $6 + 6 = 12$ can serve as the data for the times-two combinations such as $6 \times 2 = ?$).

LEARNING DIFFICULTIES

PSYCHOLOGICALLY INAPPROPRIATE INSTRUCTION

Children have difficulty learning or using mathematics because all too frequently formal instruction is foreign to their thinking.

The Absorption Model

Formal mathematical instruction, even at the elementary level, is too often based on the assumption that children simply absorb information and make a mental copy of it. Frequently, this simplistic view of learning is also the basis of special education (e.g., Reid & Hresko, 1981). Thus, school mathematics—even that for children with learning difficulties—is all too often based on a tell–show–drill approach (Suydam & Osborne, 1977, cited in Blankenship, 1984):

1. Instruction begins by *telling* a class what they need to know. Often, the teacher verbally explains the lesson. Sometimes the students are supposed to get the new information by reading their textbook.
2. Then the lesson is illustrated with examples. For example, the teacher may show how to do a procedure on the chalkboard. The concept or procedure may be illustrated further by examples and pictures in the textbook.
3. The children then imitate the teacher and practice the fact or skill until it is automatic. Predicated on the assumption that "practice makes perfect," students are regularly given extensive written assignments (e.g., Moyer & Moyer, 1985). For the most part then, doing mathematics is reduced to manipulating written symbols to obtain correct answers (Davis, 1984).

Gaps

An absorption-model approach, even when done well, fails to take into account adequately the nature of children's mathematical learning. Such an approach overlooks the crucial developmental process of assimilation and the key developmental issue of readiness. Often, the result is a gap between formal instruction and children's existing (informal) knowledge.

Gaps occur because instruction is too abstract. If the use of objects and counting are not discouraged entirely, they are usually allowed only briefly to introduce topics like arithmetic, place value, and fractions (e.g., Carpenter & Moser, 1984). Unfortunately, a highly verbal approach to instruction frequently is not meaningful to children—even when accompanied by pictures and demonstrations. For example, the reliance on textbook pictures of groups of 10 items and single items to foster an understanding of grouping and positional notation (base-ten place-value concepts) is typically inadequate (e.g., Baroody, 1987a; Hendrickson, 1983). Moreover, the written symbols and the manipulations involving these symbols often make little or no sense to children (e.g., Davis, 1984).

A gap can occur when formal instruction overlooks individual readiness and moves too quickly. Mathematics instruction is frequently done in a large group and practiced alone without direct feedback. Because children do not have the same readiness to learn a mathematical concept or skill, a lesson or exercise may not be appropriate for everyone in class. Thus, new instruction that is introduced to a group of students will probably not be assimilated by all.

THE RESULTS OF PSYCHOLOGICALLY INAPPROPRIATE INSTRUCTION

Because it does not adequately take into account the psychology of the child, an absorption-model approach often fails to foster meaningful learning, a desire to learn, mastery of basic skills, metacognitive skills, and constructive beliefs. Such an approach frequently undermines independent learning and problem-solving ability.

Rote Learning

A gap between formal instruction and a child's existing informal knowledge prevents assimilation. According to Piaget's **moderate novelty principle**, a child (or adult) cannot assimilate information that is unrelated to past experiences. That is, an individual cannot connect highly novel or unfamiliar information to existing knowledge and thus cannot interpret it. Simply put, understanding cannot be imposed. With abstract and lock-step instruction, children are forced to memorize mathematics by rote—as isolated bits of meaningless information.

In other words, a tell–show–drill regimen all too frequently fosters the development and maintenance of weak or relatively weak schemata. For most of the formal mathematics to which they are exposed, children are not given the means, the opportunity, the incentive, or the time to develop stronger schemata (Baroody & Ginsburg, 1986). That is, they are not encouraged to look for relationships between new information and their existing knowledge or between pieces of acquired knowledge. The result is that students do not develop the sophisticated representations that permit the assimilation of more advanced mathematics, flexible reasoning, or nontrivial mathematical problem solving.

Disinterest

A gap between formal instruction and children's existing knowledge can have serious affective consequences: It can undercut children's interest in mathematics, their motivation to learn it, and willingness to engage in mathematical problem solving. Piaget's moderate novelty principle describes a key link between cognition and affect. Children are naturally interested in "moderately novel" information. That is, somewhat unfamiliar situations excite natural curiosity. On the other hand, when presented with new, unfamiliar information that they cannot assimilate, children (and adults)—quite naturally—quickly lose interest in the incomprehensible information and tune it out. Indeed, many children feel frustrated and helpless when confronted with a torrent of meaningless words and written symbols. Heavy doses of practice with exercises that seem to children to be pointless can further deaden interest.

Inaccurate or Incomplete Learning

Gaps between children's relatively concrete informal mathematics and their relatively abstract formal instruction are a key reason for learning difficulties (Allardice & Ginsburg, 1983; Ginsburg, 1989; Hiebert, 1984). When introduced to formal mathematics for which they are not ready or do not understand, some children fail to memorize the meaningless information correctly or at all. As a result, they may learn concepts or procedures in an incomplete or an incorrect fashion. Systematic errors or "bugs" are symptoms of this partially correct or incorrect knowledge (e.g., Buswell & Judd, 1925; Brown & Burton, 1978; Ginsburg, 1989; Van Lehn, 1983). For instance, presented with an unfamiliar operation, children sometimes resort to using a familiar operation (Bug 1 in Table 9-2). A common error among children with little or no knowledge of the renaming algorithm is the incorrect procedure of subtracting the smaller term from the larger, even when the smaller term is the top number (Bug 2). Because children do not understand the underlying place-value rationale for the algorithm, many learn the procedure incompletely. Note that Bug 3 indicates less procedural knowledge than Bugs 4 and 5, which entail some effort to reduce. Subtraction involving zero frequently prompts other invented procedures such as Bugs 6 and 7. Example 8, consisting of a partially correct procedure and an incorrect procedure, illustrates the common case of multiple bugs.

Learning problems are compounded when new topics are introduced before a child has had a chance to assimilate more basic lessons. Because new topics often build upon previous lessons, the child gets caught in a downward spiral of failure. That is, when learning difficulties occur, a child

Table 9-2. Some Common Subtraction Bugs

(1)	53 −27 --- 80	37 −16 --- 53	(5)	203 −27 --- 86	206 −58 --- 58
(2)	53 −27 --- 34	164 −89 --- 125	(6)	128 −107 --- 1	245 −108 --- 107
(3)	53 −27 --- 36	206 −58 --- 258	(7)	208 −127 --- 101	340 −176 --- 170
(4)	203 −27 --- 276	206 −58 --- 248	(8)	103 −27 --- 26	206 −58 --- 158

(1) Adds instead of subtracts.
(2) Subtracts large from the small.
(3) Borrows without reducing.
(4) Borrows from 0, changes it to 9, but does not reduce.
(5) Skips over 0 to borrow.
(6) Subtracts $N - 0 = 0$.
(7) Subtracts $0 - N = 0$.
(8) Skips over 0 to borrow and subtracts $0 - N = N$.

has little opportunity to catch up, old problems create new learning difficulties, and the child falls further and further behind. As the gap between instruction and a child's existing knowledge increases, the chances of making sense of the mathematics for oneself decreases. Moreover, an inadequate or incomplete knowledge base is a serious barrier to problem solving (e.g., Davis, 1984).

Passivity

A gap between formal instruction and informal knowledge forces children into the role of passive recipients of knowledge and discourages independent thinking. Because understanding, exploring, questioning, and reflecting are not encouraged, a tell–show–drill approach to instruction frequently fails to foster the learning and use of task-specific strategies, cognitive learning strategies, or heuristics. Because of a focus on memorizing *the* correct written procedure, schooling often discourages children from inventing or using their own informal strategies. When mathematics is merely a basket of facts and procedures to be memorized (cf. Anderson, 1984), some children may discover that rehearsal is a useful strategy for memorizing information but learn little else about self-regulated learning. Moreover, they may not develop other deliberate strategies for facilitating learning and problem solving, such as the heuristic of evaluating new problems in terms of familiar ones.

An absorption-model approach too often fails to foster the learning of metacognitive skills or provide an opportunity to practice them. A steady diet of rote learning and meaningless drill fosters blind rule-following (e.g., Brown, 1978; Holt, 1964). As a result, even "successful" students, who have faithfully memorized their lessons, often fail to use their knowledge effectively when learning new material or solving problems (e.g., Allardice & Ginsburg, 1983). Information learned by rote frequently does not transfer, because children do not see how it is applicable to a new task. For example, because they do not understand the underlying rationale for the algorithm, many students master a carrying procedure for two-digit addition but then cannot apply this knowledge to doing three-digit addition. Even many successful students are unable to solve problems that differ at all from what they have been taught (see, e.g., Carpenter, Matthews, Lindquist, & Silver, 1984; Wertheimer, 1945). Moreover, because they do not practice self-regulatory skills like self-monitoring, many children get into the habit of depending on an authority, such as the teacher, to determine the correctness of their answers.

Debilitating Beliefs

A gap between formal instruction and children's informal knowledge can make mathematics seem incomprehensible, foreign, and arbitrary. Indeed, the way in which mathematics is taught can profoundly affect how children view mathematics, their learning of the topic, and themselves (Baroody, 1987a). When mathematics is taught in an abstract and lock-step manner, children "hear" such unspoken "messages" as

- Only geniuses can understand mathematics. Just do as you are told. You're not really smart enough to understand it.
- Mathematics is a bunch of facts and procedures. Normal children memorize it quickly. You're dumb if you can't.
- In mathematics, there is one correct method for doing things. Good children can follow directions. You're bad if you use an unacceptable procedure like counting.

Such beliefs can have a powerful impact on how children go about learning and using mathematics (Cobb, 1985a, 1985b; Pressley et al., 1989; Reyes, 1984; Schoenfeld, 1985). The destructive beliefs fostered by a tell–show–drill approach can discourage independent thinking and problem-solving ability. For example, an emphasis on memorizing written procedures teaches children that mathematics does not involve thinking and that their own ideas and strategies are not relevant or, at best, inferior substitutes for real math. Because they conclude that mathematics does not make sense, many children stop monitoring their work thoughtfully and dispense with assigned work as quickly as possible (e.g., Holt, 1964). As a result, they may not be the least bit troubled by an unreasonable answer, even when it is incompatible with what they do know (e.g., Hiebert & Wearne, 1984; Schoenfeld, 1985). For instance, children who use the small-from-large bug frequently overlook the fact that subtraction cannot yield a difference that is larger than the starting amount:

$$\begin{array}{r} 22 \\ -5 \\ \hline 23 \end{array}$$

THE CASE OF NUMBER-FACT DEFICIENCIES: A COMMON LEARNING DIFFICULTY

A weakness in basic number-combination knowledge is characteristic of children having difficulty with mathematics (e.g., Ackerman, Anhalt, & Dykman, 1986; Allardice & Ginsburg, 1983; Baroody, 1987a; Fleischner, Garnett, & Shepard, 1982; Goldman, Pellegrino, & Mertz, 1988; Hasselbring, Goin, & Bransford, 1987; Russell & Ginsburg, 1984; Svenson & Broquist, 1975; Torgeson & Young, 1983). Larger basic combinations (e.g., single-digit combinations with sums over 10) are especially difficult for children labeled learning disabled (e.g., Kraner, 1980; Smith, 1921). A related deficiency is an inability mentally to add multidigit combinations efficiently, including relatively simple facts involving 10 (e.g., 40 + 10 = ?) and multiples of 10 (e.g., 400 + 100 = ?) (Baroody, 1987a). Such children typically count on rather than efficiently recall sums for both single-digit problems (e.g., 9 + 5: "9; 10, 11, 12, 13, *14*") and multidigit problems (e.g., 40 + 10: 40, 41, 42, 43, 44, 45, 46, 47, 48, 49, *50*").

Such deficiencies are commonly attributed to insufficient practice (e.g., Pellegrino & Goldman, 1987; Torgeson & Young, 1984). This may well contribute to the problem, but it may not be the primary source of the difficulty for many. Number-fact deficiencies have also been attributed to a memory deficit (Ackerman et al., 1986; Bley & Thornton, 1981; Webster, 1979, 1980). Though it is unclear whether or not this is the primary cause in some cases, it may not be the underlying difficulty for many children labeled learning disabled.

The fundamental problem for many such children may be that they fail to learn effective strategies for memorizing consequential knowledge (Allardice & Ginsburg, 1983) and, thus, fail to develop a rich network of relationships (Baroody, 1985, 1987a; Myers & Thornton, 1977). Such children may not realize that they should look for patterns or relationships. For example, asked how he could help a first-grader learn the addition combinations, Tommy an 8-year-old boy labeled learning disabled (Baroody, 1989a) responded: "Yeah, just by telling them the answers. Make them study it." Ironically, he recommended a strategy that had not proved entirely effective for himself. His beliefs about teaching and learning the basic number combinations reflected his own tell–show–drill schooling.

Faced with the burden of memorizing many apparently isolated facts, children such as Tommy may feel overwhelmed with the chore and simply give up. For example, it may have been helpful in mastering basic subtraction facts if Tommy had learned to relate them to known addition combinations (e.g., 9 – 4 = ?: What do I have to add to 4 to make 9?) (e.g., Baroody, Ginsburg, & Waxman, 1983; Siegler, 1987). The same holds true for multidigit mental arithmetic. For example, Tommy may have been able to master adding 10 to a decade if he were helped to connect this to his existing counting (decade-after) knowledge (e.g., 40 + 10 is the decade after 40: 50) or his existing $N + 1$ knowledge (e.g., 40 + 10 parallels 4 + 1 = 5).

A SAMPLE OF COMMON LEARNING DIFFICULTIES

Oral Counting

To count to 100, a child needs to know (a) the single-digit sequence 1 to 9; (b) a 9 signals a transition (e.g., 19 signals the end of the teens and the beginning of a new series); (c) the transition terms for the new series (e.g., 20 follows 19); (d) the rules for generating the new series (e.g., the 20s and all subsequent series are generated by combining the transition term with, in turn, each term in the single-digit sequence; and (e) the exceptions to the rules (Baroody, 1989b). Among kindergartners entering school, the first component is typically intact and automatic. Many will not have the second component and, as a result, they overextend their counting rules (i.e., make rule-governed errors such as "nineteen, ten-teen, eleven-teen" or "twenty-nine, twenty-ten, twenty-eleven." Some may recognize the need for a transition but have not learned the decade term to begin the next series (e.g., they count to 29 and stop cold because they do not know that 30 is the next term). Indeed, it is not until first grade that many children recognize that the decade series ("10, 20, 30, ... 90") parallels the single-digit sequence (e.g., six + -ty, seven + -ty, eight + -ty) and master the decade (transition) terms. Some children may stop at 20 or 30 because they have not discovered the pattern of repeating the single-digit sequence with each successive decade (e.g., 20 is followed by "twenty + one, twenty + two . . . twenty + nine"). Finally, the exceptions often cause difficulties. For example, fifteen is the most commonly missed teen (e.g., Fuson, 1988). Children often overgeneralize the teen pattern ("five-teen"), skip the difficult term, or substitute something for it (e.g., "thirteen, fourteen, fourteen, sixteen").

Object Counting

To enumerate sets of objects correctly, a child must know (a) that each object in a set is labeled with one counting word (one-for-one tagging), and (b) how to keep track of counted and uncounted objects so that each object is tagged once and only once. Kindergartners typically have mastered the first component, but many have not devised effecive keeping-track strategies (e.g., Fuson, 1988). This may result in skipping one or more items or counting one or more items more than once, particularly when the set is large and/or haphazardly arranged.

Numerical Relationships

By the time they enter kindergarten, children typically have learned to use their mental representation of the number sequence in some elaborate and flexible ways (e.g., Fuson, Fichards, & Briars, 1982). Asked what comes after a number 1 to 9, most children no longer have to count from 1 to determine the successor but can automatically cite it. Citing the number before a given number is more difficult, because children have to operate on the number-sequence representation in the "opposite" direction from which the sequence was learned. Moreover, the term "before" may be relatively unfamiliar to children and assimilated (interpreted) as "after" (cf. Donaldson & Balfour, 1968). Because it may serve as a prerequisite for counting backward, a deficiency in number-before knowledge can impede the development of this counting skill. Difficulty in counting backward can, in turn, hinder the development of counting down, an informal subtraction strategy (see the subsection on informal arithmetic below).

Most children entering school can use their representation of the number sequence to determine which of two adjacent numbers indicates the larger quantity (e.g., which is more, 7 or 8?). From their experiences with small sets and numbers, they construct a magnitude-comparison rule: A number that comes after another in the number sequence is more than its predecessor (Schaeffer, Eggleston, & Scott, 1974). As children master the number-after relationships for more and more of the number sequence, they can apply the comparison rule to larger and larger numbers. However, children with relatively little informal mathematical experience or those with learning difficulties may not develop this number-comparison ability (see Baroody, 1988b, 1989c). Unfortunately, this important skill is often overlooked in the evaluation and the teaching of kindergartners. Gauging which term is "less" is even more difficult because, in part, children rarely hear or apply the term (e.g., Donaldson & Balfour, 1968; Kaliski, 1962; Weiner, 1974).

Reading and Writing Single-Digit Numerals

Reading numerals entails distinguishing among these symbols. This requires constructing a mental image of each numeral: knowing its component parts and how the parts fit together to form the whole (cf. Gibson & Levin, 1975). Children frequently confuse numerals that share similar characteristics (2 and 5 or 6 and 9) (Baroody, 1987a). For example, 6 and 9 are difficult to discriminate because both numerals have the same parts (a curve and a loop), share a part–whole relationship (the curve joins the loop), and differ only in where the curve joins the loop.

Writing difficulties, such as writing a numeral in reverse, are frequently cited as common characteristics of children labeled as learning disabled (see, e.g., Mann & Suiter, 1974; Sears, 1986). Numeral writing entails having an accurate mental image of each numeral and constructing a plan for translating this mental image into motor actions. A motor plan then consists of a set of rules that specify where to start, how to proceed, when to change direction, and when to stop (Goodnow & Levine, 1973). Without a correct or complete motor plan (a preplanned strategy), a child may, for example, repeatedly start in the wrong place and head in the wrong direction, and as a result, reverse the numeral (Baroody, 1987a).

Informal Arithmetic

Successfully solving word problems depends upon a child's ability to represent it: determine what is given, what is unknown, and how to use the given to determine the unknown. Some kindergartners and most first-graders can—without formal instruction—assimilate and model with objects the meaning of simple addition word problems such as: Joey had five marbles and he won three more. How many marbles does he have altogether? (e.g., Carpenter & Moser, 1983, 1984). A common strategy is concrete counting-all (e.g., for 5 + 3: put up 5 fingers and then 3 fingers and count all the fingers). A child who does not understand the problem or who has not constructed an addition strategy may count each set put out separately, represent only one set, or act confused.

With experience, children spontaneously abandon concrete procedures and invent verbal-counting procedures for calculating sums (e.g., Groen &

Resnick, 1977). Self-monitoring also leads children to invent increasingly sophisticated verbal strategies (Baroody, 1987a). For example, many children abandon a counting-from-one procedure (e.g., 3 + 6: "1, 2, 3; 4 [is one more], 5 [is two more], 6 [is three more], 7 [is four more], 8 [is five more], 9 [is six more]") in favor of a strategy that disregards addend order (e.g., 3 + 6: "1, 2, 3, 4, 5, 6; 7 [is one more], 8 [is two more], 9 [is three more]"), which in turn is replaced by a counting-on strategy (e.g., 3 + 6: "6; 7 [is one more], 8 [is two more], 9 [is three more]") (e.g., Baroody, 1987b; Baroody & Gannon, 1984). Though such development can be explained in terms of a cognitive drive for economy (see Baroody & Ginsburg, 1986), some researchers (e.g., Secada, Fuson, & Hall, 1983; Steffe, von Glasersfeld, Richards, & Cobb, 1983) argue that the development of counting-on is indicative of a conceptual leap in understanding number. In any case, some children, particularly those without adequate informal experience, do not make such progress in a timely fashion or, perhaps, at all (e.g., Baroody, Berent, & Packman, 1982; Bley & Thornton, 1981; Lerner, 1971).

Subtraction is often problematic for children because, in part, of their informal counting-down strategy for determining differences (Baroody, 1984). A concrete take-away or a counting-down procedure models their informal concept of subtraction as take away. (For 5 – 3, for example, a concrete take-away procedure entails representing the 5 with fingers, blocks, or tally marks and then folding down 3 fingers, removing 3 blocks, or crossing out 3 tallies, respectively.) Counting-down is a verbal procedure that for 5 – 3, say, entails beginning with 5 and count 4 (1 taken away), 3 (2 taken away), 2 (3 taken away). Such a strategy can be used with ease as long as the numbers involved are small. If the minuend (starting amount) is large, as in 12 – 9, the child has to start counting backward in relatively unfamiliar territory. If the subtrahend (number taken away) is relatively large, the child is faced with a formidable keeping-track process. With 12 – 9, for example, the child has to keep track of counting back 9 times! Many children then encounter difficulty with larger subtraction problems and grow to dislike subtraction. Many, though, invent or learn more efficient ways for determining the difference for problems like 12 – 9. For instance, they may begin with the subtrahend 9 and count 10 (is 1), 11 (is 2), 12 (is 3).

Part–Part–Whole Skills and Concepts

The elaboration of a part–part–whole concept is one of the most important developments during the elementary years (Resnick, 1983). Children need to discover that a number like 7 can be thought of in many different ways. They do not realize that a whole can be constructed from different parts (e.g., 7 can be composed from 6 and 1, 5 and 2, and so forth). Because their addition knowledge is disconnected, many children do not see 6 + 1, 5 + 2, 4 + 3, and so forth, as related, and would predict they have different sums.

Moreover, because of their incrementing view of addition, many children even view 5 + 2 and 2 + 5 as different problems (as 5 and 2 more, and 2 and 5 more, respectively) and assume they have *different* sums (e.g., Baroody & Gannon, 1984). Therefore, children have to discover that different-looking problems, such as 6 + 1 = ? and 5 + 2 = ? can actually have the same sum and that order is irrelevant to the outcome of addition (e.g., both 5 + 2 and 2 + 5 have the same sum).

Children also need to see that a number like 7 can, in turn, be a part of a larger whole (e.g., 7 + 2 = 9). An important discovery is that part–part–whole relationships connect addition and subtraction. For example, 9 – 7 = ? can be figured out by knowing what must be added to 7 to make 9 (e.g., Baroody et al., 1983). The answer can be determined by counting up (e.g., "7, 8 [is 1 more], 9 [is 2 more]: 2") or by recalling that 7 + 2 = 9. Children who have not made this connection may continue to compute differences by using a concrete take-away or a verbal counting-down strategy.

The elaboration of a part–part–whole concept enables children to solve more difficult missing-second-part problems ($A + ? = C$), such as: Joey had 5 marbles and won some more. Now he has 8. How many did he win? (e.g., Riley et al., 1983). Even more difficult for children are missing-first-part problems ($? + B = C$), such as: Joey had some marbles, and he won 3 more. Now he has 8. How many did he start with? This type of problem may be especially difficult to assimilate because of children's informal incrementing concept.

Base-Ten Place-Value Skills and Concepts

Because of their counting-based concept of number, children interpret a multidigit numeral such as 16 as 16 units and, perhaps, as 15 and 1 more. They do not think of multidigit numbers in terms of 1s, 10s, 100s, and so forth. The convention of using position to denote value (e.g., the 1 in 16 represents a 10 and the 6 represents 6 1s) is foreign to their thinking and difficult to assimilate. Children need to learn that: (a) items can be grouped, and grouped items are treated differently from ungrouped items; (b) the group size (10 in base 10) is used repeatedly to group smaller groups (e.g., 10 10s are grouped to make 100; 10 100s, 1000; and so forth); and (c) successively larger groups are arranged from left to right and the number in each group is denoted by a single-digit numeral (Hendrickson, 1983).

Because children typically begin to read and write multidigit numerals before they understand the underlying place-value rationale, they frequently make errors. For example, some kindergartners may fail to relate written numbers to their knowledge of the counting sequence and read the digits of a multidigit numeral separately (e.g., read 27 as "two, seven"). They may not recognize that the order of the digits is important and read, for instance, both 17 and 71 as "seventeen." Many first graders have not learned that zero acts as a placeholder and read, for example, 103 as "thirteen" (the zero means nothing) or "ten-three" (assimilate the unfamiliar symbolism in terms of the known numbers). Common writing errors include writing numerals as they are heard (e.g., writing "seventeen" as 71 because 7 is heard first or writing "forty-two" as 402 because the decade term is heard) (e.g., Ginsburg, 1989; Luria, 1969).

Children learn relatively quickly to recognize the 1s, 10s, 100s, and 1000s place. Unfortunately, this can be learned rotely and, hence, may represent a rather superficial understanding of place value (Resnick, 1982). Even noting place value (e.g., the 2 in 243 represents two 100s; the 4, four 10s, and the 3, three 1s) or representing a numeral with manipulatives such as Dienes blocks (e.g., setting out two flats, four longs, and three units to show 243) can be learned by rote and does not guarantee an understanding of place value (e.g., Ross, 1989a). Ross (1989b) argues that some children who correctly label, for instance, two longs and six units as 26 are simply making a "face-value error": noting two of something, not necessarily 10s, and six of something else, not necessarily 1s. She found that when 26 objects were rearranged into six groups of four items each with two left over, such children thought the 2 in 26 represented the ungrouped items and the 6 represented the 6 groups! Success on many common place-value items (e.g., see Blankenship, 1985a) may overestimate place-value understanding. In addition to Ross' face-value task, a relatively difficult task that appears to indicate some genuine understanding is a digit-correspondence task (Ross, 1989a, 1989b): The child counts, say, 25 sticks and records the number. The tester circles each digit in turn and asks, "Does this part have anything to do with how many sticks you have?"

To execute the (vertical) multidigit addition-and-subtraction algorithm, terms should be lined up from the right side so that the 1s-place digits form a single column, the 10s-place digits line up vertically, and so forth. Children who do not understand the underlying place-value rationale for the procedure may make one of several errors (e.g., Baroody, 1989b). Some may make no effort to align terms correctly. Some may be confused and align on the left at times and on the right at other times. Perhaps because they are influenced by left-to-right reading procedures, some may consistently align on the left. Alignment difficulties may appear when children have to solve problems presented in a horizontal line (Luria, 1969), copy problems from a text, record verbally presented problems, or set up word problems. Alignment-related errors are especially likely to occur when a child is required to write or copy problems vertically or do worksheet exercises in which the problems are printed vertically.

Children usually have little difficulty mastering a two-, three-, or even four-digit written addition procedure that does not involve renaming (carrying or borrowing). These step-by-step procedures are rather straightforward and entail minimal knowledge of place value. Though many children master the two-digit renaming algorithms by rote, often such learning does not transfer to problems involving three digits or more (Ginsburg, 1989). Because they do not comprehend the underlying rationale of such algorithms, many children fail to learn all (or any) of the steps (Engelhardt, Ashlock, & Wiebe, 1984). Quite often, the results are systematic errors such as those listed in Table 9-2 (e.g., Ashlock, 1982; Brown & Burton, 1978).

Geometry

The van Hiele model suggests that knowledge of geometry proceeds gradually through a series of stages (Crowley, 1987). At the intuitive level (Level 0), children learn to recognize geometric figures such as squares and circles by their physical appearance. At Level 1, children begin to learn the characteristics or attributes of the forms in isolation. At Level 2, they establish *relationships* among the attributes of a form (e.g., in a quadrilateral, parallel opposite sides necessitate equal opposite angles) and among figures (e.g., a square is a rectangle because it has all the properties of this figure). At more advanced levels, a person can construct geometric proofs and see geometry in the abstract (e.g., compare different axiomatic systems).

Elementary instruction typically focuses on the first two levels (memorizing the names and the attributes of forms). As a result, children develop partial and even incorrect concepts. For example, many children fail to identify a square as a rectangle because instruction does not help them understand that a form is defined by its critical attributes (e.g., a square has all the critical attributes of a rectangle) and how the critical attributes are related (e.g., a square is a special class of rectangles, because it is a rectangle with an additional critical attribute: four equal sides).

Fractions

Children must understand that a fraction is a part of so many *equal-sized* parts. They must learn that the more parts a whole is divided into, the smaller each part. To solve fraction problems, it is essential to define or identify the whole (Davis, 1986). (Consider the problem: The Jones Boys Gang ordered 2 pizzas each divided into 8 pieces. They ate 9 pieces. If the question is what fraction of the pieces was eaten, the whole is the total number of pieces and the correct answer is $9/16$. If the question is how many of the pizzas were eaten, the whole is 1 pizza and the correct answer is $1\,1/8$.) To add and subtract fractions, children need to understand that the fractions must have a common denominator—a common unit.

Children frequently have an incomplete concept of fractions as a part of so many (depicted but not equivalent) parts and, hence, make the kind of error shown in Frame A of Figure 9-3. Another common error is choosing as the larger fraction the one with the larger denominator. For example, children conclude that ⅓ must be bigger than ½ because they incorrectly apply their magnitude comparison rules for whole numbers (e.g., Post, Wachsmuth, Lesh, & Behr, 1985). Because they are often introduced to fractions using just one type of representation (i.e., pie diagrams in which a whole is divided into parts), children commonly fail to differentiate between a fraction of one whole and a fraction of a set of things (Davis, 1986; Silver, 1983). As a result, they become confused when given fraction problems that involve more than one thing and make errors like that shown in Frame B of Figure 9-3. Because they do not really understand the rationale underlying the procedure, children invent various procedures for performing arithmetic operations with fractions. A common systematic error is illustrated in Frame C of Figure 9-3.

Decimals

Children must learn that like fractions, decimals represent parts of wholes as well as wholes but have their own system of notation. As with fractions, they must learn the more parts into which a whole is divided, the smaller each part. They must also learn that the value of the digits is specified by their position.

Because they have no understanding of decimal representation, many children assimilate the symbols in terms of existing knowledge and make such errors as blindly using their rules for writing fractions (Frame D of Figure 9-3) or comparing the magnitude of whole numbers (Frame E) (e.g., Hiebert, 1987). Children who do not appreciate the place-value notation system but at least understand that more subdivisions imply smaller parts choose the decimal with the fewest digits (Frame F) (Resnick et al., 1989). The systematic error of overlooking the place value of the digits and is encouraging teaching practice of asking students to add same-sized decimals such as .5 + .2 (Hiebert, 1987).

IMPLICATIONS FOR ASSESSMENT

GENERAL ISSUES

Cognitive research and theory help provide direction in assessing any child. It underpins the *Standards* document (*Curriculum and Evaluation Standards for School Mathematics*) recently published by the National Council of Teachers of Mathematics (Commission on Standards for School

9. Mathematical Assessment 203

Figure 9-3. A sample of common rational–number errors.

A. Common fraction error due to not understanding that a fraction represents a part of so many <u>equivalent</u> parts.

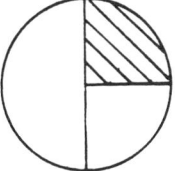

Write a fraction to show what part of the pie is shaded: __1/3__

B. Fraction error due to a failure to define the whole correctly.

For each diagram, color in ¼

a.  b. 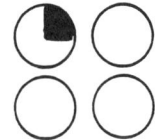 c.

C. Fraction Bug: Add across top, add across the bottom.

7/8 + 7/8 = 14/16

D. Writing a decimal as if it were a fraction with a decimal point.

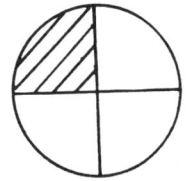

Write a decimal to show what part of the pie is shaded: __1.4__

E. Choosing as the largest decimal the number that would make the largest whole number.

Circle the letter of the largest decimal.

(a) .378   (b) .4   (c) .51

F. Choosing as the largest decimal the number with the fewest subdivisions.

Circle the letter of the largest decimal.

(a) .378   (b) .4   (c) .51

Mathematics, 1989). The *Standards* is an invaluable document for all those interested in the mathematical assessment of any child.

What is the Purpose of Assessment?

The main aim of assessment is to help educators understand what students know and to make informed instructional decisions (Commission on Standards for School Mathematics, 1989). In other words, its aim is to provide appropriate instruction for a child (cf., Blankenship, 1985a; Brownell, 1935; Denvir & Brown, 1986; DeRuiter & Wansart, 1982; Goodstein, 1984). Thus, effective assessment goes beyond categorizing children and provides information that is useful to planning instruction (Glaser, 1981; Homan, 1970; Wallace & Larsen, 1978). To achieve this, an educator must continuously build and test a theory about a child's mental state. Assessment, then, involves generating hypotheses about a child's mental structures. After this information is used to design instruction, further assessment serves to check the correctness of the hypotheses. Such an approach is sometimes called "diagnostic teaching" (e.g., Wallace & Larsen, 1978). In brief, assessment is an ongoing problem-solving process directed toward understanding a child's mental structure so that psychologically appropriate instruction can be tailored to the pupil.

What Needs to be Examined?

To gauge the nature of a child's mental structures, it is not enough to focus on external behaviors (e.g., DeRuiter & Wansart, 1982). Though it is important to note how much and what a child has mastered, assessment must examine more than product: How many and what correct answers a child produces. To gauge a child's *internal state or underlying knowledge*, it is important to determine *how* and *why*—the *process* by which—a child arrived at an answer (e.g., Bruner, 1966; Commission on Standards for School Mathematics, 1989; Glaser, 1981). In other words, assessments should address such questions as What conceptions did the child bring to the task? To what extent are they accurate and complete? What strategy did the child employ to solve the problem? What is the child ready to learn now?

In a cognitive view, it is essential to distinguish between meaningful learning and rote learning, because many students routinely master facts and procedures and can produce correct answers, without understanding relationships or underlying concepts. Examining process provides a more accurate and complete picture of a child's competence than does assessment based exclusively on noting the correctness of answers (e.g., Ginsburg, 1989). Correctness or incorrectness by themselves do not indicate how or why the child arrived at the answer (e.g., Connell, 1988). As a result, evaluation that examines product exclusively may *overestimate* a child's understanding. An example of "false success" is the child who correctly identified the form ◣ as a "right triangle," without really understanding the concept (Mason, 1989). A follow-up probe revealed that the child chose the form because "a right triangle always faces right." (The form ◿ was not considered a right triangle but a "left triangle.")

Moreover, just tallying the number of correct answers may *underestimate* a child's competence. An example of a "false failure" (or "performance failure") is a child who actual understands the rationale for a computational procedure but obtains the incorrect answer because of a momentary distraction, unclear wording, or tiredness. Finally a focus on performance overlooks invaluable information when children miss test items because they truly lack mastery. That is, in the case of a "true failure" ("competence failure"), it does not provide information about how a child's knowledge or thinking is incomplete or inaccurate.

The field of special education has been preoccupied with assessing underlying psychological processes of a more general sort. Perceptual-motor processes, in particular, have received considerable attention. The "preferred-modality" model, for example, suggests that children have varied learning styles and that instruction should match their processing strengths to compensate for their modality weaknesses. For example, the Mann-Suiter test assesses auditory, visual, tactual-kinesthetic, imagery, and language processes. For a child identified as a "visual learner" and having an "auditory deficit," a teacher would make maximum use of demonstrations, pictures, and the like and minimize verbal instruction. Though such an approach is still frequently recommended (e.g., Meyers & Burton, 1989), there is little evidence to support it (e.g., Gibson & Levin, 1975; Vellutino, Steger, Moyer, Harding, & Niles, 1977).

More recently, Cawley (e.g., 1985b) has suggested an interactive-unit model for assessing learning style and delivering instruction in an efficient manner. The model suggests 16 possible combinations of interaction between teacher and child (teacher manipulates, displays, says, or writes combined with a child manipulates, identifies, says, or writes). This is consistent with the *Standards'* suggestion to use different contexts or formats, which provides mutliple sources of information to accommodate individual thinking styles and capabilities. Though it is clearly beneficial to use a variety of formats in testing and teaching and to encourage children to respond in a variety of modes, it is not clear that educators should *focus* on modality or style strengths and weaknesses. Because an *individual's* learning or thinking style may vary with different content, contexts, and so forth, it may generally be more helpful to focus on processes underlying specific academic tasks.

At What Level Should Assessment be Conducted?

The initial level of assessment should be conducted in the classroom on an ongoing basis (e.g., Commission on Standards for School Mathematics, 1989). Classroom assessments are an indispensable component of diagnostic teaching. Teachers are in a good position to identify learning problems. Their assessment procedures are closely linked to instruction, and they are in the best position to use assessment data (Wallace & Larsen, 1978). Some children require a more detailed assessment. An intermediate level of assessment usually involves evaluating specific deficiencies in detail (Wallace & Larsen, 1978). A few (severely handicapped) children may require an advanced level of assessment—in-depth assessment by various educational and medical professionals.

What Tools Are Needed for Effective Assessment?

The *Standards* specify that assessment methods should be consistent with the purpose of assessment and that assessment should be aligned with a curriculum's goals, content, and approaches. Standardized (norm-referenced) tests compare a child's performance to other children and focus on how many correct answers a child produces. These include tests designed to gauge general ability, such as the WISC-R (Wechsler Intelligence Scale for Children-Revised) Arithmetic Test and the SRA (Science Research Associates) Primary Abilities Number Test, and those designed to gauge achievement, such as the Iowa Test of Basic Skills or the Wide Range Achievement Test. Such tests may be useful in categorizing children as, say, high or low achievers and can be useful in diagnosing a learning difficulty for the purposes of placement or special services eligibility (e.g., Tucker, 1985). However, they do not provide the kind of information necessary for planning instruction (e.g., Ysseldyke & Algozzine, 1982). The Test of Early Mathematics Ability or TEMA (Ginsburg & Baroody, 1983) is a norm-referenced achievement instrument that attempts to provide more detailed information than is usually made available by such tests. The TEMA describes a child's relative ability in informal and formal mathematical thinking and may provide some guidance for instructional planning.

Even standardized mathematical instruments labeled "diagnostic" tests may not provide adequate information for planning instruction (e.g., Cawley, 1985b; Goodstein, 1984; Underhill, Uprichard, & Heddens, 1980). For example, the KeyMath Diagnostic Arithmetic Test and the Stanford Diagnostic Math Test lack detailed coverage of computational skills and mathematical concepts (e.g., Baroody, 1987a; Goodstein, 1984; Underhill et al., 1980). Typically, on standardized diagnostic tests, understanding is measured superficially, if at all (e.g., Hayes, 1985a; Hendrickson, 1983).

Moreover, such tests often do not adequately provide for error analyses or other means for the evaluating process (e.g., Underhill et al., 1980; Wallace and Larsen, 1978). In brief, the information from standardized tests—even standardized diagnostic tests—is inadequate for classroom assessment, an intermediate-level assessment, or a case study.*

Various ability tests have been developed to diagnose learning disabilities and identify deficient underlying psychological processes. Early efforts (e.g., the Bender Visual Motor Gestalt Test, the Frostig Developmental Test of Visual Perception, the Illinois Test of Psycholinguistic Abilities) focused on uncovering deficits in sensory-motor functions such as visual, visual-motor, and auditory processes. Such test batteries have been criticized as ineffective, because they simply identify particular symptoms or inexperience for the purpose of classification (Glaser, 1981), and because they lack sound empirical support (see, e.g., Arter & Jenkins, 1979; Coles, 1978).

Various "psychological-processes" tests attempt to gauge both ability and achievement. For example, the Woodcock-Johnson Psychoeducational Battery tests such abilities as spatial relations and visual-auditory learning and achievement in areas such as calculation and passage comprehension. The K-ABC (Kaufman Assessment Battery for Children), which is based on a theory of simultaneous-successive information processing (Das, Kirby, & Jarmon, 1979), tests such abilities as hand movements and spatial memory and achievement in areas like arithmetic and reading decoding. The K-ABC and Mann-Suiter, in particular, make many explicit instructional recommendations. In general, though, instruments purporting to provide a basis for remediation and their accompanying treatment programs have yielded only limited success (Cawley, 1985c).

In recent years, there has been an effort to link assessment more closely to instruction—to make testing and teaching integral activities (Glaser, 1981; Goodstein, 1985). Indeed, "curriculum-based assessment" (CBA) has been hailed as the emerging alternative in special education (Blankenship, 1985b; Deno, 1985; Galagan, 1985). The rationale of CBA is that assessment should be done on a frequent basis and should gauge a progression of

---

*The KeyMath (Connolly, Nachtman, & Pritchett, 1971/1976) does yield subtest scores that give a rough indication of a child's ability in various areas. Moreover, item performance can be analyzed in terms of listed objectives to indicate mastery of specific skills. Unfortunately, features of the criterion-referenced format limit the interpretation of results (e.g., Cawley, 1985b). In particular, one item per objective is inadequate for evaluating an objective (Underhill et al., 1980). Some objectives are not measured effectively, and the design of others may produce false failure success (see Baroody, 1987a). The Stanford Diagnostic Math Test does contain a detailed section on interpreting scores and implementing remedial instruction, which many teachers have found helpful (Wallace & Larsen, 1978). The ability of standardized diagnostic tests such as the KeyMath and Stanford Diagnostic Math Test can be improved by examining a child's strategies while answering items, using follow-up probes, and by analyzing errors (e.g., Wallace & Larsen, 1978).

specific classroom- or curriculum-related skills (e.g., Blankenship, 1985b). This form of criterion-referenced testing is especially useful for assessing a subject domain like mathematics where hierarchies of specific skills can be delineated and it is important to evaluate specific components in a skill progression (e.g., Baroody, 1987a). Moreover, such testing can tap understanding and strategies *if* test items are designed carefully.

However, criterion-referenced tests—like standardized tests—focus primarily on product (e.g., Baroody, 1987a). Because these tests assess what is learned as well as the number of items correct, they can serve as an important starting point for the assessment of specific competencies. Nevertheless, they are not sufficient in themselves to build and test a theory about a child's mental structures. The utility of criterion-referenced tests can be expanded by, for example, observing a child's solution strategies to test items and using follow-up probes (e.g., asking a child to justify his or her response, to explain a solution strategy, to answer a related but somewhat different question). In brief, if designed and used wisely, criterion-referenced tests can be *a* valuable source of information for all three levels of assessment described above.

Informal assessment is an invaluable means for building and testing a theory about a child's mental state (Ginsburg, 1987). Teacher observations and analyses of written assignments can be a rich and practical source of information. Anecdotal records, checklists, rating scales, and teacher-made tests can also be useful for classroom-level assessment and providing a groundwork for more detailed assessments (e.g., see Wallace & Larsen, 1978, pp. 461–466). Modifying and adapting commercially made tests or inventories is another possibility and perhaps more practical than developing teacher-made tests (Goodstein, 1984). Mathematical games, which can be used at any level of assessment, provide a structured situation for observation while reducing the threat of testing and maximizing a child's motivation (cf. Allardice & Ginsburg, 1983). However, the effectiveness of informal assessment—like any kind of assessment—depends upon the theoretical sophistication of the evaluator (cf. Goodstein, 1984; Underhill et al., 1980; Wallace & Larsen, 1978). Moreover, more work needs to be done in developing observational tools that allow teachers to collect specific data quickly and easily.

One-on-one clinical interviews, which involve engaging a child in a dialogue and *probing* his or her answers, are an important means for studying children's mental structures (see, e.g., DeRuiter & Wansart, 1982, Chapter 6; Underhill et al., 1980). Though most practical at the case-study level of assessment, classroom teachers can engage children in brief interviews that may generate very useful information (e.g., Peck, Jencks, & Connell, 1989). Mathematics educators have long recommended keeping up a dialogue with children as a means for exploring mental processes (e.g.,

Brownell, 1935; Lampert, 1986). Buswell and Judd (1925, pp. 117–118) noted that: "One of the most significant contributions to the technique of diagnosis in arithmetic was made [in] 1917 by Uhl. Uhl analyzed his cases by observing the pupil and questioning him *while at work*. . . (emphasis added). The advantage of this procedure as compared with the method of analyzing test papers can scarcely be overestimated" (cf. Cox, 1975; Goodstein, 1984). Lankford's (1974) 10 questions (e.g., Tell me how you. . . . Why did you . . .?; How else could you . . .? How can you be sure that . . .?; If . . . then what?) can help a teacher get started probing a student's ideas and strategies in almost any mathematical domain (Wiederholt, Hammill, & Brown, 1983, cited in Cronin, 1985).

COMPONENTS OF EFFECTIVE ASSESSMENT

To build a theory about a child's mathematical knowledge as completely and accurately as possible, assessment efforts should collect data on informal knowledge, specific strengths and weaknesses, skill accuracy and efficiency, concepts and problem-solving skills, strategies, errors, learning potential or readiness, metacognitive skills, and affective factors and beliefs. To understand many learning difficulties, it is also essential to assess the educational context in which the child is immersed. At present, assessment of mathematical knowledge is primitive. Future efforts should consider the following:

Effective assessment examines informal as well as formal knowledge. It is especially important with children who are having difficulty learning school mathematics to evaluate informal knowledge. On the one hand, many children with low academic achievement may already know a good deal of informal mathematics that can be exploited to learn formal mathematics (Ginsburg, 1989). Too often, though, they have come to distrust their informal methods or fail to see a relationship between their informal knowledge and school mathematics (Allardice & Ginsburg, 1983). Remedial efforts should build upon a child's strengths (Underhill et al., 1980). Moreover, by noting the informal knowledge they have already learned (and may take for granted), a teacher can help build children's confidence in their ability to learn mathematics.

On the other hand, research (e.g., Baroody, 1987b) suggests that there are important individual differences in informal mathematical knowledge—even among those just entering school (Baroody & Ginsburg, 1982). For example, children vary greatly in their ability to solve simple arithmetic problems, even with objects present (e.g., Carpenter & Moser, 1983; Ginsburg & Russell, 1981; Lindvall & Ibarra, 1979). For those with weak informal arithmetic skills, it will be especially difficult to master formal skills, such as the basic addition facts. It is essential, then, to identify and remedy informal deficiencies quickly before beginning formal instruction and before the child is entangled in a spiral of failure.

Effective assessment details a child's individual pattern of strengths and weaknesses. With schooling, the range of individual differences in mathematical performance often becomes even more pronounced. Individual differences become especially apparent when number-fact training and place-value-related instruction are introduced. Knowledge of specific strengths and weaknesses is crucial for effective instructional planning, especially in the case of children who are having learning difficulties. For example, it is not adequate for an evaluation to indicate that a child has a low arithmetic achievement or a number-fact deficiency. To provide specific direction for instruction or remediation, assessment should specify what families of combinations (relationships, rules, or patterns) a child has mastered or not learned. Specific knowledge of strengths permits the educator to focus training efforts more effectively on what needs attention. Moreover, children's strengths can often be exploited by help remedy weaknesses (e.g., Hayes, 1985b).

In addition to providing clear direction for devising remedial procedures, a focus on the specific fosters a conviction that something can be done to correct the child's deficiencies (Baroody & Ginsburg, 1982). By contrast, vague diagnoses such as "minimal brain damage," "learning disability," or "low mathematical ability" do not suggest a clear or specific course of remedial treatment (e.g., Tucker, 1985; Wallace & Larsen, 1978). In addition to being of little practical value, these general labels may be frightening or prejudicial, giving the impression that the child cannot be helped.

Effective assessment evaluates accuracy and efficiency of skills. Because school mathematics routinely builds on more basic skills, it is important that a child use basic skills accurately. Moreover, because many basic skills are often combined to form more complex skills, it is essential that such skills be automatic as well as accurate. Automatic subskills reduce the load on working memory and free attention to focus on more complex tasks (e.g., Hasselbring et al., 1987; Resnick & Ford, 1981). For example, learning the multidigit multiplication algorithm is easier if two component skills (recall of basic multiplication combinations and application of the written addition algorithm including renaming) are automatic (e.g., Baroody, 1987a; Goldman et al., 1988; Kaye, 1986). However, assessment of basic number-fact knowledge often underestimates efficiency because "generous time limits" allow children to use relatively inefficient strategies to respond (Ackerman et al., 1986).

Effective assessment focuses on concepts and problem-solving skill. In addition to the mastery of basic skills, society increasingly expects and many jobs now require the attainment of comprehension and problem-solving skills (Commission on Standards for School Mathematics, 1989; Davis, 1984; Glaser, 1981). Because conceptualizing and solving problems depends upon a well-connected knowledge, it is essential that children understand mathematics and develop a rich body of relational knowledge as well as factual knowledge. Unfortunately, many children—especially those classified as learning disabled—lack such knowledge (e.g., Baroody, 1987a; Kaliski, 1962). Moreover, even when they have adequate reading skills, children labeled learning disabled have difficulty solving all but the simplest arithmetic word problems (e.g., Blankenship & Lovitt, 1976; Englert, Culatta, & Horn, 1987; Fleischner & Garnett, 1983; Ginsburg & Russell, 1981; Russell & Ginsburg, 1984).

Because effective instruction and remediation involve fostering meaningful learning as well as the acquisition of skills, assessment should not end with evaluating skill accuracy and efficiency (Brownell, 1935). Assessment should focus on concepts, even with young children labeled learning disabled (Hayes, 1985b). Greeno (1978) suggests three criteria for assessing understanding (the degree to which knowledge is well structured): (a) the accuracy and completeness of knowledge (the extent to which it *corresponds* to expert knowledge); (b) the degree to which concepts are integrated (the extent to which concepts are related in a *coherent* manner); and (c) the extent to which knowledge can be applied (the degree to which a concept is *connected* with various examples or situations) (Resnick & Ford, 1981). For example, with mental arithmetic, (a) How complete is a child's knowledge of addition patterns, principles, and rules? Does a child understand the role of zero in addition or other operations, recognize that commuted addition or multiplication combinations are equivalent, and so forth. (b) Does he or she see how the operations (e.g., combinations such as $3 + 2 = 5$ and $5 - 3 = 2$) are related? (c) Does the child connect $5 + 5 = 10$ to other situations such as the total number of fingers on both hands or the sum of 5 cents and 5 cents?

Understanding can be assessed by asking students to label concepts; identify or generate examples *and* nonexamples of a concept; use concrete models, drawings, or symbols to represent a concept; translate one form of representation into another, recognize various meanings or interpretations of a concept; identify properties of a given concept; or compare and contrast concepts (see Commission on Standards for School Mathematics, 1989, pp. 223–227). It can further be assessed by asking children to justify their responses (e.g., see Lampert, 1986), introducing situations (e.g., materials, arrangements, or examples) requiring knowledge transfer (e.g., Cawley, 1983, 1985b), using unfamiliar and nonstandard word problems (e.g., problems containing extraneous information and more than one operation), and so forth (see Resnick & Ford, 1981, pages 206–213, for suggestions regarding the assessment of integration, correspondence, and connectedness). An assessment of a student's understanding of a mathematical procedure might include recognizing when the procedure is appropriate, giving reasons for the steps of the procedure, recognizing correct or incorrect procedures, and extending or modifying a procedure to meet new demands (see Commission on Standards for School Mathematics, 1989, pp. 228–232). An assessment of mathematical problem solving might include evidence that a student can formulate a problem from, say, a list of raw data or a symbolic expression or apply a variety of strategies to solve a problem (see Commission on Standards for School Mathematics, 1989, pp. 209–213).

Effective assessment examines solution strategies. It is important to watch children's overt behavior and analyze their responses to gauge solution methods for a number of reasons (Ginsburg & Mathews, 1984). First, because children often do not do mathematics in the prescribed way, it may be helpful to know how a child informally copes with a mathematical task. This can provide insight into how the child understands the problems and what formal skills and concepts need to be taught. Second, examining strategies may indicate whether or not a child really understands a correctly used procedure or a correct answer. Third, examining a child's solution method may identify a specific unlearned step or misunderstanding that can be remedied efficiently. Fourth, examining process can reveal more understanding than an incorrect answer indicates.

Furthermore, it is important to gauge whether or not a child spontaneously invents more sophisticated strategies. Inventing a more efficient strategy is a key sign that the child is actively monitoring his or her performance and not merely responding in a mechanical fashion. Under favorable conditions, even children with severe learning difficulties can monitor their performance and invent more sophisticated computing strategies (Baroody, 1987a). Moreover, strategy transformations may result from conceptual or qualitative leaps in development and, therefore, may provide insight into the growth of understanding or thinking ability. Inefficient strategies place great demands on working memory and may absorb so much attention that a child may not hear instructions, notice patterns, or attend to other higher level tasks. Children classified as learning disabled often fail to transform existing strategies into more efficient procedures, which would reduce the demands placed on working memory and free their attention to deal with other tasks (e.g., Swanson & Rhine, 1985).

If strategy transformations do not occur spontaneously in a reasonable amount of time, efforts should focus on teaching more efficient strategies directly and assessing the effectiveness of such intervention efforts. For example, many children classified as learning disabled fail to invent thinking strategies to reason out basic number facts (e.g., Allardice & Ginsburg, 1983; Baroody, 1987a; Myers & Thornton, 1977; Swanson & Rhine, 1985). Many, but not all (e.g., see Allardice & Ginsburg, 1983), apparently can effectively be taught such strategies (e.g., see Thornton, 1978; Thornton, Jones, & Toohey, 1983; Thornton & Toohey, 1985).

Effective assessment includes an error analysis. In general, errors should be viewed as *incomplete* responses rather than "wrong" responses (e.g., DeRuiter & Wansart, 1982). Even when instruction is highly effective, it is not possible to foster the construction of entirely complete and accurate structures all at once (Resnick & Ford, 1981). Therefore, incomplete structures and the systematic errors that result are the natural products of instruction (Resnick et al., 1989). Error analyses can be an important source of information about children's underlying knowledge. That is, the nature of children's systematic errors can provide an invaluable clue to their *level* of functioning (Glaser, 1981).

Toward this end, Siegler (e.g., 1978) suggests using a rule-assessment approach: a set of problems that yield distinct responses indicating the sophistication of an underlying child's conceptual knowledge or reasoning process. A relatively simple example of this approach is illustrated by the set of problems listed in Table 9-1 to assess mental-arithmetic performance. An analysis of the *pattern of errors* can indicate whether a child is operating at an unsophisticated level (indiscriminately uses inaccurate rules), a somewhat higher level (indiscriminately uses rules that reflect some understanding of addition), or a relatively sophisticated level (discriminately uses a rule for adding zero and/or one).

Error analyses, such as a rule-assessment approach, can provide a relatively deep analysis of a child's understanding and thinking (Glaser, 1981). It can indicate where a child is in terms of the completeness of his or her knowledge and, hence, can ensure a tighter fit between a child's needs or readiness and instruction. In the same vein, systematic errors may indicate an underlying misconception or misunderstanding, provide an invaluable signal that instruction is out of synchrony with the psychology of the child, and give specific direction to remedial efforts. An examination of systematic errors is critical to elaborating a theory about the internal state of a child and planning instruction. In light of the fact that children classified as learning disabled may make more systematic errors that indicate relatively incomplete and inaccurate understanding of mathematics (see Cox, 1975), such analyses are especially important for children classified as learning disabled. Ginsburg and Mathews (1984) have developed a test that identifies error strategies in the four operations of arithmetic.

Effective assessment should gauge learning potential or readiness. Assessment should go beyond evaluating whether or not a child has mastered skills and understands concepts already taught; it should provide an indication of whether or not a child is ready for previously untaught skills and concepts (e.g., Hayes, 1985b). In assessing learning disabilities, Vygotsky (1978) distinguished between a child's existing progress (achievement) and the child's potential progress if given assistance (Brown & French, 1979). The difference is termed the "zone of potential development" (Glaser, 1981) or the "zone of proximal development" (Vygotsky, 1978). Gauging learning potential includes assessing the readiness for a specific skill or concept and can provide an indication of how quickly a child can "pick up" new material. When taught in a meaningful fashion, many children labeled learning disabled learn new material in a surprisingly quick fashion (e.g., see Baroody, 1986, 1987a, 1989a), which belies their diagnosis as organically or learning impaired. In other words, many such children do not have difficulty *learning* (Allardice & Ginsburg, 1983). Though the assessment of general learning potential and readiness for specific tasks is crucial for the design of effective instruction (Brown & French, 1979), it is often overlooked in diagnostic or screening efforts (Allardice & Ginsburg, 1983). (Feuerstein [1979] has developed a learning potential test battery for children classified as culturally disadvantaged or learning disabled. Otherwise, "there has been surprisingly little interest in investigation *learning* ability in children exhibiting poor performance in school" [Allardice & Ginsburg, 1983, p. 345].)

For example, before formal arithmetic instruction, many kindergartners, and even some first-graders, do not construct an organized informal strategy for computing sums to single-digit problems like 5 and 3 more (e.g., Baroody, 1987b; Carpenter & Moser, 1983). Many of these children would fail a test item measuring informal addition skill for no other reason than they have not had the opportunity to learn such a skill. Yet, shown a counting procedure just once or twice, some of these children quickly learn how to compute sums accurately.

In most cases, it is not particularly useful to assess readiness with tasks that gauge general cognitive capabilities. For example, though Piaget's number conservation task is often proposed as a readiness measure for number or arithmetic instruction (e.g., Hendrickson, 1983), it is clear that children learn much about these domains before they can conserve (e.g., Mpiangu & Gentile, 1970).* On the other hand, a specific assessment of previously taught skills and concepts is *an* important guide in gauging

---

*Allardice & Ginsburg (1983) note that various studies (see, e.g., Saxe & Shaheen, 1981) have reported a positive relationship between the attainment of various conservation skills and mathematical achievement but that a cause-and-effect relationship has not been demonstrated. Moreover, the theoretical relationship between task measuring general cognitive ability and specific academic task is frequently not specified or only weakly justified.

readiness, because many times such knowledge is a basis for new instruction. In cases where new material is qualitatively different or represents a qualitative leap in ability, assessment directly related to the new learning task may still be more useful than assessing general cognitive capabilities.

Effective assessment takes into account metacognitive knowledge. Children classified as learning disabled are often described as deficient in metacognitive skills, such as applying an appropriate strategy to learn new material or checking the reasonableness of answers (e.g., Allardice & Ginsburg, 1983; Cherkes-Julkowski, 1985). Indeed, in many cases, the fundamental problem is not the lack of factual, procedural, or strategic knowledge per se but in the process of *selecting* appropriate knowledge and *using* it effectively (e.g., Brown, 1978). Some research does suggest that children classified as learning disabled can learn strategic behaviors (Scheid, 1989). Given the central importance of such skills in learning new material, strategy transfer, and successfully solving problems, it is important to evaluate the metacognitive skills a child uses (Glaser, 1981; Pressley et al., 1989). For example, does a child use existing knowledge about addition to monitor and correct responses on a mental-addition task, such as "five" given for the problem 5 + 1 or 5 + 3? Does the child realize that there are patterns or rules that can make memorizing the basic facts easier (Allardice & Ginsburg, 1983)?

Effective assessment takes into account affective factors and beliefs. Evaluating personality factors (e.g., motivation, interests, and feelings) and beliefs is crucial because they can have tremendous impact on performance of children labeled learning disabled (e.g., Cronin, 1985; DeRuiter & Wansart, 1982). It is helpful to discover, for example, a child's interest so that instruction can build upon this source of inherent motivation. It is also important to uncover what beliefs a child needs to construct. Many children do not realize that it is intelligent to ask questions when something is not understood or that a key aspect of mathematics is the search for patterns or relationships. Moreover, mathematical assessment should gauge students' disposition toward engaging in mathematics (Commission on Standards for School Mathematics, 1989). This entails collecting information on their confidence, flexibility, and perseverance in doing mathematics. It also involves collecting data on their interest in and curiosity about mathematics, as well as their appreciation of mathematics as a tool for making sense of the world.

It is essential to listen carefully to students to determine what feelings and beliefs may be hindering their learning. Many children develop a fear of failure and employ protective mechanisms such as avoidance behaviors (e.g., procrastination or an unwillingness to try), which undercuts motivation and makes learning even less likely (Allardice & Ginsburg, 1983; Holt,

1964). Such cycles of self-defeating behavior are driven by destructive beliefs (e.g., only smart people are lovable, and smart people learn and respond quickly), notions taught and reinforced implicitly or even explicitly in and out of school (Baroody, 1987a). For example, children frequently are expected to memorize number facts quickly and to respond quickly on timed tests, and they are rewarded (through praise, star charts, and so forth) or punished (through some form of humiliation) accordingly. Furthermore, labeling children as learning disabled too often validates and reinforces destructive beliefs. In extreme cases, unreasonable beliefs result in math anxiety—that is, they generate so much anxiety that children become mathematically disabled (Baroody, 1987a). Particularly with children who have had a history of learning difficulties, it is essential to identify and dispel feelings and beliefs that block a child's learning. Otherwise, the pupil may well resist and foredoom remedial efforts.

Effective assessment examines the nature of a child's instruction. Assessment too often focuses solely on internal causes of learning difficulties. For example, distractibility, confusion, poor memory for facts, inability to generalize, hyperactivity, and perseveration are often cited as characteristics of children with learning disabilities (e.g., Kosc, 1974; Lerner, 1971; Sears, 1986). Furthermore, such dysfunctions are sometimes viewed as the causes of learning difficulties (e.g., Homan, 1970; Strauss & Kephart, 1955).

In many cases, though, characteristics are the *symptoms* of learning difficulties, not the cause. That is, such behaviors may result from meaningless, uninteresting, or psychologically punishing instruction. "It seems that nothing is more likely to produce . . . inattentive behavior than work that the child perceives as being beyond his comprehension" (Allardice & Ginsburg, 1983, p. 341). When instruction does not make sense to children, it should not be surprising that they become muddled or forgetful, or fail to apply their knowledge. When instruction is not engaging or when it is painful (e.g., humiliating, frustrating), some children quite understandably rebel or engage in avoidance behaviors. When assigned work makes little or no sense and it is personally irrelevant to students, it encourages thoughtless and hasty completion of assignments. "Perseveration" is further encouraged when worksheets typically focus on a single skill. Indeed, it makes some sense to figure out what is involved in the first few problems and then mindlessly use the same procedure to complete the rest of the page.

Clearly, behaviors such as inattentiveness can contribute to and further complicate a learning difficulty (e.g., Kirk & Chalfant, 1984). Thus, in assessing a learning difficulty it is essential to take an **ecological approach** (e.g., Cronin, 1985; Wallace & Larson, 1978)—to assess external factors such as the nature and pace of a child's instruction. For instance, does number-fact practice consist largely of uninteresting flash-card drills? Does the child exhibit such symptoms as distractibility when instruction is meaningful and interesting?

THE CASE OF ROBERT

We conclude the chapter with the case of Robert, a third grader who was interviewed by the first author, because it illustrates and ties together a number of important points. One day the lad came home and asked if he could stay home from school the next day. Robert was supposed to memorize 9-times combinations for homework, and he was afraid of the consequences of being unprepared the next day. Robert's mother called his teacher to point out that he had not even learned the 6s, 7s, or 8s, and that he was overwhelmed by his new assignment. The teacher responded, "You're right, the 9s are hard. We'll spend *two days* on them instead of one!" Nevertheless, Robert's mother was left with the impression that her son was well behind his classmates and that this was due to a learning disability. Now deeply worried about her son's progress and mental abilities, she sought help to determine what was wrong with her son and to see if he could be helped.

A clinical interview revealed that Robert had no difficulty recalling combinations involving 0, 1, 2, 5, or even 10 but had to compute the products of other combinations. Robert's pattern of strengths and weaknesses were, in fact, altogether *typical* of a third-grader. He knew the combinations involving 0 and 1 because of the straightforward rules underlying these "fact families." He also knew the 2s, 5s, and 10s because he was intimately familiar with counting by 2s, 5s, and 10s. Because he saw the connection between multiplication and his existing (skip) counting knowledge, he had readily mastered these combinations. Robert also had a conceptual basis for multiplication: He realized that multiplication was equivalent to the repeated addition of like terms. Moreover, he had learned that factor order did not affect outcome. (Many children quickly discover that, like addition, multiplication is commutative.)

The case of Robert is typical of altogether too many children labeled as learning disabled (cf. Baroody, 1987a, 1989a; Ginsburg, 1989). The label, in effect, blamed the learning difficulty on the child: The lad could not learn and keep up because he had a mental defect (Allardice & Ginsburg, 1983; Coles, 1978). However, Robert's learning difficulties were not due to deficiencies in his intellect—he was not cognitively disabled. The problem was created by psychologically inappropriate instruction—instruction that was inappropriately paced. Robert and his parents were the victims of anxiety caused by such unrealistic beliefs as: Basic number combinations are merely a basket of facts that all children can memorize quickly (e.g., the mastery of 9-times facts can easily be accomplished in one or, at the most, two days—without a period of informal calculation and exploration). Discussing Robert's specific informal and formal strengths, the real reasons for his difficulties, and the important role of informal mathematics in learning formal mathematics, provided the boy and his mother visible relief. In brief, the assessment provided a clearer understanding of the child's knowledge and how to help him. Equally important, it provided perspective by identifying and dispelling destructive beliefs, in part, by noting how external factors, such as the nature and pace of instruction, contributed to the difficulty.

REFERENCES

Ackerman, P. T., Anhalt, J. M., & Dykman, R. A. (1986). Arithmetic automatization failure in children with attention and reading disorders: Association and sequela. *Journal of Learning Disabilities, 19*, 222–232.

Algozzine, B., & Ysseldyke, J. E. (1986). The future of the LD field: Screening and diagnosis. *Journal of Learning Disabilities, 19*, 394–398.

Allardice, B. S., & Ginsburg, H. P. (1983). Children's learning problems in mathematics. In H. P. Ginsburg (Ed.), *The development of mathematical thinking* (pp. 319–349). New York: Academic Press.

Anderson, J. R. (1980). *Cognitive psychology and its implications*. San Francisco: W. H. Freeman.

Anderson, R. C. (1984). Some reflections on the acquisition of knowledge. *Educational Researcher, 13*(9), 5–10.

Arter, J. A., & Jenkins, J. R. (1979). Differential diagnosis-Prescriptive teaching: A critical appraisal. *Review of Educational Research, 49*, 517–555.

Ashlock, R. B. (1982). *Error patterns in computation*. Columbus, OH: Merrill.

Baker, L., & Brown, A. L. (1984). Cognitive monitoring in reading. In J. Flood (Ed.), *Understanding reading comprehension* (pp. 21–44). Newark, DE: International Reading Association.

Baroody, A. J. (1983). The development of children's informal addition. In J. C. Bergeron & N. Herscovics (Eds.), *Proceedings of the Fifth Annual Meeting of the North American Chapter of the International Group for the Psychology of Mathematics Education* (Vol. 1, pp. 222–229). Montreal: University of Montreal.

Baroody, A. J. (1984). Children's difficulties in subtraction: Some causes and questions. *Journal for Research in Mathematics Education, 15*, 203–213.

Baroody, A. J. (1985). Mastery of basic number combinations: Internalization of relationships or facts? *Journal for Research in Mathematics Education, 16*, 83–98.

Baroody, A. J. (1986). The value of informal approaches to mathematics instruction and remediation. *Arithmetic Teacher, 33*(5), 14–18.

Baroody, A. J. (1987a). *Children's mathematical thinking: A developmental framework for preschool, primary, and special education teachers*. New York: Teachers College.

Baroody, A. J. (1987b). The development of counting strategies for single-digit addition. *Journal for Research in Mathematics Education, 18*, 141–157.

Baroody, A. J. (1988a). Mental addition development of children classified as mentally handicapped. *Educational Studies in Mathematics, 19*, 369–388.

Baroody, A. J. (1988b). Number-comparison learning by children classified as mentally handicapped. *American Journal of Mental Deficiency, 92* (5), 461–471.
Baroody, A. J. (1988c). A schema model of mental-arithmetic development. In M. J. Behr, C. B. Lacampagne, & M. M. Wheeler (Eds.), *Proceedings of the Tenth Annual Meeting of the North American Chapter of the International Group for the Psychology of Mathematics Education* (pp. 36–43). DeKalb, IL: Northern Illinois University.
Baroody, A. J. (1989a). *The case of Tommy: A child labeled learning disabled*. Unpublished manuscript. University of Illinois at Urbana-Champaign.
Baroody, A. J. (1989b). *A guide to teaching mathematics in the primary grades*. Boston: Allyn & Bacon.
Baroody, A. J. (1989c). Kindergartners' mental addition with single-digit combinations. *Journal for Research in Mathematics Education, 20,* 159–172.
Baroody, A. J., & Berent, R., & Packman, D. (1982). The use of mathematical structure by inner city children. *Focus on Learning Problems in Mathematics, 4* (2), 5–13.
Baroody, A. J., & Gannon, K. E. (1984). The development of the commutativity principle and economical addition strategies. *Cognition and Instruction, 1,* 321–329.
Baroody, A. J., & Ginsburg, H. P. (1982). Preschoolers' informal mathematical skills: Research and diagnosis. *American Journal of Diseases of Children, 136,* 195–197.
Baroody, A. J., & Ginsburg, H. P. (1986). The relationship between initial meaningful and mechanical knowledge of arithmetic. In J. Hiebert (Ed.), *Conceptual and procedural knowledge: The case of mathematics* (pp. 75–112). Hillsdale, NJ: Erlbaum.
Baroody, A. J., Ginsburg, H. P., & Waxman, B. (1983). Children's use of mathematical structure. *Journal for Research in Mathematics Education, 14,* 156–168.
Blankenship, C. S. (1984). Curriculum and instruction: An examination of models in special and regular education. In J. F. Cawley (Ed.), *Developmental teaching of mathematics for the learning disabled* (pp. 29–53). Rockville, MD: Aspen.
Blankenship, C. S. (1985a). Linking assessment to curriculum and instruction. In J. F. Cawley (Ed.), *Practical mathematics: Appraisal of the learning disabled* (pp. 59–79). Rockville, MD: Aspen.
Blankenship, C. S. (1985b). Using curriculum-based assessment data to make instructional decisions. *Exceptional Children, 53,* 233–238.
Blankenship, C. S. (1988, October). *Learning disabilities: Toward the year 2000*. Paper presented at the Bicentennial Conference of the Australian Association of Special Education, Sydney, Australia.
Blankenship, C. S., & Lovitt, T. C. (1976). Story problems: Merely confusing or downright befuddling? *Journal of Research in Mathematics Education, 7,* 290–298.
Bley, N. S., & Thornton, C. A. (1981). *Teaching mathematics to the learning disabled*. Rockville, MD: Aspen.
Brown, A. L. (1978). Knowing when, where, and how to remember: A problem of metacognition. In R. Glaser (Ed.), *Advances in instructional psychology* (pp. 77–163). Hillsdale, NJ: Erlbaum.
Brown, A. L., & French, L. A. (1979). The zone of potential development: Implications for intelligence testing in the year 2000. In R. J. Sternberg & D. K. Detterman (Eds.), *Human intelligence: Perspectives on theory and measurement* (pp. 217–235). Norwood, NJ: Ablex.
Brown, J. S., & Burton, R. R. (1978). Diagnostic models for procedural bugs in basic mathematical skills. *Cognitive Science, 2,* 155–192.
Brownell, W. A. (1935). Psychological considerations in the learning and the teaching of arithmetic. In *The teaching of arithmetic* (10th Yearbook of the National

Council of Teachers of Mathematics, pp. 1–31). New York: Bureau of Publications, Teachers College, Columbia University.
Bruner, J. S. (1966). *Toward a theory of instruction.* Cambridge, MA: Belkap Press of Harvard University.
Buswell, G. T., & Judd, C. H. (1925). Summary of educational investigations relating to arithmetic. *Supplementary Educational Monographs,* No. 27. Chicago: University of Chicago Press.
Carpenter, T. P. (1986). Conceptual knowledge as a foundation for procedural knowledge: Implications from research on the initial learning of arithmetic. In J. Hiebert (Ed.), *Conceptual and procedural knowledge: The case of mathematics* (pp. 113–132). Hillsdale, NJ: Erlbaum.
Carpenter, T. P., Mathews, W., Lindquist, M. M., & Silver, E. A. (1984). Achievement in mathematics: Results from the National Assessment. *Elementary School Journal, 84,* 485–495.
Carpenter, T. P., & Moser, M. M. (1983). The acquisition of addition and subtraction concepts. In R. Lesh & M. Landau (Eds.), *Acquisition of mathematical concepts and processes* (pp. 7–44). New York: Academic Press.
Carpenter, T. P., & Moser, J. M. (1984). The acquisition of addition and subtraction concepts in grades one through three. *Journal for Research in Mathematics Education, 15,* 179–202.
Cawley, J. (1983). John Cawley's comments in D. Carnine, D. Elkind, A. D. Hendrickson, D. Meichenbaum, R. L. Sieben, & F. Smith (Eds.), *Interdisciplinary voices in learning disabilities and remedial education* (pp. 107–121). Austin, TX: PRO-ED.
Cawley, J. F. (1985a). Cognition and the learning disabled. In J. F. Cawley (Ed.), *Cognitive strategies and mathematics for the learning disabled* (pp. 1–32). Rockville, MD: Aspen.
Cawley, J. F. (1985b). Learning disability and mathematics appraisal. In J. F. Cawley (Ed.), *Practical mathematics: Appraisal of the learning disabled* (pp. 1–40). Rockville, MD: Aspen.
Cawley, J. F. (1985c). Nonmathematics appraisal. In J. F. Cawley (Ed.), *Practical mathematics: Appraisal of the learning disabled* (pp. 147–175). Rockville, MD: Aspen.
Cherkes-Julkowski, M. (1985). Metacognitive considerations in mathematics instruction for the learning disabled. In J. F. Cawley (Ed.), *Cognitive strategies and mathematics for the learning disabled* (pp. 99–116). Rockville, MD: Aspen.
Cobb, P. (1985a). A reaction to three early number papers. *Journal for Research in Mathematics Education, 16,* 141–145.
Cobb, P. (1985b). Two children's anticipations, beliefs, and motivations, *Educational Studies in Mathematics, 16,* 111–126.
Coles, G. S. (1978). The learning disability test battery: Empirical and social issues. *Harvard Educational Review, 48,* 313–340.
Commission on Standards for School Mathematics (1989). *Curriculum and evaluation standards for school mathematics.* Reston, VA: National Council of Teachers of Mathematics.
Connell, M. L. (1988, April). *What counts in mathematical evaluation?* Paper presented at the annual meeting of the American Educational Research Association, New Orleans.
Connolly, A. J., Nachtman, W., & Pritchett, E. M. (1971/1976). *KeyMath diagnostic arithmetic test manual.* Circle Pines, MN: American Guidance Service.
Court, S. R. A. (1920). Numbers, time, and space in the first five years of a child's life. *Pedagogical Seminary, 27,* 71–89.

Cox, L. S. (1975). Systematic errors in the four vertical algorithms in normal and handicapped populations. *Journal for Research in Mathematics Education, 6,* 202–220.
Cronin, M. E. (1985). Assessment techniques and practices for classroom behaviors, social/emotional factors, and attitudes. In J. F. Cawley (Ed.), *Practical mathematics: Appraisal of the learning disabled* (pp. 215–247). Rockville, MD: Aspen.
Crowley, M. L. (1987). The van Heile model of the development of geometric thought. In M. M. Lindquist & A. P. Shulte (Eds.), *Learning and teaching geometry, K–12* (pp. 1–16). Reston, VA: National Council of Teachers of Mathematics.
Das, J., Kirby, J., & Jarman, R. (1979). *Simultaneous and successive cognitive processing.* New York: Academic Press.
Davis, P. J., & Hersh, R. (1981). *The mathematical experience.* Boston: Houghton-Mifflin.
Davis, R. B. (1983). Complex mathematical cognition. In H. P. Ginsburg (Ed.), *The development of mathematical thinking* (pp. 253–290). New York: Academic Press.
Davis, R. B. (1984). *Learning mathematics: The cognitive science approach to mathematics education.* Norwood, NJ: Ablex.
Davis, R. B. (1986). *The learning of mathematics by elementary school children: Lecture notes for Elementary Education 330.* University of Illinois at Urbana-Champaign.
Deloche, G., & Seron, X. (Eds.). (1987). *Mathematical disabilities: A cognitive neuropsychological perspective.* Hillsdale, NJ: Erlbaum.
Deno, S. L. (1985). Curriculum-based measurement: The emerging alternative. *Exceptional Children, 52,* 219–232.
Denvir, B., & Brown, M. (1986). Understanding of number concepts in low attaining 7–9-year-olds: Part I. Development of descriptive framework and diagnostic instrument. *Educational Studies in Mathematics, 17,* 15–36.
DeRuiter, J. A., & Wansart, W. L. (1982). *Psychology of learning disabilities.* Rockville, MD: Aspen.
Donaldson, M., & Balfour, G. (1968). Less is more. *British Journal of Psychology, 59,* 461–471.
Engelhardt, J. M., Ashlock, R. B., & Wiebe, J. H. (1984). *Helping children understand and use numerals.* Boston: Allyn and Bacon.
Englert, C. S., Culatta, B. E., & Horn, D. G. (1987). Influence of irrelevant information in addition word problems on problem solving. *Learning Disabilities Quarterly, 10* (1), 29–36.
Farnham-Diggory, S. (1978). *Learning disabilities: A psychological perspective.* Cambridge, MA: Harvard University.
Feuerstein, R. (1979). *The dynamic assessment of retarded performers.* Baltimore: University Park Press.
Flavell, J. H. (1976). Metacognitive aspects of problem solving. In L. B. Resnick (Ed.), *The nature of intelligence* (pp. 231–235). Hillsdale, NJ: Erlbaum.
Flavell, J. H., & Wellman, H. M. (1977). Metamemory. In R. V. Kail & J. W. Hagen (Eds.), *Perspectives on the development of memory and cognition* (pp. 3–33). Hillsdale, NJ: Erlbaum.
Fleischner, F. E., & Garnett, K. (1983). Arithmetic difficulties among learning disabled children: Background and current directions. *Learning Disabilities, 2* (9).
Fleischner, F. E., Garnett, K., & Shepard, M. (1982). Proficiency in arithmetic basic fact computation by learning disabled and nondisabled children. *Focus on Learning Problems in Mathematics, 4* (2), 47–55.
Fuson, K. C. (1988). *Children's counting and concepts of number.* New York: Springer-Verlag.

Fuson, K. C., & Hall, J. W. (1983). The acquisition of early number word meanings: A conceptual analysis and review. In H. P. Ginsburg (Ed.), *The development of mathematical thinking* (pp. 49–107). New York: Academic Press.

Fuson, K. C., Richards, J., & Briars, D. J. (1982). The acquisition and elaboration of the number word sequence. In C. Brainerd (Ed.), *Children's logical and mathematical cognition: Progress in cognitive development* (pp. 33–92). New York: Springer-Verlag.

Galagan, J. E. (1985). Psychoeducational testing: Turn out the lights, the party's over. *Exceptional Children, 3*, 288–299.

Gelman, R. (1972). The nature and development of early number concepts. In H. W. Reese (Ed.), *Advances in child development and behavior* (Vol. 7, pp. 115–167). New York: Academic Press.

Gelman, R., & Gallistel, C. (1978). *Young children's understanding of number*. Cambridge: Harvard University Press.

Gibson, E. J. & Levin, H. (1975). *The psychology of reading*. Cambridge: MIT Press.

Ginsburg, H. P. (1987). *Assessing the arithmetic abilities and instructional needs of students*. Austin, TX: PRO-ED.

Ginsburg, H. P. (1989). *Children's arithmetic (second edition)*. Austin, TX: PRO-ED.

Ginsburg, H. P., & Baroody, A. J. (1983). *The test of early mathematics ability* (TEMA). Austin, TX: PRO-ED.

Ginsburg, H. P., & Mathews, S. C. (1984). *Diagnostic test of arithmetic strategies*. Austin, TX: PRO-ED.

Ginsburg, H., & Opper, S. (1988). *Piaget's theory of intellectual development: An introduction* (3rd ed.). Englewood Cliffs, NJ: Prentice-Hall.

Ginsburg, H. P., Posner, J. K., & Russell, R. L. (1981). The development of mental addition as a function of schooling. *Journal of Cross-Cultural Psychology, 12*, 163–178.

Ginsburg, H. P., & Russell, R. L. (1981). Social class and racial influences on early mathematical thinking. *Monographs of the Society for Research in Child Development, 46*, 16 (Serial No. 193).

Glaser, R. (1981). The future of testing: A research agenda for cognitive psychology and psychometrics. *American Psychologist, 36*, 923–936.

Goldman, S. R., Pellegrino, J. W., & Mertz, D. L. (1988). Extended practice of basic addition facts: Strategy changes in learning disabled students. *Cognition and Instruction, 5*, 223–265.

Goodnow, J., & Levine, R. A. (1973). "The grammar of action": Sequence and syntax in children's copying. *Cognitive Psychology, 4*, 82–98.

Goodstein, H. A. (1984). Assessment: Examination and utilization from pre-K through secondary levels. In J. F. Cawley (Ed.), *Developmental teaching of mathematics for the learning disabled* (pp. 55–80). Rockville, MD: Aspen.

Goodstein, H. A. (1985). Measurement. In J. F. Cawley (Ed.), *Practical mathematics: Appraisal of the learning disabled* (pp. 41–58). Rockville, MD: Aspen.

Greeno, J. G. (1978). Understanding and procedural knowledge in mathematics education. *Educational Psychologist, 12*(3), 262–283.

Groen, G. J., & Resnick, L. B. (1977). Can preschool children invent addition algorithms? *Journal of Educational Psychology, 69*, 645–652.

Hasselbring, T. S., Goin, L. I., & Bransford, J. D. (1987). Effective mathematics instruction: Developing automaticity. *Teaching Exceptional Children, 19*(3), 30–33.

Hayes, A. M. F. (1985a). Assessment of the severely impaired mathematics student. In J. F. Cawley (Ed.), *Practical mathematics: Appraisal of the learning disabled* (pp. 249–277). Rockville, MD: Aspen.

Hayes, A. M. F. (1985b). Assessment techniques and practices in the early years. In

J. F. Cawley (Ed.), *Practical mathematics: Appraisal of the learning disabled* (pp. 81–102). Rockville, MD: Aspen.

Hendrickson, A. D. (1983). Prevention or cure? Another look at mathematics learning problems. In D. Carnine, D. Elkind, A. D. Hendrickson, D. Meichenbaum, R. L. Sieben, & F. Smith (Eds.), *Interdisciplinary voices in learning disabilities and remedial education* (pp. 93–107). Austin, TX: PRO-ED.

Hiebert, J. (1984). Children's mathematics learning: The struggle to link form and understanding. *The Elementary School Journal, 84*, 497–513.

Hiebert, J. (1987, April). *Transition to the formal languages of mathematics.* Paper presented at the biennial meeting of the Society for Research in Child Development, Baltimore.

Hiebert, J., & Wearne, D. (1984, April). *A model of students' decimal computation procedures.* Paper presented at the annual meeting of the National Council of Teachers of Mathematics, San Francisco.

Holt, J. (1964). *How children fail.* New York: Delta.

Homan, D. R. (1970). The child with a learning disability in arithmetic. *Arithmetic Teacher, 17*(3), 199–203.

Ilg, F., & Ames, L. B. (1951). Development trends in arithmetic. *Journal of Genetic Psychology, 79*, 3–28.

Kaliski, L. (1962). Arithmetic and the brain-injured child. *Arithmetic Teacher, 9*, 245–251.

Kaye, D. B. (1986). The development of mathematical cognition. *Cognitive Development, 1*, 157–170.

Kidron, R. (1985). *Arithmetic disabilities: Characterization, diagnosis and treatment.* Tel Aviv, Israel: Otzar Hamoreh.

Kirk, S. A., & Chalfant, J. C. (1984). *Academic and developmental learning disabilities.* Denver: Love Publishing.

Kosc, L. (1970). A contribution to the nomenclature and classification of disorders in mathematical abilities. *Studia Psychologica, 12*, 12–28.

Kosc, L. (1974). Developmental dyscalcalia. *Journal of Learning Disabilities, 7*, 164–177.

Kouba, V. (1986, April). *How young children solve multiplication and division word problems.* Paper presented at the National Council of Teachers of Mathematics research presession, Washington, DC.

Kraner, R. E. (1980). Math deficits of learning disabled first graders with mathematics as a primary and secondary disorder. *Focus on Learning Problems in Mathematics, 2*(3), 7–27.

Lampert, M. (1986). Knowing, doing, and teaching multiplication. *Cognition and Instruction, 3*, 305–342.

Lankford, F. G. (1974). What can a teacher learn about a pupil's thinking, through oral interviews. *Arithmetic Teacher, 21*, 26–32.

Lerner, J. (1971). *Children with learning disabilities.* Boston: Houghton-Mifflin.

Lindvall, C. M., & Ibarra, C. G. (1979, April). *The relationship of mode of presentation and of school/community differences to the ability of kindergarten children to comprehend simple story problems.* Paper presented at the annual meeting of the American Educational Research Association, Boston.

Lunkenbein, D. (1985, April). *Cognitive structures underlying processes and conceptions in geometry.* Paper presented at the research presession of the annual meeting of the National Council of Teachers of Mathematics, San Antonio, TX.

Luria, A. R. (1969). On the pathology of computational observation. In J. Kilpatrick & I. Wirszup (Eds.), *Soviet studies in the psychology of learning and teaching mathematics* (Vol. 1, pp. 37–74). Chicago: University of Chicago Press.

Mann, P. H., & Suiter, P. (1974). *Handbook in diagnostic teaching: A learning disabilities approach.* Boston: Allyn & Bacon.

Mason, M. M. (1989, April). *Geometric understanding and misconceptions among gifted fourth-eighth graders.* Paper presented at the annual meeting of the American Educational Research Association, San Francisco.

Meyers, M. J., & Burton, G. M. (1989). Yes you can... Plan appropriate instruction for learning disabled students. *Arithmetic Teacher, 36*(7), 46–50.

Moyer, M. B., & Moyer, J. C. (1985). Ensuring that practice makes perfect: Implications for children with learning difficulties. *Arithmetic Teacher, 33*(1), 40–42.

Mpiangu, B., & Gentile, J. R. (1970). Is conservation of number a necessary condition for mathematical understanding? *Journal for Research in Mathematics Education, 1,* 179–192.

Myers, A. C., & Thornton, C. A. (1977). The learning disabled child—Learning the basic facts. *Arithmetic Teacher, 25*(3), 46–50.

Nesher, P. (1986). Learning mathematics: A cognitive perspective. *American Psychologist, 41,* 1114–1122.

Norman, D. D., & Rumelhart, D. E. (1975). *Explorations in cognition.* San Francisco: W. H. Freeman.

Palinscar, A. S. (1986). Metacognitive strategy instruction. *Exceptional Children, 53,* 118–124.

Peck, D. M., Jencks, S. M., & Connell, M. L. (1989). Improving instruction through brief interviews. *Arithmetic Teacher, 37*(3), 15–17.

Pellegrino, J. W., & Goldman, S. R. (1987). Information processing and elementary mathematics. *Journal of Learning Disabilities, 20,* 23–32, 57.

Piaget, J. (1964). Development and learning. In R. E. Ripple & V. N. Rockcastle (Eds.), *Piaget rediscovered* (pp. 7–20). Ithaca, NY: Cornell University.

Piaget, J. (1965). *The child's conception of number.* New York: Norton.

Piaget, J., & Inhelder, B. (1969). *The psychology of the child.* New York: Basic Books.

Post, T. R., Wachsmuth, I., Lesh, R., & Behr, M. J. (1985). Order and equivalence of rational numbers: A cognitive analysis. *Journal for Research in Mathematics Education, 16,* 18–36.

Pressley, M., Goodchild, F., Fleet, J., Zajchowski, R., & Evans, E. D. (1989). The challenges of classroom strategy instruction. *Elementary School Journal, 89,* 301–342.

Reeve, R. A., & Brown, A. L. (1985). Metacognition reconsidered: Implications for intervention research. *Abnormal Child Psychology, 13,* 343–356.

Reid, D. K., & Hresko, W. P. (1981). *A cognitive approach to learning disabilities.* New York: McGraw-Hill.

Resnick, L. B. (1982). Syntax and semantics in learning to subtract. In T. P. Carpenter, J. M. Moser, & T. A. Romberg (Eds.), *Addition and subtraction: A cognitive perspective* (pp. 136–155). Hillsdale, NJ: Erlbaum.

Resnick, L. B. (1983). A developmental theory of numbers understanding. In H. P. Ginsburg (Ed.), *The development of mathematical thinking* (pp. 109–151). New York: Academic Press.

Resnick, L. B., & Ford, W. W. (1981). *The psychology of mathematics for instruction.* Hillsdale, NJ: Erlbaum.

Resnick, L. B., Nesher, P., Leonard, F., Magone, M., Omanson, S., & Peled, I. (1989). Conceptual bases for arithmetic errors: The case of decimal fractions. *Journal of Research in Mathematics Education, 20,* 8–27.

Reyes, L. H. (1984). Affective variables and mathematics education. *Elementary School Journal, 84,* 558–581.

Riley, M. S., Greeno, J. G., & Heller, J. I. (1983). Development of children's problem-solving ability in arithmetic. In H. P. Ginsburg (Ed.), *The development of mathematical thinking* (pp. 153–200). New York: Academic Press.

Ross, S. H. (1989a, April). *Children's interpretations of two-digit numerals: Face value or place value?* Paper presented at the annual meeting of the American Educational Research Association, San Francisco.

Ross, S. H. (1989b). Parts, wholes, and places value: A developmental view. *Arithmetic Teacher, 36*(6), 47–51.

Rourke, B. P., & Finlayson, M. A. J. (1978). Neuropsychological significance of variations in patterns of academic performance: Verbal and visual-spatial abilities. *Journal of Abnormal Child Psychology, 6,* 121–133.

Rourke, B. P., & Strang, J. D. (1983). Subtypes of reading and arithmetic disabilities: A neuropsychological analysis. In M. Rutter (Ed.), *Developmental neuropsychiatry* (pp. 473–488). New York: Guilford Press.

Russell, R., & Ginsburg, H. P. (1984). Cognitive analysis of children's mathematics difficulties. *Cognition and Instruction, 1,* 217–244.

Saxe, G., & Shaheen, S. (1981). Piagetian theory and the atypical case: An analysis of the developmental Gerstmann Syndrome. *Journal of Learning Disabilities, 14,* 131–135.

Schaeffer, B., Eggleston, V., & Scott, J. (1974). Number development in young children. *Cognitive Psychology, 6,* 357–379.

Scheid, K. (1989). *Cognitive and metacognitive learning strategies: Their role in the instruction of special education students.* Columbus, OH: LINC Resources.

Schoenfeld, A. H. (1985). *Mathematical problem solving.* New York: Academic Press.

Sears, C. J. (1986). Mathematics for the learning disabled child in the regular classroom. *Arithmetic Teacher, 33*(5), 5–11.

Secada, W. G., Fuson, K. C., & Hall, J. (1983). The transition from counting-all to counting-on in addition. *Journal for Research in Mathematics Education, 14,* 47–57.

Share, D. L., Moffitt, T. E., & Silva, P. A. (1988). Factors associated with arithmetic-and-reading disability and specific arithmetic disability. *Journal of Learning Disabilities, 21,* 313–320.

Sharma, M. C. (1985). Interdisciplinary assessment of mathematical learning disability: Diagnosis in a clinical setting. In J. F. Cawley (Ed.), *Practical mathematics: Appraisal of the learning disabled* (pp. 177–214). Rockville, MD: Aspen.

Shuell, T. J. (1986). Cognitive conceptions of learning. *Review of Educational Research, 56,* 411–436.

Siegel, S. (1957). Discrimination among mental defective, normal, schizophrenic and brain-damaged subjects on the visual verbal concept formation test. *American Journal of Mental Deficiency, 62,* 338–343.

Siegler, R. S. (1978). The origins of scientific reasoning. In R. S. Siegler (Ed.), *Children's thinking: What develops?* (pp. 109–149). Hillsdale, NJ: Erlbaum.

Siegler, R. S. (1987). Strategy choices in subtraction. In J. Sloboda & D. Rogers (Eds.), *Cognitive process in mathematics* (pp. 81–106). Oxford: Oxford University Press.

Silver, E. A. (1983). Probing young adults' thinking about rational numbers. *Focus on Learning Problems in Mathematics, 5,* 105–117.

Smith, J. H. (1921). Arithmetical combinations. *Elementary School Journal, 10,* 762–770.

Starkey, P., & Gelman, R. (1982). The development of addition and subtraction abilities prior to formal schooling in arithmetic. In T. P. Carpenter, J. M. Moser, & T. A. Romberg (Eds.), *Addition and subtraction: A cognitive perspective* (pp. 99–106). Hillsdale, NJ: Erlbaum.

Steffe, L. P., von Glasersfeld, E., Richards, J., & Cobb, P. (1983). *Children's counting types*. New York: Praeger.
Sternberg, R. J., (Ed.). (1984a). *Mechanisms of cognitive development*. New York: W. H. Freeman.
Sternberg, R. J., (Ed.). (1984b). *Human abilities: An information processing approach*. New York: W. H. Freeman.
Strauss, A. A., & Kephart, N. C. (1955). *Psychopathology and education of the brain-injured child. Volume II. Progress in theory and clinic*. New York: Grune & Stratton.
Strauss, A. A. & Lehtinen, L. E. (1947). *Psychopathology and education of the brain-injured child*. New York: Grune & Stratton.
Suydam, M. N., & Osborne, A. (1977). *The status of pre-college science, mathematics, and social science education: 1955-1975. Vol. 2: Mathematics education*. Columbus, OH: The Ohio State University Center for Science and Mathematics Education.
Svenson, O. (1985). Memory retrieval of answers of simple additions as reflected in response latencies. *Acta Psychologica, 59*, 285-304.
Svenson, O., & Broquist, S. (1975). Strategies for solving simple addition problems: A comparison of normal and subnormal children. *Scandinavian Journal of Psychology, 16*, 143-151.
Svenson, O., & Hedenborg, M. (1979). Strategies used by children when solving simple subtractions. *Acta Psychologica, 43*, 477-489.
Swanson, H. L., & Rhine, B. (1985). Strategy transformation in learning disabled children's math performance: Clues to the development of expertise. *Journal of Learning Disabilities, 18*, 596-603.
Thornton, C. A. (1978). Emphasizing thinking strategies in basic fact instruction. *Journal for Research in Mathematics Education, 9*, 214-227.
Thornton, C. A., & Toohey, M. A. (1985). Basic math facts: Guidelines for teaching and learning. *Learning Disabilities Focus, 1*(1), 44-57.
Thornton, C. A., Jones, G. A., & Toohey, M. A. (1983). A multisensory approach to thinking strategies for remedial instruction in basic addition facts. *Journal for Research in Mathematics Education, 14*, 198-203.
Torgeson, J. K., & Young, K. A. (1983). Priorities for the use of microcomputers with learning disabled children. *Journal of Learning Disabilities, 16*, 234-237.
Tucker, J. A. (1985). Curriculum-based assessment: An introduction. *Exceptional Children, 52*, 199-204.
Underhill, B., Uprichard, E., & Heddens, J. (1980). *Diagnosing mathematical difficulties*. Columbus: Merrill.
van Erp, J. W. M., & Heshusius, L. (1986). Action psychology: Learning as the interiorization of action in early instruction of mathematically disabled learners. *Journal of Learning Disabilities, 19*, 274-279.
Van Lehn, K. (1983). On the representation of procedures in repair theory. In H. P. Ginsburg (Ed.), *The development of mathematical thinking* (pp. 197-252). New York: Academic Press.
Vellutino, F. R., Steger, B. M., Moyer, S. C., Harding, C. J., & Niles, J. A. (1977). Has the perceptual deficit hypothesis led us astray? *Journal of Learning Disabilities, 10*, 375-385.
Vygotsky L. S. (1978). *Mind in society: The development of higher psychological processes*. Cambridge, MA: Harvard University Press.
Wallace, G., & Larsen, S. C. (1978). *Educational assessment of learning problems: Testing for teaching*. Boston: Allyn & Bacon.
Weaver, J. F. (1982). Interpretation of number operations and symbolic representations of addition and subtraction. In T. P. Carpenter, J. M. Moser, & T. A. Romberg

(Eds.), *Addition and subtraction: A cognitive perspective* (pp. 60–66). Hillsdale, NJ: Erlbaum.

Webster, R. E. (1979). Visual and aural short-term memory capacity deficits in mathematically disabled students. *Journal of Educational Research, 72*, 277–283.

Webster, R. E. (1980). Short-term memory in mathematics-proficient and mathematics-disabled students as a function of input-modality/output-modality pairings. *Journal of Special Education, 14*, 67–78.

Weiner, S. L. (1974). On the development of more and less. *Journal of Experimental Child Psychology, 17*, 271–287.

Wertheimer, M. (1945). *Productive thinking*. New York: Harper & Row.

Wiederholt, J. L., Hammill, D. D., & Brown, V. L. (1983). *The resource teacher: A guide to effective practices*. Boston: Allyn & Bacon.

Ysseldyke, J. E., & Algozzine, B. (1982). *Critical issues in special and remedial education*. Boston: Houghton-Mifflin.

Ysseldyke, J. E., & Algozzine, B. (1983). LD or not LD: That's not the question! *Annual Review of Learning Disabilities, 1*, 26–28.

CHAPTER 10

Language Assessment

DORIS J. JOHNSON
PATRICIA A. CROASMUN

The purpose of this chapter is to present a series of issues and questions to be addressed when assessing language. The rationale for evaluating oral language derives from clinical observations of students with learning disabilities as well as from research. As early as the 1930s Orton (1937) reported problems with word retrieval and pronunciation of multisyllabic words. Later, various problems of language comprehension, memory, and verbal expression were described by Myklebust (1954), Johnson and Myklebust (1967); Bender (1958); de Hirsch, Jansky, and Langford (1966) and others. Such observations, along with research is psycholinguistics and work in other fields, led to the development of new procedures and tests for studying language. Within the past two decades many investigations have verified the need for studying oral language in children who are suspected of having reading problems and for early prediction (Masland and Masland, 1988). In addition, research on subtypes of reading disabilities indicates that over half of the subjects have some type of auditory language problem (Mattis, French, & Rapin, 1975; Lyon & Watson, 1981). Many of these problems persist and frequently interfere with higher levels of education, occupation, and social interaction (Johnson & Blalock, 1987; Wiig & Semel, 1984).

Like other complex forms of behavior, language can be studied from numerous theoretical perspectives (Launer & Lahey, 1981). In a review of research on language, Ingram (1976) indicated that the first investigations were diary studies such as those in the early 1900s. Later, large sample studies were done that provided normative data regarding number of words used at various age levels, number of words used per sentence, number of different words, etc. (Templin, 1957). From the late 1950s to the present, more theoretical linguistic studies have been done, beginning with the work of Chomsky (1957), whose research in syntax provided a basis for comparing normal and atypical learners (Menyuk, 1964; Lee, 1974; Morehead & Ingram, 1976). Later, theoretical advances in developmental semantics and pragmatics fostered more research on content and language usage (Bowerman, 1976; Clark, 1973; Brown, 1973; Ochs & Schieffelin, 1979). All of these investigations have contributed to the body of knowledge on language development and approaches to evaluation.

Although language can be divided and studied in various ways, many researchers and clinicians evaluate forms, content, and usage (Bloom, 1980). According to Bloom and Lahey (1978) **language forms** include phonology, morphology, and syntax, each of which is further subdivided. Phonology includes segmental (phonemes/syllables) and suprasegmental (intonation, stress, and pause) features (Bloom, 1980). Morphology is divided into the lexicon (basic vocabulary) and inflections (free and bound morphemes). Syntax overlaps with morphology and includes both inflection and word order.

Bloom and Lahey divide **language content** (semantics) into the categories of object knowledge, object relations, and event relations, all of which overlap with cognitive development. Concepts pertaining to classes of objects, attribution, action, possession, time, and causality are all included in their discussion on content (Bloom & Lahey, 1978; Bloom, 1980).

Language use includes function and contexts of language. Bloom and Lahey state that one may use language for intrapersonal reasons (i.e., vocal play or problem solving) as well as interpersonal (pragmatic) purposes. When communicating with others, the purpose may be to gain attention, request information, etc. An analysis of contexts would include both linguistic and nonlinguistic factors. These components of language are of interest to clinicians and researchers who study children in naturalistic settings and adult–child interaction. Intrapersonal processes are of interest to those who examine verbal mediation during problem solving, strategy use, and self-monitoring.

Whatever schema or theoretical orientation is used, it is essential to treat language as a rule-governed activity, not a set of skills. Therefore, we are interested in knowing whether the child is acquiring the rules for phonology, syntax, morphology, semantics, and pragmatics. In addition, when working with exceptional populations it is essential to examine both receptive and expressive components of these rule systems. Children with various types of verbal output disorders may have good comprehension but may be unable to access, organize, or even repeat words. Therefore, one cannot rely on verbal expression as an indication of a student's knowledge (Johnson, 1981).

THE ASSESSMENT PROCESS

Many excellent discussions on language assessment have been written by professionals in speech and language pathology, psycholinguistics, and learning disabilities as well as other fields (Danwitz, 1981; Geffner, 1981; Kelly & Rice, 1986; Miller, 1981; Morehead & Morehead, 1976; Schery, 1981; Scott, 1988, Snyder, 1984; Swisher & Aten, 1981; Tyack & Gottsleben, 1974; Wiig & Semel, 1984; Wood, 1982; Wren, 1985). Most emphasize that the goal of assessment should be clearly specified and that the examiner have a rationale for selecting procedures rather than simply using a list of tests. There also should be a plan for analyzing the results and conducting follow-up error analyses since most tests assess multiple functions and there are many reasons for failure (Johnson, 1987).

Generally, the diagnostician wants to know whether the child is developing language normally. This question is not answered easily since the rate of language acquisition varies. Bloom (1980) says certain children must work harder and for a longer time than others at learning language. This means that one should be cautious in using data from a single test or set of tests on a given day. It is preferable to study children over time in various contexts to learn as much as possible about their communication skills and rate of learning. A case history and discussions with parents and teachers are as essential as observations in multiple settings.

PURPOSE OF THE ASSESSMENT

There are many levels of assessment, each with a slightly different purpose. The first, most basic is *screening*, which is typically done to determine whether a child might have a problem. Screening, however, is not synonymous with diagnosis and should never be used as the basis for placement or labeling. However, the screening should be broad enough to detect most possible problems. This means that tasks are used that yield information about all rule systems relatively quickly. Clinicians might select a measure of receptive language and obtain a language sample. Some clinicians also suggest sentence repetition for speed and efficiency. In certain instances, checklists or pupil rating scales (Myklebust, 1981) can be given to classroom teachers or parents. Such scales should include items regarding both comprehension and language usage.

Because many factors may interfere with language acquisition, assessment for diagnosis and *eligibility* for services and placement is more comprehensive and should include studies of hearing, mental ability, and family history to examine possible reasons for problems. Because of the part that language plays in many intelligence tests, at least one measure of nonverbal mental ability should be used. Examples include the Performance Scale of the Wechsler Intelligence Scale for Children-Revised (1974); the Columbia Mental Maturity Scale (Burgemeister, Blum, & Lorge, 1972); the Test of Nonverbal Intelligence (Brown, Sherbenon, & Dollar, 1982); and the Leiter International Performance Scale (Leiter & Arthur, 1969). Language testing at this level should be more inclusive and, as discussed later in this chapter, should include several measures of receptive and expressive language. When problems are detected, additional studies of various learning processes such as attention, perception, and memory may be needed.

More comprehensive and precise assessment is needed for *planning intervention* since very few standardized tests have a sufficient number of items to determine whether the child has difficulty at the level of rule acquisition, rule application, or automaticity (Johnson, 1987). For example, if a child fails to include relevant information in telling a story from pictures, one might need to explore picture interpretation, word retrieval, vocabulary, and sense of audience. Similarly, errors in syntax may result from faulty articulation (i.e., inability to say particular sounds), memory, retrieval, failure to understand the underlying principle, an inability to perceive differences between words (e.g., jump, jumps) or faulty monitoring (Johnson, 1983). Therefore, more informal criterion reference measures are needed to answer questions about specific goals for remediation.

Often periods of *diagnostic teaching* are needed to determine the most effective form of instruction. For example, when teaching certain syntactic principles, one might compare the child's progress following auditory stimulation (modeling) with procedures using the printed word (reading). Because children with learning disabilities frequently have short-term auditory memory problems, reading and other visual cues may foster rule acquisition.

TYPES OF PROCEDURES

Many articles have been written about the pros and cons of using norm-referenced tests versus informal, descriptive measures (Kelly & Rice, 1986). The former are valuable because they provide the diagnostician with quantitative data to compare a student's performance with others of the same age. Often such tests are essential for classification and eligibility.

However, many tests measure only isolated facets of language in unnatural contexts. Without additional observations, one cannot be certain how the child will perform in real-world situations when multiple rule acquisition is required. Some children perform better on highly structured "stripped down" tasks when they do not have to be concerned with ideation, grammar, vocabulary, and pronunciation simultaneously. Others perform better in realistic settings because of redundancies in context. However, the types of tasks used for language sampling should be chosen carefully. We agree with Kelly and Rice (1986), who recommend both types of procedures.

ISSUES TO CONSIDER BEFORE SELECTING TESTS AND PROCEDURES

Before choosing language tests, the clinician should attempt to gain information about the child's ability to handle various types of tasks. For example, young children and some children with learning disabilities have difficulty understanding concepts such as "same" and "different." Therefore, they may fail a phonemic discrimination task, not because they have poor discrimination, but because they do not understand the instructional concept. Some have picture-interpretation problems that may reduce language comprehension or expression scores. Others may be unable to express what they know because of severe output disorders. For example, an oral apraxia or auditory-motor learning problem (Johnson & Myklebust, 1967) often interferes with their ability to speak. Hence, other modes of response may be needed to evaluate comprehension, semantics, and syntax. These same output disorders may interfere with oral reading or phonological awareness tasks. Such students can read silently and analyze words "internally" but cannot produce them accurately.

The child's overall linguistic, cultural, and educational background should also be considered. Clinicians working with non–English-speaking students should be cautious in drawing conclusions about errors.

Since language is but one form of representation, we need to determine whether children have generalized problems of symbolic behavior or specific verbal deficits. Several studies found that children with language disorders had difficulty with gesture, pretend behavior, symbolic play, and tasks requiring imagery (Kamhi, Catts, Koenig, & Lewis, 1984; Savich, 1984; Johnston & Weismer, 1983; Cicci, 1978; Cable, 1981).

Relationships between language and conceptualization should also be investigated. Bowerman (1976) says that when children acquire new vocabulary they are not learning labels for specific objects but tags for concepts or categories that represent a large set of similar yet different items. She quotes several theorists who say that learning a new word is comparable to learning a rule that specifies the conditions for using the word appropriately or correctly. Typically, these meanings must be inferred over time. One does not acquire a full concept of "dog" with the first experience. However, most standardized tests are not designed to examine depth and breadth of word meaning. For example, when children point to a picture of a dog appropriately, one does not know whether they understand "dogness" or whether they can differentiate a dog from a horse or other four-legged animals of similar size or whether they would include all types of dogs—including chihuahuas—in their dog category. Therefore, various types of nonverbal classification as well as verbal tasks should be included in the evaluation to explore possible reasons for problems. In a study of normal, deaf, and language-impaired children, Friedman (1984) found the latter had more problems with classification of objects than either of the other groups. Therefore, she concluded they have a more general deficiency in representational behavior.

In addition, studies of both reasoning and language are needed with older students and adults with learning disabilities. Stone (1987) found some adults had the concepts for a formal operations task but could not express what they knew.

We have suggested elsewhere that language may be impaired because of related or simultaneously occurring processing deficits (Johnson & Hook, 1978). Hence, the clinician may need several sessions to determine whether the problems occur at the level of input, integration, output, or monitoring (Johnson, 1983). Current research indicates that more fine-grained investigation of auditory discrimination, rate of temporal processing, and temporal sequencing should be considered in the assessment. While early studies of auditory processing were somewhat inconclusive, there is increasing evidence that many students with language learning disabilities have problems with auditory discrimination (Elliott, Hammer, & Scholl, 1989), rate of processing (Tallal, Stark, Kallman, & Mellits, 1981), temporal sequencing (Tallal et al., 1981), and memory (Kirchner & Klatzky, 1985; Tarver, Hallahan, Kauffman, & Ball, 1976; Bauer, 1979).

Finally, when choosing formal tests, a review of the manuals for information regarding reliability, validity, demographics of the sample, and possible correlations with other measures is helpful. Books on assessment, such as that by Salvia and Ysseldyke (1988) provide summaries and reviews of widely used tests. Several researchers have compared the results of two or more tests when working with language-impaired children (Friend & Channel, 1987; Mcloughlin & Gullo, 1984; Lieberman, Heffron, West, Hutchinson, & Swem, 1987). These studies are valuable for both research and service.

GENERAL FACTORS RELATED TO ASSESSMENT AND LANGUAGE SAMPLING

As stated above, since many children with language learning disabilities have both receptive and expressive problems, a careful assessment of comprehension should be conducted. Typically such a study should be done with tasks that require verbal interpretation without a verbal response. Responses usually require pointing, marking, manipulation, gesture, yes–no, or recognition. One can, of course, make hypotheses about comprehension problems from verbal responses, but errors require further analyses. For instance, the person who says "a puzzle is that water you walk through after the rain" probably misperceived the word.

The expressive evaluation includes a combination of both spontaneous and elicited language, though clinicians and researchers discuss the merits of each (Klein, 1988). The most spontaneous assessment is done by audio taping (and perhaps videotaping) the child in various natural communication settings to investigate as many components of language as possible with both familiar and unfamiliar people. Such investigations are time consuming and may be inefficient. Furthermore, if they are not conducted by skilled clinicians, one might not obtain pertinent information. However, they provide a wealth of information. In order to obtain best results, varying degrees of structure are generally imposed to elicit the desired form of language. For example, to elicit present-, past-, and future-tense verbs, one must choose relevant pictures and questions. To examine various types of discourse, the student might be asked to tell a story, give a report, tell how to make or do something, or describe something. Each of these tasks should provide data regarding vocabulary, syntax, phonology, and a particular form or plan of organization. One also can examine the person's ability to use various types of cohesive devices that link sentences and portions of text together. In all cases, the materials, setting, and questions are chosen to answer specific questions and the tasks should be age appropriate.

To obtain a representative sample of the child's spontaneous language, the sample should consist of at least 75 to 100 sentences from two to four different linguistic contexts. Wren (1980) found that even 100 utterances may not result in a representative sample of a child's language; therefore, the larger the sample, the more indicative it will be of the child's actual linguistic level. She also found that the type of task influences the amount and quality of language. For example, a pretend birthday party situation elicited the most language, whereas responses to pictures yielded the least. The entire exchange should be tape recorded and transcribed verbatim, including both the child's and clinician's utterances. A full transcription of the clinician's language provides important data for comprehension assessment. One can note the types of questions the child could or could not answer. Best results will always be obtained when the child is comfortable with the clinician, and when the materials and topics are of interest.

AREAS OF ASSESSMENT

The following discussion includes more specific rationale and suggestions for evaluating various parameters of language. Research findings are included to highlight problems that have been identified among students with learning disabilities.

SEMANTICS

The study of semantics should include an assessment of comprehension of single words, sentences, question forms, and connected discourse. Within each of these broad areas, we assess understanding of various classes of words such as concrete nouns, basic names of objects, names of parts of objects, verbs, prepositions, words representing color, size, shape, textures, space, time, etc. Understanding of grammatical relations, various sentence types, and question forms as well as more extended discourse also should be evaluated, even though there is overlap with syntax and morphology. Rate and diversity of vocabulary development should also be considered. Single "snap-shot" assessments do not provide the whole picture.

Some language-impaired children have problems acquiring labels for objects. Croasmun (1986) investigated the labeling of animals, fruits, and vehicles by $2\frac{1}{2}$-year-old language-impaired children over a period of six months and found their labeling was very inconsistent. Having named an object correctly one month, the children might then mislabel it the following month. They seemed unsure when they had acquired the appropriate label and therefore exhibited a protracted period of acquisition for these basic labels.

When 6-year-old normal and language-impaired children were taught new words either through the presentation of exemplars or through the presentation of a verbal definition, the language-impaired were found deficient in using both strategies when learning new words (Matthews, 1985). These two studies seem to indicate that language-impaired children may have difficulty learning new words and their underlying concepts and, therefore, have a limited vocabulary.

As children enter school it is important to evaluate their ability to understand the language of instruction (Carlisle & Johnson, 1989). Many do not understand terms such as "letter, word, and sound" that are used in early reading instruction (Downing, 1979). Others have problems detecting ambiguity (Groshong, 1980). Failure to understand various prepositions, or verbs such as "mark, underline, and circle" may prevent children from following instructions in the classroom. The Boehm Test of Basic Concepts-Revised (1986) and measures of oral directions assess some of these skills.

The comprehension of figurative language including slang, sarcasm, similes, metaphors, idioms, and proverbs is an area in which children with language learning disabilities have been found deficient (see Nippold, 1985, for a good review). Specifically, Nippold reported that Strand found that children with language learning disabilities were delayed in the understanding of common idiomatic expressions. Delays in the comprehension of metaphors and similes were also reported (Seidenberg & Bernstein, 1986). Although similes, which are more explicit in their comparisons since they use "like" or "as," were easier for children with learning disabilities to comprehend than metaphors, both types of figurative language were more difficult than for children with no learning disabilities (Seidenberg and Bernstein, 1986).

There are few tests for extended listening comprehension, particularly for older students. Therefore, it is frequently necessary to simulate classroom activities to ascertain whether the student understands discussions, stories, and lectures.

When a student appears to have problems, additional testing may be needed to determine whether problems occur because of perception, understanding, or memory. For example, if a student fails a two- or three-step command, the diagnostician might reduce the number of words if the problem appears to be memory, or modify the vocabulary if a comprehension problem is suspected. Similarly, if a child cannot retell a story, one may need to investigate comprehension by using more recognition and multiple-choice questions.

Word-retrieval difficulties in this population have also been well documented. German (1979) found that children with learning disabilities exhibit significantly more word-finding errors than normal children, especially with low-frequency words, while Fried-Oken (1984) reported that language-impaired children circumlocute more often, manifest longer response times, and make more naming errors than normal children. She states, "While normally developing children between the ages of 4 and 9 years rely heavily on semantic and perceptual properties of an object to recall a name, the language-impaired youngsters do not appear to identify the salient features of an object to retrieve labels" (1987, p. 206). More recently, German (1987) examined the spontaneous language samples of 7- to 12-year-old children and found that language impaired exhibited more reformulations, repetitions, and substitutions than the normal children. Other word-finding behaviors (such as fillers and starters) were seen in normal children at almost the same rate as the children with language impairment.

Formal Assessment

There are numerous tests for both receptive and expressive vocabulary. Typically, the former includes measures such as the Peabody Picture Vocabulary Test-Revised (Dunn & Dunn, 1981), and subtests from measures such as the Test of Language Development-Intermediate (Hammill & Newcomer, 1982), the Test of Auditory Comprehension of Language (Carrow, 1973) or the Clinical Evaluation of Language Functions (Semel & Wiig, 1980). Follow-up procedures may be needed to evaluate the depth and breadth of word meanings.

Expressive vocabulary is frequently studied by asking children to label pictures as in the Expressive One-Word Picture Vocabulary Test (Gardner, 1979). Such tests also measure word retrieval. Hence, one should try to determine whether the child has acquired the meaning or whether he or she has difficulty accessing and recalling the specific word.

Many vocabulary tests require the student to give definitions. Clinicians should be aware of the fact that definitions require high-level metalinguistic skills (Litowitz, 1987) in that one uses words to talk about words. Failures may result from either conceptual or semantic problems. Litowitz's studies of adults with learning disabilities indicate that a great deal of information can be obtained about both verbal and conceptual skills by analyzing definitions. She concluded that responses of the adults with learning disabilities were not like those of either young children or other adults.

Informal Assessment

Within a language sample, evidence for semantic difficultues can be gathered. The variety of word use is one area to investigate. Frequently, children exhibit limited words—not only fewer descriptors but also fewer names for objects and actions. Some use nonspecific words in lieu of specific labels. Therefore, multiple use of pronouns and nonspecific verbs such as "got" and "do" may be noted. Without further probing, it is unclear whether this pattern of expression results from a limited vocabulary or from retrieval difficulties. One way of making this distinction is to offer the child a choice of words. If the child can select the correct word, it is possible that retrieval difficulties are impeding performance. Inconsistent use of a word, hesitancies, circumlocutions, and inaccurate words may also indicate word-retrieval difficulties. Sometimes when retrieval difficulties are evident, it is helpful to classify the errors to determine the types of retrieval strategies the child is using. German (1986), Fried-Oken (1987), and Wiig and Becker-Caplan (1984) have classification systems that include categories such as phonemically related, semantically related, and functionally related substitutions, as well as circumlocutions. Fried-Oken (1987) has also proposed a Double Administration Naming Technique that can be used to differentiate a retrieval problem from a vocabulary deficit. By determining the number and types of errors made during the two test presentations, the naming deficit can be described and effective treatment goals planned.

Additional information regarding semantics can be obtained from analyzing verbal interactions and language samples.

Syntax and Morphology

Syntax refers to the way phrases, clauses, and sentences are structured, while morphology refers to the formation of new words either through the use of an inflected ending (i.e., jump, jumps, jumping, jumped) or derivational morphology. It is difficult to separate morphology from syntax because morphemes are used to construct sentences. However, some studies have examined specifically the acquisition of morphemes in both normally developing and language-impaired children.

Johnston and Schery (1976) studied the acquisition of 14 grammatical morphemes including -ing, plural -s, -ed, and auxiliary and copula verbs by 3- to 16-year-old language-impaired children. They found that the children began using many of the morphemes at the same stage of language development as normals but that the language-impaired children were at a higher language level than normal children when they began using these markers consistently. Therefore, the children exhibited the same order of acquisition, but the course of acquisition appeared to be abnormally protracted.

When Moran and Byrne (1977) studied the use of past, present, and future tenses in normal second- and third-graders, and those with learning disabilities, they found that those with learning disabilities often avoided using past-tense markers by using "did" with an uninflected form of the verb rather than an inflected form of the verb (e.g., "did walk" rather than "walked"). They also found they were three times more likely to produce an uninflected root verb than a past-tense marker, and they were more likely to use redundant markers (e.g., "sawed") than normal peers.

In terms of the development of syntax, researchers have found fewer complex sentences, elaborated verb phrases, pronouns, adjectives, and auxiliaries in the language of 3- to 5-year-old learning-impaired children than in the language of normally developing children (Johnston, 1982b). As children enter elementary school, several difficulties emerge. First, sentence formulation is often awkward. They use many sentence fragments and simple forms, and there is a repeated use of stereotypic phrases. They are also poor at judging the grammaticality of sentences and at correcting ungrammatical sentences (Liles, Shulman, & Bartlett, 1977). Donahue, Pearl, and Bryan (1982) found that children with learning disabilities say as much as their peers, but their syntax is not as complex. Even when compared with children who are at the same linguistic stage, language-impaired children use fewer complex structures (Morehead & Ingram, 1976).

While these studies describe errors in production, some learning-impaired children have difficulty comprehending language as well. Two factors seem to cause problems in the comprehension of sentences: structural complexity and syntactic compression (i.e., when there is little redundancy in the sentence) (Wiig & Semel, 1984). These factors result in specific types of sentences being more difficult for language-impaired children to comprehend. Difficulties with passive tense and questions, in particular indirect requests (Shatz, Bernstein, & Shulman, 1980); questions regarding nonobservable objects, actions, or persons; and questions containing "why," "when," and "what happened" (Parnell, Amerman, & Harting, 1986) have been reported. Wiig and Semel (1984) also reported that children with learning disabilities have difficulty comprehending ambiguous sentences. Sentences containing clauses in which one clause must be related to another, especially when temporal, cause–effect, or conditional aspects are involved, pose problems for many children with learning disabilities.

Formal Assessment

Because both receptive and expressive difficulties have been observed in these populations, comprehensive language testing should include measures of both grammatic comprehension and expression (e.g., Test of Language Development-Intermediate, Hammill & Newcomer, 1982). Receptive measures require a child to point to a picture that corresponds with an utterance (e.g., Point to, "The boy jumped"; The boy is jumping") or to manipulate objects. Expressive tasks require the child to complete or repeat a sentence. For example, the Grammatic Closure Subtest Test of the Illinois Test of Psycholinguistic Abilities (Kirk, McCarthy, & Kirk, 1968) requires sentence completion with real words (e.g., here is a dog; here are two ____). Some require sentence repetition or sentence building. Unfortunately, none of the tests use the same words on both the expressive and receptive batteries; therefore, follow-up assessment is needed.

Other tests, such as the Berry-Talbott, (Berry, 1966) require metalinguistic skills and rule application since nonsense words are used. This test requires the child to look at a nonsense figure, listen to a nonsense phrase, and complete a sentence (e.g., here is a wug; here are two ____). This task has been helpful in differentiating students with learning disabilities from normal children (Vogel, 1972; Johnson & Hook, 1978).

Informal Assessment

Because many children with learning disabilities have difficulty in this area, an in-depth analysis is required. Detailed procedures for collecting and analyzing syntax are presented by Lee (1974). The first area to investigate is the *accuracy* of the morphological markers and syntactic structures used. Subject–verb agreement, accurate use of regular and irregular past-tense markers, third person singular markers, and plurals should be investigated as well as the use of copulas and auxiliaries. Only a few errors with irregular past tenses and plurals should be present in the language of young school-age children.

Because all of the basic morphological markers of the English language have been acquired by the time a child enters school, an assessment of the child's morphological and syntactic abilities must entail more than just a judgment of accuracy. The *length* and *complexity* of the school-age child's language must also be evaluated. Unlike younger children, for whom mean number of morphemes per utterance is a meaningful measure, school-age children's syntax must be analyzed differently. When investigating the length and complexity of the school-age child's language, the base unit is a T-unit. A T-unit is defined as "one main clause plus any subordinate clause or non-clausal structure that is attached or embedded in it" (Hunt, 1970, p. 4). Therefore, a T-unit is either a complex sentence (main clause + subordinate clauses) or a simple sentence. All compound sentences are divided into separate T-units so that the length of the children's utterances will not be overinflated due to the excessive use of run-on sentences. From the T-unit, one can then determine whether the child's percentage of complex sentences and T-unit length is within normal limits. Donahue et al. (1982) and Klecan-Aker and Hedrick (1985) provide norms for T-unit length while Loban (1976) provides norms for percentage of complex sentences.

PHONOLOGY

Typically, phonology is studied by listening to spontaneous speech and by doing an articulation test. As stated above, there are many reasons why children might have phonological problems, including disorders of auditory discrimination, sequencing, and/or auditory-motor production. Standardized tests of articulation include the Fisher–Logemann Test of Articulation Competence (Fisher & Logemann, 1971) and the Goldman–Fristoe Test of Articulation (Goldman & Fristoe, 1969).

Most error classification systems indicate whether children omit, add, or substitute sounds in the initial, medial, or final positions of words, and whether the errors are rule-governed. Often children with specific learning disabilities mispronounce words but the errors are not rule-governed. Their mistakes occur more often on multisyllabic words. These may reflect disturbances of auditory perception, sequencing, or phonological coding. In other instances they may be related to output disorders. Some tend to omit syllables or sounds in both oral and written language.

Although this area is not typically the domain of the learning disabilities specialist, difficulties should be noted so that referral to a speech-language pathologist can be made when appropriate. Since school-age children can produce most sounds of our language, any errors may indicate problems. Some kindergartners and first-graders may have minor difficulty with later developing sounds such as "s," "l," "r," but by second grade any phonological errors should be corrected.

PRAGMATICS

Many diverse aspects of language are addressed under pragmatics, including topic introduction and maintenance, turn taking, formulation of ideas, ability to use language for various functions, and nonverbal aspects of language, including prosody, loudness level, and maintenance of eye contact. The primary focus of pragmatics is the child's communicative competence, i.e., his ability to make himself understood and to understand language within the context in which it is spoken.

An excellent review of the pragmatic skills of language-impaired children was written by Snyder (1984). In that review, she reported that language-impaired children may have difficulty expressing different functions of language and in the revision of utterances when asked to do so. They also may have difficulty using their fund of knowledge to organize their recall of narratives and to make inferences that relate ideas to one another. In fact, they produce a lower frequency of story grammar components and complete episodes when formulating stories (Roth & Spekman, 1986; Merritt & Liles, 1987). Differences between normally achieving children and children with learning disabilities have also been found in their ability to relate one story episode to another (Roth & Spekman, 1986). They also are not as active conversational partners and are not as assertive in conversations as their normal peers (Bryan, Donahue, & Pearl, 1981).

Receptively, the child must also be able to comprehend what is being said to him or her within particular contexts. One area of connected discourse that has received much attention has been children's comprehension of stories and story grammar (Stein & Glenn, 1979). Differences have been reported between children with language learning disabilities and normally achieving children in their recall of stories. In particular, their ability to integrate information, draw inferences, and understand relationships among story parts has been found to be deficient (Ellis Weismer, 1985; Craig & Chapman, 1987; Merritt & Liles, 1987).

There are fewer measures for pragmatics (language usage) than other aspects of language because one typically observes or interacts with the child in natural contexts. Prutting and Kirchner (1987) have published a comprehensive checklist that can be used in evaluating a person's pragmatic skills.

Several aspects of pragmatics are related to the child's ability to participate in a conversation. First, one must determine the child's ability to introduce a topic, maintain it for an appropriate period of time, and take turns during the exchange. Some children with learning disabilities will change topics frequently, add inappropriate information when contributing to a conversation, or interrupt conversational partners frequently. At other times, a child may not be sensitive to the amount of information that his listener needs to know and not inform his listener adequately. This results in the overuse of nonreferenced pronouns so the listener is unclear about the topic.

Whether the child can use language for different functions should also be determined. Every school-age child should be able to use language to express his needs, obtain information, and request information and clarification.

The child's ability to formulate his ideas into a cohesive set of sentences or discourse should be assessed. At times, a child's multiple reformulations of ideas results in the listener being unable to follow the speaker's thoughts.

We communicate much information nonverbally. Some children with learning disabilities exhibit problems in changing their tone of voice (i.e., prosody) (Crystal, 1979) and in maintaining eye contact. Others fail to respond to nonverbal cues in conversation.

In general, language should be assessed by using a combination of both standardized measures and informal language sampling. A careful study is needed because oral language forms the basis for higher level symbol systems, including reading, writing, and mathematics. Language is also the medium that is used for most new concepts that are presented in school. While we learn from experience and observation, much of schooling depends on oral language. Too often, the student with learning disabilities with reading and writing disorders is presumed to have intact oral language skills.

In special education one should not assume that a student will profit from tape-recorded lectures without an evaluation of auditory language. Finally, because the demands for higher levels of language increase with each grade level, ongoing assessment throughout junior high and secondary school is recommended. The impact of persistent problems, can be observed at work, in school, and in social situations.

REFERENCES

Bauer, R. (1979). Recall after a short delay and acquisition in learning disabled and nondisabled children. *Journal of Learning Disabilities, 12*, 596–608.

Bender, L. (1958). Problems in conceptualization and communication in children with developmental alexia. In P. Hoch & J. Zubin (Eds.), *Psychopathology of Communication.* New York: Grune & Stratton.

Berry, M. (1966). *Berry-Talbot Language Tests 1. Comprehension of grammar.* Rockford, IL: Berry Language Tests.

Bloom, L. (1980). Language development, language disorders, and learning disabilities: LD^3. *Bulletin of the Orton Society, 30,* 115–133.

Bloom, L., & Lahey, M. (1978). *Language development and language disorders.* New York: John Wiley & Sons.

Boehm, A. (1986). *Boehm Test of Basic Concepts–Revised.* New York: Psychological Corp.

Bowerman, M. (1976). Semantic factors in the acquisition of rules for word use and sentence construction. In D. M. Morehead & A. E. Morehead (Eds.), *Normal and deficient child language.* Baltimore: University Park Press.

Brown, L., Sherbenon, R., & Dollar, S. (1982). *Test of Nonverbal Intelligence.* Austin, TX: PRO-ED.

Brown, R. (1973). *A first language: The early stages.* Cambridge, MA: Harvard University Press.

Bryan, T., Donahue, M., & Pearl, R. (1981). Studies of learning disabled children's pragmatic competence. *Topics in Learning and Learning Disabilities, 1*(2), 29–39.

Burgemeister, B., Blum, L., & Lorge, I. (1972). *Columbia Mental Maturity Scale.* Orlando, FL: Harcourt Brace Jovanovich.

Cable, B. (1981). *A study of play behavior in learning disabled and normal preschool boys.* Unpublished doctoral dissertation, Northwestern University, Evanston, IL.

Carlisle, J. F., & Johnson, D. J. (1989). Assessment of school-age children. In L. B. Silver (Ed.), *The assessment of learning disabilities* (pp. 73–110). Boston: College-Hill Press.

Carrow, E. (1973). *Test for Auditory Comprehension of Language.* Austin, TX: Learning Concepts.

Chomsky, N. (1957). *Syntactic structures.* Cambridge, MA: MIT Press.

Cicci, R. L. (1978). *A study of pretended use of objects and graphic-pictorial representation in language impaired and normal preschool children.* Unpublished doctoral dissertation, Northwestern University, Evanston, IL.

Clark, E. (1973). What's in a word? On the child's acquisition of semantics in his first language. In T. E. Moore (Ed.), *Cognitive development and acquisition of language* (pp. 65–110). New York: Academic Press.

Craig, E., & Chapman, R. (1987). Story recall and inferencing skills in language/learning-disabled and nondisabled children. *Journal of Speech and Hearing Disorders, 52,* 50–55.

Croasmun, P. (1986). *A longitudinal study of the acquisition of reference skills in six two-year-old language-impaired children*. Unpublished doctoral dissertation, Northwestern University, Evanston, IL.
Crystal, D. (1979). Prosodic development. In P. Fletcher & M. Garman (Eds.), *Language acquisition*. Cambridge: Cambridge University Press.
Danwitz, M. W. (1981). Formal versus informal assessment: Fragmentation versus holism. *Topics in Language Disorders, 1*(3), 95–196.
de Hirsch, K., Jansky, J., & Langford, W. (1966). *Predicting reading failure*. New York: Harper & Row.
Donahue, M., Pearl, R., & Bryan, T. (1982). Learning disabled children's syntactic proficiency on a communicative task. *Journal of Speech and Hearing Disorders, 47*, 397–403.
Downing, J. (1979). *Reading and reasoning*. New York: Springer-Verlag.
Dunn, L., & Dunn, L. (1981). *Peabody Picture Vocabulary Test–Revised*. Circle Pines, MN: American Guidance Service.
Elliott, L., Hammer, M., & Scholl, M. (1989). Fine-grained auditory discrimination in normal children and children with language-learning problems. *Journal of Speech and Hearing Research, 32*, 112–119.
Ellis Weismer, S. (1985). Constructive comprehension abilities exhibited by language-disordered children. *Journal of Speech and Hearing Research, 28*, 175–184.
Fisher, H. & Logemann, J. (1971). *The Fisher–Logemann Test of Articulation Competence*. Boston: Houghton-Mifflin.
Friedman, J. (1984). *Classification skills in normally hearing/achieving, oral deaf, and language impaired preschoolers: A study in language and conceptual thought*. Unpublished doctoral dissertation, Northwestern University, Evanston, IL.
Fried-Oken, M. (1984). *The development of naming skills in normal and language deficient children*. Unpublished doctoral dissertation, Boston University, Boston.
Fried-Oken, M. (1987). Qualitative examination of children's naming skills through test adaptations. *Language, Speech and Hearing Services in Schools, 18*, 206–216.
Friend, T., & Channel, R. (1987). A comparison of two measures of receptive vocabulary. *Language, Speech and Hearing Services in Schools, 18*(3), 231–237.
Gardner, M. (1979). *Expressive One-Word Picture Vocabulary Test*. Novato, CA: Academic Therapy.
Geffner, D. S. (1981). Assessment of language disorders: Linguistic and cognitive functions. *Topics in Language Disorders, 1*(3), 1–9.
German, D. (1979). Word finding skills in children with learning disabilities. *Journal of Learning Disabilities, 12*, 176–181.
German, D. (1986). *Test of Word Finding TWF*. Allen, TX: DLM Teaching Resources.
German, D. (1987). Spontaneous language profiles of children with word-finding problems. *Language, Speech and Hearing Services in Schools, 18*, 217–230.
Goldman, R., & Fristoe, M. (1969). *Goldman–Fristoe Test of Articulation*. Circle Pines, MN: American Guidance Service.
Groshong, C. (1980). *Ambiguity detection and the use of verbal context for disambiguation by language disabled and normal learning children*. Unpublished doctoral dissertation, Northwestern University, Evanston, IL.
Hammill, D., & Newcomer, P. (1982). *Test of Language Development: Intermediate*. Austin, TX: PRO-ED.
Hunt, K. (1970). A syntactic maturity in school children and adults. *Monographs of the Society of Research in Child Development, 35* (Serial No. 134).
Ingram, D. (1976). Current issues in child phonology. In D. M. Morehead & A. E. Morehead (Eds.), *Normal and deficient child language*. Baltimore: University Park Press.
Johnson, D. (1983). Design for individualization of language intervention pro-

grams. In J. Miller, D. E. Yoder, & R. Schiefelbusch (Eds.), *Contemporary issues in language intervention*. Rockville, MD: The American Speech–Language–Hearing Association.
Johnson, D. (1987). Assessment issues in learning disabilities research. In S. Vaughn & C. S. Bos (Eds.), *Research in learning disabilities*. Austin, TX: PRO-ED.
Johnson, D. J. (1981, July). Factors to consider in programming for children with language disorders. *Topics in Learning & Learning Disabilities*, pp. 13–27.
Johnson, D., & Blalock, J. (Eds.). (1987). *Adults with learning disabilities: Clinical studies*. Orlando, FL: Grune & Stratton.
Johnson, D., & Hook, P. (1978). Reading disabilities: Problems of rule acquisition and linguistic awareness. In Myklebust, H. (1978). *Progress in learning disabilities, Vol. IV* (pp. 205–221). New York: Grune & Stratton.
Johnson, D., & Myklebust, H. (1967). *Learning disabilities: Educational principles and practices*. New York: Grune & Stratton.
Johnston, J. (1982a). Language-disordered children. *Language, Speech, and Hearing Services in Schools, 13*(3), 144–155.
Johnston, J. (1982b). The language disordered child. In N. Lass, L. McReynolds, J. Northern, & D. Yoder (Eds.), *Speech, language, and hearing*, Vol. 2 (pp. 780–801). Philadelphia: W. B. Saunders.
Johnston, J., & Weismer, S. (1983). Mental rotation abilities in language-disordered children. *Journal of Speech and Hearing Research, 26*, 297–404.
Johnston, J., & Schery, T. (1976). The use of grammatical morphemes by children with communication disorders. In D. M. Morehead, & A. E. Morehead (Eds.), *Normal and deficient child language*, (pp. 239–258). Baltimore: University Park Press.
Kamhi, A., Catts, H., Koenig, L., & Lewis, B. (1984). Hypothesis-testing and nonlinguistic symbolic activities in language-impaired children. *Journal of Speech and Hearing Disorders, 49*, 169–176.
Kelly, D. J., & Rice, J. L. (1986). A strategy for language assessment of young children: A combination of two approaches. *Language, Speech, and Hearing Services in Schools, 17*(2), 83–94.
Kirchner, D., & Klatzky, R. (1985). Verbal rehearsal and memory in language-disordered children. *Journal of Speech and Hearing Research, 28*, 556–565.
Kirk, S., McCarthy, J., & Kirk, W. (1968). *Illinois Test of Psycholinguistic Abilities*. Urbana: University of Illinois Press.
Klecan-Aker, J., & Hedrick, D. (1985). A study of syntactic language skills of normal school-age children. *Language, Speech and Hearing Services in Schools, 16*, 187–198.
Klein, E. S. (1988). Assessment of oral language. In J. Salvia & J. E. Ysseldyke, *Assessment*. Boston: Houghton-Mifflin.
Launer, P. B., & Lahey, M. (1981). Passages: From the fifties to the eighties in language assessment. *Topics in Language Disorders, 1*(3), 11–29.
Lee, L. (1974). *Developmental sentence analysis*. Evanston, IL: Northwestern University Press.
Leiter, R., & Arthur, G. (1969). *Leiter International Performance Scale*. Chicago: Stoelting Company.
Lieberman, R. J., Heffron, A. M., West, St. J., Hutchinson, E. D., & Swem, T. W. (1987). A comparison of four adolescent language tests. *Language, Speech, and Hearing Services in Schools, 18*(3), 250–266.
Liles, B., Shulman, M., & Bartlett, S. (1977). Judgments of grammaticality by normal and language-disordered children. *Journal of Speech and Hearing Disorders, 42*, 199–209.
Litowitz, B. (1987). Learning to make definitions. In D. Johnson & J. Blalock (Eds.), *Adults with learning disabilities: Clinical studies*. Orlando, FL: Grune & Stratton.

Loban, W. (1976). *Language development: Kindergarten through grade twelve.* Urbana, IL: National Council of Teachers of English.
Lyon, G., & Watson, B. (1981). Empirically derived subgroups of learning disabled readers: Diagnostic characteristics. *Journal of Learning Disabilities, 14,* 256–261.
Masland, R. L., & Masland, M. W. (Eds.). (1988). *Preschool prevention of reading failure.* Parkton, MD: York Press.
Matthews, F. (1985). *A comparative investigation of learning disabled and normal six-year-olds' strategies for learning new words.* Unpublished doctoral dissertation, Northwestern University, Evanston, IL.
Mattis, S., French, J., & Rapin, I. (1975). Dyslexia in children and young adults. Three independent neuropsychological syndromes. *Developmental Medicine and Child Neurology, 17,* 150–163.
Mcloughlin C. S., & Gullo, D. F. (1984). Comparison of three formal methods of preschool language assessment. *Language, Speech, and Hearing Services in Schools, 15*(3), 146–153.
Menyuk, P. (1964). Comparison of grammar of children with funtionally deviant and normal speech. *Journal of Speech and Hearing Research, 7,* 109–121.
Merritt, D., & Liles, B. (1987). Story grammar ability in children with and without language disorder: Story generation, story retelling, and story comprehension. *Journal of Speech and Hearing Research, 30,* 539–552.
Miller, J. (1981). *Assessing language production in children* (pp. 9–46). Austin, TX: PRO-ED.
Moran, M., & Byrne, M. (1977). Mastery of verb tense markers by normal and learning disabled children. *Journal of Speech and Hearing Research, 20,* 529–542.
Morehead, D., & Ingram, D. (1976). The development of base syntax in normal and linguistically deviant children. In D. M. Morehead, & A. E. Morehead (Eds.), *Normal and deficient child language.* Baltimore: University Park Press.
Morehead, D. M., & Morehead, A. E. (Eds.). (1976). *Normal and deficient child language.* Baltimore: University Park Press.
Myklebust, H. (1954). *Auditory disorders in children.* New York: Grune & Stratton.
Myklebust, H. (1981). *The pupil rating scale revised.* New York: Grune & Stratton.
Nippold, M. (1985). Comprehension of figurative language in youth. *Topics in Language Disorders, 5,* 1–20.
Ochs, E., & Schieffelin, B. B. (Eds.). (1979). *Developmental pragmatics.* New York: Academic Press.
Orton, S. (1937). *Reading, writing and speech problems in children.* New York: W. W. Norton.
Parnell, M., Amerman, J., & Harting, R. (1986). Responses of language-disordered children to wh-questions. *Language, Speech and Hearing Service in Schools, 17,* 95–106.
Prutting, C., & Kirchner, D. (1987). A clinical appraisal of the pragmatic aspects of language. *Journal of Speech and Hearing Disorders, 52,* 105–119.
Roth, F., & Spekman, N. (1986). Narrative discourse: Spontaneously generated stories of learning disabled and normally achieving students. *Journal of Speech and Hearing Disorders, 51,* 8–23.
Salvia, J., & Ysseldyke, J. E. (1988). *Assessment.* Boston: Houghton-Mifflin.
Savich, P. (1984). Anticipatory imagery ability in normal and language-disabled children. *Journal of Speech and Hearing Research, 27,* 494–501.
Schery, T. K. (1981). Selecting assessment strategies for language-disordered children. *Topics in Language Disorders, 1*(3), 59–73.
Scott, C. M. (1988). A perspective on the evaluation of school children's narratives. *Language, Speech, and Hearing Services in Schools, 19*(1), 67–82.
Seidenberg, P., & Bernstein, D. (1986). The comprehension of similes and meta-

phors by learning-disabled and nonlearning-disabled children. *Language, Speech and Hearing Services in Schools, 17,* 219–229.

Semel, E., & Wiig, E. (1980). *Clinical evaluation of language functions.* Columbus, OH: Charles E. Merrill.

Shatz, M., Bernstein, D., & Shulman, M. (1980). The responses of language disordered children to indirect directives in varying contexts. *Applied Psycholinguistics, 1,* 295–306.

Snyder, L. S. (1983). From assessment to intervention: Problems and solutions. In J. Miller, D. E. Yoder, & R. Schiefelbusch (Eds.), *Contemporary issues in language intervention.* Rockville, MD: The American Speech–Language–Hearing Association.

Snyder, L. (1984). Communicative competence in children with delayed language development. In R. Schiefelbusch & J. Pickar (Eds.), *The acquisition of communicative competence* (pp. 423–478). Baltimore: University Park Press.

Stein, N., & Glenn, C. (1979). An analysis of story comprehension in elementary school children. In R. O. Freedle (Ed.), *New directions in discourse processing: Advances in discourse processes* (pp. 53–120). Norwood, NJ: Ablex.

Stone, C. A. (1987). Reasoning and problem solving. In D. J. Johnson & J. W. Blalock (Eds.), *Young adults with learning disabilities.* New York: Grune & Stratton.

Swisher, L., & Aten, J. (1981). Assessing comprehension of spoken language: A multifaceted task. *Topics in Language Disorders, 1*(3), 75–85.

Tallal, P., Stark, R., Kallman, C., & Mellits, D. (1981). A reexamination of some nonverbal perceptual abilities of language-impaired and normal children as a function of age and sensory modality. *Journal of Speech and Hearing Research, 24,* 351–357.

Tarver, S., Hallahan, D., Kauffman, J., & Ball, D. (1976). Verbal rehearsal and selective attention in children with learning disabilities: A developmental lag. *Journal of Experimental Child Psychology, 22,* 375–385.

Templin, M. C. (1957). *Certain language skills in children.* Minneapolis: University of Minnesota Press.

Tyack, D., & Gottsleben, R. (1974). *Language sampling: Analysis and training.* Palo Alto, CA: Consulting Psychologists Press.

Vogel, S. (1972). *An investigation of syntactic abilities in normal and dyslexic children.* Unpublished doctoral dissertation, Northwestern University, Evanston, IL.

Wechsler, D. (1974). *Wechsler Intelligence Scale for Children–Revised.* New York: Psychological Corp.

Wiig, E., & Becker-Caplan, L. (1984). Linguistic retrieval strategies and word-finding difficulties among children with language disabilities. *Topics in Language Disorders, 4*(3), 1–18.

Wiig, E., & Semel, E. (1980). *Language assessment and intervention for the learning disabled.* Columbus, OH: Charles E. Merrill.

Wiig, E. & Semel, E. (1984). *Language assessment and intervention for the learning disabled,* 2nd ed. Columbus, OH: Charles E. Merrill.

Wood, M. L. (1982). *Language disorders in school-age children.* Englewood Cliffs, NJ: Prentice-Hall.

Wren, C. (1980). *The relationship of auditory and cognitive processes to syntactic patterns of learning disabled and normal children.* Unpublished doctoral dissertation, Northwestern University, Evanston, IL.

Wren, C. T. (1985). Collecting language samples from children with syntax problems. *Language, Speech and Hearing Services in Schools, 16*(2), 83–102.

CHAPTER 11

Assessment Strategies Inspired by Genetic Epistemology

D. KIM REID

During the decade preceding his death, Piaget embarked upon a new and largely unknown third phase of this career (Gallagher & Reid, 1988). The insightful and often charming accounts of child behavior recorded in his first five books brought him international acclaim and provided the foundation for a second career phase—his formulation of the logicomathematical model of cognitive development that is so widely regarded by Americans as *Piaget's theory*. During the 1970s, however, research on causality and learning convinced Piaget that children's understanding of *interrelationships* (e.g., correspondences, mappings, and morphisms) were essential to developmental progress. That awareness led him to revise his theory of equilibration (i.e., self-regulation of the effects of maturation and experience to form an assimilative base)—the central tenet of his theory (Piaget, 1978; Gallagher & Reid, 1983). This revision shifted the research focus of developmental epistemology—a more appropriate label for this body of knowledge generated by researchers worldwide—from the outcomes (e.g., whether a child is able to conserve volume) that explain the macrostructure of (stage) development to a *process approach concerned with the interplay between macrostructure and the mechanisms of change*. The impact of developmental epistemology on learning disabilities research, particularly as it relates to assessment practices, reflects this historical progression. For critical reviews of the learning disabilities research based on the logicomathematical model, see Reid, Knight-Arest, and Hresko (1981) and Stone and Michals (1986). For an extended discussion of the theoretical perspective, the reader is referred to Gallagher and Reid (1983), the only comprehensive treatment of Piaget and Inhelder's later works available in English.

What follows is a skeletal outline that highlights only aspects of the theory that have had a direct impact on learning disabilities research. Because the theory and methodology are mutually determined, there will not be separate sections describing each. Instead, a few general comments will serve as the basis for extended discussions of illustrative studies.

The process-oriented research spawned by Piaget's fresh perspective is important because it has the potential to contribute new insights about what might need to be examined in the assessments of persons with learning disabilities and about how those assessments might most fruitfully be conducted. As with any line of investigation, however, it takes time for a substantial body of evidence to accrue. Although there are increasing numbers of micro-analytic studies being published (Ackerman-Vallado, 1980; Blanchet, 1981, 1983; Karmiloff-Smith, 1979a, 1979b, 1983, 1986; Karmiloff-Smith & Inhelder, 1975; Metz, 1985; Moses, 1988; Wertsch & Stone, 1978), there are very few that have been addressed to the problems of persons with learning disabilities. Some of these are still in press (Moses, Klein, & Altman, in press). Others are underway, but have no data ready at this time to be reported (Bidell, in preparation; Moses, 1988).

DEVELOPMENTAL EPISTEMOLOGY REVISED

An adequate description of learning disabilities (indeed all of child development) requires an explanation of the interactions between macrodevelopment (changes that take place over substantial periods of time) and microdevelopment (changes that take place in short periods of time, for example, during trials on a single task). While the former typically describes the *nature* of change in broad strokes, the latter uncovers the *mechanisms* through which change occurs. Patterns of behavior common to all participants at a certain point in learning are used to infer similarities in behavioral organization. If the pattern changes in a systematic sequence, systematic developments in the organization of knowledge are inferred. If the pattern remains constant, one has evidence of stage-like developments over the course of learning.

Unlike the behaviorists, who describe learning as the result of one acquired behavior being chained to another, developmental epistemologists believe all learning to be structural, to result from successive constructions of qualitatively new organizational patterns. The existing system of interrelationships in the mental network both limits what can be learned and also provides the basis for the extension of knowledge. The network includes not only structures (representations and concepts that allow deduction) and procedures (strategies and skills), but also the ways those structures and procedures are related to task definition. A recent macroanalytic experiment, a good example of the methodology used by the Genevan school, by Pieraut-Le Bonniec (in press) on meaning and meaningful implication will clarify.

MACRO-ANALYSIS: EPISTEMOLOGICAL METHODOLOGY

Children between 5 and 13 years old were shown colored diagrams of three-sized squares constructed with rods of matching colors. The children were asked to notice that each square was defined by the number of rods per side and the perimeter by the total number of rods. Each child in turn and one of the two experimenters (E) were then given identical sets of 18 rods of various colors.

The other experimenter (E2) asked questions of the following types: (a) With your rods, could you make a small square with one rod on each side? (b) With his rods, could E make a big green square with three rods on each side? (c) With his rods, could E make a very big square without having any rods left over? The children were expected to note that this was impossible, since if the square had four rods per side, there would be two left over and if it had five rods per side, there would be two missing. When the child gave a correct answer, E2, pretending to take rods from a box behind a screen, asked, (d) Now that I have taken enough rods to make a square bigger than the ones we made before, how many do you think I have? The children were expected to say 20 or more. Finally, the children were asked, (e) If E took a big number of rods, let's say 500 or 999, how would you know if he could make a very, very big square without having any rods left over?

This study was conducted using Piaget's **method of critical exploration,** in which the children's answers to the examiner's probing questions govern the course of the very flexible procedures. The method stresses the search for the subject's sound new hypotheses, rather than the statistical significance of old hypotheses (Moessinger & Poulin-Dubois, 1981). Consequently, the experiment included a good deal of verbal interaction between the children and the examiners.

Patterns of responses were organized into several qualitatively different levels on the basis of systematic changes and constancies in the children's reasoning. As each level is described below, the emphasis will be on how structures in the mental network are related to procedures and to how both are related to how the task is defined.

LEVEL 1

The children in this group could not answer the questions hypothetically, but proceeded to make the squares before answering the questions. They discovered that they could not make a square with 18 rods, but could not state why. They knew that a square has four equal sides, but did not understand that the perimeter is equal to the combined length of those four sides, even after that had been brought to their attention. Consequently, even though they found that they had either two rods left over or two missing when they built their squares, they could not understand why one cannot build a square with 18 rods.

LEVEL 2

These children understood both that a square has four equal sides and that the perimeter is equal to the sum of the lengths of the four sides. They did not need to build the squares, but instead adopted the procedure of reasoning with numbers, for example, 4 + 4 + 4 + 4, etc. They knew that one cannot build a square with 18 rods, but like the Level 1 children, could not say why. The problem they faced, however, was a different one. These children could not relate the fact that a square has four equal sides to the properties of the whole numbers that, therefore, could possibly serve as measurements of the perimeter.

LEVEL 3

This group of children realized that the number representing the perimeter would have to be even, not odd. They answered that the square *could* be made with 18 or 22, etc. rods, because those were even numbers. The geometric properties of the square had been related to the properties of whole numbers that can represent the perimeter, but the task was still misunderstood, because the child's thinking was based on a vague sense of symmetry in squares. The difficulty of answering the question, however, was that only even numbers divisible by 4 are permissible.

Some children reconsidered their reasoning during the course of solving the problem, because they realized that not all even numbers can represent the perimeter of a square:

E2: If you can make a square with 18 rods, how many will be on each side?
C: 5..., No, that's too many. Four..., no that would mean some would be left over.

Realization that the guiding principle of evenness did not work led them to construct a new idea—that the only numbers that can serve as the perimeters of squares must be multiples of 4.

LEVEL 4

These children used divisibility by 4 as their guiding criterion. They understood a general rule that works no matter how large the number is. They did not need to build squares, all they needed to do was check to see whether the number of rods in question was a multiple of 4.

In this research Pieraut-Le Bonniec studied the development of the interrelationship between a geometric property and a numerical one as it becomes established over time. This researcher used the traditional developmental approach (i.e., students of a wide age range), rather than a longitudinal approach, but the latter would have worked equally well.

The levels of performance identified make it clear that the children's learning was not a chaining of one piece of information to another, but rather resulted from the construction of qualitatively different wholes. As the children's knowledge base (or structures) changed, so did the procedures they used and their definition of the task. For the youngest children it was a building task. As the children became more knowledgeable about perimeters, it shifted to an adding task. Children who linked the geometric and numerical properties viewed it first as a test of numerical symmetry (even numbers) and finally as a test of divisibility by 4. This example demonstrates the dissociability of knowledge (structure), procedures, and task definitions in normal development.

EMPIRICAL AND REFLECTING ABSTRACTION

It is worthwhile to examine the way developmental epistemologists characterize *abstractions* at this point, because they play a central role in explaining the findings in this and in the other studies that will be described. Piaget (1977, p. 3) insists that the development of cognitive systems results from self-organization or equilibration. Equilibration is a "process leading from certain states of equilibrium to others, qualitatively different, and passing through multiple nonbalances and re-equilibrations." States of disequilibrium result from contradictions, obstacles to assimilation, and gaps or needs, in the functionalist sense (Moessinger & Poulin-Dubois, 1981). Disturbances that lead to disequilibria are more frequent for preoperational children, since young children focus nearly exclusively on the observable characteristics of objects and actions. They find it difficult to go beyond the information given to make inferences about how and why events occur as they do.

Re-equilibrations occur because people modify repeated actions through trial and error until they attain a workable solution. Some of their regulations (activities that result in modifications) lead to compensations, others to new disturbances.

Piaget postulated that two kinds of continuously interactive abstractions, found at every level of development, contribute to the disequilibrium/re-equilibration process. The first, **empirical abstraction,** refers to the abstraction of information about properties that exist in the world—color, shape, size, mass, temperature, etc. The second type, **reflecting abstraction,** is composed of two subprocesses: **projection** and **reflection.** Projection is the transposition of an action or system of actions to a superior level, such as from performing an action to describing it verbally. Reflection refers to the reorganization of this information at the higher level. The growing conceptualization is the projection; reflection the awareness of some law or principle of a thought-reality system (Moessinger & Poulin-Dubois, 1981).

Because early abstractions emphasize empirical data, learning occurs from the periphery (of the child's mind) to the center (Piaget, 1976; 1978): success precedes understanding. Although both empirical and reflecting abstractions occur at all levels, the empirical aspects of abstraction are increasingly subordinated to the data drawn from *thinking* as the child matures. In the study described above, the children began by carrying out the task physically, relying on the empirical aspects of the problem for information. As they progressed, their hypotheses revealed better understandings of the laws governing the relationship between perimeters and the numbers that can represent them.

MACRO-ANALYTIC INFLUENCES ON THE LEARNING DISABILITIES RESEARCH

Since people who suffer from learning disorders tend to have less well-developed knowledge bases and to have difficulty implementing procedures (especially strategies) in appropriate contexts, the findings of studies, such as Pieraut-Le Bonniec's, with normally developing children led researchers to ask whether persons with learning disabilities achieve the same pattern of understandings and whether they achieve them in the same way. I, however, have been unable to locate any macro-analytic studies—developmental or longitudinal—of persons with learning disabilities that follow the process-oriented, macro-analytic Piagetian tradition.

Instead, learning disabilities researchers have applied structural methodology to a more fine-grained, micro-analytic approach, observing, within a single age group, the same elements as those addressed in the macrostructure studies—what the learners know, how they proceed, and how they define the task. Emphasis has been on an examination of the learning process itself, trial by trial as individuals solve a task.

MICRO-ANALYTIC RESEARCH IN LEARNING DISABILITIES

Studies conducted within a logicomathematical framework indicated that persons with learning disabilities evinced the same stage-like behaviors as normal persons, but with developmental delays. However, there was also some evidence that persons with learning disabilities may have been using compensatory behaviors to achieve the same levels of performance. Simultaneously, in the mainstream literature, issues regarding information-processing strategies were being raised. Consequently, the questions most pressing as the new methodology emerged were related to whether people with learning disabilities functioned in the same ways that normally achieving people did when faced with complex tasks. Because it had the potential to reveal what people *do* as they solve tasks and not just whether they perform as well as another group, micro-analytic research enabled investigators to examine the behaviors actually engaged in by individuals with learning disabilities as they solved problems and performed tasks.

TRANSITIONAL STUDIES

The transitional studies (i.e., those that bridged the logicomathematical and learning theory phases of developmental epistemology) were conducted by Reid and her colleagues. They compared not only the task performances of learning disabled and normally achieving cohorts, but also the explanations they gave for their actions and the behaviors they used that were extraneous to the tasks.

Knight-Arest and Reid (1979) examined the causal influence social interaction exerted on conservation of liquids judgments by 9- to 10-year-old learning disabled and 7- to 9-year-old normally achieving students matched for sex, IQ, and socioeconomic status. One nonconserver poured juice into differently shaped classes for two conservers. The single requirement was that all three needed to agree that the juice had been distributed fairly. The arguments the children used during their discussions were recorded. The nonconservers were retested on a conservation of liquids task one hour and again two months later. The children's justifications were recorded during both posttests. A control group practiced the conservation test without social interaction.

Results indicated that having to exchange and coordinate points of view with their peers fostered levels of structuring beyond those attained by the control group. Although the children with learning disabilities appeared to profit from the social interaction as well as their normal peers, the explanations and delayed posttest data suggested that they did not. First, they were unable to offer explanations other than those that had been voiced by their peers. Second, nearly half regressed to nonconservation responses on the delayed posttest. Finally, their performances were qualitatively different from those offered by the normal students: they appeared to have learned a specific response, rather than to have achieved a new cognitive structure. They remained at the periphery (achieving success on the task), but failed to construct mental understandings of the laws governing conservation. Consequently, when confronted with the problem two months later, they did not have a set of principles to apply.

A second and more clearly learning-oriented study (because it addressed changes in behavior over trials) (Reid & Knight-Arest, 1979; Reid et al., 1981) compared the way 10-year-old normal boys and boys with learning disabilities used "theories-in-action" to guide their attempts to balance blocks of various configurations, some of which obviously and some of which secretly had been weighted to balance off-center (Karmiloff-Smith & Inhelder, 1975). The boys were asked to tell the experimenter how things balance (their initial theories) and then to balance the series of blocks. The experimenters observed whether the boys placed the blocks in accordance with their theories (e.g., if one believes that objects balance in the middle, the initial placement of the block on the fulcrum should approximate its midpoint). They also observed whether and how the boys changed their theories as a result of the feedback they received from performing the task. In essence, what was studied was the micro-interplay between structure, procedure, and task definition. The sessions were videotaped and transcribed in the manner of psycholinguistic transcripts (Bloom & Lahey, 1978). This format enabled the researchers to analyze both action and its verbal accompaniments. Of interest was not so much the children's successes or failures, but rather the way they proceeded.

When the boys had a theory (equality of weight) to begin with (all of the normal boys, but only two of those with learning disabilities), they placed the blocks on the fulcrum near their midpoint, revealing more reliance on reflection than observables. Three of the boys with learning disabilities (but none of the normal boys), however, understood balancing in perceptual terms ("make one stay on top of the other") and five had no theories at all ("I just do it and then I find the place where it works"). These boys placed the blocks randomly, made unusually gross adjustments, and looked to the physical attributes of the blocks for explanations, understandably often erroneous explanations. The state of the materials (emphasizing empirical abstractions) guided their explanations, rather than the other way around.

As in the previous study, the boys with learning disabilities (who did not begin with a theory) were effective to the extent that they could rely on empirical abstraction as a learning mechanism. They concentrated on affirmations, displaying great difficulty in going beyond the information given. Both their actions and the states of the objects were adequately perceived, but the links between actions and states were lost to them. They did not seem to appreciate that something was to be learned from *thinking about their activity*, the reflexive aspects of abstraction.

These studies were exploratory and lacked methodological sophistication. The main difficulty, which later studies remedied, was that they did not include enough trials to study the effects of learning sufficiently, that is, to identify levels of qualitatively different performances as the task was mastered. Although the study did examine changes in knowledge, procedures, and task definition over several trials of the balancing task, most boys at the end of the study believed just what they had at the beginning.

MORE RECENT MICRO-ANALYSIS

Wansart's (in press) recent study was designed to describe similarities and differences in the way 10- to 12-year-old normal children and those with learning disabilities learned how to solve three-disk problems with various starting and ending points on the Tower of Hanoi, a children's game that involves moving a stack of disks, one at a time, from a beginning to a target peg. Since one is not permitted either to put disks on the table or to put a larger disk on a smaller one, the problem requires intermediary solutions in which smaller disks must be moved to temporary positions in order to clear a peg for the positioning of a larger disk, which will then serve as the base for a reconstructed tower. The fewest number of moves for the correct solution of a three-disk problem is 7.

Wansart applied the developmental epistemologist's micro-analytic strategies to define levels of performance over trials on a single task. Two sets of data were generated, one for the nature of exploratory behaviors and one for strategies.

The most rudimentary exploratory behaviors (what we have been referring to as procedures) reflected an emphasis on the empirical aspects of abstraction, of knowledge at the periphery. They were governed by the child's actions and the state of the materials at any given time, rather than by experimentation. Learning was by trial and error and often exhausted the possibilities available under the current level of understanding, leading the child to achieve the same results over and over.

In contrast, children operating reflexively shifted from the goal of obtaining a practical success. They searched actively for an understanding of the system that would lead to solution. Indications that they were deliberately experimenting included requests for rule clarification and comments like, "I think I've got it now."

Strategies were defined as the procedures that reflected the child's representation of the task—in the language we have been using to describe previous experiments, how knowledge base and task definition interact. The children's sequences of moves were graphed and systematic changes and constancies were studied. Five levels emerged. In this case the levels do not represent the performances of groups of children, but rather stage-like developments in the children's behaviors over time.

Level 1: Global. The first attempt was often to move the largest disk immediately to the target post, disregarding the problem constraints.

Level 2: Goal Post Resistance. The task was viewed as two separate and uncoordinated goals: putting the large disk on the target post and moving the smaller disks out of the way. This strategy led to resistance for using the target post for storage, because of the anticipation that it would block the movement of the large disk to that post.

Level 3: Subtower. Part of the problem had been solved: building a subtower of the smaller disks. At this point, however, the children did not know where to build the tower to free the target post.

Level 4: Procedural. The children were able to coordinate the building of the tower with the freeing of the target post and, consequently, were able to solve the problem—sometimes even in 7 moves. The solution was not so well understood, however, that it could be transferred and modified for other three-disk problems. They also had to be solved through trial and error.

Level 5: Representational. The solution procedures could be transferred immediately to other, similar problems involving different starting and/or target posts.

Although the children with learning disabilities exhibited the same pattern of strategies as the normal children, they did not generally advance beyond the procedural strategy. As in the second of the transitional studies, the children with learning disabilities seemed bound to the situationally specific aspects of the problem, the periphery. Wansart argued that these findings indicate a slower rate of learning that follows normal developmental patterns. Coupled with the additional finding that the children with learning disabilities engaged in active search, he concluded that characterizing students with learning disabilities as passive or nonstrategic on the basis of studies that reveal their deficiencies is a risky endeavor.

AMERICAN RESEARCH STRATEGIES

Some studies use Piagetian tasks to address similar questions, but employ research strategies more typical of American psychology than of Genevan epistemology. A recent study by Stone and Forman (in press, b) will be used to illustrate. They addressed two issues highlighted here: active problem solving and difficulties with reflective awareness.

The objective of the study was to identify different patterns of problem-solving among adolescents with learning disabilities. Data were gathered using a modified version of Piaget's bending rods task. An array of 12 rods of varying lengths, diameters, and materials and a set of weights were used to isolate the variables important to bending. Seven dependent measures related to the data-gathering methods, reasoning ability, and responses to examiner guidance of adolescents with learning disabilities were submitted to a cluster analysis and compared to performances of normal children of the same age and younger.

Four clusters were identified. The first appeared to represent normal performance (i.e., the children with learning disabilities scored within one standard deviation of the normal children's mean on all measures used in defining the clusters). The second was characterized by the unusually general nature of their conclusions, the third by a specific delay in the acquisition of the isolation-of-variables strategy, and the last by poor overall performance. (A similar study [Stone & Forman, in press, a] contrasted performances of subgroups with learning disabilities and their normal peers).

Although such studies identify groups of behavior patterns that are described as *qualitatively different*, the methods used to generate these groups are fundamentally different from those described in the macro-analytic and micro-analytic studies mentioned earlier. The theoretical perspective is behavioral in that different patterns of performance are measured quantitatively (i.e., as different patterns of high and low scores on a variety of dependent variables). In epistemological research, qualitatively different patterns of successive wholes (with respect to the organization of knowledge, procedures, and task definition) are analyzed. In addition, in the Stone and Forman work, there is no hierarchical structure to the pattern of performances, such that a subject could be expected to move from one to another as competence is achieved. In contrast, epistemological studies define hierarchical levels of either long- or short-term growth. In behavioral studies, questions and variables are predetermined, while epistemological work uses the method of critical exploration. In consequence, the behaviorist lumps a range of similar, but discrepant performances together on the basis of test scores, while the epistemologist constructs a few scenarios that must accurately accommodate the behaviors of each individual protocol. In sum, although some of the questions addressed are the same and the bending rods task was designed by Piaget, the research conducted by Stone and Forman is not "Piagetian," and the authors make no claims that it is.

IMPLICATIONS FOR ASSESSMENT PRACTICES

Several implications for assessment of persons with learning disabilities can be drawn from the research described. First, problem-solving performance should be assessed. Since they demonstrate systematic difficulty in learning to solve complex tasks, persons with learning disabilities should be observed during learning trials. These observations could be far more fruitful than test data in providing valuable insight into what the person knows about the task, the nature of the procedures used in task solution, and the level of task definition. Such observations would acquaint the examiner with information about what kinds of strategic behaviors the person *does* engage in and would militate against the prevailing "deficit" orientation in education. If an individual's patterns of changes and constancies are identified, they can serve as the basis for developmentally appropriate instructional interventions.

Second, this body of research suggests that there is a period of stagnation—a sustained preference for empirical rather than increasingly reflective activity—in problem-solving performance exhibited rather consistently by persons with learning disabilities (the same stagnation is apparent among normally achieving persons when the task is particularly complex (Moses, personal communication). This penchant to operate at the periphery could very well contribute to the cumulative deficits in verbal (but not performance) IQ that have been documented worldwide (cf., van den Bos, 1988) as persons with learning disabilities acquire semantic knowledge at a much slower rate than other members of their age group. Failure to abstract general laws/rules/principles would severely impoverish not only semantic knowledge, but also the procedures and task definitions that are so closely interrelated with them. This failure also appears on the surface, at least, to be related to the memory difficulties so clearly documented in the learning disabilities literature, because inferring depends on the ability to manipulate mental rather than physical information. When there is no opportunity to manipulate concrete materials—when reading paragraphs, for example—the failure to abstract generalities could be even more pernicious.

Consequently, it would be very important for examiners to determine what types of tasks are sufficiently easy for a given person with learning disabilities that they foster the acquisition of reflective thinking abilities and what types inhibit such performance. Proleptic teaching (Stone 1986) may then be used to induce more reproductive task approach strategies.

Finally, because reflection is both so central to problem solving and so seldom evidenced by the learning disabled, it is important when making assessments of problem-solving abilities to differentiate practical success from conscious understanding. Karmiloff-Smith (1986) has proposed a U-shaped model of development: During phase 1, children succeed at performing tasks by narrowing the distance between beginning and goal states through trial and error. When they attempt to represent their problem-solving procedures (phase 2), there are apparent performance decrements, because they try to oversimplify. Subsequently (phase 3), accuracy is restored, but with improved control—the result of the construction of explanations. What may very well be happening on our ongoing instructional assessments particularly (although it would not be unlikely that formal testing would suffer from the same problem) is that we take success as evidence of learning, when it may simply be the result of trial and error.

SUMMARY

Recent studies in genetic epistemology have been micro-analytic, examining the nature of progressions in learning across changes and constancies in individual performance over very brief periods. These studies have revealed that individuals with learning disabilities are active problem-solvers who do engage in strategic behaviors. They do not, however, operate at a level where experimentation guides performance and is used to abstract general principles that can be applied to future solutions.

Three implications for the assessment of persons with learning disabilities can be drawn from this research: First, problem solving over trials should be assessed in addition to the knowledge accumulated—the more typical practice. Second, tasks that are easy enough to foster reflective activity should be identified and used as the basis for establishing reflective approaches to more difficult tasks, perhaps through proleptic teaching. Finally, examiners should look beyond practical success for evidence that the task has been understood before assuming that it has been learned.

REFERENCES

Ackerman-Vallado, E. (1980). Etudes de relations entre procedures et attribution de signification aux instrument, dans une tache de construction chemins. *Archives de Psychologie, 48*, 59–93.

Bidell, T. (in preparation). Mechanisms of cognitive micro-genesis. Draft of thesis proposal. Harvard University.
Blanchet, A. (1981). Etude genetique des significations et des modeles utilises par l'enfant lors de resolutions de problems. Unpublished doctoral dissertation, University of Geneva, Switzerland.
Blanchet, A. (1983). Reflective abstraction and problem solving. Paper presented at the Thirteenth Annual Symposium of the Jean Piaget Society, Philadelphia.
Bloom, L., & Lahey, M. (1978). Language development and language disorders. New York: Wiley.
Gallagher, J. M., & Reid, D. K. (1983). The learning theory of Piaget and Inhelder. Austin, TX: PRO-ED.
Gallagher, J. M., & Reid, D. K. (1988). The assimilative base in Piaget's learning theory: The foundation for a model of cognitive teaching. Unpublished manuscript.
Karmiloff-Smith, A. (1979a). Micro and macrodevelopmental changes in language acquisition and other representational systems. Cognitive Science, 3, 91–188.
Karmiloff-Smith, A. (1979b). Problem solving procedures in children's construction and representations of closed railway circuits. Archives de Psychologie, 51, 35–40.
Karmiloff-Smith, A. (1983). A note on the concept of "metaprocedural processes" in linguistic and nonlinguistic cognitive development. Archives de Psychologie, 51, 41.
Karmiloff-Smith, A. (1986). Stage/structure versus phase/process in modeling linguistic and cognitive development. In I. Levine (Ed.), Stage and structure: Reopening the debate. Norwood, NJ: Ablex.
Karmiloff-Smith, A., & Inhelder, B. (1975). If you want to get ahead, get a theory. Cognition, 3, 195–212.
Knight-Arest, I., & Reid, D. K. (1981). Peer interaction as a catalyst for conservation acquisition in normal and learning disabled children. Proceedings of the 9th Interdisciplinary International Conference on Piagetian Theory and the Helping Professions. ERIC Document ED 162489.
Metz, K. E. (1985). The development of children's problem solving in a gears task: A problem space perspective. Cognitive Science, 9, 431–471.
Moessinger, P., & Poulin-Dubois, A. (1981). Piaget on abstraction. Human Development, 24, 347–353.
Moses, N. (1988). Cognitive development as reflected in the procedural behavior of adults engaged in a "tractor-trailer" task. Unpublished manuscript.
Moses, N., Klein, H. B., & Altman, E. (in press). An approach assessing and facilitating causal language in learning disabled adults based on Piagetian theory. Journal of Learning Disabilities.
Piaget, J. (1976). The grasp of consciousness: Action and concept in the young child. Cambridge, MA: Harvard University Press.
Piaget, J. (1977). The development of thought: Equilibrium of cognitive structures. New York, Viking Penguin.
Piaget, J. (1978). Success and understanding. Cambridge, MA: Harvard University Press.
Pieraut-Le Bonniec, G. (in press). The logic of meaning and meaningful implication. In W. Overton (Ed.), Reasoning, necessity and logic: Developmental perspectives. Hillsdale, NJ: Erlbaum.
Reid, D. K. (1978). Equilibration and learning. Journal of Education, 161, 51–71.

Reid, D. K., & Knight-Arest, I. (1981). Cognitive processing in learning disabled and normally achieving boys in a goal-oriented task. In M. Freidman (Ed.), *Intelligence and learning*. New York: Plenum.

Reid, D. K., Knight-Arest, I., & Hresko, W. P. (1981). Cognitive development in learning disabled children. In J. Gottlieb and S. S. Strichart (Eds.), *Developmental theories and research in learning disabilities*. Baltimore: University Park Press.

Stone, C. A. (1986). Vygotsky's developmental model and the concept of proleptic instruction: Some implications for theory and research in the field of learning disabilities. *Research Communications in Psychology, Psychiatry, and Behavior, 10*, 129–152.

Stone, C. A., & Forman, E. (in press, a). Cognitive development in language-oriented disabled adolescents: A study of problem-solving performance in an isolation-of-variables task. *Learning Disability Research*.

Stone, C. A., & Forman, E. A. (in press, b). Differential patterns of approach to a complex problem-solving task among learning-disabled adolescents. *Journal of Special Education*.

Stone, C. A., & Michals, D. (1986). Problem-solving skills in learning disabled children. In S. J. Ceci (Ed.), *Handbook of cognitive, social, and neuropsychological aspects of learning disabilities* (Vol. 1). Hillsdale, NJ: Erlbaum.

van den Bos, K. (1988, November). Problems in the cognitive development of learning disabled children. Paper presented at the NATO proceedings. Ciocco, Italy.

Wansart, W. L. (1990, March). Learning to solve a problem: A microanalysis of the solution strategies of learning disabled children. *Journal of Learning Disabilities*.

Wertsch, J. V., & Stone, C. A. (1978). Microgenisis as a tool for developmental analysis. *Quarterly newsletter of the Laboratory of Comparative Human Cognition*.

CHAPTER 12

Assessment of Metacognitive Research in Learning Disabilities: Theory, Research, and Practice

BERNICE Y. L. WONG

The theoretical construct of metacognition has found much use in learning disabilities, and receptiveness to it continues to be highly positive among both researchers and practitioners. The goal of this chapter is to assess the three interrelated facets of metacognition in learning disabilities: theory, research, and practice. Within the assessment of each facet, there will be an attempt to clarify specific issues.

ASSESSMENT OF METACOGNITIVE THEORY IN LEARNING DISABILITIES

The theoretical origin of metacognitive strategies research came from the theoretical construct of and research on metacognition. The construct of metacognition originated in Flavell's research on young children's memory processes. He invoked that construct in an attempt to explain young children's failure to maitain and generalize learned mnemonic strategies.

Metamemory, awareness of parameters that govern effective recall, was assumed to be deficient among young children, and explained their problems in strategy maintenance and generalization (Flavell, 1976). Subsequently in a seminal paper, Ann Brown (1980) related the theoretical construct of metacognition to reading. Brown stated: "Any description of effective reading includes active strategies of monitoring, checking and self-testing, whether the task under consideration is reading for remembering (studying) or reading for doing (following instructions)" (p. 456). She further elaborated on metacognitive skills of reading to include understanding task demands, identifying important aspects of a message, allocating concentration, self-monitoring, and self-questioning to ensure that reading goals are met, and engaging in debugging strategies to deal with comprehension failures (Brown, 1980, p. 456).

There is a wealth of empirical findings that attest to the vast repertoires of reading strategies and spontaneous, flexible strategy use in good or mature readers (see Baker & Brown, 1984a, 1984b, for excellent summaries). These findings led instructional researchers to focus on enhancing various cognitive and metacognitive strategies in poor readers, with the goal of improving their reading comprehension through the use of those strategies. These instructional attempts have been successful (Paris, Wixson, & Palincsar, 1986; Pearson & Gallagher, 1983). More important, some of the strategy instructional research has been effectively implemented in classrooms (Paris et al., 1986).

The relevance of the theoretical construct of metacognition and metacognitive research to special education—in particular, learning disabilities—was highlighted by Wong (1982, 1985, 1986, 1987). I sought to relate metacognition to learning disabilities because there has been an indiscriminate tendency among learning disabilities professionals to interpret performance failures in children/adolescents with learning disabilities as cognitive deficits. I felt there was a need to discern between performance failures that genuinely reflect more deep-seated processing problems versus problems that are of a strategic nature. Because metacognitive research unequivocally demonstrates that skilled reading involves decoding, reading comprehension and metacognitive skills, I felt learning disabilities professionals need to look afresh at how they interpret reading problems manifested by students with learning disabilities. Specifically, they would not be justified in inferring indiscriminately deep-seated processing deficits in any child with learning disabilities who has a reading disability. Likewise, they would not be justified in focussing exclusively on decoding and comprehension skills in remediating reading problems in students with learning disabilities.

In essence, I tied in metacognition with learning disabilities because in my view, metacognitive research broadens the perception and understanding of reading problems in students with learning disabilities and highlights the need to teach students with learning disabilities metacognitive skills in reading in addition to decoding and comprehension skills. However, I also considered and cautioned learning disabilities professionals about the limitations of a metacognitive perspective in learning disabilities (Wong, 1986). Specifically, I warned against a wholesale interpretation of failures by students with learning disabilities in terms of strategic deficits because there will be occasions when failures are caused by insufficient knowledge and/or ability. Moreover, metacognition alone does not suffice in students' maintenance and generalization of what has been learned. Students' motivation is pivotal in such maintenance and generalization (Wong, 1986, pp. 22-24).

A metacognitive framework has been used to generate comprehension-fostering research (Bos & Filips, 1982; Graves, 1986; Palincsar, 1982; Wong & Jones, 1982) and spelling in learning disabilities (Gerber, 1987; Wong, 1983). Clearly, for intervention research in which the targeted skills involve self-monitoring, self-evaluating, and self-testing, the use of a metacognitive framework is appropriate. However, the instructional needs of students with learning disabilities in more basic skills and cognitive strategies preempt and exceed metacognitive strategies. Hence, a metacognitive framework appears to be limited in its application in learning disabilities research.

Of more serious concern is Stanovich's point that linking metacognition to learning disabilities may in fact attenuate the assumption of specificity that underlies the concept of learning disabilities (Stanovich, 1986a, 1986b, 1988). The assumption of specificity holds that dyslexic individuals have a severe disability in one particular cognitive domain, typically reading, but that in other cognitive domains, they are relatively intact. It is essential that the cognitive disability be restricted to one specific area, otherwise the individual would be labeled as a slow learner or as mentally retarded. The latter type of learners characteristically have widespread cognitive deficits (Stanovich, 1986a).

Stanovich (1986a, 1986b, 1988) pointed out that recent theoretical formulations in intelligence tend to include metacognition as an integral component, for example, Sternberg's work. Thus, if metacognition is seen as a characteristic of individuals with learning disabilities it would logically lead to the conclusion that they have lower intelligence. Clearly, this conclusion would undermine the discrepancy notion, and cause the disintegration of the assumption of specificity in learning disabilities.

How can we resolve this problem? One way is to invoke Stanovich's hypothesis of Matthews effects (Stanovich, 1986b). Specifically, within his phonological core-variable model (Stanovich, 1988), Stanovich posits that dyslexic children begin with a very specific, circumscribed cognitive problem in phonological processing. This phonological processing problem impedes the child's learning to read since he or she would experience enormous difficulties in learning letter–sound associations. Early and persistent failures to learn to read inevitably create motivational problems in the young child (Torgesen, 1977). The child becomes anxious with the reading task, comes to loathe reading and develops problems with self-esteem.

In time these motivational problems generalize to academic areas outside of reading (Butkowsky & Willows, 1980) and affect adversely the child's motivation to learn in school. Because the child cannot read and dislikes reading since reading reminds him or her of his or her disability and presents perpetual frustrations, he or she ends up having substantially less reading experience outside of school. Similarly, because in remedial reading the child typically receives phonics drills or drills in word recognition rather than passage reading, he or she also comes to be much less exposed to reading than his or her peers in school (Allington, 1980). These motivational and experiential deficiencies bode ill for the dyslexic child, because many school subjects involve reading. Hence, the child's reading disability and the resultant motivational problems impede his or her learning of other academic subjects in school. Consequently (and soon), his or her academic problem would not be confined to reading. In time, as she or he ages, the dyslexic child presents a picture of more generalized cognitive and cumulative deficits.

Stanovich uses the Biblical analogy of Matthews effects to describe the generalized deficits that dyslexic individuals manifest. It's the case of the poor getting poorer as contrasted with the normally achieving child being the rich getting richer. Normally achieving children literally take off after mastering letter–sound associations or cracking the spelling-to-sound code. They begin to read much more, even average children. Independent reading for pleasure and in-class reading provide normally achieving children with reading experiences that are essential for their growth in various kinds of knowledge: vocabulary, syntax, and knowledge about the world and specific topics, e.g., dinosaurs. In turn, such growth in knowledge promotes knowledge acquisition in other related areas. Current schema theories and research in reading comprehension indicate the importance of prior knowledge in the acquisition of knowledge (Schallert, 1982). Thus, for children who learned to read, they can add much to this cognitive foundation. Cognitively speaking, they got richer. The analogy is most apt vis-à-vis skilled readers.

The Matthews effects hypothesis provides us with a potential solution for the problem of linking metacognition with learning disabilities. We can treat metacognitive problems in students with learning disabilities as a joint byproduct of their lack of reading experience and motivational problems. Metacognition about reading develops in the context and experiences of reading. An individual cannot develop metacognition about reading in a vacuum. Similarly, the self-regulatory component of metacognition depends on motivation for its deployment. As children with learning disabilities get poorer in learning, they develop metacognitive problems which are essentially, a second-order problem. In the picture of the more widespread, generalized cognitive problems they present, metacognitive problems are also present.

It is important to remember that we can avoid the problem highlighted by Stanovich only by treating metacognitive problems as a second-order problem, not a first-order problem such as a phonological processing problem, but a joint byproduct of deficient reading experiences and motivation. Seen from the perspective of the negative Matthews effects, metacognitive problems may conceivably be legitimately used to describe children with learning disabilities.

ASSESSMENT OF METACOGNITIVE RESEARCH IN LEARNING DISABILITIES

The research base of metacognition in learning disabilities appears to be surprisingly small. It seems then that the receptiveness to the construct among learning disabilities professionals reflects its conceptual appeal and its advantages in enhancing understanding of strategic problems in students with learning disabilities (Wong, 1985, 1986, 1987).

Metacognitive research in learning disabilities can readily be divided into more basic research and intervention research. To date there have been four basic research studies: Wong and Wong (1986), Englert and Thomas (1987); Englert, Raphael, Fear, and Anderson 1988); and Wong, Wong, and Blenkisop (1989). There have been three intervention studies: Graves (1986); Palincsar and Brown (1984), and Wong and Jones (1982). These studies are summarized below.

BASIC RESEARCH

Wong and Wong

Wong and Wong (1986) investigated how metacognitive knowledge of vocabulary difficulty and organization of given passages affected study time of the same passages in above average and average students and those with learning disabilities. Subjects were 17 above average readers, 14 average readers and 14 readers with learning disabilities from grades 5, 6, and 7. The investigators first interviewed the subjects individually on their knowledge of how easy or difficult vocabulary and the organized or disorganized nature of a particular passage affected the ease in studying it. Altogether, four passages were used. In two of these, level of vocabulary difficulty was manipulated. The "oyster" passage contained more difficult vocabulary such as "mollusks," "plankton," "immediate," "environment," "unexpectedly," "especially," and "maturity." In comparison, the "whooping crane" passage contained relatively easy vocabulary. Passage organization was manipulated through two alternative versions of a passage either about a fox or polar bears. Each passage contained 12 short sentences, which clustered in fours around a specific subtopic about the respective animal: physical features, food, and habitat. One version of the "fox" and the "polar bear" passages was organized so that the four sentences clustering each of the three subtopics were related to the particular subtopic and logically sequenced. In the disorganized version of the passages, thematic cohesion within each cluster of sentences was clearly lacking.

Each child was seen individually, and, depending on order of passage presentation, was given either the organized or disorganized pair or the pair with hard or easy vocabulary first. With respect to the pair of passages with hard or easy vocabulary, the child was told that two students (A and B) studied the oyster (hard vocabulary) and whooping crane (easy vocabulary) passages. Student A spent 15 minutes studying each passage. Student B spent 30 minutes on the oyster passage and 15 minutes on the whooping crane passage. The child was asked which student would remember more of the passages, especially the oyster passage, and why. To facilitate the child's response, a schematic depiction of the hypothetical students' study behaviors and the oyster and whooping crane passages were placed before the child. With respect to the organized/disorganized pair of passages, the child was told that again two students (C and D) studied them. Student C spent 15 minutes on the organized passage, and 30 minutes on the disorganized passage. Student D however, studied them for 15 minutes each. The child again was asked which student would remember more of the passages, especially the disorganized one, and why. Again, to facilitate the child's response, a schematic depiction of the hypothetical students' study behaviors and the organized and disorganized passages were placed before the child.

About three weeks after the interview, the children were again seen individually. Half the children were randomly assigned to the hard/easy vocabulary passage pair first, followed by the organized/disorganized passage pair. The remaining children had the passage pairs in the reverse order. When given the previously seen organized/disorganized passage pair, the child was told to study for subsequent recall of both passages. When given the passage pair with hard/easy vocabulary, the child was told to study for a subsequent reading-comprehension test on each passage. Within each pair of passages, the order of passage presentation was randomized. Moreover, there was a 3-minute break between passages and a 5-minute break between the two sets of passages. The child was self-paced and given unlimited time to study the passages. Also, an aide pronounced and carefully explained the meanings of key vocabulary words in the oyster and whooping crane passages. For the benefit of the readers with learning disabilities, words that might pose decoding or vocabulary difficulties were pronounced clearly and explained thoroughly. Additionally, the child was encouraged to seek help with any other decoding or vocabulary difficulties not anticipated. When ready for the recall or comprehension test, the child signaled to the experimenter. The child was told not to worry about spelling errors in written answers to the short comprehension questions. Study times in minutes and seconds were recorded with a stopwatch. The children's recall was tape-recorded and later transcribed.

The results indicated that above average readers were substantially more aware that level of vocabulary difficulty and passage organization affect the ease of studying a given passage. Examination of the children's individual protocols indicated few grade 5 children scored more than 1 point in the justification responses, which had a scoring range of 0 to 4. Those who obtained 2 points were above average. Among the grade 6 children, above average readers did very well since none had scores less than 2 points. Apart from one fifth-grade child, the average readers' performance was generally lackluster. Among readers with learning disabilities, two in grade 7 had 4 points each in justifying why the hypothetical student studying the disorganized passage a longer time would do better. Their respective responses were: "30 minutes for disorganized passage—disorganized passage would be harder to learn so would need more time," "Studied longer on the disorganized passage . . . it's harder to remember . . . need to study longer." Thus, examination of individual protocols indicated that although above average readers were substantially more advanced in metacognitive knowledge about vocabulary difficulty and passage organization, the same awareness appeared to be present in readers with learning disabilities. Such awareness, however, appeared only in two out of four of the *oldest* (grade 7) readers.

More importantly, Wong and Wong (1986) found a significant interaction between reader and passage. This finding indicated that whereas readers with learning disabilities were most sensitive to level of vocabulary difficulty in a passage, above average readers were most sensitive to the organization of a passage. Within the pair of passages with easy and difficult vocabulary, only readers with learning disabilities showed reliable differences in study times, studying the passage with difficult vocabulary significantly longer. Within the pair of passages with organized and disorganized sentences, only above average readers showed reliable differences in study times, studying the disorganized passage significantly longer.

This pattern of differential study times among above average readers and those with learning disabilities is important. The data for readers with learning disabilities challenge the ubiquitous assumption of metacognitive deficiency in reading among these students. Readers with learning disabilities apparently do possess metacognitive knowledge about one particular aspect of reading investigated, namely, level of vocabulary difficulty. Moreover, their sensitivity to differential vocabulary difficulty in the two passages led them to deploy suitable reading strategies. They studied the passage with difficult vocabulary much longer. One possible reason for these readers' possessing such metacognitive awareness may be due to their decoding problems, from which ensues an acute awareness of vocabulary difficulty in the reading materials.

With regard to above average readers, caution appears to be required in interpreting their apparently undifferentiated apportionment of study times to the passages with hard and easy vocabulary. It may not be assumed that they lack the necessary metacognitive skills. Recalling that the above average reader's mean reading grade was 9.9, it is highly likely that they found even the difficult vocabulary in the oysters passage easy. Hence, they would not show any differential studying times in studying the passages that a priori were perceived to contain respectively easy and difficult vocabulary. However, consistent with expectation, because of their superior metacognition about the role of passage organization in the ease of studying a passage, above average readers did apportion differential amounts of study times in studying the organized and disorganized passages. The data thus indicated that above average readers alone possess metacognition about the factor of passage organization, because only they studied the disorganized passage longer.

The above data lend credence to the speculation that high-order metacognitive knowledge about reading develops after readers have mastered lower-order decoding mechanics. Moreover, readers who daily struggle with decoding problems come to develop metacognition about what presents them with hurdles in their reading. It seems then that the development of metacognition in reading involves exposure to reading instruction and the individual's reading experience, and that it varies importantly as a function of levels of reading achievement. Clearly, much more research on this important issue is in order.

Englert and Thomas

Englert and Thomas (1987) provided children with two sentences that clearly signaled a particular text structure, for example, compare and contrast. The children had to add to the given sentences two more of their own. Englert and Thomas found that relative to normally achieving and low-achieving children, children with learning disabilities had significant difficulties writing sentences that conform to a given text structure. These findings suggest that children with learning disabilities lack sensitivity to text structure in their writing.

Englert, Raphael, Fear, and Anderson

More recently, Englert et al. (1988) investigated the metacognitive knowledge of children with learning disabilities about expository writing. Not surprisingly, they found these children deficient in important metacognitive knowledge about the expository writing process and other important skills in writing, e.g., text organization, self-monitoring of writing process, and use of organizational strategies to generate or group ideas. Consequently, they strongly recommend that these metacognitive, organizational and strategic skills be taught to children with learning disabilities.

Wong, Wong, and Blenkisop

Wong et al. (1989) investigated cognitive and metacognitive aspects of composing problems by adolescents with learning disabilities. Their study involved eighth- and eleventh-graders with learning disabilities, normally achieving eighth-graders, and normally achieving sixth-graders who served as a reading-age control group for the adolescents with learning disabilities. The part in their investigation that pertains to this chapter concerns their metacognitive questionnaire. Subjects had to fill in a five-question questionnaire that probed their conception of the writing process and their awareness of what writing entails. The five questions were Why do you think some children/adolescents have trouble in writing? What is writing about? How do you write? What goes on in your head when you write? and What things do you need to learn to be a better writer than you are now?

Wong et al. found that as compared with the normally achieving eighth-graders, eighth and eleventh graders with learning disabilities had a less mature/sophisticated concept about the writing process. Normally achieving eighth-graders considered writing to be a purposeful activity— to be about self-expression, which is constrained by some internal criteria of satisfaction. They considered inability to communicate what one means, and lack of planning prior to writing to cause problems in some individuals' writing. Moreover, they were articulate about their own cognitive and metacognitive processes in writing. They reported the habitual manner in which they wrote. Apparently, they systematically plan what they write by first generating ideas and then scrutinizing the ideas to eliminate unwanted ones. The remaining ones are organized and elaborated into the content of an essay. Some of the frequent elements in their verbal reports were that of seeing the shape or content of the essay in their heads prior to writing, and that of revising their initial ideas for writing.

In contrast, eighth- and eleventh-graders with learning disabilities were most inarticulate about what writing involves. Sixty-two percent of their answers on what writing is about was unscorable. They would say they did not know what writing is about, or leave a blank answer on the page, or given an irrelevant answer. Their conception of writing focused exclusively on the mechanics of writing: spelling, punctuation, and neatness, rather than on higher-order cognitive and metacognitive processes in writing. They also attributed writing problems to problems in sentence construction and in spelling. This type of explanation for writing problems conforms to their particular focus on lower-order cognitive processes in writing.

However, eighth- and eleventh-graders with learning disabilities in Wong et al.'s study did demonstrate awareness of their own cognitive processes (metacognition) in writing. They responded very clearly to the question of "How do you write?" by reporting a primitive knowledge-telling strategy in writing (Scardamalia & Bereiter, 1987). This strategy involves the writer pouring out on paper whatever comes to mind, without prior planning and indeed, without much thought. It is interesting to recall one normally achieving eighth-grader saying that writing in this manner (knowledge-telling) is what causes writing problems in some children/adolescents! Thus, the eighth- and eleventh-graders with learning disabilities in Wong et al.'s study demonstrated metacognition about their own cognitive processes that they deployed in the act of writing. However, these cognitive processes were mobilized to serve a primitive writing strategy.

Summary

The results of the preceding studies on metacognition in children and adolescents with learning disabilities debunk the assumption of ubiquitous metacognitive deficiencies in children with learning disabilities. Rather, they suggest that as compared with their counterparts with no learning disabilities, these children and adolescents possess less metacognition or a less sophisticated kind of metacognition in reading and writing.

INTERVENTION RESEARCH

Graves

Regarding metacognitive interventions, Graves (1986) reported successful metacomprehension training. More specifically, she contrasted two training conditions: one in which direct instruction in main idea identification was paired with self-monitoring training, the other provided only direct instruction in main idea identification. These instructional conditions in turn, were contrasted with a control no-training condition.

Graves found the training condition of combined direct instruction plus self-monitoring produced the best results in identifying main ideas. Moreover, trainees in both instructional conditions surpassed the subjects in the control no-training condition.

Palincsar and Brown

Palincsar and Brown (1984) taught seventh-grade poor comprehenders four strategies: generating clarifying questions in the face of text ambiguities, identifying important text elements and generating questions about them, summarizing what is read, and predicting author's themes. The instructional framework involved the notion of scaffolding, which refers to providing temporary assistance to an individual to enable successful learning, performance, or problem solving. Once the individual masters the task, the scaffold is removed. The notion of scaffolding relates directly to Vygotsky's notion of zone of proximal development which is "the distance between the actual developmental level as determined by independent problem solving and the level of potential development as determined through problem solving under adult guidance, or in collaboration with more capable peers" (Vygotsky, 1978, p. 86).

The guiding instructional principle in Palincsar and Brown was reciprocal teaching, which matches the conceptual meaning of scaffolding. Using reciprocal teaching, the teacher (experimenter in Palincsar & Brown, 1984) modeled the four strategies described earlier and then students took turn acting as "teacher." Specifically, after silently reading a designated segment of the passage, the student "teacher" predicted what would ensue in the next segment; posed a question for the group to answer; clarified points that needed clarification, and summarized the segment read.

The unique feature in Palincsar and Brown concerns the role of the teacher. She or he actively faded into the background as the students assumed more autonomy and mastery of the four strategies. The teacher deliberately ceded control of learning to the students, thereby enabling them to be truly active learners who controlled their own learning. She or he concentrated more on diagnosing the instructional needs and progress of the individual group members vis-à-vis the cognitive strategies. Such a role is not one familiar to classroom teachers. Palincsar and Brown obtained very strong data in their instructional study. Not only did students in the treatment group improve in their reading comprehension performance, they also maintained and generalized sufficiently the learned strategies to content areas in their classrooms such as social studies.

Subsequently, Palincsar continued to research the efficacy of reciprocal teaching and its implementations across various school contexts. The results indicated that reciprocal teaching is a viable intervention that enhances reading comprehension and comprehension-monitoring substantially in students. Moreover, the critical role of reciprocal teaching was pinpointed in a later study designed to enable component analysis of it (Paris, Wixson, & Palincsar, 1986, pp. 109–111).

Wong and Jones

Wong and Jones (1982) adapted a self-questioning procedure developed by Andre and Anderson (1978–1979) to enhance reading comprehension monitoring in adolescents with learning disabilities. A total of 60 eighth- and ninth-graders with learning disabilities participated in the study. A reading-age control group of sixth-graders was used. Half the subjects in each group were randomly assigned to receive a five-step self-questioning training procedure in which they learned to monitor their understanding of important textual units. Prior to this self-questioning comprehension-monitoring training, the subjects were trained to criterion on identification of main ideas (i.e., they first mastered the skill of identifying the main idea in a sentence). The steps in the comprehension-monitoring training procedure were as follows: (1) What are you studying this passage for? (2) Find the main idea/ideas in the paragraph and underline it/them; (3) Think of a question about the main idea you have underlined. Remember what a good question should be like. (A good question should target the main idea sentence and be a paraphrased version of it.) (4) Learn the answer to your question. (5) Always look back at the questions and answers to see how each successive question and answer provide you with more information.

The results indicated that training substantially increased the awareness of important textual units by adolescents with learning disabilities, as well as their ability to formulate good questions involving those units. Moreover, training enhanced their reading comprehension performance. Interestingly, training did not substantially affect the awareness of important textual units nor the reading comprehension performance of sixth-graders. Wong and Jones suggested that normally achieving sixth-graders probably had developed their own comprehension-monitoring strategies that they habitually use. Hence, the given comprehension-monitring training might well have been superfluous for them, which would account for its relative ineffectualness.

Summary

The results of metacognitive intervention have been very positive. The preceding intervention studies clearly indicate that metacognitive skills in reading can be effectively taught to students with learning disabilities, and that they brought about significant academic enhancement. Such a line of intervention research appears to be worth pursuing because there are other kinds of metacognitive skills in reading and writing that students with learning disabilities could profit from learning—for example, test-taking strategies and self-evaluative strategies. Moreover, metacognitive interventions should go beyond academic domains into the affective domain, for example, strategies to cope with distraction and initial failures at a new or difficult task (Wong, 1987; Kamann, 1989).

A caveat is necessary regarding metacognitive interventions. Training of metacognitive strategies in students with learning disabilities should follow mastery of prerequisite cognitive skills (Garner, 1987; Wong, 1988). To illustrate, training of comprehension monitoring should follow students' mastery of identification of a main idea or important sentence in a paragraph. Otherwise, students would not know on which sentences to focus their attention and monitor their understanding.

ASSESSMENT OF METACOGNITIVE PRACTICE IN LEARNING DISABILITIES

One senses that many teachers would like to be able to perform metacognitive assessments as part of their assessments of students with learning disabilities. Indeed, at conferences, teachers often ask presenters of metacognitive research if they have any manual or test for practical use in assessing the metacognitive strategies of students with learning disabilities. Of late, authors of learning disabilities textbooks too show a clear attempt to include the topic of metacognition. However, none has grappled successfully with the practical applications of metacognition. This is understandable because we have not yet attended to producing metacognitive assessment tools and curricula to help teachers of students with learning disabilities.

To date, Scott Paris and his associates (Jacobs & Paris, 1987) have developed the only metacognitive strategies assessment device in reading. In the Index of Reading Awareness (IRA), Jacobs and Paris (1987) have produced a very useful questionnaire to measure students' strategies in reading. The questionnaire is divided into four sections: evaluation, planning, regulation, and conditional knowledge, with five questions per section. It also contains multiple-choice answers. One example from each of the four sections is shown below.

Evaluation (Jacobs & Paris, 1987, p. 269)
1. What is the hardest part about reading for you?
   a. Sounding out the hard words.
   b. When you don't understand the story.
   c. Nothing is hard about reading for you.

Planning (Jacobs & Paris, 1987, p. 269)
4. Before you start to read, what kind of plans do you make to help you read better?
   a. You don't make any plans. You just start reading.
   b. You choose a comfortable place.
   c. You think about why you are reading.

Regulation (Jacobs & Paris, 1987, p. 270)
2. Why do you go back to read things over again?
   a. Because it is good practice.
   b. Because you didn't understand it.
   c. Because you forgot some words.

Conditional Knowledge (Jacobs & Paris, 1987, p. 270)
3. If you are reading for a test, which would help the most?
   a. Read the story as many times as possible.
   b. Talk about it with somebody to make sure you understand it.
   c. Say the sentences over and over.

Clearly, the IRA assessment is applicable to students with learning disabilities. It can be used for both research and practical purposes. Currently, there is only information on its use in research. However, it can be profitably used by teachers of students with learning disabilities both as a pretraining assessment and posttraining measure.

Similarly, Paris has produced the only metacognitive curricula. He has produced three sets/modules of reading and thinking strategies, one for each of the following grades: three–four; five–six, and seven–eight. There are clear merits to these metacognitive curricula, not the least is the theoretical framework and empirical base on which they were built.

The instructional principles underlying the Informed Strategies for Learning (ISL) program are direct explanation (direct instruction), metaphors for strategies, group dialogues, guided practice, and integration with content area reading (Paris et al., 1986). The uniqueness of the ISL curriculum lies in several features. First there is the explicit modeling by the teacher in the use of a cognitive or a metacognitive strategy. The second feature concerns important motivational aspects. The teacher informs the students about the rationale for learning the strategy, and provides "conditional knowledge" (Simon, 1980) on when and where to extend its application. Then in group dialogues (discussions), students get the opportunity to vent their frustrations and confusions in strategy learning. Alternatively, they can express satisfaction in learning to apply the strategy well. Such verbal outlet serves an important function for students in that they receive support and encouragement from peers in this sharing of an experience in strategy learning. More importantly, student dialogues may well indicate to underachieving students and readers with learning disabilities that strategy learning involves effort, and that judging from the satisfaction expressed by peers who master the particular strategy, that such effort expenditure is worthwhile.

The third unique feature of the ISL program concerns the use of concrete metaphors. These concrete metaphors are colorfully illustrated in big posters that are pinned on bulletin boards for instructional purposes. They greatly facilitate children's understanding of the goal of the strategies. I shall focus on a couple to illustrate their contribution to children's strategy learning. For example, in teaching understanding the goals and purposes of reading, Paris used the metaphor of "Searching for Reading Treasure." The message conveyed by the metaphor is that finding meaning in a story or passage can be as difficult and tortuous as finding a treasure chest. In hunting for meaning, the reader must be mindful of the purpose of reading (follow the direction of the hunt on the treasure map), look for clues and make decisions on which clues to pursue, as in a treasure hunt. Another metaphor is used in teaching the strategy of recognizing that different kinds of meaning can be construed from reading materials: literal, inferential, and personal meaning. This metaphor is "Turning on the Meaning" and it has a really ingenious illustration. The illustration contains three light bulbs atop three corresponding light switches. The concrete illustration capitalizes on children's familiarity with a common household item. The thought/image of switching on a light bulb drives home the activation of thought. It signals to children that they must actively construct each kind of meaning from the text. The last illustration is the metaphor of "Be a Reading Detective." Paris used this metaphor to teach students to evaluate reading purposes and text difficulty by focusing on three questions: "Why am I reading this?" (reading purpose), "What kind of reading is this?"

(genre of writing), and "What is it about?" (topic). The metaphor shows the active search for textual clues and the evaluation of evidence. The poster contains a detective scrutinizing a book for clues. It also contains questions that alert students to be vigilant in ascertaining the genre of text and the clues that support the students' genre identification. In the accompanying worksheet, students write down how they would proceed to read particular genres of books.

Apart from the instructional effectiveness, the use of metaphors liven student interest in learning the cognitive and metacognitive strategies. They truly make learning fun and hence motivate student learning.

The theoretical and empirical underpinnings, together with the well-considered, ingenious instructional designs of the ISL curriculum predispose it to success. Paris and Jacobs (1984) used the ISL curriculum in two third- and two fifth-grade classrooms. Students were taught ISL lessons twice each week for four months. As compared with children in control, noninstructed classrooms, ISL-taught children showed a significant increase in metacognition about comprehension strategies, and in criterion-referenced tasks of cloze and error detection. However, they showed no increase in standardized reading comprehension tests. In a second study, Paris, Cross, and Lipson (1984) involved 50 regular classroom teachers. They taught 20 ISL modules to approximately 800 third- and 800 fifth-graders. The results paralleled those in Paris and Jacobs (1984). Students taught the ISL strategies substantially improved in metacognition about reading, and in strategy use.

Paris' ISL metacognitive curriculum is profoundly important because it shapes future instructional research by demonstrating that the demanding criteria of qualitative instructional research can be met. It is clearly theory-based. The variables (strategies) targeted for instruction are empirically justifiable. The design of the ISL curriculum shows careful attention to teacher-effectiveness variables: explicit explanation and guided practice. Attention to students' motivation in learning is another asset of the ISL program (cf. Brophy, 1983). This is engineered through student–student, student–teacher dialogues which help foster student willingness to expend effort at learning. Such "will" to learn is vitally important in enabling a student to become a strategic learner (Paris, Lipson, & Wixson, 1983). Student motivation in learning is also ingeniously fostered by the use of concrete metaphors in the teaching of the strategies. Equally important is the fact that the ISL contains logically sequenced and interrelated strategies. Hence, students do not learn single or fragmented strategies. Rather they acquire a repertoire of thematically focused strategies, all of which lead to efficient reading. Lastly, the ISL has classroom validity. It has been successfully used by classroom teachers. Surely, this is the ultimate crucible test for any piece of instructional research!

SUMMARY

An assessment of metacognitive practice in learning disabilities suggests that practical applications may still be at the stage of being promising. This is due largely to the lack of development of metacognitive assessment tools and curricula. However, this state of affairs may not last. To date, Scott Paris and his associates have blazed the trail in developing a strategy-assessment questionnaire that is immensely applicable in learning disabilities research and practice. More important, he has developed a systematic set of metacognitive curricula for instructional purposes—the Reading and Thinking Strategies curricula. Close scrutiny of them suggests immense possibilities for use with students with learning disabilities in instructional research and actual remedial practices. Paris' strategy assessment device and curricula should serve as models for similar developments by learning disabilities professionals.

REFERENCES

Allington, R. L. (1980). Poor readers don't get to read much in reading groups. *Language Arts, 57,* 872–876.
Andre, M. E. D. A., & Anderson, T. H. (1978–1979). The development and evaluation of a self-questioning study technique. *Reading Research Quarterly, 14,* 605–623.
Baker, L., & Brown, A. L. (1984a). Metacognition skills of reading. In D. P. Pearson (Ed.), *Handbook on research in reading* (pp. 353–394). New York: Longman.
Baker, L., & Brown, A. L. (1984b). Cognitive monitoring in reading. In J. Flood (Ed.), *Understanding reading comprehension* (pp. 21–44). Newark, DE: International Reading Association.
Bos, C., & Filip, D. (1982). Comprehension monitoring skills in learning disabled and average students. *Topics in Learning and Learning Disabilities, 2,* 79–85.
Brophy, J. (1983). *Conceptualizing student motivation.* Occasional paper No. 70. The Institute for Research on Teaching, Michigan State University.
Brown, A. L. (1980). Metacognitive development and reading. In R. J. Spiro, B. B. Bruce & W. F. Brewer (Eds.), *Theoretical issues in reading comprehension* (pp. 453–481). Hillsdale, NJ: Erlbaum.
Butkowsky, J. S., & Willows, D. M. (1980). Cognitive-motivational characteristics of children varying in reading ability: Evidence for learned helplessness in poor readers. *Journal of Educational Psychology, 72,* 408–422.
Englert, C. S., Raphael, T. E., Fear, K. L., & Anderson, L. M. (1988). Students' metacognitive knowledge about how to write informational texts. *Learning Disability Quarterly, 11*(1), 18–46.
Englert, C. S., & Thomas, C. C. (1987). Sensitivity to text structure in reading and writing: A comparison between learning disabled and non-learning disabled students. *Learning Disability Quarterly, 10*(2), 93–105.
Flavell, J. H. (1976). Metacognitive aspects of problem solving. In L. B. Resnick (Ed.), *The Nature of Intelligence* (pp. 231–235). Hillsdale, NJ: Erlbaum.

Garner, R. (1987). *Metacognition and reading comprehension.* Norwood, NJ: Ablex.
Gerber, M. M. (1982). *Effects of self-monitoring training on spelling performance of learning-disabled and normally achieving students.* Unpublished manuscript. University of California, Santa Barbara.
Graves, A. W. (1986). Effects of direct instruction and metacomprehension on finding main ideas. *Learning Disability Research, 1,* 90–100.
Jacobs, J. E., & Paris, S. G. (1987). Children's metacognition about reading: Issues in definition, measurement and instruction. *Educational Psychologist, 22*(3 & 4), 255–278.
Kamann, M. P. (1989). *Inducing adaptive coping self-statements in the learning-disabled through a cognitive behavioral intervention.* Unpublished Master's thesis, Simon Fraser University.
Palincsar, A. S. (1982). *Improving the reading comprehension of junior high students through reciprocal teaching of comprehension-monitoring strategies.* Unpublished doctoral dissertation, University of Illinois, 1982.
Palincsar, A. S., & Brown, A. L. (1984). Reciprocal teaching of comprehension-fostering and comprehension-monitoring activities. *Cognition and Instruction, 1* (2), 117–175.
Paris, S. G., Cross, D. R., & Lipson, M. Y. (1984). Informed strategies for learning: A program to improve children's reading awareness and comprehension. *Journal of Educational Psychology, 76,* 1239–1252.
Paris, S. G., Lipson, M. Y., & Wixson, K. K. (1983). Becoming a strategic reader. *Contemporary Educational Psychology, 8,* 293–316.
Paris, S. G., Wixson, K. K., & Palincsar, A. S. (1986). Instructional approaches to reading comprehension. In E. Z. Rothkopf (Ed.), *Review of Research in Education, 13,* 91–128.
Pearson, P. D., & Gallagher, M. C. (1983). The instruction of reading comprehension. *Contemporary Educational Psychology, 8,* 317–344.
Scardamalia, M., & Bereiter, C. (1987). Knowledge telling and knowledge transforming in written composition. In S. Rosenberg (Ed.), *Advances in applied psycholinguistics: Vol. 2. Reading, writing, and language learning* (pp. 142–175). Cambridge: Cambridge University Press.
Schallert, D. L. (1982). The significance of knowledge: A synthesis of research related to schema theory. In W. Otto & S. White (Eds.), *Reading Expository Material* (pp. 13–49). New York: Academic Press.
Simon, H. A. (1980). Problem solving and education. In D. T. Tuma & R. Reif (Eds.), *Problem solving and education: Issues in teaching and research* (pp. 81–96). Hillsdale, NJ: Erlbaum.
Stanovich, K. E. (1986a). Cognitive processes and the reading problems of learning-disabled children: Evaluating the assumption of specificity. In J. K. Torgesen & B. Y. L. Wong (Eds.), *Psychological and educational perspectives in learning disabilities* (pp. 110–131). New York: Academic Press.
Stanovich, K. E. (1986b). Matthew effects in reading: Some consequences of individual differences in the acquisition of literacy. *Reading Research Quarterly, 21*(4), 360–407.
Stanovich, K. E. (1988). Explaining the differences between the dyslexic and the garden-variety poor reader: The phonological-core variable-difference model. *Journal of Learning Disabilities, 21*(10), 590–612.
Torgesen, J. K. (1977). The role of nonspecific factors in the task performance of learning-disabled children: A theoretical assessment. *Journal of Learning Disabilities, 10,* 27–34.

Vygotsky, L. S. (1978). *Mind in society: The development of higher psycholgical processes*. M. Cole, V. John-Steiner, S. Scribner, & E. Souberman (Eds.). Cambridge, MA: Harvard University Press.

Wong, B. Y. L. (Ed.) (1982). Metacognition and learning disabilities. *Topics in Learning and Learning Disabilities*, 2(1).

Wong, B. Y. L. (1983). Concurrent increase in knowledge and learning strategy: A new remedial instructional approach. Paper presented at the 2nd World Congress on Dyslexia, June 27–30. Halkidiki, Greece.

Wong, B. Y. L. (1985). Metacognition and learning disabilities. In T. G. Waller, D. Forrest-Pressley, & E. MacKinnon (Eds.), *Metacognition, cognition and human performance* (pp. 137–180). New York: Academic Press.

Wong, B. Y. L. (1986). Metacognition and special education: A review of a view. *Journal of Special Education*, 20(1), 9–29.

Wong, B. Y. L. (1987). Metacognition and learning disabilities. *Learning Disability Quarterly*, 10(3), 189–195.

Wong, B. Y. L. (1988). An instructional model for intervention research in learning disabilities. *Learning Disability Research*, 4(1), 5–16.

Wong, B. Y. L., & Jones, W. (1982). Increasing metacomprehension in learning-disabled and normally-achieving students through self-questioning training. *Learning Disability Quarterly*, 5, 228–240.

Wong, B. Y. L., & Wong, R. (1986). Study behavior as a function of metacognitive knowledge about critical task variables: An investigation of above average, average and learning-disabled readers. *Learning Disabilities Research*, 1, 101–111.

Wong, B. Y. L., Wong, R., & Blenkisop, J. (1989). Cognitive and metacognitive aspects of composing problems in learning-disabled adolescents. *Learning Disability Quarterly*, 123(4), 300–322.

CHAPTER 13

Assessment of Social Cognition: Review of Research in Learning Disabilities

TANIS BRYAN

Traditionally, deficits in social competence have been a marginal issue in the field of learning disabilities. This marginal status is demonstrated by (1) the absence of references to social problems in definitions of learning disabilities (e.g., P.L. 91 - 230; P.L. 94 - 142); (2) the absence of diagnostic social competence tests and procedures in psycho-educational assessments of referred children; (3) the absence of short- and long-term goals in individual education plans; and (4) the absence of training to prepare learning disability specialists to work with students who experience problems in the social domain.

Recently, however, deficits in social competence have moved from the sidelines to center stage as an issue in the definition of learning disabilities. Indeed, the most recent revisions of the definition include references to social problems in learning disabilities and seem to reflect broad based consensus among parent and professional groups. The first, developed by the Association for Children and Adults with Learning Disabilities, includes the statement: "Throughout life the condition can affect self-esteem, education, vocation, socialization, and/or daily living activities" (*Special Education Today*, 1985, p. 1). The second, developed by the Interagency

Committee on Learning Disabilities (ICLD), includes the statement: "Learning disabilities is a generic term that refers to a heterogeneous group of disorders manifested by significant difficulties in the acquisition and use of listening, speaking, reading, writing, reasoning, or mathematical abilities, or of social skills" (1987, p. 222).

In light of the increasing legitimacy of social competence as a problem in learning disabilities, it is timely to consider the extant data base concerning the assessment of such problems. Indeed, it is suggested that social learning theory and research might provide an important avenue for studying the concept of learning disabilities as a "disorder in one or more of the basic psychological processes involved in understanding or using spoken or written language" (P.L. 91 - 230; P.L. 94 - 142). Clearly, understanding spoken (or written) language requires social learning skills. Although it is likely that the developers of the definition had a more narrow application of "spoken or written language" in mind, it seems of heuristic value to apply a broader based conceptual framework of what it is that is to be understood in order to advance our understanding of learning disabilities.

The purpose of this chapter is to review research on the assessment of one component of social competence: social cognition. As recent research suggests that social cognitive skills mediate social behavior, it is most fitting that careful assessment be done of social cognitive skills in children suspected of having problems in the social domain. The chapter is limited to studies of perspective taking, moral development, and social problem solving. Other topics such as self-efficacy and communicative competence have been reviewed elsewhere (cf., Donahue, Pearl, & Bryan, 1983; Kistner, Osborne, & LeVerrier, 1988). It might be noted that various topics have not been considered in research on learning disabilities (e.g., authority or conflict relations), nor have there been attempts to test any model of social competence (cf., 1986).

SOCIAL COGNITION THEORY

The concept of social cognition represents the integration of several trends in the study of social and cognitive development (Muuss, 1982). There is no specific theory guiding the research on social cognitive behavior relations (Shantz, 1983), rather, the field represents the influence of theories from Piaget, Werner, Heider, social learning, and psychoanalytic theories. As an area of inquiry, social cognition attempts to understand the linkages between social development and cognitive development, and between social behavior and social cognition (Shantz, 1983). The study of social cognition's influence in determining behavior became a major topic of research in developmental psychology as it became recognized that the appropriate deployment of behavior is a function of knowledge about the situations in which various behaviors are to be used (Chi, Feltovich, & Glaser, 1981). Social cognition is viewed as a precursor to interpersonal situations and social problem solving (Youniss, 1975).

Although social cognition research is guided by several theories, the topics discussed here—perspective taking, moral development, and social problem solving—have been guided by age/stage models that have been heavily influenced by the work of Piaget. As a result of the Piagetian influence, the various tests of social cognition that have been developed are theory based, but have not been developed or used subscribing to the demands made by test constructors in psychometrics. That is to say, by and large, these measures have not been carefully constructed to meet the traditional requirements in test construction; i.e., evidence of test reliability and validity. It is only recently that researchers in the area have become concerned with the psychometric properties of the instruments being used to assess social cognition (cf., Enright & Lapsley, 1980; Krasnor & Rubin, 1981).

Given the recency of concern for the psychometric properties of tests of social cognition, the interpretation of data generated using these tests must be quite tentative. In addition, until more is known about the social cognition construct, it would be hazardous to consider using the results of such tests to make diagnoses at the individual level. At this time, however, in light of recent interest in the social skills of students with learning disabilities, there is an accumulating data base that provides a good start in understanding social cognitive development in samples of learning disabled students. The next sections review the studies that included samples of students with learning disabilities in their assessments of perspective taking, moral development, and social problem solving skills.

ASSESSMENT OF PERSPECTIVE TAKING SKILLS

Nine studies were located that compared students with learning disabilities and normally achieving students on measures of perspective taking. Two studies used the "apple–dog" story developed by Flavell, Botkin, Fry, Wright, and Jarvis (1968); (Fincham, 1976; Ackerman, Elardo, & Dykman, 1979). The apple–dog story examines the child's recognition that another person would view a situation differently because of a lack of critical knowledge about the situation. The child is shown a series of seven pictures that show (1) a boy walking along the sidewalk; (2) looking frightened as he sees an angry-looking dog running toward him; (3) looking over his shoulder, running from the dog, who chases him; (4) running toward an apple tree with the dog not shown and the boy's face hidden; (5) the boy climbing up the tree, the dog below barking; (6) the boy in the tree not looking at the dog or seeming frightened, the dog pictured walking across the street with its back to the boy; (7) the boy in the tree eating an apple, the dog not in the picture. The child is asked to tell the story based on the seven pictures. Then the three pictures that show the vicious dog are removed, a new person enters the room, and the child tells how the new person would tell the story.

Fincham (1976) administered the "apple–dog" story and Piagetian tests of conservation to 56 eight- and nine-year-old boys with and without learning disabilities. Subjects' scores on the apple–dog story were "2" if the story was told correctly from the second person's point of view, "1" if the story was perceptually accurate but did not maintain the perspective of the second person, and "0" if the subject was unable to switch from the first to the second person's perspective. Results found no significant differences between the boys with and without learning disabilities on the apple–dog story, or on the Piagetian tasks. In addition, point biserial correlations found that the role-taking and conservation tasks were significantly correlated for the normal group, but not significantly related in the group with learning disabilities.

The apple–dog story was also used by Ackerman et al. (1979) in a study of 20 boys with learning disabilities, 20 hyperactive, and 20 normal boys, ages $7^{1}/2$ to 10 years. Other measures administered in this study included a personality inventory, Piaget's measure of intentionality, locus of control, moral judgment, and parent interviews. Discriminant analysis did not find group differences in cognitive role taking, locus of control, or moral reasoning. Essentially this study found that boys with learning disabilities were rated more anxious and defensive relative to the other groups, and hyperactive boys were discriminated from the other groups on the basis of aggressivness. Factor analysis did not find significant relationships among the cognitive and moral development measures.

In sum, the results of two studies that used Flavell's apple–dog story found no differences in role-taking skills between boys with learning disabilities and other groups of boys. There are, however, questions that must be raised about the use of the apple–dog story. First, a one-item test does not allow for an assessment of internal reliability. In addition, no data could be found in the studies just cited, or elsewhere, concerning reliability or validity. Third, the studies are not sufficiently specific in their descriptions of the administration and scoring of the test. If, in the administration, the pictures of the vicious dog are removed from view, a child need only "reread" the pictures. The task requires little perspective taking, because the other's viewpoint has been removed. Based on face value, the results of these two studies suggest that when social perspective taking is assessed at a concrete level, making minimal demands on attention and memory, boys with learning disabilities do not differ from nondisabled or hyperactive boys.

Chandler (1973) developed a measure of perspective taking that was used by Wong and Wong (1980) to assess children's ability to interpret privileged information. This measure consists of 10 cartoon series showing a main character enmeshed in a chain of psychological events involving a cause-and-effect sequence that influences subsequent behavior. For example, one series, "Anger," consists of eight pictures showing a boy venting his anger at his little brother by blowing down a castle of cards. This was preceded by the boy's sandcastle being wrecked by a girl riding a bike through it. A second example, "Fear," consists of nine pictures showing a boy fearful to a knock at the door, preceded by his having run home after accidentally breaking a window with a baseball. Midway through each series, a second character is introduced. The second character witnesses the resultant behavior of the main character without the prior knowledge of the causes of the behavior. Enright and Lapsley (1980) report on assessments of this tests' reliability, construct validity, and external validity. The results are respectable for measures of internal consistency, temporal stability, and interrater reliability, with coefficients ranging from 0.26 to 0.96. Cluster analysis finds a homogeneous domain (common variance), and the measure appears to discriminate between emotionally disturbed and delinquent children who score lower than normal children (Chandler, 1972; 1973; Chandler, Greenspan, & Barenboim, 1974).

Wong and Wong (1980) used 3 of the 10 series to assess third- and fourth-grade boys and girls: 32 with learning disabilities and 32 without. Subjects told the story by pretending they were the main character and then repeated the story pretending they were the bystander. They were also asked what the bystander thought the main character was angry/scared/sad about. A 5-point scale was used, in which a score of 4 indicated subjects explicitly attributed to the bystander knowledge available only to themselves and a score of 0 meant the subject clearly distinguished between privileged information known only to the subject and facts that were available to the story characters. Interrater reliability on scoring was reported to be 0.81.

The results found main effects for group and sex, and a group by sex interaction. Girls with learning disabilities scored significantly lower than nondisabled girls, whereas the two groups of boys were similar. Group differences were thus attributable to girls with learning disabilities performing more poorly than their same-sex nondisabled peers. If replicable, this is of potential interest, given that a number of studies have found girls with learning disabilities to be more rejected than boys with learning disabilities on sociometric measures (Bryan, 1974; Scranton & Ryckman, 1979). Given the data on reliability and validity (Enright & Lapsley, 1980), the Chandler measure seems to be a more appropriate one to use in testing perspective taking by students with learning disabilities. The test appears to make greater demands on the child's attention and memory (for instructions) as no pictures are removed: The child must hold in mind that the second person would not have the same information as the first. The test does make demands on expressive verbal skills, thus differences between students with and without learning disabilities may be attributable to a number of factors other than, or in addition to, perspective taking.

In the next study, Horowitz (1981) employed third- and fourth-grade students: 20 with and 20 without learning disabilities. She used Piaget's Mountain Task, the Feffer (1970) Role-Taking Task, a sociometric scale, and a measure of social insight. Piaget's Mountain Task has children identify the appearance of a mountain model from different perspectives. A doll is moved around a plastic mountain and the child selects one of eight photographs showing how the mountain would look to the doll. The Feffer Role-Taking Task has the child make up a story about a picture and then retell the story from the perspective of each character while maintaining continuity between various versions of the story. The social insight measure asked children to judge how much they were liked or disliked by classmates.

It should be noted that the Piaget Mountain Task is a test of visual perspective taking, not social cognition. With respect to the Feffer measure, its psychometric properties find the test lacking. The construct is not clearly defined, the internal consistency reliability is low, and there is only one validation criterion (Enright & Lapsley, 1980). Interpretation of the results of the Horowitz study should take these problems into account.

The results found that the children with learning disabilities scored more poorly than the nondisabled students on the Mountain Task, Role-Taking, popularity, and insight. However, when IQ scores were used in analyses of covariance, groups differed only on the Mountain Task. IQ scores were significantly correlated with Role-Taking (0.48) and the Mountain Task (0.42). Questions can be raised concerning the appropriateness of using IQ in analyses of covariance since this analysis assumes the factor being covaried is randomly distributed across groups. Nonetheless, the issue of the relationship between IQ and social cognition is an important one that will be addressed in the discussion section of this chapter.

Studies conducted by Dickstein and Warren (1980) and Bruck and Hebert (1982) used the same measures of cognitive, affective, and perceptual role taking. Each measure had 10 questions. Five were egocentric and required children to respond from their own perspective; these were intended to verify that children understood the task requirements. Five were nonegocentric and required children to take into account a point of view that differed from their own. The response mode for each scale was nonverbal;

children pointed to one of three objects. The measures appear to have been developed by Dickstein and Warren (1980) for use in their study, hence no data on reliability or validity are as yet available.

The Cognitive Task measured the child's ability to predict the thoughts of others. In the egocentric questions, the child is told a short story in which there is no conflict between the information possessed by the child and the person in the story. For the nonegocentric questions, there was a conflict between the information possessed by the child and the person in the story (e.g., "Andy told his dad he was going to draw a lion in art class. When Andy got to school, his teacher told him he could draw a zebra, a giraffe, or a lion. Andy decided to draw a giraffe instead, and brought the picture home in his school bag. Point to the one Daddy will think Andy drew in art class").

The Affective Task measured the child's ability to predict another's feelings. The children pointed to one of three plastic "eggheads" looking happy or sad or showing no emotion in response to story questions. The story was worded so that there was conflict or no conflict between the affect of the story character and the child (e.g., if the child indicated she liked to take baths, the egocentric story would relate: "Sally likes to take baths. Sally's mom tells Sally it is time to take a bath. Point to the face that shows how Sally feels." The nonegocentric question would start: "Sally doesn't like to take baths....").

The Perceptual Task measured the child's ability to predict the visual perspectives of others. Children were presented with groups of toys mounted on two turntables, and a third group mounted on a rectangular platform, and two dolls. Children had to indicate the animal a doll would see when the turntable would allow both dolls to see the same animals (egocentric questions) or different animals (nonegocentric questions).

Dickstein and Warren (1980) employed 58 children with learning disabilities, ages 5 to 11, and 39 nondisabled children, ages 5 to 9. The results found no group differences on the egocentric questions, although there was an improvement across groups with age. Analysis of the nonegocentric questions finds main effects for group and age, and a group by age interaction. Although children's performance improved with age, the children with learning disabilities performed more poorly than the nondisabled group, and their rate of improvement did not match that of the nondisabled group. There was a ceiling effect for the nondisabled group by age 8 years. The children with learning disabilities, however, showed no improvement at age 10 over their performance at age 8.

Based on the findings by Ackerman et al. (1979), Wong and Wong (1980), and Dickstein and Warren (1980), Bruck and Hebert (1982) extended the study of role taking to include measures of cognitive and affective role taking, hyperactivity, and peer interactions. Subjects were 20 boys and girls with learning disabilities and 20 without learning disabilities who were administered the cognitive and affective scales developed by Dickstein and Warren (1980). In addition, parents and teachers completed the Conners Rating Scale (Goyette, Conners, & Ulrich, 1978) as a measure of hyperactivity, and the peer-interaction checklist (Paulauskas & Campbell, 1979), as a measure of interpersonal behavior with peers.

There were no group differences on the egocentric questions. On the nonegocentric questions the students with learning disabilities did more poorly than those with no learning disabilities. There were no age effects, no sex effects, and no interactions. Students with learning disabilities rated higher on the parent and teacher ratings of hyperkinesis but correlations between learning disability, sex, and hyperactivity were not significant. Using various cut-off scores, 15 to 40% ($N = 3$ to 5) of the students with learning disabilities and 2 of the nondisabled children could be considered hyperactive, thus the role-taking deficits of the group with learning disabilities cannot be attributed to hyperactivity. There were no group differences on parent or teacher ratings of peer-related behaviors. Correlations between measures found unstable relationships between the role-taking, parent and teacher rating scales. For students with learning disabilities, children with relatively high hyperactivity scores and females were found at highest risk for peer problems, at least as perceived by parents. For teachers, hyperactivity and role-taking skills were associated with teachers' ratings of peer interactions of the group with learning disabilities. But hyperactivity accounted for much of the variance between the peer-interaction ratings of children with and without learning disabilities.

Although there are no data attesting to the reliability or validity of the cognitive and affective role-taking measures used by Dickstein and Warren (1980) and Bruck and Hebert (1982), the fact that the findings were replicated is of some importance. A number of procedural differences between this and studies described earlier also may be of some importance. First, the procedure allowed for a distinction between egocentric and nonegocentric responses, thus ensuring that group differences could not be attributed to failure of students with learning disabilities to understand the task, or to memory or attention problems. Second, the method required nonverbal, pointing responses. Hence, group differences cannot be attributed to expressive verbal deficits. Third, finding that older children with learning disabilities performed much like younger students with learning disabilities, whereas nondisabled children showed the expected developmental increase in accuracy, suggests that the test is not simply measuring a developmental delay. On this test of social perspective taking, the performance of students with learning disabilities was stable across ages 5 to 11 years.

The Test of Social Inference (TSI; Edmonson, deJung, Leland, & Leach,

1974) was used in three studies that included subjects with learning disabilities (Bruno, 1981; Gerber & Zinkgraf, 1982; Saloner & Gettinger, 1985). The TSI was developed as a measure of social comprehension in conjunction with the development of a social training program for use with educable retarded persons. The TSI consists of 35 pictures selected so that inferences could be drawn about the relationship of person to person or person to object via illustrations. Children are asked to tell what the picture is about and responses are scored according to examples provided in a scoring guide. Based on studies of retarded subjects, the reliability coefficients for the measure range from 0.84 to 0.97.

The first to use the TSI with students with learning disabilities was Bruno (1981). Twenty boys with learning disabilities and 20 boys with no learning disabilities, ages 9 to 11 years participated. Based on the standard presentation, the boys with learning disabilities made significantly more errors than the nondisabled boys. There were no differences in responses to questions probing antecedent events, but there were significant group differences in inferences of causality.

The second study using the TSI was conducted by Gerber and Zinkgraf (1982). Sixty-four children with and without learning disabilities, aged 7, 8, 10 and 11 years were included in the study. Girls and black youngsters were included. Thirty of the pictures were used and subjects were asked a series of probing questions. For instance, one item shows a picture of women and a flat tire. The child is asked: "What is happening, why are all these women together, why don't they phone someone?" Responses were scored 2 points when they included two inferential statements that showed overall comprehension; one point when they showed overall comprehension, and 1/2 point when they were ambiguous, incomplete, or nonspecific. Results found that the children with learning disabilities scored lower than the nondisabled and the younger children scored lower than older children. There were no age-by-group interactions. Although the scores of students with learning disabilities increased with age, the older subjects with learning disabilities had scores approximately the same as the younger nonhandicapped group.

Saloner and Gettinger (1985) used 14 of the TSI pictures in a study of 60 boys and girls, aged 6 to 13.7: 30 had learning disabilities and 30 did not. The reliability of the 14-item test for this sample was 0.83 (Cronbach alpha). Children were given three scores. One was based on responses to specific questions (e.g., "What is the boy doing?"); one was based on responses to open-ended questions (e.g., "Look at this picture carefully and tell me about it"); and one was a ratio score based on the specific versus the open-ended questions. The students with learning disabilities scored lower than those with no learning disabilities. The group difference was attributable to their relatively poorer performance on the open-ended as opposed to the specific questions. There were no significant correlations between scores on the TSI and reading or IQ.

In sum, nine studies using five different measures compared samples of students with and without learning disabilities on perspective taking. Two studies reported no group differences (Fincham, 1976; Ackerman, et al., 1979); one reported differences only for girls with learning disabilities (Wong & Wong, 1980), one found differences possibly confounded with IQ (Horowitz, 1981), and five obtained clear differences favoring nondisabled students. The studies that failed to find group differences used measures with questionable measurement features (Enright & Lapsley, 1980), making their results difficult to interpret. Differences that were found could be attributable to a variety of factors, such as attention, listening skills, memory, and expressive language as well as poor perspective taking. However, group differences were found when the stimuli were all present (Wong & Wong, 1981), and when only pointing responses were required (Dickstein & Warren, 1980; Bruck & Hebert, 1983). Since in reality, perspective taking occurs in response to events that are fleeting in time and space, and demonstrations of understanding are likely to require verbal and/or nonverbal responses, it seems likely that the measures used in these studies provide conservative estimates of group differences. On the other hand, one could argue that in reality perspective taking might be easier; more realistic information (sight and sound) or background information on the participants may be available, or clues for how to respond may be provided by the participants or other observers. Given reliance on paper-and-pencil measures, it may be difficult to establish the skillfulness of students with learning disabilities in perspective taking. Nonetheless, to the extent that these measures capture the skill in question, students with learning disabilities who are at risk appear to be so across a rather wide span of age. Up to the highest age involved, there were no ceiling effects for students with learning disabilities.

ASSESSMENT OF SOCIAL COGNITION AND SOCIAL PERCEPTION

In this section studies that examined two aspects of social competence—social cognition and social perception—are reviewed. The test of social cognition was the Four Factor Tests of Social Intelligence (O'Sullivan & Guilford, 1976). The test of social perception was the Profile of Nonverbal Sensitivity (PONS; Rosenthal, Archer, DiMatteo, Hall, & Rogers, 1979). The Four Factor Tests consist of four multiple-choice tests, each based on a specific ability outlined in the Structure of Intellect model, and designed to measure the "ability to understand the thoughts, feelings, and intentions of other people as expressed by nonverbal behavior" (Jackson, Enright, & Murdock, 1987, p. 362). Three of the tests have been used with samples of students with learning disabilities: Expression Grouping, Missing Cartoons, and Cartoon Predictions. Expression Grouping has line drawings of facial expressions and gestures, and body postures that convey nonverbal feelings, thoughts, or intentions. In a match-to-sample design, subjects select one of four drawings that convey the same emotion as each of three identical drawings. Missing Cartoons presents an incomplete cartoon panel and subjects select the correct missing cartoon from four choices. Cartoon Predictions has cartoons that depict an interpersonal situation and subjects select which of three alternative outcomes is the most likely. Kuder-Richardson internal consistency reliability coefficients range from 0.66 to 0.82 on these measures.

The PONS measures individual differences in the ability to decode nonverbal communication. Subjects are shown a 45-minute black-and-white videotape containing 220 items, each a 2-second clip of a young woman portraying an emotional response. There are three visual presentations (face, body, figure) and two auditory presentations (scrambled speech and electronically filtered speech) shown both alone and in combination to form 11 channel categories. The subject views or listens to each clip and choses one of two descriptions as the correct description of the scenario. Studies using the PONS with students with learning disabilities have shown mixed results. Bryan (1977) found the students with learning disabilities to be less accurate, while Stone and LaGreca (1984) found students with learning disabilities to be as accurate as nondisabled children. However, in the Stone and LaGreca study extraordinary effort was made to ensure attention to the screen through instructions and incentives to students.

In the first study that assessed social cognition and social perception Axelrod (1982) administered the three subtests of the Four Factor Tests and the PONS to boys and girls in eighth and ninth grades: 54 with learning disabilities and 93 with no learning disabilities. Axelrod found that the children with learning disabilities performed worse than the nondisabled children on each measure, except for the auditory channel (randomly spliced) on the PONS. There were minimal sex effects (only on parts of the PONS) and no group-by-sex interactions. The PONS correlated significantly with Cartoon Predictions and Expression Grouping.

In the second study, Jackson, Enright, and Murdock (1987) administered the same measures to 11-, 14-, and 17-year-olds: 30 with learning disabilities and 30 with no learning disabilities. The students with learning disabilities performed worse on each measure. Significant age effects were seen, in that older subjects did better than younger subjects on the PONS, Expression Grouping, and Cartoon Predictions. There were no group-by-age interactions. Although students both with and without learning disabilities performed more accurately with age, the students with learning disabilities did not close the performance gap on these measures.

In sum, group differences favoring nondisabled students were found on tests of social cognition and social perception. These results are notable insofar as responses did not require expressive verbal skills. The results are notable also because once again group differences occurred across a wide age span, through 17 years of age.

ASSESSMENT OF MORAL DEVELOPMENT

So far this chapter has described assessment techniques that required children to make social inferences or judgments based on pictorial presentations. The stimuli used in these studies were all some type of printed material, and responses varied in demanding nonverbal (pointing) or verbal responses. In this next section we consider studies in which the assessment technique used primarily verbally presented descriptions of social conflicts, and students were required to respond verbally with conflict resolutions.

The most well known assessment device is that based on Lawrence Kohlberg's theory (Kohlberg, Colby, Gibbs, Speicher-Dubin, & Power, 1978). Briefly, Kohlberg's theory is an age/stage model with six levels of moral reasoning: (1) Punishment/Obedience (what is right is to avoid punishment); (2) Individual Instrumental Purpose and Exchange (right is doing what's best for one's own or another person's needs); (3) Mutual Interpersonal Expectations, Relationships and Conformity (what is right is performing the way that others in your group expect); (4) Social System and Conscience Maintenance (right is doing one's duty in maintaining the system); (5) Prior Rights and Social Contracts (judgments based on the basic rights, values, and legal contracts of society even when they conflict with the rules and laws of a group); and (6) Universal Ethical Principles (right is guided by universal ethical principles that all humanity should follow).

The Moral Judgement Interview (Kohlberg et al., 1978) is used to assess the developmental level of moral maturity. The Interview presents three hypothetical dilemmas involving conflicting moral issues in which the protagonist must choose to do one of two actions. The conflicting issues are (1) life versus law (should Heinz break the law to save his wife's life?); (2) punishment versus conscience (should Heinz be punished if he was acting according to his conscience?); and (3) contract versus authority (should Joe obey his father or maintain a contractual agreement?).

Fincham (1977) and Derr (1986) used the Moral Judgement Interview to compare social problem-solving skills of boys with and without learning disabilities. Fincham (1977) employed 56 white 8- and 9-year-old boys with and without learning disabilities. He varied from the standard presentation of the stories by simplifying the level of lexical, idiomatic, syntactic, and sentence semantics and the discourse elements in his use of six stories (two from each of the authority–peer, peer–ideological, and authority–deological conflict situations). He also provided subjects with sets of four pictures that portrayed each story plot. Responses were scored according to five moral judgment levels: (1) authority orientation, (2) authority-bound but emergence of awareness of reciprocity, (3) reciprocity, (4) rules for societal order, and (5) ideological. In the administration of the interview, subjects retold the story as a check on memory and comprehension. The story was retold as many times as necessary. Results found that nobody scored at level 5, and only one scored at level 4. There were no differences between groups with learning disabilities and those with none.

Fincham went to considerable lengths to eliminate other factors (in this case, language complexity in the stimuli materials) that might cause students with learning disabilities to differ from nondisabled students. At this age level, with linguistic complexity controlled, students with learning disabilities appear to be equivalent to nondisabled students. However, the age range was quite restricted, and the subjects' responses fell into only the lower three developmental levels. In addition, according to Fincham, the sample of students with learning disabilities attended a remedial school that used an "induction" type of discipline; i.e., explanations pointing to the consequences for others rather than punishment. Hence, training effects may have influenced the outcome. Fincham also makes the point that the sample might have been too young for problems in social cognition to surface using this measure, insofar as emotional and behavior problems of children with learning disabilities tend to increase with age. This latter point is supported by the next study to be reviewed.

Derr (1986) also used the Moral Judgement Interview. In this case, the subjects with and without learning disabilities were 14.3- to 18.5-year-old males. In this study, the subjects with learning disabilities performed at a lower level than the nondisabled subjects. According to Derr, the average response for the subjects with learning disabilities was between Stages 2 and 3 whereas the nondisabled males were between Stages 3 and 4. According to the Kohlberg scale the responses of the subjects with learning disabilities resembled those of nondisabled children aged 10 to 14 years. This places these subjects with learning disabilities several years behind in their development of moral judgment.

Of course we do not know what the results might have been if Derr had used Fincham's interview scenarios with reduced linguistic complexity.

Given that the same information is conveyed, studies that compare social cognitive problem solving by students with learning disabilities in response to stimuli varying in linguistic complexity would help us differentiate group differences related to linguistic versus cognitive deficits. The two studies also raise our consciousness concerning age differences in social competence. Although it is recognized that different social skills are expected at different ages, we have not begun to map the problems (or lack thereof) of students with learning disabilities at different ages.

ASSESSMENT OF SOCIAL PROBLEM SOLVING USING ROLE PLAYING

Another approach to the assessment of social cognition has been through the use of role playing. By getting students to act out how they might respond in various social situations, we hope to tap into their knowledge of social situations. Like the Moral Judgement Interview, the use of role playing is dependent on students' expressive verbal skills as well as their understanding of social situations. Hence, group differences on such measures could result from differences in linguistic skillfulness as well as social cognition.

Silver and Young (1985) used several measures of social cognition in a study of eighth-grade boys with and without learning disabilities. The measures of social problem solving included the Social Interaction Role Play Assessment (SIRPA; Waddell, 1984), the Means–Ends Problem-Solving Procedure (MEPS; Platt & Spivack, 1975), and the Awareness of Consequences Test (ACT; Platt & Spivack, 1975). Teacher and peer ratings were obtained using the Behavioral Rating Profile (BRP; Brown & Hammill, 1983) and the Junior High Class Play (JHCP). In addition, students were administered the Quick Test (Ammons & Ammons, 1962) as a measure of IQ.

The SIRPA was designed to measure the social interaction skills of adolescents. Situational themes of place, people, and types of interactions (e.g., sympathy, anger) are assessed on 15 social problem situations that are scored on a 3-point scale. The MEPS includes nine items (eight used here) that measure the "ability to orient to and conceptualize means of moving toward a goal" (p. 209). The ACT measures the degree to which an individual considers how his or her actions may affect himself or herself and others, and how others may react. The instrument uses a story-telling procedure in which a protagonist is exposed to a transgression. Responses are scored 0 for no consideration and 1 for consideration of consequences. The BRP consists of checklists completed by students, teachers, and parents, and is designed to examine behavioral adjustment scores across a variety of settings. The JHCP has students select classmates for positive and negative roles (e.g., sociability-leadership, aggressive-disruptive, sensitive-isolated, and scholarly ability).

The subjects included 44 boys with learning disabilities, 22 nondisabled boys and 22 low-achieving boys (reading or math was about the same as the boys with learning disabilities, but IQs were lower). The analyses of the results found a consistent pattern. The boys with learning disabilities scored significantly lower than the nondisabled boys but not the low-achieving group on the SIRPA, MEP, and ACT. There were no significant group differences on peer or parent ratings, but teachers rated the normal achievers higher than the groups with learning disabilities and the low achievers, who were about the same. There were significant Pearson product–moment correlations for each measure of interpersonal problem solving and Teacher Ratings on the BRP, ranging from 0.23 to –0.51.

These results are striking for several reasons. First, the group with learning disabilities performed equivalently to a low-achieving group whose IQs were lower. Thus, group differences between children with learning disabilities and nondisabled children cannot be dismissed as related to differences in IQ; on this basis, the children with learning disabilities should have performed better than the low-achieving group. Second, these results are notable for the significant correlations between teacher ratings and the measures of social cognition. Other studies have failed to find such correlations (Bruck & Hebert, 1982; Schneider & Yoshida, 1988). The relationship of social cognition to behavior is clearly important, and the reasons why significant correlations are found in one but not other studies needs further exploration and explanation. Finally, this study adds to accumulating evidence that social cognitive problem-solving difficulties are likely to be found among relatively older students with learning disabilities.

Schneider and Yoshida (1988) used five tests described by Platt and Spivack (1975, 1977), including two that were used by Silver and Young (1985): ACT and MEPS. In addition they used the Recognition of Problem Situations Test (subject articulates as many problems that people face as possible); the Optional Thinking Test (subject describes all of the actions a person could do in order to solve four hypothetical interpersonal problems); and the Causal Thinking Test (four interpersonal situations in which subject considers what might have caused a problem in the story. In addition, teachers rated students on the School Behavior Checklist.

Subjects included 30 junior high students with learning disabilities (23 males, 7 females), 30 nondisabled adolescents (23 males, 7 females), and 18 classroom teachers. The results found that the adolescents with learning disabilities scored significantly lower than the nondisabled adolescents on four of the five measures: Means–Ends Problem Solving, Recognition of

Problem Situations, Optional Thinking, and Causal Thinking. There were no significant differences on Awareness of Consequences Test. But no significant differences were found on the School Behavior Checklist, which measures social behavior problems in the classroom. Correlational analyses found low negative correlations between means–ends thinking and anxiety and academic disability and between causal thinking and hostile isolation. Sensitivity to interpersonal problems and consequential thinking were not found to correlate significantly with any behavioral factors in the group with learning disabilities. For the nondisabled group, means–ends thinking and alternative thinking correlated with teacher ratings.

The results of this study replicate Silver and Young in finding that adolescents with learning disabilities perform more poorly than their classmates on these social problem-solving skills. Schneider and Yoshida point out that the lower performance of students with learning disabilities is not likely to be related to IQ. The IQs of the students with learning disabilities were similar to those of the nondisabled students, and thus the verbal nature of the task should have affected both groups equally. Given few correlations between teacher ratings and performance, however, they raise questions about the social validity of problem-solving scales.

A third study to use role playing as a means of assessing social cognition was conducted by Pearl, Bryan, and Herzog (1988). In this study the focus was on adolescents' expectations for situations in which one adolescent requests another to participate in an undesirable activity. Students were interviewed about nine situations in which one teenager asked another to participate in an act of misconduct (e.g., stealing a car, shoplifting) or prosocial activities (e.g., shoveling snow for a neighbor). Students were questioned concerning their expectations about how the story character would request the second person's involvement, and how and why the situation would proceed if the person in the story did or did not acquiesce to the request.

Subjects included high school students from predominantly black, Hispanic, and white high schools: 100 with and 97 without learning disabilities. Eighty-four of the participants were female.

Students' responses were scored according to codes that categorized the major themes related in students' responses. Interrater reliability was at least 85% for each code. Group differences found that the students with learning disabilities expected more simple requests, while the nondisabled students expected more requests that stressed the payoff to the listener and that minimized the negatives and maximized the positives involved in the act.

A second difference was that students with learning disabilities were less likely than nondisabled students to predict that the individual would feel bad. They also showed less insight about situations in which the suggestion to engage in misconduct is made, in that they suggested fewer reasons for why someone would accept or refuse the request and spontaneously suggested fewer scenarios for what might ensue if such a response were made. Thus, students with learning disabilities differed from nondisabled students in their expectations of how a request to engage in illegal activities might be stated, and seemed to have less understanding of potential outcomes.

This study is limited in its reliance on expressive verbal skills. It is also not clear what adolescents might consider the ideal or preferred response, or the distinctions they might make concerning other adolescents' notions of appropriate deployment of such requests. Nonetheless, the study does address issues that have social validity; whether the assessment technique has social validity remains to be determined.

USING VIDEO PRESENTATIONS TO ASSESS SOCIAL COGNITION

A number of studies used videotaped presentations to assess social inferences. On the surface, the use of video presentations is very attractive because it seems much closer to reality than are paper-and-pencil tests or role playing. In reality the social scene is often complex, rapid, changing, and seldom is it made explicit what the proper mode of behavior should be. At the same time, in reality social situations often offer complete (visual and auditory inputs) and redundant information, historical and contextual cues, and feedback that signal proper responses. In this section studies that used video presentations are reviewed.

Maheady, Maitland, and Sainato (1984) used the Social Interpretation Task (SIT; Archer & Akert, 1977) and teacher ratings to compare 24 males with learning disabilities, and 24 socially/emotionally disturbed, 24 educable mentally retarded, and 24 nondisabled males at two age levels (7.0 to 11.11 and 13.0 to 17.11). The SIT is a 30-minute videotape showing 20 natural sequences of social interaction, each lasting from 30 to 60 seconds. Viewers answer an interpretive question about the people in the scene. One example is a scene showing two women playing with a baby. Viewers are asked to identify which woman is the baby's mother.

The results were that only the educable mentally retarded children made fewer correct responses. There were no differences between the children with and without learning disabilities. The children with learning disabilities received significantly lower teacher ratings than the other groups. An age-by-group interaction found that ratings got worse with increases in age, but only for the sample with learning disabilities. The scores on the SIT were not significantly correlated with teacher ratings.

Weiss (1984) used videotapes of 4- to 16-second scenes that depicted different social interactions between two or three boys: neutral, friendly, cooperative, teasing, horseplay, fighting, or angry. After viewing the scene, subjects were asked to describe it and then rate it on a scale from 1 to 7, ranging from very, very friendly to very, very unfriendly. Subjects then predicted how interactants would feel at their next meeting: happy, sad, or no special feeling. In addition, short paragraphs reporting the verbal content and describing the nonverbal expressions and actions in each scene were also used. Subjects were exposed to either the film or the written paragraphs.

Subjects included 111 black males, aged 11 to 15 years, who had been placed in a residential center. Based on ratings made by adults who worked with them, the boys were divided into four groups: aggressive with learning disabilities, nonaggressive with learning disabilities, nondisabled aggressive, and nondisabled nonaggressive. The groups with learning disabilities differed from the nondisabled groups on the unfriendly scenes and on rating how interactants would feel at next meetings. The groups with learning disabilities perceived both videotaped interactions and verbal descriptions as more unfriendly than the nondisabled groups. Aggressive versus nonaggressive designations had no significant impact. There were no group differences in the number or type of inferences expressed, however, the group with learning disabilities presented more erroneous items of information in the verbal condition. Of interest is that all groups rated the verbal descriptions as more unfriendly and predicted greater angry feelings at the next meeting. This suggests that assessment techniques that eliminate the social cues found in naturally occurring situations may elicit responses quite different from assessment techniques that use more realistic stimuli.

A third study that used videotaped stimuli was conducted by Pearl and Cosden (1982). In this case the stimuli included segments from televised soap operas that depicted an interaction between a male and a female. In each scenario the pair was discussing a topic of emotional concern (e.g., moving away, feelings of insecurity). The actual feelings were often indicated only through indirect or subtle facial, behavioral, or verbal cues. After viewing the segment, students responded to questions that required them to make inferences about the feelings of the characters, the social amenities in which they engaged, and their intentions.

Subjects included 88 males and females with and without learning disabilities in sixth, seventh, and eighth grades. The subjects with learning disabilities had a lower proportion of correct responses than the nondisabled group. Hence, using televised scenarios with both auditory and visual input that seemed analogous to real life in terms of content and complexity, the junior high students with learning disabilities were less accurate in their understanding of feelings and intention.

In sum, three studies used some type of video display to assess social cognition. These studies focused on understanding relationships, intentions, and interactions. Two of the three found the subjects with learning disabilities to perform more poorly than their peers. It is suggested that the difference in research results may stem from the complexity of the stimulus materials. The Maheady display seems concrete, or familiar (identifying who is a baby's mother) while the Weiss and the Pearl and Cosden material required students to make inferences about feelings and intentions. Notable about the Weiss versus the Pearl and Cosden studies were the samples included. In spite of using samples that differed markedly in age, race, and school placement, these studies found students with learning disabilities to perform more poorly in their comprehension and interpretation of video materials.

DISCUSSION

Interpretation of the results of studies examining the social cognition of students with learning disabilities must of necessity be concerned with the psychometric properties of the instruments being used. If we are going to be concerned with assessing the social competence of persons with learning disabilities, and providing related interventions, then we have to know something about the reliability and validity of the psychometric instruments. Unfortunately, it is only recently that there has been concern for psychometric analyses of the types of instruments used in the assessment of social cognition. At this point we must be cautious in our interpretation of research results, and recognize that it is premature to rely on these measures for individual assessment or for program evaluation. What are some of the pitfalls?

Krasnor and Rubin summarize the limitations of social cognitive assessment devices, in particular "hypothetical–reflective" measures: those that use hypothetical situations, and attempt to measure "thinking" responses (cf., Silver & Young, 1985; Schneider & Yoshida, 1988). These limitations include

1. The social goals are clearly and externally defined for the child and are not of immediate personal importance.
2. Most tests lack data concerning the sequencing of strategies.
3. Relatively narrow content areas have been sampled.
4. The verbal nature of the responses may make nonverbal strategies (e.g., frown, point) less likely to be offered.

5. Demonstration of psychometric strength for many of these measures remains weak, and reliability and normative information is rarely provided.
6. Hypothetical–reflective measures have not shown a direct relationship to the actual behavioral strategies used by the children or to observational indexes of social skill, (1981, p. 461).

There are other problems as well. The lack of normative data is not limited to a number of tests; normative data are not readily available in general. Although a number of the measures show increases in performance with age, there is really little age or sex information provided to guide interpretation of individual children's performance. Another problem that has been noted is that methods used to gather information vary widely. Even when researchers use the same measure, different test procedures may be used (cf., Fincham, 1977; Derr, 1986), different scoring procedures may be used, and there are wide differences in the reporting of analyses and results.

Third, the assessment techniques tap narrowly into social situations that children encounter, and these have been selected from an adult orientation. The narrow range of situations makes it impossible to delineate the skills necessary to solve social problems, to assess the range of a child's social cognitive skills across situations or targets, to test the internal consistency of the measures, or the generalizability of social cognitive skills (Krasnor & Rubin, 1981).

In reviewing studies that compare students with learning disabilities and groups of nondisabled students, we review the information provided about the reliability of the measures and/or the ratings. Information provided is sparse and variable; some report on interrater reliability (Wong & Wong, 1980) and some on internal consistency (Saloner & Gettinger, 1985; Jackson et al., 1987). In each case reliabilities were acceptable, but clearly, various types of reliability need to be established.

A second major issue in the evaluation of the research on students with learning disabilities is that of discriminant validity, and here we are particularly concerned with the relationships between measures of social cognition and intelligence. The question must be asked whether assessment of social cognition is just another test of intelligence. Evidence suggests that the cognitive tasks with the most validity share variance with general intelligence, but can be discriminated from it (Enright & Lapsley, 1980). Marlowe (1986) found that general intelligence, social self-perception and social skills represent independent domains, and that social intelligence appears to have two separate domains. Dodge, Murphy, and Buchsbaum (1984) assessed the relation of general intelligence to deficiencies in social cognition in aggressive children. They reported that deficiencies in aggressive children's information processing were domain specific and not accounted for by general intelligence factors.

The studies of social cognition in populations with learning disabilities that examined the impact of IQ on performance found that IQ was not correlated (Saloner & Gettinger, 1985), that the students with learning disabilities did as poorly or worse than low achieving students who had lower IQs (Silver & Young, 1985), and that using IQ as a covariate did not affect outcomes (Pearl & Cosden, 1982). Only one study using IQ as a covariate found that IQ accounted for significant differences between students with and those without learning disabilities (Horowitz, 1981). Three of four studies find IQ does not serve as an explanation for social cognitive problems in students with learning disabilities.

Similarly, problems in social cognition cannot be attributed to academic performance. Recent evidence refutes the notion that problems in the social domain are the result of poor academic achievement. Vaughn and Hogan (1988) found that sociometric measures taken as early as the second month of kindergarten were predictive of learning disability status one year later. Hence, problems in the social domain predated academic failures. La-Greca, Stone, and Halpern (1988) compared students with and without learning disabilities who had comparable reading and math achievement scores on measures of sociometric status, perceived social acceptance, and global self-worth. In comparison with comparable low achievers, students with learning disabilities were disproportionately represented among the rejected and neglected sociometric groups and underrepresented in the popular group. They also perceived their social status as lower, and their self-worth as lower.

On the whole, it seems safe to say that if children with learning disabilities do poorly on measures of social cognition it cannot be attributed to differences in verbal ability or intelligence per se or to the experience of academic failure. One general conclusion that can be made is that assessment of social cognition in persons with learning disabilities is a construct that is relatively independent of intelligence and academic achievement. This means that if students provided social cognition training show gains on these measures, it should not be attributed to the notion that the program promoted only verbal ability or general intelligence rather than cognitive role taking per se (Enright & Lapsley, 1980).

Measures of social cognition must also be concerned with construct validity. In a review of the measurement properties of social role-taking scales, Enright and Lapsley (1980, p. 662) outline 11 criteria needed to validate social cognitive measures as structural and developmental. Their work provides a framework for evaluating the construct validity of measures used with samples of learning disabled students. The 11 points follow.

1. Stages should increase with age to reflect the developmental nature of the construct.

2. Criteria should be established which clearly state the kinds of evidence necessary to support one and refute the other theory of egocentrism/decentration or operative knowing, if these two are seen as conceptually distinct.
3. It should be demonstrated that the necessary but not sufficient Piagetian stages do precede and are in part responsible for a corresponding role-taking level.
4. High internal consistency is needed to show that a child's reasoning represents a structured whole.
5. High temporal stability with no regression to lower levels is needed to support the invariance construct.
6. Criteria must be established with empirical support to show that the stages are hierarchical.
7. Cross-cultural evidence must be obtained to demonstrate the universality of the stages.
8. For the cognitive tasks, significant correlations with other cognitive role-taking scales must be obtained to demonstrate homogeneity within the domain. Affective tasks should also relate to cognitive tasks if there is a general role-taking domain.
9. For the affective tasks, significant correlations with other affective role-taking scales must be obtained to demonstrate homogeneity within this domain. Cognitive tasks should also relate to affective tasks if there is a general role-taking domain.
10. Differences on the scale between groups reflecting different levels of social adjustment would be expected to show the reasoning and behavior relationship.
11. There should be a higher within-scale or within-domain correlation than correlations between the scale and general intelligence.

In general, according to Enright and Lapsley (1980), the role-taking measures generally meet the first criterion, having shown that the age levels appear in the expected order. With respect to studies of students with learning disabilities, the expected age effects were found on the Tests of Social Inference (Gerber & Zinkgraf, 1982; Jackson et al., 1987) and on Cognitive and Affective Role-Taking (Dickstein & Warren, 1980; Bruck & Hebert, 1983). However, students with learning disabilities fail to catch up with age with their nondisabled counterparts (Dickstein & Warren, 1980; Jackson et al., 1987; Gerber & Zinkgraf, 1982). Indeed, one of the more striking findings in this review is that social cognitive differences are found between students with and without learning disabilities as late as age 18 years (Jackson et al., 1987), and may be more apparent in older than in younger students with learning disabilities (Fincham, 1977).

With respect to criteria 2 and 3 there are apparently no data for any of the role-taking measures. Criteria 4, internal consistency, cannot be assessed when the test has only one item (e.g., the apple–dog story), and evidence suggests that the other measures tap a homogeneous domain. For the criteria regarding temporal stability, hierarchical stages, and cross-cultural evidence, the measures cited included in this chapter have not been subjected to such tests.

The eighth and ninth criteria relate to correlations with other measures.

In terms of the measures cited in this chapter, Enright and Lapsley (1980) report no significant correlations between the Chandler (Wong & Wong, 1980) and Feffer (Fincham, 1976; Ackerman et al., 1978) tasks. In the studies of students with learning disabilities only a few used multiple measures and the authors were inconsistent in reporting correlations among measures. Horowitz (1981) reported the correlations between IQ and social insight (0.34), role taking (0.34) and the Mountain Task (0.42), but not the correlations between the social cognition measures. Bruck and Hebert (1983) reported that correlations between measures of role taking and peer interaction ratings were not stable. Silver and Young (1985) indicated significant correlations between teacher ratings and the social cognition measures ranging from 0.23 (means–ends) to –0.51 (SIRPA). Axelrod (1982) found correlations between the PONS and Cartoon Prediction and Expression (0.19), and between Teacher Ratings, Cartoon Prediction, Missing Cartoons, and the PONS (0.54). These fragments of information suggest that there may be some relationships between teacher ratings and performance on social cognitive measures, but this is tempered by lack of stable correlations between social cognitive measures and peer ratings. At this point, it is not possible to state that we understand the relationships across social cognition measures, or the relationships between measures of social cognition and other measures of social competence, such as sociometric status. It should be noted that attempts to show a relationship between social problem solving and observational indexes have not been successful. Krasnor and Rubin (1981) review several studies that found few relationships between peer interaction data and various measures of social cognition. The lack of correspondence between measures of social cognitive reasoning and peer interaction has created considerable controversy about the utility of social cognition assessment. Research reviewed in this chapter did not include any direct assessments or observations. Analyses of the relationship of social cognition to behavior were limited to teacher and parent ratings, and the results of these were mixed. Given the "noise" in both sets of measures, however, it seems quite premature to conclude that measures of social cognition lack external validity.

The 10th and 11th criteria are addressed by the comparisons of students with and without learning disabilities. Since overall these studies find that individuals with learning disabilities are distinguished from the nondisabled on various measures of social cognition, and that those with learning disabilities typically do more poorly than their nondisabled classmates, the results of the studies reviewed here lend credence to the validity of social cognition constructs. The results of the studies reviewed here, coupled with those on socially rejected and neglected preadolescents (Dodge, Coie, & Brakke, 1982), aggressive children (Dodge, 1980), and emotionally disturbed children (Chandler et al., 1974) certainly speak to the validity of the construct of social cognition.

Finally, what can we say about the social cognition of students with learning disabilities? Overall, although not all studies reported differences between students with learning disabilities and other groups of students, most of the studies did find differences favoring nondisabled subjects. Across a wide age span, group differences prevail. Across students in regular school settings and students in self-contained residential schools, group differences prevailed. With regard to sex, only a few studies included females in their studies, or analyzed for sex differences; their results are somewhat mixed, as Wong and Wong (1980) found females, but not males, with learning disabilities to be at risk for problems in social cognition, while Bruck and Hebert (1982) found no differences between males and females with learning disabilities; both groups did worse than nondisabled peers.

The studies also varied markedly in their stimuli and responses. Paper-and-pencil tests, role playing, moral conflicts, videotaped presentations basically all found group differences favoring nondisabled children. In terms of responses, children were asked to point to the correct response, to tell stories based on pictures, to answer questions about some presentation, to role play how they might respond in various situations. Whether the responses were verbal or nonverbal did not seem to distinguish the performance of students with learning disabilities: they did as poorly when all they had to do was point as they did when more extensive verbal responses were required.

As should be expected, several questions need to be addressed. Starting with the information processing definition of learning disabilities, we need to sort out performance on social cognition measures in terms of attention, memory, and language. The relationship of the performance by students with learning disabilities on social cognition measures to hyperactivity, reading, and more traditional measures needs to be sorted out. The social validity of these group differences clearly needs to be investigated; what does it mean, what does it predict, when students with learning disabilities perform more poorly on these measures? How does performance on social cognition scales relate to efforts to subcategorize types of learning disabilities? What role does poor social cognition play in the classroom? at home? for "survivor skills"? Why is it that older students with learning disabilities continue to have problems in social cognition? More questions than answers . . . but this is a new area of research, one that presents a challenging frontier for the understanding of learning disabilities.

REFERENCES

Ackerman, P. T., Elardo, P. T., & Dykman, R. A. (1979). A psychosocial study of hyperactive and learning disabled boys. *Journal of Abnormal Child Psychology, 7*, 91–99.

Ammons, R. & Ammons, C. (1962). The Quick test (QT): Provisional manual. *Psychological Reports.* Monograph Supplement, I-VII.
Archer, D., & Akert, R. M. (1977). Words and everything else: Verbal and nonverbal cues in social interpretation. *Journal of Personality and Social Psychology, 35,* 443–449.
Axelrod, L. (1982). Social perception in learning disabled adolescents. *Journal of Learning Disabilities, 15,* 610–613.
Brown, L., & Hammill, D. (1983). Behavior rating profile: A chronological approach to behavioral assessment. Austin, TX: PRO-ED.
Bruck, M. & Herbert, M. (1982). Correlates of learning disabled students' peer-interaction patterns. *Learning Disability Quarterly, 5,* 353–362.
Bruno, R. M. (1981). Interpretation of pictorially presented social situations by learning disabled and normal children. *Journal of Learning Disabilities, 14,* 350–352.
Bryan, T. (1974). Peer popularity of learning disabled children. *Journal of Learning Disabilities, 7,* 261–268.
Bryan, T. (1977). Children's comprehension of nonverbal communication. *Journal of Learning Disabilities, 10,* 501–506.
Chi, M. T. H., Feltovich, P., & Glazer, R. (1981). Categorization and representation of physics problems by experts and novices. *Cognitive Science, 5,* 121–152.
Chandler, M. (1972). Egocentrism in normal and pathological childhood development. In W. Hartup & J. DeWitte (Eds.), *Determinants of Behavioral Development,* New York: Academic Press.
Chandler, M. (1973). Egocentrism and antisocial behavior: the assessment and training of social perspective-taking skills. *Developmental Psychology, 9,* 326–337.
Chandler, M., Greenspan, S., & Barenboim, C. (1974). Assessment and training of role-taking and referential communication skills in institutionalized emotionally disturbed children. *Developmental Psychology, 10,* 546–553.
Derr, A. M. (1986). How learning disabled adolescent boys make moral judgements. *Journal of Learning Disabilities, 19,* 160–164.
Dickstein, E. B., & Warren, D. R. (1980). Role-taking deficits in learning disabled children. *Journal of Learning Disabilities, 13,* 33–37.
Dodge, K. A. (1980). Social cognition and children's aggressive behavior. *Child Development, 51,* 162–170.
Dodge, K. A., Coie, J. D., & Brakke, N. P. (1982). Behavior patterns of socially rejected and neglected preadolescents: The roles of social approach and aggression. *Journal of Abnormal Child Psychology, 10,* 389–409.
Dodge, K. A., Murphy, R. R., & Buchsbaum, K. (1984). The assessment of intention-cue detection skills in children: implications for developmental psychopathology. *Child Development, 55,* 163–173.
Donahue, M., Pearl, R., & Bryan, T. (1983). Communicative competence in learning disabled children. In I. Bialer & K. D. Gadow (Eds.), *Advances in Learning and Behavioral Disabilities, 2,* 49–84.
Edmonson, B., deJung, J., Leland, H., & Leach, E. (1974). *The test of social inference.* New York: Educational Activities, Inc.
Enright, R., & Lapsley, D. K. (1980). Social role-taking: A review of the constructs, measures, and measurement properties. *Review of Educational Research, 50,* 647–674.
Feffer, M. (1970, January). Role taking behavior in the mentally retarded. Department of Health, Education and Welfare, U.S. Office of Education (Office of Education for the Handicapped) Grant No. OEG-0-9-422029-0716 (032).
Fincham, F. D. (1976, September). Conservation and cognitive role taking ability in

learning disabled boys. Paper presented at the 28th Annual Conference of the South African Psychological Association, Durban, South Africa.

Fincham, F. D. (1977). A comparison of moral judgment in learning disabled and normal achieving boys. *Journal of Psychology, 96*, 153–160.

Flavell, J. H., Botkin, P. T., Fry, C. L., Wright, J. W., & Jarvis, P. E. (1968). *The Development of Role-Taking and Communication Skills in Children*. New York: Wiley.

Gerber, P. J., & Zinkgraf, S. A. (1982). A comparative study of social-perceptual ability in learning disabled and nonhandicapped students. *Learning Disability Quarterly, 5*, 374–378.

Goyette, C. H., Conners, K. C., & Ulrich, R. (1978). Normative data on Revised Conners Parent and Teacher Rating Scales. *Journal of Abnormal Child Psychology, 6*, 221–236.

Horowitz, E. C. (1981). Popularity, decentering ability, and role-taking skills in learning disabled and normal children. *Learning Disability Quarterly, 4*, 23–30.

Interagency Committee on Learning Disabilities (1987). Learning Disabilities: A report to the U.S. Congress.

Jackson, S. C., Enright, R. D., & Murdock, J. Y. (1987). Social perception problems in learning disabled youth: Developmental lag versus perceptual deficit. *Journal of Learning Disabilities, 20*, 361–364.

Kistner, J. A., Osborne, M., & LeVerrier, L. (1988). Causal attributions of learning-disabled children: Developmental patterns and relation to academic progress. *Journal of Education Psychology, 80*, 82–89.

Kohlberg, L., Colby, A., Gibbs, J., Speicher-Dubin, B., & Power, C. (1978, July). *Assessing moral stages: A manual*, preliminary edition. Cambridge, Mass., Center for Moral Education, Harvard University.

Krasnor, L. R., & Rubin, K. H. (1981). The assessment of social problem-solving skills in young children. In T. Merluzzi, C. Glass, & M. Genest (Eds.). *Cognitive Assessment*, (pp. 452–476). New York: Guilford Press.

LeGreca, A. M., Stone, W. L., & Halpern, D. A. (1988). LD status and achievement: Confounding variables in the study of children's social and behavioral functioning? Paper presented at the meeting of the International Academy for Research in Learning Disabilities, UCLA, Los Angeles.

Maheady, L., Maitland, G., & Sainato, D. (1984). The interpretation of social interactions by mildly handicapped and nondisabled children. *Journal of Special Education, 18*, 151–159.

Marlowe, H. A. (1986). Social intelligence: Evidence for multidimensionality and construct independence. *Journal of Educational Psychology, 78*, 52–58.

Muuss, R. E. (1982). Social cognition: Robert Selman's theory of role taking. *Adolescence, 17*, 499–525.

O'Sullivan, M., & Guilford, J. P. (1976). *Four factor tests of social intelligence manual of instructions and interpretations*. Orange, CA: Sheridan Psychological Services.

Paulauskas, S. L., & Campbell, S. G. (1979). Social perspective taking and teacher ratings of peer interaction in hyperactive boys. *Journal of Abnormal Child Psychology, 7*, 483–493.

Pearl, R., Bryan, T., & Herzog, A. (1988). Resisting or acquiescing to peer pressure to engage in misconduct: Adolescents expectations of probable consequences. Unpublished manuscript, University of Illinois at Chicago.

Pearl, R., & Cosden, M. (1982). Sizing up a situation: LD children's understanding of social interactions. *Learning Disability Quarterly, 5*, 371–373.

Platt, J. J., & Spivack, G. (1975). *Manual for the means-ends Problem-Solving Procedure (MEPS): A measure of interpersonal cognitive problem-solving skill.*

Platt, J. J., & Spivack, G. (1977). Measures of interpersonal problem-solving: A manual. Philadelphia: Hahnemann Community Mental Health/Mental Retardation Center Department of Mental Health Services.

Rosenthal, R., Archer, D., DiMatteo, M. R., Hall, J., & Rogers, P. L. (1979). Profile of nonverbal sensitivity test. New York: Irvington.

Saloner, M. R., & Gettinger, M. (1985). Social inference skills in learning disabled and nondisabled children. *Psychology in the Schools, 22,* 201–207.

Scranton, T. R., & Ryckman, D. A. (1979). Disabled children in an integrative program: Sociometric status. *Journal of Learning Disabilities, 2,* 402–407.

Shantz, C. U. (1983). Social cognition. In P. H. Mussen (Ed.). *Handbook of Child Psychology,* 4th ed. (pp. 495–555). New York: John Wiley.

Silver, D. S., & Young, R. D. (1985). Interpersonal problem-solving abilities, peer status and behavioral adjustment in learning disabled and non-learning disabled adolescents. *Advances in Learning and Behavioral Disabilities, 4,* 201–223.

Schneider, M., & Yoshida, R. K. (1988). Interpersonal problem-solving skills and classroom behavioral adjustment in learning-disabled adolescents and comparison peers. *Journal of School Psychology, 26,* 25–34.

Special Education Today (1985) p. 1.

Stone, W. L., & LaGreca, A. M. (1984. Comprehension of nonverbal communication: A reexamination of the social competencies of learning-disabled children. *Journal of Abnormal Child Psychology, 12,* 505–518.

Vaughn, S., & Hogan, A. (1988, February). Peer acceptance, self-perceptions, and social skills of LD students prior to identification. Paper presented at the International Academy for Research in Learning Disabilities, Los Angeles.

Waddell, J. (1984). The self-concept and social adaptation of hyperactive children in adolescence. *Journal of Clinical Child Psychology, 13,* 50–55.

Weiss, E. (1984). Learning disabled children's understanding of social interactions of peers. *Journal of Learning Disabilities, 17,* 612–614.

Wong, B. Y. L., & Wong, R. (1980). Role-taking skills in normal achieving and learning disabled children. *Learning Disability Quarterly, 3,* 11–18.

Youniss, J. (1975). Another perspective on social cognition. In A. D. Pick (Ed.), *Minnesota Symposia on Child Psychology* (vol. 9). Minneapolis: University of Minnesota Press.

CHAPTER 14

Assessing Temperament

BARBARA K. KEOGH
CYNTHIA RATEKIN BESS

Considerable clinical evidence documents the need to consider multiple contributors to the development of competence and/or to problems in behavior and adjustment. Yet within the educational arena the focus of systematic assessment has been almost exclusively on cognition and achievement. This emphasis is understandable, given that the primary task of schooling is to teach academic skills. There is increasing evidence, however, that children's experiences and achievements in school are based not only on cognitive attributes, but rather, are influenced by a range of individual and contextual characteristics. There is also evidence that children's experiences in school are best understood within an interactional framework that recognizes the bidirectional nature of pupil–teacher relationships. This perspective is, of course, consistent with a bidirectional, transactional view of child development and parent–child interaction (see Bell, 1974; Lerner, 1982; Sameroff & Chandler, 1975). It is our thesis that temperament is an individual difference attribute that contributes to children's interactions in school, and thus, that temperament warrants consideration in psychoeducational assessment. To address this topic, this chapter is divided into four major sections: definitions and conceptualiza-

---

Preparation of this paper was supported in part by grant no. HD 22944 from the National Institute of Child Health and Human Development to the Sociobehavioral Research Group, Mental Retardation Center, UCLA.

tions, a brief overview of research on temperament in schools, examples of selected methods of assessment, and problems and applications.

DEFINITIONS AND CONCEPTUALIZATIONS

Individual differences in behavioral dispositions have been recognized for centuries, although the specific dimensions or characteristics identified have varied somewhat. Rutter (1982) notes that temperamental characteristics are "abstractions, rather than directly observable discrete behaviours" (p. 2). Temperamental dimensions are presumed to have, in part at least, a constitutional basis, but are derived from observations of consistencies in behaviors, the "abstractions" capturing aspects of behavior that are not situationally specific. The interest in broad abstractions instead of the specific content of behavior has complicated definition, measurement, and interpretation. Differences in conceptualizations of temperament have yielded a number of approaches to operationalizing the construct, and the empirical data addressing temperament are not always consistent. Nonetheless, a large literature argues for the reality of temperamental differences and for the importance of these differences in children's experiences (see Bates, 1989; Dunn & Kendrick, 1980; Keogh & Pullis, 1980; Rutter, 1977, 1982, for reviews). As measurement and assessment are integrally related to definition, four well-formulated conceptualizations of temperament are presented briefly to provide background (see Goldsmith et al., 1987, for detailed discussion of these positions).

THEORETICAL PERSPECTIVES

Current interest in temperament was stimulated by the work of Thomas, Chess, and Birch and their colleagues in the New York Longitudinal Study (Thomas, Chess, Birch, Hertzig, & Korn, 1963; Thomas, Chess, & Birch, 1968; Thomas & Chess, 1977). Based on their experience as practicing psychiatrists and on their observations of individual differences in infants, these theorists equate temperament with behavioral style. Their definition emphasizes the stylistic (how) rather than the motivational (why) or the content (what) aspect of behavior. Thomas and Chess (1977) identified nine dimensions of behavioral style: activity level, adaptability, approach/withdrawal, attention span and persistence, distractibility, intensity of reaction, rhythmicity, threshold of responsiveness, and quality of mood. Presumably independent, these characteristics were found to cluster into three major groups that describe easy, difficult, and slow-to-warm-up children.

Working primarily, but not exclusively, with infants, Rothbart (1981) defines temperament as biologically based individual differences in reactivity (arousability or excitability) and self-regulation (enhancing or inhibiting processes). In work with Derryberry (Rothbart & Derryberry, 1981) she has addressed neurophysiological, behavioral, and experiential or phenomenological aspects of temperament. Although a number of the specific temperament variables studied (e.g., activity level, soothability) are similar to those proposed by Thomas and Chess, Rothbart's definition is not limited to behavioral style, but rather implicates directly predisposing psychophysiological functions.

Goldsmith and Campos (1982, 1986; Goldsmith et al., 1987) argue that temperament is best defined as individual differences in the primary emotions and arousability, and that it is identified in the expressive rather than the receptive aspect of emotion. Similar in part to Rothbart's definition in their emphasis on arousal, these theorists acknowledge that there are likely physiological or neurophysiological determinants of temperament. In empirical work they have documented behavioral expressions of temperament, describing single behavioral responses in terms of temporal parameters of latency and duration, and intensity parameters of magnitude and shape; frequency and patterning are used to describe larger response units (Goldsmith et al., 1987. In their view, temperament might be considered the "emotional substrate" of personality development.

Representing still another perspective on the definition of temperament, Buss and Plomin (1975, 1984) approach the topic from their backgrounds in personality theory and behavioral genetics. Temperament is conceptualized as a set of genetically determined personality traits or dispositions: activity (tempo and vigor), emotionality (emotional and behavioral arousal), and sociability (preference for others). Buss and Plomin argue that these temperamental traits, evident in infancy, provide a foundation for subsequent personality development, and while they are expected to vary over time and in response to environmental forces, they are also expected to show relative stability.

COMMONALITIES AND DIFFERENCES

These conceptualizations represent four influential views of temperament, and each has stimulated significant research efforts. The definitions have a number of points in common and some major differences (Goldsmith & Rieser-Danner, 1986; Keogh & Pullis, 1980). These theorists agree that temperament is differentiated from personality and from cognition and motivation; temperament includes several components or dimensions of behavior; temperamental variation is evident in infancy and serves as the foundation of personality; temperament is relatively more stable than many other behavioral or individual difference characteristics; and there is a likely biological or neurophysiological substrate to temperamental individuality. Differences among definitions are also apparent. These include the number and content of components or dimensions; the importance of genetic contributions; the nature of the relationship of temperament to motivation and to personality; the importance of regulatory or excitatory functions of temperament; and the nature of the interaction of temperament and context. On a practical level, these differences in formulation have obvious implications for assessment. Before considering various measurements, however, a brief overview of research on temperament and schooling is presented as background.

RESEARCH ON TEMPERAMENT IN SCHOOLS

Findings from a number of different research groups in different countries have identified associations between children's temperament and a range of performance/achievement indices: teacher-assigned grades (Pullis & Cadwell, 1982), pupils' performance in academic subjects such as reading and arithmetic (Hall & Cadwell, 1984; Hegvik, 1984; Martin, Nagle, & Paget, 1983; Maziade, Cote, Boutin, Boudreault, & Thivierge, 1986; Skuy, Snell, & Westaway, 1985), and teacher's instructional decisions (Keogh, 1982). Keogh and Burstein (1988), van de Werfhost (1986), and Martin et al. (1983) have documented differences in the amount and kind of personal and instructional interactions between teachers and pupils associated with children's temperamental attributes.

While associations between children's temperament and teachers' responses have been identified, the functional basis for the relationships is less clear. We suggest that temperament is best viewed as a mediating variable rather than as a main effect in teacher–child interactions. In this regard, Scarr and McCartney (1983) consider temperament an example of an "evocative" person–context correlation, as does Lerner (1982). Building on a decision-making model of teaching (Shavelson, 1976) Keogh (1982) proposed that children's temperamental characteristics contribute to teachers' perceptions of children's "teachability," and thus influence teachers' attributions and decisions about children's behaviors (and misbehaviors). In this decision model it is assumed that teachers have implicit ideas or beliefs about what pupils "ought to be like" (see Kornblau, 1982; Kornblau & Keogh, 1980), and that temperament or stylistic characteristics, as well as cognition and motivation, contribute to teachers' views of the teachability of individual children. Some children match well the adults' expectancies and views of teachability; other children have personal characteristics that are discrepant. When children's behavior and performance are consistent with teachers' views (i.e., when the "match" is good), interactions elicit positive responses; when behavior or personal characteristics are inconsistent with teachers' expectations, attributions about children's behaviors are apt to be negative, and the interactions minimal and even punitive.

GOODNESS OF FIT

The match or mismatch has been described by a number of researchers, and is usually referred to as "goodness of fit" (Keogh, 1986; Lerner & Lerner, 1983). Thomas and Chess (1977) describe goodness of fit in terms of "consonance" or "dissonance" of individual characteristics and setting or environmental properties and demands. Lerner and Lerner (1983) stress the importance of context in goodness of fit, pointing out that contextual demands in school may be related to the physical environment (e.g., crowded and/or highly structured classrooms) or to social influences (e.g., teachers' beliefs, values, and expectations about desirable behavior). The notion of goodness of fit is firmly anchored in the interaction between individuals and their social contexts, and an important assumption is that there is covariance of individual characteristics and social feedback. The goodness of fit notion has real appeal when applied to children and their social environment, including school. Windle and Lerner (1986b) note correctly, however, that despite considerable conceptual support for goodness of fit, there has been limited empirical demonstration of its power. They suggest this is due, in part at least, to the analytic methods and techniques applied, especially the reliance on cross-sectional strategies. In addition, they note that contextual demands, one component of the goodness of fit model, have not been assessed in ways that allow determination of person–context correlations. A specific problem has been the limited variance among school environments. The measurement issues in assessing temperament, thus, are not limited exclusively to the individual, but also require more careful and detailed description of the complex social environments in which interactions occur.

METHODS OF ASSESSMENT

Decisions about who and what should be assessed, the techniques or measures to be used, and where assessment should take place reflect both the theoretical orientation of the assessor and the reasons for assessment. Given the "constituencies" described in previous sections, it is not surprising that there are a number of different approaches to the measurement of temperament. Commonly used techniques include self-reports, projective techniques, direct observation, psychophysiological techniques, rating scales and questionnaires, and interviews (see Bates, 1986; Martin, 1988, for discussion). The utility of each approach varies according to the purposes of assessment and the age of those being assessed. Projective and self-report measures are obviously not useful with young children or severely handicapped individuals, as they require advanced language skills. Psychophysiological or psychobiological techniques are laboratory based, costly, and not always appropriate for the study of variables relevant to school; they are used mainly in research with infants. Direct observation is time consuming and expensive, is often restricted to discrete variables, and may have limited generalizability because of situational specificity. It should be noted, too, that temperament data are often gathered from different sources (e.g., parents, teachers, physicians, trained observers, or individuals themselves) and that assessment may occur at home or school, in research laboratories, or in physicians' offices. Thus, possible situational and informant effects, as well as the technical adequacy of instruments, must be considered.

Examination of clinical and research applications of temperament with children shows clearly that rating scales and questionnaires are among the most common techniques used. A selected listing of rating scales/questionnaires reflecting age and informant sources is shown below.

Infants and Toddlers

- Toddler Temperament Scale (TTS), Fullard, McDevitt, & Carey, 1978
- Baby Behavior Questionnaire (BBQ), Bohlin, Hagekull, & Lindhagen, 1981
- Infant Behavior Questionnaire (IBQ), Rothbart, 1981
- Swedish Temperament Questionnaire revised for 12- and 24-month olds (STQ-12, STQ-24), Persson-Blennow & McNeil, 1980
- Infant Characteristics Questionnaire (ICQ), Bates, Freeland, & Lounsbury, 1979
- Swedish 6-month Temperament Questionnaire (STQ-6), Persson-Blennow & McNeil, 1979
- Revised Infant Temperament Questionnaire (RITQ), Carey & McDevitt, 1978
- Brazelton Neonatal Assessment Scale (BNAS), Brazelton, 1973
- Infant Temperament Questionnaire (ITQ), Carey, 1970
- Nurses Scale for Rating Neonates (NSRN), Haar, Welkowitz, Blau, & Cohen, 1964

Preschool and School-Age Children

- Temperament Assessment Battery for Children (TABC), Martin, 1988
- Parent Temperament Questionnaire (PTQ), Thomas & Chess, 1977
- Teacher Temperament Questionnaire (TTQ), Thomas & Chess, 1977
- Abbreviated Temperament Questionnaire (ATQ), Garside et al., 1975
- Behavioral Style Questionnaire (BSQ), McDevitt & Carey, 1978
- Middle Childhood Temperament Questionnaire (MCTQ), Hegvik, McDevitt, & Carey, 1982
- EASI-I Temperament Survey (EASI-I), Buss, Plomin, & Willerman, 1973
- EASI-III Temperament Survey, (EASI-III), Buss & Plomin, 1984
- Colorado Childhood Temperament Inventory (CCTI), Rowe & Plomin, 1977
- Child Stimulus Screening Scale (CSSS), Mehrabian & Falander, 1978
- Toddler Behavior Questionnaire (TBQ), Hagekull, Lindhagen, & Bohlin, 1980
- Dimension of Temperament Survey (DOTS), Lerner, Palmero, Spiro, & Nesselroade, 1982
- Revised Dimensions of Temperament Survey (DOTS-R), Windle & Lerner, 1986a
- Parent Temperament Scale—Revised (PTSR), Pfeffer & Martin, 1983
- Short form of the Teacher Temperament Questionnaire (TTQ), Keogh, Pullis, & Cadwell, 1982

Given the range of techniques, the many purposes of assessment, and the multiple settings and sources of information, it should not surprise us that there are sometimes inconsistent findings. A serious problem also relates directly to the technical adequacy of instruments or scales (see Hubert, Wachs, Peters-Martin, & Gandour, 1982; Martin, 1988; Rothbart & Goldsmith, 1985, for detailed discussions of measurement issues). That there is some commonality of findings from various research groups using different assessment approaches, however, argues for the reality of temperament as an individual difference variable.

ASSESSING TEMPERAMENT IN SCHOOLS

Rather than attempting to cover in detail the many possible scales or methods, we have focused our discussion on selected instruments that have evolved from the Thomas and Chess formulation of temperament, considering first the measurement system developed by the New York group. This choice was made because of the seminal importance of the Thomas et al. work, and also because of the widespread clinical and educational applications of their formulation. Although not discussed in detail in this chapter, the extensive work on assessment by Carey and his colleagues should be noted, as these researchers have developed a number of scales appropriate for gathering parents' ratings. These include scales for rating infants (Carey, 1970; Carey & McDevitt, 1978), toddlers (Fullard, McDevitt, & Carey, 1984), preschool and primary-grade children (McDevitt & Carey, 1978), and children in the middle-childhood age range (Hegvik, McDevitt, & Carey, 1982). All of these scales are based on the Thomas and Chess definition of temperament. Each scale contains approximately 100 items describing behaviors exemplifying specific temperament attributes. The scales have reasonable psychometric properties, and test–retest reliabilities are good. However, questions of the composition of norming samples, of convergent and concurrent validity, and of interpretability have been raised (see Hubert et al., 1982; Vaughn, Taraldson, Crichton, & Egeland, 1981). The scales have had wide use in clinical practice and in research with young children (see Carey, 1982), including some efforts to relate parent-rated temperament to children's behavior and performance in school (Billman & McDevitt, 1980; Hegvik, 1984). Taken as a whole, the work of Carey and his associates represents a major contribution to the assessment of temperament.

Given that the focus of this volume is assessment in schools, the emphasis here will be on techniques that involve teachers' perceptions of children's temperamental characteristics. Four school specific methods for assessing children's temperament have been selected for brief review. All are consistent with the Thomas and Chess' view of temperament as behavioral style, but all have somewhat different emphases, formats, content, and applications.

Teacher Temperament Questionnaire (TTQ) (Thomas & Chess, 1977)

This instrument was developed as part of the New York Longitudinal Study (NYLS) and is generally comparable in format and content to the Parent Temperament Questionnaire (PTQ) (Thomas & Chess, 1977). The primary sample in the NYLS was composed of 141 children from homes of middle to upper middle socioeconomic status; other groups of differing socioeconomic and ethnic backgrounds were subsequently included. Parents were the primary source of information when the children were infants but behavioral observations and teachers' reports were added as the children grew older. Through inductive content analyses, Thomas and Chess and their colleagues defined the nine dimensions of temperament that are the basis of the (PTQ) and, with one exception, of the Teacher Temperament Questionnaire (TTQ). Each dimension is represented by eight items describing specific behaviors thought to typify the dimension (total item N = 72 for the PTQ). In the TTQ the dimension of rhythmicity was dropped, so the total number of items is 64. Items describe behaviors that are appropriate for home or school. Examples of questions from the PTQ and the TTQ, respectively, are "If my child is upset, it is hard to comfort him/her." "Child becomes easily upset when he/she loses a game." In both Questionnaires the adult rater is asked to circle the number that best describes the child's behavior (1 = hardly ever; 7 = almost always). The dimension scores are the means of the item scores. Researchers in the New York group have conducted a number of statistical and clinical studies relating temperament to a range of behavioral and academic problems (see Thomas & Chess, 1977).

Independent research on the TTQ and the PTQ raised questions about the representativeness of the norming sample and the methods of aggregating data across ages (McNeil, 1976); scoring procedures (Carey, 1970); the independence, internal consistency, and reliability of the nine dimensions (Keogh, Pullis, & Cadwell, 1980; Hubert et al., 1980); the number and organization of factors or components (Baker & Velicer, 1984; Keogh et al., 1983); the diagnostic validity of the dimensions and clinical classifications (Martin & Pfeffer, 1980), and issues of convergent validity (Billman & McDevitt, 1980; Hubert et al., 1980). Despite these questions, the TTQ has proved a useful method for assessing temperament and has been widely employed in subsequent research. The Thomas and Chess scales have also been modified to meet specific needs of other research groups.

Short Form of the Teacher Temperament Questionnaire (Keogh, Pullis, & Cadwell, 1982)

These investigators modified the TTQ as developed by Thomas and Chess in an effort to produce a form of the instrument that would be practical for research in schools. The specific goal was to reduce the number of items so that the instrument would be feasible for use by classroom teachers when rating large numbers of children. In the process of this modification the reliability of items and dimensions were assessed, the extent of agreement among raters was examined, and the factor structure was determined. The development of this instrument was based on work with over 300 (mostly white) children between the ages of 3 and 6 years and replicated with an independent sample of primary-grade children (Pullis, 1979). Preliminary factor analysis of the 64-item TTQ yielded 3 commonalities rather than 8 independent dimensions. The first, composed of the dimensions of persistence, distractibility, and activity, was called Task Orientation. The second, consisting of adaptability, approach/withdrawal, and positive mood, was named Personal Social Flexibility. The third, an essentially negative factor, was composed of intensity, threshold, and negative mood and was called Reactivity. These factors are similar to those found in subsequent investigations on the TTQ (Paget et al., 1984). Based on this factor structure, specific items representing each dimension were selected according to factor loadings. The final short form consists of 23 items representing all of the original eight dimensions (Keogh et al., 1982). Scoring is based on a 1 (hardly ever) to 6 (almost always) scale. Factor analysis of the short form confirmed the three-factor organization (Pullis, 1979; Pullis & Cadwell, 1982); internal consistency coefficients were high, and gender and age differences were consistent with those found with the original form of the TTQ. In addition, substantial agreement was found between teachers' rating of the same children with both forms.

The Temperament Assessment Battery for Children (TABC) (Martin, 1988)

The Temperament Assessment Battery for Children (TABC) consists of three instruments designed to evaluate temperament characteristics of children 3 to 7 years old in different settings. The instruments are derived from the Thomas and Chess scales developed in the NYLS. The parent form describes children's behavior occurring in the home; the teacher form is designed to document particular classroom behaviors; the clinician form is to be used in individual evaluation, teaching, or performance settings. All three forms tap six temperament characteristics: activity, adaptability, approach withdrawal, distractibility, emotional intensity, and persistence. The variables are defined similarly to the Thomas and Chess formulation, except that distractibility in the parent form refers to the ease with which a child can be distracted from inappropriate behavior, and in the teacher and clinician forms it refers to the tendency for a child to be distracted by environmental stimuli when attending to a particular activity. The parent and teacher forms consist of 48 items each, items rated from 1 (hardly ever) to 7 (almost always). The clinician form uses the same 7-point scale and consists of 25 items. Reliability and validity have been established, and relationships between the three forms of this instrument and observed behavior, intelligence, psychopathology, achievement, and teacher attitudes have been tested (Martin, 1988). Martin, Nagle, and Paget (1983) investigated the concurrent validity of the teacher form of the TABC, finding significant correlations between observed classroom behaviors and temperament characteristics of activity, adaptability, distractibility, and persistence. Relationships between teachers' ratings on the TABC, children's achievement, and social adjustment were also confirmed. Teacher's ratings on the TABC predicted reading and mathematics achievement and social adjustment.

Dimensions of Temperament Survey (DOTS)
(Lerner, Palmero, Spiro, & Nesselroade, 1982)

This instrument was designed to measure dimensions of temperament that are continuous from early childhood through adulthood and to test the goodness of fit model of temperament. The authors' conception of temperament and their item pool is based on the Thomas and Chess work. There are four forms for this measurement, three designed to be completed by adults: A questionnaire to be completed by parents describing their child, a questionnaire to be completed by adults about themselves, and a questionnaire to assess teachers' expectations and demands for students. These instruments contain 34 items and are answered either 1 (more true than false) or 2 (more false than true). The fourth questionnaire is a self-rating by children. It also has 34 items—each item true or false. The dimensions of temperament assessed with the DOTS include activity level, attention span or distractibility, adaptability or approach/withdrawal, rhythmicity, and reactivity. The instruments are unique in that they tap common dimensions across age levels. The content is similar and there are only minor changes in wording as appropriate. Factor analyses of DOTS items revealed a common five-factor model for all forms: activity level, attention span or distractibility, adaptability or approach/withdrawal, rhythmicity, and reactivity. Five scores are obtained, one for each dimension.

The Revised Dimensions of Temperament
Survey (DOTS-R) (Windle & Lerner, 1986a)

This revision was seen as necessary because of the low magnitude of relationships between temperament attributes and outcome variables, as indicated by R^2 values in multiple regression equations. Limitations included the two-choice response format, the restricted scope of some of the factors, ambiguous wording in some of the items, relatively low factor loadings of certain items, and the low reliability of certain temperament attributes for specific age groups. Revisions include an expanded four-response format, an increase from 34 items to 54 items, and minor wording changes in order better to tap the dimensions of activity level, reactivity, adaptability or approach/withdrawal, and rhythmicity. The child form to be completed by the parent, and the child (self) form are composed of 9 dimensions, while the adult self-rating form contains 10. Eight dimensions are identical for all three forms. The ninth attribute on the child and the child (self) form—task orientation—splits into two different dimensions, distractibility and persistence, on the adult form. These changes result in moderate to high levels of internal consistency for all the attributes across the age brackets, and a stronger relationship between temperament attributes and measures associated with perceived efficacy in psychosocial functioning in adolescence.

LIMITATIONS AND APPLICATIONS

Temperament is an intuitively appealing individual difference variable, as on a day-to-day basis we are all aware of stylistic characteristics of family members and of friends. Yet, despite its appeal and an increasingly large research literature that documents the reality of temperamental variation, a number of possible limitations or problems need to be considered when applying temperament constructs in psychoeducational evaluation. These are both conceptual and methodological.

Issues related to differences in theoretical formulations or perspectives and in the number and organization of temperamental attributes have already been discussed. These clearly influence how and by what methods temperament should be assessed. What must also be acknowledged is the possibility that temperament is a semantic artifact, that is, that evoking temperamental constructs does not provide new information or greater insights, but rather results only in different language for the same behaviors (Keogh, 1989). In response to this potential limitation we suggest that a substantial empirical literature, particularly studies of infants, argues for temperament as a legitimate and independent contributor to behavior. However, the possibility of the "semantic error" must be guarded against when using temperamental constructs to explain children's behavior.

A second potential limitation in applying temperament in assessment relates to the generalizability of information, and has to do specifically with questions of stability across settings and/or of informant effect. There are a number of aspects of this issue to be considered. One relates directly to the question of situational variance in behavior. Studies of parents' and teachers' ratings of temperament of the same children yield only modest correlations (Keogh et al., 1980), suggesting a number of different interpretations. Children's behavior may vary between home and school, temperament is expressed differently in different settings, parents and teachers have different perceptions of the same behaviors, and/or informant bias affects the ratings. Any of these interpretations raises questions about the generalizability of assessment findings, and suggests caution when drawing broad inferences about children based on situationally specific findings.

From a measurement perspective it should be noted, too, that bias or informant error is more likely when measurement is imprecise, e.g., when definitions of attributes and specification of rating points are ambiguous, as is sometimes the case in temperament rating scales. Thus, the technical adequacy of techniques for gathering temperament information becomes important. Finally, another aspect of potential informant effect must be considered. From a cultural perspective Super and Harkness (1986) argue that it is not just the behavior but the significance of the behavior within the context that is important. They have described a number of differences in interpretation of behavior and in the consequences of behavior related to cultural variations. While not as dramatic as the cross-cultural examples, it is reasonable that children's behavioral styles will differ in salience and in significance in particular situations. Early work in the UCLA research program (Keogh et al., 1982) suggested that temperament attributes of activity, persistence, and distractibility were especially important contributors to teachers' views of children. These attributes were less important at home, where parents were particularly sensitive to temperamental characteristics related to personal–social interactions (e.g., adaptability, approach/withdrawal). In sum, while adults' ratings of children's temperament are a useful and feasible source of information, there are threats to validity that must be considered when interpreting temperament data for clinical or research purposes.

Despite possible technical and interpretative limitations, we suggest that there are a number of sound arguments for including temperament in psychoeducational assessment. Life in school is not limited to experiences that tap only cognition. Rather, children experience a series of continuing and changing interactions with peers, teachers, and with the demands of the tasks to be learned. These interactions involve a range of personal characteristics, including behavioral style or temperament. How children approach newness and change, how they respond to classroom requirements of physical inactivity or extended demands for concentration, and how they deal with differences in teachers' management styles, may all be influenced by temperamental variation. Thus, including temperament in assessment allows consideration of an important set of individual difference variables that contribute to children's experiences in school.

There is a second major implication for assessment that follows. Traditionally, the focus of assessment has been on the child. To understand the functional importance of temperament it is necessary to consider context. In their discussion of the concept of goodness of fit, Lerner and Lerner and their colleagues (Lerner & Lerner, 1983; Lerner, Lerner, & Zabski, 1985) stress that the context of school is both physical and social. Classrooms differ in space, in arrangement of desks, in the number of pupils, and in the structure and routine of the instructional program. Classrooms also differ in teachers' expectations, goals, and values; in teachers' views about acceptable and unacceptable behavior; and in teachers' behavioral styles. These differences may affect children differently, in part because of temperamental variations. The implication for assessment, thus, is that both the individual and the context must be addressed. This is central to the goodness of fit notion, and while complicating assessment, has the potential of yielding more insightful information.

From a somewhat different perspective, we also suggest that consideration of individual differences in temperament provides adults with a different and sometimes less noxious way of interpreting children's behavior. Slow-responding, less-approaching children may be viewed by teachers as low in motivation or as indifferent to school; intense-responding, impersistent, and active children may be viewed as purposefully disruptive. Attributions about the reasons for children's behavior influence adults' responses and contribute to their decisions about what to do. Bates (1989) has found that making parents sensitive to temperamental characteristics of their children helps "reframe" parents' views of problem behavior. We suggest that sensitivity to temperament contributions to children's school performance will also help reframe perceptions of problem behaviors in schools.

REFERENCES

Baker, E. H., & Velicer, W. F. (1982). The structure and reliability of the Teacher Temperament Questionnaire. *Journal of Abnormal Child Psychology, 10*(4), 531–546.
Bates, J. E. (1986). The measurement of temperament. In R. Plomin and J. Dunn (Eds.), *The study of temperament: Changes, continuities and challenges* (pp. 1–11). Hillsdale, NJ: Erlbaum.
Bates, J. (1989). Concepts and measures of temperament. In G. A. Kohnstamm, J. E. Bates, & M. K. Rothbart (Eds.), *Temperament in Childhood* (pp. 3–26). New York: Wiley.
Bates, J., Freeland, C., & Lounsbury, M. (1979). Measurement of infant difficultness. *Child Development, 50*, 794–803.
Bell, R. Q. (1974). Contributions of human infants to caregiving and social interaction. In M. Lewis & L. A. Rosenblum (Eds.), *The effect of the infant on its caregiver* (pp. 1–19). New York: Wiley.
Billman, J., & McDevitt, S. C. (1980). Convergence of parent and observer ratings of temperament with observations of peer interaction in nursery school. *Child Development, 51*(2), 395–400.

Bohlin, G., Hagekull, B., & Lindhagen, K. (1981). Dimensions of infant behavior. *Infant Behavior and Development, 4*, 83–96.
Brazelton, T. B. (1973). *Neonatal behavioral assessment scale.* London: Statistics International Medical Publications.
Buss, A. H., & Plomin, R. (1975). *A temperament theory of personality.* New York: Wiley.
Buss, A. H., & Plomin, R. (1984). *Temperament: Early developing personality traits.* Hillsdale, NJ: Erlbaum.
Buss, A. H., Plomin, R., & Willerman, L. (1973). The inheritance of temperament. *Journal of Personality, 41*, 513–524.
Carey, W. B. (1970). A simplified method for measuring infant temperament. *Journal of Pediatrics, 77*(2), 188–194.
Carey, W. B. (1982). Clinical use of temperament data in pediatrics. In R. Porter & G. M. Collins (Eds.), Temperament differences in infants and young children. CIBA Foundation Symposium No. 85. London: Pitman.
Carey, W. B., & McDevitt, S. C. (1978). Revision of the Infant Temperament Questionnaire. *Pediatrics 61*(5), 735–739.
Dunn, J., & Kendrick, C. (1980). The arrival of a sibling: Changes in patterns of interaction between mother and first-born child. *Journal of Child Psychology and Psychiatry, 21*(2), 119–132.
Fullard, W., McDevitt, S. C., & Carey, W. B. (1978). *The Toddler Temperament Scale.* Unpublished manuscript. Temple University, Philadelphia.
Garside, R. F., Birch, H., Scott, D. M., Chambers, S., Kolvin, I., Tweedle, E. G., & Barber, L. M. (1975). Dimensions of temperament in infant school children. *Journal of Child Psychology and Psychiatry, 16*(3), 219–231.
Goldsmith, H. H., Buss, A. H., Plomin, R., Rothbart, M. K., Thomas, A., Chess, S., Hinde, R. A., & McCall, R. B. (1987). Roundtable: What is temperament? Four approaches. *Child Development, 58*(2), 505–529.
Goldsmith, H. H., & Campos, J. J. (1982). Toward a theory of infant temperament. In R. M. Emde & R. J. Harmon (Eds.), *The development of attachment and affiliation systems* (pp. 161–193). New York: Plenum.
Goldsmith, H. H., & Campos, J. J. (1986). Fundamental issues in the study of early temperament: The Denver twin temperament study. In M. E. Lamb & A. L. Brown (Eds.), *Advances in developmental psychology* (pp. 231–283). Hillsdale, NJ: Erlbaum.
Goldsmith, H., & Rieser-Danner, L. A. (1986). Variation among temperament theories and validation studies of temperament assessment. In G. A. Kohnstamm (Ed.), *Temperament discussed: Temperament and development in infancy and childhood.* University of Leiden, the Netherlands.
Haar, E., Welkowitz, J., Blau, A., & Cohen, J. (1964). Personality differentiation of neonates. *American Academy of Child Psychiatry, 3*, 330–342.
Hagekull, B., Lindhagen, K., & Bohlin, G. (1980). Behavioral dimensions in one year olds and dimensional stability in infancy. *International Journal of Behavioral Development, 3*, 351–364.
Hall, R. J., & Cadwell, J. (1984, April). *Temperament influences on cognition and achievement in children with learning problems.* Paper presented at the annual conference of the American Educational Research Association, New Orleans.
Hegvik, R. L. (1984, October). *Three year longitudinal study of temperament variables, academic achievement and sex differences.* Paper presented at the St. Louis Conference on Temperament in the Educational Process, St. Louis.
Hegvik, R. L., McDevitt, S. C., & Carey, W. B. (1982). The Middle Childhood Temperament Questionnaire. *Developmental and Behavioral Pediatrics, 3*(4), 197–200.

Hubert, N. C., Wachs, T. D., Peters-Martin, P., & Gandour, M. J. (1982). The study of early temperament: Measurement and conceptual issues. *Child Development, 53*(3), 571–600.
Keogh, B. K. (1989). Applying temperament research to school. In G. A. Kohnstamm, J. E. Bates, & M. K. Rothbart (Eds.), *Temperament in Childhood* (pp. 437–450). New York: Wiley.
Keogh, B. K. (1982). Children's temperament and teachers' decisions. In R. Porter & G. M. Collins (Eds.), *Temperamental differences in infants and young children* (pp. 269–279). CIBA Foundation Symposium 89. London: Pitman.
Keogh, B. K. (1986). Temperament and schooling: What is the meaning of goodness of fit? In J. V. Lerner & R. M. Lerner (Eds.), *Temperament and social interaction during infancy and childhood. New directions for child development.* San Francisco: Jossey-Bass.
Keogh, B. K., & Burstein, N. D. (1988). Relationship of temperament to preschooler's interactions with peers and teachers. *Exceptional Children, 54*(5), 456–461.
Keogh, B. K., & Pullis, M. E. (1980). Temperament influences on the development of exceptional children. In B. K. Keogh (Ed.), *Advances in special education: Vol. 1. Basic constructs and theoretical orientations* (pp. 239–276). Greenwich, CT: JAI Press.
Keogh, B. K., Pullis, M. E., & Cadwell, J. (1980). *Project REACH.* Technical report, University of California, Los Angeles, Graduate School of Education.
Keogh, B. K., Pullis, M. E., & Cadwell, J. (1982). A short form of the Teacher Temperament Questionnaire. *Journal of Educational Measurement, 19*(4), 323–329.
Kornblau, B. (1982). The Teachable Pupil Survey: A technique for assessing teachers' perceptions of pupil attributes. *Psychology in the Schools, 19*(2), 170–174.
Kornblau, B. W., & Keogh, B. K. (1980). Teachers' perceptions and educational decisions. In J. J. Gallagher (Ed.), *New directions for exceptional children* (pp. 89–101). San Francisco: Jossey-Bass.
Lerner, J. V., & Lerner, R. M. (1983). Temperament and adaptation across life: Theoretical and empirical issues. In P. B. Baltes and O. G. Brim, Jr. (Eds.), *Life-span development and behavior* (Vol. 5, pp. 197–231). New York: Academic Press.
Lerner, J. V., Lerner, R. M., & Zabski, S. (1985). Temperament and elementary school children's actual and rated academic performance: A test of a "goodness of fit" model. *Journal of Child Psychology and Psychiatry, 26*(1), 125–136.
Lerner, R. M. (1982) Children and adolescents as producers of their own development. *Developmental Review, 2*(4), 342–370.
Lerner, R. M., Palmero, M., Spiro, A., III, & Nesselroade, J. R. (1982). Assessing the dimensions of temperamental individuality across the life-span: The Dimensions of Temperament Survey (DOTS). *Child Development, 53*(1), 149–159.
Martin, R. P. (1988). *The Temperament Assessment Battery for Children.* Brandon, VT: Clinical Psychology Publishing.
Martin, R. P., Nagle, R., & Paget, K. (1983). Relationships between temperament and classroom behavior, teacher attitudes, and academic achievement. *Journal of Psychoeducational Assessment, 1*(4), 377–386.
Martin, R., & Pfeffer, J. (1980, March). *A report on an item analysis, reliability and validity study of the Thomas, Chess and Korn Temperament Questionnaire—Parent Form—For Children Age Three to Seven Years of Age.* Report #2. Unpublished manuscript. University of Georgia, Athens, GA.
Maziade, M., Cote, R., Boutin, P., Boudreault, M. D., & Thivierge, J. (1986). The effect of temperament on longitudinal academic achievement in primary school. *Journal of the American Academy of Child Psychiatry, 25*(5), 692–696.
McDevitt, S. C., & Carey, W. B. (1978). The measurement of temperament in 3 to 7 year old children. *Journal of Child Psychology and Psychiatry, 19*(3), 245–253.

McNeil, T. F. (1976). *Temperament revisited: A research-oriented critique of the New York longitudinal Study of temperament.* Unpublished manuscript. University of Lund, Malmo, Sweden.

Mehrabian, A., & Falander, C. (1978). A questionnaire measure of individual differences in child stimulus screening. *Educational and Psychological Measurement, 38,* 1119–1127.

Paget, K. D., Nagle, R. J., & Martin, R. P. (1984). Interrelationships between temperament characteristics and first-grade teacher-student interactions. *Journal of Abnormal Child Psychology, 12*(4), 547–560.

Persson-Blennow, I., & McNeil, T. (1979). A questionnaire for measurement of temperament in six-month-old infants: development and standardization. *Journal of Child Psychology and Psychiatry and Allied Disciplines, 20,* 1–13.

Persson-Blennow, I., & McNeil, T. (1980). Questionnaire for measurement of temperament in one and two year old children. *Journal of Child Psychology and Psychiatry, 21,* 37–46.

Pfeffer, J., & Martin, R. P. (1983). Comparison of mothers' and fathers' temperament ratings of referred and nonreferred preschool children. *Journal of Clinical Psychology, 39*(6), 1013–1020.

Pullis, M. E. (1979). *An investigation of the relationship between children's temperament and school adjustment.* Unpublished doctoral dissertation. University of California, Los Angeles.

Pullis, M., & Cadwell, J. (1982). The influence of children's temperament characteristics on teachers' decision strategies. *American Educational Research Journal, 19*(2), 165–181.

Rothbart, M. K. (1981). Measurement of temperament in infancy. *Child Development, 52*(2), 569–578.

Rothbart, M. K., & Derryberry, D. (1981). Development of individual differences in temperament. In M. E. Lamb & A. L. Brown (Eds.), *Advances in developmental psychology* (Vol. 1, pp. 37–86). Hillsdale, NJ: Erlbaum.

Rothbart, M. K., & Goldsmith, H. H. (1985). Three approaches to the study of infant temperament. *Developmental Review 5*(3), 237–260.

Rowe, D. C., & Plomin, R. (1977). Temperament in early childhood. *Journal of Personality Assessment, 41,* 150–156.

Rutter, M. (1977). Individual differences. In M. Rutter & L. Hersov (Eds.), *Child Psychiatry: Modern approaches.* Oxford: Blackwell Scientific Publications.

Rutter, M. (1982). Temperament: Concepts, issues and problems. In R. Porter & G. M. Collins (Eds.), *Temperamental differences in infants and young children* (pp. 1–19). CIBA Foundation Symposium 89. London: Pitman.

Sameroff, A. J., & Chandler, M. J. (1975). Reproductive risk and the continuum of caretaking causality. In F. D. Horowitz, S. Scarr-Salapatek, & G. Siegel (Eds.), *Review of child development research* (Vol. 4, pp. 187–244). Chicago: University of Chicago Press.

Scarr, S., & McCartney, K. (1983). How people make their own environments: A theory of genotype-environment effects. *Child Development, 54,* 424–435.

Shavelson, R. J. (1976). Teachers' decision making. In N. L. Gage (Ed.), *The psychology of teaching methods: The seventy-fifth yearbook of the national society for the study of education, 75*(1), 372–414.

Skuy, M., Snell, D., & Westaway, M. (1985). Temperament and the scholastic achievement and adjustment of black South African children. *South African Journal of Education, 5*(4), 197–202.

Super, C. M., & Harkness, S. (1986). Temperament, development and culture. In R. Plomin & J. Dunn, (Eds.), *The Study of Temperament: Changes, Continuities and Challenges* (pp. 131–149). Hillsdale, NJ: Erlbaum.

Thomas, A., & Chess, S. (1977). *Temperament and development*. New York: Brunner/Mazel.
Thomas, A., Chess, S., & Birch, H. G. (1968). *Temperament and behavior disorders in children*. New York: New York University Press.
Thomas, A., Chess, S., Birch, H. G., Hertzig, M. E., & Korn, S. (1963). *Behavioral individuality in early childhood*. New York: New York University Press.
van de Werfhost, H. (1986). Temperament and teacher-child interaction. In G. A. Kohnstamm (Ed.), *Temperament discussed: Temperament and development in infancy and childhood* (pp. 141–146). Leiden, the Netherlands: University of Leiden.
Windle, M., & Lerner, R. M. (1986a). Reassessing the dimensions of temperamental individuality across the life span: The Revised Dimensions of Temperament Survey (DOTS-R). *Journal of Adolescent Research, 1*(2), 213–230.
Windle, M., & Lerner, R. M. (1986b). The "goodness of fit" model of temperament-context relations: Interaction or correlation?" In J. V. Lerner & R. M. Lerner (Eds.), *Temperament and social interaction during infancy and childhood*. New directions for child development. No. 51 (pp. 109–119). San Francisco: Jossey-Bass.

PART III

Assessment and Intervention

CHAPTER 15

Cognitive–Behavioral Assessment and Intervention
CLAYTON E. KELLER

Cognitive–behavioral psychology, with its emphases on an individual's behaviors and thoughts, and the control the latter can have on the former, has developed as a potent approach to the treatment of personal, social, and academic problems. (See Hughes & Hall, 1989, and Kendall & Hollon, 1979, for reviews of the variety of problems that have been addressed by cognitive–behavioral methods.) This approach has been particularly successful with students with learning disabilities, for instance in the areas of increasing attention to task (Hallahan et al., 1983) and improving computational skills (Keller & Lloyd, 1989; Lloyd & Keller, 1989). Indeed a cognitive–behavioral approach fits well with orientations that emphasize the importance of cognitive and metacognitive deficits in individuals with learning disabilities (Hallahan, Kauffman, & Lloyd, 1985; Wong, 1985), as it specifically targets those deficits.

Within a cognitive–behavioral approach, assessment is especially intertwined with intervention. Some cognitive–behavioral techniques, such as self-monitoring, when used for assessment purposes, can also produce changes in behavior. On the one hand, such a result indicates one of the strengths of a cognitive–behavioral approach, namely that such relatively simple procedures can produce powerful effects. On the other hand, it makes it difficult at times to separate the parts cognitive–behavioral procedures play (Shapiro, 1984).

But separate assessment purposes of cognitive-behavioral procedures can be identified. Kendall (1981) summarized several purposes for assessing cognitions. First, the assessment of covert cognitive phenomena can provide information about their relationships to overt behaviors. Second, cognitive–behavioral assessment can provide information on how problems and coping methods develop within individuals. And, as a third purpose, Kendall suggests that cognitive–behavioral assessment can confirm both the effects of interventions designed to change an individual's cognitions and the treatment mechanism hypothesized by the intervention. All of these assessment functions are pertinent to researchers and practitioners working with individuals with learning disabilities as they lead to a better understanding both of these individuals and of ways to improve their functioning.

The purpose of this chapter is to examine cognitive–behavioral assessment techniques that have been used or would be promising to use with learning-disabled individuals. I start with a summary of a framework for conducting cognitive–behavioral assessments. I then review a variety of cognitive–behavioral methods that provide assessment information about individuals' cognitive and metacognitive abilities and processes. And I conclude with a discussion of some of the concerns with using a cognitive–behavioral method for assessment and the implications of those concerns for the assessment of learning-disabled persons.

A FRAMEWORK FOR COGNITIVE–BEHAVIORAL ASSESSMENT

Meichenbaum (1977), an important figure in the field of cognitive–behavioral psychology, suggests a cognitive functional approach as a framework for cognitive–behavioral assessment. Paralleling the behaviorist idea of examining the functional relationships among behaviors, their antecedents, and their consequences, a cognitive functional approach is also concerned with these relationships but emphasizes the role of cognitions as antecedents and consequences.

A purpose of assessment in this approach is to identify the cognitions that are involved in the functional relationships, particularly the types of cognitions that occur naturally in the relationships and the frequency with which they appear. Assessment can also manipulate the events surrounding the chain of cognitions and behaviors to examine the causal or functional connections better.

Meichenbaum suggests three types of manipulations. One is to modify the assessment or performance task in such a way that the psychological demands of the task are changed. Changing the modality of the task, providing more salient cues, and speeding up performance are examples of this type of modification. A second manipulation is to alter environmental variables that are not involved in the assessment task, such as reducing distracting stimuli or the individual's anxiety. A third manipulation is to provide the person with supports within the task (e.g., memory prompts or time to take notes) or the instructions that precede the task. The purpose of this third type of manipulation is similar to the format taken by dynamic assessments based on Vygotsky's (1986) zone of proximal development.

Akin again to a behavioral approach, a cognitive functional approach views each individual as an experiment, and the assessor takes on the role of hypothesis generator, trying to determine what cognitions are missing that will help the individual with the task and/or what cognitions are interfering with behavior. This individual orientation is especially important given the heterogeneity of the learning-disabled population.

Within a cognitive functional framework, an assessor can use a variety of methods to discover the relationships between cognitions and behavior. I now review some of those techniques.

COGNITIVE–BEHAVIORAL ASSESSMENT METHODS

Researchers have developed many techniques to gain access to an individual's covert processes when assessing cognitive strategies and metacognitive abilities or when monitoring the progress of cognitive–behavioral interventions. One way of organizing this diverse collection of methods is to consider two dimensions that are present in all of these techniques: (a) the producer of the information that forms the basis of the assessment, and (b) at what point, relative to a specific event or task, that information is produced (for this last dimension, Ericsson & Simon, 1980; Harris, 1985). Table 15-1 provides an outline of combinations of these dimensions for assessment techniques and a listing of the techniques that have been investigated and that will be reviewed in this section.

In this section I describe each of these cognitive–behavioral assessment methods, review use of the method in one or more studies, and summarize reliability and validity information for the method if it is available. Not all of these techniques have been used with learning-disabled individuals. I still include these methods because they provide unique perspectives and types of information for the difficult task of assessing covert cognitive processes, and thus represent important tools for the study of learning disabilities.

Table 15-1. Cognitive–Behavioral Assessment Techniques

I. Production by subject
  A. Before an event
    1. *Predictions*
  B. Concurrent with an event
    1. *Think aloud*
    2. *Cognition sampling*
  C. Retrospective to an event
    1. *Stimulated recall*
    2. *Interview/inventory*
    3. *Judgment*
    4. *Thought listing*
  D. Independent of a particular event
    1. *Rating scales/questionnaires*
    2. *Interview*
II. Production by others
  A. Concurrent with an event
    1. *Observations*
  B. Independent of a particular event
    1. *Rating scales*

ASSESSMENT METHODS IN WHICH THE SUBJECT PRODUCES THE INFORMATION

In most cognitive–behavioral assessment techniques, the subject of the assessment or intervention produces the cognitive information—thoughts, ideas, decisions, or strategies—that is to be collected. The techniques vary, though, in terms of when the information is collected relative to the individual's performance of a task or involvement in an event.

Methods Occurring Before the Task or Event

Researchers have asked subjects to make *predictions* about their performance in an upcoming task as a way of assessing the individuals' metacognitive knowledge about their own abilities. The individuals look at the task and make a judgment about how well they think they will do. They usually then perform the task, and their predictions are compared with their performance. (Often they are asked afterward how well they thought they did; see the *judgment* method later.) The inference behind this approach is that the individuals evaluate the demands of the task relative to some internal state of knowledge, feelings, or whatever they choose before predicting. Greater congruence between the prediction and the actual performance represents more knowledge about abilities (Keller, 1988). This prediction technique has been used in several studies with learning-disabled individuals. Loper (Experiments 1 and 2, 1984) showed nonsense words, one at a time, to learning-disabled students, and asked them to decide if they thought they could pronounce each. The students were to answer "yes," if they were sure they could pronounce the word, "maybe," if they were unsure, and "no," if they could not, reflecting a range of confidence in their decoding abilities. Slife, Weiss, and Bell (1985) showed elementary school students with learning disabilities 10 arithmetic problems, all of the same type, for 10 seconds, then asked them to predict how many they would answer correctly. A variation of this task was used by Keller (1988). And Schunk has asked students, either with learning disabilities (Schunk & Cox, 1986) or with low achievement in math (Schunk, 1981, 1982/1983), to judge their efficacy for solving arithmetic problems. The students briefly viewed sample pairs of problems. For each pair of problems they rated, on a scale from 10 to 100, how sure they were about being able to solve the problems correctly. Schunk and Cox (1986) report a test–retest reliability coefficient of 0.82 for this self-efficacy test from another study (Bandura & Schunk, 1981).

Methods Concurrent With the Task or Event

Often a researcher wants to know what an individual is thinking while involved in a task. Several methods have been used to collect these ongoing thoughts and decisions; the approaches vary in terms of whether they try to collect all relevant cognitions or only a sample of them.

Collecting All Cognitions. Simply asking the person to *think aloud* while working on a task is the main technique for collecting all relevant cognitions. The approach assumes that what the person verbalizes is what the individual is thinking, an assumption that may not always be justified as, for example, the person may not have access to the actual cognitions used in the task (Ericsson & Simon, 1980), may be saying what he or she thinks the researcher wants to hear, or may be slowing down the flow of internal, self-talk (Kendall & Hollon, 1981a). There is also the possibility that the added demand of verbalizing thoughts may affect or alter performance on the task. Keeping these cautions in mind, though, thinking aloud does represent a strong technique for gathering cognitions close in time to performance.

Thinking aloud procedures have been used for different assessment purposes. Harris (1986a) asked grade-school students with learning disabilities to think aloud while trying to solve a rigged puzzle to determine the extent to which they used task-relevant self-verbalizations or private speech. There was high reliability in identifying private versus social speech ($r = 0.98$) and in categorizing private speech into that which was task-relevant and that which was task-irrelevant ($r = 0.99$ for both).

Blackwell, Galassi, Galassi, and Watson's (1985) use of a think aloud procedure with college students solving math problems allowed them to see what cognitions were used during the solution process. Interrater agreement was high for both dividing transcriptions of these cognitions into units (97%) and categorizing the cognitions (96%). The Written Calculation and Informal Skills sections of the *Diagnostic Test of Arithmetic Strategies* (DTAS; Ginsburg & Mathews, 1984), by asking the student to explain out loud how he or she is solving the problem, also reveal the processes an individual uses during these tasks. The examiner is to categorize the strategies the student uses. The DTAS manual reports no reliability or interrater agreement figures for categorizing these strategies (Aleamoni, 1985). Keller (1988), in a study using the addition and subtraction subtests of the DTAS, had acceptable interrater agreement figures for categorizing addition strategies (88%), subtraction strategies (78%), and subtraction number fact errors (73%), but not for addition number fact errors or addition and subtraction "slips." The difficulties reliably classifying some of these aspects may have resulted from the low frequencies of their occurrences in his study.

Finally, researchers have also used think aloud methods to assess whether students have learned and are using interventions. Roberts, Nelson, and Olson (1987) measured whether their first- and second-grade students stated out loud all the self-instructions they had been taught for solving missing number problems by monitoring their statements with a checklist of strategy components. Whitman and Johnston (1983) rated the mastery of their educable mentally retarded students' use of a set of self-instructions for addition problems with regrouping by audiotaping, and then rating, the use of self-instructions while solving problems, both at the end of training and during data collection. Interrater agreement was high in both situations.

Collecting a Sample of Cognitions. Another method for collecting at-the-moment cognitions is to cue an individual to respond to a specific question or to record whatever is on his or her mind at random points within a period of time. The assumption behind *sampling methods* is that the random samples of cognitions will provide a representative picture of the cognitions of interest during the time period (Kendall & Hollon, 1981a). Sampling methods hold the possibility of less distortion of task performance than do think aloud methods and are especially appropriate when the cognitions of interest are focused and specific. Also, some sampling methods, such as self-monitoring of attention, not only assess cognitions but also produce changes in behavior. As Shapiro (1984) has noted, it is often difficult to distinguish between these two functions of the technique.

With sampling methods, the cueing can be either externally or internally generated, and the questions asked can be focused or general. For example, in a study by Hurlburt (1979), college students carried a portable electronic device that randomly generated signals. When cued by these signals, the students were to write in a notebook their thought at that moment. Similarly, Larson and Lampman-Petraitis (1989) used electronic pagers to cue children's and adolescents' reporting of their emotional state. In contrast, subjects have been trained to ask themselves specific questions (e.g., "Was I paying attention?") whenever they think of it (Broden, Hall, & Mitts, 1971). In another variation, Glynn and his colleagues used randomly presented signals on an audiotape to cue students to self-record on-task behavior (Glynn & Thomas, 1974; Glynn, Thomas, & Shee, 1973).

An extensive series of investigations of the effectiveness of this version of self-monitoring (a combination of self-assessment and self-recording) as an educational intervention was conducted by Hallahan, Lloyd, and their colleagues at the University of Virginia Learning Disabilities Research Institute (see Hallahan et al., 1983; Hallahan, Kneedler, & Lloyd, 1982; and Kneedler & Hallahan, 1984, for summaries of this research). As an intervention, self-monitoring of attention during academic work leads to improvements in attention and increases in academic productivity (Hallahan et al., 1982). As a method for assessing students' judgments about their attention, the Virginia research examined which components of the process are necessary and had these conclusions (Hallahan et al., 1982):

1. Cueing to record is necessary in the beginning but students can later be weaned from it.
2. Recording is necessary in the beginning too but can also be removed later (though then, for assessment purposes, there is no record of the students' judgments).
3. Successful use of the procedure often does not need to be externally reinforced.

The technique has been tried during independent classwork and small-group instruction (Hallahan et al., 1982), and in general education classrooms (Rooney, Hallahan, & Lloyd, 1984). The self-monitoring of attention procedure has also been used successfully by other researchers (e.g., Harris, 1986b).

Methods Used Retrospectively to an Event or After Completion of a Task

As a way to assess cognitions during a task without altering the task by thinking out loud or disrupting the task to respond to a cue, researchers can ask individuals to recall what they were thinking during the task *after* it is completed. In addition, retrospective techniques can be used in situations in which it would be impractical or unethical to use other methods to collect similar information. For example, teachers or students could not be asked to use the think aloud method to assess their thoughts during a reading lesson, but they could recall their cognitions once the lesson was over. These techniques, though, by being removed in time from when the cognitions occurred, risk inaccurate or incomplete recall of thoughts.

Guiding Recall of Cognitions. Given the difficulties in accurately recalling what one was thinking during a task or event some time in the past, researchers have developed several techniques to guide or prime this process.

One such method is called *stimulated recall*, which involves audiotaping or, more commonly, videotaping an episode or event, then playing all or portions of the tape to stimulate the person's remembrance of thoughts in that situation (Clark & Peterson, 1986). The researcher can ask questions about the person's cognitions at particular moments during the situation or the individual can stop the tape to explain what he or she was thinking at the time.

For example, Peterson and Swing (1982; Peterson, Swing, Braverman, & Buss, 1982) videotaped a direct instruction math lesson, then used a structured interview to ask fifth- and sixth-grade students what they were doing or thinking during the lesson. The students' responses were coded into five major categories: attending, understanding, reasons for not understanding, cognitive strategies that aided understanding, and perceptions of teaching processes. The researchers reported estimated generalizability coefficients of the codings ranging from 0.73 to 1.00.

A research project on mainstreaming (Hallahan, McNergney, & McKinney, 1989) used stimulated recall techniques in case studies of effective teachers of mainstreamed classrooms. The researchers showed the teachers segments of videotaped lessons when the teachers were interacting with mainstreamed, learning-disabled students; the teachers could also stop the tapes. The teachers explained what they were doing and why. These same segments were later shown separately to the mainstreamed students and nondisabled peers in the classrooms and they were asked their thoughts about the events or teachers' actions. In one case study (Herbert & Keller, 1989), for instance, both students seemed to understand the teacher's intentions to varying degrees, though the nondisabled student was more accurate in his interpretations than was the learning-disabled student.

Another approach to guiding recall of cognitive information is simply to *interview* the individual. The questions asked can be open-ended, like Harris' (1986b) social validation questions in a study of self-monitoring of attention and self-monitoring of productivity. At the end of the study, the learning-disabled students and their teacher answered questions about their preferences for the interventions, their opinions of the interventions' efficacy, and recommendations or feedback. Ghatala, Levin, Pressley, and Lodico (1985) asked second-graders open-ended questions about how they remembered more pairs of words in one list and why they used certain strategies. In addition, they also asked closed or forced-choice questions in their interviews, such as showing the students four strategies and asking them which they used to remember a pair of words or asking them which of three reasons explains why they used a particular strategy.

Asking an individual to make a *judgment* after his or her performance on a task, while not directly asking for the cognitions that occurred during the task, represents still another type of guided recall retrospective to an event. It may be, though, that individuals make their judgments based on cognitions such as feelings or thought processes that were present during the task. The judgment technique is often seen in conjunction with the prediction approach mentioned earlier and has been used to assess the metacognitive skill of monitoring performance.

Several studies have used this technique with learning-disabled students. In Loper's second experiment (1984), learning-disabled students evaluated their performance right after decoding each word in the task. The three choices were: they were definitely sure they read the word correctly, they were unsure, or they thought they did not read the word correctly. Keller (1988) used a similar procedure with addition and subtraction computation problems. And, learning-disabled students in Slife et al.'s study (1985) identified which of the 10 math problems were correct and which incorrect after they completed the set of problems.

Unguided Recall of Cognitions. One of the most common ways to collect retrospectively an individual's cognitions during a task or event in an unguided fashion is simply to ask the individual to list his or her thoughts or thoughts that were typical at that time (Kendall & Hollon, 1981a). Such *thought listings* then need to be unitized and categorized in some way.

Blackwell et al. (1985) used thought listing as one of their two assessment methods for having college students generate their thoughts while solving math problems (thinking aloud, described earlier, was the other). When using this method, they reminded the students to "Remember to write down everything you thought about in the order in which it occurred" (p. 402) right after solving the problem and without looking at the problem. They included this last instruction to avoid having the problem influence or affect the recalled cognitions. As with the thinking aloud procedure, coders could unitize and categorize these thoughts with high levels of interrater agreement.

Methods Independent of Any Particular Event

There are several types of assessment techniques that collect information about cognitions from individuals independent of performance in a particular situation. By focusing on the assessment of cognitions across situations, they provide information that is more general in nature, such as metacognitive knowledge or a measure of self-control. These approaches are also more amenable to standards of instrument development; they thus carry the potential of appropriate levels of reliability and validity. For these reasons, such methods can be valuable tools in the assessment of learning-disabled individuals and provide a more stable picture off which to reflect information about cognitions in particular situations.

Rating scales and *questionnaires* are two examples of approaches that can elicit from individuals information about cognitions across situations. The formats follow those typical for rating scales and questionnaires, yet the content of the instruments is cognitively or metacognitively oriented. For instance, Humphrey (1982) developed the Children's Perceived Self-Control Scale (CPSCS). The CPSCS is a rating scale consisting of 11 items based on a cognitive–behavioral model of self-control. A principal components analysis yielded four factors: Interpersonal Self-Control, Personal Self-Control, Self-Evaluation, and Consequential Thinking. Test–retest reliabilities ranged from 0.56 to 0.63 for the first three factors and was 0.71 for the total scale; the reliability for Consequential Thinking was 0.18, so this factor was discarded. Ratings by individual children were correlated with teachers' ratings of the children's self-control. They were also correlated with class means of classroom observations, but not with observations of individual children.

Peterson and Swing (1982; Peterson et al., 1982) developed a cognitive process questionnaire as a method in addition to stimulated recall to assess student thought processes during a particular math lesson and during other math lessons over the school year; the instrument has potential for use in other studies. The questionnaire has three subscales: Attending, Monitoring Understanding, and Specific Cognitive Strategies. Students respond on a 5-point scale ranging from "usually" to "almost never" and "don't know." The internal consistency of the Monitoring Understanding subscale is low ($\alpha = 0.22$), but acceptable for the other two subscales ($\alpha = 0.65$) and for the questionnaire as a whole ($\alpha = 0.71$).

Interviews can also be structured in such a way as to provide more general information about cognition. Zimmerman and Pons (1986) developed a structured interview about self-regulated learning strategies. For each of six learning contexts, described by a concrete example, high-school students described the methods they used in the context to participate, study, and complete assignments. If the student provided more than one method for a context, he or she rated how consistently the method was used. Coders categorized the methods into one of 15 groups (14 self-regulated learning strategies and an "other" category) with a good level of agreement (86%).

Englert, Raphael, Fear, and Anderson (1988) used vignettes of students having writing difficulties as the foundation for a structured interview assessing students' metacognitive knowledge about the writing process and text organization. Students in their study, including fourth- and fifth-grade learning-disabled students, were asked to give advice to the students in the vignettes. The researchers felt the focus on the tasks in the vignettes would be a better stimulus for producing statements reflecting metacognitive abilities than would other assessment methods, such as thinking aloud or retrospective reporting. Coders ranked responses to particular questions on a scale from 0, meaning no knowledge or understanding of the component of the writing process, to 3 for high knowledge. Agreement between two coders was above 80%.

ASSESSMENT METHODS IN WHICH SOMEONE OTHER THAN THE SUBJECT PRODUCES THE INFORMATION

While generally the subject of an assessment or intervention produces the information about cognitions, there are examples of techniques where an observer or someone who knows the person well provides the information. Granted these other individuals do not have access to the internal thought processes of the subject, they nevertheless can provide information from a different perspective, which can complement or validate information obtained directly from the person. These techniques can also be categorized by when the information is collected relative to a task or event.

Methods Concurrent With a Task or Event

The assessment method most commonly used by someone other than the subject during performance on a task or participation in an event is direct *observation*. While following standard procedures for direct observations, the focus or content of the observations changes in this situation to accommodate the covert nature of cognitions. Observations target behaviors that are seen as indicators of covert cognitive activity or of a cognitive ability.

Stevenson and Fantuzzo (1984) observed fifth-grade students to see if the students accurately used a self-control procedure that they were taught that involved self-determination and self-administration of reinforcement. The students were observed during training and treatment conditions. Observers used a behavioral checklist that contained definitions of each step in the procedure. Interobserver agreement ranged from 92% to 97%. Stevenson and Fantuzzo's method for assessing accuracy of intervention use is similar in function to the procedures used by Roberts et al. (1987) and Whitman and Johnston (1983) described in the thinking aloud section, the difference being that Stevenson and Fantuzzo relied on behaviors for their information while Roberts and his colleagues and Whitman and Johnston used verbalizations.

Humphrey (1982) used observations of children doing independent, unsupervised work during reading as one method to validate her self-control scales, the children's version of which (the CPSCS) was discussed earlier. Behaviors that operationalized self-control were "goal-directed solitary or social work during those unsupervised assignments" (p. 626) while self-control transgressions were indicated by task-irrelevant behavior, either solitary or social. The observers used a 10-second interval recording system. Overall interobserver agreement across all of the behavior categories was 87%, while agreement for individual categories ranged from 62% to 92%.

Methods Independent of Any Particular Event

Rating scales that are completed by someone who knows the individual well are another important assessment method for collecting information about cognitive or metacognitive abilities across situations. They are especially useful in situations in which the individuals, for age or whatever reason, cannot produce information about cognitions through self-report methods, such as thinking aloud or thought listing (McMahon, 1984). The raters, usually parents or teachers when children are the subjects, see the individuals in many situations and settings, and thus can examine the construct of interest based on a large accumulation of information. However, this benefit also increases the chances for sources of bias to affect the information in the ratings. Sources of bias, such as illusory correlations, difficulties assessing covariation, confirmatory bias, and the overreliance on the availability or representativeness of an event (Achenbach, 1985), are always a risk in making judgments.

There are two rating scales in particular that are valuable for the assessment of cognitive–behavioral abilities in learning-disabled individuals. One instrument is the Self-Control Rating Scale (SCRS; Kendall & Wilcox, 1979). Kendall and Wilcox designed the SCRS both to study the construct of self-control and to evaluate the effects and generalization of interventions to increase self-control (Kendall, Pellegrini, & Urbain, 1981). Teachers and parents, using a 7-point scale, rate items describing self-control, impulsivity, or both characteristics. The SCRS has high internal consistency as measured by Cronbach's alpha (0.98) and shows good test–retest reliability over a three-to-four-week period (0.84). Kendall et al. (1981) cite evidence to suggest that the SCRS is sensitive to treatment effects, yet note that changes in the SCRS need to be related to changes in behaviors.

The other instrument is Humphrey's (1982) Teacher's Self-Control Rating Scale (TSCRS). Humphrey's scale was based on Kendall and Wilcox's (1979) SCRS but is briefer (15 items versus 33 on the SCRS), uses a 5-point rating scale instead of a 7-point scale, and is based on a model of self-control (Karoly, 1977) comprised of problem recognition, commitment, protracted self-regulation, and habit reorganization. The TSCRS also parallels the content of Humphrey's Children's Perceived Self-Control Scale (CPSCS) discussed earlier. Principal components analysis showed two factors in the TSCRS: Cognitive/Personal Self-Control and Behavioral/Interpersonal Self-Control. The TSCRS and the two subscales based on the factors showed good test–retest reliability over a two-to-three-week period. The teacher ratings of self-control generally correlated with individual child ratings and with observations of the individual children during unsupervised, independent reading work (the observation technique described in the previous section).

SUMMARY

This review of cognitive–behavioral assessment methods, while discussing a wide variety of techniques that have been used or could be used with learning-disabled individuals to collect cognitive information for assessment and intervention purposes, is not exhaustive. (See Kendall & Hollon, 1981b, and Ollendick & Hersen, 1984a, for discussions of other types of methods, and specific examples of those methods, for assessing cognitive–behavioral knowledge and abilities.) Yet it highlights the potential richness of information about the cognitions of learning-disabled individuals that can be obtained, a richness that can add an important component to our understanding of these individuals and this condition.

METHODOLOGICAL CONCERNS AND THEIR IMPLICATIONS FOR ASSESSMENT

In conjunction with the potential held by cognitive–behavioral assessment methods are methodological concerns or issues about the use of these methods. I discuss three concerns in this section as examples of the types of problems faced by cognitive–behavioral assessment methods: accuracy of the assessed information, effects of the techniques on cognitive processes, and comparability of assessment methods. (See Ericsson & Simon, 1980; Harris, 1985; Kendall & Hollon, 1981b; McMahon, 1984; Nelson, 1977; and Shapiro, 1984, for discussions of other methodological issues facing this assessment approach in general and specific assessment techniques.)

ACCURACY OF INFORMATION

One issue that cognitive–behavioral assessment methods face is whether the obtained information about cognitions is accurate. Because the information sought and processes that generate the information are covert, we can never be completely sure that, for example, these are the three steps this individual used to solve the division problem. At best, with some techniques, such as self-monitoring (a form of cognition sampling), we can judge whether an individual's self-assessment agrees with the assessment of an observer. If the learning-disabled student, when cued to assess attention to task, said he or she was on-task and the observer at that same moment saw behaviors that fit the definition of on-task, we would say the assessment information was accurate. If the two sources of information did not agree, we would say the cognitive assessment was inaccurate. Yet this method of determining agreement still falls short of complete confidence about accuracy and is a technique that is not available to all cognitive–behavioral methods (e.g., thought listing or thinking aloud).

Nelson (1977) and Shapiro (1984) have reviewed the literature on factors that increase such agreement type of accuracy for self-monitoring procedures. Some of the more important factors are informing the subject that accuracy of self-monitoring is being assessed, reinforcing accuracy, and training in the assessment technique. (See Nelson, 1977, and Shapiro, 1984, for more complete summaries of the factors.) These factors, particularly the last one, may also be applicable to improving, if not the accuracy, at least the quality of the information obtained through other assessment techniques. In addition, to the extent that multiple sources of data can be used in the assessment of the cognitive area of interest and they provide congruent information, the more assurance we can take in the validity of our assessment (Harris, 1985; Ollendick & Hersen, 1984b).

EFFECTS OF ASSESSMENT TECHNIQUES ON COGNITIVE PROCESSES

Another concern about the use of cognitive–behavioral assessment methods is that the methods may alter the information obtained. That is, instead of collecting information about the cognitive processes of a learning-disabled individual at a given point, the assessment of those processes might actually change the processes as they are affected by the requirement of thinking about them or by being cued in certain ways.

Ericsson and Simon (1980) provide suggestions that may mitigate these effects. In an examination of the nature of verbal reports as data, they posited a model specifying the processes involved when an individual verbalizes information relative to the form of memory (sensory stores, short-term memory, or long-term memory) in which the information is stored. When they reviewed studies involving verbalization methods, such as thought listing and thinking aloud, they concluded that the model's following prediction was supported: "Producing verbal reports of information directly available in propositional form does not change the course and structure of the cognitive processes. However, instructions that require subjects to recode information in order to report it may affect these processes" (p. 235). While these conclusions should be investigated further, they do suggest that cognitive–behavioral assessment methods seeking information from the learning-disabled individual should pose questions or tasks that involve cognitive processes currently in use by the individual if a more direct or unaffected picture is desired.

COMPARABILITY OF ASSESSMENT METHODS

Related to the concern that assessment methods may alter the cognitive processes collected by the assessment, is the question of the comparability of cognitive–behavioral assessment methods. Just as two reading achievement tests should produce somewhat similar results if they are valid measures of reading achievement, should not the various cognitive–behavioral assessment methods collect similar information because their focus—a person's cognitions—is similar?

There are some indications of the validity of cognitive–behavioral assessment methods, for example for the Kendall–Wilcox Self-Control Rating Scale (1979) and Humphrey's (1982) self-control rating scales for children and teachers, which can begin to address questions of comparability. Much more work needs to be done in this area, though, particularly for assessment approaches that are less formalized than rating scales. There is also little research that directly tests the comparability of assessment techniques. Again, much more research is needed, as a study by Blackwell et al. (1985) suggests that methods may not be comparable.

These researchers asked math-anxious college students to think aloud while solving one set of mathematics problems and, after solving another set of problems, to list the thoughts they had during the problem solving. Thought listing took longer and students were more anxious during that assessment procedure. While thinking aloud produced more thoughts in all (about twice as many on the average) and more thoughts in some of the coding categories, particularly those related to processes involved, thought listing produced more thoughts in evaluation categories.

Noncomparability of cognitive–behavioral assessment methods may pose problems for the establishment of adequate psychometric properties for the methods, but it also can contribute to the richness of the assessment process. Each method adds a separate, complementary component to the understanding of an individual's cognitions, similar to the process of triangulation in interpretive research (cf., Erickson, 1986). In terms, then, of the implications for cognitive–behavioral assessments, note the value again of a multiple method approach (Harris, 1985; Ollendick & Hersen, 1984b), not only for dealing with the weaknesses in the collected information but also for adding to the richness of the understanding.

CONCLUSION

Cognitive–behavioral approaches to the assessment of individuals with learning disabilities provide a unique perspective for our understanding of these persons and for the support of interventions to aid them. Many assessment techniques currently exist. Researchers should continue to refine these methods and develop new approaches. Most importantly, they should also study the relationships among the methods and the contributions of the varying techniques to the assessment process, for example, within a cognitive functional assessment framework such as Meichenbaum's (1977). Such research will allow us to use the potential of cognitive–behavioral assessments fully.

REFERENCES

Achenbach, T. M. (1985). *Assessment and taxonomy of child and adolescent psychopathology*. Beverly Hills, CA: Sage.

Aleamoni, L. M. (1985). Review of Diagnostic Test of Arithmetic Strategies. In J. V. Mitchell, Jr. (Ed.), *The ninth mental measurements yearbook* (Vol. 1, pp. 499–500). Lincoln, NE: The Buros Institute of Mental Measurements, The University of Nebraska–Lincoln.

Bandura, A., & Schunk, D. H. (1981). Cultivating competence, self-efficacy, and intrinsic interest through proximal self-motivation. *Journal of Personality and Social Psychology, 41,* 586–598.

Blackwell, R. T., Galassi, J. P., Galassi, M. D., & Watson, T. E. (1985). Are cognitive assessment methods equal? A comparison of think aloud and thought listing. *Cognitive Therapy and Research, 9*, 399–413.

Broden, M., Hall, R. V., & Mitts, B. (1971). The effects of self-recording on the classroom behavior of two eighth-grade students. *Journal of Applied Behavior Analysis, 4*, 191–199.

Clark, C. M., & Peterson, P. L. (1986). Teachers' thought processes. In M. C. Wittrock (Ed.), *Handbook of research on teaching* (3rd ed., pp. 255–296). New York: Macmillan.

Englert, C. S., Raphael, T. E., Fear, K. L., & Anderson, L. M. (1988). Students' metacognitive knowledge about how to write informational texts. *Learning Disability Quarterly, 11*, 18–46.

Erickson, F. (1986). Qualitative methods in research on teaching. In M. C. Wittrock (Ed.), *Handbook of research on teaching* (3rd ed., pp. 119–161). New York: Macmillan.

Ericsson, K. A., & Simon, H. A. (1980). Verbal reports as data. *Psychological Review, 87*, 215–251.

Ghatala, E. S., Levin, J. R., Pressley, M., & Lodico, M. G. (1985). Training cognitive strategy-monitoring in children. *American Educational Research Journal, 22*, 199–215.

Ginsburg, H. P., & Mathews, S. C. (1984). *Diagnostic Test of Arithmetic Strategies.* Austin, TX: PRO-ED.

Glynn, E. L., & Thomas, J. D. (1974). Effect of cueing on self-control of classroom behavior. *Journal of Applied Behavior Analysis, 7*, 299–306.

Glynn, E. L., Thomas, J. D., & Shee, S. M. (1973). Behavioral self-control of on-task behavior in an elementary classroom. *Journal of Applied Behavior Analysis, 6*, 105–113.

Hallahan, D. P., Hall, R. J., Ianna, S. O., Kneedler, R. D., Lloyd, J. W., Loper, A. B., & Reeve, R. E. (1983). Summary of research findings at the University of Virginia Learning Disabilities Research Institute. *Exceptional Education Quarterly, 4*(1), 95–114.

Hallahan, D. P., Kauffman, J. M., & Lloyd, J. W. (1985). *Introduction to learning disabilities* (2nd ed.). Englewood Cliffs, NJ: Prentice Hall.

Hallahan, D. P., Kneedler, R. D., & Lloyd, J. W. (1982). Cognitive behavior modification techniques for learning disabled children: Self-instruction and self-monitoring. In J. D. McKinney & L. Feagans (Eds.), *Current topics in learning disabilities* (Vol. 1, pp. 207–244). New York: Ablex.

Hallahan, D. P., McNergney, R. F., & McKinney, J. D. (1989). *Improving teacher effectiveness with learning-disabled mainstreamed students* (Final Report for Grant No. 6008630227, U.S. Department of Education, Office of Special Education and Rehabilitative Services). Charlottesville: University of Virginia.

Harris, K. R. (1985). Conceptual, methodological, and clinical issues in cognitive–behavioral assessment. *Journal of Abnormal Child Psychology, 13*, 373–390.

Harris, K. R. (1986a). The effects of cognitive-behavior modification on private speech and task performance during problem solving among learning-disabled and normally achieving children. *Journal of Abnormal Child Psychology, 14*, 63–67.

Harris, K. R. (1986b). Self-monitoring of attentional behavior versus self-monitoring of productivity: Effects on on-task behavior and academic response rate among learning disabled children. *Journal of Applied Behavior Analysis, 19*, 417–423.

Herbert, J., & Keller, C. (1989, March). *A case study of an effective teacher in an inner-city mainstreamed classroom.* Paper presented at the annual meeting of the American Educational Research Association, San Francisco, CA.

Hughes, J. N., & Hall, R. J. (Eds.). (1989). *Cognitive–behavioral psychology in the schools: A comprehensive handbook.* New York: Guilford.

Humphrey, L. L. (1982). Children's and teachers' perspectives on children's self-control: The development of two rating scales. *Journal of Consulting and Clinical Psychology, 50,* 624–633.

Hurlburt, R. T. (1979). Random sampling of cognitions and behavior. *Journal of Research in Personality, 13,* 103–111.

Karoly, P. (1977). Behavioral self-management in children: Concepts, methods, issues, and directions. In M. Hersen, R. M. Eisler, & P. M. Miller (Eds.), *Progress in behavior modification* (Vol. 5, pp. 197–262). New York: Academic Press.

Keller, C. E. (1988). *Subtypes of learning-disabled students classified on the basis of cognitive processes comprising math performance.* Unpublished doctoral dissertation, University of Virginia, Charlottesville.

Keller, C. E., & Lloyd, J. W. (1989). Cognitive training: Implications for arithmetic instruction. In J. N. Hughes & R. J. Hall (Eds.), *Cognitive–behavioral psychology in the schools: A comprehensive handbook* (pp. 280–304). New York: Guilford.

Kendall, P. C. (1981). Assessment and cognitive–behavioral interventions: Purposes, proposals, and problems. In P. C. Kendall & S. D. Hollon (Eds.), *Assessment strategies for cognitive–behavioral interventions* (pp. 1–12). New York: Academic Press.

Kendall, P. C., & Hollon, S. D. (Eds.). (1979). *Cognitive–behavioral interventions: Theory, research, and procedures.* New York: Academic Press.

Kendall, P. C., & Hollon, S. D. (1981a). Assessing self-referent speech: Methods in the measurement of self-statements. In P. C. Kendall & S. D. Hollon (Eds.), *Assessment strategies for cognitive–behavioral interventions* (pp. 85–118). New York: Academic Press.

Kendall, P. C., & Hollon, S. D. (Eds.). (1981b). *Assessment strategies for cognitive–behavioral interventions.* New York: Academic Press.

Kendall, P. C., Pellegrini, D. S., & Urbain, E. S. (1981). Approaches to assessment for cognitive–behavioral interventions with children. In P. C. Kendall & S. D. Hollon (Eds.), *Assessment strategies for cognitive–behavioral interventions* (pp. 227–285). New York: Academic Press.

Kendall, P. C., & Wilcox, L. E. (1979). Self-control in children: Development of a rating scale. *Journal of Consulting and Clinical Psychology, 47,* 1020–1029.

Kneedler, R. D., & Hallahan, D. P. (1984). Self-monitoring as an attentional strategy for academic tasks with learning disabled children. In B. Gholson & T. Rosenthal (Eds.), *Applications of cognitive development theory* (pp. 243–260). New York: Academic Press.

Larson, R., & Lampman-Petraitis, C. (1989). Daily emotional states as reported by children and adolescents. *Child Development, 60,* 1250–1260.

Lloyd, J. W., & Keller, C. E. (1989). Effective mathematics instruction: Development, instruction, and programs. *Focus on Exceptional Children, 21*(7), 1–10.

Loper, A. B. (1984). Accuracy of learning disabled students' self-prediction of decoding. *Learning Disability Quarterly, 7,* 172–178.

McMahon, R. J. (1984). Behavioral checklists and rating scales. In T. H. Ollendick & M. Hersen (Eds.), *Child behavioral assessment: Principles and procedures* (pp. 80–105). New York: Pergamon.

Meichenbaum, D. H. (1977). *Cognitive–behavioral modification: An integrative approach.* New York: Plenum Press.

Nelson, R. O. (1977). Assessment and therapeutic functions of self-monitoring. In M. Hersen, R. M. Eisler, & P. M. Miller (Eds.), *Progress in behavior modification* (Vol. 5, pp. 263–308). New York: Academic Press.
Ollendick, T. H., & Hersen, M. (Eds.). (1984a). *Child behavioral assessment: Principles and procedures.* New York: Pergamon.
Ollendick, T. H., & Hersen, M. (1984b). An overview of child behavioral assessment. In T. H. Ollendick & M. Hersen, (Eds.), *Child behavioral assessment: Principles and procedures* (pp. 3–19). New York: Pergamon.
Peterson, P. L., & Swing, S. R. (1982). Beyond time on task: Students' reports of their thought processes during classroom instruction. *Elementary School Journal, 82,* 481–491.
Peterson, P. L., Swing, S. R., Braverman, M. T., & Buss, R. (1982). Students' aptitudes and their reports of cognitive processes during direct instruction. *Journal of Educational Psychology, 74,* 535–547.
Roberts, R. N., Nelson, R. O., & Olson, T. W. (1987). Self-instruction: An analysis of the differential effects of instruction and reinforcement. *Journal of Applied Behavior Analysis, 20,* 235–242.
Rooney, K. J., Hallahan, D. P., & Lloyd, J. W. (1984). Self-recording of attention by learning disabled students in the regular classroom. *Journal of Learning Disabilities, 17,* 360–364.
Schunk, D. H. (1981). Modeling and attributional effects on children's achievement: A self-efficacy analysis. *Journal of Educational Psychology, 73,* 93–105.
Schunk, D. H. (1982/1983). Progress self-monitoring: Effects on children's self-efficacy and achievement. *Journal of Experimental Education, 51,* 89–93.
Schunk, D. H., & Cox, P. D. (1986). Strategy training and attributional feedback with learning disabled students. *Journal of Educational Psychology, 78,* 201–209.
Shapiro, E. S. (1984). Self-monitoring procedures. In T. H. Ollendick & M. Hersen (Eds.), *Child behavioral assessment: Principles and procedures* (pp. 148–165). New York: Pergamon.
Slife, B. D., Weiss, J., & Bell, T. (1985). Separability of metacognition and cognition: Problem solving in learning disabled and regular students. *Journal of Educational Psychology, 77,* 437–445.
Stevenson, H. C., & Fantuzzo, J. W. (1984). Application of the "generalization map" to a self-control intervention with school-aged children. *Journal of Applied Behavior Analysis, 17,* 203–212.
Vygotsky, L. (1986). *Thought and language* (A. Kozulin, Trans.). Cambridge, MA: MIT Press.
Whitman, T., & Johnston, M. B. (1983). Teaching addition and subtraction with regrouping to educable mentally retarded children: A group self-instructional training program. *Behavior Therapy, 14,* 127–143.
Wong, B. Y. L. (1985). Metacognition and learning disabilities. In D. Forrest-Pressley, G. MacKinnon, & T. Waller (Eds.), *Metacognition, cognition, and human performance* (Vol. 2, pp. 137–180). New York: Academic Press.
Zimmerman, B. J., & Pons, M. M. (1986). Development of a structured interview for assessing student use of self-regulated learning strategies. *American Educational Research Journal, 23,* 614–628.

CHAPTER 16

Psychopharmacological Assessment and Intervention

KENNETH D. GADOW

At present, there is no psychoactive drug that is specifically recognized by the Food and Drug Administration for the treatment of learning disabilities. Nevertheless, most of the psychotropic drugs that are prescribed for childhood and adolescent psychiatric disorders are capable of affecting academic performance in some way, and academic underachievement and learning disabilities are common problems in patients for whom these drugs are typically prescribed. Many other drugs that are prescribed for common chronic childhood disorders such as epilepsy (reviewed by Gadow, 1986b) and asthma (Bender, Lerner, & Kollasch, 1988) can alter cognitive function as well.

The topic of psychoactive medication and learning disabilities is multifaceted. When drug therapy enhances academic performance, this is generally perceived as being a good thing, especially if the child was labeled as having learning disabilities by the school prior to treatment. In cases where academic underachievement is not identified as a primary target symptom, such improvement would be considered serendipitous. There are a number of potential mechanisms that could explain this phenomenon. In the case of children with learning disabilities, medication could reverse a specific defective brain mechanism that was causing the learning disability, enhance a specific compensatory process, or improve general cognitive function. When academic underachievement is secondary to a psychiatric disorder (e.g., depression, school phobia, Tourette syndrome), effective pharmacotherapy may lead to improvement in schoolwork by suppressing psychiatric symptoms. Interestingly, one of the earliest stimulant drug studies with children describes such a situation. Prinzmetal and Bloomberg (1935) administered Benzedrine (amphetamine) to four adolescents and one 11-year-old child who were suffering from narcolepsy (a disorder characterized by an uncontrolled desire for sleep or attacks of sleep during normal waking hours). The 11-year-old was failing school because he could not stay awake in class or complete his schoolwork. With medication, he was able to stay awake, his studies improved, and he was promoted to the next higher grade at the end of the school year. Whether underachievement subsequent to the onset of a psychiatric or neurological disorder should be considered a learning disability is unclear, owing to the inherent vagueness of the federal definitions of learning disabilities and emotional disturbance, and variability in the interpretation of these definitions from one school district to the next. The following examples may help illustrate some of the diversity in performance profiles that one typically sees in a child psychiatry outpatient service.

A fourth-grade boy of average intelligence and 2 years behind in reading is diagnosed by his pediatrician as having attention-deficit hyperactivity disorder (ADHD). His home environment is stable, and his parents are middle class. Although the teacher must frequently reprimand him for his inattentiveness, he is not considered a behavior problem. After receiving a psychoeducational evaluation by the school, he is labeled as having learning disabilities and scheduled to receive resource room services. A very similar boy with regard to cognitive and academic characteristics in the same district, but from a disorganized home environment and who disturbs other children in the classroom and gets into fights on the playground, is placed in a self-contained class for emotionally disturbed students.

In the first case, school personnel consider academic failure to be the result of psychological processing deficits associated with ADHD. The second child, however, is perceived as not getting along with others because of interfamilial strife, parental incompetence, and poor supervision, and his acting out behaviors are interfering with his ability to do schoolwork.

There is a third boy in this same district who was also diagnosed as having ADHD. His parents thought he was difficult to manage, and school personnel found his behavior somewhat annoying. Although his classwork was incomplete and his homework was often missing, he managed to get by academically on the basis of end-of-the-year standardized achievement test scores, which were only moderately below grade level. Because a marked discrepancy between ability and achievement could not be demonstrated, his principal did not consider him to be a suitable candidate for special education.

All three boys were treated with stimulant medication and academic productivity increased and report card grades improved.

Another facet of drug therapy and learning disabilities pertains to the adverse effects of medication on academic performance. For children who have learning disabilities prior to the onset of drug treatment, a deterioration in performance would be considered an exacerbation of preexisting symptoms. When medication impairs academic function in a nondisabled learner, this could be considered to be a drug-induced learning disability. Both are examples of behavioral toxicity. Because parents and teachers typically do not tolerate such reactions to medication, they are often short-lived phenomena. Perhaps the most at-risk group of students (i.e., those for whom this may be a chronic problem) are those with developmental disabilities, because behavioral toxicity is more difficult to detect and, regrettably, more easily "overlooked." Psychopharmacologists have not done a particularly heroic job of developing assessment measures for detecting behavioral toxicity, and school-based procedures are all but unknown.

The psychoactive drugs that are most commonly prescribed for childhood psychiatric disorders and the most likely to produce beneficial effects on school performance are the stimulants: Ritalin (methylphenidate), Dexedrine (dextroamphetamine), and Cylert (pemoline). Methylphenidate and dextroamphetamine are currently available as generic products. Treatment prevalence survey studies show that approximately 10 to 20% of the students receiving special education for learning disabilities receive psychotropic medication, typically Ritalin (reviewed by Gadow, 1986a). For these reasons, the primary focus of this chapter is on the stimulants. Presented here are summaries from more extensive reviews of the literature on (a) the short-term (Barkley & Cunningham, 1978; Gadow, 1983, 1986a) and long-term (Gadow, 1988) effects of stimulants on academic performance, (b) the relative efficacy of drug, behavioral, and combination treatments (Gadow, 1985), and (c) measures for assessing response to medication (Gadow & Swanson, 1985).

EFFICACY: SHORT-TERM STUDIES

READING

The research findings on stimulants and reading performance in hyperactive children are mixed. Medication does enhance the amount of accurate reading-related seatwork that is completed during the school day (e.g., Pelham, Bender, Caddell, Booth, & Moorer, 1985; Pelham, Swanson, Bender, & Wilson, 1980; Rapport, Stoner, DuPaul, Birmingham, & Tucker, 1985), but the mechanism of action is entirely unknown. Standardized achievement test performance, however, is affected much less dramatically. This is not to suggest, however, that everyone shares this interpretation of the research literature or that the findings from all studies are equally discouraging. For example, Richardson, Kupietz, Winsberg, Maitinsky, and Mendell (1988) reported on a study of Ritalin in hyperactive children who were underachievers in reading and who were participating in a special after-school reading program. Although the size of the drug effect was very small after 6 months of treatment, a subgroup of "good" responders (determined on the basis of teacher ratings of classroom behavior) were said to have benefited much more. Methodological and other considerations aside, the clinical implications of these findings for school-labeled learning disabled hyperactive children is unclear.

Within the past few years, three studies have been published on the use of stimulant medication with nonhyperactive learning disabled children (Aman & Werry, 1982; Gittelman-Klein & Klein, 1976; Gittelman, Klein, & Feingold, 1983). In their first study, Gittelman-Klein and Klein (1976) randomly assigned children to either Ritalin or placebo. All subjects were selected on the basis of being 2 years below reading grade level despite average intelligence, and most were receiving academic remediation in school. At the end of 12 weeks, achievement test score differences for arithmetic and spelling were trivial, but the reading score difference approached statistical significance. Teacher global ratings of reading and arithmetic performance did not discriminate between the two treatment groups. On the basis of these and other findings, Gittelman-Klein and Klein concluded that Ritalin was not an effective agent for the remediation of reading deficits in nonhyperactive learning disabled children. They also noted, however, that medication effects may be manifested only in the presence of a specialized academic intervention.

To test this hypothesis, Gittelman et al. (1983) conducted a second study in which nonhyperactive reading retarded children were randomly assigned to one of three groups: (a) reading remediation (phonics program) and placebo, (b) academic tutoring (without reading instruction) and placebo, and (c) reading remediation and Ritalin. The results indicated that although medication did enhance cognitive task performance, it did not facilitate academic achievement. Some reading achievement measures, however, did show drug effects or trends favoring the medication-treated group, suggesting that the impact of Ritalin on reading instruction was not a strong one. Quite unexpectedly, medication markedly enhanced other areas of academic skill performance (e.g., social studies), which were not part of the reading program. However, a retest of these academic skills 8 months after the termination of pharmacotherapy failed to show residual benefits. In other words, achievement test score gains appeared to fade over time after medication was stopped.

Aman and Werry (1982) administered Ritalin, Valium (diazepam), and placebo for 1 week each to 15 children diagnosed as being severely reading retarded (but with normal IQ). Medication was not found to improve cognitive functions presumed to be associated with reading disability.

In sum, although stimulant medication does not appear to markedly improve reading achievement in hyperactive (Barkley & Cunningham, 1978) or nonhyperactive learning disabled children (Gittelman-Klein & Klein, 1976; Gittelman et al., 1983) or to correct the underlying problem that is causing the reading disability (Aman & Werry, 1982), it does increase the amount of reading-related workbook assignments completed by underachieving hyperactive children. One would predict that if medication helped students to pay attention and complete more schoolwork, their reading levels would improve. At present, however, it is difficult to say with certainty whether this is true or false.

ARITHMETIC

Since Bradley's (1937; Bradley & Bowen, 1940) early studies were published, a number of other investigators have also shown that stimulant medication enhances academic productivity on classroom and laboratory arithmetic tasks (e.g., Douglas, Barr, O'Neill, & Britton, 1986; Pelham et al., 1985; Rapport et al., 1985; see also Sprague's study in Gadow & Swanson, 1985). In spite of these encouraging reports, improvement in academic achievement test performance is less dramatic. For example, of the 11 short-term studies in Barkley and Cunningham's (1978) review that employed measures of arithmetic achievement, statistically significant drug effects were reported in only one instance (Conners, Rothschild, Eisenberg, Stone, & Robinson, 1969). Interestingly, the Gittelman et al. (1983) study found significant Ritalin-induced gains on the arithmetic subtests of the Stanford Achievement Test in nonhyperactive learning disabled children, even though arithmetic skill development was not part of the intervention program.

The findings from studies on stimulant medication and arithmetic productivity are fairly consistent. Drug therapy appears to increase work output without sacrificing accuracy; however, there are only a few reports of improved performance on standardized achievement tests (Conners et al., 1969; Gittelman et al., 1983). Nothing is known about the effects of stimulants on children who have a specific arithmetic disability, with or without a concurrent behavior disorder.

SPELLING

There were 11 short-term drug studies included in the review by Barkley and Cunningham (1978) that employed either measures of spelling achievement (N = 10) or productivity (N = 1), and significant drug effects were demonstrated in only two instances (Conners, Taylor, Meo, Kurz, & Fournier, 1972; Weiss, Minde, Douglas, Werry, & Sykes, 1971). Pelham et al. (1985) reported a modest Ritalin-related increase in the proportion of words correct on weekly spelling tests, which consisted of words that the hyperactive children could not spell correctly. In a similar study, however, Cylert failed to enhance spelling performance (Pelham et al., 1980). Another investigation (Stephens, Pelham, & Skinner, 1984) of Ritalin, Cylert, and placebo revealed that stimulant drugs produced a 25% reduction in spelling errors (nonsense words) as compared with placebo. In view of these conflicting findings, no definite conclusions can be drawn about stimulant medication and spelling. Furthermore, there is no drug research on spelling disability per se.

HANDWRITING

A number of investigators have reported that stimulant drugs can enhance handwriting ability in hyperactive children (Levy, 1973; Schain & Reynard, 1975; Taylor, 1979; Whalen, Henker, & Finck, 1981) and adolescents (Yellin, Hopwood, & Greenberg, 1982). Moreover, there are a number of published handwriting samples (Levy, 1973; Schain & Reynard, 1975; Taylor, 1979) that compellingly demonstrate the magnitude of this effect. Nevertheless, poor handwriting is rarely the basis for medical referral, nor is it a clinical indication for treatment. The only published study that selected children (diagnosed as having minimal brain dysfunction) on the basis of poor handwriting was conducted by Lerer, Lerer, and Artner (1977). They found that handwriting improved with Ritalin treatment in 52% of the cases, as compared with only one child receiving placebo. In general, handwriting deteriorated subsequent to drug withdrawal, but improvement was maintained for months in children who remained on medication.

Although these findings seem exciting, neatness is only one small component of what people generally refer to as written communication skills. The latter includes spelling, sentence structure, grammar, the ability to express and organize ideas, and so forth. It is important not to underestimate neatness and legibility, but we must also realize that little is known about the effect of stimulant drugs on more serious forms of written communication disorders.

EFFICACY: LONG-TERM STUDIES

Drug studies that involve protracted treatment periods are commonly referred to as being long term. The actual time frame is arbitrary, but most investigators would probably accept treatment periods of somewhere between 6 and 12 months as a minimal criterion. There are really two subgroups of long-term studies, and they differ with regard to whether or not treatment is administered on a continuous basis up to the point of assessment. If it is, the primary objective is efficacy, and in this sense, the long-term study is comparable to the short-term clinical trial. If medication is discontinued for a substantial period of time prior to assessment, the investigation is really addressing the residual benefits of treatment and may be more appropriately referred to as an outcome or follow-up study. There are at least 11 published long-term (1 year of treatment or more) studies in which drug- and non–drug- (or minimally) treated hyperactive individuals were compared during childhood, adolescence, or adulthood with regard to academic performance. These studies represent six treatment samples, several of which were the subject of two or more research reports.

MONTREAL CHILDREN'S HOSPITAL

Weiss, Kruger, Danielson, and Elman (1975) followed three groups of hyperactive children for 5 years after initial evaluation. One group was treated with Ritalin from 3 to 6 years (mean = 4.3 years). The second group was treated with Thorazine (chlorpromazine) from 18 months to 5 years (mean = 30 months). However, in only a few cases did the treatment regimen extend beyond 2 years. The third group consisted of children who had not received medication for more than 4 months. All three groups were matched with regard to age, IQ, socioeconomic status, and gender. Because all subjects in each group were initially assessed sometime between 1962 and 1967, a diagnosis of learning disability was not rendered in appropriate cases. Therefore, the prevalence of learning disabilities in these samples is unknown.

Weiss et al. compared the three groups with regard to the number of children who had been held back one or more grades, and reported the following: Ritalin (46%), Thorazine (55%), and "untreated" (70%). The performance discrepancies were not statistically significant. A more in-depth analysis of academic achievement was conducted by comparing the difference between the Ritalin group and a therapeutically mixed (none had received stimulants for more than 6 months) hyperactive group that was matched by age at follow-up, IQ, socioeconomic status, gender, and degree of hyperactivity at initial assessment. The dependent measure was report card grades that had been converted to a 3-point scale. The results indicated that there were no significant differences between the two groups of matched pairs on academic grades in reading, language, arithmetic, French, or spelling.

Hechtman, Weiss, and Perlman (1984) conducted a 10- to 12-year follow-up of hyperactive children who received continuous treatment with stimulant drugs for a minimum of 3 years. A second group of hyperactive individuals served as an "untreated" control group. All three groups were matched on IQ and socioeconomic status, but due to differences in subject selection procedures, the stimulant-treated group was 2.2 years older than the untreated group. The results showed that the drug-treated group had completed slightly more years of education (11.0 years) than the untreated sample (10.4 years). The two hyperactive groups were also very similar in the number of grades failed in high school (drug, 50%; untreated, 46%). Interestingly, even though the untreated group was younger than the drug-treated group at follow-up assessment, more members of the former (29%) were enrolled in postsecondary education than the latter (15%).

GEORGETOWN UNIVERSITY HOSPITAL

In 1974, Rapoport, Quinn, Bradbard, Riddle, and Brooks reported the results of a study of 76 hyperactive grade-school boys from middle-class families who were treated with either Ritalin, Tofranil (imipramine), or placebo. Although teacher global ratings of academic achievement indicated a Ritalin-enhancing effect, comparisons between WRAT (Wide Range Achievement Test; Jastak & Wilson, 1984) reading, spelling, and math scores at baseline (off medication) and at 6 weeks (on treatment) were not statistically significant (see also Barkley & Cunningham, 1978). No descriptive data were provided about academic performance or a diagnosis of learning diability. A 1-year follow-up of this group of patients also failed to demonstrate a drug effect on academic achievement (Quinn & Rapoport, 1975). Of the original subjects, approximately one half received either Ritalin or Tofranil for a full year. A comparison group consisted of subjects who had shown a clinical response but whose treatment regimens were terminated for various reasons. The results yielded no statistically significant differences between the three groups on WRAT standard scores at baseline (off medication) and at the end of 1 year (on medication for drug groups and off medication for "no treatment" group).

Riddle and Rapoport (1976) also conducted a 2-year follow-up study of this same patient group and found no change in WRAT reading scores over the 2-year period for the entire sample, and a significant decrease in math scores. Of the boys who had been maintained on stimulants for the entire 2-year period, their WRAT scores were virtually identical to the test scores for the entire sample. Riddle and Rapoport noted the fact that the active treatment group was tested off medication was a major methodological problem with regard to interpreting the academic performance findings.

ROYAL OTTAWA HOSPITAL

Blouin, Bornstein, and Trites (1978) conducted a 5-year follow-up of cases selected from clinic files that were retrospectively diagnosed and classified by the investigators. Of the cases available for follow-up contact, 42 were diagnosed as hyperactive and 49 had school difficulty. In the hyperactive group, 27 had been treated with Ritalin and the remaining 15 subjects had not received pharmacotherapy. Mean duration of treatment was 1.9 years. Although descriptive information on the academic performance of the drug group was limited, at initial assessment and follow-up, differences between the hyperactive group and the school difficulty (learning or reading disabilities) group on WRAT scores were not statistically significant. In other words, many of the children in the hyperactive group were learning disabled. A comparison between drug- and nondrug-treated hyperactive subjects revealed no significant differences in academic achievement (WRAT) either at initial assessment or at follow-up. Similarly, a comparison between good and poor responders to medication (according to parental judgments) revealed no statistically significant differences in academic achievement either at initial assessment or at follow-up.

UCLA DEPARTMENT OF PEDIATRICS

Charles and Schain (1981) reevaluated a group of 98 hyperactive children who 4 years previously had participated in a 16-week drug study (see Schain & Reynard, 1975); 62 of these had participated in a follow-up study. Academic performance at follow-up was as follows: teachers judged 74% and 69% to be below grade level in reading and mathematics, respectively; 34% repeated one or more grades; 42% were in special education classes; and 24% were being tutored. In order to determine if longer treatment with stimulants was associated with a more favorable outcome, the subjects were separated into five categories: (a) drug failures and placebo successes (none treated for more than 5 months), (b) treated 7 to 23 months, (c) treated 2 to 3 years, (d) treated 3 to 4 years, and (e) still receiving medication at follow-up. Only the last group was evaluated on medication at the follow-up assessment. There were no statistically significant differences among the groups in teacher judgments of academic performance, repeated grades, or special education services.

UNIVERSITY OF IOWA

Loney, Kramer, and Kosier (1981) evaluated the adolescent status of boys who met the diagnostic criteria for hyperkinesis/minimal brain dysfunction. Each child was initially assigned to one of two staff psychiatrists, each of whom preferred a different therapeutic method, resulting in two treatment groups: stimulant medication and behavioral counseling. All but one of the drug-treated subjects received medication for at least 6 months (mean duration of treatment, 24.7 months). Approximately 80% of the children in each group received school remediation. Loney et al. used conventional stepwise regression analysis with academic achievement (WRAT scores) as the dependent measure, and eight referral variables as predictors. Treatment status (i.e., medication versus no medication) was entered as the final predictor. With this procedure, relevant referral characteristics were controlled before assessing the relationship between treatment status and academic achievement, which unfortunately, was not statistically significant.

GATEWAYS HOSPITAL (LOS ANGELES)

Satterfield and his colleagues reported on a 1-year (Satterfield, Cantwell, & Satterfield, 1979), a 2-year (Satterfield, Satterfield, & Cantwell, 1980), and a 3-year (Satterfield, Satterfield, & Cantwell, 1981) follow-up of a clinic population of 117 hyperactive children. On the basis of predicted grade-level scores (PIAT), the group was one-half to one grade level behind academically in all subjects (despite normal intelligence) before the onset of therapy, and 39% were receiving special-education services at the end of 1 year of treatment. The treatment clinic provided each child–family dyad with an individualized multimodality treatment package that included pharmacological, educational, and psychological interventions.

The 3-year follow-up evaluation compared the outcome of a treatment dropout group (less treatment) that received medication for less than 2 years (mean, 9 months) and maximum treatment group (more treatment) that was treated from 2 to 3 years (mean, 35 months). The general pattern of results was a marked deterioration in academic achievement in the group that received less treatment and improved performance in the group that received more treatment. Because the children and their families received multiple treatments, the contribution of medication to this favorable outcome cannot be determined.

SUMMARY

Eleven long-term studies of drug versus non–drug- or minimally drug-treated hyperactive children, many of whom experienced marked achievement problems, have been published. With the exception of one study (Satterfield et al., 1981), their findings uniformly support the conclusion that stimulant drug therapy does not enhance academic achievement, at least in terms of altering adolescent or adult outcome. Nevertheless, because of a number of methodological problems, the issue is not yet resolved. Moreover, there may very well be a subgroup of children in this treatment population for whom medication does have a role in academic skill acquisition.

RELATIVE EFFICACY OF DRUG, BEHAVIORAL, AND COMBINATION TREATMENTS

In an attempt to understand better the relationship between stimulant drug therapy and behavioral interventions designed to improve academic performance, I examined 16 studies that addressed this topic (Gadow, 1985). Most of the studies were conducted with hyperactive children, and only one investigation examined nonhyperactive learning disabled youngsters (Gittelman et al., 1983). In general, the academic deficits of the hyperactive samples were poorly documented. A number of different academic skills were targeted for intervention, but most researchers appeared to study whatever reading or arithmetic skills the children were engaged in at the time. Perhaps the most important distinguishing characteristic of all the academically oriented interventions was whether or not the primary objective of treatment was to increase the motivation to learn, to teach an academic skill, or both.

The behavioral interventions employed in these studies were very diverse. Process-oriented treatments, for example, included training perceptual motor skills, impulse control, self-instruction, and metacognitive skills for academic tasks. Two studies employed specialized reading interventions; one was phonics based (Gittelman et al., 1983), and the other was a combined phonics–sight word approach (Richardson et al., 1988). The behavior therapy approaches included token reinforcement, training of parent, teacher, or both in contingency management, response cost, and a combination of token reinforcement and response cost. Not surprisingly, most of the behavioral interventions in these studies were specifically targeted for academic behaviors; however, there were some exceptions (Abikoff & Gittelman, 1985; Conrad, Dworkin, Shai, & Tobiessen, 1971; Firestone, Kelly, Goodman, & Davey, 1981).

There were nine studies in which medication was directly compared with a behavioral intervention designed to help academic performance. In two cases they were equally effective or equally ineffective; the behavioral intervention was superior in four studies; and medication was demonstrated to be more efficacious in the remaining three investigations (all of which failed to show a significant behavioral intervention effect). Taken together, these comparisons suggest that effective behavioral interventions are superior to medication in enhancing academic performance.

When behavioral intervention plus medication was compared with medication alone, the behavioral intervention was found to be superior in some studies. In the remaining studies, neither was superior. Although this would appear to be somewhat at odds with the previous observation, in all instances where the behavioral intervention did not facilitate pharmacotherapy, the behavioral intervention was not found to be effective.

The combination treatment (medication plus behavioral intervention) was found to be more effective in approximately one half of the studies designed to test this question. Unfortunately, most either failed to demonstrate that the behavioral intervention was indeed effective, or they contained only a few subjects.

It must be reemphasized that the behavioral interventions in the relative efficacy studies are most diverse. Because representations of each type of treatment are limited, so too are replications. Therefore, conclusions about efficacy must be tentative. With this qualification in mind, the findings from the relative efficacy studies suggest the following.

1. Cognitive training programs are more effective when they are clearly focused on academic task performance.

2. Of the two general approaches to behavior modification, teaching caregivers how to use this strategy is less effective than direct contingency management. With direct contingency management, the therapist actually delivers the treatment or directly supervises the caregiver while he or she implements the treatment.

3. Punishment appears to be an important element in behavioral approaches for hyperactive children (see also Rosen, O'Leary, Joyce, Conway, & Pfiffner, 1984).

4. Stimulant drug therapy and contingency management *may* affect behavior in a similar way. They both appear to improve task motivation, which may explain the limited interactive effects when both are administered at effective levels.

5. Behaviorally oriented approaches that employ multiple techniques with different mechanisms of action, such as special academic curricula designed for skill acquisition that also use effective contingency management, are generally superior to contingency management alone and are probably little influenced by the addition of medication. Unfortunately, the latter are generally available only in some special education settings and are surprisingly understudied with students with learning disabilities (see, for example, Gittelman & Feingold, 1983).

ASSESSING MEDICATION EFFECTS

Investigations into the effects of psychotropic drugs on academic performance in children have been conducted for at least 50 years. Interestingly, the basic procedures for assessing treatment effects (productivity and standardized achievement tests) have remained essentially the same during this time, with some changes emerging only within the past few years. Most notable are the introduction of diagnostic reading tests and instruments designed to assess specific subskills. Perhaps the most exciting development has been the formulation and use of instructional process measures, which may help provide greater insight into the effects of drugs on academic skill acquisition. In many respects, however, pediatric psychopharmacologists have done a less than satisfactory job of exploiting the diverse array of academic measures currently available.

ACADEMIC PRODUCTIVITY

Academic productivity can be, and has been, measured in a variety of ways, including total number (or percentage) of problems, assignments, or pages of schoolwork completed, total number of problems completed accurately, or the percentage of problems completed accurately. When a specific unit of time is used, the investigator may refer to the number of problems completed per minute. It is important to give careful thought to these measures and the presentation and interpretation of drug effects. For example, an increase in the percentage of problems completed accurately concurrent with increased output would be perceived as more clinically important than a mere increase in output at pretreatment level of accurate answers.

Of all the measures of academic performance, productivity is among the most compelling because the treatment effect is so self-evident. Moreover, it is relatively easy to obtain and neither disrupts the school routine with special testing sessions nor requires a testing staff. Although it is generally assumed that if output increases so will skill acquisition and retention, the relationship between drug effects on productivity and standardized achievement test performance is unknown. Productivity measures are particularly useful in medication evaluations because they are reactive to dosage manipulations, short-term treatment effects, behavioral toxicity, and both behavior and drug therapy, and they can be used effectively in within-subject (crossover) research designs.

STANDARDIZED ACHIEVEMENT TESTS

Unquestionably the most traditional measure of academic performance in psychotropic drug research has been the standardized achievement test, particularly the Wide Range Achievement Test (WRAT; Jastak & Wilkinson, 1984). The use of a test such as the WRAT in a short-term (i.e., less than 6 months) drug study has its limitations, because the actual number of items in the test that sample concepts and skills normally acquired during a short time frame is relatively small and the standard error of measurement relatively large (Barkley & Cunningham, 1978; Sprague & Berger, 1980). Therefore, the failure to document treatment effects may be due to the insensitivity of the dependent measure. Of course, the seriousness of this disadvantage is directly related to the length of the intervention and the magnitude of the treatment effect.

Standardized achievement tests are associated with additional limitations that should be considered when they are employed as dependent measures in drug studies. First, the technical inadequacy of some tests undermines any conclusions that can be drawn about the treatment effect of drugs. For example, the most popular measure used in drug studies, the WRAT, suffers from poor reliability and validity data and inadequate standardization, in addition to limited sampling of academic behavior (e.g., Salvia & Ysseldyke, 1981; Swanson & Watson, 1982).

A second limitation relates to the types of scores derived from achievement tests. Grade-equivalent scores are commonly used to determine treatment effects; however, such scores are insensitive to true achievement gains or losses. Additional limitations of grade-equivalent scores are: (a) they are median scores, and therefore it is expected that 50% of the scores should be low (i.e., such scores cannot be used as standards of excellence); (b) such scores do not represent comparable performance across academic subjects (e.g., the same grade-equivalent score for reading and math on the WRAT may yield significant discrepancies when those scores are converted to percentile norms); and (c) such scores inaccurately represent mastery of academic material (e.g., if a child in the third grade has a grade-equivalent score of 6.2, this means that he or she accrues raw score points similar to youngsters in higher grades, not that his or her performance is like that of a sixth-grader). Another score commonly used to assess treatment effects is the percentile norm. However, an analysis of treatment effects using percentile norms is suspect because such scores have unequal units at various points on the standardization scale. For example, percentile scores at the end of the continuum would require large increments in raw scores to show percentile changes, whereas scores around the 50th percentile would require less of an increment in academic achievement to show significant treatment change. In short, if achievement test scores are to be used to assess treatment effects, a linear conversion to the raw scores may be necessary. Such a conversion may be represented in terms of z or T scores (see Swanson & Watson, 1982).

Lastly, achievement tests provide little insight into the nature of mental mechanisms that account for academic change (e.g., see Wagner & Sternberg, 1984), although this does not preclude their use for predictive purposes (see Jensen, 1981). Specifically, standardized achievement measures fail to identify the learning processes children use to enhance performance. Thus, in addition to technically adequate achievement tests to evaluate drug intervention, more refined measures or indices of cognitive processes appear necessary (see Swanson, 1985). Intervention effects can best by analyzed with such indices, and subsequent treatments can be prescribed to support educational activity or to modify detrimental, interfering activities.

There has been a trend in recent years to expand the traditional battery of measures of academic achievement to include devices that assess specific subskills in some detail. This is particularly true for studies of drug effects on reading (Gittelman et al., 1983; Richardson et al., 1988). Because tests designed to assess specific academic skills are more diagnostically oriented, they generally contain more items per grade level (or per skill) and are therefore more likely to be sensitive to short-term treatment effects.

TEACHER RATINGS

Several investigators have employed teacher ratings of academic productivity (Conners, 1972; Conners, Eisenberg, & Barcai, 1967; Gittelman-Klein & Klein, 1975; Rapoport et al., 1974). This is a somewhat exciting notion because such ratings are generally efficient and cost effective. It would be useful for someone to investigate the relationship between drug response on teacher ratings of productivity and on actual productivity assessments. There is at least one report comparing global teacher ratings of reading and arithmetic improvement and standardized achievement test performance (Gittelman-Klein & Klein, 1975), but the findings were most discouraging. However, global ratings of improvement in reading did correlate with Gray Oral Reading Test performance ($r = 0.38$, $p<0.05$). (Interestingly, the correlation between improvement on the Gray Oral Reading Test and the WRAT reading subtest was 0.03.) Because global ratings of academic improvement did not correlate with "objective achievement changes" but did correlate highly with overall ratings of behavioral improvement, Gittelman-Klein and Klein (1975) suggested that "the global academic ratings may be reflecting a halo effect from the behavior ratings, and seem invalid as independent evaluations of school performance" (p. 194). It is equally plausible, of course, that both sets of ratings tap on-task behavior and academic productivity.

ACADEMIC GRADES

Another academic performance measure that has been used in stimulant studies is academic grades (e.g., Comly, 1971). The investigator can either calculate the percentage of academic subjects that improved or assign a numerical rating for each letter grade (e.g., A (excellent) = 5, to E (fail) = 1). Although report card grades have been criticized for being tainted by subjectivity and halo effects from decreased disruptiveness, little is known about this measure in drug research. Academic grades can be used in short-term studies simply by recording letter grades for homework assignments, spelling tests, quarterly reports, and so forth.

SKILL ACQUISITION

There are very few examples of stimulant drug studies in which the investigator attempted a molecular analysis of treatment effects on academic skill acquisition. Rie and Rie (1977) conducted a Ritalin versus placebo crossover study in which hyperactive subjects were required to read (and reread) a paragraph until they could accurately answer a set of comprehension questions about its content. Trials to criterion was employed as the dependent measure. Although Ritalin did not alter the number of trials, it did produce better recall of information 2 hours after acquisition, which was interpreted to imply an effect on initial learning.

Ellis Richardson (personal communication, 1985) formulated two instructional process measures to evaluate medication effects on a child's weekly progress during a tutorial reading program, but the findings from these analyses were less compelling than those for reading tests (Richardson, Kupietz, & Maitinsky, 1987). One measure, error rate, was the number of incorrect responses divided by the total number of items presented. Error rates were calculated for both Basal Vocabulary items and Phonic Decoding items of the Decoding Skills Test (Richardson & DiBenedetto, 1985) introduced during the tutorial session and practiced at home during the previous week. A second measure was response strength, which was computed by calculating the average amount of time per item it takes a child to complete the drill decks in the tutorial reading program. Response strength is calculated for Basal Vocabulary items and Phonic Decoding items introduced during the tutorial session and practiced during the prior week.

COMPUTERIZED ASSESSMENT PROCEDURES

Another procedure that permits a more detailed analysis of the learning process with academic tasks is computerized instruction, computerized practice and drill exercises, and computerized criterion testing. One early example of the use of this technology is a study conducted by Robert Sprague and his colleagues at the University of Illinois at Urbana-Champaign (see Gadow & Swanson, 1985). They formulated an arithmetic performance test based on the Basic Arithmetic Skill Evaluation test (May & Hood, 1973), in which the child is required to solve arithmetic calculation problems presented on a computer-assisted instruction system. Hyperactive children were tested on placebo and two doses of Ritalin administered in a counterbalanced sequence under double-blind conditions. The findings showed that academic performance improved with increasing dosage, but that response latency decreased on the lower dose but increased with the higher dose. In other words, whereas accuracy improved slightly on the higher dose, there was a marked increase in the amount of time it took the children to solve the arithmetic problems, suggesting the possibility of an overfocusing of attention. The point here is that the latency measure, which is easily generated from the computerized testing procedure, provides important additional information about drug effects on academic performance.

SUMMARY

Stimulant drugs do increase academic productivity in hyperactive children and, in all probability, in children with learning disabilities. Moreover, treated children appear to be aware of this change in their academic behavior (see Gadow, 1988), which *may* lead to less stress in their lives. As Bradley (1957) noted, "medication is at best a crutch, but if in the long run it enables the child to experience success and a sense of being loved and appreciated, it is well justified" (p. 1051). It seems plausible that for some children a dramatic improvement in productivity and proficiency may even be more clinically meaningful than a modest increase in standardized achievement test performance. In addition, one of the commonly associated reasons for treatment in the first place is that the child does not complete his or her schoolwork and subsequently may not make satisfactory academic progress. Therefore, some clinicians believe that if medication makes a child more responsive to educational instruction, then it is clinically useful. After all, the education literature is replete with scientific studies that document how various strategies designed to increase task motivation improve academic productivity. Nevertheless, careful consideration must be given both to the seriousness of academic underachievement, the magnitude of the treatment effect, and the safety of the drug.

Collectively, the findings from a number of short- and long-term investigations suggest that the academic achievement test score gains associated with stimulant drug treatment are not particularly robust, long-lasting, or cumulative, which is not to say that they are nonexistent. Nevertheless, several researchers have commented that there are serious methodological shortcomings in many of these studies, which could explain the absence of clinically significant medication effects and that a "true" test of the academic skill acquisition question (as measured by achievement test performance) has yet to be conducted. Even more discouraging are the findings from outcome studies, which assess the residual benefits of drug therapy for adolescent and adult functioning. Although the research is limited, it does not appear that receiving stimulant medication for several years during childhood has a marked effect on the ultimate level of education or important education-related outcomes in later life.

Collectively, the relative efficacy studies indicate that certain academically oriented behavioral interventions are clearly superior to stimulant medication in facilitating academic performance in hyperactive, learning disabled, and hyperactive learning disabled children. Moreover, although stimulant drugs enhance a variety of learning-related behaviors (e.g., attention span) and have been shown to increase academic productivity, they do not appear to facilitate academically oriented behavioral interventions markedly unless the latter are ineffective. These findings are fairly consistent across a number of studies that vary greatly, which suggests that if a combination treatment effect does exist, it may not be clinically significant.

Since the 1930s, there has been relatively little change in the commonly used measures for assessing drug effects on academic performance in research situations. Even more disconcerting, however, is the fact that almost no effort has been made to develop and evaluate procedures for use in everyday clinical situations. There are a number of reasons for this, among them are (a) the psychopharmacologist's lack of professional training in education-related matters and preference for cognitive tasks and tests and (b) the intimidating number of logistical problems to be overcome in order to conduct outpatient studies with the public school serving as the primary data-collection site. Many educators really have not helped matters by resisting a biopsychosocial model of childhood disabilities. In addition, their lack of opportunity to learn about (or, obviously, prescribe) medication are unquestionably all-but-insurmountable obstacles to research. Anyone familiar with pediatric psychopharmacology will no doubt appreciate the almost incomprehensible irony of this situation. We have acquired a truly humbling literature on the effects of psychotropic drugs on cognitive tasks and psychological tests, and yet the typical research subject spends an infinitesimal amount of time during his or her childhood in a laboratory. This is not to deny the importance of such research, but is, rather, an appeal to broaden the database.

REFERENCES

Abikoff, H., & Gittelman, R. (1985). Hyperactive children treated with stimulants: Is cognitive training a useful adjunct? *Archives of General Psychiatry, 42*, 953–961.

Aman, M. G., & Werry, J. S. (1982). Methylphenidate and diazepam in severe reading retardation. *Journal of the American Academy of Child Psychiatry, 1*, 31–37.

Barkley, R. A., & Cunningham, C. E. (1978). Do stimulant drugs improve the academic performance of hyperkinetic children? *Clinical Pediatrics, 17*, 85–92.

Bender, B. G., Lerner, J. A., & Kollasch, E. (1988). Mood and memory changes in asthmatic children receiving corticosteroids. *Journal of the American Academy of Child and Adolescent Psychiatry, 27,* 720–725.

Blouin, A., Bornstein, R., & Trites, R. (1978). Teenage alcohol use among hyperactive children: A 5-year follow-up study. *Journal of Pediatric Psychology, 3,* 188–194.

Bradley, C. (1937). The behavior of children receiving Benzedrine. *American Journal of Psychiatry, 94,* 577–585.

Bradley, C. (1957). Characteristics and management of children with behavior problems associated with organic brain damage. *Pediatric Clinics of North America, 4,* 1049–1060.

Bradley, C., & Bowen, M. (1940). School performance of children receiving amphetamine (Benzedrine) sulfate. *American Journal of Orthopsychiatry, 10,* 782–788.

Charles, L., & Schain, R. (1981). A four-year follow-up study of the effects of methylphenidate on the behavior and academic achievement of hyperactive children. *Journal of Abnormal Child Psychology, 9,* 495–505.

Comly, H. H. (1971). Cerebral stimulants for children with learning disorders. *Journal of Learning Disabilities, 9,* 484–490.

Conners, C. K. (1972). Symposium: Behavior modification by drugs. II. Psychological effects of stimulant drugs in children with minimal brain dysfunction. *Pediatrics, 49,* 702–708.

Conners, C. K., Eisenberg, L., & Barcai, A. (1967). Effect of dextroamphetamine on children: Studies on subjects with learning disabilities and school behavior problems. *Archives of General Psychiatry, 17,* 478–485.

Conners, C., Rothschild, G., Eisenberg, L., Stone, L., & Robinson, E. (1969). Dextroamphetamine in children with learning disorders. *Archives of General Psychiatry, 21,* 182–190.

Conners, C. K., Taylor, E., Meo, G., Kurz, M. A., & Fournier, M. (1972). Magnesium pemoline and dextroamphetamine: A controlled study in children with minimal brain dysfunction. *Psychopharmacologia, 26,* 321–336.

Conrad, W. G., Dworkin, E. S., Shai, A., & Tobiessen, J. E. (1971). Effects of amphetamine therapy and prescriptive tutoring on the behavior and achievement of lower class hyperactive children. *Journal of Learning Disabilities, 4,* 45–53.

Douglas, V. I., Barr, R. G., O'Neill, M. E., & Britton, B. G. (1986). Short term effects of methylphenidate on the cognitive, learning and academic performance of children with attention deficit disorder in the laboratory and the classroom. *Journal of Child Psychology and Psychiatry, 27,* 191–211.

Firestone, P., Kelly, M. J., Goodman, J. T., & Davey, J. (1981). Differential effects of parent training and stimulant medication with hyperactives. *Journal of the American Academy of Child Psychiatry, 20,* 135–147.

Gadow, K. D. (1983). Effects of stimulant drugs on academic performance in hyperactive and learning disabled children. *Journal of Learning Disabilities, 16,* 290–299.

Gadow, K. D. (1985). Relative efficacy of pharmacological, behavioral, and combination treatments for enhancing academic performance. *Clinical Psychology Review, 5,* 513–533.

Gadow, K. D. (1986a). *Children on medication (Vol. 1): Hyperactivity, learning disabilities, and mental retardation.* Austin, TX: PRO-ED.

Gadow, K. D. (1986b). *Children on medication (Vol. 2): Epilepsy, emotional disturbance, and adolescent disorders.* Austin, TX: PRO-ED.

Gadow, K. D. (1988). Pharmacotherapy. In K. A. Kavale, S. R. Forness, & M. Bender (Eds.), *Handbook of learning disabilities* (Vol. 2): *Methods and interventions* (pp. 195–214). Austin, TX: PRO-ED.

Gadow, K. D., & Swanson, H. L. (1985). Assessing drug effects on academic performance. *Psychopharmacology Bulletin, 21,* 877–886.
Gittelman, R., & Feingold, I. (1983). Children with reading disorders - I. Efficacy of reading remediation. *Journal of Child Psychology and Psychiatry, 24,* 167–191.
Gittelman-Klein, R., & Klein, D. F. (1975). Are behavioral and psychometric changes related in methylphenidate treated hyperactive children? *International Journal of Mental Health, 4,* 182–198.
Gittelman-Klein, R., & Klein, D. F. (1976). Methylphenidate effects in learning disabilities. *Archives of General Psychiatry, 33,* 655–664.
Gittelman, R., Klein, D. F., & Feingold, I. (1983). Children with reading disorders: - II. Effects of methylphenidate in combination with reading remediation. *Journal of Child Psychology and Psychiatry, 24,* 193–212.
Hechtman, L., Weiss, G., & Perlman, T. (1984). Young adult outcome of hyperactive children who received long-term stimulant treatment. *Journal of the American Academy of Child Psychiatry, 23,* 261–269.
Jastak, S., & Wilkinson, G. S. (1984). *Wide Range Achievement Test–Revised.* Wilmington, DE: Jastak Associates.
Jensen, A. (1981). Reaction time and intelligence. In M. Friedman, J. Das, & N. O'Connor (Eds.), *Intelligence and learning* (pp. 39–51). New York: Plenum.
Lerer, R. J., Lerer, M. P., & Artner, J. (1977). The effects of methylphenidate on the handwriting of children with minimal brain dysfunction. *Journal of Pediatrics, 91,* 127–132.
Levy, H. B. (1973). *Square pegs, round holes: The learning-disabled child in the classroom and the home.* Boston: Little, Brown.
Loney, J., Kramer, J., & Kosier, T. (1981, August). *Medicated vs. unmedicated hyperactive adolescents: Academic, delinquent and symptomatological outcome.* Paper presented at the meeting of the American Psychological Association, Los Angeles.
May, L. J., & Hood, V. R. (1973). *Basic Arithmetic Skill Evaluation.* Pleasantville, NY: Educational Division of Reader's Digest.
Pelham, W. E., Bender, M. E., Caddell, J., Booth, S., & Moorer, S. H. (1985). Methylphenidate and children with attention deficit disorder: Dose effects on classroom academic and social behavior. *Archives of General Psychiatry, 42,* 948–952.
Pelham, W. E., Swanson, J., Bender, M., & Wilson, J. (1980, September). *Effects of pemoline on hyperactivity: Laboratory and classroom measures.* Paper presented at the annual meeting of the American Psychological Association, Montreal.
Prinzmetal, M., & Bloomberg, W. (1935). The use of Benzedrine for the treatment of narcolepsy. *Journal of the American Medical Association, 105,* 2051–2054.
Quinn, P., & Rapoport, J. (1975). One-year follow-up of hyperactive boys treated with imipramine and methylphenidate. *American Journal of Psychiatry, 132,* 241–245.
Rapoport, J. L., Quinn, P. O., Bradbard, G., Riddle, K. D., & Brooks, E. (1974). Imipramine and methylphenidate treatments of hyperactive boys. *Archives of General Psychiatry, 30,* 789–793.
Rapport, M. D., Stoner, G., DuPaul, G. J., Birmingham, B. K., & Tucker, S. (1985). Methylphenidate in hyperactive children: Differential effects of dose on academic, learning, and social behavior. *Journal of Abnormal Child Psychology, 13,* 227–244.
Richardson, E., & DiBenedetto, B. (1985). *The Decoding Skills Test.* Parkton, MD: York Press.

Richardson, E., Kupietz, S. A., Winsberg, B. G., Maitinsky, S., & Mendell, N. (1988). Effects of methylphenidate dosage in hyperactive reading-disabled children: II. Reading achievement. *Journal of the American Academy of Child and Adolescent Psychiatry, 27,* 78–87.
Richardson, E., Kupietz, S., & Maitinsky, S. (1987). What is the role of academic intervention in the treatment of hyperactive children with reading disorders. In J. Loney (Ed.), *The young hyperactive child: Answers to questions about diagnosis, prognosis, and treatment* (pp. 153–167). New York: Haworth Press.
Riddle, D., & Rapoport, J. (1976). A 2-year follow-up of 72 hyperactive boys. *Journal of Nervous and Mental Disease, 162,* 126–134.
Rie, D. R., & Rie, H. E. (1977). Recall, retention and Ritalin. *Journal of Consulting and Clinical Psychology, 45,* 967–972.
Rosen, L. A., O'Leary, S. G., Joyce, S. A., Conway, G., & Pfiffner, L. J. (1984). The importance of prudent negative consequences for maintaining the appropriate behavior of hyperactive students. *Journal of Abnormal Child Psychology, 12,* 581–604.
Salvia, J., & Ysseldyke, J. (1981). *Assessment in special education and remedial education.* Boston: Houghton-Mifflin.
Satterfield, J. H., Cantwell, D. P., & Satterfield, B. T. (1979). Multimodality treatment: A one-year follow-up of 84 hyperactive boys. *Archives of General Psychiatry, 36,* 965–974.
Satterfield, J. H., Satterfield, B. T., & Cantwell, D. P. (1980). Multimodality treatment: A two year evaluation of 61 hyperactive boys. *Archives of General Psychiatry, 37,* 915–918.
Satterfield, J. H., Satterfield, B. T., & Cantwell, D. P. (1981). Three-year multimodality treatment study of 100 hyperactive boys. *Journal of Pediatrics, 98,* 650–655.
Schain, R. J., & Reynard, C. L. (1975). Observations on effects of central stimulant drug (methylphenidate) in children with hyperactive behavior. *Pediatrics, 55,* 709–716.
Sprague, R. L., & Berger, B. D. (1980). Drug effects on learning performance: Relevance of animal research to pediatric psychopharmacology. In R. M. Knights & D. J. Bakker (Eds.), *Rehabilitation, treatment and management of learning disorders.* Baltimore: University Park Press.
Stephens, R. S., Pelham, W. E., & Skinner, R. (1984). The state-dependent and main effects of methylphenidate and pemoline on paired-associates learning and spelling in hyperactive children. *Journal of Consulting and Clinical Psychology, 523,* 104–113.
Swanson, H. L. (1985). Assessing learning disabled children's intelligence: An information processing perspective. In K. D. Gadow (Ed.), *Advances in learning and behavioral disabilities* (vol. 4, pp. 225–272). Greenwich, CT: JAI Press.
Swanson, H. L., & Watson, B. (1982). *Educational and psychological assessment of exceptional children: Theories, strategies, and applications.* St. Louis: Mosby.
Taylor, E. (1979). The use of drugs in hyperkinetic states: Clinical issues. *Neuropharmacology, 18,* 951–958.
Wagner, R., & Sternberg, R. J. (1984). Alternative conceptions of intelligence and their implications for education. *Review of Educational Research, 54,* 179–223.
Weiss, G., Kruger, E., Danielson, U., & Elman, M. (1975). Effects of long-term treatment of hyperactive children with methylphenidate. *Canadian Medical Association Journal, 112,* 159–165.
Weiss, G., Minde, K., Douglas, V., Werry, J., & Sykes, D. (1971). Comparison of the

effects of chlorpromazine, dextroamphetamine and methylphenidate on the behavior and intellectual functioning of hyperactive children. *Canadian Medical Association Journal, 104,* 20–25.

Whalen, C. K., Henker, B., & Finck, D. (1981). Medication effects in the classroom: Three naturalistic indicators. *Canadian Journal of Psychiatry, 26,* 385–392.

Yellin, A. M., Hopwood, J. H., & Greenberg, L. M. (1982). Adults and adolescents with attention deficit disorder: Clinical and behavioral responses to psychostimulants. *Journal of Clinical Psychopharmacology, 2,* 133–136.

CHAPTER 17

The Role of Standardized Tests in Planning Academic Instruction

DONALD D. HAMMILL
BRIAN R. BRYANT

Of the many uses of standardized tests, perhaps the most pleasing to practitioners are those that relate to academic intervention. Although diagnosticians and placement specialists value standardized tests for their ability to provide data that are useful in making identification and placement decisions, teachers generally prefer standardized measures that enable them to make concrete decisions that lead directly to improved instruction. The purpose of this chapter is to describe standardized tests and discuss how they can be used to improve instruction. We do so by describing the nature of standardized tests and the specific standardized tests that are used to plan appropriate educational programming.

THE NATURE OF STANDARDIZED TESTS

Although the importance of standardized tests is often discussed, much confusion exists as to just what a standardized test is. To clarify this situation, it is helpful first to define what a test is. *Test* is defined in *Webster's*

Ninth New Collegiate Dictionary (1987) as "something (as a series of questions or exercises) for measuring the skill knowledge, intelligence, capacities, or aptitudes of an individual or group" (p. 1218). In the broadest sense, tests take the form of traditional question-and-answer scales as well as rating scales, checklists, interviews, work samples, and observations. Tests can either be standardized or nonstandardized.

Anastasi (1988) and Nunnally (1978) describe standardized tests as having three essential characteristics: set procedures for administration, objective scoring criteria, and a specified preferred frame of reference to guide interpretation of scores. Obviously, tests that do not have these characteristics would be considered nonstandardized or inadequately standardized measures. This chapter focuses on standardized tests. Each of the three characteristics of standardized tests is described next.

SET ADMINISTRATION PROCEDURES

In order for a test to be considered standardized, instructions must be set forth that clearly describe the administration procedures. In this way, little room is left for the examiner to deviate from the prescribed procedures. Anastasi (1988, p. 25) makes the point more succinctly when she notes the following:

In order to secure uniformity of testing conditions, the test constructor provides detailed directions for administering each newly developed test. The formulation of directions is a major part of the standardization of a new test. Such standardization extends to the exact materials employed, time limits, oral instructions, preliminary demonstrations, ways of handling queries from test takers, and every other detail of the testing situation.

Such set administration procedures are crucial to all types of standardized tests, whether they are conventional question-and-answer scales, interviews, direct observations, or analytic teaching techniques.

OBJECTIVE SCORING CRITERIA

An objective system for scoring a test is essential. If the test involves questions and answers, the system must provide specific criteria for scoring the correctness of an answer. In most instances, scoring procedures are straightforward and easily defined. For example, a mathematics calculation item that reads "$4 + 6 = X$, solve for X" can have only one correct answer, 10. Any other answer would be incorrect. Likewise, when *bat* is shown to the student with the instruction, "What is this word?" only one answer is acceptable. Compare these examples with a reading comprehension question that asks, "Why do you think Mary is feeling the way she is?

(Accept any reasonable answer.)" Clearly, this example allows for a subjective judgment on the part of the examiner, a violation of the "objective scoring criteria" for standardized methods.

For other types of tests, different systems exist for objectively noting behaviors. For example, standardized classroom observation scales provide clear means of classifying different types of student–teacher interactions. Here, the author of the scale provides such a specific description of each type of interaction that subjectivity is minimized or entirely eliminated. The important aspect of such an evaluation, or any other form of standardized test, is to prepare the examiner to see the behavior clearly, to classify it according to some clearly defined system, and to record it properly.

A SPECIFIC FRAME OF REFERENCE

Well-standardized tests provide a clear indication of the frame of reference that is to be applied to the results. Such frames of reference include interpretations that are norm-referenced, criterion-referenced, or non-referenced. Each is described briefly here.

Norm-Referenced Interpretation

Gronlund (1985) describes norm-referenced interpretations as those that "enable us to determine how an individual's performance compares with that of others. This might be a local, state or national group, depending on how the results are to be used" (p. 13). Based on the performance of the comparison group, a test score or particular behavior could be described as being more or less equal to, above, or below the average. To better describe norm-referenced interpretation, three critical features will be discussed: the interpretation of raw scores, the demographic features of a normative sample, and the norm-referencing process.

Interpretation of raw scores. When norm-referenced interpretations are to be based on test performance, the raw scores (i.e., the number of items answered correctly) made by students are converted to values that represent their distance from the mean performance of the normative sample. The results are called *derivation norms*, and the procedure for computing the normative scores is relatively simple. At each age level, the raw scores made by the students in the normative sample are tallied on a cumulative frequency distribution chart. From these data, cumulative percentages are generated and percentile ranks assigned. Salvia and Ysseldyke (1988, p. 93) have described the advantages of reporting scores in terms of percentile ranks:

These unpretentious scores require the fewest assumptions for accurate interpretations. . . . They are readily understood by professionals, parents, and children. Most important, however, is the fact that percentiles tell us nothing more than what any norm-referenced derived score can tell us—namely, an individual's relative standing in a group.

The ease of interpreting percentiles makes them particularly valuable. For example, a percentile of 56 means that 56% of the normative sample scored at or below the student's score. It should be noted that the distance between two percentile ranks becomes much greater as those ranks are more distant from the mean or average (i.e., the 50th percentile).

Although percentiles provide easy interpretation, standard scores provide the clearest indication of a student's performance. Standard scores are a direct conversion from percentiles and represent a specified position in the normal curve distribution that identify the score's distance from the mean (M) of the normative group relative to the standard deviation (SD) of the distribution.

Depending upon the preference of the test developer, raw scores can be converted into a variety of standard score distributions. The most popular of these are stanines ($M = 5$, $SD = 1.96$), T-scores ($M = 50$, $SD = 10$), z-scores ($M = 0$, $SD = 1$), and deviation quotients ($M = 100$, $SD = 15$). Table 17-1 provides information that enables percentiles to be converted to a number of types of standard scores. Furthermore, the table depicts the relationship of various standard scores to one another.

Standard scores are particularly useful because they are interval data that can be combined, averaged, and otherwise manipulated statistically. They are particularly useful when comparing test scores, especially when conducting discrepancy analyses.

The test data derived from a normative group can also be used to calculate age and grade equivalents. Their use results in such statements as "Pamela reads at the 8.3 grade level" or "Lea is at the 3-year level in gross motor development." Age and grade equivalents are derived by computing the average raw score made by the normative group at a given age or grade level. Each point is recorded on a matrix that has raw scores on one axis and age or grade levels along the other axis. Points are plotted for the raw scores obtained at various ages or grades, and a line is drawn to connect the points on the matrix. In this way, the age or grade that corresponds to each raw score can be determined easily.

Age and grade equivalents are reported in test manuals because they enjoy a false reputation as being useful and easily understood. In fact, these scores are widely misunderstood, and most experts in assessment discourage their use. Such organizations as the International Reading Association (1980) and the American Psychological Association (1985) advocate abandoning age and grade equivalents when reporting test results.

Table 17-1. Relation of Various Standard Scores to Percentile Rank and to Each Other

Percentile rank	Standard Scores					Deficit
	Quotients	NCE scores	T-scores	z-scores	stanines	
99	150	99	83	+3.33	9	
99	145	99	80	+3.00	9	
99	140	99	77	+2.67	9	
99	135	99	73	+2.33	9	
98	130	92	70	+2.00	9	
95	125	85	67	+1.67	8	
91	120	78	63	+1.34	8	none
84	115	71	60	+1.00	7	
75	110	64	57	+0.67	6	
63	105	57	53	+0.33	6	
50	100	50	50	+0.00	5	
37	95	43	47	-0.33	4	
25	90	36	43	-0.67	4	
16	85	29	40	-1.00	3	mild
9	80	22	37	-1.34	2	
5	75	15	33	-1.67	2	moderate
2	70	8	30	-2.00	1	
1	65	1	27	-2.33	1	
1	60	1	23	-2.67	1	severe
1	55	1	20	-3.00	1	

Aiken (1988) and Salvia and Ysseldyke (1988) provide detailed discussions of the disadvantages of age and grade equivalents, but a few of the major problems are identified here. First, there is no such thing as a "reading level," per se, (e.g., "Denise is functioning at the 4.2 reading level"). Basal readers differ dramatically in the content of their texts at the various grade levels, and readability formulas (i.e., mathematical formulas that purport to assign grade levels to reading passages) also are erratic and differ greatly from one formula to another. Second, interpolation and extrapolation are often involved in computing these scores. Interpolation occurs when obtained points on the matrix are connected, providing an erroneous assumption that a particular raw score was actually obtained by members of the normative group. Furthermore, scores are extrapolated beyond those actually achieved in a normative sample, resulting in such "scores" as 11.6 grade equivalency, even though no one beyond the sixth grade was included in the norm group. Finally, age and grade equivalents are ordinal in nature, that is, the distance between points is not equal, a reality that prevents their legitimate use in discrepancy formulas.

The normative data just described (i.e., the generation of standard scores, percentiles, and age/grade equivalents from raw scores achieved by some specified normative group) constitutes the most sophisticated use of norms. However, other types of "norms" exist that are not derived from the performance of a normative group. Two examples of these types of norms are what we call descriptive norms and developmental norms.

Descriptive norms are those that teachers have internalized by observing children over a period of several years. Using their experience, teachers can observe their students' behaviors and make normative judgments based on their knowledge of how most people the students' ages have performed on similar tasks in the past. For example, most competent third-grade teachers with 10 years of classroom experience need no normative tables to tell them what typical behavior is for third-graders. Using their descriptive norms, teachers are able to describe an individual student's performance as superior, average, or poor.

The other type of norms that are widely used are *developmental norms*. These norms are similar to descriptive norms because they relate to behaviors that are observed to be common at generally agreed upon age levels. Unlike descriptive norms, however, developmental norms are not internalized idiosyncratically by individual practitioners or clinicians. Rather, developmental norms are based on developmental milestones that have been observed over a period of time by numerous researchers. An example would be "baby's first word," which usually occurs at 9 to 10 months of age. Thus, a 27-month-old child who utters his first word would, according to developmental norms, be exhibiting behaviors of a 10-month-old child.

Demographic characteristics of the normative group. Test developers must demonstrate that their normative group is representative of the population with which the test is intended to be used. This population may be a national group, a regional segment of the population, students in a particular school system or in a specific classroom, or perhaps a class of disabled students. The characteristics that are usually used to show representativeness include gender, geographic area, social class, race, ethnicity, urban–rural residence, age, and intellectual level.

A representative sample can be obtained in several ways. One procedure involves selecting a normative group on the basis of stratified sampling. In this way, specific school systems are targeted for inclusion in the normative group, because they represent their geographic region with regard to important demographic variables. If a targeted school system is unable to participate, an alternate site that is similar in demographic make-up is invited to become involved in the normative effort.

A second way to get a representative sample is to select schools randomly to participate in given areas nationwide. Once data are gathered, the demographic characteristics of the normative group are examined. If a particular area is found to be unrepresentative (e.g., if too few males are in the sample), the scores of participating males in the group can be weighted or more males can be tested. The key to the second procedure involves random selection, and the assumption that randomness will ensure representativeness across the key demographic variables.

The norm-referencing process. To illustrate the norm-referencing process, consider the case of 6-year-old Cari, who is suspected of having a learning disability in reading. Mr. Dunn has been given the responsibility of evaluating Cari to see if she has an aptitude–achievement discrepancy. He has selected norm-referenced measures to assess intellectual functioning and achievement, the Detroit Tests of Learning Aptitude-Primary (DTLA-P) (Hammill & Bryant, 1986) and the Reading subtest of the *Quick-Score Achievement Test* (Q-SAT) (Hammill, Ammer, Cronin, Mandlebaum, & Quinby, 1988), respectively. After administering the two measures, Mr. Dunn has determined the following:

Cari's General Intelligence Quotient on the DTLA-P was 97, placing her in the average range of aptitude. Her reading score of 62 on the Q-SAT places her below the first percentile. The difference between the scores on these two norm-referenced measures (i.e., 35 points) indicates a significant discrepancy between aptitude and achievement. Such a finding satisfies one of the criteria of a diagnosis of learning disability.

Determinations such as this can be made only with the aid of norm-referenced interpretations, which make this frame of reference useful and popular.

Criterion-Referenced Interpretation

Criterion-referencing, like norm-referencing, refers to a method of interpreting test scores. Unlike norm-referenced interpretations, which are used to compare an examinee's performance to that of a specified target group, criterion-referenced interpretations are undertaken to determine how an examinee performs in relation to mastery of content. That is, criterion-referenced assessments are "designed to provide a measure of performance that is interpretable in terms of a clearly defined and delimited domain of learning tasks" (Gronlund, 1985, p. 13).

In general, the subject matter or domain to be evaluated is clearly defined in terms of skills, tasks, or test items; and the criterion for successful mastery is specified (e.g., the examinee answers at least 90% of the items correctly). To illustrate, let us imagine that Jon is being assessed on double-digit subtraction items that involve regrouping. The following items appear on the measure:

1. 78 −29	2. 42 −33	3. 64 −28	4. 37 −19	5. 27 −18
6. 40 −12	7. 25 −16	8. 63 −47	9. 55 −19	10. 41 −18

In order to demonstrate mastery at the 90% level, Jon could miss only one problem in the set. With this frame of reference, the examiner does not need to know what other students Jon's age scored on the same items. The important question here deals with what Jon is able to do regarding double-digit subtraction that involves regrouping.

Obviously, criterion-referenced tests are meaningful with regard to instructional decision making. They can be used to identify specific instructional needs, to monitor progress in a remedial program, or to place students into a curriculum. Criterion-referenced interpretations are frequently used by teachers when they make up their own tests. For example, Ms. Jones may administer the 10 arithmetic items shown previously at the beginning of the week. After four days of drill and practice, similar items are re-administered. The students in her class that demonstrate mastery (i.e., achieve at 90% or better) can move to the next lesson. Those not achieving mastery can continue to work on similar problems until they have mastered the content.

Nonreferenced Interpretation

Similar to norm-referenced and criterion-referenced interpretations, nonreferenced interpretations are concerned with how students perform tasks that are being assessed. However, nonreferenced tests focus on identifying the strategies or systems that students use to solve problems and arrive at answers.

As one would imagine, answers that students give to problems and to teachers' questions, even when incorrect, are not always reached by guessing. Rather, most students make a decision about a problem after employing some form of strategy or logic. If teachers can determine the strategy or procedure that students use in problem solving, they can help the students "unlearn" the inefficient strategies and replace them with those that are effective.

While norm-referenced and criterion-referenced assessments are concerned with the answers that examinees give to items, nonreferenced

17. The Role of Standardized Tests in Planning Academic Instruction   381

assessments are concerned with "how" answers are derived. To illustrate, let us assume that a student correctly responds to an algebra problem, but arrives at the right answer using the "trial and error" procedure rather than using an efficient strategy. Since algebra's concepts build upon one another, the student's use of an inefficient procedure may be leading to difficulties as more complex problems are encountered. In this case, the teacher should identify that an inefficient strategy was employed in problem solving. Otherwise, the "correctness" of the problem can mislead a teacher into thinking that the student has demonstrated an understanding of the algebraic concepts underlying an item. Nonreferenced assessments can prevent such erroneous assumptions.

Another common occurrence in mathematics is exemplified by the problem "$45 - 17 = X$, solve for X." The student's answer of "$X = 32$" can reflect carelessness or perhaps an incorrect strategy. Here the student may be thinking that the smaller number is *always* subtracted from the larger number, thus demonstrating no understanding of the concept of regrouping. Such a faulty strategy must be unlearned and replaced with an effective regrouping strategy.

As a third example, consider the task depicted in Figure 17-1. By observing students as they attack the problem or by asking them how they solved it, the examiner is able to identify the strategies that were used to arrive at an answer. The problem can be solved in many ways. Some

Figure 17-1. Task: How many triangles are embedded in this picture? From D. D. Hammill (1987). Assessing Students in Schools. In D. D. Hammill (Ed.). Assessing the abilities and instructional needs of students. Reprinted by permission of Austin, TX: PRO-ED, 5-37.

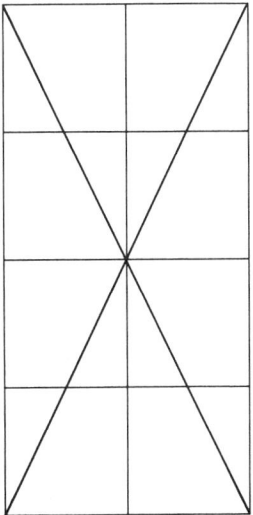

solutions are more efficient than others, but none is entirely without merit. For example, Steve solved the problem by counting the number of right angles. In contrast, Gail arrived at the solution by counting the number of smaller triangles and working up systematically to the larger ones. Glen answered the question by taking his pencil and shading each triangle after counting it. The shading helped him not to count each one more than once. Finally, Dennis started counting in the left corner and expanded to the rest of the figure. The students may or may not have come up with the same answer, but each one attempted to solve the problem in an idiosyncratic way. Norm-referenced and criterion-referenced assessments are unconcerned with the manner in which the problem is solved, whereas the nonreferenced assessment is less concerned with the final answer than with the procedure that was employed to arrive at the solution.

Some authorities consider nonreferenced interpretation to be a subtype of criterion referencing in a very general sense. They assign all interpretations that are not norm-referenced to that category, even those that apply no explicit criterion for scoring or those that use scores for purely descriptive purposes. Most writers, however, do not consider this type of interpretation as criterion referencing, but they are at a loss as to what type of referencing to call it. In fact, when Hammill (1987) first used the term nonreferencing for this type of interpretation, he stated "I called it nonreferencing, recognizing that this term is not completely satisfactory. Perhaps in time a better term will be coined, but for now this one will suffice" (p. 25). At the time of this writing, we have failed to arrive at a better term.

EVIDENCE OF ADEQUATE STANDARDIZATION

Up to this point, we have presented three key ingredients of standardized tests: set administration procedures, objective scoring criteria, and a specified frame of reference for interpreting test results. Without each of these elements, a test cannot be considered truly standardized. However, the presence of these three elements alone does not ensure that a test is adequately standardized. In order for a test to be deemed adequately standardized, evidence of reliability and validity must be available.

RELIABILITY

The documentation of a test's reliability provides important evidence of adequate standardization. Since reliability is synonymous with consistency, the lack of reliability means that a test is yielding inconsistent results.

Thus, if an unreliable test is used, students can be observed one day and identified as exhibiting particular behaviors. Observations undertaken the next day might reveal that the behaviors have vanished. In actuality, the behaviors did not vanish at all; they never existed in the first place. Rather, the observations were false-positive byproducts of the test's inadequate reliability. In short then, unreliable tests yield untrustworthy results; untrustworthy results can lead to errors in interpretation; and errors of interpretation invariably lead to producing negative consequences for the individuals who were assessed and embarrassment for the person conducting the assessment. Of the sources of error that influence reliability, the most commonly reported involve content sampling, time sampling, and interscorer sampling.

Content sampling deals exclusively with the reliability of tests, and usually refers to internal consistency reliability (i.e., the interrelationship among test items). Since the purpose of a test is to measure a certain characteristic or ability, the more a test's items relate to one another the smaller the content sampling error and, consequently, the higher the internal consistency reliability will be. The most common procedures for estimating the internal consistency reliability of a test (i.e., the amount of error that is associated with content sampling) are the split-half method, the Kuder–Richardson and coefficient alpha formulas, and the immediate test–retest with alternate forms method.

Time sampling error refers to the extent to which a person's performance or behavior is consistent or stable over a period of time. The importance of this source of error is obvious. Tests that are not stable yield inconsistent results, and remedial programs or treatments designed on the basis of such results would be suspect. The error associated with time sampling is usually estimated using the delayed test–retest with a single form method. If more than one form of a test exists (e.g., Forms A and B), the best way to estimate this source of error is by employing the delayed test–retest with alternate forms method.

Interscorer or *interobserver error* is most often used with tests that involve subjectivity in scoring, such as rating scales used to assess students' written products or speech and language samples. This source of error usually is estimated by intercorrelating the results of observations or by calculating the percentage of agreement among observers.

Most of the methods discussed in this section yield a summative statistic—the reliability coefficient. To be considered minimally reliable, the reliability coefficients for a procedure must approximate or exceed 0.80 in magnitude (Sattler, 1988). Coefficients of 0.90 or above are considered the most desirable (Aiken, 1988; Helmstadtler, 1964; Nunnally, 1978; Salvia & Ysseldyke, 1988).

VALIDITY

A test that is demonstrated to evaluate the behaviors it is supposed to measure is said to be valid. In order for a test to be considered adequately standardized, evidence of validity must be provided, usually through logical or experimental means. Three types of validity are described most often: content validity, criterion-related validity, and construct validity.

Content Validity

When discussing content validation, Gronlund (1985) describes it as "the process of determining the extent to which a set of test tasks provides a relevant and representative sample of the domain of tasks under consideration" (p. 59). Content validity is built into a test from its inception. In so doing, items, interview questions, error analysis systems, and checklists must be devised with care, ensuring that they represent adequately the domain that is being measured.

For example, the content validity of an arithmetic test could be ensured by surveying the most widely used arithmetic textbooks and selecting items that represent arithmetic problems found in all the books. Additional evidence of content validation of the test could be provided by demonstrating empirically that items on the scale satisfy rigorous statistical standards set forth during item analysis.

The content validity of a reading abilities checklist could be demonstrated by providing information that items on the checklist conform to various scope-and-sequence charts depicting reading behaviors. These charts are available in textbooks on reading and in various basal reading series used in schools.

Questions used during interviews can be examined for content validity by subjecting them to critiques by experts in the area of the interview. The reviewers could judge the value of the questions and make recommendations as to their utility. Such a nonempirical method of establishing content validity is particularly useful when accepted statistical procedures are not available.

Error analysis systems can be evaluated for their content validity by showing that the error types in question are classified in a manner consistent with current theory. For example, a reading miscue analysis that is based on the works of a noted authority would be said to have content validity.

Content validity should not be confused with face validity. Noting that a math test has adequate content validity simply because it "looks like" a math test is insufficient. Content validation is the result of careful documentation of the procedures that were employed during item development and selection.

Criterion-Related Validity

Criterion-related validation relates to the degree with which a new test either predicts future behavior (predictive validity) or predicts contemporaneous behavior (concurrent validity). Predictive validity is demonstrated by assessing current behaviors, letting an extended period of time pass (from a couple of months to several years) and then assessing similar or other targeted behaviors. The extent to which the first measure successfully predicts future performance provides evidence of predictive validation.

If concurrent validity is to be examined, performance on the new test is compared to that measured by an older, established device. If the two procedures yield similar findings, the new scale is said to possess concurrent validity.

Construct Validity

The third type of validity, construct validity, refers to the extent to which the underlying constructs of a test can be identified and how the traits reflect the theoretical models that underly the procedure. Gronlund (1985) offers a three-step procedure for demonstrating construct validity. First, several traits or constructs are identified that are presumed to account for a person's performance on the test. Second, hypotheses are generated that are based on the identified constructs. Finally, the hypotheses are verified logically or empirically.

To illustrate, the developers of a new spelling test may hypothesize that spelling should be age-related (because spelling is a developmental construct), should be related to intelligence (because spelling is a cognitive skill), and should relate to report card performance in the language arts (because spelling is one language arts component). Once the hypotheses are generated, the new spelling test would be administered to a group of students and their results compared to (a) those of students younger or older than themselves, (b) their performance on an intelligence test, and (c) their numerical grades in language arts on their report cards. If the results support the hypotheses that were formulated, the test could be said to have construct validity. Though our example pertains to establishing the construct validity of a test, the procedures advanced by Gronlund (1985) are applicable to the results of all kinds of assessment techniques.

In concluding our discussion about the nature of standardized tests, three important points should be made. To begin with, although most experts refer to standardization with regard to conventional question-and-answer scales, the principles hold for all forms of tests.

Next, we purposefully did not restrict standardized tests to those requiring norm-referenced interpretations. Whether interpretations are to be norm-referenced, criterion-referenced, or nonreferenced, the standardized instruments used to generate data that are interpretable need to possess administration and scoring instructions, generate consistent findings, and yield valid results.

Finally, tests must be thought of in relative terms regarding standardization. *Highly standardized* tests are those that have set administration and scoring procedures, have a definitive frame of reference, and provide exhaustive evidence of reliablity and validity. Tests that satisfy the essential elements of standardization (i.e., set administration and scoring procedures and a specified frame of reference) but provide only one or two studies as evidence of reliability and validity would be classified as *adequately standardized*. Tests that have set administration and scoring instructions, have a definitive frame of reference, but provide no or insufficient evidence of reliability and validity must be considered *inadequately standardized*. Having discussed the concept of standardized tests, we will devote the remainder of this chapter to describing standardized tests that are available for academic intervention.

USING STANDARDIZED TESTS TO PLAN APPROPRIATE INSTRUCTION

In the previous sections, we described the nature of standardized tests. We concluded by noting that the degree with which evidence is presented relating to the criteria for standardization (i.e., set administration procedures, objective scoring criteria, a specified frame of evidence, reliability, and validity) determines the extent to which a test can be considered standardized. The levels of standardized tests were identified as highly standardized, adequately standardized, and inadequately standardized. In this section, we provide (a) a brief discussion concerning the applicability of standardized tests for determining academic strengths and weaknesses and (b) brief descriptions of standardized instruments that are commercially available.

APPLYING STANDARDIZED TESTS FOR ACADEMIC INTERVENTION

Every test has a specified use. For example, norm-referenced standardized tests provide users with an index of performance that places a student's results along a continuum of poor to superior as compared with a normative group. Such an index is useful for identifying general strengths and weaknesses in the construct being measured, assisting multidisciplinary teams in making decisions of identification and placement, generating scores that can be used by researchers in their efforts to conduct experiments, and providing scores that can be used to determine progress in an intervention program.

Although norm-referenced standardized tests are helpful when used for such purposes, most of them are inadequate as aids in planning academic interventions. Criterion-referenced tests are better tools for this use. The reason for this is twofold. First, items in a norm-referenced test are designed to ensure variance. As Popham (1973, pp. 82–83) notes, a norm-referenced test author

> makes all sorts of concessions, sometimes subtle, sometimes obvious, to promote variant scores. He disdains items which are 'too easy' or 'too hard.' He tries to increase the allure of wrong-answer options. All this he does to produce variability

By creating items with variance, test authors ensure internal consistency of their tests and produce a scale that can discriminate between individuals with good and poor abilities in the construct being measured. Criterion-referenced tests are not concerned with variance. Instead they provide items that are supposedly within the examinee's capabilities to answer correctly.

Second, norm-referenced tests are designed to be efficient, providing as few items as possible to get the job done. These measures include enough items to sample the content being measured adequately but not enough items to completely tap a domain. Thus a norm-referenced interpretation on a geography test can be obtained with as few as 20 items. The facts about geography that a student may need to pass the sixth grade may be as many as 200. The norm-referenced test will tell the teacher who is good and who is poor in geography, but it will not include enough items to inventory specific knowledge. We strongly believe that examiners who use norm-referenced tests for determining specific instructional objectives are generally wasting their time.

SPECIFIC STANDARDIZED TESTS FOR ACADEMIC INSTRUCTION

For decades, teachers have devised and used their own tests for identifying the academic skills that students do or do not have. Of late, however, a number of tests that attempt to measure the attainment of skills in the various academic areas have become available from commercial publishers. The influx of these tests is no doubt related to the passage of P.L. 94-142 and its provision for the establishment of the Individualized Education Program (IEP). The IEP calls for providing educational goals and specific instructional objectives in each deficit area. Such a requirement is satisfied by these new tests, which often report their results in formats that fit neatly into the IEP framework.

In our search for these instruments, we found no highly standardized or even adequately standardized measures, only those that can be considered inadequately standardized. In every instance, the devices described here have procedures for administration and scoring/recording and provide for a criterion-referenced or nonreferenced interpretation. However, reliability and/or validity information are either nonexistent or insufficient. Such an oversight is unfortunate because experts on assessment (e.g., Anastasi, 1988; Gronlund, 1985) discuss the importance of technical adequacy for tests such as these. Such an oversight also demonstrates that the profession has been surprisingly lenient in accepting criterion-referenced and nonreferenced tests in the absence of standardized evidence. We suspect that such tolerance is short-lived and that test users will soon demand that authors and publishers of these types of measures provide evidence of technical adequacy. Fortunately, in the interim, test users can determine for themselves the technical adequacy of such tests (see Anastasi, 1988, Chapters 5 and 6). The tests described here are intended to provide the reader with examples of the formats, item types, and contents that educationally useful tests provide. Descriptions are provided here of the Brigance Diagnostic Inventories, the Hudson Education Skills Inventories, the Spellmaster Assessment and Teaching System, the Stanford Diagnostic Mathematics Test, and the miscue analysis procedure employed with the Gray Oral Reading Test–Revised.

Brigance Diagnostic Inventories

The Brigance Diagnostic Inventories are a series of assessment batteries that assess developmental and academic skills from birth through 18 years. The batteries are designed to measure preacademic, academic, and vocational skills while providing teachers with information that can be used to identify instructional objectives for use with individualized educational programs. As of this writing, the following batteries exist: the Brigance Diagnostic Assessment of Basic Skills—Spanish Edition (Brigance, 1984), the Brigance Diagnostic Inventory of Basic Skills (Brigance, 1983), the Brigance Diagnostic Inventory for Early Development (Brigance, 1978), the Brigance Diagnostic Inventory for Essential Skills (Brigance, 1981), the Brigance K and 1 Screen for Kindergarten and First Grade (Brigance, 1982), and the Brigance Preschool Screen (Brigance, 1985).

Although the batteries are considered to be criterion-referenced, they also provide grade equivalencies and/or developmental levels. Such "norms" are not based on the performance of a normative group, but rather rest on the association of each assessed skill with basal levels or developmental levels. As such, the inventories could be classified as employing the *consensus norms* we discussed earlier. Even though norms are provided, these tests provide the most value when their results are subjected to a criterion-referenced interpretation.

An exhaustive description of each test is beyond the scope of this chapter. Instead, Table 17-2 presents the skills areas assessed by each battery. In some instances, alternate forms are available for specific skill areas. In all instances, items were selected following a review of textbooks, basal series, and scope-and-sequence charts. According to the author, items were then reviewed by content experts to determine their value and contribution to the scales, although insufficient information is provided in the manual to use such information as support for the tests' validity.

Although Brigance recommends that administration instructions be adapted to ensure valid assessment, recommended directions for administering and scoring each item are provided. The cut-off scores for determining mastery vary from skill to skill, and an instructional objective for each skill is provided. For example, an objective accompanying the Early Development Scale reads OBJECTIVE: By (date), when presented with a list of the number words from one to ten, (child's name) will correctly read (number) of them" (Brigance, 1978, p. 205).

Hudson Education Skills Inventories

The Hudson Education Skills Inventories (HESI) consists of three batteries measuring skills in mathematics (HESI–Mathematics, Hudson & Colson, 1989), reading (HESI–Reading, Hudson, Colson, & Hudson-Welch, 1989), and writing (HESI–Writing, Hudson, Colson, Banikowski, & Mehring, 1989).

The inventories employ a "test down–teach up" model, whereby examiners test down a series of skills until mastery is achieved. At that point, instructional objectives are established for "teaching up" the skills hierarchy. Each item provides a grade level equivalency "range" (e.g., K, K–2) that reflects the placement of the item across the various basal series that were examined during item development.

Table 17-3 provides the skill areas that are assessed in HESI-Mathematics. Items in each skill area are provided to determine mastery levels. Administration and scoring procedures are provided, and a criterion-referenced interpretation is made on the results of testing. Data are recorded on the Instructional Planning Form, a sample of which is provided in Figure 17-2.

Table 17-2. Skills Assesed by the Brigance Diagnostic Inventories

BRIGANCE DIAGNOSTIC ASSESSMENT OF BASIC SKILLS—SPANISH EDITION (PREESCHOOL THROUGH GRADE 6)

Readiness
Speech
Functional word recognition
Oral reading

Reading comprehension
Word analysis
Listening

Writing and alphabetizing
Numbers and Computation
Measurement

BRIGANCE DIAGNOSTIC COMPREHENSIVE INVENTORY OF BASIC SKILLS (GRADES K THROUGH 9)

Readiness
Reading
Listening

Research and study skills
Spelling

Language
Math

BRIGANCE DIAGNOSTIC INVENTORY OF BASIC SKILLS (GRADES K THROUGH 6)

Readiness
Reading

Language arts
Mathematics

BRIGANCE DIAGNOSTIC INVENTORY OF EARLY DEVELOPMENT (AGES 0 THROUGH 7)

Motor skills
Speech-related skills

Written language skills
Math

BRIGANCE DIAGNOSTIC INVENTORY OF ESSENTIAL SKILLS (GRADES 4 THROUGH 12)

Reading
Language arts

Mathematics
Life skills

17. The Role of Standardized Tests in Planning Academic Instruction 391

BRIGANCE K & 1 SCREEN FOR KINDERGARTEN AND FIRST GRADE (GRADES K AND 1)

Personal data response	Numeral comprehension	Syntax and fluency (K only)
Color recognition	Prints personal data	Draw a person (1 only)
Picture vocabulary	Total	Recites alphabet (1 only)
Visual discrimination	Gross motor skills (grade K only)	Recognition of lower case letters (1 only)
Visual–motor skills	Identification of body parts (grade K only)	Auditory discrimination (1 only)
Counting	Follow verbal directions (K only)	Numerals in sequence (1 only)

BRIGANCE PRESCHOOL SCREEN (AGES 3 AND 4)

Personal data	Builds tower with blocks	Plurals (3 only)
Identifies body parts	Picture vocabulary	Tells use of objects (4 only)
Gross motor skils	Total	Identifies colors(4 only)
Repeat sentences	Identifies objects (3 only)	Identifies colors (4 only)
Number concepts	Matches colors (3 only)	Prepositions and irregular plural nouns

Table 17-3. Skill Areas Assessed by HESI-Mathematics

I. Numeration (NUM) (54)
   A. Terms, concepts, and symbols (6)
   B. Numeral recognition and use (19)
   C. Rote counting (6)
   D. One-to-one correspondence (3)
   E. Using number relationships (7)
   F. Place value (8)
   G. Using ordinal numbers (5)
II. Addition of Whole Numbers (ADD) (22)
   A. Terms, concepts, and symbols (8)
   B. Computation (14)
III. Subtraction of Whole Numbers (SUB) (19)
   A. Terms, concepts, and symbols (7)
   B. Computation (12)
IV. Multiplication of Whole Numbers (MULT) (16)
   A. Terms, concepts, and symbols (5)
   B. Computation (11)
V. Division of Whole Numbers (DIV) (17)
   A. Terms, concepts, and symbols (9)
   B. Computation (8)
VI. Fractions (FRAC) (41)
   A. Terms, concepts, and symbols (3)
   B. Computation (38)
VII. Decimals (DEC) (33)
   A. Terms, concepts, and symbols (4)
   B. Computation (29)
VIII. Percentages (PER) (14)
   A. Terms, concepts, and symbols (4)
   B. Computation (10)
IX. Time (TIME) (37)
   A. Terms, concepts, and symbols (12)
   B. Recognition and use of calendar time (12)
   C. Recognition and use of clock time (13)
X. Money (MON) (33)
   A. Terms, concepts, and symbols (9)
   B. Counting change and currency equivalents (11)
   C. Making change/functional applications (13)
XI. Measurement (MEAS) (38)
   A. Terms, concepts, and symbols (15)
   B. Using English measurement (11)
   C. Using metric measurement (4)
   D. English/metric computation and conversion (8)
XII. Statistics, Graphs, and Tables (STAT) (10)
   A. Terms, concepts, and symbols (1)
   B. Functional applications (9)
XIII. Geometry (GEO) (25)
   A. Terms, concepts, and symbols (1)
   B. Functional applications (24)
XIV. Word Problems (WORD) (30)
   A. Terms, concepts, and symbols (6)
   B. Strategies (11)
   C. Applied practice (13)

From "HESI-M" by F. Hudson and S. Colson, 1989. Reprinted by permission of PRO-ED.

Spellmaster Assessment and Teaching System

According to Greenbaum (1987), "*Spellmaster* was developed to help examiners quickly diagnose the strengths and weaknesses of individual students and of entire classes. The testing and scoring system allows for the identification of specific problem areas as the tests are scored" (p. 1). The assessment system is comprised of four tests. The Entry Level Tests are administered first and provide entry points (i.e., levels when testing should begin) for the other three measures: Regular Word Tests, Irregular Word Tests, and Homophone Tests.

Regular Word Tests are a series of eight graded tests that, according to the author, assess the dependable generalizations that apply to the bulk of English spellings. The Scope and Sequence chart that is the basis for the eight tests is shown in Table 17-4. As can be seen, the first two tests are based on auditory elements (i.e., those that apply when sounds and symbols have a one-to-one correspondence). Tests 3 through 6 are based on both auditory and visual elements. The author states that "these tests contain words whose sounds can be spelled in more than one way, so the correct spelling requires visual memory as well as phonic knowledge" (Greenbaum, 1987, p. 2).

Tests 6 through 8 target *conceptual* elements by including words whose correct spelling demonstrates knowledge of rules pertaining to suffixes, syllabication, and contractions. Once the appropriate Regular Word Test has been given and the student has written the words on the Student Answer Sheet, performance is scored and the results are transferred to the Spellmaster Score Form (see Figure 17-3). As can be seen, each element of a word is examined for proper spelling, and incorrect responses are circled in the shaded section of the form. The number of errors is tallied at the bottom of the form and this index forms the basis for determining whether instruction is needed.

Spellmaster is a hierarchical system, with each level leading to the next. Once each level is successfully accomplished, the next-level Regular Word Test is administered. The Homophone and Irregular Word Tests can be considered supplemental, in that they may be given at the same time as the Regular Word Tests, or they may be administered later, when regular phonic patterns have been learned.

Stanford Diagnostic Mathematics Test

According to the publisher,

the primary goal of the authors of the *Stanford Diagnostic Mathematics Test* (SDMT) [Beatty, Gardner, Madden, & Karlsen, 1985] was to develop a set of materials that

HUDSON EDUCATION SKILLS INVENTORY
INSTRUCTIONAL PLANNING FORM

Student: **Jennifer Miller** Male: ___ Female: ✓ Date of Birth: 6-9-77 Date: 11-10-87

School: **Morse Elementary** Grade Level: 5.2 or Program Level: N/A Age: 10-5

Reason for Assessment (indicate curriculum skill area of concern): Mathematics (✓) Reading ( ) Writing—Composition ( ) Spelling ( ) Handwriting ( )

Other: _____

STAGE I. ASSESSMENT PLANNING

A. FORMAL TEST DATA
- Iowa Test of Basic Skills (5-1-87) Total Math 3.1
- Woodcock-Johnson Math Cluster (11-1-87) 3.3
- WISC-R (11-2-87): Full Scale 106

B. INSTRUCTIONAL HISTORY DATA
- poor performance across all four operations
- small group and peer tutoring have been ineffective
- good attendance

Grade level of current basal texts and titles:
Mathematics _Holt Mathematics, Holt, Rinehart & Winston_
Reading _____ 1975 (5)
Spelling _____
Language (Composition) _____
Handwriting _____

C. ANALYSIS OF STUDENT WORK SAMPLES
Seems to know basic addition and subtraction facts and attempts to apply those in daily work, however multiplication is limited to use of concrete manipulatives. She fails at all attempts to do division. Samples of work are in Jennifer's classroom folder.

D. GRADE LEVEL PLACEMENT SCORES
- C A Grade Placement (5)
- Present Grade Placement (5)
- Grade Level from Formal Tests (3)
- Age Grade Equivalent Formal Tests (3)

E. ESTIMATES OF GRADE LEVEL PLACEMENTS
- Error pattern data (3)
- Teacher prediction (3½)
- Work sample analyses (3½)
- Observation data (—)
- Student prediction (5)
- Grade level of basal series (F)
- Grade in regular class (H-A-I-(F)ail) (5)
- Rate of learning (S)A-F)

F. DIAGNOSTIC HYPOTHESES
Test at high third grade or low fourth grade.

G. ASSESSMENT PRIORITIES
Addition; Subtraction; Multiplication
Division; Time; Money; Measurement
Word Problems

Figure 17-2. Sample HESI-M Instructional Planning Form. From "HESI-M" by F. Hudson and S. Colson, 1989. Reprinted by permission of PRO-ED.

STAGE II. ASSESSMENT
A. TESTING TARGETS (CHECK TARGETS ON INSTRUCTIONAL PLANNING FORM)
B. CONFIRMATION OF PERFORMANCE (RECORD ON THE INSTRUCTIONAL PLANNING FORM MASTERY OR NONMASTERY)

STAGE III. INSTRUCTIONAL PLANNING: IEP

Goal _ADDITION_
Objectives _ADD B9 (add 2,3,4, and 5 or more digit numbers w/ regrouping) ADD B10 (add cols. of numbers in which each addend has the same number of digits)_

Goal _SUBTRACTION_
Objectives _SUB B7 (subtract 1,2, or 3 digit numbers from 3 digit numbers w/ regrouping in the ones and ten's place)_

Goal _MULTIPLICATION_
Objectives _MULT B2 (recite multiplication facts 0-12 from memory) MULT B3 (orally answer multiplication facts in mixed order)_

Goal _DIVISION_
Objectives _DIV A1 (demonstrate understanding of division as a process of separating a whole group into a number of equal sized subgroups)_

Goal _TIME_
Objectives _TIME B7 (state common equivalencies related to the calendar)_

Goal _MONEY_
Objectives _MON B9 (count change and bills up to $10.00)_

Goal _MONEY_
Objectives _MON C9 (compute change to $5.00)_

Goal _MEASUREMENT_
Objectives _MEAS B8 (measure lines in inches, feet, and yards to nearest ½ inch)_

Goal _WORD PROBLEMS_
Objectives _WORD C5 (solve one-step word problems presented orally using multiplication)_

Goal _____
Objectives _____

STAGE IV. CONTINUOUS ASSESSMENT
Check after three - six weeks of direct instruction. Suggest administering the DTAS for analysis of errors and strategies (Diagnostic Test of Arithmetic Strategies)

STAGE V. INSTRUCTIONAL RECOMMENDATIONS

Addition and Subtraction:
Use CAP Program or Corrective Mathematics in small group.

Multiplication:
After oral problems use written probes of facts.

Division:
Use concrete aids to develop an awareness of concept.

Time, Money, Measurement, and Word Problems: Combine these objectives in "real life" word problems. Ask students to come up with examples. Also use example problems from Basal series at 3rd and 4th grade levels.

Table 17-4. Scope and Sequence Chart for Diagnostic Tests

	Auditory			Auditory and Visual			Conceptual	
Level	1	2	3	4	5	6	7	8
Avg. Grade Level	K–3	1–4	2–5	3–6	4–7	5–8	6–9	7–10
Consonants	b d f g h l m n p r t v y	s z w	c j k x qu			c (city) g (germ)		
Beginning Blends	dr- gr- tr- pl- fl-	sw- sp- sl- st- sm- sn- str- spr- spl-						
Ending Blends	-mp -nd -ft -lt -nt	-st -nt -if -nd -mp	-nk					
Digraphs		ch sh th ng	wh					ph (phrase) ch (ache)
Vowels	short a e i o u	short a e i o u	ai, ay, a–e ee, ea, e–e igh, y, i–e, ind oa, ow, o–e, old	u–e (cube)	u–e (rule) -y (envy)	ie (field) ei (receive) schwa (ə)*	y (system)	i (stadium) i (companion)
Vowel Digraphs				oo (pool)	oo (hood) ea (ready)			
Diphthongs				oi (join) ou (cloud) ow (down) aw (claw)	oy (joy) ew (chew)	au (sauce)		
"R" and "L" Control				ar, er, ir, ur or, ear are, ire, ore all				
Prefixes				un- re-	pre- en- mis- ex- a- in-	con- per- com-		Derivational doubling: immature
Suffixes		-s (chops)	-s (wheels) -ing -ed -es	-er -est -ly -ful -y	-tion -ive	-ent -en -ant -age	-ment -ous -ness -sion	-ance -ence -ible -able -fully -ally -ssion
Endings				-et (target) -ic (public) -al (signal) -le (poodle)		-ey (kidney)	-us (cactus)	
Open and Closed Syllables**							open: ti-ny closed: gos-sip	
Generalizations						ck, -k ch, -tch ge, -dge		
Advanced Phonics								ti (cautious) ci (social) tu (future)
Contractions							mustn't they've	
Rules								1. Dropping e: hope-hoping 2A. Doubling final consonants (monosyllabic): hop-hopping 3. Changing y to i: funny-funnier	2B. Doubling final consonants (poly-syllabic): open-opening; begin-beginner
Sample Words	lap rug flop yet mint	sang chops brush spent bathtub	mean loaded junk painting waxes	refuse smartest fired join loudly	loyal ahead expensive strangle prescribe	loosen freckle computer belief launched	skinny scaring cloudiness sympathy enormous	fortunately immortal forbidden phrase architect
Total No. Test Words	20	20	40	40	40	40	40	40

From "Spellmaster" by C. R. Greenbaum, 1987. Reprinted by permission of PRO-ED.

would serve the classroom teacher as a diagnostic tool and assist the school administrator in program evaluation (p. 5).

The SDMT is an example of a norm-referenced test that also attempts to provide a criterion-referenced interpretation. The SDMT yields standard scores that compare the students' performance to that of their peers and also provides SDMT *Progress Indicators,* which "identify specific concepts or skills with which pupils are having difficulty" (Beatty et al., 1985, p. 14). Objectives are available for each of the concepts/skills measured (see Table 17-5).

The SDMT provides an example of why providing both norm- and criterion-referenced interpretations to test results is problematic. As we noted earlier, norm-referenced tests do not tap a domain completely, thereby making criterion-referenced interpretations inappropriate. An examination of Table 17-5 demonstrates this point nicely. The first concept-skill being measured is "Whole Numbers." Only nine items are provided to measure this construct across four grades (1 to 4). Such an inadequate sampling of the domain of whole numbers makes criterion-referenced interpretations useless, although such a sampling of behaviors is entirely appropriate for the SDMT's norm-referenced interpretation.

Evidence of adequate reliability of the SDMT for making norm-referenced interpretations is provided in the technical manual. The manual discusses validity in terms of content validity only, pointing out that (a) the objectives were written to represent the content found in most curricula used in schools in the United States and (b) users should compare the SDMT items to content used in their schools. No other evidence of validity is provided.

Miscue Analysis System with the Gray Oral Reading Test-Revised

When Wiederholt and Bryant (1986) devised the Gray Oral Reading Test-Revised (GORT-R), they not only kept Gray's original method of applying a norm-referenced interpretation to the test's results, but they added a procedure for using the test to assess the reader's oral reading miscues, thus allowing for a nonreferenced interpretation. The authors use a semantic/syntactic linguistic approach to determine strategies that students employ when reading aloud. To illustrate this approach, a story read by Jonathan is provided (see Figure 17-4). His performance is analyzed with regard to five categories: Meaning Similarity, Function Similarity, Graphic/Phonemic Similarity, Multiple Sources, and Self-Corrections.

Meaning Similarity. This category allows examiners to determine the extent to which students employ comprehension strategies. For example, in line 1, the following three miscues were noted:

TEXT WORD	MISCUE	MEANING SIMILARITY
perched	sitting	1
a	the	1
for	at the	0

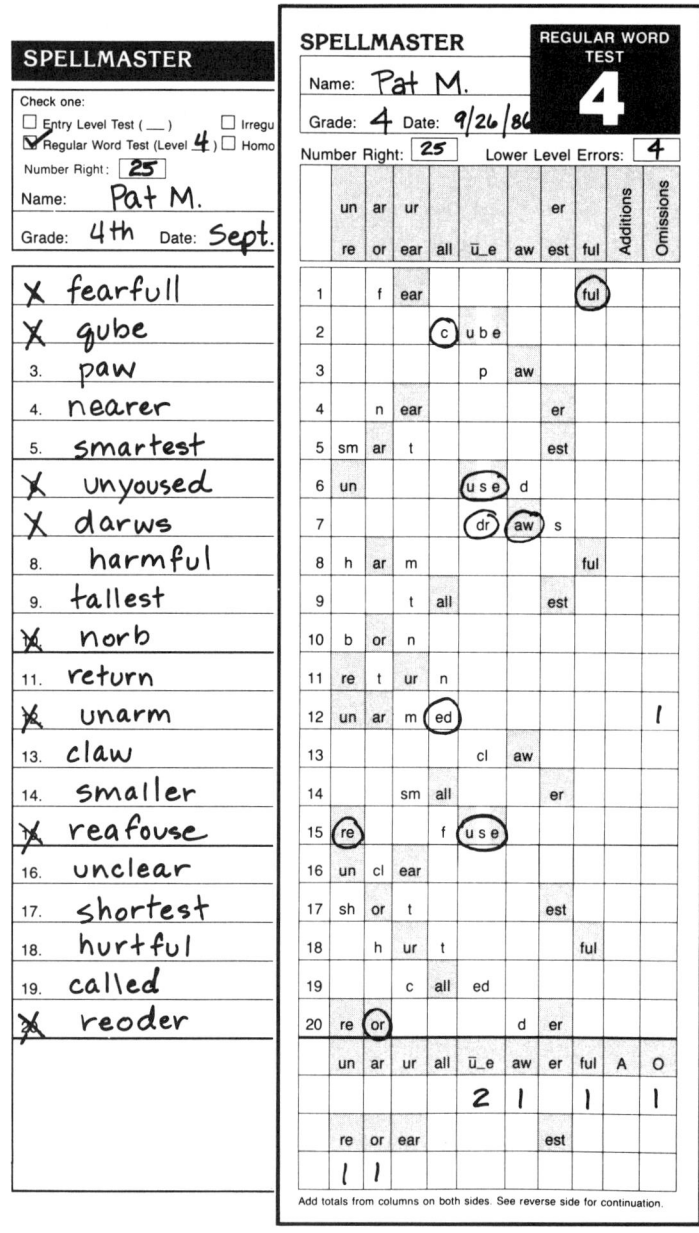

Figure 17-3. Sample Spellmaster Answer Sheet & Score Form. From "Spellmaster" by C. R. Greenbaum, 1987. Reprinted by permission of PRO-ED.

17. The Role of Standardized Tests in Planning Academic Instruction

STUDENT ANSWER SHEET — **SPELLMASTER SIDE 2** — **REGULAR WORD TEST 4**

Teacher: S. Vincent
School: Franks E
City/Town: Newton
State: Mass.

#	Student Response		oi	ou	ow	oo	ire	ore	y	Additions	Omissions
21.	store	21					st	ore			
22.	down	22		d	ow	n					
23.	wire	23			w		ire				
24. ✗	glumey	24				gl (oo) m			(y)		
25. ✗	drownding	25		dr	ow	n			ing	l	
26. ✗	spoyle	26	sp (oi)						l	l	
27.	care	27					c	(are)			
28.	shirt	28				sh	ir	t			
29.	proudly	29		pr ou d					ly		
30. ✗	fiyered	30				f	(ire)	d			
31.	join	31	j oi n								
32. ✗	smothley	32				sm (oo) th			(ly)		
33.	more	33						m ore			
34.	cloudy	34		cl ou d					y		
35. ✗	ponited	35	p (oi)(nt) ed								
36.	share	36					sh	are			
37.	pool	37			p	oo l					
38.	brown	38			br ow n						
39. ✗	dirdey	39				d	ir (t)(y)				
40.	loudly	40		l ou d					ly		

Comments:
1 sequencing
error -
10

oi	ou	ow	oo	ire	ore	y	A	O
2		2				1	2	
				ire	ore	y		
				1	2			

Table 17-5. Objectives Measured by the SDMT Red Level Subtests and Concepts/Skills. From "Stanford Diagnostic Mathematics Test—third ed." by J. L. Weiderholt & B. R. Bryant, 1989. Reprinted by permission of Austin, TX: PRO-ED.

1.0 TEST: Number System and Numeration

CONCEPT/SKILL	OBJECTIVE	ITEM CLUSTER
1.11 Whole Numbers	Demonstrate an understanding of the system of whole numbers by comparing sets of objects, by naming numbers, and by counting.	1.111 Compare Sets of Objects (Items 1–3)
		1.112 Name Numbers and Count (Items 4–9)
1.12 Place Value	Demonstrate an understanding of decimal place value by reading and interpreting numerals and by comparing and ordering numbers.	1.121 Read Numerals (Items 10–15)
		1.122 Interpret Numerals (Items 16–18)
		1.124 Order Numbers (Items 19–24)
1.3 Operations and Properties	Demonstrate an understanding of the fundamental operations of addition and subtraction and of the properties of addition.	1.31 Operations (Items 25–27)
		1.32 Properties (Items 28–30)

2.0 TEST 2: Computation

CONCEPT/SKILL	OBJECTIVE	ITEM CLUSTER
2.11 Addition Facts	Name the sums or missing addends for basic addition facts, sums to 18.	2.11 Same as Concept/Skill (Items 1–9)

17. The Role of Standardized Tests in Planning Academic Instruction

2.12	Addition, No Renaming	Use the vertical form for addition, with no renaming.	2.12 Same as Concept/Skill (Items 10–15)
2.21	Subtraction Facts	Name the differences for basic subtraction facts, sums (minuends) to 18.	2.21 Same as Concept/Skill (Items 16–24)
2.22	Subtraction, No Renaming	Use the vertical form for subtraction, with no renaming.	2.22 Same as Concept/Skill (Items 25–30)

3.0 TEST 3: Applications

CONCEPT/SKILL		OBJECTIVE	ITEM CLUSTER	
3.1	Problem Solving	Solve simple problems mentally and express simple problems as solution models.	3.11	Solve Problems (Items 1–6)
			3.12	Solution Models (Items 7–12)
3.2	Tables and Graphs	Read and interpret simple tables and graphs.	3.21	Read and Interpret Tables (Items 13–15)
			3.22	Read and Interpret Graphs (Items 16–21)
3.3	Geometry and Measurement	Demonstrate an understanding of the principles of geometry and of time and money as measurements.	3.31	Geometry (Items 22–24)
			3.321	Time Measurement (Items 25–27)
			3.322	Money Measurement (Items 28–30)

A-5 Prompt: Say, "THIS STORY IS ABOUT ANIMALS HAVING A PROBLEM. READ THE STORY TO FIND OUT WHAT THE PROBLEM IS AND HOW IT IS SOLVED."

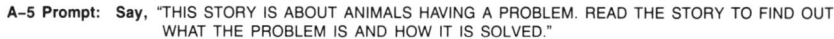

Comp. 1. (a) ___ 2. (a) ___ 3. (c) ___ 4. (c) ___ 5. (b) ___ Comp. Score ___ Rate ___ Dev. from Print ___

Figure 17-4. Example of miscue marking procedure with the GORT-R. From "Gray Oral Reading Test–Revised" by J. L. Weiderholt & B. R. Bryant, 1986. Reprinted by permission of PRO-ED.

In the first two cases (i.e., sitting for perched and the for a), the meaning of the passage is not significantly changed. The examiner would mark a "1" on the Examiner's Worksheet (see Figure 17-5) to indicate meaning similarity for each case. In the third case (i.e., at the for for), meaning is significantly changed. Thus, the examiner would use a "0" to indicate that there is no meaning similarity.

Function Similarity. Function similarity is assessed to allow the examiner to judge the extent to which the student uses appropriate grammar in reading. Again using line 1 of the example, Jonathan's miscues were analyzed as follows:

TEXT WORD	MISCUE	FUNCTION SIMILARITY
perched	sitting	1
a	the	1
for	at the	1

In all three cases, the miscues represented correct grammatical forms. Therefore, the student was given credit for function similarity for each miscue. When examining the student's performance for this type of miscue, examiners note function similarity in the context of what is read orally. That is, they are encouraged to read the sentence or phrase aloud to themselves when scoring to facilitate interpretation of function similarity.

17. The Role of Standardized Tests in Planning Academic Instruction

EXAMINER'S WORKSHEET

Student's Name: Jonathan   Form: A

NO.	LINE	TEXT WORD	MISCUE	Meaning Similarity	Function Similarity	Graphic/Phonemic Similarity	Multiple Sources	Self-Correction
1	1	perched	sitting	1	1	0	1	0
2	1	'a	the	1	1	0	1	0
3	1	for	at the	0	1	0	0	0
4	2	flown	flied	1	1	1	1	0
5	2	that	the/u	1	1	1	1	1
6	2	moment	minute	1	1	1	1	0
7	3	flew	flied	1	1	1	1	0
8	5	unable	able	0	1	1	1	0
9	5	felt	fell	0	0	1	0	0
10	6	struck	hit	1	1	0	1	0
11	6	gathered	gained	0	1	1	1	0
12	7	dropping	dripping	0	1	1	1	0
13	8	last	least	0	1	1	1	0
14	8	fill	full	1	1	1	1	0
15								
16								
17								
18								
19								
20								
21								
22								
23								
24								
25								
			Number	8	13	10	12	1
			Percentage	57	93	71	86	7

OTHER MISCUES

Type	Number
Omissions O	4
Additions ^	2
Dialect v	0
Reversals ~	0

OTHER OBSERVATIONS

Type	Check
Posture	
Word-by-word reading	✓
Poor phrasing	
Lack of expression	
Pitch (too high) or low	✓
Voice too soft or strained	
Poor enunciation	

Type	Check
Disregard of punctuation	
Head movement	
Finger pointing	
Loss of place	
Nervousness	✓
Poor attitude	
Other	

Figure 17-5. GORT–R Examiner's Worksheet. From "Gray Oral Reading Test–Revised" by J. L. Weiderholt & B. R. Bryant, 1986. Reprinted by permission of PRO-ED.

Graphic/Phonemic Similarity. The graphic/phonemic similarity category is used by the examiner to inventory the specific word attack strate-

gies employed in oral reading. Specifically, the examiner determines whether the miscue has similar affixes, roots, vowel sounds, and/or consonant sounds. In our example, no credit was awarded for the three miscues in the first line. However, the first miscue of the second line (i.e., *flied* for *flown*) received credit, because the miscue contained the same fl-blend as the text word.
Some of Jonathan's other miscues would be classified as follows:

TEXT WORD	MISCUE	GRAPHIC/PHONEMIC SIMILARITY
perched	sitting	0
moment	minute	1
gathered	gained	1
struck	hit	0

Multiple Sources. Multiple sources allows the examiner to note the miscues that fit more than one classification. The authors note that this is an optional category, but by counting miscues that fit more than one category, examiners can derive information about a student's use of multiple reading strategies. Using line 1 in the example, *sitting* and *perched* were noted as having both meaning similarity and function similarity by recording a 1 in the multiple sources column:

TEXT WORD	MISCUE	MULTIPLE SOURCES
perched	sitting	1

Self-Correction. This category allows the examiner to determine the extent to which the student uses strategies to correct miscues. The notation for the miscue in line 2 of the example indicates that the student used self-correction.

TEXT WORD	MISCUE	SELF-CORRECTION
THAT	THE/	1

Jonathan first read "the" then corrected it by saying "that." Therefore, credit is recorded in the Self-Correction column. Instead of writing the self-corrected text word, it can be more efficiently noted by writing the miscue and an arrow (see Figure 17-4). If the self-correction does not match the text word, only the first attempt is recorded. Thus, only the first miscue is analyzed as to its meaning, function, and graphic/phonemic similarity.

Once all miscues have been recorded on the worksheet, the points are summed and the totals written in the appropriate boxes at the bottom of the columns (see Figure 17-5). Below the totals are written the number of miscues that were made. The percentage of miscues for each category is calculated by dividing the number of categorical miscues by the total number of miscues. In the example, 8 of the 14 miscues were given credit for Meaning Similarity, resulting in an index of 57%, whereas 13 of the 15 miscues were given credit for Function Similarity. The resulting percentage (93%) demonstrates that Function Similarity is a relative strength as compared with Meaning Similarity. Using the miscue analysis procedure on the GORT-R enables examiners to identify strategies employed by students when they read orally. Such findings can be useful when planning intervention programs.

CONCLUSION

In this chapter, we have provided information concerning the use of standardized assessment for academic intervention. We first described the qualities that a scale must possess in order to be considered adequately standardized. These criteria included set administration procedures, objective scoring criteria, a specified frame of reference, and evidence of reliability and validity. The degree to which procedures satisfy these criteria determine whether they can be considered highly standardized, adequately standardized, or inadequately standardized.

Our search of existing standardized tests that are used for planning academic intervention (i.e., for identifying instructional objectives) led us to conclude that there is a dearth of adequately standardized instruments that are designed with this purpose in mind. Our description of instruments that are available focused on scales that are designed to assess instructional abilities in reading, mathematics, and spelling. All of the scales possessed three of the characteristics of adequately standardized tests (i.e., set administration procedures, objective scoring criteria, and a specified frame of reference). All, however, lacked evidence of reliability and validity. Such evidence can be easily gathered by users, however, using procedures outlined by Anastasi (1988), Hambleton, Swaminathan, Algina, and Coulson (1978), and others. These researchers provide guidance as to how evidence of reliability and validity can be obtained for criterion-referenced tests. Such procedures can be modified somewhat to be of use in establishing reliability and validity for nonreferenced tests.

REFERENCES

Aiken, L. R. (1988). *Psychological testing and assessment* (6th ed.). Boston: Allyn & Bacon.
American Psychological Association. (1985). *Standards for educational and psychological tests*. Washington, DC: American Psychological Association.
Anastasi, A. (1988). *Psychological testing* (6th ed.). New York: MacMillan.

Beatty, L. S., Madden, R., Gardner, E. F., Karlsen, B. (1985). *Stanford Diagnostic Mathematics Test* (3rd Ed.) Norms Booklet. San Antonio, TX: Psychological Corp.
Brigance, A. (1978). *Brigance Diagnostic Inventory of Early Development.* North Billerica, MA: Curriculum Associates.
Brigance, A. (1981). *Brigance Diagnostic Inventory of Essential Skills.* North Billerica, MA: Curriculum Associates.
Brigance, A. (1982). *Brigance K & 1 Screen for Kindergarten and First Grade.* North Billerica, MA: Curriculum Associates.
Brigance, A. (1983). *Brigance Diagnostic Inventory of Basic Skills.* North Billerica, MA: Curriculum Associates.
Brigance, A. (1984). *Brigance Diagnostic Assessment of Basic Skills—Spanish Edition.* North Billerica, MA: Curriculum Associates.
Brigance, A. (1985). *Brigance Preschool Screen.* North Billerica, MA: Curriculum Associates.
Greenbaum, C. R. (1987). *The Spellmaster Assessment and Teaching System.* Austin, TX: PRO-ED.
Gronlund, N. E. (1985). *Measurement and evaluation in teaching.* (5th ed.). New York: MacMillan.
Hambleton, R. K., Swaminathan, H., Algina, J., & Coulson, D. B. (1978). Criterion-referenced testing and measurement: A review of technical issues and developments. *Review of Educational Research, 48,* 1–47.
Hammill, D. (1987). Assessing students in the schools. In D. Hammill (Ed.) *Assessing the abilities and instructional needs of students.* (pp. 5–37). Austin, TX: PRO-ED.
Hammill, D., Ammer, J., Cronin, M., Mandlebaum, L. H., & Quinby, S. (1988). *Quick-Score Achievement Test.* Austin, TX: PRO-ED.
Hammill, D., & Bryant, B. R. (1986). *Detroit Tests of Learning Aptitude–Primary.* Austin, TX: PRO-ED.
Helmstadtler, G. C. (1964). *Principles of psychological measurement.* New York: Appleton-Century-Crofts.
Hudson, F., & Colson, S. (1989). *Hudson Educational Skills Inventory–Mathematics.* Austin, TX: PRO-ED.
Hudson, F., Colson, S., Banikowski, A.K., & Mehring, T. (1989). *Hudson Educational Skills Inventory–Writing.* Austin, TX: PRO-ED.
Hudson, F., Colson, S., & Hudson-Welch, D. H. (1989). *Hudson Educational Skills Inventory–Reading.* Austin, TX: PRO-ED.
International Reading Association Board of Directors (1980, June). Board Action. *Reading Today,* 1.
Nunnally, J. S. (1978). *Psychological theory* (4th ed.). New York: McGraw-Hill.
Popham, W. J. (1973). *The uses of instructional objectives.* Belmont, CA: Fearon.
Salvia, J., & Ysseldyke, J. E. (1988). *Assessment in special and remedial education.* (4th ed.). Boston: Houghton-Mifflin.
Sattler, L. R. (1988). *Assessment of children* (3rd ed.). San Diego: Author.
Webster's ninth new collegiate dictionary. (1987). Springfield, MA: Merriam-Webster.
Wiederholt, J. L., & Bryant, B. R. (1986). *Gray Oral Reading Test–Revised.* Austin, TX: PRO-ED.

CHAPTER 18

A Critique of Assessment Methodology

KENNETH A. KAVALE
NANCY A. MUNDSCHENK

Assessment and its trappings (e.g., test research and development) is "big business" in the field of learning disabilities. This assumption is readily documented by the findings from surveys investigating research priorities in learning disabilities (e.g., Bursuck & Epstein, 1987). Although studies of the nature and characteristics of learning disabilities lead the way, they are closely followed by assessment. Trailing by a wide margin are intervention studies that suggest that the basic diagnostic–prescriptive paradigm is heavily biased toward the diagnostic end (Forness & Kavale, 1987). There appears to be a sense of security in assessment, and its empirical foundation that makes it appear that we are dealing with a real and precise phenomenon. Quantification remains an integral part of the learning disabilities field, but what is too often forgotten is the basis for that quantification and what it actually represents. The purpose of this chapter is to explore measurement issues and determine how they affect assessment in the learning disabilities field.

THE MEANING OF MEASUREMENT

Is the concept of learning disabilities unidimensional or multidimensional? Most present conceptualizations of learning disabilities assume a multidimensional posture and this is probably preferable to unidimensional analyses for full specifications of the phenomenon (Kavale & Nye, 1985–86). Multidimensional conceptualizations of learning disabilities, however, are contingent upon the power and robustness of our measurement procedures. One assumption of this chapter is that inadequate measurement has been a major impediment to a full and complete explanation of learning disabilities.

A partial explanation for the inadequate measurement found in learning disabilities is the "empiricism" that has marked learning disabilities research (Kavale & Forness, 1985). Empiricism may be defined as an emphasis upon data collection and analysis. The focus is on the systematic collection of data but such data does not form a complete system of knowledge because the elements are not rationally connected. Empiricism implies for measurement the classic definition provided by Stevens (1951), that is, "Measurement is the assignment of numerals to objects or events according to rules" (p. 22). Similarly, Nagel (1961) defined measurement as the correlation of entities that are not themselves numbers with numbers. These definitions of measurement suggest it to be primarily an empirical, almost mechanistic process.

What is lacking in these definitions of measurement is some reference to the theoretical component of the measurement process. Measurement serves an important theoretical purpose by linking empirical indicators with abstract concepts (see Blalock, 1982). Theory in learning disabilities is concerned with concepts that are often formulated at rather high levels of abstraction. To be useful in a theoretical sense, these concepts need to be related to theory rationally and abstractly as well as empirically. In this way, there is an isomorphism between concepts and empirical indicators (measurement), a structural similarity between theoretical and observational levels. With only empirical connections (empiricism), the elements remain only partially connected and thus form essentially independent concepts that are not meshed into a conceptual whole involving a theoretical level (Hempel, 1952).

The lack of theoretical development in learning disabilities (Kavale, 1987b) forces the field to an empiricist's view of measurement. The outcome then is not more refined theoretical statements but rather a greater quantity of data and improvement in the techniques used to gather that data. Hence, the learning disabilities field devotes considerable time and effort to enhancing its measurement procedures through test development but not in techniques for anchoring these observations at a theoretical level.

CONCEPTS AND INDICATORS

Measurement is best conceived of as the process whereby abstract concepts are linked to empirical indicators. Abstract concepts (e.g., perception, intelligence, discrepancy) have been the means by which learning disabilities have been explained. Abstract concepts, however, do not possess a one-to-one correspondence with empirical indicators and can be measured in a variety of ways. For example, learning disabilities themselves have been measured through achievement indicators, memory indicators, social indicators, and the like. The overall abstract concept (i.e., learning disabilities) can be thus construed through an assortment of empirical indicators. Yet, the concept of learning disabilities is only approximated by these empirical indicators. The inherent complexity and vagueness of the concept of learning disabilities makes the empirical indicator highly variable and this makes the concept of learning disabilities essentially "open" (Kaplan, 1964) in the sense that its usage remains uncertain to some degree. Open concepts are thus never actually closed and fixed entities.

Because most concepts of learning disabilities can be neither directly observed nor measured, they can only be assessed through the use of empirical indicators that are designed to represent a given abstract concept. Empirical indicators are designed to be as specific, as exact, and as circumscribed as possible. But empirical indicators are indeterminate in the sense that they never fully exhaust nor completely duplicate the meaning of concepts. Any set of empirical indicators is, therefore, only a small subset of any number of possible indicators that might be selected. For example, consider the differences in the structure and execution of the concept of visual perception in such tests as the Bender Visual–Motor Gestalt Test, the Developmental Test of Visual Perception, the Developmental Test of Visual–Motor Integration, the Motor Free Visual Perception Test, the Revised Visual Retention Test, and the Memory for Designs Test. Given these ideational differences, there is little wonder that perceptual tests have failed generally to differentiate between groups with and without learning disabilities (e.g., Harber, 1979; Larsen, Rogers, & Sowell, 1976). Similar differences can be noted in intellectual and language assessments.

What is suggested is that both abstract concepts and empirical indicators are necessary for a useful description of learning disabilities. Concepts provide a degree of abstractness and generality for theories to make them relevant across time and setting. Empirical indicators, for their part, must be precise as well as complete if they are to represent properly their respective concepts empirically. By providing an accurate representation of concepts, empirical indicators contribute to theoretical development by highlighting the gaps that exist between theoretical formulations and observed reality. The interdependence between abstract concepts and their empirical indicators was emphasized by Greer (1969) who said, "Our creations in the world of possibility must be fitted in the world of probability; in Kant's epigram, 'Concepts without percepts are empty.' ... Percepts without concepts are blind" (p. 160).

FUNCTIONS OF MEASUREMENT

Measurement in learning disabilities can serve different purposes. Among the more important are (1) to describe learning disabilities phenomena empirically, (2) to assist in the testing of theories, and (3) to permit the differentiation between groups (with and without learning disabilities) according to the degree of certain properties they possess. None of the purposes is necessarily mutually exclusive and all have logical relevance for each of the others (see Kuhn, 1977).

The description of learning disabilities phenomena is important for cataloguing learning disabilities behaviors. Once described, it is then possible to theorize about the phenomena studied. Concepts are derived and then tested through specific hypotheses derived from the theory. The purpose of theory is to explain and predict learning disabilities phenomena, which leads ultimately to more refined explication about how groups with and without learning disabilities differ. These contrasts, in turn, lead to greater definition of the learning disabilities phenomenon.

Although description of the nature and characteristics of learning disabilities has always been important, it appears that this description has most often been associated with attempts at group differentiation rather than theoretical verification (Lyon, 1987). The emphasis on differences, however, does not add significantly to theoretical understanding but is only a more sophisticated form of empirical description. The prevailing paradigm is to compare groups with and without learning disabilities that differ along some dimension. The groups with and without learning disabilities are defined according to some criterion and then their performance on some task is measured. Any dissimilarity between the groups' performances is assumed to reveal which variables might be good predictors of learning disabilities.

The perennial problem of heterogeneity in learning disabilities samples may interfere with any interpretation, however (Kavale & Nye, 1985–1986). Although it is sometimes recognized that not all students with learning disabilities are alike, this variability tends to obscure any group comparison (learning disabilities vs. no learning disabilities) because of the potential for sizable group overlap even when the differences are found to be statistically significant (Weener, 1981).

The overlap problem is sometimes circumvented by comparing extremely different groups, that is, the 10% of samples of groups with and without learning disabilities that differ most on the variable of interest. This tactic is presumed to increase the power of the comparison because the effects of heterogeneity are assumed to be attenuated because the 10% of students with learning disabilities with the lowest scores are supposed to be more similar to each other.

The power of group comparisons is also assumed to increase by the removal of confounding variables. For example, because intelligence (IQ) correlates with many variables, knowing an IQ permits some prediction about performance on some measure. But this correlation also suggests that variation on the performance measure may also be associated with variation on the IQ measure. Group differences on the obtained measure may therefore reflect intellectual differences rather than performance differences on the task variable.

These procedures, while appearing reasonable, do not resolve the heterogeneity problem. Although group differences may emerge, the relevance of those differences are open to question. For example, if reading is the variable of interest, then IQ, socioeconomic status, family factors, school environment, and instruction explain much of the variance for both groups with and without learning disabilities. The typical learning disabilities study, however, investigates more specific variables (e.g., perceptual, linguistic, neuropsychological) and controls variables like IQ and socioeconomic status. The result is a study that necessarily examines only a small proportion of the variation in reading ability. Even if significant differences are found, the differences can explain only the variation in reading ability not explained by the other factors contributing to the total variance. Additionally, there is no insight into the relative importance of this variable in explaining the reading ability of the group with learning disabilities. Thus, the typical learning disabilities study measuring specific variables and attempting to circumvent the heterogeneity problem produces findings with very limited application, as shown in Figure 18-1.

Regardless of the sophistication of the measurement, this approach results in controversy. The learning disabilities literature is replete with a wide assortment of differences between groups with and without learning disabilities. If too much is invested in these narrowly focused studies, arguments much like the blind men who stumble upon different parts of an elephant are likely to ensue. For example, investigations have shown some groups with learning disabilities to differ on certain perceptual discrimination tasks and other groups with learning disabilities on verbal integration tasks but not vice versa. This state of affairs is readily explained if it is understood that different studies can glimpse only that aspect of learning disabilities that lies within its focus (i.e., the specific measures in the study). Unfortunately, as the focus of research studies narrows, the number of "significant differences" between groups with and without learning disabilities will probably increase. Increasing significantly also, however, will

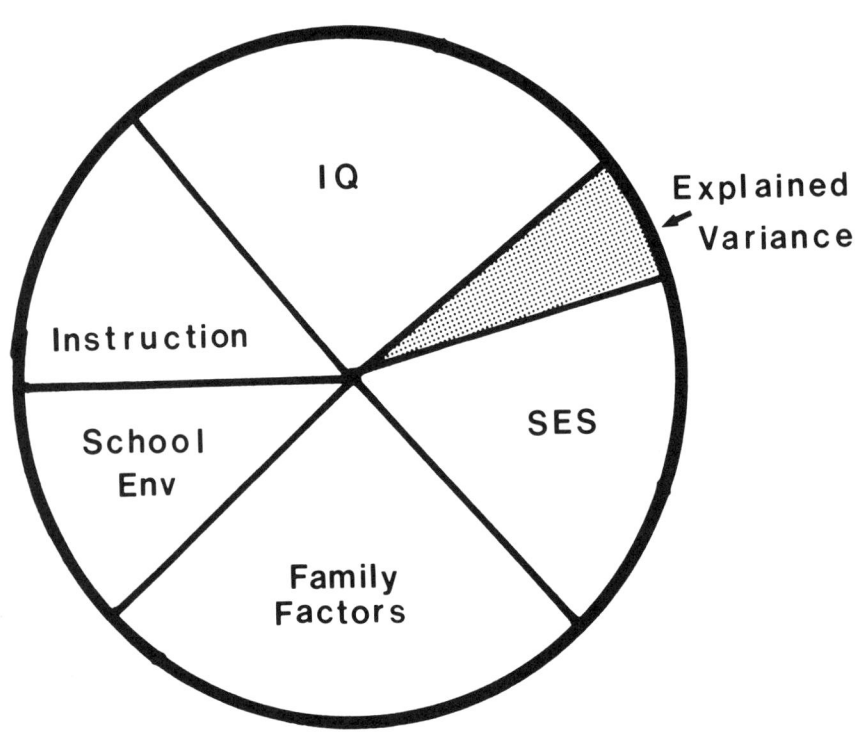

Figure 18-1. Proportion of variance in reading ability explained in the typical study of learning disabilities investigating specific variables.

be the number of blind men touching different parts of an elephant and, consequently, the number of different descriptions of learning disabilities.

MEASUREMENT AND CONSTRUCT VALIDITY

The basis for documenting differences between groups with and without learning disabilities are found in the measurements used in each investigation. But how good are these measurements? Poor measurements will certainly confound the meaning of group differences because they will not permit inferences about ability based on observed performance. Tryon (1979, p. 402) called this the "test-trait fallacy" and said it

> begins with the assumption that test scores are trait measures. The second assumption is that trait measures are basic properties of the person. It easily follows that test

scores reflect basic properties of the person. This sequence essentially converts a dependent variable into an independent variable; hence a measurement is reified into a causal force.

Thus, a test must be shown to be an appropriate and legitimate proxy for the trait (Messick, 1981). Tests are typically developed from concepts based on theoretical formulations. The weak state of learning disabilities theory suggests, however, that the associated concepts have not been fully verified (Kavale & Forness, 1985). Yet, these concepts are the basis upon which groups with and without learning disabilities are compared. To be confident in the reality of obtained differences and to avoid the test-trait fallacy, concepts need to be verified, particularly with respect to the notion of construct validity.

Construct validity is especially necessary for tests measuring traits for which external criteria are not available. Construct validation is the analysis of test scores in terms of psychological contructs (Cronbach & Meehl, 1955). If a test is designed to measure social status, for example, what kinds of evidence are necessary before it can be said confidently that the test reflects this variable? For example, if the test actually measures the construct in question, there would be an expectation for (1) some correlation between scores and independent observer ratings, (2) some differences between scores of students with high social status and those with low social status, (3) some relationship between peer ratings and test scores, and so on. There is no single criterion, as with criterion-validity, and many criteria are required to confirm what the test does and does not measure (Cronbach, 1971).

Construct validity is, of course, based on the notion of construct. Kaplan (1964) defines constructs as "terms which, though not observational either directly or indirectly, may be applied and even defined on the basis of the observables" (p. 55). Although some scientific constructs are clear-cut, learning disabilities–type constructs do not lend themselves to such exact analysis. As Kaplan (1964) suggested, "It may not be perfectly clear which direct or indirect observables determine the meaning, while there is no doubt that the meaning is determined in *some* such way" (p. 56).

Almost all learning disabilities constructs lack an exact analysis because they are not based on a powerful theoretical structure. Cronbach and Meehl (1955) discussed structure in terms of "nomological networks," which are conceived of as systems of laws showing the relationships between the construct and its various indicators. From it, the ways the indicators ought to relate to each other can be logically deduced. The network thus clarifies what the construct means and how it is likely to appear in nature.

The nomological networks in a field like learning disabilities are not, however, logically interlocking sets of definitions and statements. They are correlated directly into a law-like system in only a few instances. Instead, learning disabilities networks are structured around weak statistics (e.g., correlations, probabilities) that do not provide a full and complete rendering of the nomological network and thus leave the construct open. Attempts to close constructs with incomplete nomological networks are usually based on the use of an operational approach. A decision is made about methods, or operations, that will translate what was conceptualized into something that can be observed, or measured, in a relevant and accurate way so that different results can be assigned numerical values (Bridgman, 1927). But this leads to a situation wherein the concept of, for example, visual perception is what a visual perceptual test measures. There thus exists a confusion and confounding of concepts and test scores. If visual perception is defined as solely an empirical entity, then the operations of the visual perceptual test are merely observational and cannot enter into a nomological network.

With a majority of tests used in the assessment of learning disabilities shown to lack adequate construct validity (e.g., Bennet, 1983; Berk, 1984; Ysseldyke, Algozzine, Regan, & Potter, 1980), there is little wonder why tests used in the diagnosis of learning disabilities have come under serious attack in the past (Coles, 1978) and continues to be assailed (e.g., Davis & Shepard, 1983). Differences in the real and perceived validity of learning disabilities tests has led to widely varying diagnostic practices across school districts (Perlmutter & Parus, 1983). In turn, this variability makes it difficult to answer precisely the question, "Who is learning disabled?" which only adds to the present conceptual confusion surrounding the learning disabilities phenomenon.

THEORIES AND CONSTRUCTS

Scientific measurement is not dependent on any empirical technique but is a consequence of a well-formulated theory in which concepts are theoretically related by laws and, in turn, can be abstractly related to observable results (i.e., test scores). Operationalism in learning disabilities measurement has, in essence, bypassed the theoretical aspect of scientific measurement and has defined concepts through a solely empirical interpretation. It is for this reason that we encounter the "measurement problem" in learning disabilities. The construct validity discussed above is really undermined by an operational approach (Scriven, 1956). The question, for example, "How can we know that our attention measurement really measures attention?" is really meaningless since an operational viewpoint suggests that attention can be no more than its operations for measurement. The assessment measures attention because "attention is what it measures."

It thus makes little sense to establish more exact measurement unless it is theory based. Operationalism is simply empiricism's view of measurement that serves to produce low levels of relationship with limited scope (Lundberg, 1942). To explain these limitations, the fault is assumed to lie in the measurement problem (Duncan, 1984). Yet, this measurement problem is the result of operationalism. The result is a tautology that moves the learning disabilities field to a disorganized level of assumption and justification. Consequently, operational definitions of learning disabilities usually lack theoretical interest and technological power (Loevinger, 1957).

Operational approaches generally fail to account for the complexity-determined nature of learning disabilities. Any learning disabilities behavior may be determined by any combination of variables (i.e., A . . . Z) and may appear superficially the same when either A or Z is the primary variable. Yet an operational approach chooses the variables most easily quantified, that is, with little concern for the abstract relationships that should be used to define the concept theoretically. For example, the notion of discrepancy is often operationalized to provide rigor in definitional statements in the field of learning disabilities. The abstract notion of discrepancy is defined by the difference between expected and actual achievement. By measuring these concepts and performing a bit of simple subtraction, it is assumed that the presence or absence of a discrepancy has been demonstrated. Kavale (1987a), however, showed that the situation is not so simple; inherent problems are found in (1) the nomological network linking discrepancy with underachievement and learning disabilities, (2) the reliability and validity of measures of expected and actual achievement, (3) the influence of the measurement model on the data used to calculate discrepancy, (4) the reliability and validity of the concept "discrepancy" because of statistical difficulties (e.g., regression), (5) conceptual confusion over discrepancy as a variation (i.e., intraindividual difference) or a prediction (i.e., potential for academic achievement), and (6) the failure to include the influence of intervening variables (e.g., motivation, instruction, social/behavior status). Thus, discrepancy really represents, not the outcome of explicit theoretical deviation, but a form of psychometric engineering that disguises poorly realized conceptions (Deese, 1972).

CONCEPTUALIZATION AND QUANTIFICATION

It should be evident that conceptualization and quantification need to be better integrated if measurement is to aid the advancement of the learning disabilities field. Conceptualization refers to the theoretical process whereby constructs are given indicators, whereas quantification refers to the linkage process between the indicators and a mathematical language (numbers). Blalock (1968) suggested the concept "auxiliary measurement theory" to emphasize the point that the measurement process requires a set of theoretical assumptions that suggests that the processes of theory construction and measurement cannot be viewed as distinctly different. Many concepts in learning disabilities are difficult to observe directly and instead these concepts are inferred in terms of their presumed effects (or sometimes causes) (MacCorquodale & Meehl, 1948). Thus, attention is not observed directly but inferred from off-task behavior. Compare the distance between attention and off-task behavior to the physicists measurement of heat energy in terms of its effects on a column of mercury. Heat is thus more directly measured because the theory needed to link the postulated concept with some indicator is more tightly structured (Zebrowski, 1979). The directness also leads to simplicity in measurement in the sense that complexity is eliminated from the operations and indicators used in the process. The indirectness in learning disabilities measurement caused by a less tightly structured theoretical foundation also creates more complexity in the necessary operations and indicators. Yet, the learning disabilities field proceeds as if it were simple and direct. This is the measurement problem in learning disabilities: the attitude that clever engineering (i.e., reliable and valid quantification) can overcome basic science in the form of auxiliary measurement theories that anchor that quantification in some justifiable structure. The learning disabilities field is far too cavalier in its assumptions about measurement and too readily takes for granted that simple measures are "good" measures.

The learning disabilities field, however, must pay more attention to the measurement process because it is fraught with ambiguities and false assumptions. The physical sciences are comfortable with indirect measurement (e.g., heat, mass, electrical charge) because the assumptions required to link operational indicators to physical properties are more precise and justifiable than in learning disabilities. This is quite different from inferring memory abilities on the basis of test scores simply because the theoretical foundation is far more difficult to specify. Although the test may appear simple, the consequence is less precision in measurement because the more tenuous theoretical linkages introduce a host of unknown elements (Forge, 1987).

The unknown elements (random measurement error) produce imprecision in measurement, which tends to distort the process. However, in situations in which there is considerable variation in the independent variables, measurement accuracy is less crucial because measurement error is randomly distributed. Thus, if widely divergent learning disabilities groups are being compared and there is little question that they differ in, for example, linguistic competence of neuropsychological status, then it is much less necessary to obtain precise measures. In contrast, if the focus

18. Assessment Methodology

is on instances where the amount of change is small relative to presumed measurement error (e.g., discrepancy), then it is necessary to reduce measurement errors considerably before there can be any faith that findings are not due primarily to unreliability rather than real changes.

If, on the other hand, the focus is on disentangling the effects of even moderately intercorrelated independent variables, then more precise measurement becomes more crucial. If some variables are measured with considerable accuracy but other variables include only rough indicators, then the former will "look good" relative to the others, since the reliability coefficients of the latter will be attenuated but the coefficients of the former may well be amplified. There may thus be considerable misperception about the degree of intercorrelation among variables.

The problem of multicollinearity produces several kinds of difficulties (Goldberger & Duncan, 1973). The correlations may be so high and the intercorrelations so complex that the situation is essentially hopeless empirically. Suppose, for example, that five indicators of achievement are constructed and their intercorrelations are found in to be on the order of magnitude of 0.80 or higher. Without a clear-cut conceptualization of achievement, however, it will be difficult to determine which indicators comes closest to what is believed conceptually (see Anastasi, 1970). In this situation, the conclusion would probably be that the indicators need to be combined in a "single" variable termed "achievement" because it would be impossible to test a model in which all five are treated as distinct indicators.

On the other hand, in situations in which all independent variables are only weakly intercorrelated, although it will remain the case that the effects of each poorly measured variable will be affected (i.e., underestimated in the case of random measurement errors), this will not lead to an overestimation of the effects of the others (except in relative terms). The intermediate case, however, is far more likely. This is the case where moderate intercorrelations among subsets of independent variables exists and leads to a confusing picture empirically and great difficulty in interpreting results. In this situation, there is also the possibility for wide open debate and differing interpretation based on ideological or disciplinary biases (Duncan, 1984).

A common research scenario in this case is as follows: The investigator points to inadequacies in previous research, in which only weak to moderate relationships between a dependent variable and explanatory factors have been found. An "alternative" explanation is advanced, the relevant variables measured (imperfectly), controls for the presumed inadequate variables are introduced (also probably imperfectly measured), and then some conclusions reached that usually favor the investigator's preferred explanation. Often, however, the differences in explanatory power are slight and easily accounted for on the basis of a combination of sampling and measurement errors. The proper conclusion is that neither explanation of findings is very satisfactory.

It is precisely in situations such as these, however, that the need for careful conceptualization and measurement is greatest (Blalock, 1982). Yet these situations are frequently the subjects of serious debates where partisan perspectives replace objective research. What are the most important correlates of learning disabilities? What factors are most responsible for underachievement? What is the relationship between attention deficits and learning disabilities? These variables would all be reasonably intercorrelated and any empirical findings would be very much affected by measurement considerations. Often, the straightforward problem of assessing the reliability of each measure is compounded by theoretical ambiguities in the conceptualization, so that any series of measurement decisions will appear arbitrary and will almost certainly be challenged whenever the findings do not appear compatible with whatever theoretical position is being espoused.

What can be done in such situations? The resolution is straightforward but difficult: Such disputes and ambiguous results must be taken as signs that a more careful theoretical reformulation is needed. A series of conceptual clarifications are attempted that suggest how a more definitive empirical analysis can be made. But then another type of difficulty is encountered: Many of the variables of greatest interest are extremely difficult to quantify, even when they have been well defined conceptually. One answer is to suggest that the measurement process is both ideologically and politically biased, since any data collected are likely to be subject to constraints that are neither politically nor ideologically neutral. This is at least partially true because the variables either measured and not measured are really the result of a chance process that often makes the choices a matter of convenience (Blalock, 1974).

A second, nearly opposite, answer involves a measurement-by-fiat approach wherein the investigator selects whatever empirical indicators can be located and then simply states that these will serve as measures of some highly abstract theoretical construct. The presumed rationale is based on the assumption that for any concept difficult to measure, almost any indicator will suffice. The difficulty here lies in the fact that this method can never be criticized in a constructive fashion, aside from pointing out the arbitrariness of it. The assumptions made in moving from the theoretical construct to the operational indicator are simply left unstated. This may be true, but carried too far this assumption turns convenience into matters of principle and affords little motivation aimed at improving the measurement process (Forge, 1987).

A third answer is to sidestep the conceptual issue as being one that cannot be resolved by empirical means, turning instead to questions that can be handled by more simple (but sound) measurement. To some extent, this position is also reasonable since many interesting theoretical questions cannot be resolved empirically because of a lack of data. But pushed to the extreme, this stance may encourage investigators to confine their attention to questions that are theoretically unimportant, rather than to begin the arduous task of improving on both the conceptualization and quantification of the most important variables contained in the theory. In the extreme, this alternative leads either to blind empiricism or to matters of data availability rather than substantive importance (Ghiselli, Campbell, & Zedeck, 1981).

A constructive answer to this problem would admit the difficult nature of the problem, distinguish between the theoretically defined variables that have and have not been logically associated with empirical indicators, attempt to state explicitly the assumptions required to link the theoretical constructs with their empirical indicators, and then proceed to specify the propositions that can and cannot be tested with the obtained data. This stance admits the presence of constraints in the form of variables that cannot be measured but are retained with the understanding that certain of the linkages between constructs and indicators will be tenuous. In reality then, only certain parts of the total theory can be tested at any one time. It also makes obvious the fact that subsequent efforts must be made to fill in the remainder of the picture by paying greater attention to the variables that, for the time being, have not been measured (Merton, 1957).

THEORY BUILDING AND MEASUREMENT

Although it is desirable, in the abstract, to have learning disabilities theories that are simultaneously parsimonious, highly general, and therefore, applicable across a wide range of phenomena, it does not appear that the learning disabilities field can achieve simultaneously all three of these ideal characteristics (Kavale, 1987b).

The significant efforts at improving measurement accuracy in the physical sciences over the past 50 years is impressive but these gains have been dependent on the homogeneous properties of the phenomena studied (Zebrowski, 1979). Also, where there has been indirect measurement of these properties, the empirical indicators have been precise and usually deterministic. This precision plus the homogeneity has made it possible to define a large number of important variables in terms of a relatively small number of measured ones. It seems unlikely that this position will ever be achieved in learning disabilities.

Precision can often be attained in a field such as learning disabilities at the expense of generalizability (Suppes, 1959). One means to accomplish this precision is to create controlled (i.e., laboratory) settings in which a small sample is given simple tasks and asked to repeat them a sufficient number of times so that a reasonable degree of reliability is achieved. Another means is to select a large sample and to "count heads" with respect to easily observed or easily recordable responses. Although imperfections are present, the measurement operations will be relatively straightforward.

The problem arises, however, when there is an attempt to relate these rather sample operational procedures to more general abstract theoretical concepts (e.g., achievement, perception, cognition, attention). The twin problems of generalizability (a property of the theoretical arguments) and comparability (a property of the measuring instruments) are encountered (Blalock, 1969). If theories are to be generalizable across a variety of settings, then variables need to be conceptualized in such a way that propositions containing these variables are applicable across diverse settings. Even if generalizable, it is necessary to ask whether the comparability of measurement operations across such situations can be assessed. For example, in what sense can it be said that a measure of "attention" in a laboratory setting (e.g., the number of times a subject with learning disabilities responds only to the green light) is comparable to "attention" in a natural setting, say, the amount of goal-directed behavior during arithmetic class?

THE DIFFICULTIES AND COMPLICATIONS OF MULTIPLE CAUSATION

In a phenomenon such as learning disabilities that possesses many causal factors, it is probably the case that when only two or three are introduced simultaneously, the result will be only a small percentage of explained variance (see Figure 18-1). Furthermore, as additional variables are included, the increments in explained variance will tend to become smaller and smaller. Since this will likely hold for a variety of combinations of independent variables, it becomes difficult to reach definitive conclusions regarding which ones to eliminate. This is especially true in correlation matrices, in which the values ranges from 0 to about 0.40. Such matrices simply possess too many unknown measurement errors and sampling fluctuations to provide conclusive results (Lord & Novick, 1968).

It is, however, difficult to decide exactly where the problem resides when dealing with a relatively low percentage of explained variance. Perhaps the wrong set of independent variables was selected, or the problem may stem from poor measurement (especially random measurement errors that produce alterations in parameter estimates). Finally, it may be the case that no limited set of perfectly measured variables would yield a much higher explained variance, since there may be upward of 20 factors at work. For instance, the pattern of relatively weak correlations (in the 0.30 range) between single perceptual variables and learning disabilities found from the 1940s seems to be one reason why perceptual research has declined. In retrospect, it might be reasonable to ask why a single perceptual motor variable should be expected to predict well, given the complexity of the learning disabilities phenomenon (Vellutino, Steger, Moyer, Harding, & Niles, 1977).

This complexity also suggests that there will be a large number of equally satisfactory alternative explanations for any given phenomenon (Braithwaite, 1955). Each is probably plausible and accounts for just enough variance to keep it in the picture. If research tends to rule out any particular set of explanatory factors, another set can be created rather easily. Individual biases also enter the picture, with the result that there are likely to be several equally satisfactory clusters of explanatory variables that work to approximately the same degree. But as the number of intercorrelated independent variables increases, so does the number of reasonably plausible models that may be constructed to explain the relationships. For example, among 4 intercorrelated variables there are 6 pairs of possible linkages, with 5 variables there are 10 pairs, and so on. Drawing out the reasons why such explanatory variables may be intercorrelated becomes a major task and the assessment of these indirect effects is dependent upon the correct specification of these interrelationships (Blalock, 1982). These problems are the reason why there are seldom, if ever, dramatic breakthroughs in learning disabilities. The search for new explanatory variables usually concludes either that their explanatory power is low or that they overlap considerably with already identified variables.

There must be some chain of theoretical reasoning involved in the measurement process. This process is at times relatively simple and the theoretical linkages well conceived, so measurement is considered direct. For example, measuring the size of a table or of a span of time is sufficiently direct that is almost considered direct. Serious debate, however, ensues when learning disabilities phenomenon such as "achievement," "perception," "attention," and the like are measured.

The precise but indirect measurement in physics depends on two factors: properties that are constant in nature and a set of theoretical laws that are relatively simple and deterministic (Doebelin, 1975). Time is measured by taking advantage of the periodicity properties of a pendulum or, perhaps the earth's rotation or movement around the sun. Reliability can be assessed through repeated measurements because the property can be assumed not to be undergoing indeterminate changes. For example, a simple, precise, and deterministic law is involved in the assumption that an increase in heat energy produces an expansion of a tube of mercury. But what if this expansion rate had multiple causes? The indirect measurement would necessarily be less precise and assumptions needed to justify it would not be readily agreed upon. This is precisely the problem the learning disabilities field faces because any causal thinking is both multivariate and indeterminate. Such a situation requires simplifying assumptions but there probably is no general agreement on which to use. Measurement decisions then become more problematic and arbitrary.

THE MEASUREMENT OF LEARNING DISABILITIES: AN EXAMPLE

Suppose the goal is measuring the learning disabilities phenomenon. The first step would be to conceptualize learning disabilities by asking the question: How are they usually defined? No more difficult question could be asked and it is unlikely that any consensus will be easily achieved. The inherent difficulties in defining learning disabilities suggests that it would be very difficult to measure learning disabilities directly and, instead, learning disabilities might be best assessed through some presumed consequence (Kavale & Forness, 1985). A common and agreed upon notion in all conceptions of learning disabilities is underachievement (i.e., discrepancy) and it may provide a basis for defining learning disabilities. If it is assumed to be a single cause and a simple relationship, then the usual procedure is to infer learning disabilities on the basis of underachievement, which may be more directly observed. If achievement were the result of a single cause, then no problem exists because the strategy used would be "residualizing" (see Blalock & Blalock, 1968), that is, determining underachievement, adjusting for all other known causes, and then inferring that the adjusted causes of underachievement may then be equated with learning disabilities. But the problem becomes one of deciding which causes to include and on what basis they should be included.

Begin with the simplest situation as depicted in Figure 18-2, in which underachievement (UACH) is determined by only two factors, learning disabilities (LD) and a residual or error term (e), which if assumed to be intercorrelated with learning disabilities, can be reduced by aggregating over a large sample. This model is used, unfortunately, to infer learning disabilities, which is in effect equated with underachievement (Kavale, 1987a).

What if there were other causes of underachievement, however? The model can be expanded to include three: cognitive abilities (COG), environment (ENV), and schooling (SCH). Furthermore, suppose that the first two variables (COG and ENV) have been measured, and schooling (SCH),

18. Assessment Methodology   423

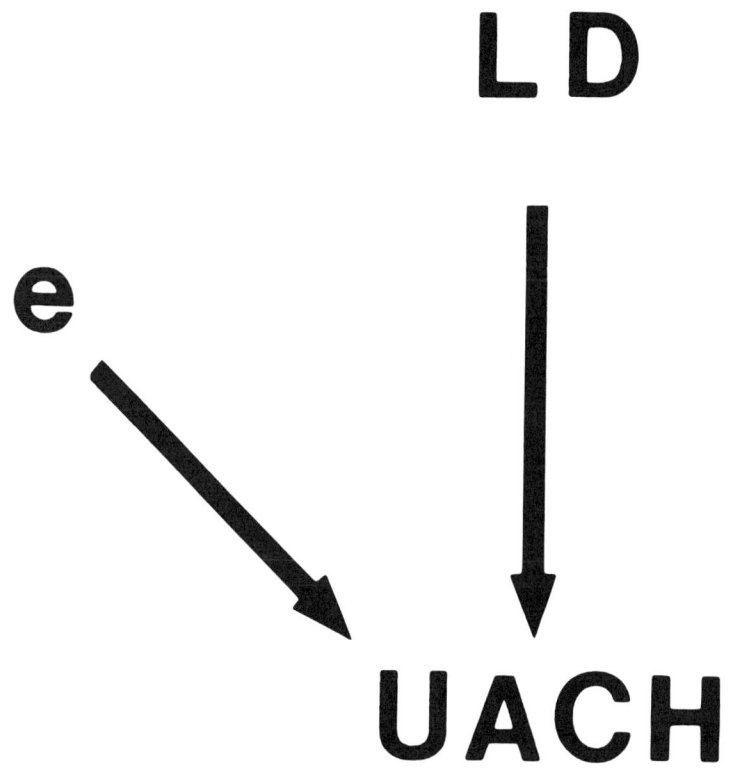

Figure 18-2. Relationship between learning disabilities (LD) and underachievement (UACH).

because it is difficult to measure, is absorbed into the error term (e). The model then would look like Figure 18-3, in which no particular causal connection is assumed between learning disabilities and either cognition (COG) or environment (ENV). In this model, it would be desirable to control or adjust for both the measured variables (cognition and environment) using adjusted achievement levels as the revised measure of learning disabilities.

This is a common measure of learning disabilities, and it requires the simultaneous controlling of all alternative causes of the dependent variable (i.e., learning disabilities) except those placed in the error term (e). After placing the unmeasured variable "schooling" into the error term, what must be assumed about it if a biased measure due to residualizing is to be avoided? What if schooling is correlated with teacher behavior, for example, in the form of referral rate? It must either be assumed that the

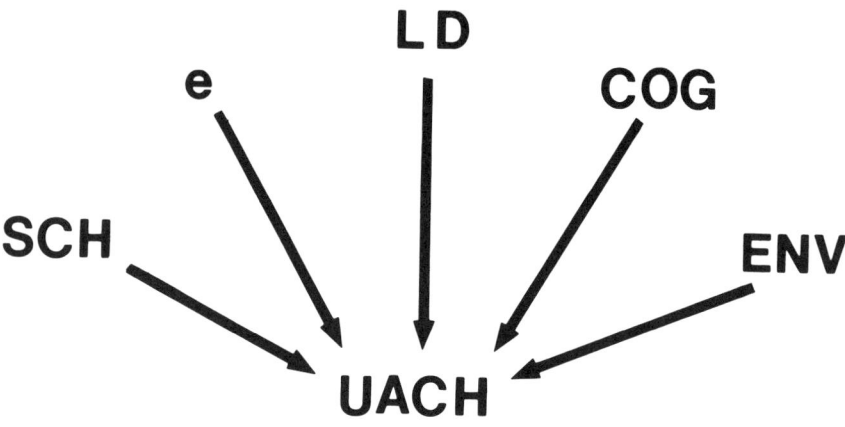

Figure 18-3. Other possible causes of underachievement. (See text for explanation of abbreviations.)

problem has gone away because the control variables, cognition and environment, have captured the schooling variable (no rationale reason to believe so) or a (nearly perfect) measure of schooling (unlikely) must be obtained and brought into the causal system as an additional control variable. Similarly, all other causes of underachievement have been assumed either to be held constant or are not correlated.

Now consider another complication, shown in Figure 18-4, in which the theoretical conceptualization presumes a causal connection between learning disabilities and the two control variables. Suppose, for example, that cognitive difficulties are believed to be the basis of learning disabilities or perhaps it is conjectured that learning disabilities are primarily the result of environmental circumstances. Should cognitive (COG) and environmental (ENV) differentials among subjects with learning disabilities now be controlled? The answer is not at all clear now.

Suppose further that neither cognition nor environment is assumed to affect learning disabilities directly but rather there are antecedent variables that may affect learning disabilities indirectly through cognition and environment. For example, assume that neuropsychological functioning (NPF) and history (HIS) (for example, genetics and cultural background) provide the basis for cognition and environment, respectively. The model must then be expanded as shown in Figure 18-5. It is not likely that the factors illustrated operate in the independent fashion shown but rather they are intercorrelated both with each other and with learning disabilities. These direct and indirect influences on learning disabilities are shown in Figure 18-6. Finally, schooling has been assumed to be a relatively inde-

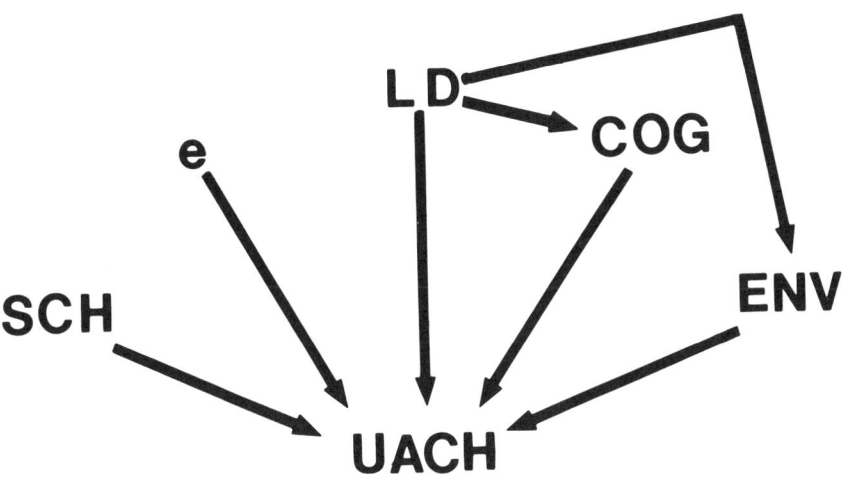

Figure 18-4. A causal connection between learning disabilities, and cognitive abilities, and environment. (See text for explanation of abbreviations.)

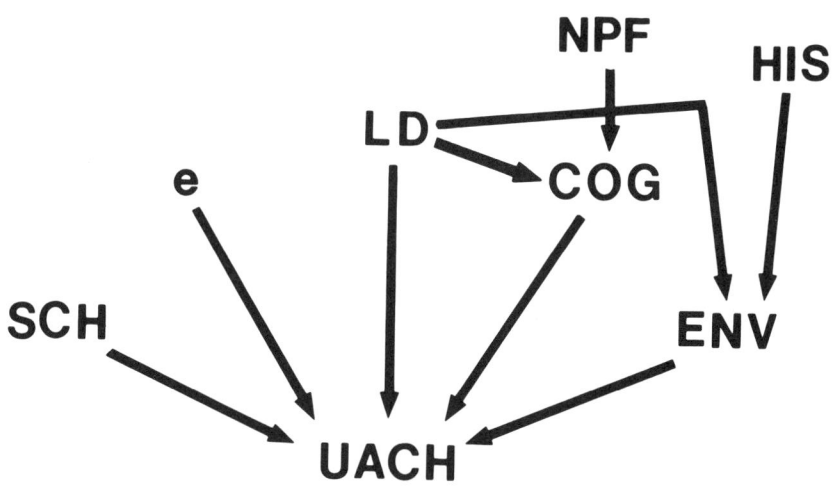

Figure 18-5. Neuropsychological functioning and history as bases for cognitive abilities and environment, respectively. (See text for explanation of abbreviations.)

pendent factor that is a consequence more than a cause. But it is likely that schooling is a primary variable in a school-based disorder such as learning disabilities so it must be considered in relation to the other variables

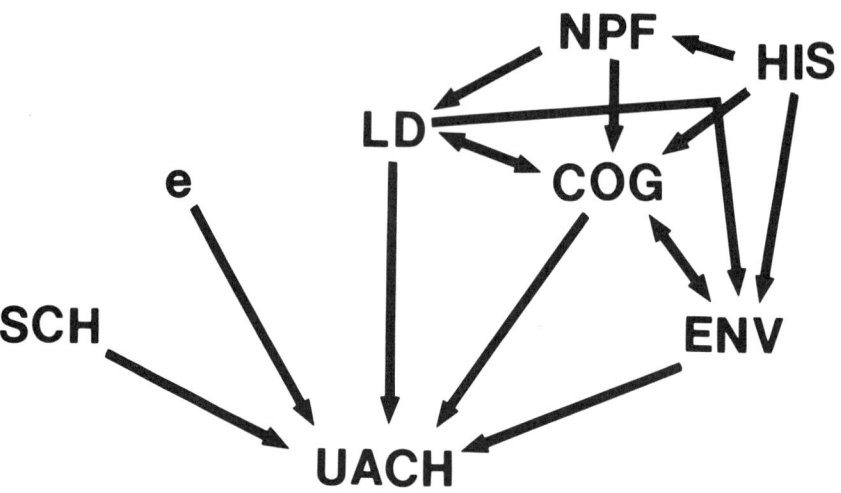

Figure 18-6. Intercorrelation of neuropsychological functioning and history. (See text for explanation of abbreviations.)

(Kavale & Forness, 1986). Such a possibility is diagrammed in Figure 18-7, which represents a far cry conceptually from Figure 18-2. Each variable presents a complex interaction that must be considered if underachievement and ultimately learning disabilities are to be measured accurately. The only independent element then is random measurement error (i.e., e) and suggests that the residualizing process may actually distort the measurement process.

MEASUREMENT AND THEORY

What are some of the implications of this exercise? First, what may have started as a relatively straightforward problem of measuring a phenomenon in terms of its supposed effects is seen broadened into a difficult theoretical problem of accounting for the complexly related causes of underachievement. Thus, theoretical and measurement issues are almost inextricably intertwined.

Second, it is obvious that the measurement process may become highly technical. It becomes much more than Stevens' (1951) classic definition of measurement as the assignment of numbers to objects or events according to rules. Measurement must also be seen as serving a theoretical function wherein it is necessary to clarify the basic concepts (Blalock, 1982). Because highly abstract concepts are used in learning disabilities, measurement

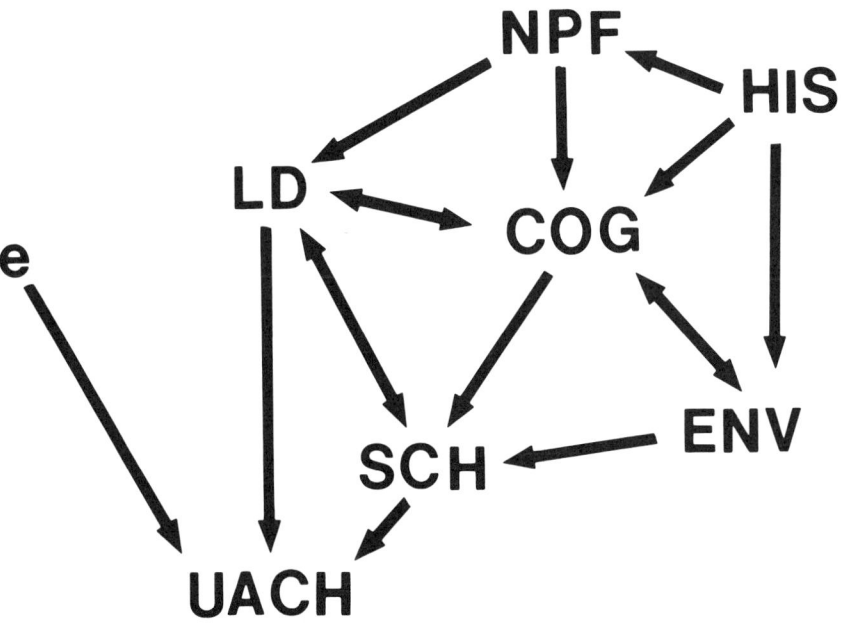

Figure 18-7. Schooling as a primary variable in learning disabilities. (See text for explanation of abbreviations.)

should be defined as the process of linking the basic concepts to empirical indicators. There is far too strong a belief that this inability to bridge the gap between constructs and indicators is the result primarily of measurement error. The learning disabilities field is too accustomed to thinking in terms of classical test theory, in which an observed score is the result of two factors (Lord & Novick, 1968):

$$X = T + e$$

Yet, this formulation is only accurate if and when measurement error is entirely random. Although this may be tenable under strict experimental design and control, it is probably not applicable in a field such as learning disabilities, in which there is likely to be not only random error but also systematic (nonrandom) error introduced by the very measurement procedures used. That is, systematic error is quite likely to be present when a set of empirical indicators measures more than the intended theoretical concept (Zeller & Carmines, 1980). Systematic errors do not conform to the statistical notions underlying random error and consequently, do not have to sum to zero. Such errors then are essentially indeterminate. Thus, for learning disabilities, classical test theory must be reformulated as follows (see Zeller & Carmines, 1980, pp. 12–15):

$$X = T + S + e$$

Unfortunately, there is no statistical theory that deals explicitly with systematic error. This means that the methods used are likely to be less elegant but more complicated than in models containing only random error. The effort is probably worth it since the resulting model will probably be more isomorphic with the nature of the error inherent in the complex learning disabilities phenomenon. Simple remedies suggesting control of perhaps one or two easily measured variables must give way to much more complex models that are capable of rectifying a large number of complications simultaneously (Blalock & Blalock, 1968). At a basic level, this means that learning disabilities theories must allow for the complete specification of rather complex patterns of interaction that includes the reasons for the intercorrelations among variables, both those measured and those that must be controlled (Kavale, 1987b). Without good measures in the first place, it is difficult to assess the adequacy of the measurement error models used. In a very important sense, the learning disabilities field will find itself going in circles.

The problem is only compounded by the ambiguities in the real world, particularly those imposed by fuzzy reality. There are very real limits, even under the best of circumstances, that interfere with measurement precision and, in turn, the ability to either confirm or disconfirm theories (Blalock, 1982).

For example, the notion of underachievement is vague and slippery (Kavale, 1987b). It becomes almost impossible to measure precisely the notion of "degree of achievement." In effect, this represents a range wherein different levels are acceptable or not. But acceptable levels of achievement exist only in a context. For example, the context involves a host of variables like outlay per pupil, urban versus rural, male versus female, teacher pay, and the like that are only at best indirectly related to the actual measurement of achievement. The usual approach here is to fall back on presumed well-established norms (e.g., 2 years below grade level) and then to measure the degree of deviance around this agreed upon but arbitrary point (Reynolds, 1981). But this is only true if we make some rather strong assumptions about the precision with which norms have been defined and the similarity of these norms across settings. In effect, the apparent precision is specious.

A second ambiguity is imposed by fuzzy group boundaries (Hallahan & Kauffman, 1977). The question: Where does learning disabilities end and either mental retardation or behavior disorders begin? Notions like a

Learning Handicapped category that combines learning disabilities, mental retardation, and behavior disorders, while appropriate perhaps for administrative purposes, does little to advance the notion of learning disabilities. The similarities among these conditions must be stressed but also their differences. With a critical examination of differences, it is then possible to speculate about what learning disabilities are. Some clarification of what learning disabilities are becomes necessary because the need to obtain learning disabilities measures only adds additional fuzziness. Group boundaries need to be defined if "contextual effects" like teacher perception or parent preferences are to be eliminated. The consequences of not doing this is the likelihood of possibly measuring something precisely but not what was originally intended to be measured. In effect, reliability checks need to be made for the question: If the appropriate boundaries are not known and arbitrary boundary decisions are made, then how sensitive is the measure to the particular decisions made? (Goldberger & Duncan, 1973). If results differ very little, then there is justification for proceeding. If they do differ, however, then it is necessary to redefine the boundaries and see whether the new choice of boundaries makes a difference in empirical findings. If it still does make a difference, then it is necessary to admit this indeterminacy.

CONCLUSION

Although learning disabilities is a multidimensional concept, problems with theoretical development have been shrouded under the argument of inadequate measurement methodology. It is this lack of theoretical development, however, that often renders ineffectual the myriad data collected on purported indicators of learning disabilities. What we have is an increasingly broad system of assumptions based on an empirical interpretation that lacks the powerful theoretical structure necessary for genuine progress in the field. This system is often represented by rather circular attempts to conceptualize through indirect measurement of variables that have not been rigorously validated. Heterogeneity in groups with and without learning disabilities increases the need for an established relationship between the construct and indicators measured. Issues of construct validity will not be resolved adequately without a sound theoretical base that synthesizes the complex intercorrelations among variables that have multiple causes. If we are to integrate our knowledge into a structure necessary for explanation and prediction, we need to identify the variables theoretically defined and linked to empirical indicators. Once this is done we can turn our attention to the indicators not logically related, and to the improvement of specific assessment methodology.

REFERENCES

Anastasi, A. (1970). On the formation of psychological traits. *American Psychologist, 25*, 899–910.
Bennett, R. E. (1983). Research and evaluation priorities for special education assessment. *Exceptional Children, 50*, 110–117.
Berk, R. A. (1984). *Screening and diagnosis of children with learning disabilities.* Springfield, IL: Charles C Thomas.
Blalock, H. M. (1968). The measurement problem: A gap between the languages of theory and research. In H. M. Blalock & A. B. Blalock (Eds.), *Methodology in social research* (pp. 5–27). New York: McGraw-Hill.
Blalock, H. M. (1969). *Theory construction: From verbal to mathematical formulations.* Englewood Cliffs, NJ: Prentice-Hall.
Blalock, H. M. (1974). *Measurement in the social sciences: Theories and strategies.* Chicago: Aldine.
Blalock, H. M. (1982). *Conceptualization and measurement in the social sciences.* Beverly Hills, CA: Sage.
Blalock, H. M., & Blalock, A. B. (1968). *Methodology in social research.* New York: McGraw-Hill.
Braithwaite, R. B. (1955). *Scientific explanation.* Cambridge: Cambridge University Press.
Bridgman, P. W. (1927). *The logic of modern physics.* New York: MacMillan.
Bursuck, W. D., & Epstein, M. H. (1987). Current research topics in learning disabilities. *Learning Disability Quarterly, 10*, 2–7.
Coles, G. S. (1978). The learning-disabilities test battery: Empirical and social issues. *Harvard Educational Review, 48*, 313–340.
Cronbach, L. J. (1971). Test validation. In R. L. Thorndike (Ed.), *Educational measurement* (2nd ed.) (pp. 443–507). Washington, DC: American Council on Education.
Cronbach, L. J., & Meehl, P. E. (1955). Construct validity in psychological tests. *Psychological Bulletin, 52*, 281–301.
Davis, W. A., & Shepard, L. A. (1983). Specialists' use of tests and clinical judgment in the diagnosis of learning disabilities. *Learning Disability Quarterly, 6*, 128–138.
Deese, J. (1972). *Psychology as science and art.* New York: Harcourt Brace Jovanovich.
Doebelin, E. O. (1975). *Measurement systems: Application and design* (rev. ed.). New York: McGraw-Hill.
Duncan, O. D. (1984). *Notes on social measurement: Historical and critical.* New York: Russell Sage Foundation.
Forge, J. (Ed.). (1987). *Measurement, realism and objectivity.* Dordrecht, Holland: D. Reidel.
Forness, S. R., & Kavale, K. A. (1987). De-psychologizing special education. In R. B. Rutherford, C. M. Nelson, & S. R. Forness (Eds.), *Severe behavior disorders of children and youth* (pp. 2–14). San Diego: College-Hill Press.
Ghiselli, E. E., Campbell, J. P., & Zedeck, S. (1981). *Measurement theory for the behavioral sciences.* San Francisco: Freeman.
Goldberger, A. S., & Duncan, O. D. (1973). *Structural equation models in the social sciences.* New York: Seminar Press.
Greer, S. (1969). *The logic of social inquiry.* Chicago: Aldine.
Hallahan, D. P., & Kauffman, J. M. (1977). Labels, categories, behaviors: ED, LD, and EMR reconsidered. *Journal of Special Education, 11*, 139–149.
Harber, J. R. (1979). Differentiating LD and normal children: The utility of selected perceptual and perceptual-motor tests. *Learning Disability Quarterly, 2*, 70–75.

Hempel, C. G. (1952). *Fundamentals of concept formation in empirical science*. Chicago: University of Chicago Press.
Kaplan, A. (1964). *The conduct of inquiry*. San Francisco: Chandler.
Kavale, K. A. (1987a). Theoretical issues surrounding severe discrepancy. *Learning Disabilities Research, 3*, 12–20.
Kavale, K. A. (1987b). Theoretical quandaries in learning disabilities. In S. Vaughn & C. Bos (Eds.), *Research in learning disabilities: Issues and future directions* (pp. 19–33). Boston: Little, Brown/College-Hill.
Kavale, K. A., & Forness, S. R. (1985). *The science of learning disabilities*. San Diego: College-Hill.
Kavale, K. A., & Forness, S. R. (1986). School learning, time, and learning disabilities: The disassociated learner. *Journal of Learning Disabilities, 1986*, 130–138.
Kavale, K. A, & Nye, C. (1985–1986). Parameters of learning disabilities in achievement, linguistic, neuropsychological and social/behavior domains. *Journal of Special Education, 19*, 443–458.
Kuhn, T. S. (1977). The function of measurement in modern physical science. In T. S. Kuhn (Ed.), *The essential tension: Selected studies in scientific tradition and change* (pp. 178–224). Chicago: University of Chicago Press.
Larsen, S. C., Rogers, D., & Sowell, V. (1976). The use of selected perceptual tests in differentiating between normal and learning disabled children. *Journal of Learning Disabilities, 9*, 85–90.
Loevinger, J. (1957). Objective tests as instruments of psychological theory. *Psychological Reports, 9*, 635–694. (Monograph Supplement 9).
Lord, F. M., & Novick, M. R. (1968). *Statistical theories of mental test scores*. Reading, MA: Addison-Wesley.
Lundberg, G. A. (1942). The operational definition in the social sciences. *American Journal of Sociology, 47*, 727–745.
Lyon, G. R. (1987). Learning disabilities research: False starts and broken promises. In S. Vaughn & C. Bos (Eds.), *Research in learning disabilities: Issues and future directions* (pp. 69–85). Boston: Little, Brown/College-Hill.
MacCorquodale, K., & Meehl, P. E. (1948). On a distinction between hypothetical constructs and intervening variables. *Psychological review, 55*, 95–107.
Merton, R. K. (1957). *Social theory and social structure*. New York: Free Press.
Messick, S. (1981). Constructs and their vicissitudes in educational and psychological measurement. *Psychological Bulletin, 89*, 575–588.
Nagel, E. (1961). *The structure of science*. New York: Harcourt, Brace & World.
Perlmutter, B. F., & Parus, M. V. (1983). Identifying children with learning disabilities: A comparison of diagnostic procedures across school districts. *Learning Disability Quarterly, 6*, 321–328.
Reynolds, C. R. (1981). The fallacy of "two years below grade level for age" as a diagnostic criterion for reading disorders. *Journal of School Psychology, 11*, 250–258.
Scriven, M. (1956). A study of radical behaviorism. In H. Feigl, & M. Scriven (Eds.), *Minnesota studies in the philosophy of science: Vol. I. The foundation of science and the concepts of psychology and psychoanalysis* (pp. 88–130). Minneapolis: University of Minnesota Press.
Stevens, S. S. (1951). Mathematics, measurement and psychophysics. In S. S. Stevens (Ed.), *Handbook of experimental psychology* (pp. 1–49). New York: Wiley.
Suppes, P. (1959). Measurement, empirical meaningfulness, and three-valued logic. In C. W. Churchman, & P. Ratoosh (Eds.)., *Measurement: Definitions and theories* (pp. 129–143). New York: Wiley.

Tryon, W. W. (1979). The test-trait fallacy. *American Psychologist, 34,* 402–406.

Vellutino, F. R., Steger, B. M., Moyer, S. C., Harding, C. J., & Niles, J. A. (1977). Has the perceptual deficit hypothesis led us astray? *Journal of Learning Disabilities, 10,* 375–385.

Weener, P. (1981). On comparing learning disabled and regular classroom children. *Journal of Learning Disabilities, 14,* 227–232.

Ysseldyke, J. E., Algozzine, B., Regan, R., & Potter, M. (1980). Technical adequacy of tests used by professionals in simulated decision making. *Psychology in the Schools, 17,* 202–209.

Zebrowski, E. (1979). *Fundamentals of physical measurement.* North Scituate, MA: Duxbury Press.

Zeller, R. A., & Carmines, E. G. (1980). *Measurement in the social sciences: The link between theory and data.* Cambridge: Cambridge University Press.

Index

Academic and Cognitive
    functioning, 139–140
Accountability and evaluating
    efficacy, 28–29
Achievement, 140–142
American research strategies, 259
Assessing
    medication effects, 362–366
    academic grades, 365–366
    productivity, 363
    skill acquisition, 366
    standardized achievement tests,
        363–365
    teacher ratings, 365
Assessment
    areas of, 236–244
    defined, 4
    domains of, 12–17
    conceptual development, 12–13
    language, 13
    mathematics, 16–17
    metacognition, 13–14
    reading, 15–16
    social interaction, 14
    temperament, 14–15
    dynamic, 75–91
    definition of, 76
    models of, 77–86
    Bransford and colleagues, 84–86
    Budoff, 80–81
    Campione and Brown, 82–84
    Carlson and colleagues, 81
    Feurstein, 77–79
    Vygotsky, 79–80
    of the environment, 53–55
    instructional, 54–55
    physical, 53
    social, 54
    ethical concerns, 35–36
    negative consequences, 37–38
    privacy, 36–37
    goal of, 2–4
    how to, 32
    conditions for, 33
    conventional vs. interventionist,
        32–33
    instructional, purposes of, 46–48
    identifying areas of instructional
        need, 46–47
    specific skill deficits, 47
    monitoring effects of instruction,
        48
    selecting instructional delivery
        procedures, 47–48
    and instructional procedures,
        86–91
    guided learning and reading,
        87–90
    in early mathematics, 86–87
    intervention research, 275–277
    Graves, 275
    Palinesar and Brown, 275–276
    Wong and Jones, 276–277
    issues in practice of, 4–12
    classification, 5–6
    issues related to tests and
        instruction, 7–8
    political and social issues, 6–7
    theory, 4–5
    and language sampling, general
        factors related to, 235–236
    of metacognitive practice in
        learning disabilities,
        277–281
    research in learning disabilities,
        269–275
    Englert and Thomas, 273
    Wong and Wong, 269–272
    Wong, Wong, and Blenkisop,
        273–274
    theory in learning disabilities,
        276
    models of, 8–9
    behavior, 11–12
    dynamic, 9–10
    neuropsychological, 10–11
    of moral development,
    perspective, 17–18

Assessment—*continued*

of perspective taking skills,
phonology, 241–242
pragmatics, 242–244
process, purpose of assessment, 231–232
semantics, 236–241
  formal assessment, 238, 240–241
  informal assessment, 238–239, 241
  syntax and morphology, 239–240
of social cognition and social perception,
  problem solving using role playing,
of the student, 48–53
  characteristics of the learner, 49
  monitoring progress, 52–53
  task performance, 50–52
    interviews, 52
    task analysis, 50
    trial teaching, 50–51
what do we want to assess, 21–29
  accountability and evaluating efficacy, 28–29
  contrasting models guiding in research and practice, 24–25
  different views of how to match instruction to
learner, 27–28
  what is to be remedied, 25–27
  who is to be identified, 22–24
what the findings mean, 33–34
  norms and standards, 34–35
  validity and utility, 34
when to, 29
  should we wait for valid tools, 30–31
  single vs. multi-stage decision making, 31
  what should precede assessment, 29–30
who decides? the politics of, 38–40
Attention, 135–136

Behavioral
  models, 11–12
  and normative assessments, comparison of, 112–117
Brain structure and related functions of, 126–127

Characteristics of the learner, 49
Classification
  research, rationale for, 61
  systems, as theory driven hypothesis, 62
  characteristics of useful, 62–67
  research on learning disabilities, interpretive necessities in, 66
  subtype research, sample selection in, 64–65
  learning disabilities, external validation of, 65–66
  variable selection, 63
Cognitive and academic functioning, 139–140
Cognitive-behavioral assessment methods, 333
  assessment methods in which subject produces information, 334–340
Comparison of behavioral and normative assessments, 112–118
Computerized assessment procedures, 366–367
Concepts and indicators, 408–409
Conceptual
  development, 12–13
  knowledge, 179
Conceptualization and quantification, 415–419
Consequences, negative, 37–38
Construct validity, lingering problems of, 161–162

Decision making, single vs. multi-stage, 31

Definitions and conceptualizations, 314–316
commonalities and differences, 315–316
theoretical perspectives, 314–315
Development, conceptual, 12–13
Developmental epistemology revised, 250–251
Differentiation of types of students, 112
Dynamic assessment, 9–10
definition, 76
models of, 77–86
Dyslexia
construct validity of the concept of, 152–154
and poor readers, evidence for differentiability of, 158–161

Efficacy
evaluating and accountability, 28–29
long-term studies, 356–360
Gateways Hospital (Los Angeles), 360
Georgetown University Hospital, 358
Royal Ottawa Hospital, 358–359
UCLA department of pediatrics, 359
University of Iowa, 359–360
short-term studies, 353–356
arithmetic, 355
handwriting, 356
reading, 353–355
spelling, 355–356
Environment
assessment of, 53
instructional, 54–55
physical, 53
social, 54
Ethical concerns, 35
Evaluation
of intervention, 22
of programs, 109–112

Follow up of students from special programs, 106–109
Framework for cognitive-behavioral assessment, 332–333

Guided learning
and reading, 87–90
and transfer in early mathematics, 86–87

Implications for assessment, 202–218
the case of Robert, 217–218
components for effective assessment, 209–217
general issues, 202–209
conducted at what level, 206
purpose of assessment, 204
tools needed, 206–209
what to examine, 204–205
practices, 260–261
Instruction
to learner, different views, 27–28
monitoring effects of, 48
Instructional
assessment, purposes, 46
delivery procedures, selecting, 47–48
environment, 54–55
need, identifying areas of, 46–47
Intelligence, deeper conceptual problems, 162–166
Intervention, evaluation of, 22
Interviews, 52
Issues
of classification, 5–6
intelligence, 162–166
political and social, 6–7
tests and instruction related, 7–8
of theory, 4–5

Language, 13
Learning and cognition, cognitive view, 179–188
formal mathematics, 183

Learning and cognition—*continued*
  informal math:foundation for
    formal math, 183
  school taught mathematics,
    183
  mathematical knowledge, 182
  personal mathematics of
    schoolchildren, 182
  preschool development, 182
  strengths and limitations, 182
  mental structures, 179–180
    affect, 180
    conceptual knowledge, 179
    metacognition, 180
    strategies, 180
  processes of change, 180–181
    assimilation and
      accommodation, 181
    integration, 181
  schema development, 183–188
    case of number-combination
      knowledge, 185–188
    developmental trends, 184
    weak versus strong schemata,
      183–184
Learning difficulties
  common, sample of, 195–202
    base-ten place-value skills and
      concepts, 199–201
    decimals, 202
    fractions, 201–202
    geometry, 201
    informal arithmetic, 197–198
    numerical relationships, 196–197
    object counting, 196
    oral counting, 195–196
    part-part-whole skills and
      concepts, 198–199
    reading and writing-single digit
      numerals, 197
    number-fact deficiencies, 194–195
  psychologically inappropriate
    instruction, 189–190
    absorption model, 189
    gaps, 189–190
  results of, 190–194
    debilitating beliefs, 193–194
    disinterest, 191
    inaccurate or incomplete
      learning, 191–192
    passivity, 192–193
    rote learning, 190
Learning disabilities
  definition and characteristics of,
    125–126
  interpretive necessities in
    classification research on,
    66
Limitations and applications,
  324–326
Long-term objective, evaluation of,
  104–105
Lovett research program, 70, 70–71

Macro-analysis
  epistemological methodology,
    251–254
  empirical and reflecting
    abstraction, 253–254
  macro-analytic influences on the
    learning disabilities
    research, 254
Mathematics, 16–17
  formal, 183
  informal knowledge, 182
Measurement, and construct
  validity, 412–414
  functions of, 410–412
  of learning disabilities: an
    example, 422–426
  the meaning of, 407–408
  and theory, 426–429
Memory, 136–137
Mental structures, 179
Metacognition, 13–14
Methodological concerns and
  implications for assessment,
  344–346
  accuracy of information, 344
  comparability of assessment
    methods, 345–346
  effects of assessment techniques
    on cognitive processes, 345
Methods, 317–324

of assessment, 317–324
  assessing temperament in
    schools, 320–324
  infants and toddlers, 318
  preschool and school-age
    children, 319
  independent of any particular
    event, 340–343
  assessment methods in which
    someone other than subject
    produces information,
    341–343
Micro-analytic research in learning
    disabilities, 255–258
  more recent micro-analysis,
    257–258
  transitional studies, 255–257
Models
  of assessment, 8–9
  behavioral, 11–12
  contrasting, guiding assessment in
    research and practice, 24–25
  of dynamic assessment, 77–86
  phonological-core variable-
    difference, 154–157
Monitoring progress, 62–63
Motor functioning, 133–135
Multiple causation, differences and
    complications, 420–422

Negative consequences, 37–38
Neuropsychological, 122–123
  assessment, 10–11
  procedures for use in children
    with learning disabilities,
    130–133
  conceptual framework for
    assessment, 127–128
  of learning disabilities, 127–128
  historical, 123–125
  perspective, 123–125
  perspective, 122–123
  procedures for learning disability
    children, 130–133
  rationale for test procedures for
    learning disabilities, 128

  test batteries, reliability and
    validity of, 128–130
  procedures, rationale for, 128
  reliability and validity, 128–130
Norms and standards, 34

Phonological-core variable difference
    model, 154–157
Physical environment, 53
Placement of youngsters at
    instructional levels, 98,
    98–100
Political and social issues, 6–7
Politics of assessment, 38–40
Privacy, 36–37
Procedure types, 232–234
  issue to consider before selecting
    tests and procedures,
    233–234
Programs, evaluation of, 109–112
Progress, monitoring, 62–63
Psycholinguistic functioning,
    137–139
Psychometric approach, 3

Reading, 15–16
Relative efficacy of drug, behavioral,
    and combination
    treatments, 361–362
Research on temperament in schools,
    316–317
  goodness of fit, 317

Schema development, 183–188
Sensory
  acuity, 133
  recognition and perceptual
    functions, 133
Severe discrepancy
  focus on, 148–150
  operationalizing, 151–152
Short-term objective, evaluation of,
    100–103
Skill defects, identifying specific, 47

Social
 cognition theory, 286–287
 environment, 54
 interaction, 14
Special programs, follow-up of
  students from, 106–108
Specific treatment planning, 22
Standardization, evidence of
  adequate, 382–386
 reliability, 382–383
 validity, 384–386
  construct validity, 385–386
  content validity, 384
  criterion-related validity, 385
Standardized test to plan
  appropriate instruction,
  386–405
 apply standardized tests for
  academic intervention,
  386–387
 specific standardized tests for
  academic instruction,
  387–405
 Brigance diagnostic inventories,
  388–389
 Hudson education skills
  inventories, 389–392
 miscue analysis system with
  Gray oral reading test-
  revised, 397–405
 spellmaster assessment and
  teaching system, 393
 Stanford diagnostic
  mathematics test, 393–397
Standards and norms, 34
Structure and related functions of
  the brain, 126–127
Students
 assessment of, 48–49
 differentiation of types, 112
Subtypes
 clinically generated, identification
  and external validation of,
  69–71
 the Lovett research program,
  70–71
 developmental classification of LD
  subgroups and, 71–72

 identification and external
  validation of clinically
  generated, 69
 identifying with multivariate
  classification methods, 67
 Yale/Haskins laboratory
  program project, 67–69
 of learning disabilities, external
  validation of, 65–66
 reliability and validity of, 65

Task
 analysis, 50
 performance, 50
  analysis, 50
  interviews, 52
  trial teaching, 50
Temperament, 14–15
Tests
 standardized, 3
 standardized, the nature of,
  373–382
  objective scoring criteria,
  374–375
  set administration procedures,
  374
  specific frame of reference,
  375–382
  nonreferenced interpretation,
  380–382
  norm-referenced
  interpretation, 375–379
  and criterion-referenced
  interpretation, 380–382
Theories and constructs, 414–415
Theory building and measurement,
  419–420
Treatment planning, specific, 22
Trial teaching, 50

Validity and utility, 34
Variable selection, 63
Video presentations to assess social
  cognition, 301–303

Yale-Haskins laboratory program
  project, 67–69

8700 Shoal Creek Boulevard
Austin, Texas 78758

Order Number 1589

ISBN 0-89079-406-5